Enrico Caruso

OPERA BIOGRAPHY SERIES, NO. 2

Series Editors
Andrew Farkas
William R. Moran

Enrico Caruso (25 February 1873–2 August 1921)

ENRICO CARUSO

My Father and My Family

by

Enrico Caruso, Jr., & Andrew Farkas

Chronologies by Thomas G. Kaufman
Discographies by William R. Moran and Richard Koprowski
Bibliography by Opritsa Popa

AMADEUS PRESS
Reinhard G. Pauly, General Editor
Portland, Oregon

ISBN 0-931340-24-1
Printed in Hong Kong
Designed by Sandra Mattielli

AMADEUS PRESS
(an imprint of Timber Press, Inc.)
9999 S.W. Wilshire
Portland, Oregon 97225

Library of Congress Cataloging-in-Publication Data

Caruso, Enrico, 1904–1987.
    Enrico Caruso : my father and my family / by Enrico Caruso, Jr. &
Andrew Farkas ; chronologies by Thomas G. Kaufman ; discographies by
William R. Moran and Richard Koprowski ; bibliography by Opritsa
Popa.
        p.   cm.
    "Caruso discography of original recordings, by William R. Moran,
and long-playing records, by Richard Koprowski": p.
    Includes bibliographical references.
    ISBN 0-931340-24-1
    1. Caruso, Enrico, 1873–1921. 2. Singers--Biography. I. Farkas,
Andrew. II. Title.
ML420.C259C3 ' 1990
782.1'092--dc20
[B]   89-17917
                                                                      CIP
                                                                      MN

Contents

Illustrations follow pages 40, 88, 128, 192, 216, 256, 336, and 432.

Dedicated to the memory of
Miss LOUISE SAER
my beloved "Lei"
who was always there

Acknowledgments

THE first word of recognition is due to my very dear friend and collaborator, the late **Enrico Caruso, Jr**. He placed at my disposal every scrap of documentation in his possession and shared with me in total candor the details, favorable and unfavorable, relating to his family and himself. His valued friendship, kindness, joviality, immense good humor, and fantastic cooking made my work a labor of love. He patiently read, and read again, each successive draft of the manuscript, offering suggestions, additions, and corrections.

In addition to Enrico, several others provided generous assistance. **Father Ernesto Balducci** of the Centro Studi Badia Fiesolana of Florence (Italy) supplied the dates of attendance of Rodolfo Caruso. **Carol C. Bhidé** (Jacksonville, Florida) made helpful stylistic suggestions. Reference librarian **Kathleen F. Cohen** (Jacksonville, Florida) tracked down the court transcripts of the Caruso litigation in New Jersey. The late **Ted Fagan** (New York), a multilingual simultaneous interpreter at the United Nations for over three decades, translated all the reviews, interviews, and correspondence from Spanish and Portuguese into English. **Doina G. Farkas** (Gainesville, Florida), librarian and linguist, translated the German texts. **Paul Karabinis** (Jacksonville) made photographic reproductions of many rare originals that illustrate this book; and his colleague, **Terry Medaris** (Jacksonville), printed them for the publisher's use. **Thomas G. Kaufman** (Boonton, New Jersey), a leading operatic chronologist, compiled the data pertaining to the careers of Ada and Rina Giachetti and Enrico Caruso and supplied the chronologies at the end of this book. **William Henry Kleckner** (Milan, Italy) researched the 1910 and 1912 Caruso litigation in Milan and obtained a copy of Rodolfo Caruso's birth certificate. **Dr. Wallace A. McAlpine** (Jacksonville) made useful suggestions about the terminology used in the chapter on Caruso's doctors. **Ralph N. Manuel** (Culver, Indiana), Superintendent of The Culver Educational Foundation, provided photocopies of the entire correspondence file relating to the career of Enrico Caruso, Jr., at Culver Military Academy. **William R. Moran** (La Cañada, California), internationally known scholar of recordings, singers, and

9

operatic history, made many valuable suggestions and compiled the complete and definitive discography of original recordings included in this volume. Sound Archivist **Richard Koprowski** (Stanford, California) supplied data on the long-playing records. **Guido d'Onofrio** (Foggia, Italy), at the specific request of Enrico Caruso, Jr., searched all the nineteenth-century records of the parochy of San Giovanniello agli Ottocalli in Naples, as well as the archives of the City Halls of Naples and of Piedimonte Matese, for the birth and death certificates of Enrico Caruso, Sr., and his siblings and also located the birth and marriage certificates of Caruso's parents and grandparents. The research of **Jim Peterson** (Clarkston, Utah) through the genealogical archives of the Mormon Church in Salt Lake City confirmed the findings of Guido d'Onofrio. **Luciano Pituello** (Milan), President of the Associazione Museo Enrico Caruso, supplied several reviews of Ada Giachetti's performances and copies of the birth certificates of Ada and Rina Giachetti. **Peggy Pruett** (Jacksonville) provided interlibrary loan assistance. **Opritsa Popa** (Davis, California), reference librarian, compiled the extensive "Caruso Bibliography." **Dr. Horacio Sanguinetti** (Buenos Aires, Argentina) shared his father's correspondence concerning the singular event of Caruso singing the prologue of *Pagliacci* and copied the text of the reviews from contemporary newspapers. **Dr. Michel Szurek** (Warsaw, Poland) located the casts and reviews of Rina Giachetti's opera and concert performances in Warsaw. **Dr. Ruffo Titta, Jr.** (Rome, Italy), allowed me access to his archives in search of material relating to the Caruso story and also gave permission to reproduce some photographs in his possession. **Robert Tuggle** (New York), Director of Archives of the Metropolitan Opera Association, shared some unpublished documents and made rare photographs available for reproduction. **K. John Westmancoat**, information officer of the British Library (London), supplied a microfilm copy of the entire Caruso clippings file held by the Library. **Marice Wolfe**, Special Collections Librarian, and **Nena Couch**, Project Archivist, at Vanderbilt University Library (Nashville, Tennessee), provided copies of photographs and correspondence from the Francis Robinson Collection.

My thanks go to these individuals for their valuable contributions to my work.

Andrew Farkas
7 April 1989
Jacksonville, Florida

Caveat Lector

L AUNCHING a biographical project at my advanced age took not only time and energy, but a good deal of faith, optimism, and a cavalier disregard for the inexorable passage of time. I commenced this project with the hope that I would be allowed to complete my work and offer it to the world as a filial tribute to the memory of my parents.

Why yet another Caruso biography?

I must advise the reader that it was neither my intent nor my objective to add another conventional biography to the ever-expanding Caruso literature that has grown to over twenty monographs. These have familiarized most readers with my father's career, and the experts all know what he sang, when, where, and how well. I have been able to contribute little to the well-documented record of his life as a singer. His voice has been described, analyzed, dissected, by genuine and would-be experts, both musical and medical. Beyond describing the effect his singing had on me, I cannot bring the reader any closer to solving the mystery of his communicative powers or the lasting appeal of his glorious voice. Although I became a singer myself and enjoyed modest success for a few short years, I do not presume to describe or explain his voice production. Just as his voice was unique and defied analysis, so too did his technique. It was the product of a throat completely free of any constriction or stress and a vocal line of emission based not on *appoggiatura* but on the column of air, combined with his particular physical structure. If his contemporaries were unable to penetrate the secret of his singing, I doubt that others trying to do so solely on the basis of his recordings can ever succeed.

As his only surviving son, I have memories of the man which go back further than any other person's. I was seventeen when he died at the relatively young age of forty-eight. Although I saw him for only short periods as I was growing up, I can contribute to the history of Caruso, the private man, details inaccessible to biographers. I am the last repository of family stories, information passed on by relatives and household staff, and anecdotes told by my father's friends and colleagues. In addition, I possess a number of documents central to the story of my parents and my brother Rodolfo, archival materials whose valuable contents deserve to be shared with the operatic public. While these memoirs range more widely than traditional biographies, I am confident that the reader will be rewarded by the new light they cast on my father's life and legacy. Although I have taken care to undergird this account with commonly known reference points, the bulk of this book, because of the nature of my sources, consists of new material. Whenever possible, I have quoted from correspondence, reviews, memoirs, and other documents, as much for the sake of authenticity as to offer the reader the thoughts and observations of the writers in their own words. Summarizing or paraphrasing a letter or a critique may be more expeditious but cannot adequately render its author's emotions or state of mind.

I have tried to keep documents and narrative in balance and to ensure continuity by a careful adherence to chronology. At times I record details which may seem trivial, yet they may provide the clue or the point of departure for future researchers trying to establish, prove or disprove, various associations or theories. I know that with my passing, the store of oral history I possess will vanish, and the documentation in my hands will be dispersed and impossible to recapture. Therefore I chose to preserve them in this book. If I have misjudged the significance of some details, I beg the reader's indulgence.

In these reminiscences, I have amplified the major incidents in my father's life, recounting certain events from a fresh vantage point, at times borrowing the words of an eyewitness. I wanted to show Caruso in the setting of his family, to show the way his actions and behavior affected the lives of others, first and foremost the members of his household. His presence was felt even in his absence; his will and wishes, perceived, expressed, or assumed, ruled the lives of those around him.

Thus my contribution is not just another traditional musical biography of Enrico Caruso, but rather a gathering of information heretofore known only to his family, meant to complement rather than to duplicate or replace the many books written about him. My father was a simple man and would be most surprised by the lasting interest in his life and the voluminous literature he generated posthumously. The critical investigations of his singing would flatter him, and he would be annoyed by the persistent curiosity about his personal life. Yet he would be the first to admit that while his studies and disciplined work made him a singer, it was the difficult, often painful experiences endured as a man that made him an artist.

In preparing this volume, I was determined to present the facts known to me with no attempt to mask or soften their less savory aspects. Biographical writings often depict their subject in the most favorable terms possible in order to ensure a revered immortality. I strongly felt that misstating facts for such an end would be dishonest and would negate the objective of my project.

Other biographies of Caruso's life and achievements typically end with his illness and death in 1921. But his story does not stop there. His legacy was borne either as a borrowed halo or as a crown of thorns by the surviving Carusos. My father earned fabulous sums with his voice and his voice alone. He died a wealthy man, leaving an estate valued at millions of dollars. It was inevitable that some of his heirs should compete for a disproportionate share of the inheritance. The litigation that followed was subject matter suitable for a soap opera. The battles were fought for high stakes, and the outcome affected the participants to the end of their lives.

My story, therefore, is also a tale of money. This recurrent theme should not be misconstrued as indicating an unhealthy preoccupation with this useful commodity. Apart from short periods of passing affluence in my adult life, I grew accustomed to impecunity. But money itself is inseparable from the Caruso story. It provided the comforts my father and his relatives enjoyed for decades. It also bought him loyalty, friendship, even affection; it was often the bond that held others in his entourage. So that aspect of his life must also be told.

A critical portion of my father's life story centers around his relationship with the Giachetti sisters: my mother Ada and her sister Rina. For want of information, the relationship between my parents has been inadequately covered in the literature. Unfortunately, I do not possess facts sufficient to do the subject justice. Still, my correspondence with my mother, my secondhand knowledge of her relationship with my father and my aunt, and the extensive research on their careers have permitted me to partially fill the vacuum about that aspect of Caruso's life. My mother is the "bête noire" of all existing Caruso biographies and is assigned the entire fault for the dissolution of their union, a persistent misperception that requires modification. However, it is not my intention to tarnish my father's image nor to whitewash my mother's memory. I have tried only to show her in a more human light, rather than as the villainess portrayed by biographers for whom the great Caruso could do no wrong.

Toward this end, I have dwelt at some length on the events of my own life. For the events of my childhood and upbringing reveal a good deal about the attitudes and behavior of my parents and relatives, while the outline of my adult years is an essential backdrop to events relating to the family, specifically my mother, my aunt, and my brother. Assuming the reader's interest in matters operatic, I may perhaps devote more space than is deserved to the details of my own brief singing career. But the distinguished name I bear made my father omnipresent in my life. It was a great source of pride, at times of reflected glory, but more often a burdensome liability.

My story deals only with my relatives, including my stepmother, Dorothy. My relationship with her was cordial yet distant while my father was alive, and I did not know her well enough to offer more than passing observations beyond the statement of facts. She played a pivotal role in the legal proceedings that followed my father's death and therefore figures prominently in some portions of my narrative.

I am keenly aware of the importance and the weight of authenticity future researchers will—duly or unduly—attribute to my account about my family. In recognition of the attendant responsibility, I have qualified my statements where appropriate. It will be obvious to the reader that events which took place before I reached the age of awareness were either recounted to me by relatives or derived from outside sources, whether or not so identified. I incorporated such materials only when I had no doubt whatsoever as to their veracity, either because they had been corroborated in the retelling by several family members, or because they were eminently plausible. I was particularly careful about unconfirmed stories, family legends, hearsay, or information obtained from dubious sources. When I was uncertain about the reliability of statements made but felt nonetheless that they bore repeating, I have warned the reader accordingly.

In many instances, I have been able to correct errors introduced by one biographer and repeated so frequently by subsequent writers that they are now accepted as facts. In the course of writing this book, I had occasion to read or reread many contemporary newspaper accounts relating to my father as well as to myself. I was amazed anew at the number of inaccuracies, the misinformation, or the pure invention they contain. The crude errors and misstatements are simply too numerous to discuss or refute. Only someone thoroughly familiar with the subject could sort out fact from fiction, and this I have tried to do. When the information I offer conflicts with published sources, it can be assumed that the contradiction is intentional, based on information which I know to be correct. Although neither my memory nor that of others in my family is infallible, and there is inevitably a small margin of error, the information given about matters of a purely personal nature can be considered definitive.

It also deserves mention that the quotations and conversations given in this account are not merely a writer's device. These short phrases and brief exchanges have been firmly etched in my memory, either by virtue of some mnemonic coincidence that helped me to remember, or due to repeated retelling by either the participants or myself.

The same is true of the excerpts taken from the recollections of my brother Rodolfo. He left behind extensive sketches prepared for the first draft of a book, along with fragments of conversations, statements, and miscellaneous data which I incorporated in the narrative at appropriate points. Rodolfo had a better way with spoken words than with the written, so I have made editorial adjustments in the passages I used. The changes are stylistic, not substantive. If this book has a ghostwriter, it is certainly my late brother.

It may be of interest to know how much of the text I wrote and how much is the work of my collaborator. Like my brother, I am a raconteur, not a writer. I spent close to one thousand hours with my friend and coauthor, Andrew Farkas, talking about my father, my family, my own life, and other topics that relate to this book. His profound knowledge of opera and of Caruso's career allowed me to refer to publicly known events without explanatory remarks or background information, and his persistent and probing questions brought forth many details that had lain dormant in my memory. Many hours of these extensive sessions were preserved on tape and then transcribed. As I examined the text, I was the first to recognize that my stories, recollections, and observations needed reorganization and polishing. Andrew provided these essential services. In addition he expended much effort verifying facts and dates of which I was unsure and gathering from other sources pertinent information missing from my archives. I reviewed and corrected the tape transcripts, all versions of the progressive drafts, and the final copy. In sum, the story is all mine; the research, arrangement, and internal structure are all my coauthor's; and the words are about half his and half mine. I accept full responsibility for all statements made and opinions expressed or implied. While only the reader can pass judgment on the final work, I must record that this book is the result of a true collaboration: intense, enjoyable, conducted in intellectual harmony with mutual understanding and respect. Andrew and I, bound by a common purpose and a deep interest in our subject, developed a profound friendship and attachment. Our different but complementary skills made this book possible.

Enriched by the experience of a long life, I believe I have been able to put the events of more than eight decades into their proper perspective. I wish to judge no one, and I can honestly say that I hold no grudge against any person, living or dead. In recounting my adversities, I have not tried to settle accounts but have merely recorded facts. I have come to understand that each of us is different, and one cannot measure his fellow men against a single norm, especially not those blessed—or cursed—with an artistic temperament. As I reflect upon the incidents in my narrative, I see that I have come no closer than before to sorting out my parents' actions, nor to solving the riddle of their relationship, the way they loved and hurt each other. I am convinced that my mother retained a deep love for my father until her death, and that his letters and actions reflect the same affection for her.

Although I never had the opportunity to know my parents as a typical child in a more usual household would, I hold a strong affection for them both, and I am grateful for the love they gave me in their own ways, albeit from a distance. At the same time I see them as the highstrung, self-centered artists that they were, living and performing under tremendous artistic, social, and domestic pressures, but above all deeply human, with the strengths and the failings of human beings. I do not judge them for their mistakes, and I cannot blame them for mine. Although my efforts to bring additional glory to the name have succeeded but little, I cherish the honor to be my father's son—a Caruso!

Enrico Caruso, Jr.
7 December 1986
Jacksonville, Florida

CHAPTER ONE

Beginnings

EVERY biography and most articles written about Enrico Caruso since his death claim that he was the eighteenth of twenty-one children, and the first to survive infancy.[1] In fact, he was the third of seven children, and his two elder brothers died at the ages of two and seven.

Pierre Key, one-time music critic of the New York *World* and author of the first full-length biography about Enrico Caruso, was largely responsible for establishing the myth surrounding Caruso's birth. In retrospect, it seems that he was the innocent victim of unintentional misinformation. He wrote that "Caruso and his brother Giovanni—speaking on different occasions—were in agreement as to the ages of their father and mother; each stated that there were twenty Caruso boys and one girl."[2] There can be little doubt that Key was quoting what the Caruso brothers had told him; after all, Giovanni was still alive at the time to refute the statement had it been untrue. It is impossible to trace which fertile mind in the Caruso family is to be credited with this invention.

Caruso is a common name in Italy. There are hundreds of Carusos in every large city. Since Enrico Caruso's name became world-famous, many a Caruso named his son Enrico.

Paradoxically, this was not the great Caruso's name. He was baptized Errico, spelled with two *r*'s in the Neapolitan manner. His
parents and his brother Giovanni always called him "Erri," as did his
closest Neapolitan friends, Angelo Arachite, Eduardo Missiano, and
others.

Thanks to the diligent, pioneering research of Caruso's admirer
Guido d'Onofrio, the Caruso lineage has now been traced directly
from original documents to the beginning of the nineteenth century.
Poring over vast numbers of musty, yellowing volumes, he has located
and photocopied all the original birth, marriage, and death certificates of the Caruso family. After decades of misinformation, these
copies have made it possible to reconstruct the following Caruso
genealogy.

Enrico Caruso's grandparents on both sides came from the small
community of Piedimonte. Over the years, the town changed its name
to Piedimonte d'Alife, and more recently to Piedimonte Matese.

The orphanage of Piedimonte, like most others, had a *ruota,* a
receptacle built into its gate or wall. This was a segmented revolving
drum with a door on each side. It helped preserve the anonymity of a
mother who wanted to give her baby up for adoption, for she could
leave the newborn in the hollow between the doors and depart unseen
and unidentified.

Francesca Venditto, the woman whose job it was to check the *ruota*
of the orphanage, found a male infant there on 20 October 1812. In the
presence of the mayor, Nicola Cenci, and two witnesses, she had the
boy registered at the *Stato Civile,* the City Hall of Piedimonte, under
the name Vincenzo Giuseppe Baldini. She probably chose Baldini as
the family name because there were no other Baldinis in the community,[3] thus the child could not be associated with any local person
by accident or insinuation. The child's birth certificate showed that he
was a foundling of unknown parentage. Vincenzo grew up to become a
laborer. When he reached adulthood, he married Carmela d'Onofrio.
Their daughter, Anna Baldini, was born on 9 May 1838 in Piedimonte
d'Alife.

Enrico Caruso's grandfather, Giovanni Caruso, was born in 1804
to Luigi and Rosa Lenna Caruso. On 3 October 1835, he married Maria
Onorata Palumbo, daughter of Pasquale and Maria Tancasia Palumbo.
They had at least two sons, Marcellino, born on 8 March 1840, and
Salvatore, both born in Piedimonte d'Alife. No other children can be
traced or verified. Salvatore's great-grandson, Enrico, is a music

Photocopy of the parochial record listing Errico Caruso's birth (*center entry*) on 25 February 1873, in Naples. Courtesy of Guido d'Onofrio.

teacher now living in Piedimonte Matese. In a village the size of Piedimonte, Anna Baldini and Marcellino Caruso must have known each other since childhood. They were married in the Church of the Annunciation in Piedimonte d'Alife on 21 August 1866. We know nothing of their courtship, nor do we know why Marcellino did not marry Anna before her twenty-eighth birthday. Of the two possible explanations, only one is plausible: Because Anna had no dowry, Marcellino had to learn a trade and have an income before he could support a wife and start a family, and Anna was willing to wait for him. The other possibility, that Anna may have been previously married and widowed, can be safely ruled out as the parochial marriage records list her by her maiden name, Baldini, and make no reference to an earlier marriage. The absence of such a notation implies that she was *nubile,* or unmarried.

The couple lived first at Via Sorgente 10 in Piedimonte d'Alife. During this time, there were no recorded births to the Carusos. Not long after their marriage, they moved to nearby Naples and settled in Via Largo Cappella Pontenuovo 59. Their first child, a son named Pasquale, was born there on 7 January 1869. The couple soon moved to Via San Giovanniello 7, and a second son, Antonio, followed two years later on 6 January 1871. The third child, Enrico—or Errico—was born at 3 a.m. on 25 February 1873.

The briefest reflection upon this chronology renders the tale about seventeen previous children a biological impossibility. Anna Caruso carried three children to full term during the six and a half years between her marriage to Marcellino in August 1866 and the birth of Enrico in February 1873. Even if she had had miscarriages or given birth prematurely, seventeen prior pregnancies are an impossibility. In the highly unlikely event that Anna had been married before, it is most improbable that she had had fifteen additional pregnancies by the time she married Marcellino at the age of twenty-eight.

Errico was baptized on 26 February 1873 at the Church of San Giovanni e Paolo, next door to the house where he was born. On March 3, Marcellino registered the baby boy as Errico at the City Hall of Naples. Because the law required that a child be registered within five days of birth, Marcellino gave the baby's birthdate as February 27 in order to avoid a fine. To this day, generally reliable reference sources give different birthdates or hedgingly state that Caruso was born either on the 25th or the 27th.[4] The entry in the City Hall register was signed by Vice Mayor Alfonso Acciardi and witnessed by Salvatore and Raffaele Morra of Via San Giovanniello 110.

It should be noted that February 1873 was a good month for singers. Dame Clara Butt was born on February 1, as was Fedor Chaliapin (whose birthdate is usually given as February 13 according to the old Russian calendar). For opera, 1873 was altogether a vintage year: Herbert Witherspoon was born on July 21, Leo Slezak on August 18, and Rosa Olitzka on September 6, to mention only the best known of more than a dozen singers born in that year.

Both of Enrico's older brothers were living when he was born. But four months later, tragedy struck, and two-year-old Antonio died on 5 July 1873. Not long afterward, Anna Caruso became pregnant again, and on 9 June 1874 she delivered another boy, Giacomo. He was baptized on the 11th and registered at City Hall on the 12th. The next child, Giovanni Giuseppe, born on 6 January 1876, was destined to live to adulthood and became the only Caruso of his generation to reach old age. He was baptized on the 7th and registered at City Hall on the 8th. His birth was followed by not one but two tragedies: Pasquale, born seven years before Giovanni almost to the day, died on 19 January 1876, and two-year-old Giacomo died on October 23 in the same year.

Yet another boy, Francesco, followed a year later, on 15 December 1877; he lived only one year and two days, dying on 17 December 1878. After him came Anna Caruso's seventh and last child and the only girl, Assunta, born on 13 August 1881. It seems that Anna Caruso did not possess a strong constitution and was greatly weakened by the seven pregnancies. The great sorrow of losing her children, one after another, wore her down emotionally. For the remaining years of her life she suffered poor health.

The modern reader may wonder what caused the high mortality rate among Caruso's siblings. They probably died of "Neapolitan fever," the collective name for typhus, typhoid, cholera, and dysentery.

Naples in those days was a filthy city without adequate sanitation. The poorest part of the populace lived in the *bassi,* the ground floors of buildings designed for warehousing, without indoor toilets, running water, or windows. Doors opening directly onto the street gave the only ventilation and were shut tight at night.

Families lived in these large rooms together with chickens and a goat or two. The livestock could not be left outside at night for fear of being stolen, and they were essential to survival. The chickens laid eggs, and the goats gave milk and occasionally a kid to be roasted for a holiday.

In the mornings, the woman of the house swept out the animal droppings and emptied the chamber pots into the street gutter. The refuse was washed away by the ever-flowing water of the street fountains or collected by the *spazzini,* the street sweepers, who dumped the contents of their carts into the waters of the port at the end of their rounds.

Cooking was done on charcoal burners set out on the sidewalk. Women cleaning house shook out dust cloths and rugs from windows on the upper floors, and debris drifted into the open pots below.

Throughout the city, the spaghetti vendor pushed his cart and charcoal burner, carrying precooked spaghetti and a container of sauce. The vendor rewarmed a portion of spaghetti in boiling water and served it on a piece of yellow corn paper, asking if the customer wanted it *co' sbruffo, o senza sbruffo,* with or without a squirt. If the buyer chose *co' sbruffo,* the vendor would take a ladleful of sauce, suck it into his mouth, and with a powerful blow spray it over the spaghetti.

The itinerant barber also contributed to the spread of disease. If his customer was old and wizened, the barber took a marble egg out of his pocket and popped it into the man's mouth to smooth out his wrinkles for an easy shave. The job completed, he removed the marble and returned it to his pocket to await the next customer.

Seafood peddlers hawked their wares with a scale slung over their shoulders and rattan trays or baskets balanced on their heads. To keep the seafood fresh, the peddlers stored their baskets dangling from a rope in the contaminated water of the port.

Herds of cows, water buffalo (*bufali*), goats, and sheep were driven through the streets by *butteri*. A housewife who needed milk called from her window and then lowered a small bucket on a string, stipulating a specific cow, sheep, or goat from the herd. The herdsman then milked the designated animal, not bothering to cleanse the udder or to rinse his own hands.

Doctors seldom washed their hands so transmitted disease from patient to patient. Hygiene, per se, did not come to Naples until the late 1920s. Toilet paper did not exist. Many street corners were equipped with *orinatoios*, with open holes at the bottom and no flowing water. The stench from these open-air latrines was unbelievable.

The streets were the playground of the *scugnizzi,* the barefoot urchins who roamed the city, as was the filthy water of the port, where they dove for coins alongside the ships that spewed their refuse into the bay. Diving in loincloths, the *scugnizzi* popped the coins into their mouths for safekeeping as they plunged again and again into the polluted water.

Is it any wonder that the people of the city died of Neapolitan fever?

The Carusos did not live in a *bassi;* their apartment was on the second floor of a two-story house on Via San Giovanniello. When Enrico was six, they moved to Via San Cosmo e Damiano 54, and two years later, to a house in Via Sant'Anna alle Paludi owned by the factory of Francesco Meuricoffre, Marcellino Caruso's employer. Marcellino was a mechanic and good at his trade. According to Key, Marcellino was promoted to the position of plant superintendent around 1881, and it is likely that the use of the house was a perquisite of his position. "My parents were not uncomfortably poor," said Caruso, trying to set the record straight in a 1920 interview for the *Sunday Express.* Although there was not enough money for fancy clothes or other niceties of life, Marcellino was a good provider. He always earned enough to put food on the table and take care of the needs of his family. He is said to have had an immense capacity for wine and often ended his day pleasantly "high." Supposedly, on one occasion, rather than pay duty on the wine he was bringing into the city, he drank the entire contents of a cask.

Marcellino was a simple man with simple aspirations. His vision for his children did not extend beyond his own limited horizon; he wanted his sons to follow in his footsteps and become mechanics. But young Enrico had different ambitions. Like most Neapolitan boys, in his younger years he dreamed of becoming a sailor. He hung around the docks with his chums or swam for hours in the Bay of Naples. At home he sang constantly, and as the Carusos lived next door to the Santa Anna Church, the organist often heard him. This older musician must have been impressed, for one day when he developed a throat problem, he sent for the boy and asked him to sing in his place. Enrico jumped at the opportunity. He received ten *centesimi* (about two cents) for singing in the Sunday service, the first money he ever earned with his fine contralto voice. It is a curiosity of nature that boy sopranos grow up to be basses, while contraltos become tenors.

"I had arrived at the age of ten before any thought was taken of my education," Caruso was quoted as saying (*The Reader,* 22 June 1907). "Of course, I knew the little things that my mother had taught me— my alphabet, and how to read the stories in a big red and blue picture book that had been presented to me on an eventful birthday." One night after he had been sent to bed early, he overheard his parents discussing his future. "My father was for apprenticing me to a mechanical engineer that he knew; but my mother insisted that I was too young to apprentice, and that it was wrong that I should have no education." The discussion ended with Enrico being sent to the *Scuola sociale e serale.* "My mother was very much pleased," he recalled.

Father Giuseppe Bronzetti's school was like many other private day schools of the period. It gave the boys a rudimentary education together with training in oratorio and choral singing, which was the principal objective of the school. The regimentation of school did not appeal to Enrico, who, according to his own admission, broke most of the school rules and lived in constant disgrace. "I was a sad trial to my parents," he recalled. "I was very noisy and lively. I sang constantly and my voice then was very piercing."[5] "I remember well how Father would pound in the mornings on the bathroom door and shout to me to stop making so much noise. Still, I continued to exercise my voice."[6]

By the age of eleven, he had developed a great love for singing. It came naturally to him and was the main source of pleasure in his life. Bronzetti's choir was often hired to perform in churches throughout the city for religious services, weddings, and other social occasions. In a short time, Enrico became the principal—and paid—soloist of the choir. Small as these first fees were, he was proud to be earning money with his voice.

To augment the musical education he received at the Bronzetti school, Enrico was sent in the evenings to study with Amelia Tibaldi Niola, a lady of considerable culture and a fine musician. She was the sister of Dr. Raffaele Niola, the family physician who, according to family lore, had delivered most—or all—of Anna Caruso's children. Miss Niola taught Enrico the fundamentals of music, *solfeggio,* piano, and correct Italian pronunciation. She abhorred the Neapolitan dialect and was determined to purify the boy's language and teach him true Italian. One evening he arrived for his lesson and absent-mindedly answered her first question in Neapolitan. "With a word of rebuke she struck me with the flat of her hand across the face, a blow so vigorous that it made my ears ring; but the resentment it aroused in me stung far more than the physical hurt I received. I remember standing there, my hand half-covering my cheek, staring at her in amazement. We went on with the lesson, and at length I went home."[7]

The boy felt humiliated and never returned. Instead, he packed his books and left the house nightly to play with his comrades in the railway yards until the lessons should have ended. After a fortnight, Marcellino happened to run into Dr. Niola, who asked why his son had discontinued his lessons.

Enrico well remembered the outcome of this chance meeting. As he later recalled: "Father did not rule my younger brother Giovanni and me with the stern hand attributed to him. We had our differences; most fathers and sons have them. I do not recall having been spanked, however, until I was about thirteen. I deserved to be."[8]

Apparently, this was not the only time Enrico suffered indignities at the hand of Miss Niola. When he recalled the incident in a letter to Dr. Niola in 1920, he received a long note from his former teacher. "You remember, in the letter you wrote my brother, the slap in your face," she wrote, "but you seem to have forgotten the strokes on your hand which I gave you with the ruler when you did not know your Gracamp *solfeggi.* Do you remember my cries of remonstrance over your veiled contraltino tones—veiled because you used to go serenading all night long?"[9]

In spite of the brevity of her tutelage, Miss Niola managed to teach Enrico a great deal about the fundamentals of music and instill in him the pleasure of being a performer rather than a listener. In 1920, recalling the pleasure singing had given him in his youth, Caruso readily acknowledged the value of Miss Niola's instruction:

> I had a contralto, not a soprano, voice, but I do not recall that it was regarded as exceptional. There was, however, the desire to sing and an indescribable enjoyment attending the singing itself. I had had no education in music beyond that given me by *Signorina* Niola during the brief time I benefited by her instruction, still there was very strong within me the musical instinct, a natural feeling for what was in good taste.[10]

Enrico's father continued to oppose his wasting so much time on music rather than devoting his energies to learning a trade and earning some money. Singing was fine in church or at home, but one had to work to earn a living. The abrupt end of Enrico's studies with Miss Niola provided a convenient excuse to take the boy out of school. In a series of interviews given in 1920 to Pierre Key, Caruso recalled that it was around his thirteenth year when he became an apprentice at the mechanical plant of Salvatore De Luca. His supervisor soon realized the boy's talent for drawing and made him a draftsman, paying him very little for exploiting this valuable skill. Caruso worked diligently, but in spite of his usefulness, he received no raises; he claimed to have received only four cents for a ten-hour workday. He discussed the matter with his father, and Marcellino suggested that he leave De Luca's plant and look for work elsewhere. His next job was at the factory of Giuseppe Palmieri. Everything mechanical fascinated him, and he was a quick study, although his wages did not reflect his abilities. The elder Caruso must have found his son a good enough mechanic by then to suggest that he join Meuricoffre. Enrico soon became so skilled that when his father fell briefly ill, the boy was able to perform his duties in his stead.

(It must be parenthetically noted that accounts of the sequence of events in Caruso's teen-age years are often contradictory. This is due to the numerous interviews the singer gave over the years to careless reporters, and to biographers who continually embroidered the stories they borrowed from various sources, including one another. The chronology here relies on the oral tradition preserved in the Caruso family and on published sources believed to be correct.)

In contrast to Marcellino, Anna encouraged her son's musical ambitions. It is said that she predicted a great future for him; but young Enrico needed little encouragement, for he continued to sing for his own enjoyment. The pianist Schirardi and Maestro De Lutio taught him his first operatic arias, and at age fourteen at the Bronzetti school, he participated in a comic opera composed by his teachers: Maestro Alessandro Fasanaro wrote the words, and Professor Alfredo Campanelli composed the music. The work carried the unusual title *I briganti nel giardino di Don Raffaele*. Enrico played the comic role of Don Tommaso, the janitor, while the chief of the brigands was acted by a very serious boy, Giuseppe Villani. Recalling the performance thirty-three years later, Caruso remarked that Villani was picked for the part because of his serious face and manner, while he, "the fun-making Caruso, was considered the best one for the timid janitor, Don Raffaele." He found it ironic that Villani became one of the most celebrated comedians in Italy, while he, "the light-hearted boy," ended up performing serious and tragic roles. He was so pleased with the performance that he kept the score and libretto, which were still in his music library at the time of his death.

On 31 May 1888, the young Caruso was engaged to sing in a service at the Church of San Severino. His mother was gravely ill, and he was reluctant to leave her bedside; but he went as planned. During the service, Anna Caruso died. It was a tremendous loss, for Enrico had a wonderful relationship with his mother, whom he adored and later described in English as "a pal."[11] He remembered: "My mother always believed in me. She called me '*tesor della famiglia*.' Yes. The 'treasure of the family.' When I am nervous onstage, for instance, when I am to sing a part for the first time and I feel my courage oozing out of the tips of my fingers, I think of my mother. She has been dead this many a year. But I think of her. Then the courage comes back to me, and I know I shall not fail."[12]

Biographers have claimed that Caruso only continued at his job as a mechanic to please his mother, and that after her death he gave it up to pursue a singing career. When he told his father of his intentions, the story goes, Marcellino predicted that he would starve as a singer. The son persisted, they had a fight, and Enrico left home and "became a wanderer." Caruso himself corrected this bit of fiction in one of his interviews with Key in 1920: "On the contrary, I did not set out from the family door until I was called to arms; I was twenty years old."[13] But he admitted: "Oh, my father did not encourage me to go on the stage. He wished me to become a mechanic like himself. Yet though he quarrelled with me when I accepted my first engagement, he was very much interested in my performances."[14]

ANNA CARUSO was the unifying force of the family more than any of them had realized. After she died, Marcellino was unable to handle the household chores and cope with his three children; he needed a woman in the house. In the fall of 1888, he was sent to Aversa to install some machinery Baron Ricciardi had bought from Meuricoffre. He found lodging in the house of Maria Castaldi, a widow. They had a great deal in common and were immediately drawn to each other. On 18 November 1888, just a few weeks after they met, they married. Although Maria Castaldi was forty-one, there is no record of her having had any children, which may explain why she was so happy to receive a readymade family in the Caruso brood. She was patient and understanding, and the children soon accepted their new mother. In a short time, Enrico grew to love her very much, and the affection was mutual; but Giovanni was forever at odds with her. This quarrelsome relationship carried into his adult years.

Initially, Enrico was so aggrieved by the loss of his mother that he could not concentrate on his work and was unable to sing. But "there came the day when I recalled how much joy my church singing gave Mother, so I returned to the choir loft. It was not a great while thereafter that I found my voice changing."[15] He was told to stop singing altogether until his voice had changed. After a brief time of transition, he was thrilled to discover that he was a tenor. Or was he? "When I reached the age of eighteen I was faced with the problem as to whether I was a tenor or a baritone," he was quoted as saying (*London Opinion,* 23 April 1910). It took some time for his voice to settle, but he never lost the baritonal timbre. Clearly, the dark tone and solid lower register were inborn, not acquired.

He began to dream of a singing career, however modest. "If anything, I was inclined to underestimate my vocal endowments,"[16] he recalled in a talk with Key. His voice was small but pleasing, and he gradually became a sought-after church soloist, eventually earning the princely sum of ten lire (about two dollars) for a service. To augment his income, he also sang in cafés around Naples, as much for the applause as for the tips he received. One Saturday night, a gentleman approached him and told him he was singing incorrectly; further, he offered to take him to his brother, who was a voice teacher. In spite of his lack of experience, Caruso had the sensibility to realize after eleven lessons that the teacher's methods were not suitable for him. Rather than ruining his voice, he discontinued the lessons, and the much-needed study was postponed.

In the summer of 1891, a pianist friend suggested that they could

make some money on the *rotonda* of the café Risorgimento, an establishment on the Bay of Naples. Each pier had a round platform, a
rotonda, where a band and a singer could perform. Here Caruso sang
popular Neapolitan songs to his friend's accompaniment. One of the
vacationers at the seaside café was impressed by his singing and struck
up a conversation with him. The young man was Eduardo Missiano,
himself a baritone, and wanted to know whether Caruso was studying
with anyone. Caruso replied that to his regret he could not afford a
teacher. Missiano came from a wealthy family and scarcely understood the restraints of poverty. He waved the matter of money aside
and insisted on taking Caruso to his own voice teacher, Guglielmo
Vergine. The audition was short and discouraging. After listening to
the light, thin Caruso voice, the Maestro passed his judgment: The
voice was "too small and sounded like the wind whistling through the
windows."[17]

Caruso recalled his new friend's reaction. "I think you are mistaken," insisted Missiano. "Try his voice again at some other time."
Reluctantly, very reluctantly, Vergine at last consented. "Very well,
come back in eight days."[18]

After the second trial, Vergine agreed to accept Caruso as a pupil.
But he issued a warning that betrayed his own doubts: "Don't expect
too much of yourself."[19]

Because Caruso was unable to pay, the Maestro drew up a contract
specifying that the young man was to pay him 25 percent of his
earnings for "five years of actual singing." Inexperienced in such matters and oblivious to the ambiguity of the phrasing, Caruso signed the
document. In return he was allowed to sit in the class, more or less
ignored, and watch the other students perform.

"There were many other pupils, many other voices stronger than
mine," he remembered. The Maestro made an especially great fuss
over a strong-voiced tenor named Punzo for whom he predicted a
bright career. Envious of Punzo, Caruso tried to force his thin little
voice to make it sound more powerful; but it did not feel right in his
throat, and he soon stopped trying.

> Vergine did not think much of my chances, but he taught
> me with skill. It was he who impressed, time and again, the
> necessity of singing as nature intended, and—I remember—he
> constantly warned: "Don't let the public know that you
> work." So I went slowly. I never forced the voice. I let it come
> in the way I believed nature wished, which was, of course, the

wise thing; but it did not tend to develop any power to the tone. I was, in my first months in the Vergine studio, still the tenor with the voice of the whistling wind.[20]

For a long time, the Maestro showed little interest in his new student. Sustained by Missiano's encouragement, friendship, and conviction that he had an exceptional voice and a great future, Caruso continued to attend the classes. He learned what he could, vocalized at home according to Vergine's instructions, and attended local opera performances to observe the great singers of the day. He later claimed that he "was often hungry but never unhappy," and that must accurately sum up those difficult years. He continued his work at the Meuricoffre factory, although it interested him less and less, supplementing his meager wages with minor singing engagements at churches, weddings, and social affairs at private homes. According to the custom of the day, he also rented out his voice to lovestruck Romeos who wished to serenade their ladies. In those days, distinguished visitors, deputations, and cabinet ministers were also serenaded. His most noteworthy engagement was at the fifteen-day centenary celebration of the Virgin of Cotrone, when he sang in honor of the Prince of Wales, the future Edward VII, who had come to Cotrone aboard the royal yacht. Years later Caruso sang for him again—at Windsor Castle.

"Quite often, of nights, I would go serenading; and very often, also, I sang with Missiano, who had a fine baritone voice. He was the one loyal believer in my future: His confidence never faltered. With a word, and friendly hand on my back, he repeatedly predicted the fine career."[21]

This was Caruso's routine between the ages of seventeen and twenty, when he was drafted into the army. After eight miserable days at the induction center in Rome, he was assigned to the Thirteenth Artillery Regiment at Rieti. Determined to keep up his vocal exercises, he sang in the large drill hall every afternoon during the free time after daily training. The surprising events that followed were often retold by Caruso with complete consistency as to detail.

One day the commanding officer, Major Giuseppe Nagliati, summoned the young recruit and curtly ordered him to stop his afternoon singing because it bothered him as he worked. But a few days later, the major commanded the recruit to meet him at a local café and took him to the house of a friend, Baron Costa, who was a great music lover. The baron turned out to be a fine musician and a good pianist and invited the young singer to practice at his home during off-duty hours. His host accompanied him on the piano, corrected his mistakes, and, according to Caruso, taught him the role of Turiddu from *Cavalleria rusticana* in five days. Considering that the entire role consists of four arias and a duet, the accomplishment is entirely credible.

Some biographers conjectured that the baron praised the abilities of the singing soldier to Major Nagliati, and this assumption was probably correct. Twenty days after Caruso began visiting Baron Costa, the major again summoned the recruit to his office.

"You cannot be a soldier and a singer too," he said. "I have arranged for your brother Giovanni to come at once and take your place."[22]

Giovanni arrived the following day to assume his brother's military obligations and thus free Enrico to pursue his career. He was deeply grateful to the major, but "he would not allow me to thank him," Caruso recalled. "Never afterward did I see Major Nagliati, though I have tried hard to find him. I owed him so much, perhaps everything, that I wished to do something to let him understand. It may be, I do not know, that but for the major I might never had been able to sing if I had to do the three years' military duty."[23]

CARUSO was discharged after forty-five days in the service and arrived home the night before Easter Sunday, 1894. He resumed his studies with Vergine and continued to sing in church, at soirées, and as a serenader. He even performed the role of Turiddu in a staging of *Cavalleria rusticana* by a local amateur group. Appropriately for the story line, his costume for the role was his own, briefly used army uniform.

The first mention of Caruso's name in print came in 1894 in the October 13th issue of *Fortunio,* a Neapolitan magazine reporting on the theatrical and musical life of the city.[24] It mentioned that "the tenor Enrico Caruso" appeared in a concert at the Teatro Excelsior, of the Rione Vomero in Naples. This was not a solo recital: Caruso shared the program with a baritone, F. M. Bonini; two other singers, Amalia and Fanny Zamparelli; and the violinist Corrado.

It seems that by this time Maestro Vergine had begun to appreciate Caruso and felt he was ready to be tested. Vergine may also have wished to see some cash flowing in from his contract. In any case, he began to use his influence to get engagements for the tenor he so underestimated at the outset. Nicola Daspuro was in the process of organizing a season at the Teatro Mercadante in Naples, and Vergine asked the impresario to listen to his pupil who had, he said, "a voice of exceptional beauty and a warm and velvety sweetness."[25] The season was fully cast, but Vergine insisted that Daspuro hear the tenor. The impresario gave in, and Caruso auditioned for him, accompanied by Vergine himself. The young man made a good impression, so Daspuro promised to engage him during the next Carnival season, which he faithfully did. After the tenor auditioned even more successfully before the conductor Giovanni Zuccani, they all agreed that Caruso should make his debut in *Mignon*. When the young singer arrived at the first piano rehearsal, he seemed a different man. Finding himself surrounded by experienced artists "nearly paralyzed his mind and throat," Daspuro wrote in his memoirs.

> He did not remember the words, he missed his cues, sang off pitch, gazed at Zuccani with a stupefied stare. In short, [it was] a real disaster. Vergine was deathly pale and his eyes were full of tears. The good Maestro Zuccani, in his turn, for a good while was very patient: He tried to guide him right and calm him ten times. But all was in vain. Caruso was in a state of total amnesia. In the end Zuccani could do no more, rose from the piano and said to Vergine:
> "Tell him yourself, Maestro, would it be possible to bring him into the performance in such a state of nerves?"
> Vergine lowered his head and did not reply.
> And then, Maestro and pupil left; they looked like two drunks![26]

Soon after this disheartening experience came an opportunity for another operatic engagement. Because his fee was to be 75 lire for four performances, Caruso regarded the première as his official debut. It seems that Domenico Morelli, a wealthy young man, had composed an opera and wanted to have it performed for a private audience. The contrabass player who used to accompany Caruso on his musical outings suggested that he audition for the composer. Morelli liked his voice and offered to sign him on. Acting upon Vergine's advice, Caruso accepted the part and sang the tenor lead in *L'Amico Francesco*. As he observed later, at the age of twenty-one[27] he made his debut playing a man of fifty, singing opposite a sixty-year-old baritone in the role of his young adopted son. The première took place on 15 March 1895 at the Teatro Nuovo in Naples. Caruso remembered the sequence of events as follows:

The general rehearsal went nicely, but the music of my part was very strong [demanding], and everyone was afraid that I would not be able to do the four performances, one after the other. But the first one went all right—great success. The second performance was the same. During the third one, just following the first act, a lawyer came to my dressing room, and said:

"I think you have a good voice, and I would like to engage you for the Quaresima [Lenten season] in Caserta; here is my Maestro, talk with him."

Immediately the contract was made, which gave me much encouragement and helped make that third and then the fourth performance of the opera successes.[28]

Historians report that the opera was a failure and that only two of the scheduled four performances took place. It is possible that across the distance of twenty-six years, Caruso remembered the events incorrectly, perhaps because the composer had paid him the stipulated fee in full. But it is a fact that he sang in Caserta during the Lenten season of 1895. Thus, shortly after his twenty-second birthday, his career as a professional opera singer began in earnest. Because he had no repertory, he had to learn each new role in record time. That he was able to do so is a testimony not only to his innate musicality and intelligence, but also to the quality of the training he received in his boyhood from Father Bronzetti and his faculty. There is no record to show who helped him with his musical homework during this period, whether it was a friendly musician from the orchestra, a colleague, a company *repetiteur,* or Vergine himself. It is likely that he received help from all these sources, always spurred forward by his own drive and by the simple, pressing economic necessity to succeed.

At Caserta he sang Turiddu and appeared in the title role of *Faust* and in *Camoens* by Musone. After Caserta, he sang Faust, the Duke of Mantua in *Rigoletto,* and Alfredo in *La Traviata* at the Teatro Bellini in his home town. Marcellino went to see his son perform, and when the box office refused him a free ticket, he paid for one. "*Va bene,*" said he, "I will pay for my seat." Caruso recalled: "I was much surprised that night to see him in the lobby when I got to the theater. 'What are you doing here, Papa?' I said. 'Oh, I have bought a ticket,' he replied. 'So sing in tune tonight, my son, or—I shall hiss.' " [29]

Despite his awkwardness onstage, the qualities of his voice made him a success with the public, if not with the critics. The extent of his popular success can be measured by the fact that a young cellist-turned-impresario, Adolfo Bracale, traveled to Naples to hear him purely on the enthusiastic recommendation of a violinist friend who had heard Caruso sing. After a brief audition, Bracale engaged him for a season at the Ezbekieh Gardens in Cairo, Egypt. In Cairo, Caruso added Edgardo in *Lucia di Lammermoor,* Enzo Grimaldo in *La Gioconda,* and Des Grieux in Puccini's *Manon Lescaut* to his repertory. The singers had only five days to learn their roles in the Puccini opera, which necessitated a good bit of improvisation. Caruso ended the ragged performance by smuggling his score onstage and propping it against the back of soprano Elena Bianchini-Cappelli. The thus immobilized Manon, unable to indulge in theatrical gestures, was obliged to expire most undramatically.

Egypt was a success and was followed by a three-month engagement at the Teatro Mercadante in Naples, where Caruso added the role of Tebaldo in Bellini's *I Capuleti ed i Montecchi* to his growing repertory. A brief excursion to Caserta to appear as Faust was followed by an engagement in Trapani, Sicily, which was to become notorious as the only time Caruso appeared drunk onstage. The often retold story deserves little mention here, since the degrading incident was not the singer's fault. On the day of his local debut, Caruso dined with his host, a baritone, and drank his usual two tumblers of dinner wine. He was accustomed to the light table wines of Naples, but the Sicilian wine was heavy and intoxicating. To his consternation and the baritone's extreme alarm, he became quite drunk. In spite of some home medications—a grog!—and a few hours' sleep, he was still tipsy when he was pushed onstage in the garb of Edgardo in *Lucia di Lammermoor.* Because of his condition, the performance began an hour late, and the audience was in a hostile mood. Caruso had no problem with the music but had trouble remembering his words. When he came to the line "*sorte della Scozia,*" he sang "*volpe della Scozia*" (the "fox" instead of the "future" of Scotland), and all hell broke loose. For once, it was a drawback to be singing in the language of the audience.

"An Italian audience knows its opera, the words as well as the music," he said, retelling the incident. "So there was an immediate disputing of what I had sung, in an unmistakable manner. It was a small riot, nor could it be quelled when the curtain had been rung down, and the impresario went before it to explain (I believe he said I was suffering from a sea voyage). There was no more for me that night. I went home and to bed, while the opera progressed without a tenor."[30] How far it progressed Caruso did not mention, but the confrontation scene of the "Sextet" and the closing fifteen minutes when Edgardo sings his farewell and stabs himself to death must have lacked a certain luster without a tenor.

The next day Caruso was "protested" by the Municipal Council of Trapani, which, in the operatic parlance of the day, meant he was "dismissed." But the following night, the audience refused to listen to his replacement, demanding the return of the "Fox of Scotland." Caruso did return and had the satisfaction of finishing his engagement, singing in *Cavalleria rusticana, La Sonnambula,* and *Malia* by Frontini.

He next appeared in Marsala as the Duke and as Turiddu; then he returned to Naples, where he was engaged by Gaetano Scognamiglio at the Teatro Bellini. Here his new role was the tenor lead in *Mariedda* by Bucceri. He sang some of the performances under the baton of the impresario himself. Scognamiglio was a fine musician who years later became a member of the Metropolitan Opera Orchestra. (He should not be confused with Caruso's Neapolitan quasi-secretary of later years, Errico Mario Scognamillo [1871–1921], who is buried beside the Caruso chapel in the Del Pianto Cemetery in Naples in a marble sarcophagus identical to Caruso's.)

Contemporary reports agree that Caruso's voice at this time was light, lyric, and short: He would often crack on the high notes. Yet when the impresario Visciani engaged him for Salerno, the conductor Vincenzo Lombardi wanted him to sing Arturo in *I Puritani,* a role with a stratospheric *tessitura.* In addition to high D's and D-flats, there is a written F above high C which the legendary Rubini sang at the world première in 1835. Omitting the high F (as probably all tenors since Rubini have done in staged performances) and taking lower options for the other high notes, Caruso still found the role too high. He said as much to Lombardi, but the conductor assured him that he would teach him how to sing properly and take the troublesome high notes.

"I began to study with Lombardi," he told Key, "yet it was not quite the same kind of study I had previously known; I mean it wasn't the same sort of instruction he gave. It seemed to be advice and demonstration . . . which gave me the conviction that I could finally learn to sing the *Puritani* with all the top notes."[31]

With Lombardi's coaching, Caruso performed well. According to Key, Fernando de Lucia, the leading tenor of the day, made a special trip to hear the young man in *I Puritani* and was lavish with his praise. Caruso's success was such that he was invited to make his debut at La Scala in Milan in Franchetti's new opera *Il Signor di Pourceaugnac.*

Visciani refused to release him from his contract, however, and he was obliged to turn down the offer.

Once he fulfilled his commitments to Visciani, he was immediately engaged, still in Salerno, by the impresario Giuseppe Grassi. He sang twenty performances of five operas, performing his first Canio in *Pagliacci* in October 1896, when he stepped in for an ailing Pagani in mid-performance. Caruso's new roles in Salerno included Fernando in *La Favorita,* Don José in *Carmen,* and the tenor part in a short work by Carlo Sebastiani entitled *A San Francisco*. He had a great deal of trouble with the "Flower Song" in *Carmen,* his voice cracking night after night on the high B-flat. Obviously, he needed more work with Lombardi. Vergine must have helped him too; he was often in attendance, keeping an eye on the young performer and collecting the 25 percent of earnings that was due him.

The Salerno season was memorable for Caruso. He was in town from June through November, long enough to become involved in a love affair with Giuseppina Grassi, the daughter of his impresario. By the season's end, they were engaged.

The next stop was again the Teatro Mercadante in Naples, where Caruso sang Alfredo in *La Traviata,* Enzo Grimaldo in *La Gioconda,* and Fernando in *La Favorita*. During the Carnival season of 1897, he sang Enzo again. In addition, he appeared in two new operas, *Un Dramma in vendemmia* by Vincenzo Fornari, and *Celeste* by D. Lamonica and G. Biondi. During this engagement, he enjoyed critical as well as popular success, and the good reviews were unanimous. *Il Mattino* of 13–14 January 1897 praised his Enzo Grimaldo, reporting that he had to encore "Cielo e mar." The reviewer observed that "Caruso proceeds with giant steps on the road to a happy future" and commended his fresh voice and beautiful timbre and the spontaneity of his delivery. On 3 February 1897, the same paper complimented his contribution to Fornari's *Un Dramma in vendemmia,* an opera remembered today solely because Caruso created the role of Beppe. The reviewer observed that Caruso's maestro, *Signor* Vergine, had reason to be pleased with his pupil's success.

Indeed, Vergine had every reason to be pleased. As Caruso recounted in a biographical sketch entitled "The Story of My Life" (*The Reader,* 22 June 1907):

> On all pay-days my Shylock was on hand to receive his percentage. The interest of the manager was eventually aroused, and I showed him my contract.

"Why," he said, "you will have to work for this skinflint for
the rest of your life. Your contract reads so that you will have
to sing for him five years of actual singing. Days that you earn
nothing do not count."

Finally I decided to see a lawyer. He advised me to stop
payment, which I did. Shylock took the case to court, and
luckily for me the courts were as wise as Portia. I was
instructed to pay twenty thousand francs besides what I had
paid, and that finished him.

The term "five years of actual singing" was the catch in Vergine's
contract. In other words, the Maestro was to receive a percentage until
all Caruso's performance time, added together, equaled five years! The
case was resolved in Caruso's favor a few years and several court
hearings later.

While Caruso was gathering laurels at the Teatro Mercadante from
December 1896 through March 1897, another young singer was
enjoying a great success at the more prestigious Teatro San Carlo: the
soprano Ada Giachetti-Botti. Whether the two met face to face during
this time in Naples has not been recorded. Probably they did not, but
they must have heard about each other through the operatic grapevine and accounts in the press. They could have attended each other's
performances on their nights off. But Caruso's renown was not great
enough to arouse a prima donna's curiosity, so it is much more likely
that the tenor went to the San Carlo to see and to learn, while the
soprano tended to her own thriving affairs.

From Naples, Caruso returned to Salerno for the second and last
time to sing again under the management of Grassi. He saw a great
deal of Giuseppina, but since his last visit he must have discovered that
one can enjoy female companionship more abundantly without the
restricting bonds of holy matrimony. He had changed his mind about
marriage and broke off the engagement. This was the first time he got
cold feet on his way to the altar, but certainly not the last; in later life
he made almost a habit of it. The father of the bride, who had already
made preparations for the wedding, reacted predictably to this turn of
events, and Caruso was only too glad to bid farewell to Salerno.

The next was his first truly prestigious engagement: He was
invited to participate in the festive inaugural season of the Teatro
Massimo in Palermo, Sicily. As his artistic stock rose, so did his fees.
For singing a dozen *La Gioconda*s in forty-five days, he was to receive
2,750 lire. He obtained the engagement on the recommendation of

Maestro Leopoldo Mugnone, who had heard him sing the role of Enzo Grimaldo in Naples, and who was to conduct the *Gioconda*s in Palermo. Soon, however, Caruso was romantically involved with one of the ballerinas from the "Dance of the Hours"—a dancer in whom Mugnone also took an interest; thus he became the conductor's rival.[32] The fact that Mugnone's wife, mezzo-soprano Maria Paolicchi-Mugnone, was also a member of the company placed no restraints on the conduct of the Maestro. Apparently, his casual attitudes were shared by his wife. During a rehearsal, Mugnone heard Maria's coquettish giggle coming from one of the loges, where she was enjoying the company of several young men. He must have been familiar with that giggle, because he stopped the orchestra and in a loud, clear voice called out: *"Maria, non mi far tanto la puttana costassù!"* ("Maria, stop playing the whore up there!")

The ballerina's unconcealed preference for Caruso made Mugnone nasty. During rehearsals, he made the tenor's life miserable in every way, hoping that Caruso would reach a breaking point and quit the company. Mugnone underestimated the Carusian tenacity. As a final move, the conductor went to the impresario and said that Caruso was not good enough to sing at the theater in the festival season. But the impresario thought otherwise.

"Well, you recommended him and we must let him go on" was his firm reply.[33]

Caruso appeared as scheduled and sang so well in the general rehearsal (the Italian equivalent of an opening night) that the conductor himself rapped on the desk with his baton and shouted "Bravo!" The tenor excelled in all twelve performances of the opera, and by the time he was to leave for Naples in mid-June, he and the conductor were friends again. In fact, it was Mugnone who obtained Caruso's next engagement at Livorno, singing Alfredo in *La Traviata* opposite the soprano Ada Giachetti.

"Look here, rapscallion," Mugnone said to him, "you are going to sing with the most beautiful woman I have ever known. Be careful not to fall in love with her."[34]

By some coincidence, Mugnone had a photograph of Ada in his luggage when he made this remark. It was a picture Ada had given him as her benefactor, in all likelihood when the conductor passed through Naples during the Carnival season. Now he showed the picture to Caruso. The tenor agreed that the lady was very beautiful. As for not falling in love with her, he made no promises.

CHAPTER TWO

Ada Giachetti

MOST books about Enrico Caruso devote a negligible amount of space to the two women around whom the better part of his adult life revolved. These were the Giachetti sisters: Ada and Rina.

In the Caruso biographies, Ada is variously represented as a third-rate singer whom even Caruso's personal fame and influence could not propel into the limelight, or as an older woman and trollop in search of adventure. Rina Giachetti is usually dismissed with a couple of confused sentences conveying misinformation passed from one writer to the next. As a rule, the other members of the Giachetti family are not mentioned at all, although the Caruso story is inseparably intertwined with theirs. For in the private life of Enrico Caruso, one cast of characters was dominant: the Giachettis.

Guido Giachetti was born in 1851.[1] He was a state employee, an agent of the Department of the Treasury. His was a middle- or upper-middle-class family, which at one time had substantial real estate holdings. Guido owned farmland and a large old house outside Florence known as La Villa alle Panche. He married Giuseppina Guidalotti, by whom he had three children: Ada, Enrico, and Rina. All three were born at the Palazzo dello Strozzino on Via dei Serragli in Florence.

Very little is known about Enrico Giachetti, the middle child and only boy. Ironically, only the mysterious circumstances of his death have come down to us. It seems he went to Kenya as a young man. According to one of his comrades, who told this story to the family, one afternoon he returned to his tent for a siesta in keeping with Italian custom and to escape the heat of the mid-day African sun. Before he lay down on his cot, he placed his pistol on the camp table beside a siphon of seltzer water. The rays of the sun, magnified by the bottle, focused on the pistol, causing it to fire, and the bullet killed him instantly. Whether he truly suffered such a freak accident or was the victim of a homicide has never been established.

Ada was the oldest child. She was born at noon on 1 December 1874 and baptized Vittoria Matilde Ada Giachetti. According to all reports, she was a lovely child and a beautiful young woman. Rina described her as having luminous grey eyes and golden blonde hair that grew darker as she reached adulthood. She was vivacious, always exuberant, and, according to her sister and others who knew her, temperamental and prone to occasional hysteria.

The youngest child, Rina Emilia Luisa Giachetti, was born on 25 August 1880. She had thick, chestnut-colored hair and dark eyes and was just as beautiful as her older sister. Guido took great pride in his girls and was always pleased to be seen with them. Because of the six years' difference in their ages, Rina looked up to her older sister, and Ada assumed a protective attitude toward the younger girl. They were quite close when they were young and in their teen-age years, and apparently there was little competition between them. By the time Ada was fully grown and a married woman and mother, Rina was still a young girl.

As a treasury agent, Guido was sent on assignments around the country. His trips sometimes lasted for weeks, occasionally for months. On one of these temporary assignments, he rented an apartment and hired a housekeeper, Teresa Da Vela. As such things happen, proximity led to intimacy, and Teresa became pregnant. Their son was born in the fall of 1900, shortly after King Umberto I was assassinated on July 29. In memory of the late king, they called the baby Umberto. Because Guido was married but not to the child's mother, the baby was registered as Umberto Da Vela, and in place of the father's name, the birth certificate showed "n.n.," the abbreviation for the Latin *non noto*, "not known."

In countries where church and state are less inextricably intertwined than the Catholic church and the Italian state, a couple who realize that their marriage was a mistake can dissolve their union and begin new lives. With the divorce rate as high as it is today, it is almost impossible for most Westerners to identify with the mores and ethics of nineteenth-century Italy. Divorce simply did not exist there until 1970. Two persons bound by matrimony lived and died in that holy state, whether theirs was a happy union or an unbearable yoke. Because it was obviously absurd to force two incompatible people to spend their lives together, society, forced into hypocrisy by the church, tacitly accepted separations, affairs, and second families. Depending on the extent of the openness of an "arrangement" and the social standing of the individuals involved, such a liaison could attain a degree of respectability, so long as it was reasonably permanent.

Italian law drew a clear distinction between legitimate, illegitimate, and natural children. If a child was born in wedlock, he was legitimate. An illegitimate child was one born to parents married not to each other but, as often happened, to someone else. If only one of the parents was married, "n.n." was used on the birth certificate in place of his or her name. In addition to protecting the married parent from proof of adultery, this legal provision spared the child from being branded as illegitimate. By this legal twist, the baby became a "natural" child, provided that one parent recognized it as his or her own. Going a step further, the law acknowledged that the impaired legal status was not the child's fault and, as a protection, prohibited any research into the maternity or paternity if it endangered his legal standing as a natural—as opposed to illegitimate—child.

For many years, "n.n." was the progenitor of thousands of Italian children.

Giuseppina Giachetti must have known about her husband's transgression, but as a respectable and devoted wife was expected to do, she stayed with Guido. When she died on 11 June 1909, Guido, apparently a man of principles, married Teresa Da Vela. Their son became Umberto Da Vela–Giachetti and finally had a home with both his natural parents. Guido and Teresa lived in harmony until the end of his life in 1935.

Music must have played an important role in the Giachetti household. Both girls showed a musical inclination early in life, and the family encouraged musical interests. According to Rina, Ada's first singing and piano lessons came from their mother and grandmother, both of whom were very musical. Whether Giuseppina or her mother had formal musical training is not known. The fact that they did not

Exterior and interior
of the church in
Piedimonte d'Alife
(now Piedimonte
Matese) where
Caruso's parents,
Marcellino Caruso
and Anna Baldini,
were married in 1866.
Courtesy of Guido
d'Onofrio.

Left, Marcellino Caruso, drawn by Enrico Caruso in August 1905.
Above, Anna Baldini, Caruso's mother. Print from a pastel portrait.

Above, Maria Castaldi, Caruso's stepmother; *right,* Assunta Caruso, Caruso's sister. Enrico Caruso made both drawings in 1905.

Guido Giachetti, father of Ada and Rina.

Giuseppina Guidalotti, Guido's first wif
and the mother of Ada and Rina.
Photography G. Brogi.

Teresa Da Vela, Guido's second
wife and the mother of Umberto.

Three-year-old Ada Giachetti.

The house on Via dei Serragli
where Ada and Rina Giachetti
were born.

ENRICO CARUSO

An early postcard photograph of Enrico Caruso. Photography Miani.

Young Enrico Caruso drawn by Fortunino Matania, a Neapolitan artist who later achieved fame as an illustrator and painter.

Postcard photograph of Caruso sold in Buenos Aires during his seasons there.

Ada Giachetti
in Buenos Aires
in 1901.

Two photographs of Ada Giachetti probably taken at the studio of the painter Filippo Galante in Buenos Aires in 1901.

Fourteen-month-old Rodolfo "Fofò" Caruso in Milan, 1899.

Enrico Caruso in 1900. Courtesy of Adria Firestone.

Villa alle Panche ("Le
Panche") at Castello near
Florence, the estate Caruso
purchased in 1904.

Ada Giachetti at Le
Panche in 1904,
awaiting the birth of
Enrico, Jr.

Ada Giachetti with Enrico, Jr. ("Mimmi"), and Rodolfo ("Fofò") at Le Panche, ca. 1906.

Six-year-old Rodolfo Caruso in the uniform of the Collegio Cicognini. Photography Brogi.

Enrico, Jr., ca. 1908.

The young Caruso as Turiddu in Mascagni's *Cavalleria rusticana* (Caserta, 1895).
Collection, Alexander Eddy.

Caruso (*second from left*) with friends at Salsomaggiore. Titta Ruffo is standing at left in the back row. Baritone Eugenio Giraldoni is seated second from right. Courtesy of Dr. Ruffo Titta, Jr.

The same party on the steps of the Pensione Speranza in Salsomaggiore, with Caruso at center. The two "statues" on the pillars are baritones Giraldoni (*left*) and Ruffo (*right*). Courtesy of Dr. Ruffo Titta, Jr.

ruin the young girl's voice demonstrates that they had at least some competency. When Ada reached the student years, she enrolled in the *Istituto Musicale di Firenze,* where she became the pupil of Maestro Ceccherini,[2] the singing teacher of both Eva and Luisa Tetrazzini. Although she was a dramatic soprano, her technique was solid and her voice flexible enough to sing *coloratura.* She could easily cope with Leonora's *cabaletta* in *Il Trovatore* and Violetta's florid music in the first act of *La Traviata.* She was an excellent musician, a fine pianist, and a quick learner. The 31 March 1893 issue of the newspaper *Il Trovatore* reported that she substituted on short notice for an indisposed Alice Bianco, who was to sing the role of Serpina in *La Serva padrona* at the Philharmonic of Florence. Although the performance was a success, this role was notably absent from her repertoire in later years. Remarkably, she must have prepared it for a single performance.

One evening Ada and her mother visited the Philipson family in Florence. Another invited guest was the conductor Leopoldo Mugnone. Inevitably, the conversation turned to opera, singing, and the bright future the young woman hoped to have once she made her debut. Ada was invited to sing for the gathering, and Maestro Mugnone was sufficiently impressed by the impromptu audition to offer her then and there a stage debut under his direction. After a short discussion with her mother, Ada agreed. She spent the following month studying the role of Amelia in Verdi's *Un Ballo in maschera* with Mugnone.

When the opera went into rehearsal, word of the young singer began to spread in the community. While she sang Verdi inside the theater, Mugnone sang her praises outside, until all musical Florence anticipated a special performance. On 7 January 1894, the night of her debut, the Teatro della Pergola was filled to capacity. Everyone wanted to hear this exceptional debutante who at a young age could attempt such a difficult role. Naturally, the entire family was at the theater. Backstage, Guido wished his daughter well before the performance. He was proud, excited, a bundle of nerves, and could not understand why Ada was so calm. Decades later, Rina vividly recalled the exchange between father and daughter.

"Don't you feel nervous?" Guido asked Ada as he parted the curtain slightly to show her the full auditorium.

"It seems to me as if I were to sing in my own house," Ada replied.

Neither bravado nor the inexperience of youth lay behind her remark. She had been singing as long as she could remember, for her own enjoyment and for the pleasure of family and friends. She had

Pregiatissimo Signore,

R. TEATRO PAGLIANO

Domenica 7 Gennaio 1894, alle ore 8 pom.

PRIMA RAPPRESENTAZIONE STRAORDINARIA

dell' Opera in 4 atti del M.º VERDI (Proprietà G. Ricordi e C.)

UN BALLO IN MASCHERA

ESECUTORI:

ADA GIACHETTI
(AMELIA)

ADA BONNER   PAOLINA GOVONI
(OSCAR)   (ULRICA)

ANTONIO BAGGETTO   F.co BORTOLAMASI
(RICCARDO)   (RENATO)

LEOPOLDO CARNESECCHI   LUIGI MANZUOLI
(SILVANO)   (UN GIUDICE)

Maestro Concertatore e Direttore d'Orchestra

LEOPOLDO MUGNONE

Sostituto Direttore, ARTURO BOVI - Altro Maestro, TOMMASO BICCHIERAI
Istruttore del Coro e Suggeritore, L. BIANCHI - Direttore della Banda sul Palco, G. MARTINI
Ispettore di Palcoscenico, CLEMENTE GIACHETTI.
70 Professori d'Orchestra – 80 Coristi d'ambo i sessi – 24 Bandisti – 36 Comparse.
N. 16 Ballerine – Coreografo **Giovanni Oro**

Ingresso Lire **UNA** – Loggione Cent. **50**
Militari e Ragazzi pagano la metà.
Poltrone L. **5** — Posti distinti L. **2** (oltre l' ingresso)
PALCHI: Ordine I e II L. **20** – Ordine III L. **10** – Ordine IV L. **5**.

*La vendita dei Palchi, Poltrone e Posti distinti, si fa al Camerino del Teatro ed al
Negozio Piattellini in Croce Rossa.*

Martedì 9, QUARTA ed ULTIMA RAPPRESENTAZIONE *LA GIOCONDA*.

Mercoledì 10, Seconda Rappresentazione dell'Opera
Un Ballo in Maschera.

Quanto prima l' Opera in 2 atti del M.º P. A. TASCA **(Nuova per Firenze)**

A SANTA LUCIA.

Poster advertising Ada Giachetti's debut, in Florence. Courtesy of
Associazione Museo Enrico Caruso, Milan.

often sung arias, duets, and entire operatic scenes at the conservatory and had performed *La Serva padrona* the previous year. As far as she was concerned, the only difference between these performances and her impending debut was the larger audience, and that was a welcome change. Mugnone had coached her well, she knew the role, her voice was in excellent shape—why should she worry?

She had a spectacular success. The first-night audience loved her Amelia, and the local press echoed their approval. The 8 January 1894 *Gazzetta dei Teatri* carried this review by a certain "Federico":

> Verdi's old work has revealed to us an artist whom in my humble way I would strongly recommend to all the able *impresari*. I am referring to the debutante Ada Giachetti who faced the test and triumphed. Her warm, beautiful, secure voice will please everywhere. This lovely beginner received a most flattering baptism last night and was recalled a dozen times on stage. She delivered the substantial role of Amelia in an enviable manner even scenically.

After eighteen performances of *Un Ballo in maschera,* she took on the role of Marguerite—or rather, Margherita—in twelve performances of Berlioz's *La Dannazione di Faust,* again under the baton of Mugnone. Impressed by her musical talent, enthusiasm, and personal appeal, the conductor took a special liking to Ada. He enjoyed working with her and helped her to become established on the Italian operatic circuit. The performance of 11 April 1894 at the Teatro della Pergola went well, and the reviewer "Federico" of the *Gazzetta dei Teatri* praised her Margherita, together with the Mephistopheles of Mario Sammarco.

Her debut gave a definite direction to her life as an artist and coincided with another, more personal turning point. On 28 April 1894, shortly after launching her stage career, she married Gino Affortunato Paolo Botti in Fiume. Their marriage certificate shows that Ada was nineteen and Gino Botti twenty-two. According to an article in *The New York Times* of 3 August 1921, Botti was "a singer who had taken up a banking business"; but Rina Giachetti recalled that he came from a wealthy family of manufacturers. This is all the information we have about Gino Botti. We don't know how he and Ada met, how long they were engaged, where the couple spent their honeymoon, or whether the union was initially a happy one. Ada, a typically fertile Italian woman, soon became pregnant. Their son, Lelio, was born in Florence ten and a half months after the wedding, on 12 March 1895.

Ada continued to sing in the first few months of her pregnancy, which may have been a mistake. She attempted the title role of *Aida* for the first time at the Teatro Pagliano in Florence. On this occasion, the reviewer of the *Gazzetta dei Teatri* devoted a long passage to her.

> *Signora* Giachetti made her debut a short while ago in *Ballo in maschera* and I said then that the young lady had a bright future ahead of her. Without a doubt she maintains that promise, but the desire to advance her career faster than she should made her take on a role that, in my view, was beyond her power. I noticed that even though this young lady is an intelligent singer, she could not make me forget other performances of *Aida* in which the title role was not sung by a celebrity.
>
> This notwithstanding, the likeable (*simpatica*) artist was applauded after her first and third act arias and the final duet.

Following the series of *Aida*s, no other engagements can be traced for several months. Perhaps the critique of her Aida was a sobering experience. Rather than jeopardizing the good impressions of her debut, Ada wisely left the stage to await the birth of her child. With the resilience of youth, very soon after giving birth, she resumed her career at full force.

BY coincidence, she had the opportunity to prove her mettle by returning to the stage in the title part of *Aida,* the very role in which the critics had panned her. She sang it several times in October 1895 at the Politeama of Carrara, this time to positive critical response. A telegrammatic notice published in the *Rivista Teatrale Melodrammatica* of October 28 reported an "immense success" and stated unequivocally that "Giachetti-Botti [was] the heroine of the evening."

In December she appeared as Alice in *Falstaff* at the Teatro Dal Verme in Milan. A Milanese newspaper, possibly the *Corriere della Sera* (the preserved clipping is unidentified), dated 26 December 1895, wrote of her: "Giachetti-Botti was a revelation in the part of Alice, so much so that she had to repeat the passage of the last-act trio which in all other theaters passed unnoticed. Beautiful voice, very beautiful woman, great intelligence and great self-possession. A real *find*."

The 28 December 1895 issue of *Il Trovatore* fully seconded this judgment. "New to the Milanese stage was Giachetti-Botti, who, having overcome an initial nervousness, ended by fully asserting herself, and earned a great, unexpected success. Alice, admirable for a beautiful and agile voice, perfect diction, vivacious action, and personal charm, was especially applauded in the second and third acts."

Elsa in *Lohengrin,* her next assignment at the Teatro Dal Verme, was a less fortunate undertaking. The reviewer of the *Gazzetta dei Teatri* dismissed her with one sentence in the 27 February 1896 issue: "Giachetti was good, however I prefer her in the role of Alice."

From Milan, Ada traveled to Sicily. The Palermo engagement at the Politeama under the direction of her mentor Leopoldo Mugnone was an unqualified success. She sang Margherita in Boito's *Mefistofele,* partnered by Francesco Navarini in the title role.

> Giachetti-Botti delivered her role very well (*benissimo*), interpreting the prison scene in particular with the necessary dramatic power, greatly moving the audience that brought forth a real ovation and the insistent demand for an encore. Giachetti is a very fine artist; her voice is sweet, even, brilliant, and trained by excellent schooling. (*Gazzetta dei Teatri,* 9 April 1896)

After several repetitions of the Boito opera, Ada performed in Puccini's three-month-old *La Bohème,* in the presence of the composer. Adelina Stehle took the part of Mimì, and her husband, Edoardo Garbin, sang a stupendous Rodolfo. A notice in the *Gazzetta dei Teatri* of 30 April 1896 reported that Puccini was deliriously acclaimed by the audience, that Mugnone gave an exceptional interpretation of the score, and that "Giachetti-Botti [was] an incomparable Musetta." Composer and artists received forty-five curtain calls. *La Bohème* had an enormously successful run, and on April 29 a banquet was given in honor of Puccini, who became the darling of Palermo.

Giachetti also sang the title role in Bertini's *Ninon de Lenclos* and earned praise as well as extra income with her own benefit performance of *Mefistofele.* It was the custom in those days, in both the legitimate and the lyric theaters, to reward the outstanding artists of the company with a benefit performance. The actor or singer collected the profits of the evening, which meant that the monetary rewards were in direct proportion to the artist's drawing power.

The 6 August 1896 issue of the *Gazzetta dei Teatri* carried a brief notice about Giachetti: "This most worthy artist, who takes giant strides toward becoming a celebrity, has signed an excellent contract for the Fermo fair" where she was to sing her first Mimì at the Aquila theater. According to the *Gazzetta dei Teatri,* it was a successful portrayal. "Giachetti-Botti's splendid Mimì was greatly acclaimed throughout the opera. In the third act she moved the audience to indescribable ovations." In Fermo, she also had a benefit night; after *La Bohème,* Ada and the tenor Gianni Masin sang the duet from Gomes's *Guarany.* She was showered with "exceptional applause, a profusion of flowers, and many valuable gifts. Following the performance they accompanied her home in a torchlight parade amidst cries of: 'Viva Mimì!' " (*Gazzetta dei Teatri,* 17 September 1896).

After Fermo came Ada's first engagement in Bologna, where to excellent reviews, she sang both Margherita and Elena in six performances of *Mefistofele.* The critic of the *Gazzetta dei Teatri* wrote on 29 October 1896:

> Without exaggeration or partiality and in all truthfulness, *Signora* Ada Giachetti-Botti was the linchpin of the performance. Her beautiful and imposing figure, adorned by grace and youth, lends itself marvelously to the incarnation of Margherita and Elena. Naïve and virginal Margherita conquers with her beautiful voice, with her florid song full of melancholic love. With what exquisite sentiment did she interpret the famous *nenia* ["L'altra notte in fondo al mare"] which she had to repeat to enthusiastic applause! Her voice penetrates and moves the depths of the heart, so that one cries and throbs along with her.
>
> Her somber and bewitching Elena has sensuous warmth, and the heroine of Troy seems to palpitate with new life.

Apparently, she scored a great personal success, and the opera succeeded as well. The management of the Brunetti theater of Bologna extended the run for six more performances. Subsequent reviews were no less flattering and effusive in their praise for her delivery of the double roles.

From Bologna, she went to the prestigious Teatro San Carlo in Naples, where she repeated her success as Alice in *Falstaff.* The excellent cast included Arturo Pessina in the title role, Antonio Pini-Corsi as Ford, and Virginia Guerrini as Mistress Quickly. After this came her first Santuzza in *Cavalleria rusticana* opposite Fernando de Lucia in the role of Turiddu and Pini-Corsi as Alfio. "Giachetti-Botti, ideal Santuzza in figure, voice, diction, passion, forced to repeat the narrative," stated the first telegrammatic announcement of the performance in the *Gazzetta dei Teatri* of 11 February 1897. *Il Mattino* of

February 15–16 reported that *Signora* Ada Giachetti-Botti had to repeat the aria and the duet with Fernando de Lucia, and that she was warmly received "because she sings and acts the part with much passion and great effect."

During the Naples season, she also took part in a benefit concert with Guerrini and A. Pane. They performed the trio from *Il Matrimonio segreto,* and Guerrini and Giachetti sang the duet from *Semiramide.* In the latter, they sang the *cadenza* of the famous Marchisio sisters with "such fusion of their voices and with such perfection" that they earned "most warm and enthusiastic applause," reported the *Gazzetta dei Teatri.* Ada was also the featured artist at a great reception at the house of *Donna* Luisa Maria Capozzi, who invited "the flower of Neapolitan society." Here she sang several arias, and "the *romanza* from *Andrea Chénier* brought forth [such] frenetic applause that she was obliged to repeat it" (*Gazzetta dei Teatri,* 11 March 1897).

Ada next sang the title role in the local première of *Maruzza,* a contemporary opera by Pietro Floridia. The work, successful elsewhere, had a mixed reception at the San Carlo. Yet the reviewer wrote that "Giachetti-Botti, of the luscious voice, was a bewitching Maruzza" (*Gazzetta dei Teatri,* 15 April 1897).

In May and June of 1897, Ada had no engagements. According to the custom of the time, the *Rivista Teatrale Melodrammatica* carried an announcement that the soprano was "available," the term used to convey that the artist was looking for a job. The notice gave her address in Florence, where she presumably remained during this period. The Lisciarelli management then signed her to appear at the Teatro Goldoni in Livorno in July and August in a series of performances of *La Traviata* and in Puccini's *Manon Lescaut* and *La Bohème.* Her partner in *Traviata* was to be a promising young beginner, Enrico Caruso.

LIVORNO was almost home for Ada. The Giachettis maintained an apartment on the Viale Regina Margherita, and Giuseppina joined her daughter there. Gino Botti, who apparently did not travel with Ada, was probably attending to business commitments elsewhere. The third family member to arrive was Ada's sister Rina. She was recovering from a recent illness, and her doctor had recommended bathing in the sea to accelerate her recovery.

Ada was already in town when Caruso arrived. He needed to find accommodations; but remembering his exchange with Mugnone, he decided to call at once upon his beautiful leading lady. He found only her mother at home. *Signora* Giachetti was very kind to the visitor, especially when he mentioned that he had come to pay his respects because Maestro Mugnone spoke so highly of Ada. Because of the role the conductor played in launching Ada's career, his name was the best possible introduction for Caruso. *Signora* Giachetti asked the tenor whether he had found a place to stay, and when he said he had not, she suggested that he rent a room in their apartment. In his turn, he invited both mother and daughters to dinner at a nearby *trattoria*. Later that afternoon, he met both sisters at the same time.

Seventeen-year-old Rina fell in love with the handsome young tenor at first sight. She was happy to have him as a lodger and gladly waited on him hand and foot. Years later she fondly recalled how she attended to all his needs, washing his clothes and ironing his shirts and pants. Rina's youth, charm, and unconcealed devotion pleased and flattered Caruso, and he began to court her. They went for long bicycle excursions in the countryside around Livorno. On one of these trips, Caruso made amorous advances, but Rina, with commendable fortitude, refused to yield to his charms. As she later said, she confessed that "she loved him deeply and she would be happy to unite her life with his, but only in holy matrimony." In short, she made it clear that there could be nothing between them without benefit of clergy.

Caruso balked. He had just wriggled free of a matrimonial engagement to Giuseppina Grassi and was reluctant to make another commitment so soon after that sticky affair. It is possible, too, that charming as young Rina must have been, his feelings for her were not strong enough to warrant an irreversible commitment to marriage.

Rina, perhaps overly confident of his interest in her, gave Caruso time to think it over, which proved to be a mistake. Having sufficiently recovered from her illness, she returned temporarily to Florence to take her final examinations at the Conservatorio Cherubini. She completed her courses *cum laude* and received her diploma in singing.

In the meantime, *La Traviata* went into rehearsal at the Teatro Goldoni, and Caruso began to work daily with his leading lady. As was his habit then and later, he sang at half-voice in rehearsals. (Conductors and fellow artists resented this so greatly that he found it necessary, when he joined the Metropolitan in later years, to stipulate in his contract that he was not obliged to sing at full voice during rehearsal.) Apparently, Ada had never heard him onstage, and she was very disappointed in his voice. At the time, she was a more accom-

LIVORNO

R. TEATRO GOLDONI

La sera di Mercoledì 7 Luglio 1897 a ore **9** precise
Prima Rappresentazione
dell'Opera in 4 atti del Maestro Comm. G. VERDI

La Traviata

(proprietà RICORDI)

PERSONAGGI

Violetta Valéry	*Sig.*ra	**Ada Giachetti-Botti**
Flora Dervoix	»	AMELIA BIADI
Annina	»	N. N.
Alfredo Germont	*Sig.*r	**Enrico Caruso**
Giorgio Germont	»	**A. Pini-Corsi**
Gastone Visconte Letorieres	»	PILADE LOTTI
Barone Douphol	»	A. SELVAGGI
Marchese D'Obigny	»	N. N.
Dottore Grenvil	»	N. N.

Coro di signori e signore amici di Violetta e Flora
Mattadori — Piccadori — Zingare

BANDA SUL PALCOSCENICO

Maestro Concertatore e Direttore d'Orchestra

Cav. VITTORIO PODESTI

PREZZI D'INGRESSO

Platea L. **2** - Posti distinti L. **2** (oltre l'ingr.) - Poltrone L. **5**
(oltre l'ingr.) - Palchettone L. **2** (oltre l'ingr.) - Terrazza L. **1**
PALCHI: 1° e 2° ord. L. **20** - 3° ord. L. **10** - 4° ord. L. **5**.

Poster for the first performance of *La Traviata* in Livorno, the first time Enrico Caruso and Ada Giachetti sang together. Courtesy of Associazione Museo Enrico Caruso, Milan.

plished and better-known artist and considered him beneath her level as both a singer and an actor. In fact, she asked the conductor Vittorio Podesti to have him replaced. "If you think I am going to ruin my reputation singing with this little *tenorino,* you must be out of your mind!" she supposedly said. It was only because of the conductor's faith in the young man that she relented. The "little *tenorino*" acquitted himself far beyond her expectations. Ada reaped the larger share of critical acclaim for *La Traviata,* but her leading man was also well received.

The review in the *Gazzetta Livornese* of 9 July 1897 was lavish with praise for Ada and very complimentary about Caruso.

> *Signor* Caruso, tenor, has a voice and method that have become very good. He is an absolute master of the stage and singing, able to intone sweetly, with bittersweetness, much that is so doleful and sad in those pages.
>
> In sum: a performance deserving praise.

The *Rivista Teatrale Melodrammatica* of 15 July 1897 carried a telegram from Livorno describing the first and second performances of Verdi's opera as an "immense success." According to the telegram, "Giachetti triumphed over the exciting memory of Gemma Bellincioni. She showed herself a most intelligent artist, interpreting the difficult role of Violetta with attention to the smallest details [in her] delivery. Splendid voice, amazing agility, correct diction, masterful acting." The telegram also praised the warm and ringing voice of the "young tenor Caruso, an artist with a brilliant future."

The July 12–13 issue of the *Gazzetta Livornese* gave Ada even more accolades and proclaimed that Caruso's singing at times "recalled the most celebrated interpreters of the divine score: recalling Bancardi and Stagno." More performances and more reviews followed, all glowing. In reviewing Ada's Manon, the *Gazzetta Livornese* of 6–7 August 1897 commented that "this chosen and distinguished actress-singer, whose gifts of face and figure are equal to her powerful and noble voice, clear and vibrant . . . is by now numbered among the finest of the lyric theater in Italy."

The 15 July 1897 issue of the *Gazzetta dei Teatri* quotes the critique of the *Telegrafo* with respect to Ada Giachetti:

> The success of this enchanting artist was a veritable triumph. She pleased in every respect: voice, singing, action, dramatic expression, intensity of feeling. One can also add the

ideal beauty of her person, and with such an entity of quality no one can marvel at the enthusiastic reception and warm ovation of the public. *Signora* Giachetti-Botti is not only a good singer but a superb actress as well. Her stage presence, gestures, could be the envy of the best performers of the legitimate theater. Furthermore, she is most beautiful, with a splendid personality; her deportment, dignified walk, and posture on the stage were all beyond reproach. Her voice has been trained in a strict school; but in her singing one can find great artistry, much passion, a touch of affectation.... *Signora* Giachetti sang the entire evening in a way to make no one long for any of the great queens of the lyric stage; she demonstrated in many ways that she belonged among them. For instance, in the last scene of the first act and in the entire fourth act, she sang and acted to perfection, so much so as to make one think that she would be a *Marguerite* in the prose version to rank with the best.

Because of the company's success, the impresario wanted to stage *La Bohème*. He had the necessary talent in his troupe, but Caruso had never sung the role before. The tenor coveted the role, not only for artistic considerations but also because he would sing it with Ada. Caruso recalled the circumstances:

> The Livorno engagement commenced for me with *Traviata,* and such was my reception by the audiences that after 15 days of singing the impresario asked me if I knew the *Bohème* of Puccini. I answered that I did, to which he said: Soon the consent of Ricordi will come, making it possible for you to sing in this opera, and when it does I will make for you a contract for another month at the same price, 1,000 lire.[3]

The music-publishing firm Ricordi owned the copyright to *La Bohème* and, together with the composer, had the right to approve or disapprove the cast. In reply to the impresario's proposal, they wrote, "We do not know who Caruso is."[4] The impresario suggested another alternative to Caruso: to visit Puccini at his nearby villa and ask for his permission. The tenor, in turn, proposed that if he got Puccini's approval, he would sing the performances for the fee of 1,000 lire; if not, and if the impresario allowed him to go on anyway, he would sing for living expenses only, which amounted to 15 lire a day.

Two weekends later, a friend invited him to go hunting and took

him to a house on a nearby lake. They entered, and to his surprise he
met Puccini. This historic meeting has been incorporated in many
biographies, about both Caruso and Puccini, and altered or inflated
according to the writer's whims. The version used here is the one told
by Caruso himself and preserved by Pierre Key in 1920.

> The Maestro said:
> "People have told me much of you, *Signor* Caruso, but
> never have I had the pleasure of hearing you sing. Won't you
> sing for me?"
> I said quickly:
> "Yes, Maestro."
> "Do you know anything from my *Bohème?*"
> "Yes. I can sing for you from that opera, but don't expect
> me to put the high C in the romance."
> Puccini replied:
> "It is, perhaps, that you do not look enough at the score,
> because a point in the bar which has the high C shows the
> singer may or may not take it at his pleasure."
> "Oh yes," I answered, "I know that, but it is the custom for
> everybody to put in that high C."
> "Never mind," said he, "sing me well all the aria, and I
> don't care for the high C, because generally the tenors sing
> badly the aria in order only to sing the high C."
> Caruso sang, and after the aria Puccini said to the friend
> who brought him:
> "Tell the impresario I approve that Signor Caruso sings in
> my *Bohème*."[5]

Caruso got the role but earned only 15 lire a day: The impresario
maintained that he had visited Puccini on his own accord and not on
the order of the manager. This was another valuable, if costly, lesson to
Caruso about the *modus operandi* of impresarios. Under the circumstances, he accepted the terms, and his rendition of Rodolfo fully
vindicated Puccini's faith in him. In addition to his determination to
build a reputation, he was eager to impress both the composer and his
leading lady. On 28 August 1897, after the fifth performance of the run,
the critic for *Il Trovatore* declared that "the tenor Caruso was a revelation in the part of Rodolfo. Singing, musical and dramatic expression,
and a truly beautiful voice are the gifts of this young artist." In the
same paper, another reviewer wrote enthusiastically:

We have heard and already admired the tenor Caruso in *La Traviata*. But in *La Bohème* he surpassed all our expectations. It is impossible to give a better rendition of the role of Rodolfo scenically or lyrically. His most pleasant, flexible, young voice that arrives with the greatest ease at the high C-natural never tires and is never tiring.

A high C-natural with the greatest of ease in 1897? This review is revealing in several ways. It not only shows the artistic growth of Caruso and the vocal mastery he had been able to attain, but it also suggests that the tenor with the "short voice" Ada encountered at the first *Traviata* rehearsal had made dramatic progress in a very brief time in the realm of singing technique. In all probability, the aria had been transposed a semi-tone down, a frequent practice of which the reporter was perhaps unaware. Even so, a resounding B-natural is more of a feat than posterity has usually accorded to the twenty-four-year-old Caruso. It was certainly a long way from the nightly crack on the high B-flat in *Carmen* only a year before.

As usual, Ada's reviews were glowing. The same reviewer for *Il Trovatore* called her "a splendid creature, with a rich, fresh, pleasing voice and good singing method," and continued:

> The beautiful Giachetti-Botti, an artist to her very soul, with only three or four years of experience finds herself well advanced into her career. She plays the part with such exquisite feeling that leaves nothing, absolutely nothing to be desired! She infuses all the sentiment, grace, perfumed, sweet melancholy that the delicate creature requires.

Other newspapers joined the chorus of praise. "Giachetti-Botti has conquered the most elevated position for her art and she is of great and true value" (*Tirreneo*). "*Signora* Giachetti-Botti exceeded the most flattering predictions and expectations" (*Corriere Toscano*). "Puccini's *Bohème,* the third triumphant success for the celebrated Giachetti-Botti, ideal Mimì, exquisite singer, passionate actress, perfect artist" (*Gazzetta dei Teatri*).

The Livorno season was an absolute triumph in every respect. Ada gave yet another benefit performance, and the long reviews, all flattering, were collected and republished in the *Gazzetta dei Teatri* of 16 September 1897. The review of the *Corriere Toscano* began as follows:

> The beautiful and intelligent artist to whom the public of the Goldoni gave such a solemn demonstration of enthusiasm

last night, sang through the entire summer season without interruption for two long months in three operas, in which she had ample opportunity to show her eminent qualities of singer and actress. Powerful in *La Traviata,* dramatic in *Manon,* passionate and fascinating in *La Bohème, Signora* Giachetti-Botti demonstrated her various qualities, able ingenuity, and facile assimilation of the most correct singing method and a congenial artistic temperament which allow her to pass from one *genre* to another, bringing to the interpretation of the various characters an entirely personal note of grace and sweetness. That is why after two months of arduous work, after three operas in succession in which the power of her voice never failed for an instant, *Signora* Giachetti-Botti last night had the supreme satisfaction of seeing herself celebrated and being thrilled by the tumultuous, sincere admiration.

The 12 August 1897 review in *Il Trovatore* was no less effusive, praising "Violetta, Manon, Mimì, triple creation of the illustrious artist." Caruso's reviews were also very good, and Ada was happy to admit that her concerns about singing with an unknown tenor were unfounded. Puccini took the trouble to see for himself how his erstwhile visitor was performing Rodolfo. August 14 was the last performance of *La Bohème.* The *Gazzetta Livornese* of 27 August 1897 reported on this special evening honoring Puccini. The composer received many gifts, and after the third act there was a veritable rain of red and yellow cards paying tribute to his talents. It was described as an "unforgettable evening" and an "unforgettable success. The tenor Caruso was in full control of his resources. The *Signora* Giachetti-Botti was incomparable.... At the exit of the theater Puccini acknowledged a warm demonstration and was accompanied home by a local band, a number of torch-bearers, and an immense wave of people."

During the series of *La Bohème*s, Ada's attitude toward her tenor underwent a profound change. All who knew him in those days agree that Caruso embodied youthful exuberance, gentleness, infectious high spirits, and animal magnetism in extreme degree. These charms simply could not—and did not—escape Ada's attention.

No evidence remains to tell us whether the initial meeting between Ada Giachetti and Enrico Caruso was anything more than casual. But Rina has her own interpretation of subsequent events. According to her, Ada at first had no romantic interest in Caruso, considering him quite provincial. However, the growing affection between Caruso and herself did not pass unnoticed. Ada was first a bit surprised and later annoyed at being overlooked in favor of her younger sister. The soprano became interested in Caruso, and he responded. While Rina was in Florence, the passionate onstage relationship of Alfredo and Violetta, Rodolfo and Mimì, continued offstage with equal intensity. Upon her return to Livorno, Rina was confronted with the shocking turn of events and left with no choice but to accept the situation as *fait accompli.*

Ada broke the news herself. Reminding Rina of her youth, she counseled her to forget the tenor; but the sisterly advice could not soften the blow. Rina was devastated. Caruso was her first love, with all the attendant sweetness, intensity, and heartache. She could not bear to remain in Livorno and returned to Florence gravely ill and emotionally depleted.

Forty years later, in an interview for a Brazilian newspaper, Ada Giachetti recalled the moment of falling in love:

> At first I was reluctant to sing *Traviata* with him [Caruso]: His voice was short (*sua voz era curta*), undeveloped. . . . No one could foresee Caruso's future, but finally I agreed and did sing Violetta to his Alfredo. . . .
>
> At times the splendor fades and passes from the earth, but the memory of love remains, fixed, in the shining paths that signalled its glory. In the third act of *La Traviata,* when the violins weave their sublime music, the theater is gripped by a profound silence. The harmonies draw forth one's very soul— Violetta is enveloped in a supreme moment of emotion. Her voice becomes a truly divine instrument, blending with the orchestra. That night I felt that the young tenor was something more in my life than just another operatic Alfredo.
>
> "It is a strange thing, you know, I was never concerned about singing with anyone before, but then I had also never loved anyone before. Verdi's music was the crucible of our nascent love. (*A Noite,* Rio de Janeiro, 4 March 1938)

Ada and Enrico were elated by their joint success. If they fell in love during *La Traviata,* their mutual attraction blossomed into a passionate affair during *La Bohème.* The fact that they were living under the same roof only combined opportunity with desire. Presumably their involvement became deeper than either had intended, and there was no ready solution for the situation. Perhaps they did not know whether they wanted the love affair to last; but it is clear that Ada was not ready to break up her marriage. Thus the liaison had to be concealed from Gino Botti.

As Livorno was a small town, it could not support more than two months of opera, and the season came to an end when audience receipts no longer covered expenses. In late August, *Signora* Giachetti moved back to Florence, and Ada returned to Fiume. Because Caruso was paid only 15 lire for each performance of *La Bohème,* he finished the season at Livorno with no money left to support himself. He had to go somewhere between engagements, so the Giachettis invited him to stay at their home in Florence for the interim. Whether they knew of the passionate affair between the tenor and their daughter is uncertain, although Giuseppina was surely not blind to the romantic developments. Caruso stayed with the Giachettis for eight days, and they lent him 50 lire, which was enough to get him to Milan. It is a reflection on his economic condition of that period that he carried all his clothing and other belongings in a large paper bag. Caruso repaid the 50 lire as soon as he could, and he never forgot the hospitality and kindness Giuseppina and Guido had shown him. In 1920, in the last year of his life, he commented that "from time to time I am still giving back to the family which loaned me the fifty lires I so much needed in those early days, many, many, and many fifty lires."[6]

The fact that Ada was married in Fiume suggests that this was Botti's home town and their permanent home as well. Who took care of baby Lelio during Ada's frequent absences is unclear. Rina makes no reference to the baby being either with Ada or with their parents. It is most likely that Lelio was routinely left with Gino Botti's mother.

Ada and Caruso saw each other again in Fiume and, according to unconfirmed reports, sang there together. Caruso then had to move on to Milan, where he took a cheap room in a boarding house. Again in need of money, he went to the impresario Edoardo Sonzogno after three days to ask for an advance against his performances. Sonzogno was very kind and gave him the money he needed.

In Milan, Caruso sang in five different operas. Turiddu in *Cavalleria rusticana* was the first role he ever learned, and Canio in *Pagliacci* he had sung already. But he also took part in two world premières, both given in November 1897: Giordano's *Il Voto* and Cilea's *L'Arlesiana*. Ignoring previous agreements, Sonzogno insisted that in addition to the operas he had prepared, Caruso should learn the tenor role in Massenet's *La Navarraise* (or *La Navarrese,* as it was given in Italian) for the local première only five days away. This is a relatively short, two-act opera, and most of the music is sung by the soprano in the title role. Still, it was a grueling assignment, and Caruso studied day and night. Two days later, in the first rehearsal, the conductor, Maestro R. Ferrari, said, "I cannot go on, he doesn't know anything." In two more days came the general rehearsal. Caruso arrived wearing his hat, and Marguerite de Nuovina, the soprano, snatched it off his head and cast it away.

"When you sing with a lady, take off your hat!" she commanded. [7]

Caruso behaved like a gentleman and said nothing. After the rehearsal, Sonzogno predicted a great success for De Nuovina and a fiasco for Caruso. But just the reverse was the case: According to Caruso, "the audience cared more for my smooth style of singing—the voice being rather light then—than for the screaming of Madame X. From this moment I went on with success in the entire Sonzogno repertoire." [8]

During Caruso's absence, Ada probably spent the Christmas season with her husband and infant son. But soon after the holidays, she traveled to nearby Trieste to sing in *Falstaff* and *Mefistofele*.

The under-rehearsed first performance of *Mefistofele* was a disaster for all concerned except Ada. The 20 January 1898 *Gazzetta dei Teatri* gives the following cryptic introduction to selected excerpts from reviews: "This celebrated artist was the only one who, in a disastrous evening, held high the prestige of the Teatro Comunale, earning a decidedly triumphant success." The reviews quoted by the *Gazzetta* confirm this summary:

> We were sincerely pleased by the attractive and charming *Signora* Ada Giachetti [*not* "Giachetti-Botti"!] who is truly worthy to tread the stage of our grand theater for the velvety softness, the brilliance and solidity of her voice that does not betray the slightest effort. She offered us an intelligent and passionate interpretation of the role of Margherita, to which she gave most delicate contours and shading, a nobility of *portamento* and refinement. She was thunderously applauded after the *nenia* and in the death scene, saving more than once during the evening the vessel headed for certain shipwreck. The audience took advantage of each pause in the storm, directing at her special, warm applause. (*Il Piccolo della Sera*)

The critic was not exaggerating. Another reviewer for *La Sera* passed the same verdict, phrasing his displeasure more bluntly: "It is painful to speak of the rest of this unwanted, unrequested *Mefistofele:* It was a shipwreck from which only Giachetti saved herself."

WHILE in Trieste, Ada received a letter from her aunt in Florence suggesting that the sea air would be good for Rina, who was still in poor health, and that she should travel to Trieste and stay with Ada. The soprano agreed, and her sister soon joined her. Apparently, the girl's presence did not interfere with her commitments, for Ada continued to appear in *Mefistofele,* which, from the second performance on, went much better. The run continued to be reviewed by the majority of the newspapers. The *Piccolo* "could not but confirm the flattering judgment passed on Giachetti after the first performance";[9] the *Mattino* found her "outstanding"; the *Triester Zeitung* declared that "if she continues at this rate, she could be rightfully called the star of the future."[10] The *Indipendente* and the *Osservatorio Triestino* were also lavish with praise for her voice and her singing and acting ability.

After performing Margherita and Elena, Ada returned to her acclaimed interpretation of Alice in *Falstaff.* The reviews were very good. The first one published by the *Piccolo* gushed to the point of embarrassment, and the second, though more restrained, was still excellent.

> *Signora* Ada Giachetti as Alice was deliciously mischievous; flaunting a vivacity of superb quality, a most graceful flirtatiousness; always gay, lively yet moderate in posture and movement, revealing also an elegance and delicacy in her singing and the pearly ringing of her *fioriture.*[11]

The reporters of the *Indipendente* and the *Mattino* were equally generous with superlatives. However, the most profoundly admiring review was the one reprinted in the *Gazzetta dei Teatri:*

> A most laudable colleague and sharing in the honors was *Signorina* [*sic*] Ada Giachetti, who interpreted the role of Alice. To speak of her we would have to borrow the entire theatrical vocabulary, the most superlative, and we would still find ourselves falling short of the truth. In our previous issue we have said that when *Signorina* Giachetti sang in *Falstaff* in Milan, Verdi embraced her, deeply touched, and said that he had not heard a comparable interpretation. And these words of the illustrious composer are the best proof of this noble artist, and how all critics should bow to her. After the undisputed success that Miss Giachetti had in *Mefistofele,* now is added the clamorous triumph in *Falstaff.* (*Gazzetta dei Teatri,* 10 February 1898)

The accolades continued throughout the run, culminating in a benefit performance in which Ada sang "the adorable part of Alice, in which she fears no rivals. . . . They paid homage to the noble artist with twelve colossal bouquets, two valuable pieces of jewelry, and a superb fan."[12]

In *Falstaff,* Ada was partnered by the baritone Antonio Scotti, who sang the amiable dipsomaniac of the title. Ada was a young, lively, and beautiful woman, often the object of male attention, so it is not surprising that Scotti tried to court her. But Rina described the situation differently, saying that "Ada had a crush on Scotti." She maintained that the two singers sent frequent *billets-doux* to each other using her as the innocent go-between. We have only Rina's word for this more-than-friendly interlude; yet considering Ada's apparent proclivity for flirtation together with Scotti's well-earned reputation as an immensely charming ladies' man, the idea of such a flirtation does not strain the imagination. Rina also claimed that in the end she found the situation unpleasant and refused to serve as their *postillon d'amour,* but "because of her love for Caruso, the cause of her deepest suffering, [she] never mentioned it to him."[13] One must draw one's own conclusions as to Rina's motives for silence. In view of the deep friendship that developed later between Scotti and his fellow Neapolitan, Caruso, it must be recorded that at this time the two had not yet met.

This incident suggests that Botti had reasons to be jealous even before Caruso came on the scene. Obviously, Ada no longer loved or respected him. We will never know exactly how Botti failed to measure up to Ada's expectations of a husband or why she became disillusioned with him so early in their marriage. Ada's world was the theater, and if Botti was indeed trying to pursue a singing career, he left no mark whatsoever in the annals of the contemporary lyric stage, which made him a poor match for an ambitious young prima donna. But it is more likely that he was involved in manufacturing and commerce, as Rina believed, and thus lived in a world apart from the theater. In any case, due to Ada's engagements and Botti's commitments elsewhere, the couple spent more time apart than together, a circumstance rarely conducive to marital fidelity. Botti must have known that all was not well between them, yet he was disinclined either to leave or to share his wife.

Caruso spent the Carnival season of 1898 in Genoa. Under Sonzogno's management, he sang in Leoncavallo's *La Bohème* and in Bizet's *The Pearlfishers—I Pescatori di Perle*—with Giuseppe de Luca at the Teatro Carlo Felice during January and February. Afterwards, as he was scheduled to sing with Ada in Trieste in early April 1898, he rejoined her in March. Rina was still with her sister when the tenor arrived in town, and both women were anxious to see him again. Ada could not go to the railway station to meet him, and so, placing considerable trust in the emotional fortitude of her younger sister, she sent Rina to meet Caruso. They had not seen each other since Livorno, and this meeting, in Rina's words, "was like oil on the fire." All the tender emotions that she had tried so hard to suppress flared up again at the sight of her dear Enrico. As time went on, her torment grew. Seeing him, being near him, yet knowing of his relationship with Ada caused her more pain than she could bear.

While Rina was suffering from lovesickness, Caruso found himself in the unenviable position of falling deeply in love with both sisters at once. It appears that his feelings for both were genuine, passionate, and uncontrollable. Grasping the implications of this emotional triangle, one can have no doubt that Ada, with her considerable feminine powers, did all she could to maintain her hold on Caruso. The younger sister was hopelessly outmatched. After all, Rina was a virgin and determined to remain so until she married, while Ada was a willing mistress in the full bloom of womanhood. It was an unbearable situation for Rina, who finally announced that she had decided to go away. Caruso, perhaps feeling guilty about the situation he had created and torn by conflicting emotions, was disconsolate. Rina has described a confrontation of gigantic proportions, when Caruso threatened suicide, drew a revolver, and fired at his head. According to her account, *Signora* Giachetti was present. Fortunately, she was able to push aside the weapon, and the bullet went astray.

This melodramatic story sounds entirely apocryphal. Nonetheless, it deserves mention, because it appears in Rodolfo Caruso's handwritten notes taken during an interview with his Aunt Rina in 1948. But there is no evidence of a self-destructive streak in Caruso's character. If he ever contemplated suicide, in this writer's opinion, it would not have been for his inability to choose between two women. He gave ample proof in the years ahead that he loved them both, but not *that much.*

After things calmed down, Rina again planned to depart, in the hope that by forcing the issue, she could bring Caruso to understand the depth of her love and to reconsider his choice. But her hopes were in vain. Even if he had been inclined to change his mind, it was too late by then to do so: Ada was five months pregnant, carrying Caruso's child.

UNDER the circumstances, it must have been exceptionally unnerving for Caruso and the visibly pregnant Ada to fulfill their long singing engagement in Fiume. In April and May, they appeared together at the Comunale in *La Bohème, La Traviata,* and *Mefistofele.* Astonishingly, the soprano continued to perform into the eighth month of her pregnancy. Botti knew that his wife was expecting, but he didn't know that the child was not his. Ada delayed the inevitable confrontation until the end of the season. Once she had made her difficult avowal, she returned to Florence to her parents' house. Having dishonored her marital vows, she did the only honorable thing: She sought a separation. Botti, who had followed her to Florence, would have none of it. He vehemently opposed the idea, threatening to keep Lelio and never to let her see her son again. The encounter became violent, and Botti struck the pregnant Ada several times. If he had any hopes of changing his wife's mind, they now evaporated; for Ada was not the kind of woman who could be forced to stay with a man she no longer loved. She was prepared to leave with nothing but the clothes she was wearing. According to Caruso's letter to Puccini, written shortly after these events, she did just that.

Botti's reaction to the situation is understandable, especially in the context of nineteenth-century Italy. For an affluent young man from a good family, losing his wife to a second-rank tenor was a social disgrace of such magnitude that he could never expect to live it down. He did not want the reputation of being a cuckold, but in the end he had no alternative. Ada was pregnant, and given her nature and temperament, she must have coldly informed her husband that she did not intend to hide the fact that he was not the child's father. Botti's choice was no choice at all. He was forced to accept the lesser disgrace and separate from the wife who had betrayed him. After Ada and her tenor settled down together, Botti tried to harass them from time to time, until Caruso reportedly paid him a large sum of money to stay away permanently, which he did. If this story, kept alive in the Caruso family, is accurate, then the cuckolded Botti in effect sold his wife to Caruso. He did carry out his threat, however, and kept little Lelio away from his mother. Losing her son was the price she had to pay for joining her life to Caruso's.

With this major obstacle cleared, the lovers could finally be together. Cut off from Botti's support, Ada had only what she had saved from her engagements, which was very little. Nor did Caruso have enough money to set up a household. The couple could have moved in with Ada's parents in Florence, but their profession necessitated that they stay in the center of operatic activities, and that meant Milan. It was also essential for them to maintain a semblance of affluence and rent an apartment with a so-called good address. The apartment house of their choice was Via Velasca 1. To help the lovers settle in Milan, Guido pawned the family table silver (which had originally belonged to his wife Giuseppina), and Rina contributed her gold chain, a medallion of the blessed Madonna, and other articles of value. The apartment was spacious enough for the immediate family, and Via Velasca became home for the Carusos until 1903.

There, on 2 July 1898, their first child was born. He was named Rodolfo after the hero of Puccini's *La Bohème,* the opera that had brought his parents together. Caruso registered his birth on July 4 at the City Hall of Milan. He identified himself as the father but stated that his child was born of an *unwed* woman whose name was unknown. Accordingly, in place of the mother's name, the birth certificate showed "n.n.," for "not known." The boy was baptized on July 7; his godparents were Rina Giachetti and the conductor Giovanni Zuccani. His full name was Rodolfo Marcellino Giuseppe Caruso, but his father, with his flair for nicknames, called him Fofò from the first day of his life. The nickname stuck, and he was never called by any other name within the family. Although Ada was in remarkable physical condition, she took a few months off after the delivery. The birth of Fofò was a joyous event for the whole family. *Signora* Giachetti joined the Carusos in Milan to look after the household, taking Rina with her. Rina adored the baby, showering all her love for Caruso on his infant son, and she mothered the boy from the day he was born. She was happy to look after him; and when Ada's milk dried up and his mother could no longer breast-feed him, the baby would take the bottle only if Rina held it next to her naked breast, making the infant think he was taking the maternal nipple.

Soon after little Fofò's birth, Caruso returned to Livorno for a short engagement. This was followed by a series of performances at the Teatro Lirico of Milan, which included the highly successful world première of *Fedora* on 17 November 1898. Giordano composed the opera for the husband and wife team of Roberto Stagno and Gemma Bellincioni. Tragically, a few months before the première, Stagno died of a heart attack. A replacement was needed in short order: a tenor who could satisfy both composer and prima donna. Giordano's publisher, Edoardo Sonzogno, asked Bellincioni to go and hear Caruso, which she did. She found the tenor acceptable and recommended him for the role of Loris. The world première of *Fedora* became the turning point of Caruso's career. He recalled that "although people did not expect me to have much success, it turned out to be one of the best in my career.... After that the contracts descended on me like a big rainstorm."[14] Following that performance, he was in constant demand to the end of his days.

After a few months' rest, Ada sang *La Bohème* in Turin; then, with Caruso, she prepared for her first Russian tour. Both singers gathered their share of laurels in St. Petersburg. The tenor appeared in five operas; and Ada sang in *Un Ballo in maschera, Ruslan and Ludmila, Tannhäuser,* and *Cavalleria rusticana.* Ada was in stellar company: Her partners in these operas were Luisa Tetrazzini, Mattia Battistini, Vittorio Arimondi, and the tenors Francesco Marconi and Angelo Masini. She appeared with Caruso only in *Cavalleria,* singing Santuzza to his Turiddu. The *Gazzetta dei Teatri*[15] carried reports of their successes, concluding that "one can say of Giachetti that she is one of the most successful acquisitions made by the management of the Conservatoire theater."

The season went well for both singers, and they returned to Italy enriched artistically as well as materially. In his biography of Caruso,[16] Key mentions that the tenor was summoned to sing in a special concert at the St. Petersburg palace of Tsar Nicholas II. At the conclusion of the concert, the Tsar thanked him and presented him with a pair of gold and diamond cuff links. Because Key's source of information was Caruso himself at a time when he found it difficult to talk about Ada, he failed to mention that she also sang in the concert, and that her gift from the Tsar was a pair of Fabergé eggs.[17]

AFTER the couple returned to Milan, Caruso appeared during the Lenten season in *Fedora,* with Bellincioni in the title role. Whether Ada was engaged elsewhere at this time has not been established.

The third musician in the family, Rina, was still a music student. In the spring of 1899, she was studying voice with Carlo Carignani, a well-known voice teacher in Milan whose wife, Carlotta, ran a *pensione* for artists. One day Rina was at home alone, practicing and singing for her own pleasure, when the doorbell rang. The caller, a *Signor* Monari, identified himself as an impresario. Assuming that he was looking for Caruso, Rina invited him in. There was an embarrassed silence, then Monari asked if it were she whom he had heard singing through the open windows. Rina answered in the affirmative. Monari then told her how impressed he was with her voice and asked whether she would be prepared to sing in public. She responded with an enthusiastic "yes!" The impresario proceeded to offer her a contract to make her debut in *Carmen* at Zara. But Rina was still a minor, which meant that Monari had to have her parents' permission in order to engage her. Guido was not in Milan, and her mother was away from the house at the moment, so she asked her visitor to come back for the necessary approval.

Brimming with excitement at the prospect of singing onstage, Rina told the family what had happened. To her utter disbelief, neither her mother nor Caruso would consent to her plans. Among other objections, they were convinced that Rina was too young to launch an operatic career with its attendant travels, hazards, and responsibilities. They refused to give their permission for her to go.

Rina was aghast. She had great faith in her abilities and felt that she was ready. Perhaps she also had a psychological need to show her sister, as well as Enrico, that she was somebody, a talented young artist with a good voice and a promising future. Now opportunity had literally knocked on her door. She stood firm and insisted that she be allowed to go to Zara. When the argument reached a deadlock, she told Caruso and her mother flatly that she was ready to begin her career, with or without their consent. If they persisted in their refusal, she was prepared to leave without permission.

Caruso flew into a rage. He yelled at her, saying that in her father's absence he felt responsible for her, and that because of that responsibility he would never give his consent. If she wanted to go so badly, very well then, no one would hold her back; but if anything happened to her, he, Caruso, could not be held responsible.

Finally a compromise was reached: Rina could go to Zara to make her debut, but her mother would accompany her. This seemed acceptable to everyone concerned. Upon Monari's return, Giuseppina Giachetti signed the contract, and mother and daughter left for Zara soon afterwards.

Rina made her debut as Micaela in *Carmen* on 5 April 1899. Before the performance began, she confided to Campodonico, the mezzosoprano who sang the title role, that she was positively terrified.

"Don't worry, dear," said the older singer. "I will give you some medicine that will calm your nerves."

She opened a bottle of champagne, and the two fortified themselves with the entire contents of the bottle. Rina's fears vanished, and she sang splendidly. The telegrammatic notice on the performance, dated April 6, mentioned her briefly: "Giachetti praiseworthy Micaela, had to repeat the *romanza*" (*Rivista Teatrale Melodrammatica,* 8

April 1899). She also sang Olga in *Fedora,* and probably Musetta in *La Bohème*. Rina may have been pleasantly high on champagne at her debut, but she was completely intoxicated with the applause that was finally hers. She later remembered having had a "clamorous success," adding that her conduct at Zara and thereafter was above reproach in every respect. She did not have any amorous adventures, though not for want of opportunity.

At the end of the Zara season, Rina returned to Milan. The dispute about her debut had strained her relationship with Caruso and her sister, and she did not wish to rejoin the family at Via Velasca. With her earnings, and the hope of more to come, she rented her own apartment. Mother Giuseppina moved in with her, not so much for Rina's protection as to safeguard her reputation.

The news of Rina's successful debut at Zara opened doors. Almost immediately after her return to Milan, she was invited to sing in *La Serva padrona*.[18] According to all signs, Rina Giachetti was on her way to an operatic career. The family was also ready to smooth over hurt feelings and to reestablish a close relationship. According to Rina, it was Ada who "relentlessly sought a reconciliation." When at last the sisters made peace, the motivating factor for Rina may have been her desire to see her nephew Fofò as often as she wished.

CHAPTER THREE

The Americas

IN the summer of 1899, Caruso was booked, for the first time, to perform at the Teatro de La Opera in Buenos Aires. Concurrently, Ada
received an offer to sing in Chile. Caruso did not want her to make the
trip alone, and when he suggested that Rina accompany her, Ada
obtained an engagement for her sister. The tour was to last about four
months. Little Fofò stayed with his Grandmother Giuseppina in
Milan.

Sailing in April on the *Regina Margherita,* Caruso arrived in Buenos
Aires on May 7. His first performance was in *Fedora* on May 14. No
sooner did Caruso land in South America than the lovers began an
exchange of picture postcards.[1] When they were apart, they enjoyed
sending each other one or more cards daily with brief comments about
the day's happenings or just a brief note of love. A typical message was
written by Ada on May 12, using their pet names for each other: "*Un
bacio al mio Ghigo dalla sua Coccolina.*" ("A kiss to my Ghigo from his
Coccolina.")

The Giachetti sisters' Chilean debut was in July, and they sailed to
South America two months after Caruso. The young women were left
entirely to their own resources. It speaks for their enterprising spirit as

well as their powers of endurance that they were willing to undertake such a journey, which, in those days of primitive travel, was fraught with danger. After an uneventful Atlantic crossing, they reached Tierra del Fuego. What had been a pleasant voyage to this point became pure nightmare when they sailed into the Straits of Magellan. The difficult passage lived up to its reputation, and the ship, tossed and shaken by violent waves and enveloped in thick fog, was in constant danger of breaking up on the rocks. During the crossing, the women were in a state of terror; they suffered from seasickness that did not abate until they disembarked in Santiago, grateful to again set foot on *terra firma*.

Upon their arrival, Rina—and Ada too, to a lesser extent—began to wonder whether she had been overly confident in undertaking the journey. She found herself in a rude and scarcely civilized world. It was the period of the Yukon Gold Rush, and many adventurers stopped at Santiago after rounding Cape Horn to tempt fate at the gambling tables or simply to rest before continuing the journey to the frozen wilds of Alaska. The would-be gold miners, as well as the lucky few returning from the Yukon with new-found riches, seized the opportunity to live it up, and the city was in ferment. It was a life without check or restraint, the very opposite of the refined, orderly life to which the Italian women were accustomed. Everywhere, they encountered gentlemen excessively eager to serve them; yet the fiery and predatory glances that came their way put Rina in an unprecedented state of anxiety. Up to that point, she had known only the quiet, almost bucolic life of Tuscany, where she was sheltered from anything coarse or unpleasant. She soon realized that with or without Ada at her side, she had to fend for herself.

In her recollections of this period, Rina mentioned that the trip, and the unusually close circumstances of their daily lives, brought the sisters closer to each other than they had been in years. They could even discuss secrets of the heart—specifically, the deep love they both felt for Enrico. For a while, a tender and sincere harmony reigned between them.

During this tour of the "Gran Compania Lirica Italiana," Ada sang the female lead in *Mefistofele, Mignon, Andrea Chénier, La Bohème,* and *Aida*. Rina performed Micaela in *Carmen,* Venus in *Tannhäuser,* Inès in *L'Africana,* and Musetta in *La Bohème*. In the Santiago and Valparaiso performances, Anita Occhiolini was the Musetta, and the only joint appearance of the sisters was in *La Bohème,* at Concepcion, where Ada sang Mimì and Rina sang Musetta. As far as we know, this was the only time the Giachetti sisters sang together.

The critics were kind, especially to Ada, who was the prima donna of the company and had the starring roles. After her first appearance in *Mefistofele,* one reviewer wrote:

> Now I come to the beautiful *Signora* Giachetti *pour la bonne bouche.* The last are the first, as the saying goes; and in all truth Giachetti, in the role of Margherita and Elena, was what one can call ideal. Her success was real and pure fanaticism; and I can honestly say that Giachetti is an artist of uncommon merits. Beautiful, [with an] even and powerful voice, she sings as few do, and in *Mefistofele* there has not been anyone here to equal her either as a singer or as an artist. Giachetti therefore will be the "encore" of the season, I am certain. The public anxiously awaits her in other operas. In *Mefistofele* she was as great as she was sublime, especially in the quartet and the *nenia* of the prison scene. She could not have had a greater ovation than the one she received, having to repeat both pieces with her colleagues and alone.
>
> What can be said of the "Classic Sabbath"? A true Grecian type, equal to a statue of Pheidias resplendent in gold and precious stones taken from the depths of an enchanting garden, majestic and beautiful, singing to the shining moon with a voice from Paradise, eliciting applause and [demand for] an encore for the inspired piece.
>
> In conclusion: Giachetti has shown herself a truly noteworthy artist. (*Gazzetta dei Teatri,* 24 August 1899)

The same paper reported on her later appearances in equally glowing terms. Thomas's *Mignon* created a furor, "due to the enchanting interpretation of the protagonist by Ada Giachetti."[2] She sang with "a velvety and angelic voice," and to her "uncommon artistic attributes is added the poetry of her singing, equal to her ideal appearance." In Ada Giachetti, the critic continued, "we have a star rising on the horizon of art whose rays will illuminate the best theaters of the world." Her "Non conosci il bel suol?" ("Connais-tu le pays?") stopped the show.

In *Andrea Chénier,* she seems to have had a still greater success. According to the reviewer, "in the strongly drawn dramatic parts she has no rivals. . . . The composer and the librettist could not have found a more effective Maddalena to give a *verismo* interpretation of the poetic heroine and the drama. She was a true revelation."[3] *La Bohème* was declared by the Santiago reviewer "perfect and incomparable because of *Signora* Giachetti, one of the most sublime Mimìs I ever heard, both as an exquisite singer and as an actress." Celebrated above the rest of the cast, she was "the queen of the evening." *El Sur* of Concepcion of 5 October 1899 found her "an enchanting Mimì... adorable in her passionate phrases of love." Finally she sang the title role in *Aida,* in which it was said that "the simple dignity of her comportment produces around her something indefinable, and her voice continuously expresses faith, love, hope, courage. This is Ada Giachetti. An Aida as sublime as great. A true revelation of art! And thus a clamorous success." (*Gazzetta dei Teatri,* 19 October 1899)

Unfortunately, Ada had to cancel several performances due to illness. When she returned to the stage in the role of Mimì, the critic for the *Gazzetta* rejoiced, declaring her the "supreme attraction" of that opera, and her "Mimì absolutely without rival for the impetus of passion, the color of phrasing, and the spontaneity of accent."

Rina was also well received. The Valparaiso *El Mercurio* of 5 October 1899 commented on her "admirable impersonation of Venus" and went on to say that "she was tender, voluptuous, sang with exquisite freshness, and she moved with a certain timidity that was most seductive; genial and free, she translated into her singing with remarkable clarity all the feeling of that turbulent and restless soul with the true majesty of a royal bard." She also made a good impression in *La Bohème.* The 5 October 1899 *El Sur* review said of Rina that "Musetta's entrance was most suggestive. The beauty of the young artist charmed the public."

If the artistic aspect of their sojourn in Chile was eventful, so too was their social life. Soon after the performances began, a certain Daniele Concia showed himself eager to be of service to the older sister. The proffered assistance was "not without certain dangers," as Rina observed, and she implied that her sister was ever willing to take such risks. At the same time, a Carlo C. began to pursue Rina, who begged her sister for help in rebuffing the insistent suitor. Instead, Ada encouraged her to accept his ardent courtship. In later years, Rina unequivocally stated that her sister fully intended to leave her "to the mercy of fate in a country where all were strangers and where a woman alone was constantly threatened," and that Ada's motivation for this most unprotective stance was resentment for the younger sister's sentiments toward the man in her life. In the end, Rina's resistance eroded. Perhaps her suitor was charming and irresistible; perhaps he was determined and forceful; possibly, he was violent. In any case, after his persistent advances, Rina gave in.

Ada had an unexpected reaction to this turn of events. In Rina's words, when she confided in her sister,

> the latter had almost an outburst of joy and a glow in her eyes. In a detailed letter she told Enrico Caruso what happened in a manner to definitely alienate his affections from the younger sister. [Rina] in this upheaval (*trambusto*), torn by conflicting feelings, began to hate her seducer with all her soul. A tragedy might have followed if the conclusion of the season and the thought of returning home had not ended everything.[4]

Rina left no description of her relationship with Ada after this traumatic experience, nor did she mention whether Ada sought to comfort her. It is possible that Rina was unaware of the letter Ada wrote to Caruso until the sisters' return to Italy. Thus there was probably no marked deterioration in their relationship until they arrived home. Ada then told Caruso the details of Rina's affair, which upset him greatly, as could be expected in this age when feminine purity was considered a sacred virtue. The episode brought about an estrangement of the sisters that lasted, with occasional brief reversals, to the end of their lives. Ada must have seen Rina as a constant threat to her own relationship with Caruso, even when Rina no longer lived under the same roof. As subsequent events proved, Ada's apprehensions were well founded. Caruso never lost his roving eye, and Rina blossomed into a most attractive young lady and a talented artist with a fine voice. As long as she was unattached, she was a temptation for any man. Although Ada's unfeeling attitude toward her sister and her betrayal of a confidence can scarcely be excused or condoned, her motives are all too understandable.

Despite the passage of four months, the memory of the tumultuous voyage through the Straits of Magellan was still vivid, so the sisters, following the example of other singers and orchestra members of the company, decided to return to Buenos Aires by land, over the Andes. They learned that they could travel by train from Santiago to the first mountain range; from there, it was a three-day journey on muleback to the Argentine railway line that ran east to Buenos Aires. Traveling with them was a servant girl named Raffaella, an affectionate, solidly built woman from Trieste who wanted to go back to Italy and became as devoted to Rina as a watchdog.

The train ride was pleasant, but all too short. Although the distance they had to travel by muleback was not long, the roads were little more than paths cut across that terrifying mountain range. It was spring at sea level, but the mountains were still dominated by winter. Led by an Indian guide, the party had to negotiate passes in the Andes at elevations of more than 12,000 feet, their progress hindered by snowstorms and blizzards. They were forced to make frequent stops along the way at *posadas,* wooden structures that served as post office, rest house, inn, and tavern, all in one. The journey was dangerous as well as uncomfortable. At times, the party found itself on a path that was just a slippery ledge cut into the mountainside. When several mules carrying some of the baggage lost their footing and fell hundreds of feet into a gorge, Rina refused to go further on muleback. Seeing that she was at the verge of exhaustion, the guides bound her to a sled and pulled her over the snow toward the valley. In the evening, they reached a *posada* where they spent the night wrapped in chinchilla furs, wonderful pelts that were still plentiful and inexpensive in the region.

The *posada* they reached that first night had a single large room. All the travelers crowded around the fire and passed the night on straw mattresses. The young women stayed apart and avoided the mattresses for fear of bedbugs, spending a restless night on wooden benches at a distance from their companions.

They continued the journey the following day in intense cold and bright sunshine. Under a profoundly turquoise sky with a few white clouds, they trekked over the blinding spread of snow on paths as treacherous as those of the day before, past high peaks beset by raging gales. At the *posada* where they stopped the second night, they met a band of rough men—*gauchos,* peddlers, and adventurers—who were traveling in the opposite direction. The latter were amazed to find three young women in those godforsaken mountains. As they assessed the situation in the communal hall, it didn't take them long to realize that the women were without an escort and were thus easy prey. The men, no doubt anticipating some adventure, became increasingly vulgar and rude. However, one of them, with a great deal of tact and courtesy, offered to protect the women. The sisters were surprised to learn that the name of this gentleman was Caruso. What is more, he bore a close resemblance to Enrico Caruso—so close that they were convinced he must be a near relative of their loved one. When they quizzed him about his origins, he became evasive, so that his parentage was never clarified.

The man placed himself at their disposal, taking a particular liking to Rina—or so she later claimed. His gallantry notwithstanding, the women spent the night filled with fear. Having obtained at this *posada* a little room all to themselves, the three women barricaded themselves inside, piling against the window and the door every piece of furniture they were able to move. Several times during the night, they heard the doorknob turning as though someone were trying to enter. At last dawn broke, and they could resume their journey.

The rude party of men proceeded toward Chile, but the mysterious *Signor* Caruso interrupted his journey to accompany the ladies back to Buenos Aires. There they spent a couple of days, taking excursions in and around the city, before their departure for Italy. Once aboard ship, the ladies found a large bouquet of the rarest red orchids in their cabin with a note of *bon voyage* from the mysterious cavalier. The note said that he did not ask nor expect anything in return for his assistance, but he was only too gratified that he could fulfill his chivalrous duty (this was 1899!) and was happy to have been of service.

From that day on, neither Rina nor Ada heard anything further from their singular escort. When they recounted their adventure to Enrico, he was unable to cast any light on the identity of the other Caruso.

The return voyage was relaxing and without incident. After twenty-one days at sea, with stops at Madeira and Lisbon, the Giachetti sisters arrived in Genoa and from there returned to Milan.

CARUSO had already returned home from South America. Upon landing in Naples, he had gone straight to his father's house. Reminiscing about this meeting, Caruso recalled:

> He was very pleased with my success.
> "So they applaud you, do they, Enrico?"
> "Yes, Father."
> He nodded and smiled. I was glad but sorry too; I missed not being able to see my mother there to be pleased, too. If she had lived, I know just how she would have met me when I came into the house; speaking not so much with words as with her eyes . . . and her hand on my shoulder. It made me sad to think she could not have remained the few years longer so she might have known.[5]

When Ada finally returned to Italy, she and Caruso had a happy reunion. But Caruso had achieved international fame, and an orderly life was no longer possible for him. He soon had to leave again for Russia. He and Ada had performed together in St. Petersburg the year before; but in 1899–1900, he was scheduled to make the trip alone. The couple found the separation unbearably long, following so soon on the heels of their respective South American tours. Caruso dispatched affectionate postcards daily to Italy, and Ada replied frequently and in kind. Each tender message was a little gem reflecting not only the love they shared but also the degree to which thoughts of each other filled their waking hours.

Early in 1900, Ada and Aurelia Arimondi, wife of the bass Vittorio Arimondi, decided that writing was not enough and determined to join their husbands in Russia. They took the train from Milan to St. Petersburg, a long and fatiguing journey under the best of circumstances, and especially so at the height of winter. To complicate matters, their train was derailed en route and arrived half a day late. Caruso, desperate for news of Ada, dashed out of his hotel without his overshoes in the sub-zero Russian winter. The women arrived safe and sound in late afternoon, but Caruso paid the price for his impulsiveness. He was barely able to finish that night's *Mefistofele* and came down with a bronchial pneumonia that put him out of commission for the whole month of February. Vittorio Arimondi tried to cheer him up with a series of humorous postcards, each captioned with a line from *The Barber of Seville*. The slight humor lay in the incongruity of the quotations.[6]

Caruso resumed his place in the repertory, again as Faust in *Mefistofele,* on 28 February 1900. On the same day, he wrote a postcard to Ada (who was still with him in St. Petersburg): "My beautiful love, when I have grown old and you are still young and beautiful as now, I imagine that if I finish my career well, you will crown me with laurel. Let's hope it will be so. Greetings and kisses, your Chico" (pronounced "Kiko"). Although Ada was to travel with Caruso to Moscow, she wrote to him in advance from St. Petersburg. "May your life be always strewn with flowers. This is the wish of the one who loves you more than anyone else in the world. I kiss you," she wrote on March 6. The same day she sent a card bearing the image of a "lucky spider" and wishing that his future might be woven, like the spider's web, with golden thread. Two more cards bore the same date. "My loved one," Ada wrote, "Love me always and I will do everything possible to make your life less hard. I kiss you affectionately, your little wife [*sposina*] forever, Ada." Even before they left Russia in early April,

Ada began to send cards to Via Velasca in Milan, so that Enrico would be greeted by her messages of love. On March 14, she wrote from Moscow: "Dear Enrico, I love you so much, and you? Very, very much, I know. I kiss you many, many times, your Ada."[7]

Caruso had less than a month to recover from the Russian winter and enjoy a breath of Italian spring before leaving for another winter season in the southern hemisphere. From May 10 until the end of July 1900, he sang in Buenos Aires.

WITH an ocean between them, the lovers accelerated their daily exchange of postcards. Ada's first card may have been waiting for him upon arrival. "My love, how was the trip? Was the sea always calm? Let's hope it was. Are you well? Our Fofò is fine and every day becomes more mischievous" (22 April 1900). Ada wrote three more cards the same day, asking in one of them, "Enrico dear, will you send me postcards? You know it is a holiday for me when I hear from you. Write every day so that I receive news from you often. I kiss you, Ada." The following day she wrote that his telegram had arrived and brightened her day. The short messages of love and caring seemed to make the days pass faster. On May 9, she wrote simply: "Dearest Ghigo, a kiss from your Fofò and a thousand from his *mammina*. Ada."

Caruso kept up the correspondence on his end. The long separation was difficult for him; he could hardly wait to be on his way home. "In 7 days I will embrace you, Chico," he wrote on a card on which he sketched the Buenos Aires harbor; on another, he wrote: "See you soon, never to leave you. Kisses, very much your own (*tuissimo*), Enrico," and below another sketch, the pet name "Chico."

The world première of *Tosca* took place on 14 January 1900. On the basis of earlier communications with Puccini, Caruso expected to be invited to create the role of Mario Cavaradossi, but the composer granted this honor to Emilio de Marchi instead. Caruso was hurt, but he did not complain and harbored no grudge against Puccini then or later. At least he had the satisfaction of knowing that he was not bypassed for artistic reasons. De Marchi was the lover of Hariclea Darclée, the soprano chosen for the title role; and Puccini, who apparently considered the services of a world-class prima donna paramount to the opera's success, succumbed to the demands of his Tosca. Caruso chose to avenge the slight by becoming the best possible interpreter of the role. In the fall of the same year, he sang Cavaradossi for the first time in Treviso at the Teatro Sociale, with Ada in the title role. The first performance on 23 October 1900 was a resounding success, as the reviews amply testify.

"The tenor Caruso sang unsurpassably," reported the *Gazzetta dei Teatri* of 1 November 1900. "*Signora* Ada Giachetti was greatly acclaimed; she was superbly beautiful, a faithful interpreter of her part. She was a perfect Tosca." Because Tosca is possibly the ultimate vehicle for a female singer—a prima donna playing the role of a prima donna—Ada had the larger share of accolades in the Treviso papers. The *Adriatico*[8] found her in full control of the new role and possessed of a "beautiful voice, rich, congenial, her manner of singing passionate, suggestive, befitting the drama of the part." The reviewer also described in great detail her exquisite costumes—which were her own—in each of the three acts. The *Gazzettino*[9] praised her for "the totality of her feminine beauty, gifted with a magnificent and powerful voice, and uncommon intelligence. The notes came harmoniously and with ease from her throat. But what power in the high notes and what finished schooling this chosen artist shows!" The *Gazzetta di Venezia*[10] observed: "As a singer she has a robust and beautiful voice, clear and brilliant, and she phrases with artistry. Top honors are due to her and the tenor Caruso."

Subsequent performances brought further praise for the pair, and again, Giachetti was singled out for her contribution. The 1 November 1900 *Gazzetta dei Teatri* called her "a perfect Tosca," and a week later the November 8 issue of the same newspaper introduced selections from assorted reviews with a summary of the soprano's past successes, concluding that "with the interpretation of Tosca, Giachetti has reached the zenith."

Beginning on 17 November 1900, Ada and Enrico sang another successful series of *Tosca*s in Bologna. Here they were partnered by Eugenio Giraldoni, creator of the role of Scarpia; the ubiquitous Mugnone conducted. Audiences as well as critics were most enthusiastic. After one performance, Caruso had the satisfaction of hearing Puccini comment that "never before had this role been better sung."[11] In the case of the one-year-old opera, this praise was significant only in the implication that Caruso sang the role better than Emilio de Marchi, the Cavaradossi of the world première. Puccini's unequivocal statement to the press may well have been a pacifying gesture toward the tenor and a public admission that the role should rightfully have been his.

The November 18 issue of *Il Resto del Carlino* reviewed the *prima* (opening night) of *Tosca* at the Comunale in Bologna. "The protagonists were most admired as actors and as singers. After the first act, Puccini was called out once. 'Vissi d'arte' was very well (*benissimo*) sung by Giachetti, but the opera was much discussed and found, at times, inferior to the tragedy of the subject." Curiously, the 22 November 1900 *Gazzetta dei Teatri* lumped Caruso together with Giraldoni (Scarpia) and Nicolai (Angelotti) in the same sentence, stating merely that they showed themselves to be "distinguished artists worthy of great elogies," but singled out Ada:

> La Giachetti, with her beauty, elegance, and most precious vocal gifts, was an incomparable Tosca who immediately conquered the public with her exquisite interpretation. She delivered superbly her entrance, the duet with Cavaradossi, the scene with the knife, and all solo numbers.

Probably neither Caruso nor Ada realized at the time that, having attained a certain "zenith" with her new role, Ada was soon to conclude the first phase of her career. Indeed, the twelve Bologna *Tosca*s were her last extended engagement. In six short years, she had made an excellent name for herself, and there is no doubt that she could have risen to still greater heights. But she gave it all up for the man she loved.

According to all reports and her own statements, her retirement came about upon Caruso's insistence. "He never allowed me to sing again! I left the stage and went on to follow his always rising road to glory," she said in a 1938 interview for *A Noite* in Rio de Janeiro. Caruso's insistence that she fulfill the traditional role of wife and mother precluded the pursuit of an active career. Another factor in his thinking could have been his reluctance to share the limelight with Ada, who was becoming a celebrity in her own right. "In this household, I do the singing," he is reported to have said at various stages of his life. It is doubtful that Ada Giachetti could have attained the preeminence among sopranos that Caruso reached among tenors. Yet, had she persevered in her career, she would certainly have achieved a secure position among the female singers of the first rank.

The winter of 1900 brought Caruso's debut at La Scala of Milan—in Caruso's words,

> the "terrible La Scala" which scares all the artists. My contract for this theater was for four months, with 50,000 lire for the season. Here, also, I found the hard time, because, despite all my successes, some people were not sure of my ability. . . . I

realized quickly enough that the feeling in and about La Scala was against me. Somebody said that I was "not well." Somebody was "not sure" of my ability. Somebody else said that 50,000 lire was "an enormous price" for me. In such an atmosphere I began my work at what was the most critical period of my career.[12]

He was to make his debut in *La Bohème.* The rehearsals began badly. Caruso sang at *mezza voce,* as was his habit, and took the high C of the *romanza* "Che gelida manina" in falsetto. The conductor, Arturo Toscanini, asked if the tenor could sing this C "a little stronger" from the chest. Caruso said yes, he could, and Toscanini wanted to hear it. Caruso replied that he "didn't feel like doing so then because it was not necessary."[13] Toscanini, growing exasperated, suggested that they transpose the aria a semi-tone down. Caruso agreed, but, as he told Pierre Key,

> Toscanini was no more successful in hearing my high B-natural in the "Che gelida manina" than he had been during those times we had sung it in the original key, for I used the falsetto when we came to the high note, which left my conductor as nonplussed as before.[14]

The altercation between conductor and singer was at last resolved. But on the day of the general rehearsal or *prima,* instead of the short rehearsal Caruso expected, Toscanini pressed the company to rehearse the entire opera and then began again with Act I. It was nearly five o'clock by the time Caruso could go home, "desperately tired from all my singing at that long 'small' rehearsal. My moments of rest were short, for at half-past seven the *avvisatore* came with the carriage to take me to the theater."[15] At nine sharp, the troupe recommenced in earnest in front of an audience. Caruso, who had sung most of the rehearsal at full voice to the satisfaction of all concerned, was exhausted and did not sing well. The critic of *La Perseveranza* of 27 December 1900 wrote: "Miraculous things have been said about the tenor Caruso. The assembly of La Scala expected a great deal of him. But the outcome did not correspond to the expectations."

The following morning, Caruso awakened with a fever, and he was bedridden until the opening night of the season. La Scala was to open with *Tristan und Isolde,* but the production was cancelled due to the illness of the Tristan, Giuseppe Borgatti, and they decided to open with *La Bohème* instead. Caruso felt he was not up to the task; but the

director, Giulio Gatti-Casazza, spent two hours arguing with him until
he finally yielded to the pressure. He sang Rodolfo in the opening-
night performance, and he earned the success he deserved. "The
public did not, of course, appreciate how difficult was my position,"
Caruso recalled. "Only the artist knows what a task it is to appear when
he is ill, as ill as I was that night. Perhaps, had I myself realized my exact
condition, I might not have yielded. But as everything turned out, it
was the thing to have done."[16]

In spite of the mishaps surrounding his debut, 1901 started out
exceedingly well for Caruso, and he sang one opera after another at La
Scala. In January, he took part in the world première of Mascagni's *Le
Maschere*. In February, he enjoyed one of his greatest successes in a
revival of *L'Elisir d'amore*, a performance which elicited the un-
restrained admiration of the conductor Toscanini. In March, he sang
Faust with Fedor Chaliapin in the title role of Boito's *Mefistofele*. In
retrospect, it was a greater honor for Caruso to partner the great basso
than vice-versa. This was Chaliapin's first engagement outside his
native Russia and his first appearance in the role. His colossal personal triumph overshadowed the accomplishments of any other cast
member, then in Milan as on all occasions thereafter.

It must be noted that according to the *Rassegna Melodrammatica*,[17]
Ada was also engaged at La Scala for the 1900–01 season. Diligent
research has failed to turn up the date of her debut or subsequent performances, although we do have Caruso's word (in a letter written to
Pasquale Simonelli in 1903) that Ada sang at La Scala. It is probable
that either she sang minor parts, or she took over the roles from
leading singers and thus was not included in the standard annals of the
theater.

A few weeks' rest followed the La Scala season; then, in April 1901,
Caruso and Ada sailed to Buenos Aires. He was to sing at La Opera (the
current building of the Teatro Colón was constructed in 1908). The
curiosity of the season was his first and only excursion into the
Wagnerian repertory. According to the critiques, his performance of
the title role, in Italian, in three *Lohengrin*s was a qualified failure. The
reviewer of *La Prensa* had this to say in the 7 July 1901 issue:

> [Caruso] sounded somewhat insecure in the opening aria
> "Mercè bel cigno gentil." The duet "Rispondi Elsa" was
> better. . . . The greatest merit is to be given to the idyllic love
> duet of Caruso and Miss D'Arneiro, which was the highlight of
> the evening for the artists. . . . The famous aria of the last

scene, "Da voi lontano in sconosciuta terra" [the "Gralser-zählung"], the true hallmark of every tenor, is always awaited with great interest by the audience. Many believed that Caruso would live up to the expectations. Unfortunately, this was not the case; we don't know whether it was for a lack of self-confidence or because he did not have his voice fully under control, but it is certain that the "Racconto" did not come up to expectations, or even close to it.

This single excursion into the Wagnerian repertory apparently sufficed for Caruso. The Paris correspondent for the *Daily News* once asked him whether he would ever sing Wagner. "Later, much later," he said. "When my voice is aged, I shall be able to shout as loud as I like. Then I shall be able to put in my repertoire *Tristan, The Meistersinger,* and *Siegfried*."[18] This tongue-in-cheek comment is perhaps less reflective of Caruso's concept of how Wagner's music should be sung than of the performing style of contemporaries whom he had heard in these roles.

Ada traveled to South America with Caruso, in part because she had an engagement at the Politeama in Buenos Aires. She was scheduled to appear in *Mefistofele* but canceled at the last minute for "reasons of health," according to the newspapers. With this withdrawal from the season, she effectively retired. Nine years were to pass before she returned to the stage, and then she did so as much by necessity as by choice.

Ada had two pregnancies between 1900 and 1903, which may help to explain her canceled performances in Buenos Aires and her subsequent withdrawal from singing altogether. Both children died at birth. No exact information is available, but it has been mentioned in the family that one child, a boy, was born with a "cowl" (a sometimes fatal "veil" of tissue) over its face, and the other, also a boy, was strangled by the umbilical cord during birth. The deliveries took place at home with the assistance of a midwife, for no one went to a hospital in those days except for an operation or to die.

By this time, the offers kept coming without any effort on Caruso's part. As he added new roles to his repertoire, Ada, who was an accomplished pianist, assisted him musically. It is notable that Caruso's conquest of his problems with high notes coincided chronologically with the beginning of his relationship with Ada. Indeed, it was well known in the family and the closest circle of friends—although never publicly acknowledged by Caruso—that Ada had taught him a great deal about singing technique. In later years, he was increasingly reluctant to give credit to anyone for his accomplishments, claiming that his early training notwithstanding, it was he who had taught himself to sing. It is quite possible that having learned the rudiments of singing, he discovered for himself the method best suited to his particular physical and vocal equipment and thus improved upon what he had been taught. All the same, it is beyond any doubt that without Vergine and Lombardi, he would not have developed into the singer he became; and it is equally certain that he received many pointers and finishing touches from Ada Giachetti.

With Ada's retirement from the stage, their lives took on a degree of normalcy. Ada spent most of her time at home, helping Caruso with his music and entertaining frequently as befitted the life companion of the foremost up-and-coming tenor of the generation. Needing some artistic outlet, she began to paint. During their months in Buenos Aires, both she and Caruso spent many hours at the studio of Filippo Galante, an Italian painter Caruso had befriended during his previous engagements in Argentina and who in turn had taught the singer a great deal about painting and modeling. Now Galante worked with them both, and they learned much about the craft and techniques of painting.

In addition to her obligations as lady of the house, Ada looked after little Fofò. He was a healthy, active infant and soon became quite a handful, requiring constant supervision and getting into mischief even then. In his later years, one of his favorite stories about his childhood dated back to the time the family spent at the apartment on Via Velasca.

I remember my first well-deserved spanking when I got drunk for the first time in my life. Father loved Tuscan wine because it had a low alcohol content. It was transparent ruby and fizzled almost like champagne. He had it sent up from Florence in cases of half-liter bottles. I was barely three and a half, but I was unusually lively and often beyond the control of the members of the household, which, at that time, consisted of my parents, Uncle Giovanni, Grandmother Giuseppina, and a factotum cousin of Mother's. One day, rummaging through the apartment, I stumbled upon the loft where these cases of wine were kept. At the sight of the inviting containers, encased in straw with red, white, and green streamers, I recalled the taste of the well-watered-down wine which on the rarest occasions I was allowed to sip. I swear my mind was innocent, but the devil guided my hand, and I found myself holding one of those little bottles. Furtively and unobserved, I managed to reach the dining room. Once there, I grabbed a piece of cheese from a buffet and hid myself under the table, which was covered with a large cloth that reached almost to the ground. How I managed to remove the tightly packed cork I don't know; perhaps I used a corkscrew, but I must have been precocious to figure out its use at three and a half. I settled as best as I could against the center post of the oval table and began to nibble on the cheese and sip the wine, which tasted just fine. Past that I have no recollection of anything.

Accustomed as they were to my noisy presence, running around or getting into some mischief, the complete quiet of the house reminded the family that I ought to have been there. Grandmother was the first to look for me. She knew my kind, and the silence made her suspicious.

"That boy is up to something," she said, and in a loud voice she began calling me. "Fofò! Fofòo! Fofòooo!"

She paused for a reply, but there was only dead silence. Alarmed, Grandmother called Uncle Giovanni and Mother, and they began to search through the house, calling my name. Nothing. In the meantime, Papa came home from a rehearsal at La Scala. When he was told what happened, he thought I might have slipped out unobserved and, crossing the street, been the victim of an accident. He flew down the stairs and asked the doorman if he had seen me, then proceeded to check in the stores on our street. Nobody had seen me, not even the two *carabinieri* doing their rounds, so he returned home. A sense of despair took hold of the family. Then Uncle Giovanni passed through the dining room and heard a little snorting grunt, like the sound of labored breathing. Standing still, he looked around to find the source of the sound and concluded it could only come from under the table. He tip-toed to the table, and lifting the cloth, he discovered my respectable person propped against the large center post of the table, blissfully asleep like Noah after discovering the juice of grapes, the empty flask tightly clasped to my chest and cheese crumbs all around. Naturally, I was pulled out from under there to the great relief of all concerned, but I was also spanked and scolded. I heard little of their recriminations, because I proceeded to sleep for twenty-four hours, as I was told afterwards.[19]

When Fofò was old enough to attend kindergarten, he was sent to the best one in Milan. Ada used to fix a little lunch basket for him. Thus from early childhood, he spent his days among other children and was rarely alone. Some sort of truce must have prevailed between the sisters at this time, because Fofò later remarked: "I also remember that I often visited Auntie Rina, who lived in a lovely apartment on one of the boulevards of Milan. She was so much like Mother that I was never sure if I should call her Auntie or Mamma."

Because of his heritage and his life among musicians, Fofò had a good ear and was quite musical as a child. One incident was especially revealing.

> I remember as if it were yesterday the time my father took me to his dressing room during the world première of Franchetti's *Germania* (11 March 1902) and beat with his finger on the dressing table the rhythm of "Questa o quella" from *Rigoletto*. Without hesitation, I attacked the aria, perfectly in tune. The artists who were there rewarded me with more or less welcome kisses.

Fofò was three and a half years old at the time. Although he was in his mid-teens before he heard his father in a performance, this tale indicates that Fofò must have heard Caruso's daily practice and subconsciously retained the melodies.

The première of Alberto Franchetti's *Germania* was a festive event. Puccini, Giordano, D'Annunzio, Giacosa, Floridia, and other celebrities were present in the audience. In the judgment of the reviewer of the *Corriere della Sera* on 12 March 1902, "Caruso did not appear suited to deliver efficiently his role, which calls for outbursts and power of voice." The audience thought otherwise. In fact, it was his delivery of the role that prompted the recording technician of the Gramophone & Typewriter Company, Fred Gaisberg, to offer him a contract to record ten selections. The recording venture turned out to be an immediate commercial success.

The next milestone in the Caruso career was his debut in London. According to *The New York Times*, "it was Scotti who carried to Caruso in Italy the invitation to sing in London."[20] Covent Garden wanted to make it a festive occasion, and they cast him opposite Nellie Melba in *Rigoletto*. The reporter for *Monthly Musical Record* wrote:

> The only brilliant night of the season was on May 14, when Mme. Melba made her re-entrée as Gilda in *Rigoletto,* and *Signor*

Caruso his debut as the Duke. I have heard Melba sing better, but her beautiful voice and ease of singing were refreshing to tired ears. *Signor* Caruso is a typical Italian tenor. He reminds one of Tamagno, De Lucia, and De Marchi, and yet he is greater than any of these. He has much of Tamagno's force, but none of his brazen-throated hardness of tone. It was splendid to hear runs sung with such steady energy."[21]

Some time before, Maurice Grau, managing director of the Metropolitan Opera, opened negotiations with Caruso, only to leave them unfinished, possibly due to his declining health. Now negotiations were resumed by Grau's successor, Heinrich Conried, a Viennese actor and manager who was to take over the management of the Metropolitan beginning with the 1903–04 season. The man who was to be the catalyst in the matter was Pasquale Simonelli, President of the Italian Savings Bank of New York. He knew Caruso and had heard him in Italy very early in the singer's career. He called on Conried and persuaded him to follow the outlines of the original contract proposed by Grau. It was a business venture for Simonelli, as Caruso later confirmed in a letter: "*Signor* Simonelli received his percentage as any other agent would for the five years while the contract with Conried was in effect. After the contract expired, Caruso never again paid a fee or a percentage to anyone."[22]

By the time Conried began negotiating with Caruso through Simonelli, he had heard a great deal about the tenor from Antonio Scotti and from opera lovers in New York. In addition, he had listened to Caruso's recording of "Vesti la giubba," which Simonelli had brought to him, and he was impressed by what he heard. The same was true for Simonelli, although he could hardly recognize the voice he remembered. After a steady exchange of letters had brought him closer to Caruso, the bank president ventured to say as much. The tenor's response was straightforward: "I can well understand that you did not recognize me in the phonograph, because my voice has undergone an extraordinary development, and everyone who heard me in the early days of my career marvels how my voice could have gone through such an evolution."[23]

According to the tenor himself, the "evolution" of the Caruso voice began in St. Petersburg at the Conservatory, where "very much against the will of my teacher ... I first sang Radames in Aida. I attribute much of the help I got at this time to the singing of Radames. It was a great help because it developed and consolidated my voice, and really was responsible for making secure my high C, which I had been previously afraid to 'put.' "[24]

The Metropolitan contract was settled in the spring of 1903, and Caruso asked for a steep advance. On March 9, he wrote to Simonelli from Lisbon:

> First of all, my heartfelt thanks for your kind services on my behalf with Mr. Conried, [and] I will be happy to thank you in person and to compensate you as it is my duty. . . . Mr. Conried must have found my conditions regarding the advance a little bold, but given what happened to me with Mr. Grau, it was justified that I should protect my interests.

The singer went on to describe the multitude of offers he had been receiving and turning down. He was telling the truth: By the end of 1902, following his London season and thanks to the public reception of those first, celebrated G&T recordings, Caruso was in constant demand internationally. He could have lived in the most obscure corner of Europe, and the impresari would have found him. There was no longer any need to live in Milan, and he longed for a quiet retreat where he could forget about the pressures of his career.

Pursuant to the Metropolitan Opera contract, an advance of 25,000 lire was deposited in Caruso's account on 5 April 1903. With this money, he bought the majestic old Villa alle Panche, or Le Panche for short, the country estate at Castello, eleven miles from Florence, that belonged to the Giachetti family. It needed modernization, and the Carusos could not occupy it until a great deal of construction work was completed. In the meantime, the tenor gave up the apartment in Milan and moved to Florence, where he and his family took up residence in the Via della Scala until Le Panche was ready to receive them. Their prolonged absence from Italy, the coming summer season in Buenos Aires, and Caruso's Metropolitan engagement allowed time for the workmen to prepare the country home.

Although Caruso and Simonelli had a falling out over business matters later on, they kept up a lively correspondence in 1903 and for many years thereafter. Caruso kept the New Yorker informed about his movements. From Lisbon, he was going to Monte Carlo "and then to Paris for the big Verdi Gala [*serata*], then on April 29 I will leave for Buenos Aires." He also expected to "give a few extra performances in Rio de Janeiro."[25]

The Verdi Gala that was to take place at the Paris Opéra was a fundraiser for a Verdi monument. However, the event was abruptly canceled. The 5 April 1903 issue of *Le Figaro* announced that the Gala would not take place as planned because "Messrs. Tamagno and Caruso, who have promised their services, are unable to be in Paris at the specified date." No further explanation was given, and one can only regret that Francesco Tamagno, on the eve of his retirement, could not symbolically pass on the baton to the supreme Italian tenor of the next generation. Because of the cancellation, Paris had to wait another year for Caruso's local debut.

For his part, Simonelli kept Caruso informed about forthcoming events on the New York musical scene. These involved Alessandro Bonci, the tenor whom the operatic world of the time held to be his rival. Responding to the news that Bonci was to be engaged in New York, Caruso wrote Simonelli quite candidly on June 15: "I don't hide it from you that I don't look favorably upon Bonci being engaged, not that I am afraid of him as an artist, because I am Caruso and he is Bonci and there is an abyss between us, but because he is not a decent fellow. I hope his engagement is after mine, and I would like you to keep me informed about it."

In early April, Caruso wrote to Simonelli from Monte Carlo:

> In the meantime, I inform you that my wife is a most distinguished lyric artist, having tread the boards of the best theaters, such as Scala and Dal Verme of Milan, San Carlo in Naples, Massimo in Palermo, Imperial in Petersburg, and the principal Italian and South American theaters. At the moment, you can well understand that there is no need for her to sing considering that I alone suffice, however for North America I would make an exception. Her stage name (if you wish to be informed) is Ada Giachetti.

Were these words inspired by Ada? Was Caruso relenting in his opposition to her pursuit of a career? The only thing certain is that Caruso had second thoughts about broaching the subject, to which he returned briefly in a letter of September 9: "One day I wrote to you about my wife, [but] later I regretted it."

Apart from professional concerns, Caruso turned to Simonelli for help with personal matters. In a letter of 9 September 1903, he asked Simonelli to find accommodations for him, Ada, a maid, and a valet. In his next letter, written from Rio de Janeiro on September 19, he returned to the matter of housing. "Considering that I don't know the customs of the country, I must rely entirely on you. Should I stay at a hotel? Well then, let's go to a hotel. Should I live in a house? I will live in a house. Who could better advise me than you?" Caruso specified that he wished to have "an apartment with southern exposure, consisting of a drawing room to receive visitors, a dressing room, a bedroom with two beds, one with a double bed, and additional bedrooms for others."

The South American engagement was followed by a short rest in Florence; then Ada and Enrico sailed on the ship *Sardegna* and arrived in New York on 11 November 1903. Fofò was left with Rina, as he later recalled:

> When in 1903 Papa and Mamma were in New York, I spent the entire winter season in Naples with Auntie Rina, who never let me out of her sight. Because of this, I had to swallow for eleven nights, almost in succession, that many performances of *Tosca,* in which she was highly acclaimed. This gave me such an aversion for this opera that I have avoided it ever since. I cannot say that I don't enjoy the main arias, but I became overly familiar with the plot and action.

Enrico Caruso's association with his European impresario, Emil Ledner, dates from this period. Their correspondence began even before the singer left for his first North American season; Ledner was to handle a series of concerts for him in Europe at the explicit request of Metropolitan Opera director Heinrich Conried. As it turned out, Ledner became Caruso's exclusive manager from this time forward, serving in this capacity until the outbreak of World War I.

Initially, there was a question about the number of performances Caruso was to sing in his first season at the Metropolitan. The singer said to Ledner, "Director Conried fears that there will not be enough interest in me for forty performances." He added: "If I really fail to please enough to sing forty times, I will leave whether I have a contract or not; and if I fail, I will leave after my first appearance."[26]

Caruso did not fail, nor did he create a furor. The gala audience liked the new tenor in the opening night *Rigoletto* on 23 November 1903.[27] Richard Aldrich gave a fair assessment in a sober, front-page review in *The New York Times* of November 24.

> It signalized the first appearance of the most important of Mr. Conried's new artists, one upon whom much will depend during the coming season—Enrico Caruso, who took the part of the Duke. He made a highly favorable impression and he went far to substantiate the reputation that had preceded him

in this country. .... His voice is purely a tenor in its quality of high range, and of large power, but inclined to take on the "white" quality in its upper ranges when he lets it forth. In *mezza voce* it has expressiveness and flexibility, and when so used its beauty is most apparent.

Neither this reviewer nor any other in New York could know that the evening inaugurated what posterity would regard as the Caruso era of the Metropolitan Opera House. Caruso's first American season has been discussed and documented in every major biography. In short, after a few performances, New York audiences grew to like him and accorded him his fair share of applause. The arrival of a much-heralded new tenor completely overshadowed the fact that the opening night *Rigoletto* was also the house debut of conductor Arturo Vigna, who remained with the Metropolitan for four seasons.

Outside the Opera House, the Carusos made many friends in New York. Because they knew very little English, they were largely limited to Italian artistic and social circles, and Caruso was often dependent on the assistance of friends. One who was always ready to help was Antonio Scotti, who later recalled an incident revealing of Caruso's open, honest character.

> I remember after the first big triumph at the Metro-politan when the critics wanted to see him and he asked me to act as his interpreter. One of them asked Caruso to tell them about the time early in his career when the audience in [Sicily] hissed him, and Caruso said after I had translated the question for him:
> "Tell them I was drunk."
> I was horrified.
> "Fool," I said. "You can't say things like that in America for the papers. If you do you will always be known as the drunken tenor."
> So I told them that he was ill at that performance and that was the truth. But the young tenor, new to America, thought that by saying he was drunk he could most quickly and satis-factorily explain his failure.[28]

While in New York, Ada was introduced as Mrs. Caruso and treated accordingly. The notion that she was married to Caruso was so firmly established then and on her subsequent visits that as late as 1908, the usually astute New York reporters referred to her as Caruso's wife.

Ada as well as Enrico spent the entire 1903–04 Met season in New York. Life in the American metropolis was a new experience for them both, and they enjoyed the attention the prominent members of the Italian colony lavished on them.

One relationship that dated from this time had long-term consequences. After attending Caruso's Metropolitan debut, Marziale Sisca, publisher of the Italian-language newspaper *La Follia di New York,* sent the tenor a congratulatory note and requested a photograph to be published in *La Follia.*

"I am sorry I cannot oblige you with a photograph," Caruso wrote to Sisca on 10 December 1903, "because at the moment I don't have any. In case a sketch I made of myself will do, I enclose it for you." Sisca printed the autocaricature in the next issue of his paper. He also began to pay periodic visits to Caruso, and a friendship developed. When Sisca invited Caruso to attend the annual banquet of the Italian Chamber of Commerce, the latter amused himself and the guests by drawing caricatures. Inspired by the excellence of the drawings, Sisca used them to illustrate his article about the banquet. Thus began Caruso's weekly contribution of drawings to *La Follia,* which continued until his death. As Sisca later acknowledged: "Circulation rose vertiginously, winning readers even among those who did not know Italian, but who bought the paper because of Caruso's caricatures."[29]

Returning home from America, Caruso stopped in Paris to make his debut in the French capital. His debut role was the Duke in *Rigoletto,* as in his debut at the Metropolitan Opera the previous winter and at Covent Garden the year before. One reviewer wrote: "If he does not have the elegance and distinction of a Jean de Reszke, Caruso possesses a facile and light tenor voice, without a doubt the most attractive [to be heard] at the moment: He had to encore 'La donna è mobile' three times!"[30]

The major event of the year in the Carusos' personal lives was Ada's fifth and last pregnancy. The narrator of the present reminiscences—who was apparently predestined for life in America—was conceived during that first season in New York. Following their return to Italy, Ada and Enrico told Fofò that "Mamma had bought him a little brother."

With the vigorous assistance of a midwife, I came into this world at 7 a.m. on 7 September 1904, in the bedroom of the newly furnished villa, Le Panche.

Ada Giachetti, soprano, and Enrico Caruso, tenor, became my parents.

Caruso in 1903 in his
Metropolitan Opera debut
role, the Duke of Mantua
in Verdi's *Rigoletto*.
Photography A. Dupont.

Jean de Reszke, the
aristocratic tenor whose
memory shadowed Caruso
during his first seasons in
New York.

Soprano Emmy Destinn and Enrico Caruso, ca. 1905.

Maurice Grau, manager of
the Metropolitan Opera
(1900-04). Photography
A. Dupont.

Heinrich Conried,
manager of the
Metropolitan Opera
(1904-08).
Photography A. Dupont.

Postcard photograph of conductor Leopoldo Mugnone, addressed to Titta Ruffo in Odessa, Russia, in 1905. Courtesy of Dr. Ruffo Titta, Jr.

Caruso and friends at Montecatini. Caruso, drinking, is third from right; at far left is conductor Leopoldo Mugnone.

Four pen and ink caricatures by Enrico Caruso, drawn on postcards bearing the "Collezione Caruso" imprint. *Top, left to right,* Caruso and conductor Alberto Vigna; *bottom, left to right,* baritone Antonio Scotti and soprano Marcella Sembrich. These were the cast and conductor at Caruso's Metropolitan Opera debut in 1903.

Eight self-caricatures of Caruso singing, expressing various emotions, captioned by himself.

Top, from left: Sostenuto con calma, sustained with calm; *Allegrezza rubando,* stolen gaiety.

Bottom, from left: Vibrato giocoso, jocular vibrato; *Strazio,* torment.

Top, from left: Soavissimo, most sweetly;
Furioso agitato, with agitation, fury.

Bottom, from left: Marcando con tristezza,
accentuating with sadness; *Annotato triste,*
indicating sorrow.

Pen and ink self-caricature drawn by Caruso on Hotel Shelbourne stationery in Dublin, 1909.

Two postcards of Caruso's self-caricatures.

CARUSO'S SERIES OF POSTAL CARDS

Signor Enrico Caruso
Copyrighted 1908 by Marziale Sisca

SIGNOR CARUSO AS SKETCHED BY HIMSELF

CHAPTER FOUR

At Le Panche

MY arrival was perfectly timed for my globe-trotting father, and he was at Le Panche when I was born. On 8 September 1904, he wrote to his friend "Don Pasqualino" (Pasquale) Simonelli:

> I have been waiting and am still waiting for the news of the birth of a baby in your house, but I am the first to give you such news. In fact yesterday morning at 7 a.m. after a terrible night came to the world a beautiful baby boy who, thank God, did not harm the mother who is now resting after her labor. And what labor it was! I hope you have received my telegram, and I am now waiting for you to reciprocate with the good news that your wife had a successful delivery.

My birth certificate states that "*un tale Enrico Caruso si presentò davanti la prefettura*" ("a certain Enrico Caruso appeared before the magistrate"); my mother's name was shown as "n.n." My baptism took place in the chapel of the villa and must have been a festive event, because Fofò distinctly remembered the celebration that followed, when he filled himself with sweets to his heart's content.

I was destined to carry my father's name and baptized Enrico

Roberto Giovanni Caruso. Rina Giachetti and Roberto De Sanna (hence the Roberto) were my godparents; Giovanni came from my uncle or, perhaps, my great-grandfather. Despite this broad selection of names, Father called me "Mimmi" from the day I was born.

Some biographers have suggested that just as my parents named my brother Rodolfo after the tenor hero in *La Bohème,* the opera in which they were appearing when they fell in love, they nicknamed me after the leading female character of the same opera. The truth is that the name Mimì is unrelated to the word *Mimmi.* In Italian, *il mimmo* or *il mimmi* means "the little one" or "the baby." The term can be used for boys or girls: My Uncle Enrico Giachetti's little daughter, named Rina after my aunt, was known in the family all her life as "Mimma," which is the feminine form of the Italian for "baby."

I was a welcome addition to the family. Fofò recorded that "the birth of my baby brother brought great happiness to Father and a good deal of joy to me as well, because I immediately set about to take advantage of the newcomer and make him a part of my games as a delightful playmate."

By the time my parents returned to Italy from New York, most of the remodeling at Le Panche was finished, so they could move into their new and spacious home. Father supervised the completion of the work, but somehow it did not progress as quickly as in the past. Father realized why the pace had slowed when the construction foreman came to ask him to close the windows when he practiced in the mornings. It seems that as soon as he began to sing, all the workmen put down their tools and just listened until he was finished.

Father actively involved himself with the renovations and with the planting of the gardens. As Fofò recorded, Father once said, "Next to my wife and my music, I love flowers." A hired gardener, Emilio Tani, kept the parks and flower beds neat at all times.

Fofò recounted an amusing incident from this period.

Father devoted himself with all his passion and artistic inspiration to the design of new construction that was completed only gradually, some of it still unfinished when we moved in. He spent a lot of time with the laborers, often working alongside them, and he especially enjoyed offering suggestions to the painters and decorators and giving them a hand.

The grounds took up most of Father's attention. Because the terrain was flat and he liked hills, he had an artificial hill raised in the garden. He designed paths, parks, flower beds. He had a beautiful hothouse built for tropical flowers which was a marvel of the times. We also generated our own electricity for the house. The mechanic in charge of the large, fuel-driven motor was to have taught Father to drive the car he had bought only recently. Until then we had only horsedrawn carriages. Mamma was somewhat skeptical about Father's automobilistic aptitude.

"You are a great tenor, but I just don't see you as a driver."

He took Mother's teasing in good humor and, partly for the sake of his self-esteem, decided to learn to drive. The garden road had a long, straight avenue lined with an endless row of potted chrysanthemums before it curved away. With the mechanic at his side, Papa maneuvered the car, then with great jerking jumps amidst a burst of backfires, the Britzia Zust took off. Mother, I, and other spectators prudently followed Papa's progress from the top of the little hill freshly planted with trees and shrubs.

All went well as long as the avenue was straight. Where the curve began, he was irresistibly drawn to the row of vases on the right and demolished every last one, sending them into a thousand fragments and rolling over all the poor chrysanthemums. We saw him stop the car. We did not hear the words but saw Papa gesticulating at the mechanic who, in turn, responded just as energetically. The car turned around and with another four or five leaps and jerks took off again. The nice row of pots on the other side suffered the same fate as the rest. Arriving at the point of departure, Papa got out. From that day on he never drove again. I think this was due to Mother's merciless ribbing. But I felt mortified for him.

With each birthday, Fofò became even more mischievous and found new ways to get into trouble at Le Panche. The villa had an imposing curved walnut staircase. This was designed by Father, who had it covered with a light-colored carpet that ran down the middle. The carpet left an indelible memory in Fofò's mind, just as Fofò left an indelible memory on the carpet. He narrates:

One day my father, who always took an interest in my studies, ordered me to do my homework. I was to remain in my room on the second floor, but I thought I would be more comfortable downstairs on the glassed-in veranda, where I could see the garden and the white sheepdogs I liked so much. This way I could study and keep an eye on my favorite animals. I bundled up my books and notes, took the inkwell and the pen (there were no fountain pens for kids in those days), settled on the veranda, and began to study. All of a sudden I heard my father's powerful voice from the stairs.

"Who got this carpet dirty with inkspots?"

I was struck dumb and stayed quiet. Papa continued to grumble and in a moment called me by name.

"Rodolfo!"

Not "Fofò," oh boy! When Papa called me by my full name, it meant he was very mad.

"Rodolfo . . ."

"Papa? You're calling me?" I said in a small voice.

"Come up here!"

"Coming."

I tried to get up from the table, but my legs were weak. I finally moved and went to the bottom of the stairs. At the top, on the landing, stood Papa, furious. He launched an attack:

"Did you spill the ink?"

"Me?"

I must have had a dumb expression on my face because Father said immediately:

"Come up here!" I did, with reluctance. "Show me your hands."

Oh, horror! They were covered with ink, and I wasn't even aware of it.

"I told you to study and not to run around!"

"But Papa, all I wanted . . ."

I ducked just in time to avoid a slap. I turned and dashed downstairs because I saw in my father's eyes a whole cloudful of slaps about to rain upon my head. Papa was in slippers and came after me. I made it to the glass doors of the veranda without being caught. I ran across the garden to an iron gate that was erected to separate the park from the fields. When I was outside I looked back and saw Papa, who, having lost his slippers on the staircase, was not prepared to cross the gravel of the garden barefooted. I heaved a sigh of relief; but after I watched him reenter, I did not have the courage to go back into the house. It was mid-day and I was hungry, and as it was threshing time, I went to look for the peasants. I found them sitting in the middle of the field under a tree, about to start eating. When they saw me approach, they asked:

"*Signorino,* would you care to join us? We don't have beefsteak, just good beans cooked in oil and fresh bread. Make yourself at home."

At first I did not know whether I should accept, but my appetite was growing and it was easy to give in. I ate the heartiest meal of my entire youth.

The hours passed and I was still afraid to go home. My rebellion, which after all was but an escape from a good spanking, seemed out of all proportion. The moon rose and I stayed outside. Finally a servant came to look for me, reassuring me about the paternal reactions. I was given a cold meal and I ate alone. Shortly afterwards Papa came in and with a good-natured cuff said:

"Try to be more careful. I don't like dirty and careless people."

He kissed me, and with that we sealed the peace.

Although my father was very strict with me, in my childish way I worshipped the ground he walked on, and because of that I was very sensitive to anything that had to do with his person. I accepted reprimands or spankings from my father, which were given as deserved, because I never saw a trace of uncontrollable rage in his face, but rather an expression of sadness. My mother on the other hand had manifestations that were rather shocking. As a matter of fact, I remember that the earliest beatings I received from her were accompanied by terrible screams, even if the offense was minor.

Once in Milan, as we were leaving the dentist's office, I found in the empty waiting room a little girl's purse, obviously forgotten by another patient. It had a few small coins in it. To me it seemed a fortune, because until that time I had never owned a cent, and thus I furtively hid this find without telling anyone. We returned to Le Panche from Milan, I with my treasure beside me. I had my own room, and when we arrived I prudently hid my treasure in a chest of drawers under my shirts. One day, tidying up my belongings, Mamma discovered it. She called me and demanded to know where I found it. After some hesitation and unsure of what I had done, I ended up by telling her the whole story. At that moment Mamma gave me two powerful slaps across my face that made me dizzy, then picked me up and stretched me out on the bed, pulled down my pants, and gave me such a beating with all her strength that I began to howl savagely. She never stopped screaming: "You are a thief! You are a thief!" My father and the other relatives ran in and literally had to drag my infuriated mother away.

I was five years old.

Another serious incident occurred a short time later. I don't remember for what transgression she tied me tightly to the well at Le Panche, and with the rope struck me several times with the expression of one possessed. My father fortunately heard her demented screams and ran to my rescue. He had to give her a resounding slap to end her hysterics. These incidents, in contrast to the severe but serene punishments meted out by my father, may explain my respect and sentiments toward him.

FOFÒ was happy to have a little brother, but his joy was short-lived. Within a month after my birth, Mother sent him to the Collegio Cicognini at Prato. For some reason, even before I arrived, there was never a close, loving relationship between Mother and Fofò. The lack of rapport was underscored when he was sent to the boarding school, in his words, "by Mamma, against my father's advice, because she did not know how to restrain my vivacity." He ascribed this decision exclusively to Ada, who, to his way of thinking, did not want him around. I cannot imagine in what way a child of six could have interfered with her life, considering that she had servants to control the boy's "vivacity." But then, the one role at which she consistently failed was that of motherhood.

Fofò was terribly miserable and homesick, and from the moment he arrived at the Cicognini, he did nothing but cry. The director of the school took the boy into his own home and family to calm him, but to no avail. In the end he notified Father that he should come and get his son or else the boy was going to sob himself to death. Six-year-old Fofò was simply too young to be abruptly transplanted into the cold and impersonal setting of the quasi-military school. In his own words,

> Besides living with my parents, one of my pleasures was to be able to have breakfast with them; buttered toast with coffee, in bed if possible. At the school we had to rise at five in

the morning, wash and dress in a mad hurry to go into an enormous refectory where we had to gulp down from heavy clay mugs a little milk barely darkened by some so-called coffee and slices of hard, day-old bread. It was just too horrible for me.

Father must have come home briefly between his Berlin and London engagements and made the trip to Prato to collect Fofò. Remembering the incident, Fofò repeated that "Papa was happy to liberate me, because the idea of the boarding school was not his at all but Mother's. In the midst of embraces and caresses I said good-bye to the majestic mass of the *collegio* and went home. He came for me driving a fiery horse harnessed to a sulky. I always admired his skill at handling horses."

Fofò was ecstatic to be at home again. The dreadful experience left a lasting impression, and he must have made an effort to remain on his best behavior. After this, there was no further attempt to send him to a boarding school for another two years. He received private instruction at home and could again enjoy an easy-going family life. We two got along well; Fofò enjoyed having me around and played with me as if I were his own live toy. He recalled:

> The time passed and my little brother began to toddle around. Mamma had brought me a little pedal-driven automobile with two seats from Paris. I was overjoyed, Father incomparably less so, because that thing was to the detriment of my studies; in addition it endangered my little brother, who greatly enjoyed these rides as a passenger on the seat behind me. I must have had a sense of responsibility already at that age, because for fear of losing him over a bump or ditch, I strapped him in like a little salami, while he just smiled and happily clapped his hands. In fact, one day I took a curve too fast and we turned over, giving him a nice bump on his head which earned me a good spanking. But those were happy years, because my parents were together and happiness radiated from Papa's face.

There can be no doubt that my parents were happy together. I was too young to store up memories, but Fofò had many recollections of this period. He told me that I was loved and babied. Father often played with me and used to walk the property carrying me on his shoulders. He made a few futile attempts to sketch me, but like most toddlers, I was too restless to sit still. Fofò, on the other hand, was old enough to take orders, and much to his displeasure, he was often used as a model.

Papa loved to paint and model in clay. I remember extensive sittings that made me long to roam with my companions, the children of the gardener and the peasants. Instead, he held me captive for long hours in a large room he turned into a studio. It had Indian arms, trophies from Borneo, Japanese swords and daggers, grotesque Japanese masks, and a stuffed crocodile whose open mouth filled me with terror. I always passed in a wide circle around it. Papa demanded that I stay immobile, which was contrary to my hyperactive nature, and every now and then I ruined a pose because I was unable to recapture the posture that had inspired his imagination. Papa then seemed to me like a slave driver, and I could not understand his melancholic and displeased expression. To be sure, working on me required the patience of Job, which was not one of Papa's virtues. In the end the clay head was finished, and even to my undeveloped artistic sense, it seemed rather successful. In fact, later on I had to admit it was a minor masterpiece.

SOON after I was born, I was placed in the care of a wet-nurse, Giulia Focosi, who was the wife of Eduardo, the customs agent of the district. For Italian women, breast-feeding was a form of contraception, as a woman rarely ovulates so long as she is producing milk. Giulia, with her imposing stature and generous bosom, breast-fed me for over fifteen months. The wet-nurse freed Mother to travel with Father to New York for his second Metropolitan season.

By this time, Ada had apparently given up all hope of resuming her career. As she later recounted:

[Caruso was to appear in *La Bohème,*] and he was to sing it with Nellie Melba, an Australian soprano from Melbourne. At the last moment, however, she fell ill and the impresario, who knew me by name, asked me to replace her, offering me two thousand dollars per night, but Caruso would not permit it. He resisted all my appeals and prayers as well as those of the impresario. But every night thereafter, following each performance of *La Bohème,* with a charm that was so typical of him, he would hand me the two thousand dollars as a gift!   (*A Noite,* Rio de Janeiro, 4 March 1938)

Apart from the pardonable exaggeration of the fee (inflated either by Mother's memory or by the over-zealous journalist wanting to make a good story better), this vignette is revealing of Caruso's attitude. At this stage of his career, he surely did not fear that Ada's success would eclipse his own. It is more likely that he did not want it said that Ada obtained an engagement because she was "Mrs. Caruso." Mother obeyed his wishes, but she harbored a deep resentment.

During this second New York season, the Carusos rented a house and gave Italian dinners for their circle of intimates. Mother fulfilled her obligations as hostess, behaving as expected of a Metropolitan tenor's wife. *The New York Times* referred to her as "Mme. Caruso" and described her as "a handsome woman with dark eyes and hair."[1]

Father sang *Faust* and *Carmen* in French for the first time. During the summer, he had taken formal lessons for three months, and he now claimed to have mastered French "sufficiently at least for the purposes of opera."[2] In the years ahead, he gained a speaking fluency in the language.

After Conried ended his second Metropolitan season, he felt secure enough about the company to take it on its first major cross-country tour. The stops included Boston, Pittsburgh, Cincinnati, Chicago, Minneapolis, Omaha, Kansas City, San Francisco, and Los Angeles. Caruso's letters and postcards kept his friends in New York informed about the details. He had to maintain a rigorous performance schedule while coping with serious health problems. Mother, worried about him, joined him on the tour. On 10 March 1905, he wrote to Simonelli from Boston: "After *Lucia* and *Pagliacci* this evening [is] *Gioconda,* and I hope to have the same success in spite of my 'mumps.' I hope it won't develop into anything, because it could have bad consequences for everybody. My wife is here precisely to look after me. Tomorrow we depart for Pittsburg [*sic*]." Luckily, his condition cleared up by the time they reached Chicago. It had no ill effect on his singing, and he proudly reported to Simonelli on March 23: "Here too, in Chicago, the success was colossal, because everybody thought that Caruso was Conried's *bloffe* [bluff]; instead I showed them at my first appearance. I am satisfied because things are going well, and the stress did not affect either my voice or my health. The 'mumps' have gone, and everybody says that they made my voice more beautiful."

Simonelli, however, must have read some unflattering reports about Caruso in the newspapers and sent them on to him. In reply, Caruso wrote from Minneapolis on March 26: "My success in Chicago in *Lucia, Pagliacci,* and *Gioconda* was simply phenomenal and will be remembered for many generations. Apropos that correspondent, one can see he was not in the theater and has not even read the critique because it began thus: 'Caruso Is King'—'Caruso Has Stolen All Hearts'—'Caruso Wounderfull' [*sic*] and so on."

On April 1, Caruso wrote from Kansas City: "Success all along the line (not the railway line, although most of the time we are on top of it)." But his progress from success to success could not alter the fact that traveling and singing day after day as if on a road show was strenuous work, and he was glad when the tour ended. Upon his return from the West Coast, he sang his farewell to New York in a benefit concert at the Waldorf Astoria and then sailed for Europe. On May 13, he was back in Paris appearing in *Fedora* with Lina Cavalieri in the title role and Titta Ruffo lending added distinction to the cast. Soon after, on May 22, his two-month engagement in London began.

At the end of July 1905, Caruso traveled to Ostende, Belgium. He sang the Duke in *Rigoletto* and gave a concert on August 3 and 6 respectively. Then, finally, he could go home to Le Panche to relax—by working. From Naples, where he visited his parents and Giovanni, he wrote to Simonelli: "I keep working on my large homestead because there is always something to do."[3] In search of an artistic outlet besides sketching, he turned to sculpture. "I have begun to model a whole head of my Fofò, and I hope that it will turn out well."[4] At this stage of his life, Caruso considered himself no more than a talented amateur in the visual arts, and he dismissed Simonelli's compliments. "You are teasing me saying that you hope to have a bust made by me," he wrote on August 13. "I only doodle, which kind friends find pleasing, however I know they are just little things [I do] to pass the time." In the same letter, he mentioned that "the King of England has sent me a magnificent photograph of himself in a fitting silver frame with his monogram, and also on the photograph 'Edward VII Rex.' "

In an age when major artists are booked several years in advance, one cannot help but smile when catching a glimpse, through my father's correspondence, of the inner workings of such an important opera house as the Metropolitan at the turn of the century. Caruso wrote, for instance: "I have not seen Conried, but I expect him any day to discuss the operas to be given during the next season. For sure there will be Puccini's *Manon,* but *Iris*—I don't believe so."

In the fall of 1905, Mother returned with Father to New York. A large picture of my parents aboard ship, in the company of Johanna Gadski, Heinrich Knote, Andreas Dippel, and Scotti, was published in the 12 November 1905 issue of *The New York Times*. I believe it is the only photograph I have ever seen of my parents together.

This season firmly established my father as a Met artist, and when it ended, he joined the company on its second cross-country tour. The second stop was the New National Theater in Washington, D.C., where Father sang Edgardo in *Lucia di Lammermoor* on 23 March 1906, and Canio in *Pagliacci* on March 24. It was a particularly warm night, and Caruso spent the intermission in the alley by the stage door, cooling off and entertaining one of the porters with his stories. Suddenly, the doorman appeared informing him that "the President is here and would like to meet you." Caruso thought it was a joke and sent back the message that the President should wait. He continued with his stories, and when he finally reentered the theater,

> I nearly die, then. Inside by the doorman stands—who you think? T. R. Himself! He stands there, he is hot, he is not in a dress suit, he smile his fine smile at me, and grasp my hand.
> "Mr. Caruso," he say, "I hear you are ver' busy in the alley, so I wait for you!"
> What can I do? "Mr. Presidente . . ." I stammer, but I can say no more. My heart aches. All the time I am acting foolish in that alley, I could have been talking to T. R.![5]

Father greatly admired President Roosevelt, and in a reversal of the normal procedure, it was the singer who asked his distinguished caller for an autographed photo. Roosevelt was happy to oblige and the following day sent a framed photo of himself, duly autographed and dedicated "to Enrico Caruso."

Taking a cue from the President, Washington society focused its attention on the visit of the Metropolitan Opera artists. As reported in the 8 April 1906 issue of the *New York Sun,* one enterprising automobile agent took advantage of the surge of interest. One day he stopped Father and Pol Plançon in the hotel lobby and told them that a wealthy and distinguished Washingtonian had placed his automobile at the disposal of *Signor* Caruso and his friends. Since they had time on their hands, Caruso and Plançon proceeded to take in the sights for an hour and a half. They were chauffeured by the agent, who made sure that they traveled the most fashionable thoroughfares and were widely recognized. The sales gimmick worked: The agent was inundated with orders for the particular car—if it was good enough for

Caruso, it was good enough for a number of wealthy admirers. The agent reinforced the popular misconception by claiming that he was "shipping two cars to Caruso's place in Italy."

After Washington, the company performed in Pittsburgh, Chicago, St. Louis, and Kansas City before traveling all the way to the West Coast, where the tour ended in an unexpected climax. On April 17, they performed *Carmen* at the Grand Opera House in San Francisco. Members of the cast retired late and on April 18, rose earlier than planned: It was the morning of the San Francisco earthquake.

Fofò, left at Le Panche in the care of Luisa and Giuseppe Guidalotti, learned about it within hours. He narrates:

> My parents were in America, my baby brother with his wet-nurse, *Signora* Focosi, and I lived alone at the villa Le Panche with a relative named Luisa, Mamma's companion, who took care of the household. Giuseppe Guidalotti, Mother's cousin, served at that time as Father's administrator in charge of his properties; he later married Luisa. One night we were dining in one of the little parlors when all of a sudden the telephone rang. Guidalotti went to answer it. I remember well his violent reaction. He hung up and with an upset expression said:
>
> "San Francisco has been destroyed by an earthquake and now is in flames."
>
> Luisa began to cry. I didn't understand anything about this excitement until Guidalotti said to me:
>
> "You know, your Papa was singing in that city, and we have no news of him."

A day or so later, word reached Le Panche that Father was safe. Because he was Caruso, the most colorful figure of the Metropolitan troupe, stories blossomed around him. Some were plausible, some were preposterous, and most were contradictory. If one article claimed that Caruso lost all his costumes when the Grand Opera burned to the ground, there was another to quote him as saying that "all my belongings were saved. Fortunately my stage costumes were at the hotel and not one was lost."[6] It is impossible to separate fact from fiction. Adding to the supply of half-truths, and strictly on the strength of the source, I offer what my brother preserved of Father's tale about the terrifying experience.

When he returned to his hotel, he took a bath and went to

bed. After a few hours of sleep (he knew afterwards that it was 5:13 in the morning), he felt the bed move as if someone were shaking it. Thinking that it was his valet, he said:

"Martino, I am tired, let me sleep."

And he went back to sleep. In a few minutes the bed shook even more violently and a wardrobe with a mirrored door fell on the foot of the bed, breaking the mirror into smithereens. Papa sat bolt upright and saw the walls swaying, while large chunks of plaster fell off the ceiling onto the radiator pipes. Water from the broken pipes began to fill the room. The twisting walls caused short circuits and electrical fires, and the smell of burnt rubber filled the place. For the moment Father was unable to move, his reflexes paralyzed by the swaying and his throat tightened by fear. The earthquakes he had heard about since his boyhood flashed through his mind: Vesuvio, Etna, Stromboli, Lisboa, Guadalupe ... Then the infernal shaking stopped and he finally screamed: "Martino! Martino!" And the reply came: "*Signor* Enrico! *Signor* Enrico!"

In the next instant his faithful Martino burst in from the adjoining room. In that terrible danger they held onto each other, waiting for a few more seconds. There were no further shocks, so they feverishly started to pack. They hastily threw into two trunks the most necessary clothing and valuables. Once they had done that at lightning speed, they rushed down on the interior fire stairs because the elevators had stopped working. They dragged the trunks from landing to landing while smoke began to fill the stairwell. Once in the lobby, they each dragged a trunk across to the entrance and were out in the open. Martino, concerned about the costumes that were left at the theater nearby, turned to Father:

"*Signor* Enrico, I'll run over to the theater to see how things are."

Father stayed with the trunks on the sidewalk. There were many collapsed houses all around, flames were rising here and there, but the multi-story hotel still stood, thanks to its steel structure. There were cracks in its facade, and water gushing from the broken pipes on each floor gave the impression of an immense cascading waterfall. A subsequent shock finally cut off the water entirely. Papa stood there all confused, trying to decide what to do next. With a few friends who had joined him in the meantime, they began to work out plans for their escape. An unidentified lady approached him, exclaiming with malicious wit:

"Well, *Signor* Caruso, perhaps you have brought the volcanic temperament of your Vesuvio this far?"

Papa didn't even deign to respond with a comeback; in those moments he was in no mood for levity. This however distracted him for a few seconds. He turned back to the trunks. He couldn't believe his eyes. There was only one left! Looking around he was amazed to see about a hundred steps away a pig-tailed Chinaman trotting jauntily with the trunk on his shoulder as if he were minding his own business. Springing in pursuit of that character, Papa drew his revolver and fired two shots in the air. The effect was amazing. The Chinaman, frightened by the shots and Father's yelling, dropped the trunk, and "putting four feet to the ground," vanished in a flash.

Martino returned with the news that the theater was in flames, and the costumes were going up in smoke. Because their lives were saved, all that was now meaningless.

An American gentleman placed an automobile at their disposal. Carrying their modest luggage, they crossed many streets engulfed in flames. They left San Francisco and took refuge on a hill where they camped out for the night. They appeased their hunger with a few cans of sardines and crackers, but when they wanted to slake their thirst, they found that the mineral-water bottles [in the car] had been filled with gasoline as a precautionary measure, and they had neglected to bring along drinking water. [In fact, there was none to be had.] To quench their thirst during the night, they tried to drink the nauseatingly oily and warm water from the radiator.

In the morning they managed to board the ferry to Oakland and took refuge in the villa of friends.

In the meantime the city continued to burn. On the third day a train was assembled in Oakland for New York. As a memento of the terrible experience, Father kept the old-fashioned wing collar torn from his shirt; it was stiff from having been soaked through with sweat, and black with soot. He wrote the date of the disaster on it and carried that collar with him from San Francisco to New York.

It is a well-known story which bears repeating that among the belongings Father salvaged from his hotel room was the photograph of President Roosevelt. When he reached Lafayette Park, he wanted to get inside an enclosure guarded by soldiers to rest for awhile, but, as he later said, he was told he

> looked strong enough to go on. Suddenly a soldier said: "What's that you've got?" and there, under my arm, unconsciously I carried the autographed photograph of President Roosevelt, three feet square. Whereupon the soldier said: "Any friend of Teddy's goes inside," so I had a good grass bed till daylight when friends took me in.[7]

The Metropolitan artists left by train, and within a few days they were back on the East Coast. While it is clear that Mother did not travel with Father to San Francisco, I have been unable to establish whether she remained in New York. It is possible that when he left on the cross-country tour, she sailed for England by herself. In any case, she met him in London, and it must have been a great relief to her when she could embrace him again.

Caruso returned to Europe from New York, but he had two more months of singing ahead of him before he could go home to Italy. Within four weeks of the San Francisco earthquake, he was performing at Covent Garden. In London, he sang twenty-nine performances of eight operas in addition to two concerts; then he spent the month of August in Ostende, Belgium, presenting eight recitals at the Kursaal. Finally, at the end of August, he returned home for a month of well-deserved rest.

During this period, he purchased a very large estate with a sumptuous villa at Lastra a Signa, outside Florence, a newsworthy event reported on 11 August 1906 by *Il Mondo artistico,* among other papers. The villa, named Bellosguardo, originally belonged to the Pucci family; Father bought it from the current owners, whose name was Campi. Although the villa was not truly in disrepair, he spent a great deal of money modernizing and improving it, redesigning the gardens and cleaning and repairing the fountains.

In the region, there was a holiday called *La Festa dei Pucci* when, one day a year, the gardens of Bellosguardo were opened to visitors. The local people could come up, picnic in the park, and wander about as they pleased. When Father bought the villa, he had the best intentions of maintaining the tradition. But during the next *Festa,* the visitors literally destroyed the garden, trampling the flower beds, ripping out plants, and taking whatever they desired as souvenirs. Father was annoyed and hurt at being thus repaid for his hospitality, and he forthwith abolished the annual event. To signal his displeasure, he had a twelve-foot-high wall built around the perimeter with broken glass embedded in the concrete on top.

The summer of 1906 was eventful at a personal level as well.

In London, Caruso's leading lady in three operas, *Tosca, Aida,* and *Madama Butterfly,* was Rina Giachetti. Inevitably, he and Rina saw a great deal of each other, and Mother was helpless to prevent it. The resentment she felt toward Father for forbidding her to pursue her own career must have reached a high point when she saw her husband and her sister playing love scenes onstage. Beyond the fact that all the glamor of the operatic stage, as well as the applause and accolades showered upon Rina, could well have been hers, Ada always had the lingering suspicion that the feelings between Rina and Caruso might erupt into a torrid love affair.

In 1906, it finally happened.

CHAPTER FIVE

Rina Giachetti

IT was ironic that the temporary suspension of Mother's career coincided with the beginning of Aunt Rina's. The sisters' careers meshed nicely during their joint South American tour, Rina's first major engagement. Once past her apprenticeship, Rina seems to have moved from success to success, without notable setbacks or failures, just as her sister had done half a decade earlier.

"Ada Giachetti was a little, mediocre Italian opera singer," wrote Emil Ledner in 1922;[1] and Vincent Seligman, comparing the sisters in 1938, gave the verdict: "Ada was never as good an artiste as her sister Rina."[2] The only thing these two distinguished gentlemen and generally reliable biographers have in common is that neither of them had ever heard Ada Giachetti sing. This is scarcely surprising since, until her retirement, Ada sang mostly in Italy. Rina had the longer career and performed in several European and South American countries; thus she had more time and opportunity to build an international career. Irrespective of any other feelings Rina may have nurtured about her older sister, she spoke to Fofò with admiration about Ada as a singer and an artist.

Ada's malicious letter to Caruso from Chile evidently accomplished her objective: She succeeded in disillusioning him with respect to her younger sister, and Rina's disgrace as a deflowered woman was compounded by his rejection. Rina reacted predictably, with a newfound determination to make it on her own. She broke with her family and, soon after her return from South America, accepted an engagement at the Teatro del Liceo in Barcelona. On 22 April 1900, she first appeared in the role of Olga in the local première of *Fedora,* opposite Stehle in the title role and Garbin as Loris; later in the season, she sang Micaela in *Carmen* and Musetta in *La Bohème.* Although it is a small role, her Olga in *Fedora* attracted enough attention that she was invited to repeat it a month later in Vienna. This time the cast was headed by Gemma Bellincioni, creator of the title role, and Fernando de Lucia, one of the most celebrated divi of the day. The reviewers found the "outstanding Giachetti an excellent Olga."[3]

In the fall of 1900, she sang in *La Bohème* at Casalmaggiore; and after the turn of the year, she faced the highly critical Naples audiences in the Carnival season of 1901, where she was surrounded by outstanding singers. Here she sang Colombina in Mascagni's *Le Maschere* opposite the distinguished tenor Giuseppe Anselmi, and Musetta in *La Bohème,* with Angelica Pandolfini as Mimì and De Lucia as Rodolfo. However, during this Naples engagement, just as Ada had done before her, she graduated from Musetta to Mimì. She first sang the role on 23 February 1901, partnered by De Lucia as Rodolfo. Following several performances of these two operas, she appeared in *Fedora,* again with De Lucia, who made something of a specialty of the role originally created by Caruso. Two of the three operas were conducted by Leopoldo Mugnone, the man who appeared and reappeared in the careers of the Giachetti sisters and, according to unverifiable rumors of the day, in their bedrooms as well.

During Rina's first Naples engagement, the impresario of the prestigious San Carlo Opera House, Roberto De Sanna, began to court her. He was a distinguished gentleman, good-looking and educated, with a thorough musical training, and highly respected in artistic circles. He fell in love with Rina and, as she put it, "offered her his protection." Being in a state of emotional collapse over Caruso, she accepted De Sanna's courtship. "A conjugal relationship was born, and they lived as man and wife," Rina later said, for several years. They never married, in all probability because De Sanna already had a wife, a plausible assumption that cannot be ascertained. De Sanna's "protection" was of great value to Rina in the early years of her career; at the same time, she must have had outstanding natural gifts which she developed and perfected. She was able to hold her own in the company of the foremost artists of the period, and enthusiastic reviews greeted each successive performance.

De Sanna engaged Caruso to sing at the San Carlo in 1902. After almost two years of separation, Rina and her idol met again. Rina remembered that they "made peace, but a certain coolness prevailed," no doubt due to her liaison with De Sanna.

Yet they had to make peace, for artistic if not for personal reasons. Cast as the lovers in Massenet's *Manon,* they were to sing together for the first time. According to an effusive telegraphic report in *Rassegna Melodrammatica* (22 January 1902), it was "an extraordinary success for Rina Giachetti, unsurpassable protagonist, greatly applauded during the entire role, greeted by innumerable calls. Caruso surprised us, enthused us with beauty of voice, unsurpassed artistry; twice repeated the 'Dream,' encored the invocation to God in the third act, was judged an incomparable Des Grieux." The review of *Il Mattino* stated with more detachment that Rina "was able to make excellent use of the range and limitations of her voice. She has achieved a real success. The curtain calls after each act with Caruso, must have encouraged Giachetti and dispelled for the subsequent evenings that little panic that every first night puts in the voice of singers."[4] The *Tribuna* declared her "a beautiful, admirable Manon, singing her entire role with gusto, intelligence, and freshness of voice."[5]

Rina was incapable of hiding from the audience that she was half frightened to death to sing at the side of Caruso. The February 14 issue of the *Rassegna Melodrammatica* devoted a long article to her, analyzing objectively the "perfect antithesis" of the two singers. Calling Rina alternately *Signora* and *Signorina* Giachetti, the reviewer observed that she was "apprehensive and trembling before her debut," while Caruso was "feeling sure of himself. Although she sang the second-act aria, 'Il picciol desco' ('Adieu notre petite table'), with artistic sentiment and delicacy, the paying public was silent." There was applause at the end of each act, and finally "a great, most warm and insistent applause at the end of the last act which must have pleased *Signorina* Giachetti because, having sustained the entire act with her singing, that applause signified her victory over the preconceived diffidence of a public whose severity did not allow her to overcome her fear and better demonstrate her diligent preparation and interpretative zeal."

In March 1902, she sang Musetta in Leoncavallo's *La Bohème* in the presence of the composer. She had a "clamorous success"[6] in the role. The second performance was an even "greater triumph,"[7] and she had to repeat the "Waltz Song." At the end of the month, she sang with the famous Catalan tenor Francisco Vignas in Massenet's oratorio, *Maria Maddalena;* and in April, she appeared in the same composer's *Cendrillon,* in which she was "an excellent protagonist."⁸ She closed her Naples engagement with *Mefistofele,* in which she was again partnered by Vignas.

In the late fall of 1902, she went to Torino to interpret Puccini's Manon. The *Gazzetta di Torino* singled her out from the rest of the cast, and the *Gazzetta del Popolo* found her "a great lady and the absolute mistress of a stupendous voice."⁹ She also appeared in Minhejmer's *Mazeppa,* in which she "had the opportunity to display once again the grace and seductive qualities of her beauty and virtuosity."¹⁰ On December 27, she triumphed in *Germania* in Florence at the Pergola, earning excellent notices. It was her first engagement in her home town and in the very theater where Ada had sung, and she must have had a special sense of triumph. Continuing her engagement in Florence, Rina appeared in *La Bohème,* again as Mimì, a role she seems to have permanently added to her repertory after abandoning Musetta. The reviewer of *Fieramosca* wrote: "*Signora* Giachetti is the possessor of true vocal treasure which she pours forth unsparingly, whereas in the role of the afflicted Mimì she should . . . use more *mezza voce,* those *sfumature* of which she gave such beautiful example in the phrase 'Addio senza rancor,' that earned her such warm applause."¹¹ The *Nazione* found her interpretation "true, full of feeling," adding that "she sang the role with much grace, refinement," and her "beautiful, warm voice of good range was used with much intelligence."¹²

Her first Tosca also was extremely well received. The *Gazzetta dei Teatri* (31 January 1903) reported that "Rina Giachetti has surpassed all expectations. She showed herself in every phrase an actress-singer of great worth"; not surprisingly, she had to repeat "Vissi d'arte." She received "great ovations" as Puccini's Manon, and her benefit performance of *Tosca* was a gala event, the *Corriere Italiano* recording that she received an "infinity of flowers" and "many jewels."¹³ *La Nazione* even listed by name those who sent her gifts and flowers, among them *Cavaliere* Roberto De Sanna. She was described as "beautiful . . . most elegant and esteemed . . . an excellent singer" and said to have received over ten curtain calls amidst "a copious rain of flowers" for "having conquered the favors of the public" in her "real successes in *Germania, Bohème,* and *Tosca.*"¹⁴

Her *Tosca* at the Teatro Dal Verme in Milan earned her the "enthusiasm of the public that deeply appreciates her most beautiful vocal and dramatic interpretation" (*Rassegna Melodrammatica,* 7 May 1903). *La Sera* wrote that "[she has a] secure voice, well placed, penetrating, the facility to bend it to the demands of singing, limpid diction, fine dramatic instinct, which make Giachetti a Tosca to rank with the best one can hear."[15]

At the Teatro Manzoni of Pistoia in July 1903, she was "a vibrant Ricke"[16] in *Germania* opposite Francisco Vignas.

Rina's powers of interpretation matured with each performance. By the time she opened with *Tosca* in Naples in December 1903, the *Rassegna Melodrammatica* could report an "extraordinary success."[17] On this occasion she was partnered by Emilio de Marchi, creator of Cavaradossi; the role was taken in later performances by Anselmi and Amedeo Bassi. De Marchi was also her leading man later in the season when she had a "triumphal success"[18] as Valentine in Meyerbeer's *Gli Ugonotti*. She outdid herself in the role and, as her voice warmed up, improved from act to act, giving her all in the difficult showpiece, the last-act duet. "She conquered with [her] acting [and] beauty of voice that was judged extraordinary in the fourth act."[19] She also appeared as Stephana in Giordano's *Siberia,* as Amelia in *Un Ballo in maschera,* in the title role of *Adriana Lecouvreur,* and in Acts II and III of *Poliuto* at the side of Francesco Tamagno, the creator of the title role of Verdi's *Otello,* in the final season of his career.

By 1904 Rina was an established artist. The 31 March 1904 issue of the *Rassegna Melodrammatica* published a bouquet of her reviews from a wide selection of newspapers. *Il Pungolo* praised her vocal refinement and grace.[20] According to the critic of *Roma,* she sang Stephana in *Siberia* with "soul, artistry, and feeling."[21] *Il Mattino* recorded that "this young artist in her brief and rapid career has passed from success to success, making a name for herself in such diverse repertory [and] always more genial in her art of singing and dramatic intelligence."[22] A later telegram signed by "Laplaca"[23] called her an "ideal Amelia" in *Un Ballo in maschera,* the opera in which she earned the most applause. In *Adriana Lecouvreur,* she reportedly received "a standing ovation," had to repeat "Io sono l'umile ancella" and "Povero fiori," and showed herself to be "an excellent actress, effective, a delicate singer, accomplished, delightful."[24] According to *Don Marzio,* "the most beautiful palms and the most beautiful wreaths await Rina Giachetti, who truly, in the exact value of the word as it is used in art, interpreted the role of Adriana."[25]

She next traveled to Warsaw and conquered audiences with her debut role of Tosca. The May 11 issue of *Kurjer Poranny* praised the extensive range of her "perfectly trained, beautiful voice." According to the custom of Italian singers of her generation, she stepped out of role to acknowledge "with a graceful smile and continuing bows" the applause that obliged her to repeat "Vissi d'arte." Apart from this liberty that clashed with local tradition, the reviewer conceded that "Miss Giachetti's acting cannot be faulted at all, except perhaps that her movements are slightly heavy and she has a limited ability to change the expression of her beautiful face and huge black eyes." Her Scarpia was Eugenio Giraldoni, creator of the role, who had sung it in Bologna less than four years earlier with her older sister and Caruso. The Warsaw critics' generous praise for the baritone is best reflected in a single sentence in the same review: "What was said about Mr. Giraldoni, that he is an incomparable Scarpia, turned out to be true."

A review in the May 11 issue of *Kurjer Warszawski* was even more complimentary of Rina. It stated: "To sing Tosca after Bellincioni, who, as is well known, is a great exponent of this role, is an apparent act of uncommon courage. But Miss Giachetti belongs to the small group of exceptional singers who can compete with the stars of the operatic world for the palm of primacy and are not afraid of comparisons. . . . She is indeed one of the best singers who ever visited us." The review also praised her diction, her acting abilities, and the beauty, power, expressiveness, and excellent training of her voice.

While in Warsaw, Rina gave several joint recitals with Giraldoni and gathered more laurels in *Aida, Manon,* and *Cavalleria rusticana*. After one of her particularly successful performances, the waiting crowd—in the best European tradition of opera enthusiasts—unhitched the horses from her carriage and pulled it through the town to her hotel. Poland was then under Russian rule, and Jews were often subjected to harassment by the authorities. Due to her dark ringlets and aquiline nose, Rina was taken for a Jewess, and as Rina later recalled, the ovation she received was mistaken for a politically motivated demonstration by the local Jewry. Fortunately, the night ended without an unpleasant incident.

After Warsaw came London. She made her London debut on 17 October 1904, quite fittingly at the side of Caruso, who played her lover in Puccini's *Manon Lescaut*. The October 18 issue of the *Times* reported:

> The interest of the performance depends largely on the interpretation of the two roles which count, those of Manon and Des Grieux, and it would not be easy to find two better-

fitting exponents of the parts than Mme. Giachetti and M. Caruso. The former has many of what in England are regarded as the defects of present-day Italian operatic singing, notably a persistent vibrato; but even those whose pleasure is interfered with by this defect must have realized much from the personal energy of her acting. Every ounce of her ability was utilized, and utilized to real advantage, so that her first appearance was a very distinct success. M. Caruso was in fine voice after a slightly husky start, and rose to a height that even he has rarely touched in the scene at Havre Harbour. Here his acting and his singing were full of that particular kind of extravagant emotionalism which counts for so much in modern opera; that is, the singer accomplished precisely what he himself sought to accomplish, and his efforts were rewarded by the salvoes of applause with which they were greeted.

Rina's next London assignment was again Puccini, the title role of *Tosca*. "Report of the exceeding excellence of Mme. Giachetti's Tosca had, of course, preceded her, but it was in no way exaggerated as such things usually are," reported the London *Times* on October 20. "In far better voice than on Monday [i.e., October 17], or because she had 'found' the house, Mme. Giachetti sang with something like rare distinction, while her acting was of the kind too seldom seen on the operatic stage. Her horrible scene with Scarpia in the second act was most vividly portrayed, and in the last act again her expression of the varying emotions was of the highest order."

The reviews of her other roles were just as flattering. In *Cavalleria rusticana,* "the Santuzza of Mme. Giachetti was very dramatic";[26] and in *Adriana Lecouvreur,* she "was quite satisfactory in the title part, and the fault was certainly not hers if [the part] seemed a little wanting in sincerity and depth of expression."[27] When Adelina Patti paid her a visit backstage, the great diva was exceedingly complimentary. As a token of her esteem, she sent Rina an inscribed photograph of herself.

On November 10, Rina sang one performance of Marguerite in *Faust*. She closed her London season as Desdemona in Verdi's *Otello;* the title part was taken by V. Duc, and Victor Maurel, creator of the role, sang Iago. According to the *Times* review of November 28, "Mme. Giachetti sang and acted with that excellent spirit so characteristic of her." According to all indications, by the end of her first London season, Rina Giachetti was accepted as a singer of the first rank.

THE Covent Garden season had confirmed Rina's artistic standing as a prima donna of international caliber. From London, she returned to Italy. Her first major assignment was Alda in the Naples première of *Rolando di Berlino* in January 1905. This was a role Emmy Destinn had created at the world première on 13 December 1904. Indeed, Rina's repertoire often paralleled that of the famous Czech diva; then and after, particularly in London, she often took over Destinn's roles in the course of a season.

Rolando was Leoncavallo's latest attempt to recapture the success that had eluded him since *Pagliacci*. The opera was written expressly for the Royal Court Opera of Berlin, for the pleasure of Kaiser Wilhelm and the glorification of the Hohenzollern dynasty. It was to have been a vehicle for the reigning star of the Court Opera and darling of the royal court, the young American soprano Geraldine Farrar. The work enjoyed only a brief *succès d'estime,* mostly due to the circumstances of its provenance. Regardless of the opera's subject matter, Italy was curious to hear Leoncavallo's music. The Teatro San Carlo management wanted to be the first to mount the opera.

In the days after the performance, every Neapolitan paper reviewed *Rolando di Berlino,* and all agreed that Rina was excellent in the role of Alda. "Among the performers Rina Giachetti is the very first (*primissima*)," wrote the critic of *Il Pungolo,* "[with her] supple voice, fresh, ingratiating, delicate art of singing, notable extension, moving phrasing. The public triumphantly acclaimed the young artist." *Il Mattino* commented on her "ingratiating and penetrating voice," calling her an artist who "continues to rise, strengthened by superb schooling." The *Rassegna Melodrammatica* reported that "Rina Giachetti showed herself with the qualities of a celebrity, giving an extraordinary presentation of Alda; her most effective acting and singing were full of verve, warmth, passion. She was triumphant, [there was an] indescribable acclaim, general applause." *Il Giorno* singled out her *romanza* "Splende la luna," which she had to repeat, as "exquisitely sung, shaded with intensely passionate phrasing." *Roma* praised her pure lyric soprano voice, her singing technique, and her excellent interpretation.

With her success in *Rolando,* Rina reached a level of celebrity in Neapolitan musical circles that deserved special recognition. Following a concert, Matilde Serao, the most respected female journalist of the day, wrote an effusive piece in the 11 February 1905 issue of her newspaper *Il Giorno.*

She could really be called Victorious! From the moment her beautiful figure, so full of suggestive grace, appeared on the platform of the Sala Maddaloni, a shiver passed through the audience, and everybody understood that she was a Queen of the celebrations, a Queen who carried the royalty of her exquisite art that shone from the magnificent eyes even before she raised her golden voice in the religious silence, to embroider with the softest weave of notes a human throat could sing, the sweet aria of Mignon, "Non conosci il bel suol" ["Connais-tu le pays"]. A queen, Rina Giachetti, because no crown is more beautiful and more radiant than the laurel she is going to triumphantly gather on the principal stages of Europe, to wreathe her beautiful brow and black tresses. And when the acclamation of the public erupted like a formidable explosion, demanding an encore, the kind artist sang the delightful aria "In quelle trine morbide" of *Manon Lescaut,* putting into it all the refinement of her art, all the purity of her voice, all the warmth of her feeling, in a marvelous fusion.

The author of this florid tribute, Matilde Serao, was a successful novelist and journalist. Born in 1856, in 1884 she married the equally famous writer and journalist Edoardo Scarfoglio, who was four years her junior. Among the many accomplishments of these two literary figures was the founding of the Neapolitan newspaper *Il Mattino*. In 1904, Serao separated from her husband and began publishing her own newspaper, *Il Giorno*.

With perfect hindsight, one may ponder whether she would have penned this accolade to Rina Giachetti had she known that within a few years, the lady would become her estranged husband's mistress.

THE year 1905 brought Rina's first Portuguese engagement. She performed the soprano leads in *Manon Lescaut, Fedora, Tosca,* and *Cabrera* by Menendez, at the Teatro San Carlo of Lisbon. In every role, she enjoyed a warm reception, and her appearance in the Portuguese capital was another artistic success. In *Tosca,* particularly, she had inspiring partners—Edoardo Garbin and the baritone Mario Ancona—and the critics acknowledged the excellence of her interpretation. *O Secolo* called her a "brilliant and notable interpreter of the role of Tosca," and *O Mundo* praised her "first-class singing," stage presence, and acting.[28] By this point in her career, she had accumulated spectacular costumes, and her gold-trimmed, crepe de chine costumes commanded special attention. Some of her performances were attended by the royal family, the king and queen and Don Alfonso, the crown prince.

After Lisbon she was ready to conquer the South American operatic centers. She spent the summer months—the winter season in this part of the world—appearing in six operas in Buenos Aires and Montevideo. Three of the six roles were new to her repertory: Fidelia in Puccini's *Edgar,* the soprano lead in Leopoldo Mugnone's new opera *La Vita Bretone,* and the title role of Catalani's *Loreley.*

Rina was acclaimed in her debut role as Puccini's Manon in the Argentine capital, and she enjoyed an even greater triumph as Tosca. It seems that she perfected her interpretation of the role from season to season. The reviewer for *La Prensa* gave his unreserved approval.

Miss Giachetti once again proved herself a master artist in the use of vocal brushwork that she had already shown in *Manon*. In the singing filigree work of last night's performance she was outstanding. She sounds and shades admirably, using her *mezza voce,* which effectively whispers and thus preserves all the expressive intensity of the phrases, without distorting them with unexpected sonorities or rhythmic alterations which would vitiate the general character of the musical line.

Her exquisite "playfulness"—if one can use that expression—in the first-act duet with the tenor [Anselmi] was greatly appreciated, especially the insinuating inflections of the "Non la sospiri, la nostra casetta." Obviously, apart from the great interest with which the stage action was followed, it was understandable that everyone was impatiently awaiting the moment of "Vissi d'arte," the emotional and melodious highlight of the score.

And here again, Miss Giachetti eclipsed all the memories one might have retained of previous versions. It may have been sung before with more voice, but never with more art nor finer diction. At the aria's end she was thunderously applauded and obliged to repeat it.

Our congratulations cannot be limited to the lyrical side of the singer's art, for her stage presence and her handling of the drama were a not-distant second to her vocal prowess. (*La Prensa,* 8 June 1905)

Rina must have been pleased with the abundant recognition by the public and the press. In the span of a few years, she had attained artistic maturity, and the critiques suggest that during this season she was in magnificent form. One success followed the other, and her third Puccini heroine, Mimì, also earned undivided praise.

> Miss Giachetti endows the role of Mimì with poetry and delicacy, and admirably embodies that exquisitely sensitive creation of Murger's imagination. She does, in fact, possess all those rainbow-like shades of the dawn with which Rodolfo compares her, and at times even the radiant shadows of twilight, with its own sudden flashes of the dying light that flickers on the horizon.
>
> Her first-act "Racconto" was superbly embroidered and she brought out all the composer's intentions, which earned Miss Giachetti the audience's ovation. A similar response from the public occurred after the third-act duet and the death scene, the latter performed with the simple naturalness expected of a weak light that is imperceptibly extinguished. (*La Prensa*, 19 June 1905)

Puccini was pleased too. He presented Rina with a photograph of himself bearing the dedication *"Alla carissima Rina Giachetti, vita ed anima di Tosca—Manon—Mimì, l'aff.mo suo G. Puccini, ricordo di B. Aires.* 12-7-1905." ("To dearest Rina Giachetti, life and soul of Tosca—Manon—Mimì, her most affectionate G. Puccini, in memory of Buenos Aires, 12 July 1905.")

The fourth Puccini work of the season was the composer's first opera, *Edgar*. It was a curiosity and treated as such, the singers, including Rina, earning only passing compliments. "Playing the part of an enchantress" in the title role of *Loreley,* she was said to "[imbue] her role with all her enchantments. She gently shaded her singing and made the dramatic aspect of her role, which is mostly understated, believable."[29]

Leopoldo Mugnone conducted her every performance. Inevitably, he asked her to sing the soprano lead in his own opera, *La Vita Bretone*. The opera had a mixed reception: The artists and the composer-conductor received curtain calls, while at the same time, the audience threw paper and other objects onstage. Both Rina and Giovanni Zenatello gave their best efforts. One critic commented that "Miss Giachetti performed marvels of expressiveness, but to no avail. It was obvious that the public refused to be won over."[30]

The tally of the Buenos Aires season showed that Rina sang twenty performances before the company moved on to the Teatro Solis in Montevideo. She opened again with the role that had become her calling card, Manon Lescaut, and the reviews were as enthusiastic as the month before.

> Miss Giachetti was an unsurpassable Manon, thanks to her voice, her talent, and the sincerity with which she infused the role. From the moment of her *romanza* in the first act, it was obvious that she is not only a singer with a beautiful voice and perfect training, but also an intelligent actress who feels intensely and can well express the naïveté, the passion, and the anguish of the three stages in the life of Manon. . . . Moreover, and recalling the many Manon Lescauts we have heard here, we feel obliged to state that Miss Giachetti possesses not only exquisite artistry but also the necessary sensitivity and tact to impersonate such characters as the famous heroine of Prévost's novel. One sees in her the vibrant "sacred fire" of musical inspiration, so that she is not only the singer striving to remain within the created *tessitura,* but also to imbue every note with all the color and life they seek to express. Miss Giachetti only recently began her artistic career; with the qualities she already possesses one can augur well for her brilliant future on the lyric stage. (*El Dia,* 21 August 1905)

The other opera Rina sang in the Uruguayan capital was *La Vita Bretone,* which did not give her the same opportunity as Puccini to earn outstanding reviews. Nonetheless, there could be no doubt that her South American tour was an unqualified success.

AFTER South America, Rina appeared in London, this time without Caruso. Her leading man in three out of four operas was Giovanni Zenatello, who was a very fine singer but not Caruso's equal, and thus gave Rina more opportunity to shine. Her reception was good, and she was invited to participate in a command performance at Windsor Castle. At a reception following the concert, the soprano was presented to King Edward VII. The King was most charming and asked her when she would be singing again at Covent Garden.

"Tomorrow night, Your Majesty," she replied.

"Indeed?" exclaimed the King. "How will you be able to arrive in London in time?"

She told His Majesty that she was obliged to take a coach later in the evening. When the King heard this, he placed a special train at her disposal so that she could travel comfortably through the night. In memory of the evening, Edward VII sent her a personally dedicated photograph in a silver frame.

In January 1906, following the London season, Rina returned once more to Spain, with an invitation to sing at the royal court on the occasion of the visit of Wilhelm II of Germany. As she entered the salon at the appointed hour, she asked one of the glittering officers, who was about to light a cigarette at a candelabra, where she might deposit her coat. When the man turned around, Rina realized she was in the presence of His Majesty, the King of Spain. Eager to be of service, His Majesty gallantly removed the coat, which was made of the very chinchilla furs that had given her warmth and comfort during her trek across the Andes on muleback six years earlier. Then Queen Victoria of Spain joined them, lavishing her compliments on the singer. According to Rina, the Spanish royals had heard her several times in London, both in the theater and at a command performance at Buckingham Palace.

After her recital, Rina was presented to the German Emperor, who asked her if she had sung *Rolando di Berlino*. She answered that she had created the role in the Italian première of the work the previous year at the Teatro San Carlo in Naples. When the Emperor expressed an interest in hearing the opera sung in Italian, Rina telegraphed to Naples to have *Rolando* restored to the repertory and advised the management that the German Emperor planned to attend the performance in about fifteen days. Regrettably, an ill-timed eruption of Mount Vesuvio caused the cancellation of the royal visit, and the performance did not take place.

Rina returned to Covent Garden in the fall of 1905, to the enthusiastic welcome of both audiences and critics. The *Times* wrote of her first *Manon Lescaut:* "*Signora* Giachetti made a most welcome reappearance in the title role; and though her voice appeared at first to have lost something of its roundness, this defect disappeared in the later acts when she sang quite beautifully and acted with the sincerity and conviction that characterized her performances last year."[31] In the days that followed, her success as Tosca was even greater.

> The performance of *La Tosca* [*sic*] on Wednesday evening can rank with any that have been given in previous seasons at Covent Garden.... Last year *Signora* Giachetti and *Signor* Sammarco made a great effect in the opera, but both sur-

passed themselves last night. The former scored an enormous success in the second act, which brought forth one of those outbursts of applause which, bad enough in early Verdi and the like, entirely spoil the dramatic effect of such a scene as that which precedes the stabbing of Scarpia; and the latter was more sardonic than ever, while both sang quite superbly. *Signor* de Marchi, too, is a very fine Cavaradossi—he was the first in the opera—and still improved the position he has made for himself here this season. (*The Times,* 13 October 1905)

Rina's interpretation of this role must have been truly exceptional, as in the following days almost every important newspaper carried a review of the performance. According to the *Daily Telegraph,* she "sang with great assurance the emotional scenes of Tosca." The *Daily News* wrote: "One of her major attractions is her balanced moderation. She knows how to obtain the maximum effect." The *Yorkshire Post* praised her realistic impersonation of Tosca and her superb dramatic effects. The *Westminster Gazette* considered her especially well suited for the role; and the *Morning Post* judged her vocally and histrionically an excellent Tosca. The *Observer* felt her Tosca ranked with that of any previous interpreter of this role. The *Globe,* the *Sunday Times,* even *Sporting Life* carried reviews, all of which were flattering. Puccini himself was in the audience at the second performance on October 19. The October 21 *Il Mondo artistico* reported that the composer was called onstage after Act II, causing "real delirium."

Following *Tosca,* Rina assumed the title role in a third Puccini opera, *Madama Butterfly*—a role she took over from Emmy Destinn. The *Times* critic was less enthusiastic about her interpretation of Cio-Cio-San and on October 25 wrote that "if Mme. Giachetti, who succeeds Mme. Destinn in the title-part, is not an artist of quite the calibre that is wanted for the mixture of tragedy and comedy, she sings the music well, and makes a laudable attempt to be Japanese in her manner." The critic's failure to muster more enthusiasm should not have chagrined Rina overmuch, for in the following season the same writer offered a single sentence in appreciation of Destinn's great interpretation: "Mlle. Destinn, as Mme. Butterfly, sings and acts the charming part with distinction" (28 May 1906). There must be times when even a critic runs out of superlatives, not to mention the singular choice of the word "charming" to describe this heroine who commits hara-kiri before the final curtain.

Rina's last appearance of the season was in *Mefistofele;* she sang both Margherita and Elena. Although the audience liked her, the two roles were not congenial to her, and she failed to win critical acceptance. The *Times* reviewer wrote: "If Mme. Giachetti as Margherita cannot compare with Nilsson, Calvé, or even with Miss Macintyre in sincerity, charm, or emotional power, she was yet quite adequate, and the lovely song in the prison scene and the famous duet in the classical Walpurgisnight were well sung."[32]

It was regrettable that Rina did not end her Covent Garden engagement on a more glowing note, but overall the season was overwhelmingly positive. The year 1905 was busy and rewarding for her, and in purely vocal terms, it was quite possibly the high point of her career.

RINA returned to the Teatro San Carlo in Naples, where she sang Cio-Cio-San in *Madama Butterfly*. Her next assignment was the title role in the world première of D'Erlanger's opera *Tess*. The first performance on 10 April 1906 was a great success according to the *Rassegna Melodrammatica,* which proclaimed Rina an "incomparable protagonist, bringing the part to life with passion and sweetness [and receiving] an extraordinary ovation."[33]

A week after the première of *Tess,* Rina made her Monte Carlo debut in the dual role of Margherita and Elena in *Mefistofele*. The cast was exceptional: Francesco Marconi sang Faust, and the great Fedor Chaliapin took the title role.

After Monte Carlo she returned to Naples for more *Madama Butterflys*. The 22 May 1906 review of *Rassegna Melodrammatica* called hers "one of the most beautiful, caressing, and robust voices to be heard today on the great stages." The critic added that she sang "with security, elegance, and feeling. . . . She was recalled several times at the end of each act."

Next came Covent Garden, where her first assignment, on 9 June 1906, was *Tosca,* with Caruso. The *Times* review on the 11th implies that she overacted, while at the same time granting that Sardou's melodrama warrants an emotional approach. There was also some indication that Rina's voice was not at its best during the entire season. The critic wrote:

> *Signor* Caruso was in splendid voice, and sang the part of
> Cavaradossi in perfect style; *Signor* Scotti as Scarpia repeated a
> familiar triumph, and it is difficult to see how the parts could

be better played or sung. Mme. Giachetti's voice is not of the kind which commands universal admiration, but she sings the music with much intelligence; and if her acting is the kind that used to go by the name of "transpontine," it is necessary to remember that Sardou's idea was purely melodramatic, and that it is Puccini who has raised the piece to a really artistic level, so that it is hardly blameworthy to exaggerate a little in the title-part.

Rina's only Aida, on June 25, elicited no comment: "On Monday *Aida* was given, with Mme. Giachetti in the title-part, Mme. Kirkby-Lunn as an admirable Amneris, *Signor* Caruso as an incomparable Radames, and *Signor* Sammarco as a most vigorous Amonasro."[34]

The cool critical reception must have compelled her to make a special effort in her final role of the summer season. Her Butterfly of July 12 was reviewed in the *Times* on July 16.

Mme. Giachetti has played the part of Madama Butterfly here in the autumn, but she too is less familiar to us in the part than Mlle. Destinn. Vocally she is not so beautiful, her voice is not so rich and full, but her splendid intelligence enables her to make use of every scrap she possesses, and she has an astonishing variety of color; in her acting she is more varied and subtle than Mlle. Destinn—not more impressive, perhaps, but more complex; and she certainly succeeds in giving us a most interesting study.

Before the season ended, she scored a critical triumph with her last Tosca on July 18.

As to La Tosca—well, if we have to see a woman writhing in agony on a sofa while her lover is being tortured in the next room, we would rather see it done by Mme. Giachetti than by anyone else; at every moment in the play she is acting well; and when, after the murder, she puts the candles down by the dead man's head and slinks like a cat from the room, she gets a thrill out of her audience that ought to satisfy even M. Sardou himself.[35]

It seems that Rina spent the balance of the summer relaxing then returned to London for a busy fall season. She sang nineteen times in four operas in nine weeks. On October 6, she opened the season with *Madama Butterfly*. The review of the 8th[36] again found fault with her

Royal Opera Covent Garden

THE GRAND OPERA SYNDICATE, LIMITED.

Manager .. .. .. M. ANDRE MESSAGER

Secretary and Business Manager, Mr. NEIL FORSYTH

THIS EVENING'S PERFORMANCE.

Monday, June 25th, at 8

VERDI'S Opera

AÏDA

(IN ITALIAN)

Il Rè	... ...	M. ARTUS
Amneris	... ...	Mme. KIRKBY LUNN
Aïda	... ...	Mme. GIACHETTI
Radames	... ...	Signor CARUSO
Ramfis	... ...	M. JOURNET
Amonasro	... ...	Signor SAMMARCO
Un Messaggiero	...	Signor ZUCCHI
Conductor	...	Signor CAMPANINI

Stage Manager   ... ...   M. ALMANZ

Royal Opera Covent Garden program listing of the cast of *Aïda,* 25 June 1906.
Rina Giachetti sang opposite Caruso. Courtesy of Covent Garden Archives.

voice, though not with the delivery of the role: "If *Signora* Giachetti's singing was not in itself very beautiful, her whole interpretation of the part of Butterfly was so genuine as to enlist unreserved sympathy." Referring to the same performance, *Il Mondo artistico* reported on October 11, with some exaggeration, that Rina had performed the last act of *Butterfly* with such passionate anguish that the audience no longer knew whether her suicide were real or merely staged: They were relieved to see her rise and acknowledge her ovation with a smile.

The Tosca of Rina Giachetti was by this time the accepted standard in London. The *Times* critic said as much in his October 16 review of her first appearance in the role in the autumn season, on 13 October 1906.

> In her portrayal of La Tosca *Signora* Giachetti is unrivalled; her acting is so fine and so compels attention that we forget the tremolo in her louder notes, and simply accept everything she does. She was in exceptionally good voice Saturday, and with *Signor* Sammarco to support her as Scarpia made the second act thrill us as we have seldom been thrilled before.

Her Adriana Lecouvreur earned her a simple mention, and the review of her fourth role of the season, the title role of *Fedora,* again complained about her singing:

> *Signora* Giachetti's dramatic powers find an excellent opportunity in the title part. She is not a Sarah Bernhardt, and there is little or no suggestion that at any time she is trying to entrap Loris; but she has plenty of vigor, and does not hesitate to give all that she possesses. Vocally her performance was quite satisfactory, making allowance for the quality of tone which is seldom agreeable in loud passages.[37]

The critiques of both London seasons of 1906 imply that Rina's voice was beginning to show wear and that she was having problems with her high notes. By the end of the autumn season, she was clearly tired, and the critics did not hesitate to say so.

> The popularity of *Madame Butterfly* prompted the Covent Garden management to give it more times than planned. In the Saturday matinée [of November 24] with *Signor* Zenatello and *Signora* Giachetti in the principal parts the performance could not fail of its effect, even though it must be confessed that the upper notes of Mme. Giachetti's voice sometimes sounded painfully worn.[38]

RINA'S vocal problems during this time may be attributed in part to stress and personal crises.

In May 1906, De Sanna resigned his administrative post at the San Carlo, explaining that he was overwhelmed by the burdens of the position and his various other commitments. A report in the 22 May 1906 *Rassegna Melodrammatica* surmised that the decision could also be traced to "the bitterness brought on by those vicious people who carp and criticize without knowledge of what a heavy burden the management of the Teatro San Carlo is; perhaps disagreements with the city fathers had something to do with it, over which the press many times voiced its views." Augusto Laganà, former impresario of the Teatro Massimo of Palermo, was elected by the governing board to replace *Commendatore* Roberto De Sanna, who continued to organize the London seasons of Italian opera for another year.

Rina did not sing again in Naples after De Sanna's resignation—at least there is no record of any further appearances at the San Carlo. Whether she declined to sing there out of loyalty to the departing director or she was too closely identified with him and was no longer welcome, we do not know. In view of her past triumphs, her excellent reviews, and the successful engagements in London, Madrid, Rome, and eventually at La Scala, it seems clear that she won her place on the international operatic circuit on her own merits. De Sanna's influence may have helped her on the road to artistic glory, but the credit for her achievements belongs to Rina herself.

Her liaison with De Sanna ended around this time, for reasons that remain unclear; Rina offered no explanation in her interview with Fofò four decades later. De Sanna was apparently in good health, for he remained professionally active for some time and lived for another eight years. (De Sanna died the night of 28–29 September 1913.) One can surmise that the end of their relationship had something to do with Caruso.

According to Fofò's notes, Rina placed the beginning of her liaison with Caruso in London and dated it from 1905. However, if the affair started in London, the correct date must have been 1906. Had it begun in 1904, the lovers would have contrived a meeting somehow, somewhere the following year, but in 1905 their paths could not have crossed: Caruso sang at Covent Garden from May through July, and Rina appeared there in October. She spent the entire summer in Buenos Aires and Montevideo, performing from the first week of June to the end of August.

But in 1906 they sang together. They were with the same company and saw each other often. Rina's feelings about Caruso had never changed, and as he made quite obvious by his subsequent actions, she had never lost her attraction for him. It was predictable—if not inevitable—that Rina and Enrico became lovers.

Consummating their long-time love for each other must have had enormous emotional meaning for them both. Enrico had many love affairs, for women were only too eager to be seduced by Caruso. But Rina was someone very special: Rina represented a suppressed desire, a great, unfulfilled passion held in check for nine years. For Caruso, this was not a flirtation or a casual interlude, but a kind of honeymoon with a first love. The fact that it had to remain a secret could only lend it spice.

Rina, too, must have felt a flood of emotions when she found herself in her dear Enrico's arms after all those years of yearning. In her mind, she had always had first claim on him. She maintained, and rightly so, that Ada had behaved most unscrupulously in turning Caruso away from her, and she deeply resented her sister's manipulations to keep them apart. Rina would have been less than human if her love affair with Caruso had not filled her with a sense of victory.

It was, however, an affair that could lead nowhere. Caruso, with his contradictory nature, could be amazingly callous about women while at the same time adhering to a certain code of ethics. No matter how many women he bedded over the years, he loved my mother deeply and unconditionally. Because of Fofò and me, he did not even contemplate leaving her. From the very beginning, he treated Ada as his wife, the Italian wife of an Italian husband: a woman to love, to support, to be proud of, and to be faithful to except when there was an opportunity to the contrary. And Caruso never missed an opportunity.

After their brief affair, the lovers had to part. Rina, enriched by tender memories, found herself alone once more.

CHAPTER SIX

Enter Cesare Romati

AFTER London, Caruso had one more engagement to fulfill, a repeat of his highly successful and lucrative concerts at the Kursaal in Ostende, Belgium. He gave only two concerts a week, and so his stay at the resort was like a vacation. He could eat, drink, and relax, swim at his pleasure, and enjoy his friends, the Gutekunsts from London.

Father usually drank only wine, and that in moderation; but this year in Ostende, he made the costly mistake of indulging in too much champagne. Long afterward, he told Fofò about the incident, perhaps to warn him against the dangers of drinking and gambling. If that was his objective, the moral of the story was entirely lost on my brother, but fortunately he found the tale worth preserving:

One evening [Caruso] found himself in the Kursaal at Ostende with three strangers who, on their part, knew who he was. They may even have followed him for some time. To make a long story short, after some conversation, in between a few off-colored jokes, they managed to make Father drink several bottles of champagne, even though he never drank in excess. The champagne destroyed the iron control he always had over his actions, and without knowing what he was doing, he found himself at a green table, playing baccarat. The champagne entered his bloodstream, and at a certain point he passed out.

The following morning, he was awakened by his valet and informed that a gentleman wished to speak with him. Papa excused himself, saying that it was an inopportune time, that he was tired and did not want to receive anyone. The caller was insistent, claiming that it was a very serious matter. Reluctantly, he got up, slipped into a robe, and after freshening up a bit, went to the salon. There was a gentleman he did not know, dressed in black with top hat in hand, looking for all the world like a second in a duel. When asked whom he had the honor of addressing and for what purpose, the man identified himself as the collector for a private bank and showed him a promissory note for 60,000 francs, then about $11,000.

"Monsieur Caruso, c'est à vous cette firme ici?" ("Is this your signature, Mr. Caruso?")

Papa, amazed, took the piece of paper, examined it, and had to admit that the signature was his, although the text above it was not written by him. He asked what obligation the piece of paper carried. At that point the official explained that he, Monsieur Caruso, had played baccarat the night before and lost. Carrying neither cash nor a checkbook, he had settled his gambling debt by signing an I.O.U. to a gentleman, drawn on that private bank.

The blood rushed to Father's head. He understood that he had fallen into a crude trap, but in that morally indefensible situation he had no recourse, especially since the signature was indeed his, even if the figure was not in his handwriting. He paid, with a bad taste in his mouth, swearing that he would never again gamble in a casino, or with strangers for money. He kept his word all his life.

THAT Ada was always suspicious of Rina can be taken for granted. Accepting that the liaison between Enrico and Rina began in 1906 in London, it would appear that Mother soon became aware of it. In fact, according to some sources, she came upon her sister and Caruso *in flagrante delicto.*[1] The shocking discovery made her realize that nearly a decade of scheming to keep Father and Rina apart had failed. This must have accounted for her decision not to return with Caruso to New York for the 1906–07 season. She could easily have traveled with him: I was looked after by my first governess, a German lady, and Fofò was old enough to be left with our grandparents. For the first time in eight years, Mother and Father were to be apart for at least six or seven months.

Father did not seem particularly aggrieved by this turn of events. Perhaps he thought that the long separation would help to induce Mother's forgiveness. Besides, he had to ready himself for his European tour, which began with his first appearance in Vienna. The opera chosen to introduce Caruso was, once more, *Rigoletto*. In addition to having to meet the high expectations of the sophisticated and judgmental Viennese audience, he would have to hold his own opposite his great compatriot Titta Ruffo, who was making his own local debut in the title role. The gala event was duly exploited by the administration, and ticket prices were raised for the benefit of the pension fund of the Royal Court Opera.

The event was heralded in the press long before the actual date of 6 October 1906. The singers' movements were covered by reporters eager for news, and in spite of the elevated ticket prices, the performance was sold out. The cream of Viennese society was in attendance.

On the night of the performance, Caruso and Ruffo, old friends by then, arrived at the theater together in a closed *fiaker* around six o'clock. Fortunately for all concerned, all went as well or better than expected, although Selma Kurz, as Gilda, started with some intonation problems which, in view of her exceptional abilities, must have been due to nerves. Caruso reaped his share of laurels, but *Rigoletto* is, after all, a baritone opera, and the *Neues Wiener Tageblatt* declared Ruffo the hero of the evening.[2] The applause, the standing ovation of the screaming, roaring, stomping audience, would not cease, and the curtains had to be parted again and again. Finally the stage manager said to Caruso: "Yell 'Auf Wiedersehen!' " In spite of his total lack of knowledge of German, Caruso got the idea and began to shout "Auf Wiedersehen!" to the audience. "There was another round of thunderous applause, and finally quiet."[3] The following day, Caruso received official notice that Emperor Franz Josef I had bestowed the title *Kammersänger* upon him. Not since 1883 had a singer received such a distinction after a single appearance.

FATHER must have been pleased with himself as he sailed for New York, and he was most likely in a light, carefree mood. Then, a short while before the Metropolitan's opening night, the notorious "monkey house" incident took place. This ludicrous event in Father's life had reverberations in the international press.

Father was staying at the Savoy Hotel overlooking Central Park, where he often went for a stroll. One afternoon, in the monkey house at the Central Park Zoo, a woman claimed that he had tried to molest her. A policeman, who said he had been watching him and had seen the incident, arrested Caruso and took him to the police station. When the case came before the judge, the woman, Mrs. Hannah Graham, failed to appear in court.

On November 26, only a week before his first performance of the season, a reporter cornered him during rehearsal at the Met and posed several questions about the case. Father lost his temper. "He said a few uncomplimentary things about the judicial system which would permit a public man—he might even say a world-famous man—to be humiliated, escorted through the streets like a felon, and flung into a cell on the unsupported words of a woman; an elderly woman, he said, not particularly good-looking."[4]

Although Father was quick to assert his innocence, he was terrified of the effect this incident might have on his American career. He dreaded his first *La Bohème,* fearing a demonstration against him. Under the circumstances, he must have been especially pleased when the press touted his gallantry in yielding the distinction of opening night to the returning prodigal daughter, Geraldine Farrar, who was to make her Metropolitan debut after five enormously successful years at the Royal Opera of Berlin. Of his eighteen seasons with the Metropolitan, this was the only opening night in which he did not take part.

Caruso should have had more faith in the loyalty of his New York public. When the curtain parted, he was standing at the window with his back to the audience. Then applause broke out, and as one reviewer put it, "Caruso turned, his face flushed with excitement, and, after bowing to the audience, went back to the window. Hereupon the applause broke out afresh in greater volume than before."[5] The spontaneous, all-forgiving ovation brought tears to his eyes, and he was almost unable to sing. "I needed this relief," said *Signor* Caruso after the performance, "for my nerves have been horribly strained during the last few days. My gratitude is unbounded, and I shall never forget the sympathy displayed by the people of New York. I feel that my vindication is complete."[6]

Rina Giachetti in 1905.

Rina Giachetti in London.

Rina Giachetti as Margherita in Boito's *Mefistofele*, ca. 1905.

Rina Giachetti and Giovanni Zenatello in Puccini's *Madama Butterfly* at Covent Garden, 1905. Photography Langfier. Courtesy of Covent Garden Archives.

Views of the villa Bellosguardo at Lastra a Signa, outside Florence. Caruso purchased the estate in 1906.

The gardens at Bellosguardo.

Enrico Caruso in 1907. Photography A. Chickering.

The interior of Bellosguardo. *Above,* main entrance on the ground floor.
Below, formal dining room, ground floor.

The interior of Bellosguardo. *Above,* billiard room, looking into the down-stairs art gallery. *Below,* the art gallery on the second floor: cabinets with snuff boxes, antique watches, coins, bronzes, glass ampules.

Enrico Caruso's bedroom at Bellosguardo.

The bedroom of the mistress of the house at Bellosguardo.

Guido Giachetti in the late 1920s.

Guido Giachetti at work in the library of the Fascist Party headquarters in Florence, ca. 1930.

A Mishkin portrait of Caruso inscribed to Guido and Teresa Giachetti.

Caruso in the garden at Bellosguardo with Enrico, Jr.

Renovations at Bellosguardo. On the terrace listening to the Victrola are (*seated, left to right*) Teresa Da Vela Giachetti and Rina; (*standing*) Rodolfo; Caruso; (*seated at right*) the composer Leoncavallo; and (*far right*) accompanist Bruno Bruni.

Enrico, Jr., with his governess,
Miss Louise Saer, in London, 1909.

Enrico, Jr., visiting his father
on the deck of the oceanliner
Kronprinzessin Cecilie in
Southampton, October 1909.
The caged poultry in the
background would be used
for passengers' meals.

Caruso aboard the *Kronprinzessin Cecilie* with soprano Frances Alda and bass Andrès de Segurola (*at Caruso's left*), 1909.

Caruso, Alda, De Segurola, 1909.

Andrès de Segurola, 1909.

Caruso contemplating a photograph of Enrico, Jr., ca. 1910.

A pastel portrait of Enrico, Jr.

Rodolfo in the uniform of the Badia Fiesolana, ca. 1909.

The Caruso brothers, "Mimmi" and "Fofò," at Bellosguardo.

Painting of Enrico, Jr., by an English artist.

Rodolfo Caruso, painted by Carlo Stragliati.

The Caruso family in
1916: *from left,* Rodolfo,
Rina, Caruso, and
Enrico, Jr.

Enrico, Jr., in London, 1913.

A formal portrait of Caruso displaying his decorations, inscribed to Rina Giachetti: "To my dear Rinuccia [little Rina] with affection. Ghico, Berlin, 1913."

Caruso in evening dress complete with top hat, the outfit that reminded
Enrico, Jr., of London coachmen. Courtesy of Francis Robinson Collection,
Special Collections, Vanderbilt University.

Caruso with cigar. Photo Dührkoop, Berlin.

A dapper Caruso in a white linen suit and two-tone shoes.

Au souvenir des jolies
Jours a Frankfurt
Octobre 1909 à
piccola bambolina

Top left, Else Trauner, Caruso's German friend, in Frankfurt, 1908. Photography Eduard Blum. *Top right,* Else Trauner in Frankfurt, 1909. *Bottom,* Else and Caruso at the Englisher Hof in Frankfurt, 1909. Courtesy of Nanne Bruns.

Enrico Caruso. The signature "Meffert" in the corner could be the photographer's or that of Caruso's long-time mistress, Mrs. Mildred Meffert.

An elegantly dressed Enrico Caruso.

A Caruso portrait by Mishkin. Courtesy of Francis Robinson Collection, Special Collections, Vanderbilt University.

The Giachetti sisters, Rina, *below,* and Ada, *opposite.* Photography Bragança.

Ada Giachetti's passport photo, ca. 1912.

The portrait Enrico Caruso gave to Ada in 1917.

Caruso singing at Sheepsheads Bay, New York, 1918. Courtesy of Francis Robinson Collection, Special Collections, Vanderbilt University.

Caruso's secretary, Bruno Zirato, *left;* his friend, art dealer Amedeo Canessa, *center;* and Caruso, *right,* on Fifth Avenue, New York, ca. 1918.

"Mugging" had a special meaning for Caruso, and a photo automat was simply irresistible. Courtesy of Francis Robinson Collection, Special Collections, Vanderbilt University.

Judge Baker of the Yorkville Police Court fined him $10—this in spite of the fact that a Dr. Adolph Danzinger, a New York lawyer and formerly American consul general at Madrid, gave a sworn testimony that "he entered the monkey house at the same time as did *Signor* Caruso. He did not see Caruso speak to or annoy any woman. No woman spoke to *Signor* Caruso or struck him as Mrs. Graham is alleged to have done in the presence of policeman Kane."[7] After an unsuccessful appeal, he paid the $10 fine in May 1907. A year after the verdict, in February 1908, his accuser, Mrs. Graham, and her half-sister, Mrs. Stanhope, were found fighting in public and arrested for disorderly conduct. They were fined a penny each, and the courtroom crowd, which included many Italians, seized the pennies as souvenirs, chanting "Caruso is vindicated!" When Caruso learned of the arrest, he commented that it would go far toward clearing his character.

The story went down in operatic history as the "monkey house affair" and was picked up by every major European newspaper. Most Europeans were amused and surprised that the Americans should make such a fuss about such a ridiculous incident. Even if the accusations against Caruso were true, which most people found hard to accept, the international reverberations were unwarranted. When Puccini heard about it, he wrote to his friend, Sybil Seligman, on 20 November 1906: "Did you read in the papers about Caruso? I believe that the whole thing was a put-up job by some hostile impresario."[8]

Compounding Father's problems was his concern as to how Ada might react to the news. On 20 November 1906, the *Daily Telegraph* reported that "the tenor cabled *Signora* Caruso in Italy advising her to pay no attention to any unpleasant reports regarding him that might reach her." Given Mother's volatile and jealous nature, the news reports were bound to have an explosive effect. More than anyone, she could no doubt imagine that the accusations of misconduct were true. Although she professed to the newspaper reporters that she had complete trust in her "husband," Ada probably regarded this adventure as yet another transgression by her philandering tenor. When Caruso returned to Italy at the end of the season, he must have met with bitter recriminations. From the bits and pieces of information that could be assembled about this period, it seems that by the end of the summer of 1907, the rapport between Ada and Enrico had changed substantially. The fact that Caruso was engaged to sing with Rina must have further aggravated the situation at home. Rina's presence at Covent Garden may have been the main reason Mother decided to take up residence in London during the engagement. Whether or not she succeeded in keeping the lovers apart during this period is anybody's guess. She rented an elegant house in Ealing, a suburb of London, and the family stayed there from May until August 1907, except for Fofò, who was left in Italy with our grandparents, Giuseppina and Guido. For obscure reasons, Fofò never accompanied us to England.[9] Perhaps, as Fofò believed, Mother simply did not want to have him around.

Mother had servants to take care of the household. I was a month short of my third birthday, and my German governess had just left us. One afternoon the doorbell rang. The maid ushered a tall lady in through the French doors of the veranda. She was Miss Louise Saer, an applicant for the vacant position. I remember her first visit as if it were yesterday. She wore a Gibson girl outfit, a white, high-waisted blouse with leg-of-mutton sleeves, a black belt, black skirt, and black shoes. I was hiding behind the balustrade at the bottom of the stairs. Mother appeared at the top landing, the *voile* of her beautiful gown floating behind her as she descended the stairs. The sun filtered through the windows enveloping her entire person in a golden halo of soft sunlight; she was as beautiful as an apparition. She said to me in Italian that the lady was to be my new governess. I raised one hand and, pointing at the visitor, said, "*Lei?*" ("She?")

From that day on, Miss Saer was "Lei" to me, and I never called her by any other name.

This incident is my only recollection of my mother. I was very young when she vanished from my life, and to my lasting regret, I have been unable to resurrect further memories. Only after my sixth year do the images I have from my childhood grow more numerous.

WHEN Father finished his London commitments, I think we went to the seashore in Italy and then to Signa, presumably to check on the progress of construction work at Bellosguardo. Father's correspondence with Marziale Sisca from this period discloses that he didn't set foot at Le Panche during his holidays. At the end of the summer, we went to Le Panche and Father left for a European tour. Mother did not accompany him on the tour, and for reasons we can only guess, she did not go with him to New York for the 1907–08 Met season. Significantly, perhaps, it is clear that Cesare Romati, a handsome chauffeur, was already employed at Le Panche when Father left for America in the fall.

After a stopover in Milan, Father went to Germany. His European impresario, Emil Ledner, joined him, and they proceeded to Budapest, the first stop of the tour. Here he sang Radames in *Aida* at the Royal Opera House on 2 October 1907. It was the most enigmatic performance of his life. Emboldened by his fame, the management made this a benefit performance and, for the first time in the theater's history, raised the ticket prices threefold—an invitation to disaster. The Hungarian audience expected a vocal miracle, but Caruso was not a miracle, just an excellent tenor. Disappointed in their expectations, the audience did not applaud after his "Celeste Aida," and only after the Nile scene did they warm up to him at all.

At his next stop, in Vienna, reporters asked Caruso to comment on the Budapest *Aida*. The news of the fiasco traveled as far as the Austrian capital, and the reporters were determined to spread it beyond national boundaries. Within a couple of days, the story had made its way to the English newspapers via Austria. According to the *Daily Telegraph,* "in consequence of the evident indisposition of the artist the public were generally disappointed, and after the first two acts no one applauded. . . . At the close of the opera, when the applause became louder, *Signor* Caruso refused to come onstage. On reaching his dressing room he burst into tears and said he had never experienced anything like it." [10]

Father had to take a stand on the matter, and he chose to exhibit righteous indignation. The Viennese correspondent of the *Mail* quoted him in the October 5 issue:

> What the Budapest newspapers say, declared *Signor* Caruso, is throughout lies and misrepresentation. One says that I was ill, and another actually adds that before I appeared [I] had to have morphia injected. Of course not a word is true. I was as well as ever, and sang my best. If the public, as some Hungarian newspapers affirm, was really disillusioned, it was, I think, in consequence of the exorbitant prices. Thus a box cost 16 pounds ($80) which is far too much for Budapest.
>
> I am also reproached that I did not especially acknowledge what applause was given to me. I could not, for the lady who sang with me would not accept a recall. Did they expect that after singing the great aria I would stand upon my head?

Privately, Caruso agreed with Ledner that the Budapest *Aida* did not go well at all. But the extent of the unfavorable reception was unwarranted. The performance is generally considered an inexplicable fiasco, the last outright failure of Caruso's career. Fortunately, not only his repeat of the role in Vienna two days later, but all the other performances of the tour went very well. He was loath to admit a failure, and in a letter of 17 October 1907, he wrote to Sisca from Hamburg: "Like here, I had my success in Leipzig, Vienna, and Budapest. I hope to have it in Berlin and Frankfurt as well."

On 13 November 1907, Caruso arrived in New York on the White Star liner *Oceanic*. His fellow passengers included several celebrities, among them Geraldine Farrar, Antonio Scotti, and Riccardo Stracciari. Speculations appeared beforehand in the New York newspapers that Caruso, having been fined $10 for a misdemeanor, could conceivably be refused entry to the country under American law. When reporters asked him about the "monkey house affair," "*Signor* Caruso politely but firmly declined even to discuss the question beyond saying that the appeal still stood." He added indignantly that "nowhere else in the world but in America could an artist have been badgered by so ridiculous an incident."[11]

From a professional standpoint, the season progressed as was to be expected; on the private level, however, it was more complex. All was not well between my parents, and since Mother was four thousand miles away, Father led the gay life of a bachelor. One of his more widely publicized involvements dated from this season.

According to later reports by the press, it seems that in early 1908, while attending a matinée at the Garden Theater in the company of Lina Cavalieri, Caruso, looking down from his box, spotted a beautiful lady in the orchestra section. He kept eying her. After the performance, they were introduced by a mutual friend. She was Mrs. Mildred Meffert, at the moment separated from her husband. The latter may have been a former Metropolitan tenor who sang the roles of the Shepherd in *Tristan,* Mime in *Rheingold,* and Heinrich in *Tannhäuser* during the 1898–99 season, although this identification is unconfirmed. In the course of the conversation, Father asked Mrs. Meffert if she would be at the opera the following day, a matinée of *Tosca.* They met after the opera, and he asked if he might call on her. Thus began an affair that was destined to be more lasting and more dramatic than Father's casual dalliances. Years later, Meffert claimed Father had told her that if something should "happen between *La Señora* [*sic*] and me, it shall be my great happiness to marry you. But now I cannot for the children's sake. She is their mother. She deserves from me some semblance of respect."[12]

Meffert claimed that this promise of marriage took place on 3 April 1908. The "*Señora*" (actually *Signora*) was Mother, of course. Father, with singular dishonesty, was playing both ends against the middle: He was not married to Mother and had no intention of marrying Mildred. But he enjoyed his newfound lover. He called her "my little Princess" and shortened her name to "Mil," pronouncing it "Meel." Meffert called him "Baby," and that is how he signed the *billets-doux* he wrote her. (In collectors' hands, there are love notes to other women where he signed himself as "Henry.")

Following the 1907–08 Metropolitan Opera season, Caruso went on an extended tour of American and Canadian cities, traveling as far west as Chicago and north to Montreal. He was only thirty-four, and his capacity for work was at its peak. He enjoyed singing and performing and felt in the best of vocal health. Treated like a world-class celebrity, he met an enchanted public wherever he went, and the reviews were always excellent. The public could hardly wait for his new records, and money poured in. His fees, possibly the highest in the business, were rising. He had a beautiful new mistress in New York, Mother was waiting for him in Europe, and he may even have had a tryst lined up somewhere with Rina. He must have felt on top of the world when he left New York on 21 May 1908 aboard the S/S *Kaiserin Augusta Victoria,* bound for London.

This was his last carefree transatlantic crossing for several years. Some of his close friends were on board, among them his accompanist Tullio Voghera and Father Tonello. The priest was an old friend of Father's who was often invited to celebrate mass in the little chapel at Le Panche. Caruso once gave him a beautiful gold watch, but not long afterward he noticed that the good priest was unable to tell the time without a clock nearby. Father asked what had happened to the watch, and Tonello admitted that because the church needed money for repairs, he had pawned it.

Father bought Tonello another gold watch. But this time he had engraved on the back: "*Da non essere impegnato!*" ("Not to be pawned!")

According to Tonello, Caruso planned to complete his engagements in London and Paris and then go to Naples to visit his father Marcellino, who was in poor health. It was not to be. On the fourth day of the trip, a wireless message arrived: "Prepare Caruso for the sad news of his father's death."[13]

The captain decided that the priest should break the tragic news to Caruso. When Father Tonello was handed the cable, Caruso teased him that he was such an important personage that he alone received a cable that day. It took the priest all day and the best part of the evening to gather up enough courage to carry out his sad duty. As Father wrote to Sisca upon his arrival in London on 2 June 1908:

It is useless to describe to you my grief upon receiving the fatal news. As soon as Father Tonello uttered my poor father's name, in a flash I knew that he had died, because I could have never expected the news of improvement but only of worsening as his condition was very bad, thus from the news I guessed that he was dead, and so it was! Poor old man! Dying without having his children around him! It is said that God is just—but why not wait a few days? No sir! I must carry some great sin on my shoulders and have to pay for it by never seeing my father again! It was just like that with my mother! I cried, but I had to take hold of myself because of the obligation to think of those who remain, whose condition is not bright because [I have] a feeble-minded (*stupida*) sister and an almost imbecilic (*quasi incretinito*) brother. I will go to Naples as soon as I can and put everything in order.

He went on to complain bitterly about the burdens of his profession, and the fact that he had a mansion, not a home, where he could not live in tranquility "because I live with a woman who is not legally mine. Should I die tomorrow, my children would not inherit this place or anything that is mine, because they were born outside the law." He added that he was thinking of renouncing his Italian citizenship and assuming another nationality in order "to assure a future for my children who otherwise would end up having nothing."

In addition to wanting to ensure that Fofò and I would inherit what he had "accumulated in the many years of work," he wanted to legalize his relationship with Mother. In the winter of 1907, Gino Botti had threatened to institute proceedings against Mother, and Father had reportedly paid him a large sum of money—perhaps not for the first time—to induce him to change his mind. No doubt Father had had enough of people trying to extract money from him under every possible pretext. At the same time, Mother had had enough of the ambivalence of her marital, social, and legal status, and it is most likely she who proposed to Father that they move to the United States and take up American citizenship. This would have removed her from the jurisdiction of Italian law, she could have obtained a civil divorce from Botti, and she and Father could finally have married.

Caruso had the entire 1907–08 New York season to consider, and perhaps reconsider, this course of action. It is doubtful that he had taken any steps by the time he reached London. Although he wanted to do the right thing for Mother and for us, he was in no particular hurry. He was a patriotic Italian, and to renounce his Italian citizenship was a tall psychological hurdle to clear. He may have had other motives for procrastination, but this alone was sufficient to prevent him from acting with his customary zeal. When he arrived in London that summer, the matter was still in the planning stages, although it was probably around this time that he instructed his lawyers in Milan, Nicola Vetere and De Simoni, to explore the matter.[14]

Although he was in deep distress over Grandfather Marcellino's death, Father set aside his personal tragedy and participated on 30 May 1908 in a benefit concert given under the patronage of His Majesty King Edward VII at the Royal Albert Hall. He sang superbly; it seems that the emotional crisis had left his voice intact. But word of his loss had reached the King. "I was called to his box," Caruso wrote to Sisca on June 2, "and he expressed his condolences and sympathies for the loss of Papa, and his thanks and appreciation on his part and everyone else's for having sung in such a moment of grief, and his regrets over not having me this year at Covent Garden."

Mother met him in London at their apartment. This suggests that she was still undecided as to whether their union could be salvaged. But she was distant and cool and pressed him about the issue of their citizenship and the move to the United States, her divorce and their marriage. Once he and Ada were face to face, he had to answer questions and listen to complaints and recriminations. His responses or explanations must have been unsatisfactory. Whether or not rumors about his involvement with Mildred Meffert had reached Mother, this confrontation must have shown her that Caruso was not going to change his way of life with respect to other women.

What specifically gave Mother the impetus for the drastic final step is not known; in any case, she decided what to do next. She did not go with Caruso to Paris, and as soon as he left London, unbeknownst to him, she and her chauffeur headed for Le Panche.

Father sang the Duke in *Rigoletto* at the Opéra on 11 June 1908, in the distinguished company of Nellie Melba and Maurice Renaud. It was a benefit performance, the proceeds going to the Dramatic Authors' Fund. According to a letter to Sisca of June 2, he planned to "go down to Italy on the 12th to take care of everything and everyone." He probably went to Naples to be with his bereaved stepmother and brother, but by the end of the month, he was back in London. When he returned to Ealing, he found the house empty. He assumed that Mother, in another fit of temper, had asked Romati to drive her on some excursion. His own relationship with her was strained, and their need for each other greatly diminished. In general, he found her attitude unreasonable. A passage in a letter to Sisca dated 2 July 1908 is a direct reference to her demanding ways: "Apart from the sorrow over the loss of my poor father I don't want to torment my soul anymore for others who on top of it are not even grateful." At any rate, his movements and his correspondence indicate that he had no premonition of impending domestic doom nor concern about Mother's sudden departure. He went about his business as if nothing unusual had happened. In the same letter to Sisca he mentioned: "I have done a private concert already and I have only one or two more to do. I will let you know later where you can reach me; in the meantime you can always write to me care of *Signor* G. Vecchiettini, 12 Via S. Frediano, Florence." He added, not without pride:

> Last night I went to hear *Otello* at Covent Garden. I was in a box. After the first act word got around that I was in the theater, and all the binoculars were directed at the box. All of a sudden, that great mass of people erupted into a storm of applause and screams in my direction, giving me an extraordinary demonstration. It was a most emotional moment. One could see that this people still love me.

As time went on and he did not hear from Ada, he became suspicious. Because she traveled by car from London to Florence, Mother needed a considerable head start to carry out her plans. It is most unlikely that she had confided in anyone who might have alerted Father to the truth of the situation. Contrary to the claims of many biographers, it appears that when Father headed home to find out for himself what was going on, he did not yet know what to expect. Without advising anyone of his plans or his anticipated arrival, he set out for Florence. When he arrived at Le Panche in the second week of July, he found the villa empty except for the gardener.

Mother had run away with the chauffeur, Cesare Romati.

CHAPTER SEVEN

Exit Ada Giachetti

F OFÒ described Romati as a "fairly good-looking, muscular man."
He added: "I used to admire him for his knowledge of the car and
his driving skill which in those days were extraordinary qualities in a
man." He admitted that Romati was always kind to him, yet, as he said,

> [I] always harbored a certain resentment because I saw
> him behaving with too much familiarity with Mamma.
> Furthermore, I felt a special aversion toward Romati, because
> he was responsible for the death of my little fox terrier, Gypsy,
> which I loved very much. He didn't do it intentionally, to be
> sure. It happened during an automobile ride in our Daimler
> double phaeton. Like other cars in those days, it had no doors.
> I was sitting next to him on the front seat with the dog on my
> lap. It was a lively little animal, and while driving with one
> hand, Romati was teasing her with the other, pretending to
> throw a ball for her to catch. The dog jumped out of my arms,
> fell on the aluminum running board, slipped off, and ended up
> beneath the rear wheel. Romati refused to listen to my
> protestations and to those of Mamma and the others in the car,

claiming that we were on an incline and he could not stop, and left the little corpse lying in the middle of the road. My dislike of him stemmed from this incident.

This small tragedy must have occurred in 1907, when Fofò was home for the summer holidays. The year before, shortly after his eighth birthday, he was considered old enough to be sent again to a boarding school, this time permanently. He entered the Badia Fiesolana on 8 October 1906.

This school was a former monastery converted into a boarding school for boys and run by the Scolopian fathers, a branch of the Jesuit order. Fofò hated the place. Years later he described it as a severe, forbidding structure, "roosting like a hawk on a cliff. It had the air of a fortress ready to spew forth an army in assault on the neighboring Villa de' Pazzi, the place where the plot was hatched that cost Giuliano Medici his life."

There were over a hundred boys at the Badia, ranging in age from six to eighteen. It was one of the best parochial schools in the area, where well-to-do families sent their unruly offspring to acquire knowledge and discipline. Fofò had a difficult time there. He was not from a titled family; being the son of a famous opera singer counted for nothing among his classmates. He had to fend for himself, relying on his strength and his fists. Taking their cue from their parents, the boys teased Fofò mercilessly, calling him names and taunting him about the fact that his father and mother had never married. He recalled:

[I] knew nothing of that, but the malicious tone of my companions gave rise to such an instinctive reaction in me that, without knowing whether I was telling a lie or not, I claimed to have seen Mamma's wedding dress in one of the wardrobes, and what is more, I [said I] was there at their wedding. I told this incongruity with such bitterness and rage that I might have killed if I could have laid hands on any of them. I almost did. One of my schoolmates, meaner than the rest, was taunting me with his sarcastic remarks, influenced, no doubt, by the gossip and malicious remarks of his parents. He gave me a shove as if by accident. He should not have done that. I jumped on him in a flash, pinned him down with my knees, and strangled him until his tongue hung out. Fortunately, my classmates and the preceptor managed to drag me away by force, otherwise I would have choked him to death.

Hardly anyone visited Fofò during the school year. He was allowed to come home only for the Christmas and Easter holidays. Why Mother abandoned him so completely is inexplicable, especially considering that Fiesole is very close to Florence, and she had a car and a chauffeur at her disposal. At least Father kept in touch by mail, writing letters from New York and "a postcard almost every four or five days in his clear, calligraphic handwriting." Miserable Fofò could hardly wait for the end of the school year when someone from the household would show up to liberate him for the summer.

IN early July 1908, Fofò was expecting Father to come and take him home for the summer vacation. He was petrified to face him just then, because his report card showed a bad grade in mathematics. As he put it, "I had the urge to flee in fright from my father's stern look. I never had had corporal punishment from him, but one word of reproach sent me into an abyss of mortification."

Just as the boys were about to leave for their usual afternoon walk in the countryside, Fofò was called to the Rector's sitting room, where parents could visit with their little darlings once a week. Terrified, he slowly began the descent on the grand stairway to the conversation room. At first, he was hesitant to enter.

[He] first peeked through the glass in the door to gauge Father's mood, to see in his face whether he had spoken to the dean yet.

I was shocked. My father's head was resting on the Rector's shoulders and he was shaking with sobs. I could not understand it! I always thought of him as thundering Jupiter; benevolent, but thundering just the same. All my courage left me, and with trembling knees I went to meet him. I thought that this time not even the Almighty himself could save me; if Papa is so upset about my grades, I will have to pay dearly for those tears.

Being a child, this was the only explanation I could think of, considering how much interest my father had taken in my studies and what satisfaction my good grades would have given him. I decided to confront him and take my punishment. I entered. I will never forget the picture before my startled eyes. Papa lifted his head from Father Brattina's shoulder, and I saw his anguished face. His eyes, almost unrecognizable, showed a man nearly gone out of his mind.

To my amazement, he rushed to me the moment he saw me, threw his arms around me, and clasped me to his chest. He kissed me as never before, and in a voice choked by violent sobs, he kept repeating:

"Mamma has left us . . . Mamma has left us . . ."

For a moment I could not understand anything. Then, almost as in a dream, I put my arms around his neck and hugged him with all my strength, kissing his cheeks with frenzy. The stubble of his day-old beard hurt my lips. Yet this slight pain made me want to return my father's embrace. Suddenly, Father pulled himself together and taking me firmly by the hand said:

"But we will find her; and you are coming with me."

While a rickety taxi carried us through the winding lanes of the smiling slopes of Fiesole toward the city of Florence that lay below, I was turning over in my head Father's words "Mamma has left us" and all that had transpired just a few minutes before. As soon as we reached Florence, Father became a demon in motion. He had to visit innumerable offices to make the necessary arrangements for our trip. Every official solicitously offered his assistance to facilitate the issue of a passport. Father explained to me that we were going to Nice, where Mother had gone and had taken my brother with her. I had left the *collegio* in my uniform, so we rushed through several stores where I was outfitted with civilian clothes. One last trip was to the Cook travel agency to buy tickets for the sleeping car, and soon afterward we were at the train station awaiting our departure.

All these events should have been overwhelmingly happy and fantastic for me. It was my first time traveling in a sleeping car, a most interesting novelty. But as I examined every detail in the compartment, all its equipment and the utilization of every bit of space, inevitably my eyes fell upon Father's pale face and his glistening eyes as he sat in silence at the corner window seat.

The train started to move and gain speed, and I watched the streets and houses grow sparser. Every now and then, the piercing whistle of the locomotive called me back to reality. Once past city limits, the express train maintained a constant speed. The regular break in the rails set up a rhythm which gradually set me daydreaming. I leaned against the window and watched the telegraph poles pass faster and faster against the receding green landscape. Their succession had a hypnotic effect on me, almost leaving my mind completely detached from my body. . . . Mamma! Although it was almost a year since I had seen her, I had her clearly in my mind. . . . A jolt and the screeching of the brakes brought me back to the present. I glanced at my father. Two bright tears were rolling down his cheeks from under his half-closed eyelids. Poor Papa. He must have been suffering. He seemed to have aged by several years. A deep furrow ran across his forehead, and a light tremor made his hands tremble as they lay crossed on his lap. A nauseating, bitter taste came to my mouth, and my throat tightened. I jumped up and flew to the neck of my father, who was taken aback, and I showered him with kisses, something we had seldom done outside of wishing good morning or good night. Father embraced me, and as the train gained speed after the brief stop in Pisa, he began to speak.

"The greatest misfortune that can happen to a child is now happening to you. I am suffering greatly, but for the moment you are not fully aware of your loss; your little heart does not yet know what you have lost."

His tears began to flow copiously. I was very confused; I had always regarded him as a man of steel.

"I too have lost my mother, whom I adored when I was young. She was the best woman in the world, and her memory is still bright in my heart. But she was taken from me by Him to Whom one cannot command, perhaps to take her place in heaven among the best. But your mother has left you, to go with someone else."

I thought it over, and finally I posed the question that had weighed on me for several hours and which I had been unable to formulate.

"Papa, why did Mamma leave us?"

Father's face contorted violently. He clasped me to himself and kissed me, then sat me down next to him and calmly began.

"In all good conscience, I cannot tell you why all this is happening. You are ten years old, but life in the *collegio* and the moral instructions of the Scolopian fathers have opened up your mind and soul. Thus I consider you a young man and I can confide in you as in a man. For some time, I have been receiving anonymous letters in New York—at least they were unsigned—which spoke without respect of your mother, claiming that she had been treating our chauffeur, Romati, with too much intimacy. . . . I never paid attention to these base accusations, and although they upset me, I continued my work in New York, as you know."

"I did not have a care in the world until I reached London," he continued, "where I received the news of the death of your poor Grandfather Marcellino, and found the house at Ealing empty.[1] And it was quite a shock when I arrived at the villa and Emilio, the gardener, told me there was no one at home. For the moment, I did not understand what he was saying, and I entered. There I had another surprise. In the hallway stood five or six trunks, packed and ready. Amazed, I asked Emilio what those trunks were doing there. Emilio said: 'Master, *Signora* Ada gave me orders to send them to the railway station in Nice.' You can imagine, Fofò, how the doubts that had been creeping into my heart turned into cruel reality. I still did not want to believe it. I pressed Emilio to explain what he meant. He told me that two days earlier, following the receipt of a telegram whose contents he did not know, Mamma hastily made arrangements for her departure. She sent ahead some of the trunks, and taking Mimmi with her and a Miss you don't know [the governess, Miss Saer], she set out by car with Romati at the wheel. She left instructions to have the rest of the packed trunks shipped. I searched the house for some clue. I now had the proof of everything those anonymous letters had said and I had refused to believe.

"Emilio followed me, seemingly wanting to say something, trying to decide whether he should or not. Annoyed because I wanted to be alone, I asked him sharply what it was he wanted to say. He then said with an air of great embarrassment: 'You see, Master, I was supposed to send to the *Signora* a small jewel case with her jewels in it; she forgot to take it just as she was leaving. What should I do with it?' I told him to give it to me and not to ship anything.

"I decided immediately to come and get you, hoping that together we will catch up with Mamma and convince her to return with us."

These words were incomprehensible to me. The train entered the first of many tunnels on the line along the seashore from La Spezia to Genoa. We had to close the windows in order to keep the compartment from filling up with smoke. The darkness that enveloped us in each tunnel sent me trustingly closer to my father. He placed an arm around my shoulder and drew me to him. We remained silent, absorbed in our own thoughts. Every so often I would feel the hair on the back of his hand as it passed lightly over my cheek, and the light tickle gave me the sensation of the most welcome and sweetest caress.

I fell asleep and woke up in the turmoil of the station of Genoa. It was dark already. At that moment, the chief steward of the dining car came from compartment to compartment calling in a stentorian monotone, "Dining car, first call!" We were alone in our compartment, and when he saw Father so absorbed in his thoughts, his face contorted by suffering, he decided not to insist, much to my disappointment. I had never eaten in a dining car. With all the tension, my appetite had grown rather than diminished. As the man was about to withdraw, Father returned to reality and asked:

"Do you want to eat?"

"As you wish, Papa."

We were given two tickets for reserved seats, and after awhile we headed to the dining car. It was a great novelty and diversion for me. After a short while, all eyes turned toward our table. The word had spread that the tenor Caruso was in the car. I remember as if it were yesterday that at our table sat two ladies, probably English, who must have been torn between the conflicting impulses of wishing to engage such an illustrious man in a conversation, and remaining indifferent and reserved in the manner of the true British. In the end, they made my father more nervous than ever. He was always courtesy personified but now, unable to communicate, surely must have given the impression of being something of a bear. Poor ladies. If they could only have imagined what was going through my father's mind, they would have blushed for their artless attempts at conversation.

Papa did not touch his food. I believe he only came with me because I would not have been able to manage by myself. After the meal, we returned to our compartment where we sank into deep silence. My youth conquered all the wild thoughts that crowded my young mind; I closed my eyes and only awakened at the border town of Ventimiglia. The bureaucratic routine of border crossing was the merest formality for us. A French train took us from Ventimiglia to Nice, where we arrived around one o'clock in the morning. We settled in a hotel whose name I do not recall, near the Place Massena on the Promenade des Anglais. I was happy that I could sleep that night in the same room with my father, although we had a suite with two bedrooms and a sitting room.

In the morning, Father made a few phone calls, probably to the police, and around ten he called me.

"Fofò, you know that Mamma has your brother with her; she doesn't know yet that we have arrived. Go to the garden at Place Massena right outside and see if by chance you can find Mimmi. If you do, bring him to me immediately."

This had to be just a wild guess on Father's part, but an intuitive one. Children then, as today, were often taken to a park to play. Indeed, Miss Saer had a fetish about parks: Because a child of four could not be ordered to sit still all day long, I had to get out of the house and be allowed to run around. The park at Place Massena was the logical place to send Fofò to look for me. Fofò felt he had been entrusted with a mission of great importance and was determined to perform it as was expected. After systematically combing the entire length of the park, Fofò found me. He ran to me calling my name, and I must have had some vague recollection of my brother, because I trustingly gave him my hand. He began to drag me toward the hotel. Fofò narrates:

> I heard a strident feminine voice I didn't know call Mimmi amidst a cascade of words in a foreign language. For the moment, I wanted to go even faster, but as I heard the volume and energy of the voice increase and the swish of skirts getting closer, I decided to stop and turn around. In front of me towered a blond lady of indeterminate age. Her face was severe but beautiful. She was dressed all in white with a long and very narrow waist, and an enormous straw hat. Although I did not have much experience in such matters, I immediately took her for an English lady. Without losing her self-control, she first spoke to my brother, who did not let go of my hand, then calmly, but not without some trepidation, she asked me a multitude of questions in a language I did not understand. Not knowing how to explain myself, I made her understand with

gestures that I wanted to take my brother to Papa. I repeated the word "Papa" I don't know how many times, motioning with my hand in the direction of the hotel. For a moment she hesitated, then she signaled me that she would follow us.

The triumphal trumpets of *Aida* could not have adequately proclaimed my glory as I presented myself to Father, like an officer to his superior: "Mission accomplished!" To tell the truth, Papa was amazed at the speed with which I carried out my assignment.

I REGRET to say that my first faint recollection of the whole series of events is playing in the public gardens at Nice and being led by the hand by Fofò to the hotel. But I do remember most vividly that when he brought me to the hotel suite, Papa was sitting at the dressing table in a robe. I had no idea who he was: He was a total stranger to me. He opened his arms and repeatedly called to me, but instead of going to him, I clung to Miss Saer's skirt. Father was in a terrible state, nervous and irritable. He called me again, this time impatiently. Sensing the immense tension, I began to bawl at the top of my lungs. Lei tried to quiet me, but I would not stop shrieking. Finally, Father had enough. He came over and struck me lightly on the hands, not harshly, but strongly enough to get my attention. No one had ever struck me before. It was such a great shock that it accomplished its purpose: I stopped crying.

Surprisingly, this incident is the very first recollection I have of my father.

Fofò continues his narrative:

Father left my brother and me to an affectionate reunion, and spoke to the mysterious English lady for over an hour in the sitting room. When they finally emerged, he introduced her to me saying:

"This is Miss Louise Saer. She will take care of Mimmi from now on. You will obey her in all that concerns him."

After the introduction, Father told us not to leave the hotel any more unless he accompanied us. This ruined my plans because I already expected to run along the seashore with my little brother and have a wonderful swim. It seemed unfair. Having found my brother, the whole story of Mamma left my mind.

That evening, after the Miss and Mimmi had retired to the
other room, Father said to me:

"I have had Mamma notified of my arrival; she will
probably come here in the morning. Even if she would not
have wanted to come, now she will for sure, because Mimmi
did not go home to her. Don't set foot outside the hotel unless
I say so."

I had a restless night, and I dreamed of blonde children,
one, two, a hundred, a thousand, until they became legion and
I awoke with a jolt, covered with sweat. Day came. The hours
passed, and I saw my father become increasingly nervous and
tense. Naturally, so did I. The only happy one was my little
brother, who cheerfully knocked over the building blocks I
dispiritedly stacked for him without much joy or enthusiasm.

Around ten in the morning, we heard a car stop in front of
the hotel. Our suite was on the first floor overlooking the
street. One of the windows was to the side of the hotel
entrance. It was summer, and the venetian blind covered the
open window to let in the sea breeze and to diffuse the bright
sunlight and the intense reflection of the blue sea in the Gulf
of Nice. It allowed a view to the streets without being seen. At
the sound of the automobile, both Father and I rushed to the
window. I had the same apprehensions as he, without being
fully aware of the reason for it. I saw Mamma get out of a taxi,
beautiful as an angel, but her face had a very aggressive expression. Father told us to go in the other room with Miss Saer and
not to make a sound.

I soon heard Mother's excited voice demanding furiously:
"Where is Mimmi?"

I don't know what Father replied because they kept their
voices low, but gradually their tone grew louder, and I heard
Father say:

"Ada, come back to me! You must do it for the love of our
children."

I could not make out Mamma's torrent of words; her voice
was hissing with rage. All of a sudden I thought I heard a thud,
and I could no longer contain myself. My heart beating with
suspense, I opened a small crack in the door, enough to see the
scene that made the blood rush to my head and made me
pledge all my love to my father forever. He had dropped to his
knees in front of Mamma. He was clasping her knees. His face

was so contorted that my heart ached for him. I was afraid that he would go out of his mind. He was yelling, his bloodshot eyes full of tears, his voice choked with pain:

"Ada, Ada . . . Don't leave us . . . Don't leave your little ones . . . Don't ruin our entire existence . . . Remember our love . . ."

Mamma stood erect, listening to him without saying a word, her eyes glowing with anger and her lips trembling from emotion. There was a moment of silence.

Then she unleashed her fury. She pushed him away, hurling demented words at him I could not comprehend. She said that she was tired of I don't know what, that she had found another ideal, that she had her rights as a mother, and she spoke of a past that was finished. Confronted with that fury, Father slowly rose. His face turned hard; all signs of weakness left his expression. In a determined and cutting voice, he said:

"You will never see your children again."

I don't know what happened after that, because with gentle force, Miss Saer pulled me away from the door. I started to tremble with fear and panic. We could still hear Father's threatening voice through the door:

"I will kill him like a dog!"

Then we made out from his enraged tone that he made Mamma believe he had sent us away somewhere. We heard the door slam, and there was dead silence. The rumble of the automobile under our window told me that Mother had left. That was the last time my little brother heard our Mamma's voice, and it was the penultimate occasion for me.

A great storm of nature had passed, and we left our room. Almost tiptoeing, as if not to disturb the silence, we went to our Father's side. I was aware of what had taken place, and my brother in his innocence was attracted to his *Daddy* [*sic*]. Papa was slumped in the armchair, holding his head between his hands and breathing heavily. He wasn't crying, but his face had a painful grimace (*una smorfia*) that later became a part of his Pagliaccio. He embraced us tenderly yet almost savagely. I remember his words:

"You don't have a mother any more, but I will be everything for you two."

So it was. From that day on, I had a deep love for my father that took precedence over all else in my life.

The day passed as if we were all in a diver's bell. Only my brother let out joyful squeals, happy to have the whole salon full of playthings I hastily gathered for him. Father stayed close by, except for a few moments when he had discussions with some people, probably detectives. We dined in the living room, but none of us had much appetite; even my brother felt the weight of the atmosphere.

That night I again had nightmares. I awoke exhausted in the morning, and I was surprised to see my father fully dressed. As soon as he saw me open my eyes, he said:

"Get up, get dressed, and come with me. We are going to bring Mamma back. We will try to persuade her, and you be very nice to her."

This instruction went against my inclination, because in this conflict, I was siding entirely with Father. As soon as I was ready, he called Miss Saer and, as far as I could make it out, ordered her not to leave the hotel with Mimmi. She promised, and Father seemed reassured. Before leaving the room, I saw him take a large revolver from his valise and put it in his pocket. I finally understood. "I will kill him like a dog" must have referred to the detestable chauffeur, Romati. An automobile was waiting for us at the hotel. We rode the whole length of the Promenade des Anglais, turning onto the coastal road that goes to Cap Martin. Papa had a piece of paper in his hand, and on it the address of the villa where Mamma had taken refuge with Romati.

At a given moment, he curtly ordered the car to stop and told the driver to wait there. We walked down a long road in the middle of a park that ended in a small square with a graceful little villa surrounded by trees. Papa made me stay behind him and on the alert. We reached the entrance of the villa. Father drew his revolver and tried the door handle. It was unlocked, and several windows on the garden side stood open. We entered a [large room] that took up almost the entire ground floor. No one was there. Papa ran upstairs, calling "Ada! Ada!" I looked around, and on a small table near a chaise longue I saw a half-empty box of chocolates and a few novels by Salgari. For the moment, I forgot the emotional drama of which I was a part and took an immediate interest in these novels, which were my favorites. In the meantime, Father slowly came down the stairs, with a lost look. He took me by the arm, and together we searched the house from basement to attic. Not a soul. In the garage we found the Renault Mamma had bought and for some reason abandoned.[2] Papa gathered up the few things of value that for him represented personal effects left behind by Mamma. I, on my part, took possession of the four or five books by Salgari. Downcast, we returned to Nice. Back at the hotel, Papa asked me to leave him alone, and locked himself in his room.

With pantomime signs, I managed to explain to Miss Saer all that had happened. When I came to the part about the revolver, she became very upset. After a little while, I saw her head for Papa's room and discreetly knock. Father did not want to open at first but then faced her, asking what she wanted. I saw Miss Saer almost push him back, with determination, and enter the room. I don't know what she said, but it seemed to me as if she were gently reprimanding my father. At the end of that encounter, I saw my father embrace her as one would embrace a mother, and quietly cry on her shoulder. Then slowly he detached himself, took the revolver out of his pocket, and gave it to her. Miss Saer took it, returned to her room, and securely locked it away in her valise.

There was an air of catastrophe all around us, and despite my age I sensed its gravity. During the rest of the day, we stayed close to Father. Watching him, I felt like crying, and my stomach was upset. I often took his hand, tearfully brought it to my lips, and kissed it. He was deeply demoralized.

That evening, Father and Miss Saer had a long discussion. She then began to pack the few pieces of luggage that were left at the villa, her clothing and my brother's. The next morning, she left for England with Mimmi; Father and I headed back to Florence. But he did not want to go back to Le Panche. We moved to the house at Signa which he had recently bought, and where we spent so many happy days together later on.

HAVING failed to make Mother change her mind and return to us, Father had to plan for the future without her. It meant he had to completely restructure his life. He hated change, and a dramatic upheaval of this kind must have had a terrible effect on him. From Nice, he went to Florence to make arrangements for Fofò's immediate future. Because he would have nothing to do with the Giachettis for the moment, he took my brother to Naples to stay with relatives. But poor Fofò was sent back to the Badia as soon as it reopened in the fall. Father had his own belongings removed from Le Panche and never lived there again. He may have gone back once or twice to check on the property, but to the best of my knowledge, he avoided it from then on, leaving it in the charge of Emilio Tani.

Father was probably still in Italy when he received a letter from Mother dated 23 July 1908. She begged him to forgive her for what she had done, adding that she could no longer reciprocate his affection and that she hoped the children born of their union would give him the strength to forget her. She also hoped that Father, who had always been good to her, would remain so in the future; and she asked him to indicate whether she could expect any help from him or she should try to find gainful employment and perhaps return to the stage. She said that she had already abandoned "him," meaning Romati, and closed the letter as she began it, begging her "good and generous Enrico" to forgive her, because in the final analysis, it was he "who had been the cause of it all."

Father's response, if any, has not survived the years. He probably received this letter in his last days in Florence as he was putting his affairs in order. After he had accomplished what he could under the drastically changed circumstances, he traveled to London, ending the most tumultuous fortnight of his life. On 28 July 1908, he wrote from the Hotel Cecil to Sisca:

> I return to London after 15 days of vicissitudes: I believed that after all the work done in America it would be given me to rest and relax here in old Europe at my leisure with the family, but I was mistaken.
>
> It would be too long a story to narrate all that happened between the 10th and the 25th of this month. Suffice it to say that there is no affection left for me in the world. I have nothing left but two poor creatures to whom I must devote myself body and soul. If it were not for these two poor innocents who belong to me, I would have put an end to my life by now.
>
> They have broken my heart in the prime of my life! I have cried so much, but my tears have served for nothing.
>
> I hope that in time my poor heart so roughly crushed will heal and life will be brighter for me.

Losing Ada was the one sorrow from which Caruso never

recovered. She was the great love of his life, the companion of his youth, the helpmate of his early struggles and witness to his rise to world renown. More than all these, she was the mother of his children and the lady of his house. It was not only wounded pride and the blow to his male ego that made him suffer so, but the fact that he had been deserted by the only woman he had ever loved unconditionally. In addition, Ada had humiliated him, made him the laughingstock of the world, by leaving him for a chauffeur in his employ. Wounded, insulted, embittered, he fought back any way he could. On 13 September 1908, he wrote to Sisca from London: "All my affairs are being put in order, and who will have the worse of it is the woman who forgot everything, because I arrived in time to take *everything* from her, leaving her with the shirt on her back."

Yes, Ada Giachetti left Caruso's life as she had come into it: with nothing of her own but her clothing.

"Putting his affairs in order" involved Miss Saer and me. Father rented an apartment in London, at 13 Clarendon Court, Maida Vale, which was to be our home for several years and his own *pied-à-terre* during his visits to England. For reasons I never understood, Father decided to leave Fofò in Italy, thus condemning my poor brother to a most unhappy and lonely existence. Fofò recalled:

> At the end of that unfortunate summer, Papa sent me back to the Collegio alla Badia Fiesolana, giving strict orders that I was not to see any relatives, including Uncle Giovanni, unless I was accompanied by his administrator Giuseppe Vecchiettini. He also left instructions that I was not to be allowed close to anyone in the Giachetti family. This was the beginning of a black period for me, because while the other boys always had visits from close and distant relatives, I had to wait for the return of my father from America for his summer rest to have the benefit of a little familial affection. Vecchiettini took me out for the major holidays, Christmas and Easter, to let me enjoy a bit of freedom and fun. But he was not Mamma, Papa, or my Aunt Rina. In short, he was not a relative.
>
> However, even though I was sequestered year in and year out in the austere *collegio,* I had two or three months of intense joy each summer when Papa returned to Italy for his vacation.

BY late July, the tragic turn in Father's private life began to receive attention in the international press. Reporters wanted a statement from him, and he knew full well he would have scarcely a moment's peace until he gave one. He told them what they expected to hear, rearranging the facts to save face as best he could. In a special cable from London, a reporter stated that Caruso was actually

> glad that his wife [*sic*] left him. . . . Life with her was impossible. I told her so several weeks ago. I expect my wife to be a woman who can sympathize with me—a woman of ability, of understanding, of appreciation. . . . A month ago in Italy I told her how she had fallen below the expectations I had formed of her, and bade her begone. . . . The woman did not come up to my standard and I have no regrets. She has gone off with somebody on her own level. (*The New York Times,* 14 August 1908)

Of course, the press had a field day with the story. By the time the next special cable (from Rome) reached *The New York Times,*[3] he had decided to turn all the skeletons out of the closet. He "publicly declared in the newspapers that she is not his wife," that he had never been married; and he openly admitted that Ada had "eloped . . . with his chauffeur."

Having organized our lives, Father returned to Naples to visit his stepmother Maria and his siblings Assunta and Giovanni. It must have been painful for him to tell his closest relatives what had happened. Predictably, they all saw matters through his eyes; Giovanni, in particular, never forgave the entire Giachetti clan for what "they" had done to his brother.

Father also sought some badly needed rest and diversion. He traveled to Tunis with friends, roaming the streets dressed as an Arab. When he returned to Naples in the same garb, preceded by a well-placed rumor that a high Turkish dignitary was arriving in Naples to negotiate the extradition of a Turkish refugee, he was treated with great respect. Much to his delight, he had deceived even the Neapolitans. He then invited all and sundry to dine with him at one of his favorite restaurants in Posillipo, making a special point of being seen in the best humor, joking and conversing with the locals. The performance was straight out of *Pagliacci:* Beneath the clowning lay the agony of losing Mother. Father was so deeply wounded in his manhood that he had to prove to the whole world he did not care that Ada Giachetti had left him.

Then, as later, he could not understand Mother's drastic and improbable action. Vincent Seligman recorded that Mother was "an extremely attractive woman and Caruso was still very much in love with her at the time she left him; in the previous year we had travelled out to Italy with him, and I remember how, directly he caught sight of her on the platform at Milan, he had leapt out of the train whilst it was still moving, and thrown himself passionately into her arms."[4]

Another friend of Father's, the Dutch actor Lou Tellegen,[5] also commented on his love for Mother. He recorded in his memoirs:

> That grown-up child, Enrico Caruso, lived not far from me and came to see me frequently. . . . I had a great veneration for that big boy, because he was such a baby, and God had given him so much that the gift was too colossal for his comprehension. Such a sentimentalist! Such a rich nature wasted upon superficial whims and ambition! What a child he was, that man with his broad shoulders and enormous chest, crying like a baby when his first wife left him.
>
> "How could she?" he wailed. "How could she desert *me,* the greatest tenor in the world, for a chauffeur?" It made no difference that the chauffeur was handsome. Enrico could not comprehend that any woman could leave him, "the greatest tenor in the world," and he wept floods on my shoulder. Darling man! Heavenly boy![6]

CHAPTER EIGHT

Final Rift

I have been trying to solve the puzzle of my mother's conduct for seven decades, yet all I can do is sift and resift the facts.

Two months before my fourth birthday, Ada Giachetti left the foremost tenor of the world and ran off with his chauffeur. I don't believe that she was insensitive or stupid, though I can find a whole string of adjectives to describe her: She was jealous and vengeful, rash, impulsive, emotional, sensual, irresponsible, and sometimes irrational. She was all these, yet Father loved her, and she him.

I have no doubt that my parents loved each other in the best, old-fashioned sense of the word. They were together for eleven years. Which of the two made the greater contribution to the union is difficult to say, but the sacrifices were all made by Mother. Father insisted that she give up her career and devote herself to him alone. He saw no reason why she should not travel with him if he so wished or stay home, take care of the children, and be there when he returned from his trips.

There is no sensible explanation of why Father would not allow her to sing in at least a few performances every season, with or without him. Her reviews show that she was good enough to be engaged on her own merits. My parents could have become an operatic duo, following the example of several singing husband and wife teams of their century, from Ludwig and Malvina Schnorr (the first Tristan and Isolde) through Mario and Grisi, Heinrich and Therese Vogl, Roberto Stagno and Gemma Bellincioni (creators of Turiddu and Santuzza in *Cavalleria rusticana*), Nikolai Figner and Medea Mei-Figner (the first Hermann and Lisa in the *Queen of Spades*), to their exact contemporaries, Adelina Stehle and Edoardo Garbin, Giovanni Zenatello and Maria Gay. The two pregnancies Mother had between Fofò and me should have delayed her pursuit of an active career only temporarily. Grisi had six children during her career, Ernestine Schumann-Heink had eight, and it has been recorded that Patti's mother sang the title role of *Norma* the night before Adelina was born! When Mother accompanied Father to America, he didn't let her accept a single engagement. In addition to the opportunity of replacing Melba in *La Bohème,* according to family lore, she was offered other roles as well, among them Violetta and Tosca. Father supposedly said at different times in different ways: "In our family Mrs. Caruso takes care of the home and the children; I do the singing."

Did she leave Caruso because, in her heart, she longed to return to the stage? This she could have done regardless of my father's protestations. If he had stood in her way and forced her to choose between him and her calling, she could have gained the world's sympathy for giving up the great Caruso for love of her art. By running away with a lowly employee, she only reaped scorn. She must have been able to anticipate this consequence.

Questions of career to the side, why would a woman abandon two children and a life of luxury at the side of a celebrated artist and compatible companion, a man not difficult to live with so long as he was treated as the head of his household and allowed the prerogatives of men of his era? Did Mother want to get even for his philandering? Was she truly, physically and emotionally, tired of him? And after Caruso, what kind of life did she expect to have with Romati? Apparently, the two had planned to open an automobile dealership financed by the sale of her jewelry, which, along with her clothing, she considered rightfully hers. Beyond that, how would they live? Romati, too, was married, and she was only trading one concubinage for another.

Why, then, did she do it?

Two statements made by Ada—one publicly, one privately—are as close to an explanation as we shall have. In a 1938 interview with a reporter for *A Noite* in Rio de Janeiro, where she was then living, she said:

[Caruso] had a weakness he never overcame: He was a ladies' man and he never fought against temptation! He would give himself to all, and it was this that finally came between us. Violent outbursts, wounded feelings! One day we even came to blows so that we separated and I returned to the stage in Italy.

In a letter written to me in the late 1930s, she offered more personal reasons and named the person she considered the cause of all her misfortunes: her sister Rina.

Father sang with Rina in Naples in 1902, and in London in 1904, 1906, and 1907. Their professional commitments obliged them to spend a great deal of time together—circumstances hardly conducive to domestic harmony given Mother's jealous nature, Rina's unconcealed attraction to Caruso, and his susceptibility to feminine charms. In addition, sibling rivalry must have extended into the domain of singing. Not only was Rina's career blossoming before Ada's eyes, but her sister was singing her—Ada's—repertory at Covent Garden, often partnering her *de facto* husband in roles she herself could well have sung with him.

When Ada became aware of his dalliance with Rina in 1906, she chose not to accompany him to New York; she may have been only too glad to have an ocean between them. However, the following summer, the three of them were together again in London, where Father and Rina sang in the same cast. The circumstances must have placed the relationship under further strain, to a degree that can be judged by the fact that Miss Saer once mentioned she had heard loud exchanges after several performances and, though she did not understand much Italian at the time, had heard Rina's name in the course of the quarrels.

Mother's affair with Romati began after the 1907 Covent Garden season. She returned to Italy before Caruso, who traveled later in the company of the Seligmans. In Milan, Mother told Father she had done something which would perhaps displease him. "What you do is well done," he answered.[1] She then told him she had purchased a forty-horsepower automobile. The car was parked in front of the hotel, and the hired chauffeur in the driver's seat was Cesare Romati. Whether Romati or the automobile came first into Ada's life can never be established, but in either case, the result was the same. It is hard to tell whether the affair began like any other, because of the mutual attraction of two people, or whether this was Mother's way of repaying Father for his infidelities. It happened, and according to the rules of social conduct, it was impossible to justify.

At first, Father was unaware of the developments. After he returned to New York, Mother made several long trips in her new car with her good-looking chauffeur. They drove to Nice, where she asked Caruso to send her 10,000 lire, and later she requested 10,000 more. Father sent her the money.[2] The requests for cash continued, and he sent many 1,000-lire banknotes—to Nice, to Milan, to London. Apparently, Ada and Romati made a grand tour of southern Europe; but this could not go on forever, and Mother must have known she had to make a choice.

Was the choice freely made? There is evidence that sometime before 1912, Ada told Caruso Romati had been sent by a "secret society" to eliminate him, and that only by becoming Romati's lover could she save him.[3] I doubt that Father was able to accept this statement at face value.

It is hard to tell whether Mother had a plan, whether she had thought through what she was about to do and where it might lead. It is equally difficult to know whether it was motherly love that prompted her to take me with her on her flight to Nice, or whether I was there to ensure Father's continuing magnanimity. Although she took Miss Saer and me with her for the moment, I have no doubt that when I was old enough to be accepted at a boarding school, Miss Saer would have been dismissed, and I would have met the same fate as my unhappy brother.

FATHER left for his German tour at the end of the summer. He performed his familiar roles in *Rigoletto, La Bohème,* and *Pagliacci* in Wiesbaden, Frankfurt, Bremen, Hamburg, Leipzig, and Berlin. After the events of the summer, every performance of the last two works must have caused him indescribable pain: *La Bohème* for its memories, and *Pagliacci* for the relevance of its plot.

The story of two recording mysteries, preserved by Leonard Petts, former Archivist of E.M.I. Music Ltd., must be mentioned here, because they fall chronologically in this period.

One of these concerns a single recording allegedly made on 8 October 1908. It is the first entry in the weekly recording sheets of the Gramophone Company (formerly the Gramophone & Typewriter Company) for that day. A handwritten entry made in London by Fred Gaisberg's brother, Will, shows a single ten-inch recording thus: "8972e 8-10-08 ANG [or AUG] CARUSO Rigoletto: La donna è mobile (Verdi)." The other recordings made at the studio that day were 8973e–80e, all by the Black Diamonds Band. The bound files of recording sheets, complete only from 30 September 1908 onwards, have survived, and the entry has recently been confirmed by British discographer Alan Kelly.

Who ANG—or AUG—CARUSO may have been is a puzzle. It was not Enrico Caruso who made this record in London on 8 October 1908. The night before, on October 7, he sang *Pagliacci* in Frankfurt, and his next performance, in Bremen, took place on October 11. (According to Petts, Fred Gaisberg, who could have recorded Caruso in Germany, was in Scandinavia in September 1908 and from there went to Egypt and other parts of the Middle East.) The performer who recorded the *Rigoletto* aria that day was not *Enrico* Caruso. I wish I could cast further light on the matter, but satisfactory answers to the remaining questions will have to come from professional discographers of the period.

The second "lost" recording allegedly made by Caruso would have preceded the mysterious *Rigoletto* excerpt.

New Year's Eve of 1908 was a gala event in London. The *Daily Express* reported that "never before have the London hotel managers spent money so lavishly on decorations and entertainments."[4] The papers carried a tally of the number of guests at major hotels: The Savoy entertained two thousand; the Princes', one thousand; the Carlton and the Waldorf, eight hundred each; and the Ritz, five hundred. To make the occasion more festive and to capitalize on the breadth of exposure it provided, the publicity department of the Gramophone Company installed a record player in the restaurants of the main hotels which, precisely at midnight, reproduced the Westminster chimes and the striking of Big Ben. The record, GC-9423, was a ten-inch Black Label Pre-Dog.

But the best of what the gramophone had to offer was reserved for the Covent Garden Ball. The *Daily Chronicle* filed the following report:

> Five thousand tickets were sold for the fancy dress ball at Covent Garden. . . . The auditorium had been lavishly decorated for the occasion by Mr. Frank Rendle, the lessee of the house, and not the least conspicuous adornment was an immense electric illumination bearing the figure 1908, which at midnight was changed—in semi-darkness—to 1909. The New Year was welcomed in by singing—by the means of a private gramophone record—of "Auld Lang Syne," the soloist being Enrico Caruso, who had volunteered this melody to Mr.

Rendle during the summer when he was in London on holiday.[5]

Personally, I would interpret this as an error in reporting: Perhaps they played a Caruso record and another artist's recording of "Auld Lang Syne." None of the standard Caruso discographies has mentioned the recording until recently. John R. Bolig places it "circa August 10, 1908,'[6] which date, in the absence of a cited authority and in light of the missing recording logs for August, is dubious at best. Some eminent discographers strongly doubt that the record was ever made.

AFTER Ada left him, Caruso felt free to do as he pleased. Like a sailor with a girl in every port, it seems that he singled out a lady for his attentions in each city where he sang. Language was not a barrier: He was quite fluent in French, English, and Spanish. According to Emil Ledner, it was usually the women and girls who pursued him. Ledner wrote:

> I could never understand it! His personality was really not suited to stir interest. The sensuality of his voice, his theatrical temperament might have indeed exercised a strong appeal on a certain breed of women. But there were many women whose social position should have given them the greatest restraint and who in spite of it tried, often with downright insistent means and deeds, to get close . . . and beyond. Caruso was not fond of "adventures" . . . even less of really elegant women bestowed with charm and personal appeal . . . on the contrary. Often enough when we found ourselves in the company of graceful, beautiful and truly desirable women he would whisper in my ear: "My Ada!! No one can compare to her." One had to know "Ada" to fully appreciate this sentiment. . . . [Here we should mention that Ledner remembered Ada as "a little, chubby, downright fat Italian woman."][7]
>
> Due to the fact that Caruso did not speak a word of German, [and] that all letters passed through my hands, I have nipped in the bud and destroyed "follies," not harmless "derailments," that have become apparent and some that were just developing.[8]

One of Caruso's friends in Germany was a young operetta singer, Else Trauner. In my collection, there are two charming photographs of this lovely lady. On the back of one is written in ink: "*Au souvenir des dernières minutes à la gare de Francfort s/M—Else Trauner*" ("In memory of the last minutes at the railway station of Frankfurt"), "Frankfurt a/M—Oktober 1908." They met again a year later. The other postcard photo, which shows Else's image framed in a heart, bears the penciled inscription: "*Au souvenir des jolis jours à Frankfurt*—Octobre 1909—Else." ("In memory of the lovely days at Frankfurt.") Below, also in pencil, are the words "*piccola bambolina,*" which means "little doll," presumably Caruso's pet name for Else. According to her former neighbor, Miss Trauner was a charming, educated woman from a good family. Born in Frankfurt on 29 April 1887, she was young, attractive, fluent in at least two languages, and a singer who appeared in Hanau, Altenburg, and Erfurt, so Caruso must have appreciated her company.

Father and the young singer met by chance at the railway station in Frankfurt. Else was accompanying her aunt to Berlin, and when she found herself face to face with Caruso, on impulse, she offered him the rose she was carrying. Father in turn invited her to his compartment, and by the time the train reached Berlin, the two had established a good rapport. They often met socially, and Else soon became his interpreter about town. Miss Trauner must have made him forget his woes, because as she recalled in an article: "He was an especially cheerful person and always ready to joke."[9] She attended his performances and heard him in *Aida, Carmen, Rigoletto, Bohème, Tosca,* and *Pagliacci*. In the same article, she wrote: "He was not only a great singer but a great actor as well, who lived his roles with great intensity. I remember that after a performance of *La Bohème,* he was unable to acknowledge the ovations because he was emotionally too spent." He must have been overcome by the powerful memory of Livorno and thoughts of Ada of which Miss Trauner was unaware.

The liaison continued on Caruso's subsequent German tours. In a letter of 17 January 1976, Else wrote to her niece, Mrs. Ilse Trauner Mittermair: "You know about my, one can say, friendship with the great singer." The pair took special delight in escaping Ledner's vigilant eyes, on one occasion sneaking off to the local fairgrounds to an international airship exhibit. They also went on excursions together, once to Königstein in the company of Italian friends and the Dutch baritone Anton van Rooy. Father's affection for Else was obvious, but again he managed to avoid a commitment. Mrs. Mittermair often heard her aunt say in later life: "Enrico adored me so much he wanted to marry me, but the war made it impossible."[10] It appears that in spite of the other attachments Father maintained in New York and developed in Italy in 1911 and 1912, he let Miss Trauner go on hoping for a permanent arrangement until the outbreak of the war.

Her relationship with Caruso left a lifelong impression on Else. Although she continued to sing for her own pleasure, she gave up her career after she married a young officer, Bernhard Kleinsteuber, in June 1917. Her husband must have been remarkably tolerant and understanding, because her music room became a virtual Caruso shrine. Gifts, medallions, a gold and enamel locket made in Paris in the form of his self-caricature, several drawings, and other memorabilia were prominently displayed on the piano. The walls were lined with photographs of Caruso, including an inscribed photo of the two of them taken in front of the Englischer Hof in Frankfurt in October 1909. Else also kept his love letters until the end of her long life; she died in 1985 at the age of 98.

According to Ledner, other women could not console Father for his loss.

> He could not get over Giachetti's betrayal for many, many years, maybe never. [She had never disappeared] from his life, thought, feelings. After that episode in his life, the day before *Pagliacci* or *La Bohème* was to be presented was invariably a frightful one for Caruso, for myself, and for everyone associated with him. During and after the presentation of either of these operas, he would have fits of violent weeping, followed by a fever that lasted for several hours. He saw in Nedda the living, and in Mimì the dead Giachetti. This feverish emotion never left him and often became almost unendurable. Finally he had to stop giving *Pagliacci* for a whole season."[11]

During this period, Caruso began to complain of headaches, which soon became so severe that he could barely cope with the pain. In Ledner's words:

> I never thought it possible for a human being to suffer so intensely and yet perform his duty, the way he did at that time. For weeks he would be subject to periods of intense pain almost every day. The three physicians who attended him in these crises were unable to give him relief. I often saw Caruso, in these moments of torture, press his head against the brass rods of his bed and beat his forehead with his fists. I cannot comprehend even today how he mustered up the resolution and iron energy to fill his three engagements in Berlin—to slip

out of the Hotel Bristol in his dressing-gown, in the very worst
of one of these crises, take his automobile to the opera house,
and then sing *Aida, Carmen* and *L'Elisir d'amore*! One always
spoke of the extremely critical Berlin audience! No audience
in the world would have treated the visibly sick artist with
more loving understanding and indulgence. Caruso appeared
each of the three evenings of his engagement, singing
unusually tastefully and acting with powerful effect; but it was
not Caruso. In each case I begged him the day before he
appeared, and even on the day of the performance, to cancel.
But my persuasion had no effect upon his iron will. "If I do not
appear, I shall make hundreds of enemies. Many of the tickets
had been bought from speculators. Every man who gets back
only half what he paid at the box office will become my enemy.
I absolutely do not want people to talk about my illness." You
could never move him from that position. I never thought it
possible that a human organism could survive such quantities
of aspirin, pyramidon, and similar drugs as he swallowed.
When we left Berlin, I took along approximately 20 bottles of
aspirin. For years these headaches remained unconquered. He
wrote in 1914: "Even though my health is good, my headaches
never leave me"; and in February 1915: "My head and brain
aches have become an affliction that is affected by every
change in the weather. When it rains and the temperature
drops, I get this heavy pressure in the brain and these pains torment me. The only way I can treat them is with German
aspirin. Please send me again several bottles."[12]

During Caruso's European tours, Ledner, going beyond his role as
manager, became his secretary, press agent, travel companion, nurse,
confidant, and, in Berlin, his host. It was not an easy job. Caruso's mail
alone could number fifty to sixty pieces daily in a variety of languages.
Ledner handled the business correspondence and all letters in
German. He and Caruso would hold a "correspondence conference"
each morning, after which Father vocalized, took an hour-long walk,
and read his copy of *Il Corriere della Sera,* which roughly completed his
daily routine. According to Ledner, "he was then faced with empti-
ness and utter boredom," which he often tried to relieve with such
pastimes as pasting snapshots or postcards in a book, playing solitaire,
or going to a movie. Occasionally Ledner would entertain him with
German anecdotes whose point Father did not understand, or Caruso

would tell him Italian anecdotes whose point escaped Ledner.

> Outside his artistic profession it was impossible to keep
> [Caruso] occupied in any fashion. He was always gracious,
> always friendly, but idle. . . . Living with him daily and being
> constantly in his company, especially in view of the fact that
> German was completely excluded as a means of communica-
> tion, made excessively heavy demands upon a person's head,
> nerves, patience and endurance. . . . He was a peculiar com-
> bination of generosity and extreme pettiness. The
> unpredictable Neapolitan traits of his character were often
> irritating and embarrassing. His education was scanty. During
> all the years that I spent with him I never saw a book in his
> hand. I never was able to persuade him to visit a museum or a
> picture gallery, and rarely a theater. The notable sights that
> strangers cross the ocean to see had not the slightest interest
> for him.
>
> Yet he possessed a keen, though narrowly defined mind.
> He had the polish and manners of a great, popular, admired
> artist; but he never posed. He possessed much natural tact,
> and excellent taste regarding costumes and dressing. He com-
> bined a certain worldly wisdom with being domineering and
> stubborn, and was immovable once his mind was made up. He
> could be cordial and kind, and indulgent for the blunders and
> mistakes of others; but he could also be immensely unjust. A
> person who would get into a fight with him always got the
> worst of it. He never would admit that he was wrong, no
> matter what his refusal to do so might cost.[13]

There is little to add to this brief portrait, except to say that the
comments are right on target. Ledner made valuable observations
about still other facets of Caruso's personality. Father always insisted
on staying at the Palace Hotel in Hamburg, where he was given the
same apartment year after year, arranged precisely as he had left it the
year before.

> He was a perfect fool about children, and had taken the
> two little daughters of the hotel proprietor to his heart. He
> exchanged postcards with them during the winter, sang little
> songs to them in his reception room, played short scenes from
> Italian farces for them, performed magic tricks, and when in
> Berlin, he nearly pillaged novelty shops along Friedrichstrasse

for magic tricks. Every year he gave a magic show in the private apartment of Mr. Paegel [the hotelier], always exhibiting a number of new tricks.[14]

I am grateful to Ledner for preserving these vignettes, which show a side of my father I did not know, for he never sang songs or put on magic shows for the entertainment of his own children.

THE German tour took most of October. After that, Caruso sailed to New York for one of his most challenging opening nights, a performance of *Aida* on 16 November 1908. It was a special occasion, for it was the house debut of soprano Emmy Destinn as well as the inaugural performance of the new artistic management team of the Metropolitan: Giulio Gatti-Casazza and Arturo Toscanini. The rehearsals gave Father the opportunity to take sweet revenge on Toscanini.

> Although having in my contract a clause in my favor which stated I was not obliged to give my full voice at any rehearsal, I nevertheless sang for Toscanini's benefit in the first rehearsal of *Aida* with all the voice I had. This so surprised and pleased him as well, that he asked me why I did so.
>
> "Once you catch me," I replied, "because I don't give you voice enough; now I have my pleasant revenge in hearing you say to me 'Don't sing so loud.'"[15]

Father had to give his best on opening night, and he did. The following day, November 17, Richard Aldrich wrote in *The New York Times* that Caruso, in the part of Radames, "sang with probably more power, with more insistent dwelling on the highest tones, with more prodigal expenditure of his resources than even he has achieved before."

The accolades of the press notwithstanding, the events of the summer of 1908 had left their mark. In the previous year, toward the end of 1907, Caruso was so grossly overweight that he had to do something about it. Though he did not actually diet, he ate less. No doubt his emotional upheavals also affected his appetite, so that he began to shed excess pounds. When a slimmer Caruso appeared in Berlin a year later, the difference was so noticeable that the local papers made special mention of his "Adonis-like figure." It was also reported that "the critics find that the tenor's dramatic ability has vastly improved since he was last in Berlin."[16]

Upon his return to New York in November 1908, his friends noticed a change in him, physically as well as emotionally. Although he was always prone to changing moods, in this period he was mostly gloomy and depressed, with little trace of his usual carefree self. Still in search of a hotel where he could feel comfortable, he moved to the Hotel Knickerbocker. Owner James B. Regan and the management bent over backwards to accommodate him in every possible way. They succeeded in making him feel at home, so that he made the hotel his New York base until it was sold in 1920.

Caruso's emotional state did not improve with the passage of time. In addition, something did not feel right in his throat. In December 1908, he canceled two performances, a most unusual occurrence in his career to that point. When he did sing, his voice sounded unchanged; thus his complaints to friends were ascribed to nerves, moods, depression, or hypochondria. Then, to make things worse, in the last week of January 1909, Ada Giachetti unexpectedly appeared in New York.

She was accompanied by a small man with a dark beard whom reporters identified as "Giagnanni." (The correct spelling of his name was probably "Giannini.") Neither his identity nor his relationship to Mother is known. The pair took rooms in the Hotel Knickerbocker near Caruso's suite. Not knowing what to expect and fearful that he might refuse to see them at all, on Tuesday morning, January 26, they lay in wait for him in the corridor.[17] When Caruso emerged from his apartment, they gave him a nasty surprise. After exchanging some harsh words, the three went to the reception room at the end of the hall. Mother had come to ask for money. She used the worst possible approach: She made demands. After a few minutes of heated discussion, Caruso stormed out of the room and reported to the hotel administration that the woman living on the same floor was annoying him. The management took his side and politely but firmly asked Ada to leave. Embarrassed by what had occurred, she showed no resistance and left with her companion. They moved to the Hotel Navarre.

Realizing her grave tactical error, Mother wrote a long letter to Father on January 27. She apologized for what had happened the day before and asked him to meet her and peacefully talk over her request. Father agreed and went to see her with his lawyer. She asked him to return her jewelry, which he flatly refused to do, but he did agree to help her financially, provided that she would accept no singing engagements in North America. He gave her a large sum of money at the time and promised to continue to send monthly checks. This amounted to granting alimony to the woman who had never been his wife and who had deserted him. She asked him to forgive her and apparently he did; a few years later, he claimed in court that he had given Ada his forgiveness on three separate occasions.

Having thus accomplished her objective, Ada was ready to leave New York. Before sailing on the French liner *La Lorraine* on January 28, she wrote to Caruso once more, thanking him for his generosity, and "blessing and kissing her Enrico."

FATHER was greatly upset by Ada's visit. Pierre Key maintains that he wept during their private meeting. There is no reliable record to indicate whether the possibility of a reconciliation was mentioned by either of them.

However, Caruso had no time to feel sorry for himself. The next morning, the day of Ada's departure, he dutifully took the train to Philadelphia, where he sang Manrico in *Il Trovatore*. In his emotional state, the fact that he could sing at all is a testimony to his remarkable will power and professionalism.

This highly charged episode came on the heels of an emotionally draining six months. Caruso felt the strain and canceled several more performances before the season was over, singing only forty-four of his scheduled sixty-five appearances. In a letter of April 2 to his brother Giovanni, he wrote that he had not sung for a month and a half and was terribly nervous about his upcoming performance, adding that perhaps he should take a year's rest in Italy.

Caruso sang Radames on April 7, and he should not have. *Musical America* pronounced a verdict: "It now appears that it was a grave mistake to have had Caruso sing the last time, when he appeared in *Aida*. He had not sung since the 4th of March."[18]

Father knew something was drastically wrong with his voice but insisted that it remain concealed from the public. His physician, Dr. Holbrook Curtis, forbade him to accept any professional engagements for the next six months. "He is nervously exhausted and needs a complete rest,"[19] Dr. Curtis told the newspapers.

The staff of *Musical America* were not to be misled. The magazine summed up his unpleasant experiences, among them "the sensational arrival of the woman with whom he had been living for some years, and the great strain imposed upon him by the work of the season, when he has sung sometimes as often as five or six times a week."[20] The reporter continued:

[It is] very questionable whether the great tenor will ever be himself again, which would be regretted the world over, not only because Caruso is incomparable in many parts and has a magnificent voice, but because he is a liberal, kindly, well-disposed man, generous to a fault—and in that, a great contrast to some foreign singers and musicians, who come here to get every dollar they can and take it away with them to Europe, while they damn this country. Caruso has always had a good word for America and the American people. There never was an artist who appealed to him without meeting with a kindly and generous response.[21]

Because Father could not finish the season, Oscar Hammerstein, the impresario of the rival Manhattan Opera Company, agreed to lend Giovanni Zenatello to the Metropolitan to sing the "Caruso roles" during the upcoming tour. His only stipulation was that the programs had to carry a note that Zenatello's appearances were by courtesy of Mr. Oscar Hammerstein. Gatti-Casazza had to swallow his pride and comply with the condition. But Gatti had Andreas Dippel, his comanager (for the time being), write a letter of acknowledgement on 9 April 1909. "I wish to thank you," Dippel wrote, "in the name of our company for the spirit of cooperation shown, and you may rest assured that we shall heartily reciprocate whenever an occasion shall present itself."[22]

On 14 April 1909, Caruso sailed for England on the *Mauretania*, terribly worried about his health, his voice, his career, and his future. The dogged persistence of the usual troupe of reporters was an added aggravation. They zeroed in on the condition of his voice, speculating in print and putting forth the opinion that he had serious vocal problems, hence the many cancellations. Father vigorously denied that anything was wrong with his throat and made every effort, while he was in London, to appear as healthy and carefree as he possibly could. He finally left London and went directly to Milan to see the renowned throat specialist Professor Della Vedova. The doctor had removed a node from one of his vocal cords a few years before. After an examination, he diagnosed a recurrence of the affliction on the other cord. Operating on the world-famous Caruso in 1909 was a matter of great delicacy, both in terms of the surgery itself and in terms of the adverse publicity Father desperately wanted to avoid.

The informational hide-and-seek continued in Milan. Caruso tried to quell the rumors about his voice and, at one point, even told reporters that his so-called illness was a figment of the imagination of the press. In spite of his efforts to conceal his movements, on 26 May 1909, the Central News Agency reported from Rome that *"Signor* Caruso, the famous tenor, today entered the private hospital of Della Vedova at Milan for the purpose of undergoing a slight surgical operation on the larynx." The following day, however, a Milan correspondent emphatically denied that an operation had taken place. He had seen the singer, who had said: "It is true that here in Milan I have been to see a throat specialist for five minutes, and that probably I shall go again. I want to take care of my voice. That is all, and it is the pure truth."[23]

In the meantime, the state of Caruso's health became an international news item. The home office of the *Daily Telegraph* began to badger the paper's Milan correspondent with telegrams: "How is Caruso after his operation?"

The reporter went directly to the clinic to interview Della Vedova. The professor was willing to speak about anything except the throat of the celebrated singer.

> To every question he replied with a polite smile, and the words:
> "I cannot say; you will understand it is a professional secret."
> "Are you treating Caruso?"
> "I cannot say."
> "Have you operated on him?"
> "You will understand . . ."
> "Was the operation successful?"
> ". . . professional secret."[24]

The diligent reporter pursued his story through other avenues and finally tracked down the correct information.

> Caruso has really undergone an operation. Every arrangement was made for the maintenance of the profound secrecy. The operation was performed in the morning, when the clinic is closed to the public. Professor Della Vedova was assisted by three colleagues, who, in all probability, swore an oath to keep silent. . . . He had, as a matter of fact, already entrusted his harmonious larynx to the professor three years ago, and now he had to undergo at the same hands an operation which was, so to say, the *pendent* of the former. It was a question of two

symmetrical operations. Three years ago it was the right vocal cord; now it was the turn of the left. . . . He has sung for so many as nine evenings in succession, a prodigious performance, which is to be explained only by the robustness of the famous tenor, and the 1,000 pounds which were the adequate compensation for each evening's efforts.[25]

After the cat was out of the bag, the newspapers could ferret out the details. It was reported that Caruso had undergone an operation on his vocal cords, and the London papers carried the news the following days. Professor Della Vedova performed the operation assisted by three other throat specialists. During the operation, the hospital was closed to the public. The 4 June 1904 issue of the *Chronicle* commented: "Whereas there is a chance of Caruso recovering his former freshness, he never again will be able to subject his voice to the overstrain put upon it during the last few years without incurring disastrous consequences."[26]

After the danger of hemorrhaging had passed, Caruso moved back to the Hotel Cavour in Milan, where he spent a period of convalescence under the professor's daily supervision.

There are contradictory reports about when and how many times Della Vedova operated on Father's vocal cords. It seems safe to assume that there was at least one previous operation for the removal of nodes, which probably took place in 1906. We do know that for restoring his vocal health and earning power in 1909, Della Vedova charged him 60,000 lire, the equivalent of $12,000.

When Caruso saw Della Vedova's bill, he hit the roof. He refused to pay, claiming the fee was exorbitant. The matter was taken to court where, under the judges' influence, Della Vedova let common sense prevail. The honorarium was reduced by half, and Father paid it.

A sidelight to the operation was the presence of my brother in Milan. In 1906, Mother and Grandmother had taken Fofò to the Milan Exposition, which celebrated the opening of the Simplon Tunnel, at that time the longest tunnel in the world. The exposition was located on a large meadow which later became the central park of Milan. A row of benches had been set out for visitors, and Fofò made a sport of jumping over them. He misjudged the height of one, and the tip of his shoe got caught on the bench. He fell flat on his face and broke his nose. Dazed by the fall, he had to be carried to the first-aid station, where the doctor worked high up in his nostrils to repair the damage. The septum did not heal properly, and he could not breathe well, taking in air mostly through his mouth. Once in Milan, Father decided that Della Vedova should operate on Fofò's nose and on his own vocal cords at the same time, so that father and son could convalesce together. Apart from the unpleasantness of the surgery, Fofò was happy to spend so much time with Father. In his memoirs, he mentioned an incident from the period:

> [I] became an accomplice of Papa in a little *peccadillo* concerning the strict orders of Professor Della Vedova. The doctor came on a daily visit to see us, usually in the late afternoon. However, one morning around eleven, as Father was blissfully smoking a cigarette, he was alerted that, completely off his accustomed schedule, the professor was on his way for the visit. I happened to be in the room where Papa was periodically checking my homework, and I suddenly saw him all confused.
>
> "Fofò," he said excitedly, "the professor forbade me to smoke. Don't you let on that I have been smoking!"
>
> He removed the pack of cigarettes from his vest pocket, ran to the wardrobe, and hid it on top of the cornice. He then dashed to the bathroom like a guilty little boy, and I heard him rinse his mouth with a mouthwash made by Dr. Weymann which Papa used for oral hygiene. In the meantime, the professor entered the room. Finding me there alone, he proceeded to examine me first. This look at my nasal passages gave Father enough time to pull himself together and return to the room with a big smile and a "Greetings, Professor" delivered at a few meters' distance, since he was unsure whether he had eliminated all the telltale smell of tobacco. I must admit that this complicity gave me a slight edge in my relationship with my father.

ANOTHER, much graver incident occurred during Father's stay in Milans in June 1909. Mother was in town, and she wanted to see him. She was staying at the Hotel Excelsior, an artists' *pensione* run by Carlotta Carignani. It is likely that in an attempt to rebuild her voice, Ada was taking lessons from Carignani's husband, Rina's former teacher.

She announced her visit, and Father braced himself to see her for the first time since the stormy encounter in New York a few months earlier. The agreement they had reached had brought about some sort of truce, and they could face each other now without bitterness. However, this encounter, as engineered by Mother, changed all that, and the misadventure left a lifelong impression on Fofò. He writes:

> One of the most dramatic moments of my life occurred in this same period of Papa's operation. It cemented, once and for all, the emotional tie between us.
>
> Taking advantage of Papa's presence in Milan, Mamma contacted Father at the hotel. Naturally, he was all excited. When he told me that I might be able to see Mamma again, his eyes shone with joy and he had a broad smile on his face the like of which I had not seen in a long time. The morning Mamma arrived I was told to stay in my room, and thus I could not witness the meeting of those two tormented souls. After a while Father called me in. My heart was beating with an undefinable emotion which was anything but the joy of embracing again one's own mother. She covered me with kisses and clasped me to her bosom. I am ashamed to say that I felt tense and did not reciprocate those kisses. She noticed it and increased the effusive outpouring of her maternal affection.
>
> "You will go out with Mamma and you will have lunch with her," Father said. "I will come and get you later; now go, get dressed."
>
> I went to my room. As in a movie, visions of Nice passed in front of my eyes, then the *collegio* where I had been confined, and my father's utter despair at the separation. I was not very enthusiastic about leaving him, even temporarily. I had developed a deep affection for Papa, and I would have unhesitatingly given my life to save his. Perhaps he never imagined the extent of my love for him, and to my sorrow he measured it only by my studies and my report cards. But these were considerations that I began to understand only much later when we became friends, and after death separated us.
>
> When I was ready, Mamma took my hand, visibly happy, maybe too happy, so much so that my subconscious told me to be on the alert. I was eleven and a half, not tall but robust because of the sports and quasi-military life at school. We left the hotel and took one of the beautiful, horse-drawn carriages that were quite common in Milan in those days.

"First we'll go for a nice ride, and I will take you to the park where you broke your nose three and a half years ago," Mother said.

The carriage went on a long excursion of the Milanese boulevards and passed under the trees and through the meadows of the park. I watched Mamma from the corner of my eye. She was so much like Auntie Rina, but there was something hard about her. Perhaps she was a little more beautiful, if that were possible, because Auntie Rina *was* beautiful. But while every time I was with my aunt I felt joy in my heart, with Mother I became tense. As a matter of fact, I sat on the edge of the carriage cushion as stiff as if I had swallowed a broomstick. Mamma did not stop talking, but my mind was back at the Hotel Cavour. It was almost noon by the time we returned to the center of town. We left the carriage and went on foot along the Corso Vittorio. As we passed a toy shop, Mamma stopped and asked:

"Do you see anything you like? Would you like a train? A ship? A camera?"

I thanked her and said that I did not want anything, not to be contrary or discourteous, but because I was really not used to toys after the years in the *collegio*. At school our amusements were much tougher: soccer, horseback riding, fencing, boxing. Mamma had apparently forgotten that when she put me in a boarding school for the first time, I was barely six years old. We continued on the street, and I remember as if it were today that we entered a delicatessen and bought various cold cuts I liked so much. This I easily accepted, because at school we weren't lucky enough to have them. She forced on me a box of chocolates I considered unnecessary because I did not care for them.

Finally we arrived at a house and went upstairs to a floor which was occupied entirely by singers. We went straight to the dining room. Several tables were already occupied; a little table was reserved for Mamma. There were many people, men, women, typical theater folks. Among the women there was a great fluttering of houserobes and much decolletage, locks of hair in ringlets more or less blonde, more or less real. The men also wore long hair, fancy waistcoats, smooth faces. They all made a fuss over me, especially a lovely lady dressed in a very brief negligée. She made a delightful impression on me.

Mother noticed it and gave me a lecture, telling me that I should stay away from the lady because she was not a proper person and should not be frequented. I kept quiet and was not expansive with any of them. We finished the long meal and passed through a sort of smoking lounge where I was the object of curiosity to the female artists living there. There was one who seemed to be Mother's friend, very young, probably not more than twenty. She, too, was dressed rather freely, so much so that looking at her, with the still innocent eyes of a youth barely into puberty, I found her deliciously salacious.

I thus spent a pleasant afternoon. Then all of a sudden Mamma became nervous.

"Fofò, I am expecting some businessmen. They are to be here shortly and I must talk to them. It is better if you go to my room and wait for me there. Come."

She took me by the hand and led me to her bedroom. She kissed me, told me to wait, and left. But when she closed the door, I heard her turning the key. It made me curious, if not exactly suspicious. I tried the door; I had heard right, it was locked.

I looked around the room. It had drapes, a large bed without a footboard, a canopy of sheers coming down from ceiling height in rich folds enveloping half the bed. Nice armchairs in flowered silk upholstery gave a sense of comfort. On the dresser was a beautiful, engraved silver toilette service I instantly recognized, having seen it at Le Panche. On a charming little desk with many fetching articles was a photo of Papa, but on the dresser was another that filled me with revulsion. It was a photo of Romati, the man I hated as the cause of all the unhappiness of our family. Even today this photographic polyandry remains an enigma to me; it was a reflection of Mamma's unfathomable character.

Without knowing the cause, I suddenly grew alarmed. The building had quieted down after the noise of the meal and the chitchat of the siesta. I could clearly hear the sound of a bell. After the passage of time, I rightly expected the arrival of my father. I put my ear to the door and heard Father's voice, asking:

"Where is Fofò?"

"Oh, he left about half an hour ago," Mamma replied. "He said he knew the way quite well, and he preferred to go by himself. Why? Haven't you seen him?"

"I came by cab from the hotel only five minutes ago," said Papa. "He hadn't arrived yet. Very well, I will wait for him at the hotel."

With my heart in my throat, I began to comprehend what was going on. I panicked and began to scream:

"Papa! Papa! Here I am!" banging my fists on the door. I stopped to listen and heard the front door to the stairwell slam closed. I understood, in despair, that Papa believed what Mamma had told him and had left, leaving me in her hands. At lightning speed I backed up a few paces and ran against the door with my shoulder. It did not open, but a second assault of my shoulder used to the rough game of football forced it open, just as Mamma was coming down the corridor. She tried to bar my way, but like a good player, I dodged her. I ran down the corridor to the door with Mother on my heels, yelling:

"Fofò, stop! Fofò, come back here!"

I paid no attention. With trembling hands and my entire body taut as a blade, I grabbed hold of the doorknob, in terror of being caught by Mamma. After seconds that seemed like centuries, I managed to tear the door open just as Mamma's nails ripped my clothes as she tried to stop me.

The stairway had four ramps with a landing at each level surrounding a central well. One could see the entire staircase through the wrought-iron balustrade. Papa stood on the second landing listening, suspicious of all the commotion Mother was making with her screaming. All in one breath I dashed down the twenty steps to the next landing. I stopped halfway between my parents. Father watched me without uttering a word. Mamma had stopped on the top landing, and looking at me with flames shooting out of her eyes, she kept on screaming:

"Fofò, come back up here, or you will never see your Mother again!"

I had a moment of indecision because Mamma's appeal really shook me. In my heart raged a storm beyond my comprehension. Papa continued to watch me without saying anything. After a few seconds, I slowly began to walk down the stairs, step by step, turning to look at Mamma once or twice. When I reached the landing where Papa stood, he put a hand on my shoulder, and together, in silence and without turning, we descended the steps. Mother yelled again something that sounded like a threat, then entered the apartment slamming the door behind her.

She was right. I never saw her again.

CHAPTER NINE

England

WHILE Fofò lived through this turbulent time in Milan, I was completing my first year in England with Miss Saer. Accustomed to being surrounded by a full household of relatives and servants, I found it a drastic change to have only Lei as my companion. Although I was her charge even at Le Panche, I must have been used to seeing my mother every day—she must have played some role in my daily life. Even so, from the time Lei was hired, I have no memory of any interchange with Mother, of playing with her or being held by her. I do remember seeing women around when we moved back to Le Panche in 1907 after the London season ended, but I don't know who they were. One of them had to be Mother, and at that early age, I must have had her image imprinted on my mind. I don't know what explanation I was given for Mother's absence after she left in 1908, but I kept waiting for her return or expecting to find her. "Where is Mother? When is she coming back to see me?" I would ask. For years after she left, I had a strong desire to find her. Time and again, in a hotel lobby or a railway station, I would walk up to an attractive lady who was wearing a dress or a hat that reminded me of her, and I would ask: "Are you my mother?" The lady would gaze at me in bewilderment, and

Miss Saer would apologize and lead me away.

This went on for a long, long time, until I must have realized that Mother was gone, and I was not going to find her.

Father continued to return to Italy every summer. Italy was home, and after he finished his work in America and England, he always returned there to relax and be reunited with his family, the Carusos. He would notify Miss Saer of his plans for the summer, and she would make the necessary arrangements to take me to him wherever he wished.

The summer of 1909 was the first Father spent in Italy without Mother, but he was not alone. After his return to New York, the affair with "Mil" Meffert had blossomed. It lasted fully five years, and if her later claim can be accepted, she either saw him or heard from him daily during the months he spent in America. He lavished her with gifts (over the years, he gave her $10,000 worth of jewelry) and gave her an annual allowance of $7,000. Meffert later said that she "was very happy and unhappy. For there was the woman who was known as his wife," and unless she chose to sever the relationship, he could not, "for she was the mother of his children."[1] But when the news came that " 'La Señora' had eloped with a chauffeur I wept tears of joy. I sank upon my knees and thanked God for freeing my beloved from the bonds honor had forged upon him. Happy as a girl in her betrothal days, I made plans for my bridal. I fully expected that when he returned that summer from Europe we would be married."

The "girl in her betrothal days" was to be sorely disappointed. True to form, Father "evaded. He made excuses," complained Meffert. "Torn with terror at his strange attitude, I began to plead. I reminded him of his promises. I questioned him. I wept. He shrugged his shoulders. He refused to talk. He gave no sufficient reason. I nearly went mad."

Meffert further stated that toward the close of the 1909 opera season, Caruso said that following a tour of the United States, he would come back to New York and marry her. She made this claim in 1914, but the facts show that her memory was playing tricks on her. There was no tour, because that was the year Father developed vocal problems and canceled his scheduled Metropolitan performances long before the season ended. He may have decided to sail to Europe on the spur of the moment, but Meffert's complaint that he left New York without notifying her is hard to accept. As a matter of fact, once his operation and convalescence were behind him, he sent for her and proceeded to entertain her lavishly at various resorts and hotels. He introduced her to friends as his intended wife. Later in the summer, Mrs. Meffert lived with us at Bellosguardo, where she tried to win us over. Fofò and I were told to call her *"Mammina."*

I have no recollections from this summer, and my only source of information is a short paragraph in Fofò's memoirs.

> The first year after Mamma's departure, Papa arrived in Florence accompanied by a beautiful, blonde American lady, whose name I don't remember. She was very nice to me, but I noticed that Miss Saer, who came over from England with my brother, remained quite reserved, keeping even Mimmi at a distance from that beautiful woman. We made wonderful excursions to all points of the Gulf of Naples and other parts of Italy. We even touched Signa, but stayed there only briefly. The more nervous Papa became, the more kind and affable the lady would be. Finally, one day she left for America alone. Father was to leave in August on a tour through the major cities of Europe.

Mildred Meffert was the first of several *mammina*s Father brought home in the coming summers. They were all very nice to us, each in turn hoping that if we, the children, grew attached to her, she might become a permanent member of the family. But Father was in no mood to get too firmly attached to anyone, and every summer we had to get used to a new *mammina*.

At the end of July 1909, Miss Saer and I returned to England, and Father went to Ostende. He sang some concerts at the Kursaal beginning August 1. He was testing his voice for the first time since the operation, in a small place and with just three numbers on the program. The engagement went well, and he then gave several full-length concerts in the British Isles, ending the tour in London. It was much wiser to test the endurance of his voice in the provinces, away from the major musical centers, and a good deal safer to face the audiences and critics of Blackpool or Newcastle, or even Edinburgh and Dublin, than those of London. The concerts were successful, and Father was satisfied with his voice, as was the public. He wrote to Sisca from Blackpool on 31 August 1909:

> I have done three concerts and with great success. All they talk about in England is Caruso and his voice. The malicious [ones] would have been glad if I really had lost my voice, but it's all the same to me, because even if I had lost it, I don't

depend on anyone. One of these days I will have to stop, but when I do, they can say what they want because I will laugh at it as I am laughing now.

In order not to overtax his voice, he had two assisting artists with him: a Devonshire soprano, Elisabeth Pender-Cudlip, and a Metropolitan Opera colleague who doubled as a quasi-secretary, Armand Lecomte. By the end of the tour, Caruso felt secure enough to face the London public, and he gave his penultimate recital in the Albert Hall on September 18. He sang "Celeste Aida," "O Paradiso," and the duet "Solenne in quest'ora" with Armand Lecomte, and he gave five encores, including "Vesti la giubba."

The critics were pleased. One paper reported: "We may add that the insinuating, appealing, velvet-like voice is in better condition than ever, its absolute evenness—no less than its roundness and resonance—compelling the admiration of the ordinary musical person as well as of the *cognoscenti*."[2] Lecomte's solo number was the *Pagliacci* "Prologue," and Miss Pender-Cudlip sang Micaela's aria from *Carmen*. Tullio Voghera accompanied the vocal solos on the piano. The concert was rounded out by Thomas Beecham conducting the Beecham Orchestra. It was a great success, and according to Thomas Quinlan, organizer of the concert, the huge Albert Hall was sold out, and 4,000 people had to be turned away.

My memories begin to grow more numerous after the Italian holidays of this summer. On September 7, my fifth birthday, Father had to be in Edinburgh, but he sent me a huge teddy bear and several large boxes of chocolates. He stayed with us at the apartment at Maida Vale before and after his tours and whenever his next concert was only a train ride away. At home he was always relaxed, and we often played together; we would romp on the carpet in the parlor, or I would sit on his back and play "horsie." In the mornings, I used to go to his bedroom, climb into his bed, and sit on his stomach: Lying flat on his back, he would toss me high in the air with his powerful diaphragm. We laughed and giggled together; those were happy mornings for us both, and I enjoyed being with my father. Because I was still a small child, he was entirely uninhibited in showing his affection. I understood only decades later that, true to his word, he tried his best to be both father and mother to me.

David and Sybil Seligman met Father shortly after his Covent Garden debut in 1902. They became close friends, and he was a regular visitor at their home. Their house on Upper Grosvenor Street was large, dark, and very Victorian, with heavy drapes, large furniture, and a Tiffany lamp hanging over the dining-room table. Their son, Vincent, mentioned Father's visits in his book *Puccini Among Friends,*[3] recalling how his mother used to coax Caruso into giving impromptu after-dinner concerts. Father took me along once in a while. On one occasion, we were riding in a cab to a birthday party at the Seligmans'. Father put his arm around me, and I dozed off during the long ride. In my sleep, I drooled on his beautiful embroidered vest, leaving a large damp spot on the yellow floral design, but he didn't budge until I awakened. Only then did he wipe himself with his handkerchief. Spoiled little brat that I was, I repaid him by being terribly peeved because the birthday child received a beautiful watch from him and I did not. Father took the trouble to reason with me that I was not old enough to have a watch, but at the ripe old age of five, I was not about to let reason control my emotions. I also remember that there were many people in the room, and they listened to a cylinder recording— not a platter—of my father's voice and discussed it afterwards.

This must have been one of the Anglo-Italian Commerce Company cylinders, Father's only commercial cylinder releases predating his exclusive contract with Victor. Father was a gentleman and a wise businessman and would not have compromised his commitment or his contract. It has been claimed that he made some cylinder recordings for Gianni Bettini, the recording entrepreneur active in turn-of-the-century New York.[4] But by the time Caruso was established in New York, Bettini had moved to Paris; if he ever recorded Father's voice, it had to be there. In light of his exclusive contract, however, any recordings made by Bettini must not have been musical recordings suitable for release. Responding to an inquiry by William R. Moran, Victor Bettini, Gianni Bettini's son, wrote that Caruso, who was a lifelong friend of his father's, "often came into his office and sang through his machine and yet there is no evidence of such recordings! I used to have them in the unfortunately destroyed material stored in France."[5] It must be borne in mind that when Victor Bettini wrote this, he was past eighty, and the cache of his father's cylinders had been destroyed two and a half decades earlier.

In those early years in London, Father was gentle and kind even when he had to play the role of disciplinarian. Once I put a ball through one of the six glass panels of the studio door in the apartment at Clarendon Court. To hide the damage I had done, I nailed the curtain to the door, fully expecting it to pass unnoticed. When Father came home, he called me to his room.

"What did you do?" he asked.

"Nothing, Papa."

"Did you put those nails in the door?"

"No."

"Mimmi, you had better tell the truth, or you will go to bed without supper," he said sternly but without raising his voice. I thought it over and confessed.

"All right, I see it was an accident. You told the truth, so you are forgiven. But remember: You must always tell the truth, no matter what the consequences may be."

And that was the end of it.

Immediately after his British tour, Father went to Germany for a month then on to the United States. He could not stop in London, but he wanted to see me again. He sailed on the *Kronprinzessin Cecilie* from Bremen, and he cabled Miss Saer to meet his ship in Southampton. We arrived the day before the ship was to dock. Miss Saer hired a hansom cab, and we went from guest house to guest house until we found one that was both cheap enough and respectable enough to meet Miss Saer's standards.

When the ship arrived, we went on board. In those days, the ships carried live poultry to feed the passengers, and Father took a picture of me standing on the deck in front of a long row of cages filled with chickens.

Father embraced and kissed me, and we spent several hours together. He chatted at length with Miss Saer, but as I was not quite six, he could not carry on anything resembling a conversation with me. I remember that he asked how I was spending my days, what games I played, whether I had received the gifts he sent. I also remember that I was so frightened by a sudden blare of the foghorns that we had to go ashore, to Father's annoyance. I am left with the impression that he was glad to see me and made a sincere effort to keep me entertained. To me he was still little more than a friendly stranger, and the burden of refashioning his image in my mind into that of a father was entirely his. He tried his best; he was charming and kind. Intuitively, he did the right thing in trying to see me at every opportunity, no matter how briefly. With each visit, he reinforced his role in my life, and by the end of the following summer, I had accepted him as my Papa.

MY life in England was entirely routine, with very few highlights. Miss Saer would take me every day on interminable walks to the park in

Cricklewood, or to Regents Park to feed the swans, or to Hempstead Heath where I sailed my boats. The pride of my fleet was a battleship Father had sent for Christmas, whose cannons actually fired pistol caps. He sent me toys regularly, but only this and the huge birthday teddy bear stand out in my memory. I was showered with toys on holidays and special occasions, and my Christmases were simply spectacular. Every year I promised myself to stay awake all night to see Santa, but I would fall fast asleep. When I awakened, the bedroom floor would be covered with packages. I doubt that I ever knew exactly which toy came from which of Papa's friends or my faraway relatives.

On Sundays we would go to an Episcopal low church. The first time we went, Lei failed to tell me what to expect or how to behave. When they passed the plate with many coins on it, I took one and said "thank you." Of course, she corrected my *faux pas* on the spot and gave me a coin to put on the tray.

I also recall a few unusual events, such as Kaiser Wilhelm riding in a carriage with Edward VII on a state visit, the funeral of King Edward VII, the coronation of George V, and the Lord Mayor's inauguration. When I grew older, Lei and I went to the British Museum, to Kew Gardens for lessons in botany, and to Madame Tussaud's.

Miss Saer's guiding principle was to keep me walking so that I would see, learn, absorb, and exercise at the same time, and sleep well at night. Wherever we went, we went on foot. She would not dream of wasting money on a cab, so when we absolutely required transportation, we took the trolley or the bus. When we came to town from Cricklewood to visit Papa at his hotel, he always gave Miss Saer a gold sovereign (worth about five dollars) to pay for the cab back. Ever-frugal Lei would put the coin in her purse and thank Father; but as soon as we were out of the hotel, instead of hailing a cab, she would flag down the Willesden–Cricklewood bus at the Marble Arch. Then the next day, she would march me down to the post office and have me deposit the sovereign in a postal savings account she had opened for me.

Papa always hired a hansom cab or a landaulette, driven by a coachman in a top hat. One night Antonio Scotti came to pick him up; they were going to a dinner or some social function. Of course, they were dressed in evening clothes, complete with cloak and top hat. I took one look at them and said: "Oh, Papa, you look so handsome, just like the coachman!" Scotti burst out laughing, and Father grunted something. I didn't understand what was so funny, for I meant exactly what I said. Another time, I complained that Father was always leaving me. He explained that he had to work to earn money, otherwise I would have nothing to eat. That was a reasonable explanation, until the next time. When I asked again where he was going, he said: "I am going to sing for your dinner."

My bedtime was seven o'clock. Lei would kiss me on the cheek and hold my hand until I fell asleep. What she did afterwards I don't know; probably she took care of herself, did some household chores, sewing, knitting. Sometimes she had visitors, always women. Occasionally her sister Margaret would stay with us for a few days and keep me entertained with fantastic tales and adventure stories. After I learned to read, I would often lie on the bear rug in front of the fireplace and read by the light of the fire.

In spite of my unusual upbringing, I was a well-adjusted and happy child. I wanted for nothing, and I didn't know how life could be different. I wasn't shy, had no inhibitions, and had no problem meeting other children when I went each day to play in the park.

Vincent Seligman wrote that "as far as he was able to do so, Caruso remained faithful to his promise to devote himself to his boys. . . . Caruso came over to see [Mimmi] whenever he could, and his letters to my mother are full of expressions of gratitude for the kindly interest which she took in his poor motherless boy. He also announced his intention at one time of sending his elder boy, Rodolfo, 'to school with Vincenzino'; but eventually he decided to leave him in Italy under the care of his Aunt Rina."[6] Besides Mme. Seligman, other friends of Father's visited me from time to time, among them Mr. and Mrs. D. Nuñes da Costa and Otto and Lena Gutekunst. Father was a frequent visitor at their homes. My favorite was Mrs. Bertha Nuñes da Costa, a beautiful woman in her late twenties, who treated me as if I were her own child. I grew very attached to her. She never forgot a holiday or a birthday, and she came by weekly or more often, always laden with presents. The Da Costas loved children but had none of their own, and they used to give extravagant Christmas parties for all their nieces and nephews and other young friends. Mr. Da Costa, a wealthy lawyer or stockbroker, would dress up as Santa Claus, and we would all gather around a gigantic Christmas tree, its base buried in presents.

IN the spring of 1910, Gatti-Casazza and Toscanini took the Metropolitan ensemble to the Paris Opéra on its first international tour. By then, Caruso was so closely identified with the Met that such a visit was unimaginable without him. Lei and I joined him in Paris. We stayed in one room of his large hotel suite but spent little time with him. I don't remember whether I was taken to any of his performances.

The change of locale had no effect on our daily routine. We went on the usual walks and spent the best part of each day in a park. In England, I had contacts with other children at the playground. It was the natural thing for children of my age to walk up to a group and join in, and on our outings to the Bois de Boulogne, I expected to do the same. To my consternation, I was rebuffed. I was dressed in the English style, and as soon as the local children realized that I not only looked different but couldn't speak their language, they would have nothing to do with me. Lei tried to console me, but I felt rejected. I learned only later that this was par for Paris; these little brats grew up into the rude and inhospitable Parisians who consider subhuman everyone who cannot speak flawless French.

While in Paris, I met with two celebrated ladies. When Miss Saer, who was usually reticent and shy, found out that "Madame" was in residence, she was determined to meet her. "Madame" was of course Madame Sarah Bernhardt. We went to her apartment, and Lei sent her the message that Enrico Caruso, Jr., son of the world-renowned tenor, would like to pay his respects. The maid let us in, and we were led to Madame's bedroom. She was sprawled across a large four-poster bed. By that time she was old and ill, with a wooden leg, and in great physical discomfort. Lei was duly awed in the presence of the legendary tragedienne, but to me she was just a fragile old figure. She was very gracious, but to my present regret, I don't remember what she said to me nor what I mumbled in response.

The other great lady I met in Paris was Geraldine Farrar. She was a close friend of Father's. (According to rumors, she was an intimate friend, though I can neither confirm nor deny this.) She was always exceptionally kind to me, even decades after Father's death. As it happened, while Father sang at the Opéra, Farrar and Scotti were performing *Tosca* at the Opéra-Comique. She was staying at the Elysée Palace Hotel, and it was only natural that Papa should visit her. One day he said to Miss Saer:

"Please dress Mimmi up nicely. Put on his best clothes—we are going to see a lovely lady."

The large suite had a *jardin d'hiver,* and a second door opened into the apartment proper. Geraldine was indeed a lovely lady, and I was quite taken with her. It was not so much her physical beauty but her effervescent, magnetic personality that was so captivating. She greeted Papa then turned to me.

"So you are Mimmi! I am so happy to meet you!"

Then, looking me over, she added:

"What a big boy you are, and how nice you look. Now why don't you sit here and play with these nice dolls while your daddy and I have tea."

This much said, I was left alone to play with a staggering collection of beautiful dolls. I sat on a rattan chaise longue perfectly bored for about two hours, wondering why it took Papa so long to drink his tea. I was too young to give much thought to this social call, and it wasn't until many years later that I put two and two together. Did Father take me along in order not to compromise Geraldine? Did he leave Lei home because he did not want to embarrass her? There may have been a perfectly innocent purpose to our visit too. Papa wanted Geraldine to meet me and see what a nice boy I was. He felt that I needed a mother, and I learned much later that there was a possibility of Gerry's mother adopting me. Nothing came of that, but I often wondered what my life would have been like if in my sixth year, I had become "*Mammina*" Farrar's little boy.

AFTER the Parisian engagement was over, we traveled with Papa to Italy. As usual, Father had his retinue with him. They traveled second-class, while he, Miss Saer, and I traveled together in two first-class compartments. He greatly appreciated Lei's dependability and the fact that she took such good care of me, and he always treated her as an equal and with the respect due to a lady. I also believe that he was a little bit in awe of her, perhaps on account of her prim and proper British deportment.

I enjoyed the train trip and our meals in the fancy dining car. At our first dinner, I found a chocolate bar on the table. It was an advertising gimmick for Suchard chocolates, and I was terribly disappointed to find a piece of wood inside.

"Take it with you and put it under your pillow," suggested Papa, "and see what happens."

I did as told, and wonder of wonders! By next morning, it had turned into a piece of real chocolate. Since I shared a compartment with Lei, such miracles could easily happen.

Father was in a splendid mood during the whole trip and entertained us both as best he could. He passed the time playing with me, conversing with Miss Saer, drawing quick sketches of the landscape, and dozing off from time to time. He also read magazines, mountains of magazines. I don't recall ever seeing him with a book in hand, but he was a voracious reader of Italian magazines and newspapers.

In the dining car, they served us a large bowl of fresh cherries. Papa found a cluster of three. He put the bunch in his mouth, ate the cherries, then with his tongue tied the three stems into a knot. Miss Saer was greatly amused, and I was more fascinated than if he had sung a dozen high C's. Papa untied and rinsed the stems, and I spent the rest of the day trying to tie them in my mouth. When I finally succeeded, I had a greater sense of accomplishment than if *I* had sung a high C! When I tired of the cherry stems, I asked Papa to sing me "La Marcia Reale." He sang some of it to please me, but I was not impressed at all.

As we approached Italy, the weather became warm. In those days before air-conditioning, all one could do against the heat was open the windows, but sometimes even that was not enough. So Father contrived to hook his cane to the eyelet in the curtain and prop it outside the window. The curtain acted like a sail and blew fresh air into the compartment. It did help with the heat, but after a few hours of such ingenious ventilation, we were covered with dust and soot and had to scrub ourselves clean in our tiny washbasins. Father sprinkled cologne on his big handkerchiefs and handed one to each of us, so that we were able to freshen up a bit.

This was the first time I slept in a *wagon-lit*. I still recall lying on my tummy in the morning, looking out the window at the magical panorama that opened up before me. The train was high in the Alps; on one side were snow-capped mountains, and far down on the other was a beautiful lake with a small island in the middle. The finishing touch to this picture was a little steamer cleaving a blue-and-white wedge across the mirror-like surface of the lake.

A cholera epidemic broke out in Italy in the summer of 1910. The east coast of the peninsula was spared, so we went to Rimini for the summer to avoid exposure to the disease. Father rented a villa near the shore. The beach had golden sand and was lined with several rows of little cabanas—wooden cabins with multicolored canvas tops and striped awnings. For the *Festa dello Statuto* (Constitution Day), Papa gave a big dinner party. The highlight of the evening was to be a fireworks display he had ordered, with multicolored rockets, pinwheels, and Roman candles. The show was spectacular, but no one took into account the evening breeze. One or more rockets were blown back toward the shore and fell, still burning, on a cabana. In a flash, the wooden structure caught fire, and the wind carried the flames from cabana to cabana. Within minutes the entire beach was ablaze with the most spectacular fireworks, completely out of control. The spectators instantly formed a fire brigade back to the villa, but in spite of their vigorous efforts, the cabanas burned to the ground. Father had to pay a tidy sum for the destruction; at least a hundred cabanas went up in flames.

I was not quite six years old when we were at Rimini, and I was inexperienced at the fine art of building sand castles. All I could do was fill my little bucket with sand and turn it over, as if making a mudpie. Papa decided that I needed some instruction. He showed me how to build a fort with walls, battlements, watch towers, a moat, and a bridge.

"And now," he said, "for a background, we are going to build Mount Vesuvio."

He stuck a broomstick in the sand and piled sand around it. When the "mountain" was about five feet high, he burrowed with his hand into the base until he reached the broomstick. He removed it and shaped a crater at the top. He then filled the hole with wet straw and lit it. The burrow at the base worked like a flue, and the slow-burning straw emitted clouds of smoke.

"*Ecco il Vesuvio!*" declared Papa triumphantly.

I was thrilled. At that time I knew Vesuvio only from pictures. But ever after, seeing the real mountain in Naples, I remembered that happy day in Rimini when Papa built a volcano just for me. He had a grand time doing it too. He also made sand sculptures, dragons, Neptune with sea horses, and dolphins. The bathers and strollers stopped by to admire his artwork; but to him it was just play, like drawing caricatures. We took it for granted that Papa could do such things, never marveling at his bursts of creativity.

This summer at Rimini is memorable for another reason: I learned to swim under rather traumatic circumstances.

I was deathly afraid of the sea. Papa, having grown up literally *in* the Bay of Naples, could not understand how a son of his could be so petrified of the water. He would take me in his arms and wade in. The moment the water hit my fanny, I would start to scream. He would ignore my hysterics, hold me tight, and dip me up to my neck until I got used to it. I gradually relaxed and splashed around, but I clung to him for dear life. He encouraged me to learn to swim, but to no avail.

After many futile efforts, he had had enough.

The Adriatic at Rimini is very shallow, and one must wade far out into the sea to swim. Once Papa invited a few of his friends boating, and we rowed out some distance.

"Mimmi, will you swim today?" he asked.

"No, Papa, I am afraid."

He nodded and said nothing. He had a mischievous twinkle in his eye which I did not know how to interpret. A few minutes later, catching me in an unguarded moment, he picked me up and threw me in the water. He then jumped in to help me, though as it turned out, this was unnecessary. It was a sink or swim situation, and after the first moment of terror, I started to paddle. Screaming, spitting, I managed to stay afloat. When I realized I was not going to sink, my fear of the water disappeared. I was finally willing to learn to swim, and once I did, I became a veritable waterbaby like Papa, spending entire days in the sea.

I became aware of Father's special place in the world during the weeks at Rimini, when I first noticed the immense respect he commanded from everyone who came in contact with him. When we returned to Clarendon Court, the impressions of the summer must have been on my mind. We had one of those old-fashioned bathrooms with a large washbasin on a lily stand and a faucet on each side. It was too high for me, and I had to use a little step stool to brush my teeth. I distinctly remember that on my sixth birthday, as I finished brushing my teeth, I turned to Miss Saer and asked:

"Why am I Caruso's son?"

This incident was not part of the family lore that was repeated to me after I grew up. It did not have to be, for it remained clearly etched in my memory. I knew that my father was a famous and important man; I saw the adulation of the public in the theater and the respect he encountered wherever he went. So how did it happen that I became his son? The remarkable thing is that this thought occurred to me when I was only six. It has haunted me ever since. To this day it puzzles me that I am the son of this great and wonderful artist.

WE returned to England, and Father went on a tour of Belgium and Germany. It was a tour riddled with accidents. During *Carmen* in Frankfurt, on October 4, he hurt his knee badly as he dropped to the ground beside the body of the dead Carmen. Then, on October 11 in Munich, after a curtain call in *La Bohème,* he struck his head against a piece of iron-framed scenery with such force that he sank unconscious to the floor. When he came to after a considerable time, he insisted on finishing the performance. No announcement was made, and the audience was unaware of the mishap. Fortunately, the German tour brought special honors as well. On 22 October 1910, Caruso sang at the Potsdam Palace, and Kaiser Wilhelm II conferred upon him the title of *Kammersänger*.

While he spent the month of October singing in Europe, his lawyers were busy defending him in court. In June 1909, soon after her attempt to kidnap Fofò had failed, Mother brought a lawsuit against him in Milan.

Among numerous other witnesses, Father called on his old friend and colleague from the Metropolitan, the basso Andrès Perello de Segurola. I have been unable to confirm whether two separate civil actions were involved or only one. Relying on family lore, the corroborating evidence of De Segurola's unpublished memoirs, and scanty newspaper coverage, I can only confirm the substance of her suit. Mother tried to gain custody of Fofò and me. She accused Caruso of having violated the civil code, because in applying for Fofò's birth certificate, he had claimed that the child was born from his union with an unmarried woman (*nubile*). This was not the case; thus he had lied to the authorities.

Ada's accusation backfired. The judge supposedly said: "Madame, you are not the mother of these children. *Your name* does not even appear on their birth certificates."

De Segurola recalls that Vittorio Molco, their mutual friend and Caruso's attorney, summoned him to Milan to appear in court as a witness for the defense. In their first conference, Father said: "Andrea dear, I want you to keep in mind something I have already recommended to my friend, Molco. I want my sons by all means, but I beg you to avoid as much as possible humiliating Ada in your depositions. I shall be grateful to you both if you do it. I love her in spite of all. I can't help it."[7]

Mother also alleged that while she was a resident of the Milanese *pensione,* the Hotel Excelsior, its proprietor, Carlotta Carignani, in complicity with Father and acting upon his instructions, withheld a letter addressed to her which contained a contract from Oscar Hammerstein offering her $10,000 to sing at the Manhattan Opera House in New York. Finally, she claimed that Father had appropriated her jewelry and refused to return it.

The defense asked that the case be dismissed for lack of evidence on the part of Ada Giachetti, that Caruso be absolved for the false statement he had made about the marital status of the mother of his sons, and that Giachetti be turned over to the jurisdiction of the tribunal of Milan for defamation of character. The lawyers argued in and out of court until 1911, when a decision was finally handed down. In the words of the Milan correspondent for the *Chronicle:*

> The investigation of the case, which has been before the courts since June 1909, showed unblushing bribery and corruption on the part of the witness, *Signor* Turco Micalizzi, a New York journalist. The latter retracted his original testimony, wherein he stated that artists and others had seen Caruso flourishing the letter of contract in his hand in a New York restaurant. He declared that he had organized this false evidence at the instigation of Ada Giachetti, her chauffeur, and a theatrical agent named Loria, by whom he had been offered a 1,000 franc tip and a lucrative situation. The magistrates have denounced all parties to this conspiracy, and the Procurator-General will proceed against them, on the ground of perjury and calumny.[8]

Father was acquitted of all accusations. The matter could have ended there, but he realized he was the victim of a conspiracy and filed a countersuit against Ada and her cohorts for libel.

Another problem Caruso had to settle in 1911 concerned his tax status in England. Because he maintained the apartment at Maida Vale, the tax assessor of London decreed him a London resident and slapped him with a huge tax assessment. Father was incensed. In a fit of pique, he had the Maida Vale apartment emptied. He ordered some of the furniture shipped to Italy and gave the rest away to friends and acquaintances. He instructed Miss Saer to rent an apartment for us in her name, but sensible and frugal Lei convinced him this would be a useless expense, since I could go to live with her family. Father agreed, so Lei and I moved in with her two unmarried sisters, Lillian and Bridget, at 48 Chichily Road in Cricklewood, London.

Whether it dated from this time or before, my first recollection of the Saer family is a big dinner gathering. The only brother, Reverend John B. Saer, acted as the head of the household. His sons, Jack and Harold, and a daughter named Margaret were there, but I don't remember a Mrs. John Saer; perhaps she was no longer living. And there were Miss Saer's five sisters, each wearing a blouse of a different color. The bright colors made a lasting impression on me, and I began to call each sister by the color of her blouse. From that day on, they were Red, White, Blue, Green, and Black to me. I remember the given name of three of them: Lillian was White, Margaret was Blue, and Bridget was Red. And, of course, there was Louise, my own Lei.

The Saer family came from Canarvon, Wales, not far from Harlech. Louise, my dear governess, was a bright, well-educated woman. Being strictly British, she seldom showed her feelings. Outwardly she always sported a stiff upper lip, but I saw her crying alone many times at night, when she thought I was asleep. She must have borne some deep sorrow; I never dared to ask her about it. Somewhere in the back of my mind, there is a tale about a love affair and a fiancé lost in the Boer War.

During all the years I knew her, she had no male friends or callers—not one. She never married and devoted the best years of her adult life to looking after me. Though she cared for me and loved me, she was never demonstrative. She comforted me, carried me around, even cuddled me and kissed me good night, but somehow there was always an invisible barrier between us. I am convinced that in her perception, she was an employee, and I her employer's son. I don't remember ever running up to her, throwing my arms around her neck, and saying, "Lei, I love you!"

I continued to live in virtual isolation with the Saer women. I had no friends who came to visit, and I never went to other homes to play. My only playmates were the children I met at the playground.

Our domestic routine at Chichily Road never varied. White kept house and did the cooking. Red was a schoolteacher and my personal tutor in the afternoons; I had lessons with her after she came home from school. She taught me English, literature, mathematics, geography, Greek and Roman history and mythology, and English and world history, but very little about the sciences. Although she was a very loyal British subject, she condescended to teach me the story of the insurrection of the colonies against the Crown in 1776. It is small wonder that I became very British in the process. When I informed Father that I intended to grow up an Englishman, he had a hard time trying to explain to me that he was Italian and I was Italian, though I happened to live in England. I boldly told him that *he* might be Italian, but I was not. Luckily, he had a good sense of humor and saw the lighter side of the issue, otherwise he might have shipped me straight home to make an Italian patriot of me.

Red knew how to make the lessons and my homework a challenge instead of a chore. For instance, she turned my history lessons into an interesting game. She would tell me to lay out the Relief of Lucknow, the Battle of Waterloo, or the Battle of Hastings. Using the toy soldiers Mrs. Da Costa had brought me by the hundreds, I would recreate the battle formation according to the historical model, then explain the troop movements and the outcome of the battle.

When we were in England, I insisted on speaking English to Papa, and he humored me as best he could. I once complained about his funny way of talking and suggested that "Papa should go to school to learn how to talk." But when we were in Italy on vacation, the tables were turned. I must have remembered enough Italian from my early childhood to pick it up quickly. I had an authentic English accent, however, and I often mispronounced the double consonants. My brother took great delight in mimicking my speech. In 1911, we spent the summer in Marina di Pisa; and once, while running along the curved shoreline, I took a shortcut to a boat over what I thought was land covered with green moss. In a flash I fell through a thick layer of algae into the water. They fished me out and took me bawling to my father.

"Papa, io credeva thuto thera," I sobbed in accented, broken Italian. I meant to say that I thought it was solid ground. But I mispronounced the words, failing to stress the double consonants in *tutto* and *terra*. My dripping little figure covered with green muck was ridiculous enough, but my Italian statement simply brought down the house. Fofò exploded laughing and couldn't stop. "Thu*t*o the*r*a," he howled, leading a general outburst of hilarity. "Thu*t*o the*r*a, thu*t*o the*r*a!" Shaken by the experience and soaked to the bone, I failed to see the humor of it all; and the more they laughed, the more distressed I became. Finally Papa motioned to Miss Saer to take me away and clean me up.

By 1911, I had grown beyond the cuddly age. Papa stopped babying me, and our playing together ceased. After I reached puberty, I don't remember him ever embracing me. He must have hugged and kissed me, at least when we met or said good-bye each summer, but it happened so seldom that I have no recollection of it. Treating me without much gentleness may have been his idea of making a man out of me, but instead it left me with a series of unpleasant memories. At Marina di Pisa, for instance, I fell and skinned my knee badly. Miss Saer took me to Papa:

"Mr. Caruso, Mimmi just fell and hurt himself."

Father took one look at me and said: *"La prossima volta te lo faccio dall'altra parte!"* ("The next time I will do it to the other one!")

It was his way of telling me to be more careful and not let it happen again, but the lesson was lost on a bawling seven-year-old looking for comfort and sympathy.

In August 1911, Father had a minor accident: His car collided with a

Caruso as the Duke of Mantua in Verdi's *Rigoletto*. Photography A. Dupont.

Caruso as the Duke of Mantua.
Photography Bert.

Caruso and soprano Lina
Cavalieri in Giordano's *Fedora,*
Paris, 1905. Courtesy of Dr.
Ruffo Titta, Jr.

Caruso as Fernando in Donizetti's *La Favorita*, 1906. Courtesy of Metropolitan Opera Association.

Caruso as Raoul in Meyerbeer's *Les Huguenots,* 1906. Photography Burr McIntosh.

Caruso as Mario Cavaradossi in Puccini's *Tosca*. Photography A. Dupont.

Four poses as Canio in Leoncavallo's *Pagliacci,* showing the evolution of the character over the years. Photography A. Dupont (*top left*), Bert (*bottom left and top right*), and Mishkin (*bottom right*).

Enrico Caruso
„Bajazzi"

6034
Verl. Herm. Leiser, Berlin-Wilm.

Caruso as Des Grieux in Massenet's *Manon*. Photography Mishkin.

Caruso's classic pose as Radames in Verdi's *Aida*. Photography Bert.

Caruso as Don José
in Bizet's *Carmen.*

Caruso as Rodolfo
in Puccini's *La Bohème.*
Photography Mishkin.

A kilted Caruso as Edgardo in Donizetti's *Lucia di Lammermoor*.
Photography Mishkin.

Caruso as Enzo Grimaldo in Ponchielli's *La Gioconda*. Photography Mishkin.

Caruso as Dick Johnson, a role he
created in Puccini's *La Fanciulla del
West* in 1910. Photography Bert (*left*)
and Mishkin (*below*).

Caruso as Riccardo in Verdi's *Un Ballo in maschera,* 1913. Photography Mishkin.

Caruso in the title role
of Saint-Saëns' *Samson et
Dalila*, 1915.
Photography Mishkin.

Caruso as Jean de Leyden in Meyerbeer's *Le Prophète,* 1918.

bus in Anticoli. I wasn't with him but only heard about it. The press picked up the story, mentioning that both vehicles were badly damaged, and that "Caruso helped the chauffeurs for several hours to repair the damage. In his car he was carrying three bronze busts by Cifariello: of Italian actress Adelaide Ristori, the Prince of Bavaria, and one of himself."[9]

In the winter of 1911, after his return to America, Caruso suffered the loss of one of his dearest friends, Eduardo Missiano. The baritone sang small roles at the Met, thus they saw each other fairly often. On December 6, Missiano suddenly became ill at dinner and died within a few minutes. Caruso was contacted and asked to come to his friend's house, but it was too late. Father was struck by the strange coincidence that the last time they performed together at the Met, Missiano, as the jailer in *Tosca,* had sung: "You have only one hour left [to live]."

Missiano was very dear to Father, who never forgot how much he owed to him and what his friendship had meant in those early years in Naples. The day after the baritone died, Father was quoted in the papers as saying:

> Missiano is the best friend I ever had. But for him I might have been still singing at some concert hall in Italy. As long ago as 1892 he and I used to swim together at one of the Italian seaside resorts. I was always in good spirits, and loved to sing. He told me that my voice was unique; but I always laughed and said I sang because I couldn't help it. Missiano reproached me for not studying, until, to please him, I went to a Neapolitan singing teacher, Guglielmo Vergine, who shrugged his shoulders and exclaimed, "Caruso, your voice is all wind."
>
> After that Missiano kept quiet, but not for long. He said Vergine must be crazy, and insisted on my seeing Vergine again. I did and Vergine took me up. Five years ago I found Missiano in poverty in Naples and brought him to the Metropolitan Opera House, where he has been singing small parts ever since.

IN 1912, Lei and I again went to Paris to meet Papa. He was singing with the Monte Carlo Opera on its second tour to the French capital. The season opened with Chaliapin taking the title role of *Mefistofele* opposite the Faust of Dmitri Smirnov. I was taken to see Papa in *Rigoletto.* Antonina Nezhdanova sang Gilda in her only engagement outside Russia, and the title role was sung by Father's friend, the immortal Titta Ruffo. What was undoubtedly one of the most stupendous performances of the period was nothing more than an evening's diversion for me. To my lasting regret, I remember nothing of the musical aspects of the performance, and I have only superficial recollections of the evening. I remember Papa straddling a chair and playing solitaire while singing "La donna è mobile," and on the final flourish of the aria, tossing the whole packet of cards on the table. I also remember that in the altercation between Sparafucile and Maddalena, to punctuate his outburst, the bass Giuseppe Torres de Luna threw his long knife on the table; it landed upright, the blade quivering for seconds. But what amused me most was the kidnapping of Gilda. One of the courtiers carried her down a ladder from the second-story window. The bundle in his arms did not resemble the soprano at all, in shape, form, or—most emphatically—in weight.

While Caruso was in Paris, his lawyers were again diligently at work. They were trying to settle a lawsuit for breach of promise brought by a young woman named Elsa (or Elisa) Ganelli. It was one of those messy entanglements that Father got into from time to time.

Ganelli was a pretty, nineteen-year-old salesgirl. Father met her in a department store on the Corso Vittorio Emmanuele in Milan in 1909 and was quite smitten. An intimate correspondence developed between them, and he proposed marriage. By the end of the year, the rumor began to circulate, in print, that he was contemplating a simultaneous wedding and retirement from the stage. In Frankfurt, he told Ledner about his wedding plans. Ledner's level-headed reaction was: "I know your engagements. They happen at least once a year."[10] But Father pretended to be offended and forbade any unkind remark. "I love Miss Ganelli. She is a respectable, honest girl, pretty as a picture. I induced her to give up her job immediately and I will marry her next year, after I return from New York."[11] He even insisted that the engagement party should be held not at the hotel but at Ledner's home.

The following year, he sent 10,000 francs to Miss Ganelli to buy a new wardrobe and join him in Berlin, properly chaperoned by her father. The pair arrived, "the daughter, indeed a beautiful young lady, the father an elderly, somewhat tallish gentleman, both freshly outfitted,"[12] according to Ledner. Miss Ganelli behaved quite naturally, but her father, unaccustomed to the style of dress, was obviously uncomfortable.

He had a particularly hard time with the top hat, upturned collar, and the gloves. . . . They stayed isolated in their hotel suite, and they saw Caruso only at the theater, in the living room, in the dining room, or at common walks. Caruso behaved impeccably, treated Miss Ganelli like a great lady, pretended to be very much in love, all the while being reserved, spoke a lot about his plans for the future, about the wedding next spring, and of the miserable interval until then.[13]

Complying with Caruso's wishes, Ledner invited a group of prominent people to his home for a formal dinner and announced the engagement to the guests. After about ten days in Berlin, the Ganellis returned to Italy, and Father went on to Bremen. An hour before his ship departed for New York, he handed Ledner the text of a telegram and asked him to read it in order to be informed. The text read, approximately: "Nothing can become of our wedding. After mature deliberation I must give up, must cancel our private, not yet publicized engagement. Let us both forget all that has happened."[14]

Ledner was stupefied. "This telegram should be sent?" he asked. Father was nervous and seemed embarrassed. "Please do not ask much now. I am sick and tired of this story."[15] Ledner sent the telegram as instructed. Caruso explained his change of heart in an interview in the 30 May 1911 issue of the *Daily Mirror:*

But when she and her father came, I found I had made a mistake, because they were very ordinary people. They stayed in Berlin a few days, and I gave her 2,000 marks and went to America. Afterwards I explained to her that I could not marry her, or anyone, and asked her to let me have my letters back, and said I would send those she wrote to me. I stopped writing. But she? No. She went on.

When I went to Paris she and her mother came, and her mother told me she wanted to give her daughter to me, but I said "Go away," but also that I would give 1,000 francs for my letters back.

The Ganellis began to bombard Caruso with letters which he left unanswered. Pasquale Ganelli, the girl's father, made statements in the Italian papers and threatened to publish Father's love letters unless he bought them back at a very high price. Caruso refused, and they filed suit for breach of promise on 22 June 1911 in Milan. Father wrote to Ledner on July 9: "Miss Ganelli has taken me to court in order to have me sentenced to pay 250,000 lire [$50,000] on grounds of material and moral damages. In reality it is not she who is suing me but her father, that friendly gentleman. I know this type of lawsuits. It is only an attempt to get at my fortune."[16]

The lawsuit was conducted with extreme acrimony on both sides. A large number of documents were presented, including a packet of Caruso's letters with repeated proposals of marriage. When it was over, Father cabled Ledner: "The Ganelli lawsuit ended with a complete victory for me."[17] The court "deplored" his conduct toward a respectable girl, but as there had been no improprieties, the case was dismissed, and Caruso was ordered to pay Miss Ganelli 10,000 lire for her legal expenses.

CHAPTER TEN

Engagement, Trial, Peace

IN 1912 my aunt reentered our life.

The last time Father and Rina sang together was during the summer and autumn seasons of 1907 at Covent Garden. Vocally, she was not in the best of health, and her reviews became increasingly "mixed." The critics did not hesitate to report on her vocal difficulties. When she was teamed with Caruso, her shortcomings were all the more conspicuous. Her first appearance in 1907 was as Tosca, on June 13. Two days later the *Times* critic wrote:

> On Thursday *Tosca* was given before a very large audience, and with Mme. Giachetti in the title part. She is very possibly right in preferring the ultra-melodramatic way of acting it; . . . Mme. Giachetti's singing was perfectly successful until she came to the trying passage in the last act, where the soprano and tenor sing in unison with little or no accompaniment. Here every note, and the transition from one note to another, showed up the defects of Mme. Giachetti's method in contrast with that of *Signor* Caruso, who sang the music of Cavaradossi to perfection. *Signor* Scotti is nowhere better

suited than in the part of Scarpia, and he sang and acted it as admirably as ever.

Rina's next opera, *Cavalleria rusticana* on June 27, was judged "a considerable improvement on the first performance of this season [on June 9 with Scalar as Santuzza], as Mme. Giachetti sang with a good deal of point and acted with all her wonted intensity as Santuzza." Then came *Fedora,* again with Caruso at her side. This enjoyed the best reception of the three.

> It seemed all the more a pity last night [July 3] that there was not more opportunity for continuous singing, as *Signor* Caruso was playing the part of Loris, and playing with immense vigor and sincerity, always on the point, as it seemed, of breaking out into a torrent of lyrical song if only the composer would have let him. There was some compensation from Fedora (played now, as it was in the autumn, by Mme. Giachetti), as she has one or two charming airs and does not have to rely merely on the intensity of her acting.[1]

But Rina's vocal problems persisted. One can only surmise that either she had a premature vocal decline due to imperfect training, or she did not find a competent teacher to correct her technical defects as they developed. Commenting on her Mimì in *La Bohème* upon her return to London in the fall, one reviewer wrote: "The last scene of Act I was on the whole sung with refinement by *Signor* Bassi and Mme. Giachetti, though, needless to say, Mme. Giachetti's final notes had not the effect which the passage can have."[2]

On October 10 she repeated her celebrated Tosca, paired for the first time with Giuseppe de Luca. Rina was an accomplished actress by this time, and she had the ability to adjust her interpretation to the temperament of her new Scarpia. "To record that last night's performance [of *Tosca*] was a notable one is to pay a high tribute to the work done by *Signor* De Luca and Mme. Giachetti,"[3] wrote the *Times* critic on October 11.

> The acting of each in the second act was the more impressive that it was never exaggerated, indeed the quietness of *Signor* De Luca's representation of his part is one of its remarkable features. Both, too, used such opportunities as are given to them for genuine musical effect; *Signor* De Luca's voice was at its best in his soliloquy at the beginning of the second act, and the applause which Mme. Giachetti aroused by her

singing of the song "Vissi d'arte," though ill-judged, was a spontaneous appreciation of an artistic piece of singing.

Rina closed the London season with a successful *Germania*. In December, she repeated her Tosca in Madrid and also at the Monte Carlo Opera. In the latter theater, she also sang Musetta to Selma Kurz's Mimì. The special attraction of the performance was Chaliapin's Colline, a role he added to his repertory in 1897; but this was the first—and probably the only—season that he sang the role outside Russia.

From this point on, Rina had few engagements. She took part in the Carnival season at the Teatro Costanzi in Rome in the spring of 1909. In addition to her old standby, Cio-Cio-San in *Madama Butterfly,* she added two new roles to her repertory: Maddalena in *Andrea Chénier,* and the title role of *Rhea* in the local première of Samaras's opera; all three operas were conducted by Giorgio Polacco. She returned to the Costanzi at the end of the year for a series of performances of *La Bohème* and *Mefistofele,* both conducted by Pietro Mascagni. Finally, on 28 March 1910, she made her debut at La Scala in Milan in *Rhea*. The critique of the 4 April 1910 *Rassegna Melodrammatica* praised her performance, but not without reservation.

> Rhea [was] performed by Rina Giachetti, she of the luscious and shapely figure, of the insinuating and lovely voice which carefully molded the most delicate musical modulations. On the first night she did not seem to be in full control of her resources, but during the second performance her voice glowed with more brilliance and vibrancy, giving the part of Rhea a much appreciated vividness.

The opera failed to please and had only three performances. Thus, according to the annals of the theater,[4] Rina sang only three times at Milan's prestigious La Scala. Whether she appeared anywhere after this engagement is not known, but no further engagements can be traced. It is possible that, having reached La Scala and feeling entirely secure financially, she decided to bring her singing career to a close. She may have been influenced in her career decisions by her involvement with the next man in her life—Edoardo Scarfoglio.

GRANDFATHER GUIDO was heartbroken when Ada left Caruso. He loved my father, not like a son-in-law, but like a son, took great pride in his success, and wanted him to be happy. He also realized the suffering Ada had caused him.

I don't know whether my father and my grandfather stayed in touch after 1908. However, after the Ganelli affair was finally over, they had a man-to-man talk. I don't know when and where this took place, but I do know the essence of their conversation. Guido told Father that it was time he settled down: He had two children to consider, and they needed a mother and a permanent home. Grandfather added that Rina was unmarried and at the moment unattached. She was family, and she would make a fine companion and a good mother. It was his opinion that Papa should marry Rina and finally make a home for us all. Guido didn't have to remind Papa how much Rina loved him, for that was never a secret.

Father took some time to think this over. Considering their history, it would have been a logical step to make his relationship with Rina permanent. But his love life never followed a logical pattern. Although Rina, on one side of the Atlantic, must have held some hope of marrying Caruso, just as Mrs. Meffert did on the other, they were both to be disappointed.

Rina was without a romantic attachment in 1912. As was to be expected, De Sanna had his successor in her life: She became the mistress of Edoardo Scarfoglio, the powerful publisher of *Il Mattino*. Born in 1860, he was twenty years older than Rina and was married to, but separated from, the famous journalist Matilde Serao. The exact duration of Rina's involvement with Scarfoglio is uncertain; whether it was a long-time arrangement or a brief affair is anybody's guess. Nor do we know the reason for their parting. It is possible that Rina could not measure up to the considerable intellectual powers of either her lover or her legitimate predecessor in his life, the cultivated Serao. The only thing certain in view of later developments is that the affair did not last beyond 1911.

Guido's reasoning made sense to Father. It is not known whether Rina or Caruso took the initiative in rekindling the relationship, or whether Grandfather arranged a meeting between the two, but they began to see each other again in 1912. Rina needed no encouragement; she had been in love with Father since her teens. The renewed liaison became common knowledge, and at a big engagement party in Montecatini, Father announced his intention to marry Rina. I believe the party took place sometime in July of 1912.

Although I must have seen Rina when I was a toddler, my first recollection of her dates from 1912, just before the engagement. Papa, Miss Saer, Fofò, and I were staying at the Hotel Cavour in Milan, in all likelihood because Papa was working with his lawyers in preparation for the trial against Mother. Rina came to visit and brought me a toy submarine which she and I proceeded to launch in the bathtub. I had no concept of beauty then, yet she struck me as an extremely attractive, well-dressed lady, buxom, with a narrow waist, carrying with her an overpowering cloud of perfume. It was also the first time that I saw a stunning sample of her collection of large hats. Papa was not in, and Rina visited with me for about an hour. I did not warm up to her at all. This may not have been her fault; I was not an affectionate child by nature or by upbringing. Apart from my search for a mother, I was distant and unconcerned with other people. With the exception of Mme. Da Costa, I could not warm up to anyone until I was a grown man. If Rina liked Fofò more than me, it didn't matter at all. I don't think an impulse of jealousy ever crossed my mind.

From Milan our party proceeded to Montecatini, the rich man's resort a few miles from Florence. The curative powers of its wells were world-famous, and it attracted the sick and healthy alike. During the season it had an almost carnival atmosphere with all sorts of attractions for the amusement of the guests, from gambling casinos to visiting companies which presented various types of entertainment. We settled in at the Hotel La Pace, where the engagement party took place. It was a big affair, which included all Father's vacationing friends and invited guests in addition to the immediate family. Mugnone was there, the attorney Ceola, and several prominent composers: Giordano, Mascagni, and possibly Puccini, though I am not sure. I was too young to attend the big event, but Fofò was present, and according to his reports it was a sumptuous affair.

There was great excitement, and everyone in the party seemed extremely happy, particularly Auntie Rina. She was finally going to have the man she had loved all those years, practically from the day she set eyes on him fifteen years before. Probably the same was true for Father. He was going to have restful and happy off-season months in Italy in a familial setting. Being a man who liked order in his life, he must have looked forward to having a family and a home again.

The long road from engagement to wedding was never trod by the betrothed. The party was newsworthy enough to be picked up by the press; and when the news reached Mother, she did not hesitate to let them know how she felt about the engagement. She is said to have sent a telegram to Caruso which said in essence: "If you marry Rina, I will kill you both."

My source for this information is Fofò, who learned about the telegram from Rina herself. Although Father may have had his usual attack of cold feet on the way to the altar, Rina maintained that her sister's threat had a great deal to do with the permanent postponement of the wedding. Rina loved my father enough to acquiesce to his wishes and stay with him regardless of her legal or social status. Unlike Mother, Rina was never known or regarded as *Signora* Caruso but always remained *la Signorina* Giachetti.

When Fofò realized a summer or two later that there was not going to be any wedding, he was heartbroken. To his way of thinking, this would have been an ideal marriage, restoring the family life we had lost when Mother left us. Fofò hated our mother and in her place lavished all his affection on Auntie Rina. After all, it was Rina who had taken care of him when he was a baby, and as a toddler, he had spent more time with her than with Mother.

ONCE the engagement was announced, life took on as much normalcy as the routine of a summer resort would allow. In the mornings, Fofò and I were dragged to the spa and ordered to drink the horrible water. I tried my best to sip as little as possible and spill the rest. But Papa, Rina, Mugnone, and their friends would guzzle the horrid stuff, convinced—like every visitor to Montecatini before and since—that it could cure all ailments and restore their corpulent bodies to health.

The spa had an active night life, and we saw several performances given by visiting companies. I remember the operettas *Bal Tabarin* and *The Merry Widow*. There was also a *Pagliacci,* which Father took us to see. When it was over, he went backstage to compliment the artists. I remember nothing of the performance, but I still recall the expression of the tenor—whoever he was—when he realized that Caruso himself had been in the audience.

On these occasions, Rina put on her finery. To the Italian eye, she was a strikingly attractive woman, and she knew how to accent her best features. She had abundant, rich black hair which her maid brushed every morning until it had a sheen that sparkled in the sunlight. She had it set with a curling iron in long ringlets in the style of Princess Eugénie. Her gowns were beautiful, often cut very low to emphasize her full breasts; and she always wore a few pieces from her large and valuable collection of jewelry. She had a narrow, corseted waist and ample hips. Although she was of average height, her flowing gowns made her seem taller than she really was. She looked lovely on my father's arm, and her proud carriage reflected her satisfaction at being the fiancée of the famous tenor.

IN September 1911, Italy's political leaders decided to invade Tripoli and declared war on Turkey. The hostilities lasted longer than expected. By the middle of the following year, the older generation of reservists had to be mobilized. Uncle Giovanni was recalled to service. Rina, Fofò, and I went to Naples to see him on his way to Tripoli. His immediate family were there: my Aunt Bettina and my cousins, Marcello and Anna. I remember Giovanni in his khaki uniform as we rode in an open car, his long rifle in hand with the *pomo d'oro* stuck in the barrel to keep out the sand. As we watched the troops from Grandmother Maria's balcony, they sang:

> *Tripoli, bel suol d'amore,*
> *Sarai italiana al rombo del cannone!*

(Tripoli, beautiful land of love,
You will become Italian at the cannon's roar!)

Luckily, by October 1912, Turkey was ready to acknowledge defeat and peace talks began. Uncle Giovanni once again returned from war unscathed.

This was my first trip to Naples. I was fascinated to finally see Papa's city, Mount Vesuvio, and the panorama of the bay. This was also the first time I remember meeting my step-grandmother Maria Castaldi Caruso and my paternal aunt, Assunta. Because Fofò often stayed in Naples with our relatives as a child, he came to know the two women while he was growing up, and he was very fond of Assunta. She was a fragile, melancholy woman, gentle and quiet, and perhaps mentally retarded. Somebody had warned me: "Watch out, your aunt is crazy!" The remark must have frightened me, because I didn't want to go near her. She tried to be friendly and with outstretched arms said:

"Mimmi, come to Auntie!"

"I don't want to. You are crazy!" I replied.

Poor Assunta began to cry, and at that moment Fofò slapped me so hard that I just about went flying across the room.

"Don't you ever say that again to your aunt! Apologize and kiss her hand!"

I did, and she patted me on the head. My fear gradually disappeared, and we got along well during our visit. She lived with my step-grandmother in the apartment Father had bought for his parents. Southern Italian custom prescribes black dress for five years after a close relative dies, and since Grandfather Marcellino had died in 1908, both women were dressed in mourning. The somber clothing seemed to match the women's personalities and the ambience of the apartment. I remember the heavy furniture and the dark red curtains, which made the rooms dark and oppressive.

Assunta never married. She had been a sickly child, probably due to infantile malnutrition and because she was the last child of a forty-four-year-old woman already worn out from child-bearing. In her adult years, she was never healthy. Father always provided for his sister's welfare, but I don't know whether he felt any deep affection for her. I never heard him speak about her, while she was alive or after her death. The 1908 letter to Sisca with its despairing reference to his "feeble-minded" sister[5] shows that he had no illusions about her mental capacities. Key wrote about Caruso and Assunta that "he had shown her a constant tenderness throughout her somewhat melancholy life."[6]

At summer's end, Father traveled to Milan, and Miss Saer and I returned to England to pass another uneventful year at 48 Chichily Road.

THE Milan trial of October 1912 was the countersuit Father had brought against Ada, Romati, and their two coconspirators, Gaetano Loria and Vincenzo Micalizzi Turco, who had made libelous statements against him in 1910. Father must have realized that the journalists would seize the opportunity to delve into his private life, but he was determined to clear his name no matter how painful the process. The reporters did not fail to mention that in the course of the trial, tears welled up in Caruso's eyes more than once. To endure the emotional trauma of confronting his rival and hearing Romati "describe his intimate relationship with Giachetti in a manner similar to Boccaccio's,"[7] as one reporter put it, was the price he had to pay.

The Caruso trial was the free circus of Milan. The court overflowed with spectators. Of the four defendants, only the former chauffeur, Cesare Romati—now described as an "aviator"—and Micalizzi Turco were present; Gaetano Loria and Ada Giachetti were not, despite the fact that the trial had been adjourned in August due to

Ada's absence. On account of the adjournment, Caruso had to cancel two guest appearances in Berlin.

The proceedings unearthed a great deal of dirt. The charges were straightforward. Ada Giachetti was accused of defaming the character of Enrico Caruso and slandering both Caruso and Carlotta Carignani; Micalizzi Turco was accused of perjury and bribery of the witness Savoia in the 1910 trial; Romati and Loria were charged with complicity in the felony of slander.

The court reviewed the accusations made by Ada Giachetti in 1910. She had alleged that Caruso intercepted and withheld a letter mailed to her from New York by Gaetano Loria. The letter supposedly contained a contract for Giachetti to sing at Oscar Hammerstein's Manhattan Opera House in New York. She had further alleged that Caruso stole jewels belonging to her and worth 300,000 lire (about $60,000), an accusation repeated in an interview, spiced with invectives, given to Antonio Alogne of the *Corriere della Sera*. In another document, also read in court, Giachetti accused Carlotta Carignani, owner of the *pensione* Excelsior, of duplicity, claiming that while she encouraged Ada's relationship with Romati, she secretly kept Caruso informed.

Caruso's principal defender, the attorney Valdata, presented a document signed and dated by Ada Giachetti on 26 June 1909, in which she declared that she had no claims against Enrico Caruso, "neither entitled to the restitution of the jewelry nor for any other reason." In the same deposition, Giachetti pledged "to abstain from appearing in public in North America practicing her art."[8]

There was a long succession of witnesses. Micalizzi Turco testified that he was destitute when he met Loria and Romati, and that Loria had offered him money to declare in court that he had heard Caruso had in his possession a thick letter addressed to Giachetti. At the time, he said, Romati gave him one Napoleon (a gold coin), and later, "from time to time, 5, 10, 20 and 30 lire."[9]

At this point in the trial, like the surprise witness in a courtroom drama, Caruso's attorney Giovanni Ceola made his deposition. He said he had learned from the lawyer Ugo Marcora that Caruso had received an offer to have the action concerning Ada's purloined letter halted for a price of 200,000 lire (about $40,000). Ceola decided to get to the bottom of the matter, went to Paris, and arranged to meet Loria. Unaware of his identity, Loria confided that Caruso had wronged him and that he was using Giachetti to take his own revenge. Loria also told Ceola that the organizer of the original plot against Caruso was Rossi-

Crivelli, Romati's lawyer. Not surprisingly, Rossi-Crivelli was not present at the 1912 court hearing. Loria boasted that he had nothing to fear in the matter because he would be no more than a witness for the defense, stating that he personally had mailed the notorious letter with the contract to Giachetti.

Ceola had heard enough, but he had the presence of mind to see Hammerstein, who also happened to be in Paris. Hammerstein told Ceola he would never have engaged Giachetti for the simple reason that he did not care for her as an artist. In his deposition, Ceola described Loria as a crook and a thief of the first order, with links to the Italian criminal organization the Black Hand.

Ceola firmly stated to the judge: "It is my impression that the letter was never written."[10]

Why did Loria hate Caruso so much? The explanation was provided by Richard Barthélemy, composer, singing teacher, and Caruso's accompanist for over a decade. Barthélemy testified that one day Loria had approached him, insisting on being introduced to Caruso. Loria, who claimed to have a command of several languages, wanted to become Caruso's secretary and virtually begged to be hired, saying he would be satisfied with very little just to be close to such a great artist. Caruso, the proverbial "soft touch," took the man into his employ. It soon became obvious that Loria was unsuited for the job, and he was fired. That, apparently, was Loria's grudge against Caruso.

A succession of witnesses disclosed various lurid details. Giuseppe Guidalotti, a lawyer, former overseer at Le Panche, and Giachetti's cousin, stated that when he became aware of the intimacies between Ada and her chauffeur, he insisted that Romati be dismissed. But "Giachetti was unable to be without Romati,"[11] and he was rehired. Romati, aware of Guidalotti's animosity, threatened and assaulted him and was arrested for the attack.

Emilio Tani, gardener and superintendent of Le Panche, confirmed the intimacies between Giachetti and Romati. Another witness, Gino Filiberti, a former servant of the Caruso family at the villa, told of surprising Romati one night as he entered Caruso's bathroom and then his bedroom, where Giachetti slept. The incident earned Filiberti his immediate dismissal.

Tumiati, co-owner of the Hotel Cavour, told of occasions when Caruso would lock himself in his room out of fear following scenes he had with Giachetti. Attorney Nicola Vetere testified that he and his colleague, Dr. De Simoni, were charged with initiating proceedings for a divorce on behalf of Ada Giachetti against her husband Gino

Botti, in order that Ada could marry Caruso. Vetere soon learned about the intimate relationship between Giachetti and the chauffeur, however, and thus made no further efforts to obtain a divorce. Vetere added the previously undisclosed detail that Giachetti had wanted to start an automobile dealership, which would have enabled her to live like a lady—so she said—without having to depend on Caruso. However, he remarked, "Romati has become an aviator in the meantime."

Several witnesses made depositions to the effect that Romati was a dubious character, had a bad reputation, and was living on his wife's money while he was at Salsomaggiore. Others spoke on behalf of the plaintiff and testified to Carignani's affection toward Giachetti while she was staying at the *pensione* Excelsior in Milan.

Caruso's chief defense attorney, Valdata, stated that the present action did not begin as a legal action by Caruso against the mother of his children, but rather as a response to Giachetti's action against the father of her children. Valdata stressed that although Giachetti had since 1907 betrayed Caruso with one of his servants, he had thrice forgiven her; as she persisted in the betrayal, the attorney said, it became necessary, for Caruso's own dignity, to break all relations. At the same time, Caruso had provided her with an allowance that was undeniably generous after such an offense. In conclusion, Valdata asked that the offenders be punished, requesting—unquestionably at Caruso's suggestion—that Giachetti be given a suspended sentence.

Caruso's second defender, Giovanni Porzio, delved into the relationship between Giachetti and Romati and their plan to force Caruso to pay a large sum of money through a scheme that implicated his honor and dignity. A lawyer named Cardinali spoke on behalf of Micalizzi Turco, then a lawyer named Romita spoke on behalf of Romati. The latter asked that his client be absolved, concluding that Romati lacked the organizer's mind that would have been necessary for the architect of the elaborate scheme to discredit Caruso.

The court retired to deliberate. The suspense in the courtroom was intense. At a late hour, the tribunal returned, and the presiding judge, *Commendatore* Maestri, read the sentence.

Ada Giachetti was found guilty as charged of defamation of character for having alleged that Caruso misappropriated her jewels and that he and Carignani wrongfully intercepted her correspondence. She was sentenced to one year in prison and ordered to pay a fine of 1,000 lire ($200).

Vincenzo Micalizzi Turco was found guilty of perjury, but in view of his retraction of the statement made earlier and other extenuating circumstances, he was sentenced to only three months and twenty-six days in prison.

Cesare Romati and Gaetano Loria were found guilty of bribing witnesses. Romati was sentenced to one year and fifteen days in prison, and a previous suspended sentence was revoked. Loria was sentenced to eleven months and twenty-three days in prison.

Because of the Italian Amnesty of March 1911, the prison sentence of each of the accused was reduced by three months, and Giachetti's fine of 1,000 lire was reduced to 100 lire.

Due to insufficient evidence, Giachetti, Loria, and Romati were found not guilty of the charges of slander; and for the same reason, Loria was absolved of the charge of perjury.

All the accused were then sentenced to pay damages to Caruso and Carignani, in amounts to be settled in a separate action, in addition to the court costs, which were set at 1,000 lire.

Thus the celebrated lawsuit came to an end, or almost to an end. The defendants, unwisely, appealed the verdict. The Court of Appeals not only upheld the decision, it "increased the penalties inflicted by the lower court."[12]

It is my understanding that although Mother was not present at the trial, she was in Milan. Immediately after being informed of the verdict, she left Italy for South America, which was her only alternative to imprisonment. She settled in Buenos Aires and never again set foot on Italian soil.

Her romance with Romati had been short-lived. Perhaps, when she found herself involved, with her former lover, in the countersuit initiated by Caruso, she chose not to face either Romati or Caruso in the courtroom. Thus, though Romati himself appeared at the trial, she was represented only by attorneys. We do not know how long Romati and my mother were together. It is certain that Romati did not go with her to South America once the trial was over. He continued to rely on his old tricks, trying to con money out of women under the pretext of love and prospects for a lucrative future. The Milan correspondent for the London *Chronicle* wrote on 27 December 1912:

> [Cesare Romati], who was recently condemned at Milan to ten months' imprisonment as the organizer of a perjury plot against the great tenor, was again arrested today on a serious charge.
>
> While on bail pending his appeal, Romati made the

acquaintance of a young lady of good family at Gallarate. After a promise of marriage, he persuaded her to sell some property for the purpose of financing a grand school of aviation for the upper classes, which he said he was commissioned to organize. No sooner had the money been obtained than Romati prevailed upon the girl to leave her home and run away with him to Varese, where, till shortly before Christmas, they stayed at the lady's expense.

Romati, according to the young lady's statement, then excused himself, saying he must spend the Christmas season with his family at Brescia. When, however, some days elapsed without any tidings of him, and she discovered that on leaving her he had taken 100 pounds from her cashbox, she came to Milan and gave information to the police. Romati, when arrested, was apparently in hiding at Varese, only a few streets from where he abandoned the girl. This afternoon he was brought to Milan Prison in irons.

I am convinced that Father did not withhold Ada's jewelry out of pettiness. If she had meant to keep and wear the jewels, he would gladly have let her have them. However, he was not about to provide a financial base for Ada and her lover as they established a business together. He had given Ada, as his common-law wife, every material comfort, but he was loath to do the same for her lover as well.

Years later I asked Emilio Tani, who was then my own gardener at Le Panche, to tell me the truth about the jewels. Reluctantly, at first, he told me what had happened.

As the lovers were leaving Le Panche, they loaded the car in a hurry. Because they were taking Miss Saer and me, they had a good deal to carry. The last thing Mother brought down to the car was her jewel case. While she stopped for a moment to adjust her big bonnet and the scarf around her neck, she handed the jewel case to Emilio to hold. At that moment, Romati called to her and honked the horn, hurrying her. Forgetting all about the case, she turned and ran to the car, leaving the jewels in Tani's hands. Romati drove off, and they did not realize what had happened until it was too late.

"What was I to do?" said Emilio. "When the *Commendatore* came home, I handed the jewel case over to him."

CARUSO'S return to Covent Garden in May 1913 after a four-year absence was the most anticipated event of the season. He arrived in town in mid-May, accompanied by his valet and his secretary of the moment, Felice Caramanna. Lei and I and several of Father's friends met him at Victoria Station; I was happy to see him, and Papa embraced me. We drove in several cars to the Savoy Hotel, where Caruso was surrounded by a waiting crowd, including reporters. They all wanted some statement from him, and he was willing to talk about anything they asked.

Their questions were wide-ranging. The *Daily Telegraph* mentioned that when Caruso was eighteen years old, he was in doubt as to whether he was a tenor or a baritone, adding his comment that "the matter has been settled some time ago."[13] The article continued: "Caruso never forgets to acknowledge his indebtedness to Major Nagliati... and, above all, to his illustrious teacher, Guglielmo Vergine." In addition to respectable reportage, some of the journalists got carried away and wrote ludicrous fabrications. I like best the confused passage in an unidentified clipping of 17 September 1913 that describes Le Panche as "another of [Caruso's] country houses which is situated six or seven miles from Bellosguardo. This is called 'Belvedere' and is surrounded by sixteen farms, each containing a piano." This bit of creative journalism always made me conjure up the image of the semiliterate tenant farmers of Cercina coming home after a full day's work in the fields and attacking the keyboards with the vengeance of a Horowitz.

Caruso opened on May 20 with *Pagliacci* opposite Carmen Melis as Nedda and Mario Sammarco as Tonio. He "held the house hypnotised," in the verdict of one critic. The writer added that the Caruso voice "may not be quite as ringing as it was—it seems to have altered a shade in colour, to have lost a tithe of its resilience—[but it] is still, as it has ever been, the best voice in the world. . . . It was, in fact, a Caruso night of Caruso nights."[14]

I heard him sing in his Albert Hall concert in 1909, but my solitary memory of the event is that every time Father came onstage, I exclaimed aloud: "That's my daddy!" Miss Saer had a hard time keeping me quiet. That was the only recital of Father's I ever attended. The first opera performance of his I can recall with any clarity is the *La Bohème* he sang with Melba in 1913. Father was staying at the Savoy, and we came to town from Chichily Road in Cricklewood. Miss Saer, as usual, refused to hire a cab, and we took a bus to the theater.

The papers said that Father was a wonderful Rodolfo and praised both his Mimìs—first Melis, later Melba. "His singing of 'Che gelida manina' was a masterpiece of finely ordered singing. The sustained notes were splendidly resonant; the half-voice of silk-like quality, while in the duets [with Carmen Melis] his voice pulsed and throbbed."[15] Unfortunately, all that was lost on me; I was bored until the little band came on in the Montmartre scene and Musetta sang her famous waltz. But I must have been impressed, for I asked Papa to teach me to sing. Amused by my request, he sat me on his lap, and the lesson began with "La donna è mobile." It was to no avail. The more I tried, the worse I sang. Either I had no voice at all, or I could not carry a tune. I was sorry I had asked, and probably Papa was too. Soon, to our mutual relief, he gave up the effort; we were both discouraged and decided that singing was not for me.

This was the one and only singing lesson I ever received from my father. When I mentioned this incident to a journalist many years later, he felt obliged to write that I received my first voice lessons—in the plural—from my father. While technically this was correct, it strained the truth beyond all limits.

IN 1913, a small book entitled *How to Sing* appeared, its title page naming Enrico Caruso as its author. Father did not write it and had no advance knowledge of its publication. To make matters worse, it turned out that whole chapters of the book had been lifted from *L'Art du Chant Technique* by Mme. Meyerheim, a well-known singing teacher active in Paris, who brought suit against the publisher and against my father. The incident was picked up by the world press.

Of the many articles on the subject, perhaps the most vivid summary was that written by Avery Strakosch. It first appeared in *Musical Courier* and was later reproduced in full in the 13 February 1915 issue of *Opera News* (no relation to the magazine of the same title published by the Metropolitan Opera Guild). Strakosch offers a revealing glimpse of Father, the soft touch.

> One hears much of Caruso and his generous acts. I had a chance to get a glimpse of his goodness. A young writer entered and asked Mr. Caruso if he would sign an autobiographical article. He shook his head and said, "No, I cannot."
>
> "Why not?" asked the aggressive young party, not losing hope.

"It is a long story."

"Tell it to me."

"Well, many times in the past have I signed articles. Some time ago I received from different friends many books—always the same book. It was entitled 'How to Sing, by Caruso,' and my personal signature was in the book.

" 'This is very strange' I think to myself. I looked carefully and found the publisher is one of London. When I returned to London, I searched for the publisher. At last I found him. He knew nothing of the dishonest author or authoress. He said the book had been purchased from America. I departed.

"Suddenly a woman rushes over from Paris, a singing teacher, I believe, and begins suit against me and calls me a plage."

"A what?"

"You not know what a plage is?"

"Oh—a plagiarist?"

"Exactly. She says that 'my' book is a copy of what she wrote and published ten years before. Well, I had other engagements and left London. Now when I return, I have to go to court and prove, yes, actually prove that I did not write that infamous book!"

An angry Caruso was not an awe-inspiring sight, so the aggressive young thing assumed an air of innocence and answered assuringly, "But, Mr. Caruso, I am not that kind."

"No, I cannot give my signature."

The A. Y. T. still lingered. One could see that determination was her watchword.

"Shall I be frank? Well, it is this way—as this article stands, I get fifty dollars for it. With your signature I get two hundred and fifty dollars for it."

That was, to use an American expression, "some ultimatum." It was also a psychological moment—a few moments before, he had been speaking of his former poverty. The heart of Caruso was touched.

"All right, I give you my signature," he replied in quiet desperation.

BY the end of the London season, Father was ready for a rest. After his last *Bohème,* we went to Italy, this time to Livorno, where we moved into Villa Rina, Auntie Rina's property. This was a pretentious, three-story building in typical Mediterranean style, with formal gardens in front and back, situated on the Viale Lungomare Carducci between Ardenza and Antignano, a stone's throw from the beach. The nine-foot entrance had French doors with "R. G." emblazoned on the large glass panes. There was a spacious foyer, which opened to the left onto a large Louis XIV parlor. To the right was a formal dining room where as many as twenty-four could comfortably be seated. At the end of the foyer was the stairwell to the two upper floors. Beyond this was a *jardin d'hiver,* then, on the left, a bath and a storage room. There was a butler's pantry between the kitchen and the dining room. To the left of the stairs was a bedroom used by Guido and Teresa. In the rear of the garden was a large paved rectangle covered with awnings which we called the "California room"; in good weather we often ate our meals there.

The master bedroom and an adjoining bathroom on the second floor were Rina's quarters, which Papa shared in the summer. Fofò's and my bedroom was on the same floor, as were a small sitting room and Miss Saer's room. The music room with Rina's Bechstein concert grand piano was also on this floor. Miss Saer shared a large bedroom with my cousin, little Rina or "Mimma," the daughter of Mother's deceased brother, Enrico. According to fine family tradition, she too was conceived on the wrong side of the sheets. Uncle Enrico acknowledged the child and gave her his name, but she was another child whose birth certificate showed "n.n." in place of the mother's name. After Uncle Enrico died, Guido and Teresa took her in, deeming this situation better for the child than remaining with her mother, who was poor and uneducated. Thus little Rina acquired a family, a home, and the nickname "Mimma" and lived with us at Villa Rina. Her mother worked in the neighborhood and occasionally came to visit. These visits were always short, because the woman was visibly ill at ease; yet she was grateful that the Giachettis took such good care of her little girl.

The top floor repeated the pattern of the one below. The center room was a study for the family, and the other rooms were used by Umberto, the son of Guido and Teresa, and the servants.

Auntie Rina spared no expense to make the villa comfortable. She wanted to give Papa a wonderful home for his summer vacations. Although we invariably wound up in early fall at Signa, I think it gave Rina a great deal of satisfaction that Father seemed to feel more at home at Villa Rina than at Bellosguardo. This was not surprising, for hers was a large country house furnished with excellent taste that showed a feminine touch in every detail, whereas the villa at Signa had heavy, somber furnishings, and the dimensions of the rooms were simply overpowering. Bellosguardo was a palatial residence, Villa Rina a home.

Whether we stayed in Livorno, at Signa, or at Le Panche, it was like living in a family boarding house with an aunt in charge. The dinner table had ten permanent place settings. When Papa was in residence, he sat at the head of the table, and Rina sat to his right. Then there were my maternal grandparents Guido and Teresa, their son Umberto, Fofò, myself, Miss Saer, my cousin Mimma, and Giselda (known as "La Gella"), a Giachetti relative and companion to Rina. Those family dinners were routine affairs that gave us no particular sense of togetherness. I can still see my aunt serving spaghetti: She always took a large linen napkin, spread it across her ample bosom, tucked its two corners under her armpits to hold it in position, and served from the large bowl with broad, determined motions. Few words were spoken. Father was never good at small talk except in the company of his Neapolitan cronies. At the family table, he was quiet, and when we would talk too much, he would admonish us: *"Si viene a tavola per mangiare e non per chiaccherare."* ("One comes to the table to eat and not to chitchat.") Not surprisingly, we could finish a four-course meal in twenty minutes.

At home we were trained to *"capire a volo"*—to anticipate Father's wishes: He would look at one of us and command with his eyes. One soon learned to decipher the lift of an eyebrow or movement of the eyes and hand him the salt, the water pitcher, or the parmesan, whatever he commanded. This was more a game of wits than a demonstration of his control over us, so none of us ever resented it. When Father was in an especially relaxed mood after dinner, he would line up the half-filled water glasses, wet his fingers, and play them like a glass harmonica. With a little rearrangement of the contents of each glass, he could build the semblance of a scale and play a simple tune. His face would take on a childlike intensity as he concentrated on the piece, and he would beam an enormous smile when we applauded his performance.

A certain evening routine also evolved in Livorno. I was expected to say good night to Papa, my grandparents, and Rina, kissing each of them on the cheek. This was more a ritual, a tribute to figures of authority, than a show of affection. I have no recollection that they ever kissed me in return.

IN the summer of 1913, the family spent a few weeks at Salsomaggiore, a popular Italian spa famous for the curative powers of its waters. The hot springs and steam rooms were supposedly beneficial for anyone suffering from respiratory problems. Although we had a car, we went by train. In those days, Italian roads were so bad that it was usually wiser to travel by rail. Besides, the car was not big enough to carry Father, Rina, Fofò, Lei, myself, *and* the luggage.

On our way to Salsomaggiore, we stopped in Bologna. We were enjoying the rich contents of the picnic baskets one could buy at the station when a trainload of convicts pulled up and stopped beside our compartment. They were a sad sight. The prisoners were chained together, and a *carabiniere* stood guard at each end of the car. Without a moment's hesitation, Father left his seat, got off the train, and bought all the cigarettes at the station's tobacco shop. He had them delivered to the *carabinieri* to be distributed among the prisoners. A round of cheers went up for Papa that equaled in enthusiasm that of any operatic audience—cheers that he found, as he remarked, even more rewarding.

We all had a good time in Salsomaggiore. Father, who was in a jolly mood, was more talkative than usual and told stories to amuse us. Assuming that Miss Saer's Italian was sufficiently inadequate, I was too young to understand, and Fofò was old enough to hear, Papa entertained Rina with bawdy jokes. Children, however, have long ears, and a couple of his jokes stuck in my memory. A particularly gross one was about a man who sold his soul to the Devil. When the Devil came to collect, the man's wife, not wanting her husband to burn in hell, struck a bargain with the Devil. She said that in the pitch-dark cellar of the house, she kept an animal never seen by anyone. If the Devil could not guess what it was, he would have to let her husband go. She then went to the cellar, stripped naked, stood on all fours, and, dropping her head below her shoulders, let her long hair hang down like a tail. The Devil was dumfounded and came upstairs cursing. "It has a long tail, but its behind has teeth, it has two udders in the wrong place, and there are two throats but no head!" Even funnier than the joke's crude humor was Father's inimitable sketch of the strange beast, which I managed to have a look at.

In September, Papa left for a series of performances in Austria and Germany. Then he returned to New York, Fofò to the Badia Fiesolana, and Lei and I to Cricklewood, where I spent the usual monotonous months waiting to be reunited with Father.

ON 23 December 1913, the Met performed *La Bohème* in Philadelphia with Caruso as Rodolfo and Frances Alda as Mimì. The role of Colline was sung by the Spanish bass Andrès de Segurola. The performance was responsible for one of the most curious events in Father's career. Many years later, on 2 December 1946, De Segurola spoke of the performance, recording the story on an acetate disc in the KMPC studio in Beverly Hills.

According to De Segurola, he woke up hoarse on the morning of the performance and went to his throat specialist for a treatment before boarding the train. When he joined Caruso in his drawing room on the train for the usual poker game, the tenor said:

"How are you going to sing, Andrea? You are absolutely hoarse! How are you going to sing 'Vecchia zimarra?'" Then he jokingly added: "Don't worry! I will sing it for you."

And he began to sing the aria, imitating the voice of a basso *cantante.*

Before the performance, Caruso prepared an inhalation for De Segurola. In the first two acts, as the basso recalled, "[I sang] not at all well, but at least I filled my role." Colline does not appear in the third act, so he stayed in his dressing room reading the paper. When he was called for the fourth act, he tested his voice—and no sound emerged! He ran to Caruso, who asked the stage manager to hold the curtain and gave the basso another inhalation, but to no avail. De Segurola went onstage but "could not utter a single tone." He began to panic, convinced that a scandal was inevitable. In full view of the audience, he grabbed Papa by the lapel and said:

"Enrico! You have to sing for me! You did it on the train, you are going to do it here."

Now it was Caruso's turn to panic.

"No, I can't, I can't! I don't remember the words, Andrea, don't, don't...!"

"Say yes! You are going to do it!"

And when conductor Giorgio Polacco gave the sign for the aria, Caruso started to sing.

"But not as a tenor!" exclaimed De Segurola on the disc, still awed by the memory. "As a basso *cantante,* with the most beautiful voice that sounded like a cello. It was an experience I will never forget! We went wild about his feat and insisted that he make a record. A few days later, Calvin Child gave me a copy of it."[16]

Frances Alda, eyewitness to the incident, recorded her version for issue on the flip side of the record in 1948. By and large it agrees with De Segurola's account.

The Caruso brothers, Enrico and Giovanni, strolling down Fifth Avenue, ca. 1910. (The men behind them are unidentified.)

Caruso signing autographs in Germany, ca. 1909.

Caruso with his European impresario, Emil Ledner (*at Caruso's left*), in Berlin, 1909. Note the forceful Caruso stride.

Caruso with his "boss"
Giulio Gatti-Casazza of
the Metropolitan
Opera aboard the *Kaiser
Wilhelm II*, 1913.

Caruso holding soprano Frances Alda
(Mrs. Giulio Gatti-Casazza)
on the ship's railing, 1913.

...uso clowning with a dog aboard ship, 1913.

Caruso with a bust of himself, probably in the studio of Filippo Cifariello. Reproduced from the collection of the Library of Congress.

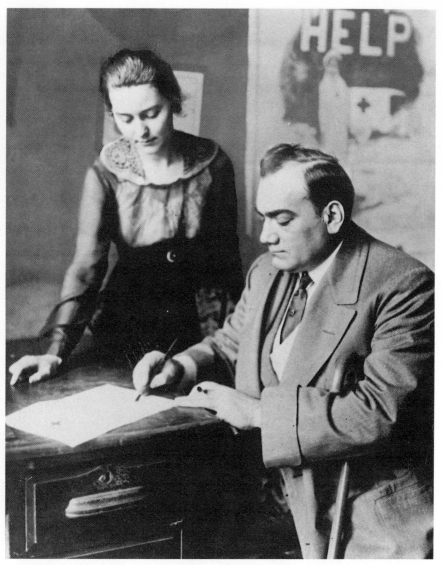

Caruso adding his name to a list of sponsors of his favorite charity, the International Red Cross. Courtesy of Francis Robinson Collection, Special Collections, Vanderbilt University.

Antonio Scotti as Scarpia in Puccini's *Tosca*. The inscription reads: "To Enrico, with affection. Totonno, New York, 1910."

Caruso with his closest friend, baritone Antonio Scotti, ca. 1907.

Large cabinet photo of Caruso, inscribed to "Dear Titta Ruffo, in memory of the memorable evening of *Rigoletto* in Vienna, 6/10/1906. Enrico Caruso." Courtesy of Dr. Ruffo Titta, Jr.

Titta Ruffo in the title role
of Verdi's *Rigoletto.*
Courtesy of Dr. Ruffo
Titta, Jr.

Left to right,
Hipólito Lázaro,
Enrico Caruso, and
Titta Ruffo in their
dressing room
following the double
bill of Mascagni's
Cavalleria rusticana
and Leoncavallo's
Pagliacci in
Montevideo, 1915.

Titta Ruffo and Enrico Caruso listening to the Victrola, 1914. Photography Underwood and Underwood. Courtesy of Metropolitan Opera Association.

oprano Geraldine Farrar bidding
rewell to Berlin in 1905.

Geraldine Farrar as Juliette in
Gounod's *Roméo et Juliette* in
Berlin, ca. 1904. Photography
Gerlach.

Caruso and Geraldine Farrar in Bizet's *Carmen,* ca. 1914. Photography Mishkin.

Later, in 1914, Caruso himself told the story to M. Incagliati, reporter for *Giornale d'Italia*. According to Caruso's account, as the crucial moment of the aria approached, he asked De Segurola:

"How do you feel?"

"Terrible," the bass replied.

"Give me the coat," Caruso said. "I will sing it for you."

"And to the surprise of all," Caruso went on, "especially of Maestro Polacco, who thought I had actually gone mad, I attacked the popular aria, which I had to encore amidst a storm of applause."[17]

Caruso's somewhat embellished version was not reflected in the press. Neither the Philadelphia newspapers nor *Musical America* noted that it was Caruso who had sung the bass aria, nor that it had been repeated.[18]

APART from this historic *La Bohème,* Caruso's stay in New York was uneventful until a burst of drama toward the end. Mildred Meffert, his mistress of five years, brought charges against him for breach of promise. Once again, all the details were aired in the press.

Mrs. Meffert was separated from her husband at the time she met Father in 1908. After their liaison began, "her husband tried to effect a reconciliation, but his effort failed solely on account of Caruso,"[19] declared her lawyer, Irving E. Ziegler. Then followed the summer of 1909 which she spent with Caruso in Europe; after her return, her husband obtained a divorce. It appears that soon after the divorce, Mr. Meffert died in an automobile accident.

Mildred Meffert was not only a beautiful woman, attractive enough to catch Caruso's roving eye, but she was educated in a convent and was an accomplished musician, she spoke several languages, and she had traveled extensively in Europe. Caruso showed her countless attentions and seemed to love her very much.

However, "Mil" made a grave tactical error: After Caruso's separation from Ada in July 1908, she began pressuring him to live up to his promises and marry her. But Enrico Caruso could never be pressured into anything, least of all marriage, and her insistence began to wear on his patience. Prone to histrionics, she once threatened suicide. After a stormy quarrel, she snatched his revolver from a drawer and ran out of the room crying, "I cannot bear it. Farewell!" Father ran after her and tore the gun out of her hand, possibly as much from determination to avoid a scandal as from compassion. He must have been greatly annoyed that his lovely and accommodating "Mil" had turned into a hysterical shrew. His sudden infatuation with Elsa Ganelli in 1911 may have been partially triggered by a desire to extricate himself from the entanglement with Mrs. Meffert. But when the Ganelli affair fell apart, he continued the relationship with "Mil" until March 1913, eight months after he announced his engagement to Rina! On Christmas Eve, 1912, he handed Mildred Meffert a check for $500, a most generous gift for the time. The check, which still exists, was no doubt accompanied by other presents.

There is no record of whether Caruso simply stopped seeing his "Mil" or there was a dramatic parting. The lovers began to confide in their mutual friends about the situation, and someone told Meffert that Caruso was afraid she might use his love letters against him. That, apparently, gave her the clue as to how she could fight back.

On 22 April 1914, she brought suit for breach of promise, asking for $100,000 in damages. "Enrico Caruso has left me a brokenhearted woman, one of the tarnished toys with which the pathway of his life is strewn," she declared in an interview. Her lawyer added that "her association with the tenor has made impossible her return to her family." [20] In her complaint, Mrs. Meffert stated that because of Father's promise of marriage, she had "refused the attentions of all other men and discarded all prospects of a settlement in life." She alleged that on 3 April 1908, Father had promised to marry her. In support of her claim, she was prepared to submit a hundred or so handwritten love letters and postcards, which Father had signed variously as "Enrico Caruso," "Baby," "As Ever, Baby," and "Your Loving Baby." The letters, from New York City and Europe, were addressed to "Mil" and were filled with terms of endearment.

Father should have learned by this time never to put into writing what he did not wish to have read in a court of law!

Father's lawyer, Alfred F. Seligsberg of Wise & Seligsberg, tried to settle the suit out of court. He offered Meffert a fair sum of money (various reports put it at $1,500 or $3,000) for returning the letters, but Meffert's counsel rejected the offer. Shortly after the summons was served, Father went on the Met tour to Atlanta. Meffert's attorney, Ziegler, followed him to discuss the case, but Caruso simply turned over all negotiations to Seligsberg. When the tour was over, Father packed his bags and left for Europe. In the end, Meffert did settle out of court—for $3,000, according to one source, and for "more than twelve times $3,000," according to her lawyer. As part of the settlement, she returned all Caruso's love letters, which he supposedly destroyed.

Father's appearance at Covent Garden in 1914 turned out to be his last London season. I was ten years old and able to enjoy the spectacle of opera, and I was taken to see him in *Aida, Madama Butterfly,* and again in *La Bohème*. Now that I was familiar with the plot of *La Bohème,* I enjoyed it more than in the previous year. Father had taken one of the upper-tier boxes for us. Since Miss Saer was a governess rather than a maid, the social etiquette of upstairs-downstairs London allowed her to dress well. She was tall and decked herself out specially for the opera, piling her blonde hair high on her head. At the last curtain call, Papa looked up toward the box and, putting his hand to his lips, threw me a kiss. All eyes turned in our direction. I was not tall for my age and was scarcely visible in the box. The spectators could see only Miss Saer. It was not surprising that the next day, a London paper carried the headline: "Caruso Blows Kisses to Unknown Blonde in Box."[21]

Miss Saer kept that newspaper clipping for years.

CHAPTER ELEVEN

War Years

AT the beginning, the summer of 1914 was peaceful and enjoyable despite ominous rumors about the imminence of war. The Covent Garden season ended in late June with *Tosca,* and we traveled to Italy for our usual summer vacation. Father was eagerly looking forward to a much-needed rest. He was forty-one, and his capacity for work had not diminished; but the cumulative effect of a very full season had taken its toll. For the first part of the summer, we went directly to Villa Rina in Livorno, where Father was least likely to have to face a stream of visitors. This summer, however, excruciatingly painful headaches overshadowed his vacation. He had suffered from headaches for years, but now they began to increase in frequency, and they were getting worse. The headaches were to stay with him the rest of his life, growing more painful each year. They were not migraines; the muscles on the back of his neck would become hard and stand out like two iron bars, stiffened in a terrible cramp. I can still see him, moaning prostrate on the rattan chaise longue in the *jardin d'hiver,* with Rina massaging the back of his neck. After a long, long time, the muscle tension would ease, and hours later the pain would subside.

In order to relax, Father began to paint again. He made caricatures of the entire household—family, friends, visitors, servants. When my turn came, he looked at my head this way and that and finally settled on my profile. I sat patiently, waiting for the results. I was disappointed when I saw the finished sketch, for he drew me with a long neck. But I had to accept the unflattering reality that the caricature looked just like me. On the bottom of the picture, Papa scribbled, "MIMMI BY HIS FATHER." Then it suddenly occurred to me that I did not have a picture of him, and I asked him to draw me one. I had never asked for a sketch of himself, and Papa seemed pleased. He began to draw and paint. It was fascinating to watch his deft work with the brush—he used it as others would use a pencil. In bold strokes, he created a remarkable likeness of his own face. When he finished the outline, he filled in the flesh tones with watercolor. The whole self-portrait took him only minutes, and when he handed it over, young as I was, I had no doubt that I was holding in my hand one of his best self-caricatures. Since it was made for "domestic consumption," he did not sign it. Then, as an afterthought, he wrote with white crayon his "EC" in the corner and added the date: 1914.

RINA and Papa were very happy together. Rina was deeply in love and delighted to have him all to herself (in a manner of speaking). Her main preoccupation was his comfort and happiness. They were quite affectionate, but they never acted like lovebirds. Papa called her "Rinuccia" ("little Rina"), and she rarely called him anything but "Ghico" or "Chico." When I asked her why she called him that, she explained that it was the diminutive for "Enrico." She must have known what she was talking about, but I have never heard anyone else use this name for the Enricos I have known, including myself. "Ric" or "Rico," yes—but "Ghico"? Never. It is most likely that this, and "Chico" along with "Ghigo," was a pet name the Giachetti sisters had given Papa, for Mother often addressed him thus in her postcards and other correspondence.

Obviously enjoying each other's company, Father and Rina were together most of the time. They played double solitaire in the *jardin d'hiver,* went to the beach, visited with friends, or went to the races. We often ate at a restaurant on the beach that Papa especially liked, possibly because its seaside setting reminded him of Naples. On many occasions, we drove to Antignano or Castiglioncello outside Livorno. Most Sundays, we went to church, usually without Father. I distinctly remember the moment one Sunday morning after Mass when a jealous

husband tried to shoot his wife, who was with another man, and hit
Pietro Mascagni instead, severely wounding him in the head. The
Maestro was just leaving church and walked into the line of fire. Fofò
and I went to pay our respects after Mascagni came home from the
hospital.

When Father was in residence, many famous people came to visit.
The house was always full of celebrities whose names meant very little
to me at the time, and Rina and Father often took me along when they
visited their friends. Thinking back on these encounters, I am sorry I
was too young to appreciate them, or at least to preserve the details of
the experiences in my memory. When we visited Leoncavallo, I didn't
want to go inside the house with the adults, so I played in the garden
until it was time to go home. I must have behaved badly, because
Father and Rina didn't bother to take me along to Puccini's at nearby
Torre del Lago. I recall visiting Mascagni more than once; his villa in
Livorno was two villas down from Rina's.

Occasionally we would go to see the Carusos in Naples, Grandmother Maria and Aunt Assunta. Uncle Giovanni and his family would
join us; then family and friends would go to dine at Castellammare or
Posillipo.

We were in Livorno when the war broke out. Under the provisions of a war clause, Ledner, who had an exclusive contract with
Father until this time, was obliged to cancel his engagements for the
fall of 1914. Father was not accustomed to managers canceling on *him,*
and a tense exchange of letters followed. In the end he realized that the
developments were entirely beyond Ledner's control and expressed
his willingness to waive what he considered his "justifiable claims, in
order not to mar our friendship."[1]

Another singer whose engagements fell victim to the outbreak of
war was Caruso's friend and colleague at the Met, Andrès de Segurola.
He was to appear in a series of *Don Giovanni* performances at the Mozart
Festival in Salzburg organized by Lilli Lehmann. Not knowing where
to reach De Segurola, Lehmann sent a telegram to Caruso asking him
to advise the bass of the cancellation if he knew of his whereabouts.
The telegram was addressed simply to "Enrico Caruso, Famous Tenor,
Italy." It reached Papa with no difficulty.

Father, who apparently knew that De Segurola was in Milan,
managed to contact him and invited him to spend a week with us. He
had a grand time with Papa, as he later recalled in his memoirs.

Although Italy remained neutral for the time being, it was decided
at a family council that it was best for Miss Saer and me to stay in Italy.

Father felt that in the adversities ahead, the family should be together. Because the war was expected to be over in a few months at the most, the possibility of moving to America with Papa did not even come up. No one foresaw that the hostilities would last so long; and in the end, Lei and I remained in Italy five years, from the summer of 1914 until August 1919.

ON 19 October 1914, Caruso sang a benefit performance at the Costanzi in Rome. It was a wonderful opportunity for the entire family to see him perform. We stayed at the Hotel Flora and were terribly excited about the whole affair. Father did not take it lightly either. He had not sung in Italy since 1903, and he knew the Italian public would judge him mercilessly.

The gala event was conducted by Toscanini. It began with the *William Tell* Overture, followed by Act II of *Madama Butterfly,* with Lucrezia Bori and Giuseppe de Luca, and Act III of *Ernani,* with Mattia Battistini and Egidio Cunego. The highlight of this operatic songfest was a complete performance of *Pagliacci,* which Caruso performed with Bori, De Luca, Angelo Bada, and Riccardo Tegani. The performance fulfilled all expectations, and Toscanini, for once yielding to the pressure of the public, allowed "Vesti la giubba," a Caruso hallmark, to be encored. The audience went absolutely roaring wild; I have never heard anything like it before or since. At the age of ten, I finally began to enjoy opera. I was caught up in the ovation and reacted with the rest of the audience, applauding madly. Auntie Rina stopped me immediately.

"We are family. The family does not applaud," she admonished.

The performance had a still deeper effect on Fofò. This was the first—and only—time he heard Father in the theater, and the experience left a lifelong impression. Fofò wrote:

> As far as Father's voice and artistic efforts were concerned, I was like the proverbial shoemaker's son who went barefoot because his father made shoes for everyone else. During the years I spent with him, I had few opportunities to hear him sing. When I could have heard him almost daily, I was too small to formulate an idea of his artistry, and in my boyhood I met Papa only during the three months of the year [when] he came to Italy to rest. During this period, he continuously studied and reviewed his repertory, which made his

vacation anything but complete relaxation. I knew his voice
well, even though while studying he would never open up
except on the rarest occasions.

Then came the benefit performance in Rome given for
the aid of Italian refugees who had escaped from the regions of
the military conflict. It was a terrible experience for me.
Through my binoculars I saw his hand tremble as he struck the
big drum upon his entrance in *Pagliacci,* and in that moment I
hated the stage, the theater, singing, everything. I was seized
by such anxiety that I spent the entire performance in the
antechamber of the box covering my ears. I removed my
hands only when the noise told me that the shouting,
applauding, and arm-waving audience was according my
father a triumph the like of which I had never seen. It was
about eleven years since he had last sung in Italy, and there had
been malevolent comments about the condition of his voice.
Hearing that ovation, I was in tears with joy and emotion, and
enormously proud of my father, not so much for his success as
for having disproved the malicious rumors. But this experience was such a strain on my nerves that I swore never to hear
my father sing again, to see him at the mercy of the public, the
victim of the terrific strain of a moral obligation toward his
audience.

The October 20 issue of the *Messaggero* reviewed the great evening
at the Costanzi, referring to the malevolent rumors:

> Various legends were spread about that dared to claim that
> the passage of time had not spared his marvelous vocal cords,
> and Caruso was no longer the artist whom we once acclaimed
> with such enthusiasm. Last night's test dispersed the slightest
> doubt about the merits of the singer, because in the triumph
> accorded to him with the unrestrainable outburst of the
> crowd, he has once again emerged, just as eleven or so years
> earlier, as the greatest among all the tenors on the interna-
> tional musical scene.

The review went on to analyze Caruso's singing, remarking on the
warmth of his "prodigious voice," which had become heavier,
although "the velvet remained fresh." The critic praised his expressive phrasing, the conviction and moving passion of his delivery, and
the refinement that had brought his artistry to the point of "incom-

parable perfection."

Franco Raineri, reporter for the *Giornale d'Italia,* generously praised Father's acting, adding:

> But the voice! "Ridi Pagliaccio!" [was] the moment of yesterday's performance that will remain indelibly with everyone. A moment too brief [which] the great mass of the public wanted to relive.... We don't remember ever hearing, or seeing, such applause. The entire audience [rose to] their feet, clapped their hands, screamed frenetically, and Caruso, moved, really moved—as those standing close by can attest—pointed at his heart, profoundly upset and shaken by this powerful manifestation accorded to him by an Italian audience, for the first time after so many years![2]

THE Rome *Pagliacci* came late in the fall. When it was over, Papa barely had time to say good-bye to us before he had to leave for the Metropolitan season in New York. He took an express train to Naples and from the train station went directly to the harbor, where he visited briefly with his stepmother, Maria, and his sister, Assunta, at the pier. Then a motorboat whisked him off to the waiting ship, the *Regina d'Italia.* When Father came on board with Armand Lecomte (his "man of affairs" at the time), Mario Fantini (his valet), and another servant, he met De Segurola, who had sailed from Genoa. Years later, around 1934, the basso told me a story about the trip, a tale also recounted in his memoirs.

> As soon as we saw his motor boat approach, all the passengers waved their handkerchief to him. "A marvelous sight from the distance," he told us afterwards. When he stepped on deck, debonair as always, we greeted him with a tremendous ovation. The evening before the ship was to dock in Gibraltar to take on coal, finishing our usual poker game, Caruso said: "Andrea, let us have lunch together in Gibraltar tomorrow. You will find some place where we can have a *paella* I like so much."
>
> We did just that, and after lunch we went for a carriage ride. It was hot, the horses' hooves raised a lot of dust, and we got quite thirsty. The coachman suggested a nearby tavern, and we crossed *La Linea,* the boundary between the English

possession and Spain. We soon found the place, a colorful spot
that looked like a set straight out of *Carmen*. We ordered some
cold *gassosas* (soft drinks). While we were waiting for the
drinks, we noticed some colorful posters announcing the
coming *corridas*. One of these showed a toreador dressed in his
resplendent costume. Enrico asked me if I knew who he was. I
did not, so I asked the host, who could have played Lillas Pastia
without makeup or costume. My innocent question made him
explode.

"Who is that?" he shot back. "Are you Spanish?"

When I answered in the affirmative he became quite
upset.

"What, *Señor*? You are Spanish and you don't know the
great toreador, the famous Guerrita? Guerrita, the bravest,
most daring *torero* in all of Spain! *Carramba,* he earns ten
thousand pesetas for every bullfight!"

I translated his fireworks to Caruso, whose reaction was:
"How much is ten thousand pesetas?"

"About two thousand dollars," I answered.

"Well, tell the *hombre* I get more than that for one appearance, and I don't have to face bulls! Some cows once in a while,
but I don't have to kill them!"

I translated for the excitable proprietor Caruso's remark.

"Very funny," laughed the innkeeper, shaking his two-
hundred and fifty pounds of jelly. "No, *Señor*! Nobody in the
world makes as much money as Guerrita!"

"It's the truth!" I confirmed it for Enrico. The man paused
for a second, then, shaking his fat finger at Enrico, he
exploded:

"*Madre de Dios,* you are Caruso!"[3]

MY lessons with Red in England must have given me a solid academic
foundation. When I entered the public school in Florence, I was ahead
of my classmates in every subject except Italian and Latin. I then
finished three years of Italian in one, and by the end of the second year,
I was doing very well in Latin too. Because of the circumstances, I grew
up fully bilingual, without a foreign accent in either language, except
that my English was "Veddy, veddy British, don't you know, old chap."
All in all, public school was a pleasant change after the long sessions
alone with Red, and the daily exchanges with classmates of my own age
helped me learn the skills of relating to others.

At home, my only companions were my brother and my Uncle Umberto. (Umberto was two years younger than Fofò, but the quirky ways of our family made him an uncle to us.) Rina rarely talked to me, and we never had conversations. Even Lei would instruct me or talk *to* me rather than talking with me. No one asked me about my days or wanted to see my report card, so long as my schoolwork was passing. During my first year at Livorno, I asked Rina if I could have a bicycle—both Fofò and Umberto had theirs. She promised that if I passed my exams, she would buy me one. I did—she didn't. From that day on, I never trusted promises. Papa would talk to me occasionally, but I did not have much interest in him at that time; thus our relationship did not make giant strides. Once I complained that I never got any praise, only scoldings.

"Why should I praise you?" said Papa. "You did well, there is nothing to say. When you do something wrong, you'll hear about it."

I was the child who wasn't there, until I got into mischief. Then I was punished, usually by Aunt Rina. She was determined to control us, and in the end she did. I remember her yelling at me:

"*Se non ti pieghi, ti spezzo!*" ("If you don't bend, I will break you!")

So I bent for a while. Whenever I did anything wrong, the dramatic soprano voice would echo around the house.

"Mimmi! Come here!"

"Yes, Auntie."

"Did you do such and such?"

"Yes, Auntie."

Pow! Her hand would fly across my face faster than the eye could follow. She always wore a couple of rings, and the back of the metal would clonk against my cheekbones. After the blow, one was supposed to say "*Grazie, Zia*" ("Thank you, Auntie"), otherwise there came another blow from the opposite direction, backhand. I took the cuffs manfully for a few years but resented them greatly, because very often Fofò or Umberto had pulled a prank and left me holding the bag. By the time I was nearly thirteen, I had had enough. Once, as I stood before Rina aware of what was coming, I instinctively lifted my arm to shield my face. Her flying arm struck my elbow with such force that she hurt herself badly, and her arm swelled up. In the end she had to go to Salsomaggiore for mudpacks to bring the swelling down. She realized from the experience that I was too old for that kind of punishment, and she never struck me again.

I must have known my paternal grandfather and maternal grandmother, but I have no memories of them. Marcellino died in 1908, and

Giuseppina in 1909 when I was five and already living in London. So the only grandparent I remember was my maternal grandfather, Guido Giachetti. He was a crusty old gentleman and lived on to old age in good health. We spent many years together under the same roof. We got along well, although the traditional grandfather-grandson relationship never developed between us. He was much too strict and serious for my taste, and I was much too immature for him. He called me hard-headed and stubborn because I never did what he bade me do. I took offense at the usual insignificant things, and my grandfather, in the way of adults, never understood why. For instance, I resented that I was not allowed to whistle, because in his opinion only ruffians whistled.

His second wife, Grandmother Teresa, ran the household and was in charge of the maids. I can still hear the keys of all the cabinets, closets, and pantries jangling on her belt. Guido took care of the maintenance and repair work around the house. The large garage of the villa had a small apartment upstairs which served as Guido's workshop. He was very creative and made all sorts of useful things and gadgets for the house: chicken coops, rabbit hutches, bookshelves, gunracks, even a "corker" that made the cork slide *into* the bottle more easily. He felt responsible for the physical functioning of the household. "*Ci penso io!*" ("I'll take care of it!") was his standard phrase. In everything he did, Grandfather Guido was very precise. His tools were hung on hooks on a board attached to the wall, with the outline of every tool drawn on it to ensure that each was in its proper place. After Italy entered World War I, he mounted huge maps on the walls in his workshop. Here he kept track of advances and retreats with pins bearing tiny black-and-yellow flags for the Austrian troops and the tricolor for the Italians. One could follow the troop movements as the front line undulated back and forth on his maps. Guido also read a great deal; he was a well-informed, educated man. He spent the last decade of his life as the librarian of the Florence *fascio,* the Fascist Party headquarters.

With her parents looking after the household, Rina was able to lead a life of leisure. She had everything a lady of her status could wish: an elegant villa, beautiful clothes, jewelry, carriages, automobile, servants. Everything she owned she had earned with her singing with the exception of her marvelous jewelry collection, which was made up largely of gifts from past admirers and from Father. To put it plainly, Rina was the kind of woman who appreciated being appreciated by the men in her life, in material as well as physical and emotional terms.

Rina unquestionably had a prima donna's flair and presence, but she commanded respect by behaving like a lady rather than a prima donna. She was always well dressed, even around the house. I remember her magnificent hats, each larger than the next. She spent her time shopping, visiting friends or entertaining at the villa, or going to the racetracks. We also used to go to the local baths, the Bagni Pancaldi, or the Bagni all'Ardenza, where natural swimming pools formed by reefs were washed by continuously flowing sea water. Father loved to soak there. He swam too, but with more vigor than style, and for only short distances. Exercise for exercise's sake was anathema to him. After a good swim, we would dry ourselves, put on our *accappatoio* (a hooded terry robe) and sandals, and go to the restaurant on the *rotonda,* the large platform at the end of the pier.

Father liked to be photographed at the wheel of an automobile, but he never learned to drive. Thus, in spite of his bad experience with a chauffeur, he always had to have one in his service. The driver in his employ before and during the war was Fulvio Fava, who was also an excellent mechanic. Puttering in the machine shop of the garage, he designed an automatic transmission for the Lancia. When Father came home for the summer, Fava asked him to finance his invention. It would have cost some 3,000 lire (about $600). Papa was not interested in business ventures and turned the request down.

Fava was employed year-round. He drove Rina to visit her friends in the neighborhood or to shop in Florence. When we heard the air-powered horn of her big Fiat at the outskirts of Livorno, we knew that dinner could be served in thirty minutes.

Rina was always surrounded by rich young men who would fawn over her, much to her delight. Also, with or without Caruso, she liked to entertain. People floated in and out, appearing and disappearing as in a sideshow. I remember only a few of them: Malenchini, the mayor of Livorno, whose villa was next to Rina's; the lawyer Ceola; a family named Saccorotti, who had two pretty girls, Lidia and Giovanna. I also remember a wonderful Jewish couple named Fontanella, who played a vital part in Rina's life in later years.

My aunt's speaking voice was very rich and distinctive, suggesting the voice of a trained singer. When she got mad at one of us and began to shout, her penetrating soprano could be heard a mile away. But, like Papa, she was soft-spoken most of the time.

Thinking back on the years we spent with Rina, I find it inexplicable that music played almost no part in our lives. We did have a Victrola which I used more than anyone else, listening to "my kind of music"—loud and bombastic military marches. Once, a fresh batch of Caruso records arrived from America, and Rina played them for her friends. Everyone praised them, but the music was completely lost on me. At my young age, my taste leaned to Sousa and Pryor; I thought "The Stars and Stripes Forever" was the finest piece of music I had ever heard. There was a beautiful piano at the villa, but I don't think I ever heard Rina practicing at the keyboard. (This was my domain, for I was forced to take piano lessons.) She never spoke about singing or did vocalises, although sometimes she gave impromptu recitals to her local admirers and friends. Undoubtedly she still had a fine voice, but at close quarters and to my inexperienced ears, she sounded like a screeching hen.

Whenever Rina's guests made polite remarks about her singing and suggested that she should resume her career, she would wave them aside with the words: "*Sono tempi passati.*" ("Those times are gone.") Her life as a singer was a thing of the past. We never knew why she had abandoned her career in her thirtieth year, presumably at the peak of her powers. The subject simply did not come up, neither while we lived under the same roof nor at any time later. It may be that my aunt's singing was chiefly a way of showing Ada that anything she could do, Rina could do better. Perhaps it was just a means to earn a good living and amass wealth. Once Rina had the material things she wanted, she was no longer interested in "working." Her earnings were well invested. In addition to the house in Livorno, she had land holdings, a farm, and another small villa in Fiesole above Florence. Another possibility is that Rina developed vocal problems that were simply too difficult to overcome. And yet, the end of her career closely coincided with the renewal of her liaison with Father; and Fofò wrote that "Rina gave up her career to make a home for Enrico's children." If this is correct, Father brought to a premature end two outstanding careers: my aunt's as well as my mother's.

LE PANCHE was refurnished to accommodate the family group. Although Father avoided the villa, it was to be our home base in the winter while he was gone. Bellosguardo was too big, and workmen were again busy with renovations and refurbishings ordered by Papa. Because of Rina's intervention, Fofò was finally allowed to leave the hated Badia and attend the *liceo* in Florence instead.

I think the years he spent under Rina's guardianship were the happiest of his life. He loved Rina, perhaps more than a young man should love an aunt, and the two were very close. Fofò was Rina's pet and could do no wrong. She bought him the best clothes, paid his debts, gave him the biggest portions. When Rina took a bath, the maid would line the tub with a sheet. Rina would immerse and cover herself, then Fofò would pull up a chair, and they would have a long chat while Rina soaked. It was surely not the customary thing to do, but ours was a most unusual family, with not one average, normal person in it with the possible exception of my grandparents, Teresa and Guido.

CHAPTER TWELVE

Buenos Aires

T HE winter came and went. In spite of predictions to the contrary, the war showed no signs of ending. The possibility that Italy would enter the war became an inevitability, and our apprehensions grew daily.

The year 1915 was a busy one for Papa. He returned to Europe twice, first to sing at Monte Carlo in March and April, and then in September to sing at the Teatro Dal Verme in Milan. Sandwiched between the two engagements was the South American season in Buenos Aires and Montevideo from May through August. So, in effect, he spent the whole year working; apart from the long sea voyages, only the month of October was a time of rest.

Upon his arrival in Buenos Aires, Father settled at the Hotel Plaza. Shortly thereafter he received a cable telling him Assunta had died of tuberculosis on 1 June 1915. His sister's death must have been a blow he had to overcome in order to give his best to the Argentinians. He had not been heard in Buenos Aires in twelve years, and this was to be his first appearance at the new Teatro Colón, which had opened in 1908. It was a gala season with a stellar roster. In addition to Caruso, the list of tenors included such illustrious names as Bernardo de Muro and

Hipólito Lázaro. Among the ladies were Adelina Bertana, Gilda Dalla Rizza, Amelita Galli-Curci, Rosa Raisa, Tina Poli-Randaccio, Hina Spani, and Geneviève Vix. The lower male voices were represented by Mario Sammarco, Giuseppe Danise, and Titta Ruffo, often called the "King of the Baritones" or the "Caruso of Baritones" in my father's lifetime. De Segurola described Ruffo's voice as "phenomenal" and compared "the amazing volume of his voice to the imposing mass of Niagara Falls—no end in sight."[1]

The two operatic superstars held each other in high esteem. Critics often commented that when they sang together, it was like a singing contest, and it may have seemed so to an audience. The two did not try to impress each other, but in order to live up to each other's expectations, they had to give their utmost. This clearly comes across in their recording of "Sì, pel ciel" from *Otello,* that paragon of recorded duets made a year earlier in 1914, which has never been surpassed for sheer vocal opulence. Listening to that record, time and again I must remind myself that while Ruffo was the veteran of many *Otello* performances, Caruso never sang the title role in his life; yet his rendition of the music is as artistically ripe and interpretatively correct as the delivery of the formidable baritone. Posterity should be grateful that this excerpt has survived. The other selection recorded at the same session, the *Gioconda* duet, was unsatisfactory, and the matrices of the multiple takes were destroyed.

At the age of forty-two, Father was still in full control of his vocal powers; yet facing Ruffo again, the only singer who could be regarded as his equal in the Italian repertory, must have been a challenge as well as an artistic pleasure. The thirty-eight-year-old Titta Ruffo was in his absolute prime and was a favorite with the Argentine public, which was clearly reflected in the reviews. In *Pagliacci,* Caruso and Ruffo were paired in their best roles, and the result was a predictable triumph for both artists. At the Colón, they sang only Act I as part of a gala performance, but on August 16 they performed the complete opera in Montevideo. This was the only time they ever appeared in the entire work together. Poor Hipólito Lázaro, who sang an excellent Turiddu in *Cavalleria rusticana,* was but a minor attraction in what became a curtain-raiser to the main event of the evening. This is painfully underscored by the treatment accorded a backstage photo taken after the performance showing Lázaro, Caruso, and Ruffo together: In most reproductions, this famous picture is cropped, with Lázaro omitted as if he were a blemish.

ON June 18, apparently before Ruffo arrived in town,[2] Caruso was scheduled to participate in a benefit performance at the Colón in Buenos Aires, an endless operatic orgy of which the first act of *Pagliacci* was the main attraction. This was the occasion of an incident unique to his career. Fortunately, the events were recorded from the diverse vantage points of at least two professional reviewers as well as a competent amateur eyewitness.

The incident was briefly described in the June 19 issue of *La Prensa*. *La Nación* of the same day devoted much more space to it, and the portion of the review relating to Caruso is worth quoting in full.

> The festival organized yesterday at the Teatro Colón for the benefit of the Pious Society of the Ladies of Mercy achieved such a level of artistic success, due to an unforeseen event, that we can safely say it can hardly be expected ever to recur.
>
> It was, in fact, an extraordinary occurrence. An audience, as select as it was numerous, gathered to hear an interesting music program that, if not novel, was at least assured outstanding execution. Orchestral numbers were to be played by the Municipal Orchestra conducted by Maestro Malvagni, vocal selections by the principal artists of the lyric company of the Teatro Colón: Mmes. Vix, Dalla Rizza, Frascani, Raisa, Spani, Melza [i.e., Melsa], and Messrs. Genzardi, Lázaro, Berardi. There were also dance numbers on the program, . . . the first act of *Pagliacci* sung by Mme. Roggero [i.e., Ruggero], and Messrs. Caruso, Sammarco, Caronna, and Nardi, with an act of *Aida* to end it all.
>
> Such a program in itself would have augured a successful evening, had it not been for a fortuitous event that infused added enthusiasm into an evening not without its measure of surprise.
>
> Part of the program had been completed with most encouraging results. . . . The first act of *Pagliacci* was about to begin when *Señor* Lázaro appeared in front of the curtain to announce that *Signor* Danise, the baritone who was to sing the role of Tonio, was indisposed. A shudder swept through the audience, which feared that the act might have to be canceled, but *Señor* Lázaro continued, saying that *Signor* Caruso had agreed to sing the prologue of the work. The excitement at such a happening was enormous. The public applauded, and

Señor Lázaro can safely consider his own the ovations that followed his brief announcement. . . .

With score in hand, which if not indispensable was at least helpful, *Signor* Caruso sang the famous selection, and was able to give it such meaning and deliver it with so much heart and soul in his proper *tessitura* that it was fully comfortable for the beautiful voice and capable diction of the artist. The audience hardly waited for the final notes before bursting into clamorous applause, shouts of approval, and acclamation. The ovation lasted so long that when the curtain finally rose, there were still sounds of it in the hall.

The performance of the work itself went much as we have already reported in the past. The audience was once again indulgent toward some of the singers and recognized the true worth of Caruso's final aria, acknowledging his inimitable ability to bring into the trite phrases of the "Ridi Pagliaccio!" the anguished and desperate feelings flowing from the actions of the character. Another ovation greeted him, and he had to take six curtain calls. . . .

Thus, the audience enjoyed a rare treat that could be duplicated only with great difficulty: the prologue of *Pagliacci* sung by Caruso. The event, which may well turn out to be unique, was truly a dream come true.

This remarkable episode was witnessed by a young university student and future professor, Florentino V. Sanguinetti. In a letter to his friend Hiram Fontana in Rosario, Argentina, he recapitulated his experience in great detail. The letter is significant not only because it is the account of a knowledgeable listener, but also because it was written immediately after the event, when Sanguinetti was still under the spell of strong first impressions. In addition to describing the surprising events, it was meant to tell his friend what to expect when Caruso later appeared with the Colón ensemble in Rosario. Sanguinetti wrote:

19 June 1915. 1 a.m.

Dear Hiram:

A few days before coming here I received your kind letter, whose answer I postponed until I might have something interesting to tell you. So, still possessed by the profound impressions gathered only a few hours ago when listening to the supreme harmonies of Caruso, I will try to convey some of this to your soul, eager to enjoy the art of that rare human privilege. The kind of spectacle given at the Colón you will know from the newspapers. Along with the rest of the audience I arrived there, ready to hear the great tenor, the program confected for the occasion being incidental. The emotion was intense, and all fell silent when the tenor Lázaro appeared and announced that because Sammarco was ill, *Signor* Caruso, in a glowing gesture of comradeship and consideration, was prepared to perform in his stead. You can imagine the amazement of the audience and the noisy chatter that swept through the hall before the orchestra attacked the first notes of the immortal prologue—and no one can describe the anguish of the moment when Caruso, with great control and raising the register, uttered that "Si può?" [making this one] of the unforgettable nights.

His voice is as dark as a baritone's, but above all, his was such a noble gesture, his feeling and acting were so deeply felt, and he put such warmth into the role that before the end, the final chords were drowned in a formidable ovation. The rest of the act of *Pagliacci* did not offer greater enchantments, and only Caruso, without makeup and acting very natural, dominating all with a detailed perfection, gave color and movement to the scene, confronting the impatience of the audience which anxiously awaited the final ineffable aria: and then came the *romanza*. And Caruso sang, and I can only say that there are no words nor means to describe those moments.

Tears poured down the faces of the audience. All breasts burned with fervid emotion. Fingers curled and uncurled and little by little, as the scene rose to its climax, so the listeners rose to their feet, finally bursting out with frenetic enthusiasm at Canio's last sob.

When you have lived through such an unforgettable quarter hour, you will be able to appreciate the well-deserved prestige of the artist and feel the most tender sensations of your lifetime. I followed with my opera glasses, my ears, and my soul the voice of Caruso, and I believe that God has bestowed on an exceptional throat the added boon of a superior spirit and intelligence. Caruso feels, weeps, sings, shouts, and curses humanly, that is, effortlessly, naturally, and with inimitable realism. He performs the second part of "Vesti la giubba" with beauty, talent, and a sense of nightmare, all fantastic. One has to watch his acting to realize that no one can match him at singing from the heart, at incarnating his role with the real gestures of the character. In the theater, even in the presence of the great tragedians, I have never felt as true a sensation as that of today. I actually shared the cares and the pain of the clown, and I throbbed with his indignation and wept for his misfortune. . . .

The voice of Caruso is full-bodied, velvety, possessing an enchanting smoothness and an open range that is free, without the embarrassments of a Lázaro or a De Muro, who show the effort it takes them to sing in a timbre they still do not control. Caruso sings fluently, simply, never losing that freshness and charm that connoisseurs relish. He phrases so correctly and with such complete purity that although I do not really know Italian, I can recall the majority of the words of the libretto.[3]

This vivid report conveys the magnificence of the Caruso voice, vintage 1915. One factual detail, however, requires explanation. The reviewer for the June 19 *La Prensa* wrote that Caruso had volunteered to sing the prologue for Giuseppe Danise, while according to Sanguinetti, he replaced Mario Sammarco. This discrepancy is explained by the son of the writer, Dr. Horacio Sanguinetti, in an article that appeared in 1979 in his magazine *Ayer y Hoy de la Opera:*

The first act of Leoncavallo's opera according to the program was to be sung by Caruso, Mme. Roggero, and the baritone Sammarco. At the last moment Sammarco became ill, and they rushed to recruit Danise to replace him. But he also was unwell, and although he was willing to mark the role, combining singing with miming gestures, he did not relish tackling the prologue, a perilous showpiece. "I will do it," said Caruso, so that when Hipólito Lázaro came onstage to announce the change, the audience, at first fearing cancellation, gave free rein to its joy.[4]

In what key did Caruso sing the piece? Unaltered, as written, or transposed into the tenor range? Independently, both the reviewer for *La Nación* and the author of the private letter indicated that the aria was transposed. If this conclusion is correct, it speaks for the musicianship of the Municipal Orchestra players that at a moment's notice and without prior rehearsal, they could execute the transposition to the satisfaction of the demanding audience of the Colón.[5]

THE season that started so well was marred by an old specter: In the third act of *Lucia di Lammermoor,* Caruso cracked on a high note. In the main, the gallant Argentine audience and the critics simply noted the mishap and forgave him. An undated newspaper clipping in my collection, probably from *La Prensa,* gave this assessment:

> [Caruso's delivery] possessed admirable expression, and he sang with rare eloquence. His Edgardo was outstanding for its spontaneous emotion, for the inner feelings that imbued the singing—and we arrived at the last hurdle, the "Tu che a Dio." The first phrase emerged with moving charm, with an accent of sorrow and in a voice that glowed. A few measures into the aria itself, a crucial note failed horribly! The hall shuddered in an exclamation of surprise and pity. The tenor continued to sing but [was] unable to clear a frightening threat of a frog [in his throat].
>
> To some ears, the last inflection of voice that fades away with Edgardo's last breath did sound suspiciously like a croak. Then the curtain came down, and applause broke out which recalled the tenor twice to the footlights. However, at his second curtain call, some whistles, which had previously been weak, suddenly shrilled over the heads of the audience like a whiplash. At that, the hall, which was already emptying out, reacted: In the boxes, the stalls, and the balconies, the public, following the lead of the ladies present, protested against the insulting catcalls and applauded loud and long, but Caruso refused to return.
>
> We too applauded, out of respect for an illustrious artist whose career has been so glorious for Italian art and because we considered that an insignificant misfortune, that proves nothing, should not be allowed to tarnish or eclipse all the talent that the artist had brought to his performance of the role as a whole. Because it was that talent that counted and not a single doubtful note.

One group of ladies in the audience were so outraged at the incident that they sent Caruso a testimonial letter of support, insisting that they wanted to hear him in *Lucia* again and were quite certain he would be "a sublime Edgardo."[6] It was rumored that the catcalls were perpetrated by the claque accountable to the impresario Walter Mocchi, and at his signal. An anonymous letter Father received lends credence to that supposition.

Buenos Aires, 28 July 1915

Most kind and great Caruso,

I cannot remain silent about the vicious act the management has done to you.

I can assure you that the adverse criticism of this evening was inspired and paid for by that fine pair of oxen, Mocchi and Da Rosa.

I am a friend of yours, an insider to all that happens in the theater, and cannot sign myself otherwise than

Napoli [Naples]

Although it is strange to think that an impresario would campaign against his own star, this was entirely in Walter Mocchi's character. Perhaps the impresario wanted to get even for the high fees he had to pay Caruso, or perhaps he was simply in a malicious frame of mind. Whatever the reason, Mocchi thrived on intrigue and was the proverbial "snake in the grass." Two decades later, he denounced the other star of his company, Titta Ruffo, to the fascist authorities in Italy. The baritone was briefly incarcerated, on an order of arrest personally signed by Mussolini.

The engagement in Buenos Aires had its drama on a personal level as well. Mother had settled in this city, and she and Father met for the first time since the Milan trial of 1910.

AFTER Ada Giachetti returned to Italy from New York in January 1909, the cash payment she received and Caruso's promise of a monthly check enabled her to devote the year to rebuilding her voice and preparing to resume her career. Her first engagement of note was during the Carnival season of 1909–10 in Genoa. On December 29, she sang Maddalena di Coigny in *Andrea Chénier* at the Teatro Carlo Felice. Her other appearance in this season was as Ania in Franco Leoni's *Tzigana*. In 1910 she sang in Vienna, and before the first Milan trial of the same year, she appeared in Athens. She spent the winter months in São Paulo as the leading singer of the Italian Lyric Company, performing the title roles of *Aida, Tosca,* and *La Gioconda;* Leonora in *Trovatore;* and Amelia in *Un Ballo in maschera*. The company was second-rate, but in all probability this was the only engagement she could obtain at the time. Being the featured prima donna of the troupe and singing all the plum roles, she had no reason to complain.

Unfortunately, the ten-year hiatus in her singing career and the inevitable aging process had taken their toll; she was unable to rebuild her voice to its former glory. It is also possible that she had not allowed herself enough time to fully retrain her voice. In any case, on a wet, inhospitable evening, she opened the São Paulo season with *Aida* on 23 December 1910. The reviewer for *O Estade do São Paulo* praised her performance but observed that the audience reception was reserved.

> The honors of the night went clearly to *Señora* Ada Giachetti, who sang the title role. The artist, it is true, does not have a voice of outstanding freshness, but on the other hand it is velvety and full-bodied, even throughout its range, unwaveringly on key, and handled with great artistry. In the course of the opera, she brought to bear all these qualities.... The public might well have been more generous toward the artist by applauding her with greater warmth, but we are certain that at future operas it will remedy this fault. (*O Estade do São Paulo,* 24 December 1910)

If Ada's Aida failed to earn her much-needed recognition, her Tosca was even less successful. The critic for the same paper wrote that "although she did not sing the role as well as she had sung Aida, she still shone, especially in the first-act duet with the tenor. Her 'Vissi d'arte' did not get the applause it deserved because of an unjustified indifference of the public" (2 January 1911). She enjoyed a better reception in *Il Trovatore:* "She sang the part of Leonora excellently," wrote the music critic for *O Estade de São Paulo.*[7] But the review of *Un Ballo in maschera* lumped her with Adalgisa Minotti, who sang Oscar, mentioning only that the two were "well cast and earned the applause the public gave time and again to the two ladies."[8] As Gioconda, "she brought an impressive dramatic quality to the part as was to be expected, and used her supple and velvety voice to great effect."[9] The "Suicidio" of the last act was much applauded, but the audience did not call for an encore.

Ada then repeated her Aida and Gioconda at the Teatro Apollo in Rio de Janeiro and also appeared in *Africana.* Her next role was Santuzza in *Cavalleria rusticana* at the Palace Theater in the same city. Concluding her engagement in Rio in early March, she traveled to Buenos Aires for a series of performances at the Teatro Nuevo—not at the prestigious new Teatro Colón. She opened again with *Aida,* and her reviews were similar to those she received in São Paulo.

> *Señora* Giachetti, the main star of the company, was

received with flattering enthusiasm. She possesses a graceful figure and an elegant carriage as well as good stage presence. Her voice is sonorous in the middle register and has no vibration in the upper, which may make it appear at some points a trifle tremulous (*temblorosa*), but this may well have been due to nerves that are always to be expected on an opening night. However that may be, she is an artist of great talent who will always be heard with pleasure, and she earned the best ovations of the evening. (*La Prensa,* 17 March 1911)

Other roles followed, among them Santuzza. In the latter, the *La Prensa* critic reported, Ada "confirmed the warm reception she had received on opening night";[10] but soon afterward, she became indisposed due to some illness, and a soprano named Migliardi had to take over the role.

Her next stop was the Urquiza in Montevideo, and she also appeared at La Plata, Rosario, Mendoza, Santa Fe, and Cordova, singing in *Aida, L'Africana,* and *La Gioconda,* and possibly performing other roles in her repertoire. She then returned to Buenos Aires, this time to the Teatro Coliseo, where she sang several performances of *La Gioconda, Aida,* and *Cavalleria rusticana.* In all likelihood, there were other performances in this year and the next, but the only appearance that could be traced is a *Carmen* at the Teatro Coliseo in Buenos Aires on 13 November 1913. On this occasion, Ada's Don José was the twenty-eight-year-old Aureliano Pertile. *La Prensa* reviewed the performance on the following day, saying that "*Señora* Giachetti successfully performed the difficult title role both vocally and as far as characterization is concerned. The public applauded her as much as the tenor Pertile."

It must be mentioned that Ada was offered the role of Carmen in Naples as early as 1897. As she later told an interviewer, "I studied Carmen, and I really wanted to sing that role, but as the day of the performance drew near, a strange fear took hold of me, and I did not sing Carmen in Naples" (*A Noite,* Rio de Janeiro, 4 March 1938). Ironically, Carmen was the last new role Ada undertook and possibly the last performance of her career, which came to an end near her thirty-ninth birthday.

Reading between the lines of the reviews, which were mixed, one must conclude that her voice had lost its bloom. She had trouble with her top notes, and she may have developed a wobble. It is also possible that her voice had become heavier and that it was artistic exigency that had led her to explore new repertory with a lower *tessitura*. Short-term solutions were Carmen and the return to the *verismo* role of Santuzza. It would be interesting to know whether she retired from the stage for a second time—probably in the year 1914—because of a lack of engagements or because she herself recognized that she had reached a stage of irreversible vocal decline.

Eventually she became a voice teacher, but she did not give up singing entirely. The flamboyant British impresario Joseph Fenston writes in his autobiography that in the 1920s, he encountered a "grand old lady" singing "Vissi d'arte" in a cabaret in Buenos Aires. He praised her singing and asked, "You have been an opera singer, no?" She told him with pride: "Yes. I am Giachetti."[11]

BY 1915, Mother had clearly retired from the stage. She was living alone in Buenos Aires and depended on Father for financial support.

It would be interesting to know which of my parents took the initiative in arranging to meet. Their encounter must have been deeply emotional for them both. It has come down to us in the family that Mother told Father she had wanted to leave Romati soon after the break, but the chauffeur had "threatened to kill Caruso and the children." Romati's connections with the Italian underworld made Mother believe he would carry out his threat. She did not dare to tell Father about it, and that is why, when he followed her to Nice to seek a reconciliation, she could only say that she did not want to be with him any more.

How true this assertion was and how much of it Caruso believed we will never know. It seems that he and Mother made peace and saw each other often while he was in Buenos Aires. Papa told her about the family, but when he mentioned his intention to marry Rina, she violently opposed it. He tried to reason with her, explaining that Fofò and I needed a mother and a home. The idea was unacceptable to her, and she repeated her earlier threat:

"Marry if you must . . . anyone but my sister. If you marry Rina, I will kill you both."

Despite Ada's opposition, it is hard to understand why Father did not marry Rina. Undeniably, he loved her, felt comfortable with her, and liked to have her around. They were both single, and there were no legal obstacles to the marriage; yet he kept postponing the final step. Was he afraid that Ada's dramatic reaction might be more than an empty threat? Did he nurture a secret hope that he might still be reconciled with Ada? For a Roman Catholic Italian citizen, as he knew full well, marriage was an irreversible step, and its finality must have frightened him. Perhaps he simply felt that marriage would limit his freedom when it came to important affairs of the heart.

In spite of their disagreements, my parents parted as friends. In later years, they stayed in touch through correspondence. Father's letters were affectionate but not tender, written in a tone one would use with a trusted friend rather than a lover or wife.

Although I don't know whether Mother attended his performances in Buenos Aires, it stands to reason that she did—in all likelihood, she attended every one. I have often wondered what passed through her mind as she sat in the elegant auditorium listening to the familiar, caressing voice. Did she find its beauty changed? Was Caruso singing better? Were his interpretations deeper, truer?

Did that voice allow her, if only for moments, to return in spirit to the happy years they spent together in their youth?

CHAPTER THIRTEEN

Life in Florence

THE family spent the summer of 1915 at Villa Rina, waiting for Father's return. I had no idea what was happening in Buenos Aires, but Auntie Rina must have known that Ada lived there and that Father would almost certainly see her. If she was apprehensive about the outcome of such a meeting, she did not allow this to show in her behavior. Rina was quite sure of her Ghico's affections.

Father's last performance in Buenos Aires was on 30 August 1915. Upon his return to Italy, he had to go straight to Milan to take part in two benefit performances of *Pagliacci* at the Teatro Dal Verme with Luigi Montesanto, Claudia Muzio, and Armand Crabbé; Toscanini conducted. *Il Corriere della Sera* reported on September 24 that "Caruso has returned to us after many years of absence with a heavier voice and a timbre that has grown purer and more manly, with a much greater breath control, with greatly increased resources of expression; in sum, with a new totality in his singing, of a highly dramatic quality." Three days later, the same newspaper reviewed the second *Pagliacci*, commenting on the phenomenal volume of Caruso's voice, the dramatic emphasis of his phrasing, his facial acting, and the minute details of his gestures.

With this benefit behind him, Papa was finally able to come home and relax. It was too late in the year to enjoy the seashore, so we all went to Bellosguardo for the month of October. Later, when Father left for America, we moved back to Le Panche.

The rumors of war became fact: Italy entered the war against Austria-Hungary on 24 May 1915. Already, before the war, the lower classes hated the *"signori"*—the moneyed upper class—for their economic ease. Now, because they believed it was the *signori* who had forced them into war, the hatred grew. The fact that the lower classes suffered most of the casualties while the rich served mostly as officers did not help the situation.

The villagers showed their hatred any way they could. In 1913 we were returning by open car from Uncle Giovanni's house on the Vomero through the poorer section of Naples. Someone threw a spiny cactus pear at us and hit Rina. Papa stopped the car and yelled in Neapolitan: *"Fessi fetenti, non avite crianza!"* ("Stinking asses, you have no respect!") By the following year, the situation had become so bad that when we went for a ride, Father, Fofò, and Fava, Father's chauffeur, all carried handguns and a rifle. The conditions brought on by the war polarized Italian society even more than before.

The winter of 1915 was particularly severe, and I came down with double bronchial pneumonia. Auntie Rina called in a well-known specialist in pulmonary diseases, Professor Galileo Pierallini, who was chief of staff at the *Ospedale di Careggi per i tubercolotici*, the tuberculosis hospital at Careggi. Antibiotics did not yet exist, and he issued the standard orders of the day: Confine the patient to bed, paint the chest twice daily with iodine tincture, and apply to the chest and back hot poultices made of boiled linseed. It was a time when doctors made house calls, and the good professor dropped in to see me every day. Eventually I recovered, and the family gained a new friend in Dr. Pierallini.

Auntie Rina also had medical problems around this time. She was bedridden for a week or so, and Grandmother Teresa looked after her. The rest of the family took turns staying with her to keep her company, and I went to her room several times each day. Once, upon returning from school, I walked into the room unexpectedly and heard Teresa say to Rina, *"Sarebbe stato meglio se tu l'avessi avuto."* ("It would have been better if you had had it.") I distinctly remember both the phrase and the tone of Teresa's voice, which set my mind to work. Better if she had had what? A child? Had she had a miscarriage or an abortion? In either case, the child could only have been Father's.

I could never verify my assumption. Fofò said nothing; either he knew no more about Rina's condition than I did, or his loyalty to Rina was so strong that he would not tell what he knew.

BY the end of 1915, we began to feel the effects of the war. It became increasingly difficult to obtain enough anthracite coal to heat even the essential rooms at Le Panche, and we had to shut off most of the forty-odd rooms to conserve fuel. Early in the new year, the government confiscated our two automobiles. So that we would not be entirely without "horsepower," they left us one of our four horses. With our means of transportation gone and the severe shortage of heat, life was difficult at either of the damp, cold villas. Following that winter, Rina concluded that it was too much trouble to maintain either residence for the time being. In early 1916, she rented an apartment for us on the fourth floor of a large *palazzo,* an apartment building, in Florence on Piazzale Donatello. She took several truckloads of furniture, linen, silverware, dishes, and fine china from Le Panche. To make certain that we were well supplied with food, she brought from the farms at Signa smoked hams, sausages, olive oil, wine, and flour, all of which were stored in the attic. From Naples she ordered cases of Pasta di Gragnano—some of the best pasta in all Italy—along with hundreds of cans of tomatoes grown in the volcanic soil on the slopes of Mount Vesuvio.

To make the apartment more homelike, she ordered embroidered curtains bearing the Caruso family coat of arms from *Le Sorelle Navone,* one of the finest emporiums in Florence. With Father's money and her own excellent taste, she created a lovely, warm home for us for the long winter months.

The war dragged on and on, and life in Italy became increasingly difficult. In 1916, Fofò had his eighteenth birthday and became eligible for the draft. Military life did not appeal to him even in peacetime, and he had no intention of being killed for king and country. Rina's circle of friends included many high-ranking officers, among them General Mario La Chantain. With his help, Fofò got a deferment in 1916. He then plotted to become permanently unfit for military service. He had been robust and heavyset all through his teens; now he decided to lose weight in a hurry. Emulating our inglorious Roman ancestors who, after a heavy meal, repaired to the *vomitatorium,* Fofò would retire to the bathroom, stick a finger in his throat, and induce vomiting after every meal. Unheeding of Rina's commands, pleas, or threats, he kept up this routine for so long that he ended up looking like a skeleton. For a long time afterward, he could not keep anything on his stomach. To his utter disbelief, he was drafted within a year. He had ruined his health for nothing.

IN the 1915–16 season, the Metropolitan revived *Samson et Dalila* by Saint-Saëns. Opening night was 15 November 1915, and Caruso shared the title roles with Margaret Matzenauer. The revival was a great success. The critics observed that Caruso's voice, which was heavier and less lyric yet richer than before, was ideally suited for the role. They also singled out his acting, which had improved from season to season: He had reached new heights in this role. These successes were the result of long hours of study and practice, as Father worked unceasingly to live up to his reputation.

The season had a moment of comic relief which made headlines. It happened during the *Carmen* performance of 17 February 1916.

Returning from her recent Hollywood triumph as a silent-screen Carmen, Geraldine Farrar—now Mrs. Lou Tellegen—indulged in some overrealistic stage business. In the first act, she fought viciously with the chorus girls; at another point in the drama, she slapped Caruso with unnecessary vigor. He was taken aback by the resounding blow. The opportunity to get even with his pugilistic partner came in Act III, when Carmen is trying to get away from the enraged Don José. Caruso held Farrar's wrists in an iron grip; as she struggled ferociously to get away, he suddenly let go. The lady landed with a thump on her backside. Following his return home, Papa reenacted the scene to our great amusement. The numerous articles and books which relate the incident mention that Farrar's response to Father's protestations was to announce that "if Caruso did not approve of her impersonation, the management might engage another Carmen."[1] When Caruso was told of her reaction, he responded, "No, we can prevent a repetition of the scene by getting another José."[2] Somehow, the two singers made peace, because neither withdrew from the production, and the opera was repeated a week later without a cast change.

Caruso sang often during the season and accompanied the Met on its tour to Boston and Atlanta; his reliable services to the company were recognized and acknowledged by the management. But the constant hard work and the necessity of remaining consistently in peak form put him under a heavy strain. He was exhausted by the time he sailed for Europe in May 1916.

Few lay people realize the tremendous physical and emotional demands of a singing career. Father performed three, four, sometimes five times a week, working ten or eleven months of the year. During the last few years of his career, he scarcely had a vacation. By 1916 he was so overworked that he decided to spend the entire summer relaxing at Bellosguardo.

Worries about his health may have contributed to this decision to take a true vacation. During the past season, Father had suffered dizzy spells that attacked without warning.[3] He had consulted with several doctors, but none came up with a satisfactory diagnosis. One had suggested that he go on a diet (probably to lower his blood pressure), and Father shed over twenty-five pounds by the season's end. He liked being lighter and more agile, and he grew back his on-again, off-again mustache—a sure sign of a new and improved self-image.

In spite of the war, the never-ending improvements at Bellosguardo were progressing, and the villa grew more luxurious each year. All the members of the Livorno household spent most of the summer there. We had many visitors: friends, relatives, colleagues, house guests who stopped by or stayed several days. They usually came by train from Florence. The *sottofattore* (the assistant caretaker) would meet them at the Signa railroad station with the *calesse* and bring them to the villa on the hill. Papa frequently entertained his guests with his latest recordings. I have a snapshot taken at that period showing Grandmother Teresa, Aunt Rina, Fofò, Papa, Leoncavallo, and Maestro Bruno Bruni on the terrace, listening to a Victrola. In the background can be seen part of the construction in progress.

At the beginning of the summer, Papa tried to forget all about singing. He loved to work with his hands and often did, side by side with the workmen. He also read magazines, sketched, and painted. He would draw anything: the family, the sheep, workmen, guests, clouds floating in the azure heavens. It was wonderful how he could transform the most mundane subjects into fantastic images. He worked very fast, getting his first impressions down on the drawing pad so as not to lose the feeling of the moment. Time and again, he would make a quick sketch, look at the finished drawing, grunt with satisfaction or disapproval, show it to me—then crumple the paper and throw it away. None of us saw Papa's sketches as anything important.

Papa paid a great deal of attention to his properties. He loved his land, his villa, and all the fruits of his labors. In the summer, he would cover the estate on foot, enjoying every tree and shrub. He took a special interest in his tomato garden; the plants were all brought from Naples. And how good the tomatoes were! We used to eat them right off the vine, one after the other. Papa would walk down each row, inspecting, pruning, picking, eating.

Father's endeavors to improve his properties didn't always work out as planned. For instance, someone had suggested that he should increase his wine production. The idea appealed to him, and in preparation for storing the wine he expected to produce, he ordered over a dozen huge oak wine casks from the Rhineland in Germany, which were delivered sometime before the outbreak of the war. The casks were so enormous that they had to be assembled on the premises: They were twelve or fourteen feet in diameter, perhaps more, and proportionately high. Had Father turned all his land holdings into vineyards, he could not have produced enough wine to fill a fourth of them. As it turned out, none of these mammoth vats ever held a drop of wine. After they sat on the property a few years, Father realized his mistake. With Neapolitan ingenuity, he had them fitted with doors, windows, and flooring and gave them to the tenant farmers, whose housing was in poor condition. They were glad to move in.

PAPA loved Fofò and me, but he was strict in his demands for obedience. He never had to discipline us "manually" as Auntie Rina did or as Mother used to do with Fofò when he was a child. One look or an "Ehi!" was sufficient to control us. There were times, however, when I tried his patience sorely. I remember that he used to read his papers in the formal English garden or on the nearby terrace. My room was directly above on the top floor. I used to play one Sousa march after another by the open window, then repeat the whole stack of records. They were so loud that you could almost see the tin horn of the Victrola vibrate. Father would tolerate it awhile then explode. The famous voice would rise above the din of the gramophone.

"*Ehi! Smetti la! Chiudi la finestra costa sopra!*" ("Hey! Stop it! Close the window up there!")

I closed the window, and in a hurry.

Papa continued to suffer from his headaches. It seemed that neither rest nor activity had any influence on their frequency or duration. When they came, he simply had to endure the pain until it passed, which took longer and longer. He kept popping the aspirins Ledner sent him from Germany through Switzerland; if they did not make the headaches go away faster, at least they made the pain more bearable. Massaging the stiffened tendons on the back of his neck no longer seemed to help. Still, Rina would apply massage until the crisis passed. None of the doctors Father consulted knew the cause of the spasms, and no one could give him relief. My own guess is that the headaches and neck spasms, like leg cramps, were due to some circulatory problem, perhaps brought on, or aggravated by, incessant smoking. Papa did use a holder with a bit of cotton inserted to act as a filter, but he smoked like a chimney, one cigarette after another. I often saw him light up a fresh cigarette from the butt of the previous one. He would smoke his first cigarette in the morning with his first cup of black espresso coffee and smoke the last one just before he closed his eyes at night. Oh, I am certain there were intervals when he did not have a cigarette in his hand—after all, one could hardly make love with a burning weed in one's mouth!

In the second half of the summer, Father's accompanist, Bruno Bruni, came from Florence for a daily visit. Papa was preparing for the revival of Bizet's *The Pearlfishers,* and he and Bruni spent the morning hours working on the score. They went over the music of Nadir, the roles in Father's repertory that he was to sing in the forthcoming season, and various songs. Father took these sessions very seriously. Regardless of the music or the type of vocal exercise, he never opened up and sang at full voice. He vocalized *mezza voce, piano, pianissimo, piano, mezza voce*—never *forte*. His objective was to keep the breathing and singing apparatus in shape so that the various organs would not "forget," while taking care not to overtax the "instrument."

By this time, of course, singing was second nature to Caruso. "He sang naturally," wrote the critics; but the Caruso voice was the result of untold hours of study, practice, and training: first with Vergine, then with Lombardi, later with my mother, and finally by himself. His progress could be compared to the career of an Olympic swimmer. First, there is the boy who likes the water. If he shows aptitude, he is enrolled in a swimming class; then he graduates to the care of an Olympic coach. After months and months of practice, he swims before a grand audience and wins. "Swimming comes naturally to him," say the spectators, taking for granted the lifetime of training that led to the championship. A lifetime of hard work made Father a champion in his field. He did his vocalises every day of his life, even during vacations.

When he was preparing for the season or for a tour, he would go over his repertory. Often he would repeat a phrase over and over, changing the inflection, the tone, or the breathing until he got it right—until it met his own standards. Father was a perfectionist in the purest sense of the word: He worked very hard to make his delivery of each note, each phrase, each line, as good as he could possibly make it. In his own words:

> I wish people generally might know how hard I have worked to gain such vocal abilities as I possess. They say that I sing as I do because I have the voice; they think for me that is easy. It may appear so, I hope it does, for the artist should always conceal from his audience all evidence of physical effort. To gain such technique demands the constant effort; the exercise of the muscles, day after day for many years, until they respond at once to the will and have been developed to that point where sudden and very great effort never imposes a strain that cannot be met. If people only could be close enough to see my hands tremble during the delivery of some very physically exacting phrase, they wouldn't say I sing easily.[4]

AFTER lunch, which was the main meal of the day, we always took a siesta to replenish our energies. To this day most of Italy strictly observes this traditional mid-day rest. As the late Noël Coward put it, only "mad dogs and Englishmen" would exert themselves in the heat of the mid-day sun. Only in Milan, the fast-paced business capital of the country, do the people ignore this age-old custom. "Oh, the Milanese aren't civilized!" was the explanation facetiously offered recently by Dr. Ruffo Titta, Jr.[5]

At Bellosguardo we usually retired after our noon meal to our cool room, behind open windows and closed shutters, and rested until three or four o'clock. Sometimes Bruni stayed for lunch and siesta, then he and Father worked an hour or so more in the afternoon. Around five, when it began to cool off, we would go down to the *Sirena,* the fountain with the siren, and enjoy *merenda,* a light afternoon snack, under the shade of one of the great oak trees in the park. We would have watermelon or cantaloupe with smoked ham or prosciutto, pears, and *pecorino* cheese—a hard, sharp cheese made from sheep's milk—and enjoy the cool evening breeze. Aunt Rina was in seventh heaven when her Ghico was at home, and, except when he was in the grip of a headache, Papa seemed happy and content.

I enjoyed being with my family and finally getting to know Fofò. He acted the part of the big brother and played often with Umberto and me. The war and all the other problems of the world seemed far away from Signa, and we spent an idyllic summer together.

The rest was good for Papa. By fall he seemed rejuvenated and eager to face another season. I was growing up, and I enjoyed having him with us for a longer period than usual. This was the first time I can recall feeling truly sorry when it was time for him to go. I distinctly remember thinking that I had to wait another eight or nine months until I would see him again. As we said good-bye, I was hoping that the time would pass quickly.

Father did not come back to Italy for three years.

CHAPTER FOURTEEN

Dorothy Park Benjamin

FOLLOWING Father's departure in the fall of 1916, we returned to our apartment on Piazzale Donatello for the winter, and Auntie Rina rejoined her large circle of Florentine friends. There were the Fontanellas; the Berardi family; Miss Nathan, an English retiree; General La Chantain; Major Brambilla; the Coppedé family; the Pintacudas; the Bigiavis; and, of course, the lawyer Ceola and the Saccorottis. Most of them were quite wealthy, or at least well-to-do; Auntie Rina preferred to associate with people of good financial standing. She gave many formal dinner parties and soirées, and twice a week she invited four friends to play poker—always the same four. When I asked her why no one else was allowed into that poker game, she explained it was "because this way the losses and the winnings even out." I remember only three of the four permanent members of the group: Miss Nathan, Dr. Pierallini, and a youngish lawyer by the name of Levi.

One weekend Levi was dining with us. We had a typically Italian meal, spaghetti, *saltimbocca alla Romana,* salad, and fruit. The fruit was followed by a delicious *torta.* Mr. Levi did not touch the meat but enjoyed the pastry so much that he asked Rina how it was made.

"You take two dozen eggs, fresh cream . . ." Rina began.

"Oh, *Dio mio!*" Levi gasped; then he ran to the bathroom, and we heard the telltale sounds of vomiting. I could not understand it. When he returned, we all had espresso and conversed as if nothing had happened. Only later did someone explain that Levi was an orthodox Jew, and his dietary laws forbade him to eat eggs on the Sabbath. In those days, there was no thought of religious differences, and social boundaries were seldom drawn on religious grounds. Miss Nathan, as I recall, was also Jewish.

Rina held her games in the parlor, and the men played cards in the dining room. Guido often played chess with Fofò and checkers with me. On non-poker nights, he had his friends over for a game of *scopa, scopone,* or *bazzica.* Grandmother Teresa would clear the dining table and bring in four tumblers, two half-gallon flasks of chianti, and a tray of Toscani cigars. Grandfather and his friends would play and smoke until the wine gave out. It took them about four hours to empty both flasks—then they knew it was time to quit.

I was attending the *ginnasio* Galileo Galilei, within walking distance, on Via Cavour. Fofò continued at the *liceo* and took private English lessons.

Dr. Pierallini, who had entered our circle to combat my pneumonia the winter before, became a frequent visitor. He was a handsome bachelor, successful, affluent, and only a few years older than Rina. We enjoyed his company and always made him welcome, whether on social or professional calls. When Rina felt even slightly indisposed, she would send me to get the good doctor, who lived on Via San Gallo just ten blocks away. If he was not at home, I would leave word with his servants; if he was, he would smile and say:

"Tell your aunt I will be over in a little while."

This went on throughout the war years, and I was amused by the number of times my aunt required the attentions of a pulmonary specialist.

WE were hoping to see Papa again in 1917, but transatlantic travel had become far too dangerous thanks to Kaiser Wilhelm's submarines, which indiscriminately torpedoed not only battleships but passenger and merchant marine ships as well. Quite by accident, I witnessed one of these attacks in the summer of 1917. From a top-floor window in Villa Rina, I saw a submarine torpedo a freighter outside the port of Livorno. The freighter took on water and began to tilt but managed to reach the safety of the port.

I spent the summer hanging around Fofò—until he was drafted—and Umberto. Being bilingual, I was able to serve as guide and interpreter when convalescing British soldiers were billeted in a villa near ours.

At the time we settled in Livorno, Miss Saer knew very little Italian and was at our mercy linguistically. Fofò and Umberto made her the butt of many coarse jokes and played some inexcusable pranks on her. They were older and stronger than I, and it was useless to try to stop them. Miss Saer would ask the Italian word for some common object, and the boys would supply the most vulgar noun they could think of. The next time Miss Saer asked someone to pass the "salt" or the "vinegar," there would be an explosive roar of laughter. The game was discovered before long. Auntie Rina gave the boys a pair of her celebrated slaps, and they behaved—until the next time. I still shudder to think what my poor governess must have said to the shopkeepers when she walked into a store to make some innocent purchase.

Although Miss Saer had the typical Anglo-Saxon attitude of expecting the whole world to learn English, she soon learned enough Italian to speak tolerably well. She never mastered the nuances of the language, however, and would occasionally come up with outrageous statements. Her nephew, Jack Saer, when he served with the British Air Force, came to see her on leave in late 1917 or early 1918. He was probably the first Briton with whom she had spoken in years. When Auntie Rina asked her if she had enjoyed herself, she expressed her elation in correct Italian with this memorable line:

"Tanto piacere sentire propria lingua in bocca ad altri!"

This is a perfectly proper statement at first glance: "What a pleasure to hear one's own language in the mouth of others!" However, *sentire*, "to hear," also means "to feel"; and *lingua*, "language," also means "tongue." The mere thought of substituting these two words in her sentence sent the whole family into convulsions.

IN 1917 Father spent the summer months—the South American winter—in Buenos Aires. He returned to the Teatro Colón and again saw Mother. On this neutral ground, it seems they were able to face each other as friends. In fact, when the company sailed across the Rio de la Plata to perform at the Teatro Solis in Montevideo, Papa asked Mother to come along. This took more courage than he had usually shown in the past, for he surely knew that he invited the ridicule of his colleagues by associating with the woman who had jilted him for a chauffeur before the eyes of the world. He must have had strong feelings for Ada. It appears, too, that he had plans for continuing the relationship. As Ada remembered:

> We met in 1915 in Buenos Aires for the first time since our separation and remained friends thereafter. We met again in the Argentinian capital in 1917 on perfectly friendly terms. I lived there for eighteen years. On that second occasion, we arranged to meet again in New York in five or six months, but fate willed it otherwise. . . . We never saw one another again. As I said, Caruso was a ladies' man.   (*A Noite,* Rio de Janeiro, 4 March 1938)

It is hard to know how seriously Father contemplated a reconciliation with Ada, an act that would have caused more than the usual share of complications. He would have had to tell Rina that their relationship had come to an end and he had decided to go back to her older sister, thus delivering the same blow to Rina for a second time in her life. Considering his experience in such matters, it is unlikely that this was what held him back. Upon reflection, he must have realized that it was one thing to meet Mother in faraway Argentina and quite another to bring her to the United States.

New York was not only his artistic headquarters but his home for two-thirds of each year. He was a celebrity to everybody, from the shoeshine boys to the prominent families of the Golden Horseshoe. His every move was reported in the press. Ada's return to his life would have made headlines, and he would have had to suffer through endless interviews. He could not have kept the two sisters on different sides of the Atlantic as seasonal mistresses. Although such an arrangement would not have gone entirely against his grain, the women in question would never have agreed to it. He would have had to stay with Mother year-round if a reconciliation were to work at all. That would have meant obtaining clemency from Italian officials for her prison sentence and traveling with her to Italy in the summers.

It is also possible that after what had happened between them, Mother would have felt uncomfortable living with Father in the public eye. Marriage was impossible as long as Botti was alive, although, had he been determined enough, Father could have gotten around this problem by obtaining a Mexican divorce or by relinquishing his and Ada's Italian citizenship—another move that would have echoed around the world in the press. In any case, the events of 1918 made reconciliation a moot issue.

Self-caricature of Enrico Caruso, drawn in 1914. Photography © Lawrence Victor Smith 1990.

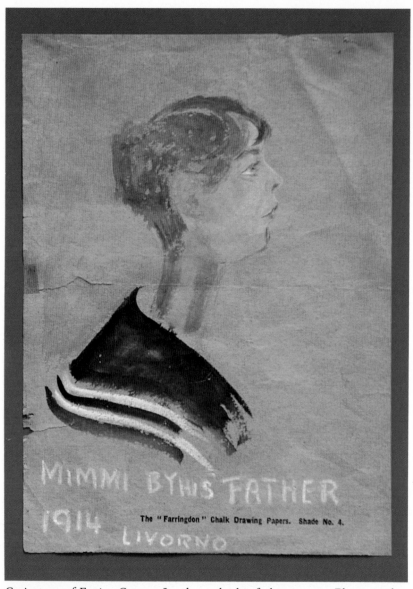

Caricature of Enrico Caruso, Jr., drawn by his father in 1914. Photography
© Lawrence Victor Smith 1990.

Painting of Ada Giachetti on the *belvedere* of the villa Bellosguardo at Signa, signed and dated A. Galli, 1907. Courtesy of the Associazione Museo Enrico Caruso—Centro Studi Carusiani, Milan.

Dr. P. M. Marafioti (*left*) and a
Moroccan customs officer (*below*),
watercolors by Enrico Caruso. Note
the initials *EC* at the bottom of this
and the following watercolors.
Photography Paul Karabinis.

Assunta Caruso (*left*) and a self-
caricature (*above*), watercolors
by Enrico Caruso.
Photography Paul Karabinis.

Watercolors of unidentified men and women by Enrico Caruso.
Photography Paul Karabinis.

Oil portrait of Titta Ruffo (*left*), Enrico Caruso, and Fedor Chaliapin (*right*), painted by the Polish painter Tadé Styka in Paris, May 1912.

Enrico Caruso as Canio. The bronze statue was made by Angelo Arachite, Caruso's sergeant during his brief military service. Arachite, Caruso's lifelong friend, became a successful sculptor, popular in Naples. Photography © Lawrence Victor Smith 1990.

A portrait head of Enrico Caruso, unsigned. Silver on artist's clay lining.
Photography © Andrew Farkas.

In addition to having to cope with his colleagues' reaction to Ada's presence in Montevideo, Father was not in his best form; he was probably suffering from another spell of his excruciating headaches. In the concluding performance of *Carmen,* he had a rough start then suffered one of those vocal mishaps he always dreaded. The 27 August 1917 issue of *El Dia* observed, not without indulgence, that "in the first act, Caruso had two physiological mishaps (*contratiempos fisiologicos*) which affected one high note in the middle and another in the high registers. But within his interpretation of the role, these were some-what akin to the memory of two flies on a Velásquez canvas." The reviewer referred to other occasions of such "vocal accidents," adding that two other singers of the cast suffered from "similar accidents." But a Caruso was not allowed to have accidents, and his colleagues did not let him forget it.

Father's next engagement was in Rio de Janeiro. He wrote Mother several times. The letters, which were handed down to me, reflect a brooding, sad, aging, hard-working man, who still enjoyed the excite-ment of a performance, but less and less the trappings and pressure of being the major operatic attraction of the day.

Rio de Janeiro
9 September 1917

Dear Ada,

Your letter was immensely welcome, because from the moment I arrived here to this day I have been in a state of indescribable agitation! Let me explain. After what happened at the last evening in Montevideo, the duration of the trip was an atrocious pain, because, besides being aware that my rude colleagues and impresari blamed me for your having come to Montevideo, I could read on all the faces the derision in my regard. You can imagine my agony! You cannot understand it, because in [the period of] my life passed with you, I never took things so seriously; but since the moment my heart was pierced, every little thing makes me suffer so much.

Upon my arrival here I found a terribly hostile ambience and the critics wanted to classify me as an old wreck, notwith-standing the success I had at my debut with *Pagliacci* in the theater. For over a week my mind has been tormented because in the theater I am applauded, yet the critics say I am old and that it is time for me to retire, leaving a good memory of the past. One can see that they are playing a game, because the public becomes delirious when I sing. I made my debut in *Pagliacci;* [it went] well in the theater but badly with the critics, who said that I am no longer what I was some fourteen years ago. What jackasses. I know that too, but the difference is that I sing better today than I did then.

The second opera was *Carmen,* and it was an even greater success in the theater and a little better in the press. I sang the second *Pagliacci* today, and it seems that the gentlemen of the press found me better than the first evening. From all this it appears that the press is against the management, and to kill Enesta, they want to kill me. As for myself, I am caught in between and try to fight, and I hope that in the end they will find me to be right.

I am sorry to hear that you have been indisposed, but I hope that by the time this reaches you, you will have recovered completely.

I will wire you [money] tomorrow to send me some Adams cigarettes, and before I leave here, I will send you another few thousand pesos I have left over.

Live a tranquil life, because even though you have done me *much, so much wrong,* I could never forget things that only death can erase.

Try to choose your friends from among mine so that I may live more peacefully.

A warm salutation,
Enrico

This is the letter of a man who confides his cares to an intimate friend. I am certain that Father supported Mother all those years not only out of a sense of obligation toward "the mother of his children"— his standard phrase in referring to Ada—but also out of a deep-rooted desire to know that she was secure and free from want. His feelings for her were a part of him, permanent and ineradicable. Mother's profound regrets in later life showed that in spite of the wounds she and Father inflicted on each other, their emotional bond remained strong.

A few days later, Father wrote again.

Rio de Janeiro
19 September 1917

Dear Ada,

I have received your telegrams and your letter of the 13th current, as dated on the post-office stamp. However, I have received nothing [else], neither the shoes nor the cigarettes. In any case I thank you for your trouble.

I am glad to hear that the cure is good for you, but I cannot say the same of myself because at this very moment as I write to you, I suffer the most atrocious torments! It has been four days since this ailment returned and would not leave me! Imagine how I suffer, having to sing at the same time. I have the urge to kill myself. I can't take it any more. I hope today is the last, because when this pain comes it lasts about four days, and I thus hope that today is the last one. . . .

The public here understands my work, and the critics are beginning to [as well]. In *Tosca* and in *Elisir* I made them euphoric, and they said that when I leave they will carry me in triumph. Tonight I sing the last act of *Elisir* for the benefit of the Italian Red Cross. Tomorrow is *Bohème* and Saturday *Manon* of Massenet, and Sunday night [the] 23rd I leave for S. Paulo where I will remain until October 10.

Be good to me and take care of your health.

With many warm thoughts,
Enrico

Father's headaches continued to plague him, and his comment about having to sing at the same time—and, it went without saying, having to give his best to convince the critics he was not yet a broken-down wreck—was the agonized cry of an artist nailed to the cross of his own reputation. In the hostile atmosphere in which he found himself, he had no friend to turn to, and so he continued to correspond with Ada. Rina was too far away; in any case, at this moment in their lives, he may have been disinclined to carry on an intimate exchange of letters with her.

Rio de Janeiro
15 October 1917

Dear Ada,

I received all that you have sent in due course: letters and package, and in good order. I received today the one you sent to S. Paulo which was forwarded to me here.

I take this opportunity to answer the questions you asked. First of all, as you can see I am here to sing more performances; I have given 13 with *Carmen,* and there will be another one tomorrow, it will be *Manon* by Puccini. So much for not being liked!!! The theater is sold out at exorbitant prices and they made 140 contos, which is 200,000 lire.

At S. Paulo things went quite well, and at the benefit evening for the Red Cross I received a beautiful diamond worth about six contos.

Last night I sang Massenet's *Manon,* and because I sang it in French it was the end of the world, but I won because I did sing in French, and I was applauded more than on any other evening. The end of the world came because Pardo was ill and hospitalized, and Dalla Rizza took her part and thus she sang in Italian and received the replies from Crabbé in the same language.

Tomorrow it will be all over and then on November 12 it starts all over again in N.Y.

I leave on the *Saga* on the morning of the 17th and I hope everything will go well.

My headache is gone and I think that certain things I eat must eliminate it. As soon as I am in N.Y. I will start the cure again with precision.

I am sending you a prayer offered on the occasion of the first communion of Mimmi who has been confirmed.

Ciaò. Stay well and accept my many good wishes,

Enrico

[In the margin] I enclose a thousand-peso note that was left over. Write to New York Hotel Knickerbocker.

It can be taken for granted that Mother wrote to Father in New York. It is less certain whether he wrote back to her. He probably enclosed short notes with the checks he sent. Then the checks continued, and in all probability the notes stopped.

AFTER the disappointment of not seeing Papa in 1917, we were hoping to see him the following summer. Germany was close to defeat, and transatlantic travel was supposedly less dangerous; but Father decided once again to stay in New York. The success of the silent films

Geraldine Farrar had made for Jesse L. Lasky's Famous Players prompted the producer to offer Caruso $200,000 for two silent feature films. It was too much money to turn down.

According to contemporary accounts, Father took film-making very seriously and had a lot of fun at it. He completed the two films—*My Cousin* and *A Splendid Romance*—in six weeks during the summer of 1918, but only the former was released; it did so poorly at the box office in America that the second film was withheld. The paying public made it clear that Enrico Caruso was an opera singer, not a silent movie star. Yet in England both films played, and even *A Splendid Romance* did fairly well. But Caruso on the silent screen just wasn't Caruso. One movie house tried to turn the film into a talking picture. The cinema correspondent for the *Daily Express*[1] reported that at the screening of *My Cousin* in London's Cathedral Hall, Caruso's soundless, on-screen rendition of "Vesti la giubba" was accompanied by a recording of his voice, and "the synchronization between sound and picture was practically perfect." But another reporter abhorred the resulting effect and expressed the hope that no one would pursue the crazy idea of making talking motion pictures.

During this period, Father's letters were infrequent. We in Italy knew of his excursion into films, but we were completely unaware of any other consideration that might keep him in New York. He let us know only that he would not be returning home.

In 1918, when summer came, we moved to Villa Rina to spend the hot months at the seashore. One morning in late August, the Livorno paper carried the banner headline: "CARUSO SPOSA AMERICANA!" ("Caruso Marries American Woman!") The news caught us totally unprepared.

OF course, the facts were soon available, from every source except Caruso himself. It seems that in early 1918, he met and was captivated by an aristocratic young American, Dorothy Park Benjamin. After a short but stormy courtship, they were married August 20 at the Marble Collegiate Church in New York. In late March 1919, to please Caruso, Dorothy converted to Roman Catholicism, and immediately after the baptism, he married her again in the Chapel of the Blessed Virgin at St. Patrick's Cathedral in New York.

Dorothy's father was responsible for the storminess of the courtship.

Without a doubt, Park Benjamin was a brilliant man. His father of the same name was a well-known poet, lecturer, and newspaper publisher and an associate of Horace Greeley. Dorothy's father, then Park Benjamin, Jr., was educated at Trinity School in New York and at the U.S. Naval Academy at Annapolis. He graduated in 1867 and made several cruises with Admiral Farragut. Following his resignation from the Navy, he studied for a year at the Albany Law School and was admitted to the bar. Intrigued by the scientific advances of his time, he then enrolled at Union College, where he majored in science and received his Ph.D. in 1871. He embarked on a career as a specialist in patent law, becoming the most prominent practitioner in this area and a close friend of many scientists and inventors, including Thomas A. Edison. Too versatile and many-faceted to limit himself to the practice of law, he served as associate editor of *Scientific American* from 1872 to 1878 and was editor-in-chief of Appleton's *Cyclopedia of Applied Mechanics*. He also published many articles on scientific subjects and authored several books, among them *The Early History of the Naval Academy* and *The Early History of Electricity*.

To a man of such formidable intellect, Caruso was no more than a singer, a well-paid operatic entertainer. That he was at the top of his profession was commendable but by no means constituted credentials sufficient for a son-in-law. When Caruso asked for Dorothy's hand in marriage, Benjamin was astounded. Such a development didn't even occur to him. It seems that he vacillated for a while, but his final answer was a definitive no. He demanded and expected total obedience, and the matter was closed as far as he was concerned; it didn't cross his mind that Dorothy would disobey him.

A contemporary clipping (7 September 1918) from an unidentified London newspaper states that when Caruso asked for his daughter's hand, Park Benjamin replied: "I object to you because of the difference in the ages of my daughter and yourself; the difference in nationality; and principally because of your artistic temperament." An additional, unspoken objection was rooted in the difference in their social standing. Pride in the family name was reflected in the names of at least three of the five children: the elder son, Park Benjamin, Jr., and the younger son, Romeyn Park Benjamin; even Dorothy was named Dorothy Park Benjamin. He could not allow his daughter to marry one of the hundreds of slum-born Carusos who happened to raise himself above all the rest, thanks to a wondrous pair of vocal cords and years of hard work.

When he received word of the marriage, Benjamin said in an interview:

I can hardly answer for the whole family—we haven't had time to think. The thing is done now, and cannot be helped, and we shall probably make the best of it, and although we do not think Dorothy is wise, this is her home. There is no mystery why we did not go to the wedding—we were not asked![2]

The Benjamin house was never again Dorothy's home; for her father pushed her out of his life, emotionally and legally. In Dorothy's memoirs, Park Benjamin emerges as a rigid, authoritarian man, demanding unconditional obedience of those dependent on him. In fact, in his will dated 11 May 1920, he left his five children "the sum of $1 each and make no further bequest to them because of their long-continued, persistent, undutiful and unfilial conduct toward myself."[3]

Dorothy's mother, Ida E. Benjamin, suffered from ill health and was sent by her doctors to a sanitarium in rural New York before Dorothy's eleventh birthday. There she died in 1922, separated from the family and remaining an invalid over many years. Dorothy, cast into the role of housekeeper and hostess for her father, took her mother's seat at the dining table and became the frequent focus of Park Benjamin's violent and often unreasonable temper.

Caruso's friends were puzzled by his marriage, and I have it on good authority that most of them thought Dorothy a poor choice as a wife, the age difference being the least of their concerns.

Why, at last, did Caruso marry? Perhaps, in his middle age, after all his many affairs, he was ready to settle down with one woman. But a more plausible explanation was tendered by his old friend Pasquale Simonelli, who quoted Caruso as saying to him: "*Voglio una donna che sia mia!*" ("I want my own woman!") He meant that he wanted a woman who was not "shopworn," who had not previously been someone else's wife or mistress. Yet I am convinced that Father was much happier with "women of experience." It is possible that Caruso had learned of Rina's close friendship with Dr. Pierallini and that the specter of the past gave him the determination to act before life repeated itself, leaving him publicly jilted by both Giachetti sisters. Rightly or wrongly, he made up his mind as to the direction his private life should take, and his plans no longer included Rina.

Why Caruso married is unclear, but it is a matter of record how the marriage came about. In 1917, Maestro Fernando Tanara, one of Father's accompanists in New York, and his wife were expecting a child. As Tanara recalled for the *Daily Express* in May 1934:

"If it is a boy, Tanara," Caruso said, "I will be godfather.
But if it is a girl—nothing doing. There are already too many
women in my life. They are a nuisance."

It was a boy, but all the same, it did bring another woman
into Caruso's life. And she stayed, becoming Mrs. Caruso and
the mother of Gloria.

A rich and beautiful young American, Miss Dorothy
Benjamin, had heard Caruso sing and wanted to meet him. She
persuaded my wife to ask her to the christening ceremony.
Caruso was attracted immediately. He flirted outrageously.
Next day he invited her to lunch. Miss Benjamin went.

When in love he forgot everything. He was also
irresistible. Miss Benjamin found him so.

Whatever his motives, his marriage was a tremendous blow to all
of us at home. True to form when it came to women, once more Father
behaved like a cad, this time with Rina: He let her find out about his
marriage from the newspapers. I don't have all the facts and I sincerely
hope I am wrong, but to the best of my knowledge, neither before nor
after the fact did he ever contact Rina to offer her an explanation, an
apology, or a good-bye. It well may be that she did not lead a blameless
life during my Father's long absences. Yet considering his endless
dalliances, he could hardly point an accusing finger, least of all at the
woman to whom he had publicly announced his engagement six years
before but whom he declined to marry. In spite of his conduct, Rina
loved him unconditionally, and there was nothing she would not have
done for him.

Auntie Rina was terribly hurt. She was the stoic type; she did not
complain. If she cried, she cried in private. But she was very downcast,
and we all sided with her, feeling she had been terribly wronged. In
impotent fury, we turned all the pictures of Father in Villa Rina against
the wall.

The news of Caruso's marriage reverberated through the musical
world. Puccini wrote to Sybil Seligman from Viareggio on 31 August
1918: "Caruso? But is it true? Heaven knows how badly it will affect 'X';
she has been behaving in Italy as though she were the wife of the great
tenor and the guardian of his son."[4]

"X" was of course Auntie Rina.

A month later, on September 24, in another letter to Sybil
Seligman, Puccini took a mean swipe at Rina:

I've had Caruso's wedding invitation. The news of the

marriage here came like a thunderbolt; by order of the authorities everything was sealed up—and so, from a Princess, 'X' was thrown into the streets, to which, if the truth must be told, she always belonged. It's the way of the world."[5]

Puccini, of course, was the pot calling the kettle black: He himself had many highly publicized extramarital affairs and apparently had the morals of an alleycat.

Although at fourteen, I wasn't mature enough to understand the full implications of this turn of events, I did realize that the relative balance and harmony of the life I had known for the past four years had come to a sudden halt.

My instinct proved correct. At the time of his wedding, Father cabled his administrator, Giuseppe Vecchiettini, in Florence: *"Mettete sigilli alle case."* ("Seal the houses.") Vecchiettini, aware of our family history, must have thought to himself: "Here we go again."

Fortunately for Rina, she had a furnished apartment's worth of belongings in her possession, which she kept for herself. I believe she was entitled to this "settlement." She had been my father's woman for the last six years, and she had cared for his children. Even if she did not wait for him like Penelope, she had loved him deeply since she was a young girl, and she would gladly have stayed with him all her life. But he never took her to America, most likely because he was reluctant to introduce her to New York society as the aunt of his children, the sister of the woman who had left him. During the years of their liaison, Rina was partially supported by my father; now she refused to be put out on the street like some retainer taken off the payroll. She kept whatever was under her control.

Between her long-term relationships with Roberto de Sanna, Edoardo Scarfoglio, and my father, Rina must have had many suitors. Almost certainly, she and Dr. Pierallini were having an affair. They were close friends, they liked each other, and Father did not come home to Italy after 1916.

After Caruso's marriage to Dorothy and his break with the Giachettis, Rina did not let the grass grow under her feet. A year later, on 15 December 1919, she married Dr. Pierallini. She was on top of the world. She was in the prime of life, her husband was a successful professional man, they had several valuable properties between them, and she had finally achieved respectability. She spent a beautiful decade with her husband, living like a queen and having everything she ever wanted. She made only one mistake: She played the stock market on margin. In the 1929 crash she lost everything, or almost everything; she had to sell her properties to cover the margins. Shortly afterward, Pierallini died, and Rina was left alone.

IN addition to ordering the villas sealed, Papa instructed Vecchiettini to remove us from the Giachetti household. Fofò had been inducted by this time, and at the moment he was on the Trentino in the Alps, with the Third Engineers under General Di Gennaro. Fortunately, the war was almost over, and he came through his military service unscathed. After the Italian victory at Vittorio Veneto, the armistice with Austria was signed on 3 November 1918. Fofò was still at the front when he received a picture of Dorothy inscribed "To Fofò, his new *Mammina*." A few days later came another photograph from Father; the inscription read: "To my dear son Fofò, his devoted Father." After this came silence. Fofò remained isolated and ignored.

With my brother in the Italian army, Vecchiettini had to concern himself only with Miss Saer and me. He moved us to a suite at the Hotel Paoli on the Lungarno in Florence, and we reverted to our old routines. Life with Lei was the norm of my childhood, and I accepted the situation without difficulty. But Miss Saer deserves admiration for the way she adjusted to the most abrupt and irrational changes.

I continued to attend school and in my free time guided American and English soldiers around Florence. One day passed like another. Occasionally Fofò came back on short leaves.

An epidemic of Spanish influenza struck in 1918. When I got it too, Lei was terribly worried. I had only a light case and recovered, but tens of thousands died of the disease all over Europe. Without hesitation and putting her own life in danger, Lei took care of me day and night. Luckily, she did not get the potentially fatal disease.

In the past, Father had sent me greetings when he wrote to Rina. Now that I was on my own, it was necessary to correspond with him directly. Correspondence in later life cost me no effort, but certain obligatory family letters in my teens were pure agony. Whenever Auntie Rina was away from home, Miss Saer saw to it that I wrote to her, and my letters dripped with phony clichés about how much I missed her. It was much easier to write to Papa. Although I was never deeply attached to him, I missed him. Besides, I wanted to hear about the changes in his life and to know what his plans were for me.

I waited for a letter from Papa in vain. Finally, in December 1918, I wrote to him, for some inexplicable reason, in English.

My dear Papa,
I have been expecting a letter from you, but perhaps you are busy and have not time to write.
I know, Papa, that you have made a change in your life, but I hope it will make no difference to Fofò and me, and that there will always be the same affection between us as before.

I then told him about my studies and about the schools being closed because of the influenza epidemic. I closed with:

We are all rejoicing because of the Italian victories and we hope soon to have peace, and then you will be coming home to see us.

> With very much love, dear Papa
> from your son,
> Enrico

Father replied on 1 January 1919. As was his habit in his correspondence, he wrote in his characteristic strong hand on the corner of my letter "Rp 1/1/19," *Rp* standing for *risposta* (reply). His letter was kind and reassuring, and although he made it clear that we were not to join him right away, I contemplated with increasing optimism what the future might hold. Letters traveled by ship and took over two weeks to reach their destination. My next letter, again in English, is dated 15 February 1919:

My dear Papa,
The arrival of your letter was a great joy to me not having heard from you for more than four months.
I know from you about my new *Mammina,* if I can call her so—for the present I will call her sister for I have heard she is young, and as you say very adorable and I hope that we shall get along well together.
I am very sorry indeed that I cannot come to America but as that is your will: *Fiat voluntas tua.* I must abide by it, but I am longing for the time of your arrival here so that after many years we will meet and embrace each other again, and I hope, dear Papa, that you will never leave us, or else take us with you.
In the meantime I will study and try not to lose the year.
I am well and waiting for you.

I closed the letter asking for his permission to buy a bicycle. I don't remember what his answer was, but I did not get the bicycle. He received my letter on 4 March 1919 and replied the following day. As I recall, he wrote that I should be patient and wait until we met again. Cut off from all relatives but Fofò, I was again left in limbo.

CHAPTER FIFTEEN

From Signa to New York

A T the end of the 1918–19 season, Caruso renewed his Met contract for another three years. In late spring of 1919, I received the exciting news that Papa was finally coming to Italy for the summer and bringing Dorothy with him.

They sailed from New York in late May, arriving in Naples the first week of June. Father took his bride to meet his stepmother Maria, then his brother Giovanni and his family. After spending a single day in Naples, the newlyweds proceeded north to Genoa. Arrangements were made for the Caruso family to join us a short time later at Bellosguardo. Dorothy later wrote:

> [Enrico] was anxious to go on and meet his son, Enrico—
> or Mimmi, as his father called him. . . . With Mimmi was his
> governess, Miss Saer, who had brought him up and to whom, I
> am sure, he owed his perfect English and his beautiful
> manners. It was quite evident that Enrico was immensely
> proud of this son of his.[1]

For my part, I looked forward to the visit with a mixture of apprehension and curiosity. Had Papa's attitude changed toward us because of his marriage? What would my new stepmother be like? Would she like us?

I had not seen Father for three years. When he last saw me in 1916, I was a boy of twelve, and now at fifteen I was a young man. I worried about what he might say or ask about Rina; but this was unnecessary, for he never asked about anyone in the Giachetti family. He had closed that chapter of his life permanently.

Miss Saer and I went to Genoa to meet Papa. It was a happy and affectionate reunion. Over the years we met and said good-bye many a time, but I doubt that either of us was ever happier to see the other. Only Fofò was missing, but he was still in the service and unable to get away. Later, when he could, he joined us at the villa.

Papa was very pleased at my mastery of Italian. Whereas before we sometimes had to mix English with Italian, now we could carry on a conversation entirely in Italian. He was also amazed at how much I had grown, and secretly I was amazed at how much he had aged in three years. He had lost some of his hair and acquired many new wrinkles. But he was still vigorous, bursting with energy, his old jovial self, and visibly proud to introduce to us his young wife. Dorothy was all smiles and positively charming.

They arrived with a mountain of luggage. The large trunks were sent on to Florence by train, and we continued by car. Miss Saer and I rode in the car with Papa. I sat next to Dorothy, and Lei on the jump seat facing us.

Then a curious thing happened. Ever since I could remember, I had longed for a mother. Every child I knew had one except Fofò and me. Rina had never showed me any affection at all. When Father first set up house with her, I showed that I accepted the arrangement by addressing her as "Mamma." Brusquely, she told me: "*Non son tua madre, non mi chiamar 'Mamma'!*" ("I am not your mother, don't call me 'Mamma'!") My hope of finding a surrogate mother remained unfulfilled, and I still had no one to whom I was closely attached except Miss Saer. But ours was the relationship of child and governess, and Lei always typified English reserve. For someone with her background, it was improper to show too much emotion.

Then, all of a sudden, there was Dorothy. She was a young, attractive, elegantly dressed woman: my father's wife. There was something motherly about her despite her youth, probably because of her large frame and height. She was the closest thing to a mother I could ever expect to have. As I was sitting next to her, in a sudden surge of emotion I cuddled closer, and she responded by putting her arm around me. I put my head on her shoulder and gave her a big, contented smile.

And then I glanced at Lei. I saw indescribable hurt in her face. It took me years to fully comprehend what she must have felt at that moment. There she was, the only person in the world who had looked after me for the past twelve years, the one who took care of me when I was ill, the only one to show me any warmth and affection—then this strange woman appears, and I so readily accept her! For my dear Lei, it must have been the most agonizing moment in all the years she spent with me. From the distance of almost seven decades, I can still see her pained expression.

The caravan wound its way down to Signa, and we settled in at Bellosguardo for an unusual summer. Within a couple of weeks, relatives arrived from all over Italy and were quartered in various parts of the villa. In the end, the Carusos, the Iacolettis (Giovanni's inlaws and relatives), and heaven knows who else swelled the number of residents to twenty-one. I never counted them, but Dorothy, who remained an outsider because of her limitations with the language, did.

My hopes about finding a mother in Dorothy did not materialize. Our relationship at Bellosguardo remained cool and formal. As she recalled: "When we reached Genoa and found him [Mimmi] waiting for us, I was embraced by a tall, handsome boy of fourteen, who, somewhat to my dismay, called me mother."[2] Dorothy, who was twenty-six, was too young to be a mother to a boy of almost fifteen. That summer at Signa, a rapport of sorts developed inevitably. In fact, Dorothy and I were quite friendly until after my father's death. Besides Papa, I was the only person in the entire household equally at home in English and Italian. Miss Saer knew some Italian, and Martino Ceccanti, Father's former valet, now an overseer at Bellosguardo, knew some English; but when Dorothy needed on-the-spot translations, I was the one who supplied them.

Among the many relatives at Bellosguardo that summer, only Giovanni's children, Anna and Marcello, were close to my age. When Marcello and I exchanged family photographs forty years later, he recalled this time together.

> How many memories your photograph has awakened in my heart! I saw myself again as a boy in the paradise that was Bellosguardo; the respect and fear we had for my dear departed uncle, because with our childish mentality we did not understand that he was the dearest and kindest being that

existed in the world, and we held him in abject fear. We feared
his every word, every gesture, every glance.[3]

Another person I remember fondly from the summer is my
Grandmother Maria. After Assunta died, Grandmother lived alone.
She was a wonderful old lady with a dignified presence. She rarely
spoke and never smiled or laughed, but, like a true Neapolitan, she
said everything with gestures. Father always paid special attention to
her.

"*Mamma, come vi sentite?*" ("How are you, Mamma?") Instead of the
familiar "*tu,*" he always used the formal "*voi*" with her, the Italian form
of "you" signifying the greatest respect.

With a wave of the hand, she would indicate "so-so."

"*Cosa volete, Mamma?*" ("What would you like, Mamma?")

She would form her hand in the shape of a cup, signaling "drink."

"*Mamma, volete un po' di spaghetti?*" ("Mamma, would you like some
spaghetti?")

She would put her thumb under her chin and say "Tsk!" meaning
"No, I am full up to here."

Grandmother Maria could not stand Giovanni. Throughout the
summer, they had loud quarrels in their worst Neapolitan dialect. The
cascade of angry words was completely out of character for my
taciturn grandmother. Because at that time I did not know enough
Neapolitan, to this day I don't know what they were fighting about.
One day, when we returned from a shopping trip to Florence, we came
upon the two of them in the midst of a terrific row. Giovanni was so
enraged he was speechless. After standing a moment in trembling
silence, he grabbed his straw hat and bit a large piece out of the rim.

Grandmother loved my father as much as she disliked Giovanni,
and the feeling was entirely reciprocal. She was very proud of him; at
mealtimes she was only too happy to sit and look at her favorite son.
The fact that they were not blood relatives did not seem to matter to
either of them. Being warm and expansive by nature, she often
embraced and kissed Papa. Because I was the son of her Enrico, she
was very affectionate with me too, and I always got my share of hugs
and kisses. For Maria I was not in the way, and I liked this old grandmother of mine.

I don't know what Maria thought of Dorothy. The two women
could not communicate, which was probably just as well as their
mentalities were galaxies apart. The rest of the family did not dare to
say anything negative about Dorothy to Papa, nor behind his back in

my presence. The only person who showed thinly concealed animosity was Giovanni. It was understandable, considering that his livelihood—the supply of money he received regularly from his wealthy and generous brother—could depend on the attitudes of this strange American woman and the directions in which she influenced her husband.

Grandmother outlived Father by many years; she died in 1939 at the age of ninety-two. In later life, I visited her occasionally when I was in Naples, but I did not maintain strong ties with the Carusos. They were a small part of my life while I was growing up, and my attachment to them was never profound. I did not find Giovanni likable and saw his children too seldom for a bond to form between us.

ONE morning I stood by as Papa opened the mail. A long envelope had some interesting U.S. stamps, and I asked if I could have them for my collection. Papa explained that one never removed stamps from U.S. mail, because the stamp on the envelope was the guarantee that the letter was under the protection of the United States government. If there was anything derogatory or threatening in the letter, the U.S. postal inspector could be called in to prosecute the sender.

I was surprised. Who would want to write anything threatening or derogatory to my father? Smiling at my naïveté, Papa told me he had a whole collection of threatening letters he had received over the years. The one that had caused the most trouble was sent to him in New York in 1910 by the Black Hand, an Italian criminal organization specializing in extortion. They demanded money and threatened to kill him if he did not pay. He notified the authorities and was immediately given police protection and a handgun for his own protection. A police escort accompanied him to the Brooklyn Academy of Music for a performance of *La Gioconda*. During the show, forty-three policemen were stationed in the chorus, on the catwalk above the stage, in the stalls, and in the galleries. The police even insisted that Father carry a loaded revolver in his pocket. He returned to his hotel under police escort, and two detectives remained on duty outside his rooms. To catch the blackmailers, Martino volunteered for the dangerous assignment of delivering the money to the specified place in Brooklyn. There was a police stakeout, and the extortionists were caught. From that day on, Martino, whom I had regarded as merely an excellent valet, was my hero.

The long, rectangular upstairs salon at Signa was lined with cabinets. Behind inlaid glass doors were Papa's collections of bronzes; glass ampules from Pompei and Herculaneum; Greek and Roman coins; old snuff boxes; erotic statuettes in bronze, gold, and silver; and antique watches. One day I walked into the room and found him sitting at the table with the watches spread out on a velvet mat before him. They were beautiful pieces, all decorated—some enameled, some cloisonné, others engraved. He was obviously enjoying his treasured pieces for the first time in years. I sat down across from him, feasting my eyes on the beautiful objects. Father did not seem to be in the mood for conversation, so I did not talk either.

As he opened the lid of one of the watches, it chimed. He looked at me with joy, and we smiled at each other like two children playing with wonderful toys. Encouraged by the smile, I reached out to pick up one of the watches. My hand was still hovering in mid-air when he let out a shout, his eyes wide with horror:

"Non toccare! Non toccare!" ("Don't touch!")

I withdrew my hand instantly, stiffening in my seat, and continued to sit quietly.

He picked up the next piece and accidentally dropped it on the marble floor.

I never dared to ask what happened to the watch. Fearing a volcanic eruption of Father's temper, I jumped to my feet and fled from the room.

Father always had to be doing something. He read magazines, sketched, or joined the workmen who were repairing the road that led to the villa. Although he was powerfully built and muscular, he was not a strong man and he never exercised. But soon after he arrived at Signa, he got into working clothes and began carting loads of gravel in a wheelbarrow. He also did some digging, planting flowers and bushes. Though he was unaccustomed to manual labor, he really worked and had the blisters on his hands to prove it.

But what he seemed to enjoy the most that summer was sitting for hours in the hot, unventilated room in the gallery adjoining the chapel, working on the *presepio,* the Nativity scene. He didn't mind the heat or the flies circling his hot pot of foul-smelling fish glue. Some time earlier, at the Paris Exposition, he had purchased an exquisite collection of several hundred figurines dressed in the style of the peoples of Palestine: Arabs, Moors, Jews, Saracens, Palestinians, all in wonderful costumes. The figurines ranged in size from two or three inches to twelve inches or more, and the details and workmanship were exquisite. Each figurine was hand-painted and graced with a unique and appropriate expression. The little figures were over a century old, and some had been damaged as they were moved from country to country. Father hired an artist, an aged man who no doubt needed the money, to restore his precious statuettes.

There were also animals—donkeys, camels, sheep, and oxen with carts—and some huts and houses. The "stage" for Father's Nativity scene was a large platform about fifteen feet wide and seven feet deep. It took up most of the room, leaving about a four-foot walk space in front for visitors who came to view his masterpiece. Father built the landscape himself, carving sheets of cork into trees, hills, rocks, cliffs, roads, and background scenery. Every time the old man would try to help him with the construction, he would gently nudge him aside:

"*Lassa fa' a 'mmé, ce pens'io.*" ("Leave it to me, I'll take care of that.")

After the stage was set to his satisfaction, he began to position the hundred or more figurines. The large ones would go in front, the smaller ones further back, and the tiny ones at the rear. This ingenious arrangement gave the whole scene the illusion of perspective and depth. Father worked for hours on end in his smock, having a wonderful time all by himself. Thinking back on it, I can see that the little room beside the chapel was just about the only place that summer where Father could enjoy some solitude. No one bothered him there—only Dorothy or I sat with him at times and kept him company. We would take turns visiting him for short periods and watching him work with great intensity. Fascinated as I was with his work and happy as I was to be with him, I could not take the heat, the flies, and the smell of the glue for long. Neither could Dorothy. He must have chuckled to himself after we quietly disappeared, leaving him alone, just as he wished. Considering the beauty of the *presepio* and the time and energy invested in it, it was a tragedy that in the end Father was not given the time to enjoy his creation.

FOFÒ was finally able to join us, and he too met the new *mammina*. I think he liked her, although he made Dorothy uncomfortable. The sudden acquisition of yet another "son," and a twenty-one-year-old adult at that, required a good deal of psychological resilience. In addition, as we were told soon after Father's arrival, Dorothy was pregnant. She must have found very few moments that noisy summer to adjust to her new condition and the prospect of motherhood.

After two years in the service, Fofò was elated with the freedom and congeniality of the family circle. Having Father with us compen-

sated for the conspicuous absence from the villa of his beloved Aunt
Rina. As his military leave grew short, he decided to make the most of
the opportunity to talk with Father. One day the entire family was
having lunch. Father sat at the head of the table, Fofò on his right, and
Dorothy at the opposite end. For some reason, Fofò chose this
moment to bring up a matter he had been contemplating for some
time. Perhaps he thought that in this setting, in front of all our relatives, Father would be more likely to accede to his request, or at least
less likely to flatly refuse it. He told Father that he considered himself
an adult and wanted to be on his own, to start some business and to get
married. As he went on, his voice took on an edge, and he sounded
almost arrogant. He concluded his little speech by saying that Papa
was so rich that money meant nothing to him, and he commanded:
"Mi voglio sposare e mi devi dare un milione!" ("I want to get married and
you must give me a million [lire]!")

Without a moment's pause, my father said: *"Ti do' un milione!"* ("I'll
give you a million!") and with the back of his hand slapped Fofò across
the face with such a blow that he went flying off the chair to the floor.
My brother was no weakling, so Father must have given him quite a
whack to knock him off his chair. Fofò was speechless, Dorothy
shocked, and the whole gathering stunned. Somebody helped Fofò
up, and Father embraced him but showed no regret for having struck
him.

"You shouldn't talk like that to your father," he said.

I think he was right. Fofò had spoken disrespectfully. Something
in his tone of voice had smacked of an ultimatum, and as I have said
before, Father did not respond well to ultimatums. He had to show
who was boss, as much to teach my brother a lesson as for the benefit
of the whole family sitting in his house, at his table, eating his food, all
of them supported by his money.

I don't know what followed, because the ever-tactful Miss Saer
immediately rose from the table and led me away. "Come along,
Mimmi, let's go to our room," she said. I didn't dare protest, so off we
went. My brother may have broken down crying after that, because
Dorothy made the comment in her book that Fofò was "given to
weeping bitterly at table."[4] In fact, in my experience, Fofò never wept
at the table, bitterly or otherwise. If he broke down on this occasion
after I left, it must have been out of humiliation, frustration, and the
pain of having been slapped by the father he adored. Dorothy, who
couldn't understand the conversation, simply had no idea what was
going on, and Father may never have told her the details.

Besides, my brother was a stoic. He *never* cried. Once, in a game, he skinned his palms—I remember that blood was pouring from his hands. Grandfather Guido treated the wound by pouring iodine all over it. No matter how it stung, Fofò did not let out a squeak, and not a tear came to his eyes. He had learned self-control in the *collegio*, where he had to be tough to survive. If he had dared to cry, the other boys would have ridiculed him and called him names.

In the end, Father did not give Fofò the money. I don't think he opposed the marriage, but he knew that Fofò was not ready to start a business and may have suspected that he was not the working type in the first place, certainly not yet. He was a *"figlio di papà"* ("daddy's boy") then, and so he remained for the rest of his life, as long as his resources allowed.

WHAT promised to be a happy reunion with Father and a peaceful summer vacation for us all was jarred by a series of natural and political disturbances. First came a small earth tremor, followed within a day by a real earthquake. The old part of the villa was sturdy enough to withstand the quake, but the walls of the new section cracked in several places. At the same time, there was a terrific hailstorm that broke windows, overturned statues in the garden, and tore trees out of the ground. The storm at Signa was a terrifying experience, but the damage was even greater in Florence proper, only nine miles away. More thunderstorms followed, weaker than the first, but strong enough to keep us locked in the villa and to handicap the efforts in Florence to find shelter for the homeless and to clean up the rubble in the streets. Amidst the devastation, there were riots and strikes, and the people were hungry. One day a large crowd of women and children came to the gates of Bellosguardo asking for food. Father listened to their plea and ordered the servants to give them all the bread we had baked for the day, also coldcuts and fruits. Afterward he said that he felt good about helping the poor and hungry.

His satisfaction was short-lived. Word got around that there was food to be had at the villa. Not much later, a crowd of some three hundred men returned to the gate, many of them armed. Vecchiettini, the administrator of Bellosguardo, came running, asking what to do. Father ordered him to let the men in. The crowd marched toward the villa, followed by empty wagons. They unceremoniously demanded all the flour, wine, oil, and bread we had. Father protested, but in vain. The leader of the rabble told him that they were going to take what they wanted, by force if necessary. When Vecchiettini tried to resist, they threatened to hang him on the spot and seemed fully prepared to carry out this act. Father was more angry than frightened; in fact, as he faced the mob, I understood why Fofò called him "a man of iron." But he was also a pragmatist. Realizing there was nothing he could do against three hundred angry communists, he agreed to their demands, with the stipulation that they leave enough food for the household. He made sure that they did, but they still carried off most of the foodstuffs, the livestock, and Father's prized poultry, including four peacocks. For good measure, they commandeered our two cars to help carry away the loot. A day later, the leader brought a small amount of money which he claimed were the proceeds from selling the food. He promised to return the cars later, which he did before the end of the summer.

Dorothy, now in the sixth month of her pregnancy, surely did not need all this excitement. She was terribly lost through the whole summer, unable to communicate with the people around her, with nothing to do all day and nothing to read. The bulk of Papa's library was at Le Panche, and even there, the books were almost exclusively in Italian. So Dorothy spent her days chatting with Martino Ceccanti, Father's former valet and now employed at Bellosguardo, or me, sunbathing, wandering around the property, or playing with the animals. Before the mob took them away, we had chickens, turkeys, rabbits, goats, sheep, and peacocks (brought to Signa by Rina) on the property. Dorothy was afraid of the larger animals but enjoyed watching the strutting peacocks, their magnificent tails displayed in a giant fan. She also loved to stroke the white Belgian hares, marveling at the softness of their fur. Once Father found her sitting with a large rabbit on her lap and went wild at the sight.

"No, no, Doro, don't do! The baby will have long ears and a harelip!"

In the midst of the disturbances, Father had to go back to work. His accompanist, Bruno Bruni, began his daily trek from Florence to Signa. Papa was preparing for the Metropolitan's revival of Halévy's *La Juive,* and time was getting short before the première. The routine was the same as in years before. Bruni came in the morning, and he and Papa practiced until lunch. Then, after the inevitable *siesta* and depending on Papa's mood, they would often continue until late afternoon. Father practiced behind closed doors; as it was his habit to sing *mezza voce,* we barely heard him. To be frank, the whole family simply ignored his singing. Now, if he sang some *real* music, Neapolitan songs or arias from some Italian opera, that would have been a different matter. But *La Juive*? Who cared about that?

As I remember it, Papa had planned to stay in Italy until the end of August, but he changed his mind. He decided to cut his ill-fated "vacation" a couple of weeks short and leave in mid-August. To my indescribable joy, he decided to take me with him to America. Of course, Miss Saer would travel with us.

Before we embarked at Genoa, I had the opportunity to visit the Boy Scout headquarters. Because I was the son of Caruso, I was given the V.I.P. treatment. As the leader showed me around, I was surprised to see racks with at least two dozen rifles arranged in neat rows. Although the Boy Scouts was supposedly a non-military organization, the scouts were being trained to handle firearms as early as 1919. It was a reflection on the atmosphere of the country that made Mussolini's takeover a few years later not only possible but politically necessary.

Italy was in turmoil after the First World War. Street fights and shootings were common, and vandalism rampant. The communists, capitalizing on the situation, incited the populace to anarchy. Everyone hated the rich, and the have-nots often resorted to violence and theft. One particularly dangerous practice evolved during this period: Hooligans would stretch a strong, thin wire across the road at a level that could decapitate an unsuspecting driver. This happened so often that drivers had to install a *tagliafilo* on their cars as a safety measure. This was a serrated, wire-cutting blade mounted between the front bumper and the top of the windshield that could snap the wire. Such a device once saved Fofò's life. Wherever we went, we traveled armed, because a volley from our guns would scare away any would-be thieves. There could be no doubt that Italy, like Germany, needed a strong leader, and it was the great misfortune of both countries that they fell victim to mad and evil dictators.

MY first trip to America was aboard the *Giuseppe Verdi*. It was a fine ship, recently refurbished after serving in the war as a troop carrier. The American soldiers affectionately called it the "Joe Green," translating Verdi's name into English. I enjoyed the trip, although there wasn't much to keep me occupied. Because we made the trip well before the fall season was to begin in New York, there were no celebrities except Caruso on the ship. I made friends with some of the passengers and asked them to sign my autograph book. I must have made a nuisance of myself; borrowing a line from *La Bohème,* the conductor Giulio Setti wrote in my book: "*Mimmi è una civetta che frascheggia con tutti!*" ("Mimmi is a hussy who flirts with everyone!"), making a pun on my nickname and the name of Puccini's heroine Mimì. My relationship with Dorothy remained friendly but without warmth. I was too old to be entertained with games and too young to be treated as an equal. Dorothy felt duty-bound to concern herself with my welfare, but that was the extent of her interest in me while Father was alive.

Papa let me hang around with him, which I was only too happy to do. It was wonderful to spend time with him after the long separation of the war years. The people on board had the good sense and courtesy not to annoy him with their constant attention, yet he could never pass unnoticed, and everyone greeted him with great deference. He was in good spirits and willingly engaged in conversation; on a couple of occasions, he even let himself be coaxed into singing. The crew also gave him very special treatment. Pasta dishes were not the usual fare for first-class passengers, but the chefs in third class prepared some of his favorite Neapolitan dishes and sent them up to him. He loved *calle e trippe all'aglio ed olio* (tripe and gelatinous gristle with garlic and oil), *calzone di calamari* (pizza dough made into a pocket and stuffed with baby squid, chopped parsley, and garlic), and of course *spaghetti alla napoletana*.

Papa could come and go on all parts of the ship as he pleased—even the captain's bridge was not off limits to him. The captain did all he could to make Father feel welcome, and the two often engaged in lively conversation. Once, not wanting me to feel left out, the captain turned to me saying he had heard I was a real autograph hound. How many signatures did I have from my famous father? Papa and I looked at each other in amazement. He was Papa to me, not the great Caruso, and it never occurred to either of us that his signature belonged in my little book.

"Shouldn't you give an autograph to your son, Mr. Caruso?" the captain asked.

"I don't have my book with me, Papa," I said.

"Never mind," said Father. "Here is an autograph for you."

He had a broad platinum ring studded with seven diamonds. We called it the ring of the week, because each perfect diamond had a different color, crystal clear, white, yellow, red, blue, violet, and black, and each day Papa would turn it to wear a different color on top.[5] At this point he made a fist, and with one of the diamonds, he signed his name on the window pane of the captain's bridge.

"I am honored, Mr. Caruso," said the captain, "especially since your boy can't take that signature with him. To have Verdi's name on my ship and yours on my bridge—I couldn't ask for more!"

When the good ship "Joe Green" was finally salvaged, I wonder if anyone was aware of that unique memento on the bridge.

During one of our strolls on the deck, I heard Papa singing snatches from *La Juive* in French. I asked him how he learned French and whether it was a difficult language. There was nothing to it, he assured me, and he decided to teach me some French on the spot. We started with the simplest phrases, which I repeated after him as best as I could. Soon we came to "*tu es*" ("you are").

"*Too es,*" I pronounced it, making the French *tu* sound like the same word in Italian.

"No, no, no! *Tu,*" said Papa, "not *too.*"

"*Too.*"

"*Tu!*"

"*Too.*"

"Look, Mimmi," he said, puckering his lips. "*Tu!*"

"*Too.*"

Papa lost his patience and raised his voice.

"*Senti, figlio mio, fa la bocca da culo di gallina. Tu!*" ("Listen, my son, shape your mouth like a chicken's ass! *Tu!*"

And there my French lessons ended. Many years later I spent some time in Paris in the company of a lovely French girl. She taught me quite a bit of French, and Papa would have been proud of the rapid progress I made mastering her tongue.

WE docked in Jersey City on 3 September 1919. New York was hidden in the mists of a downpour. The rain did not deter the flock of reporters who came to meet the boat and surrounded Father as soon as they caught a glimpse of him. To lengthen their reports, they described his and Dorothy's attire in minute detail:

> Caruso wore a smart-looking blue serge norfolk suit, a gray double-breasted waistcoat, tan oxford shoes with broad silk laces, a blue-and-black silk cravat and a pearl pin, with green velour hat lopped up on the left side in cavalier style. Mrs. Caruso looked very well indeed, and wore a blue tailored suit and a hat set with peacock feathers. She was a little disappointed when a friend informed her that her parents had not forgiven her marriage to the tenor and were not among the

crowd waiting at the top of the pier in Jersey City to welcome her home.

Word of the uprisings in Florence had reached New York, and Papa was asked about the Florentine mob that took our food. He told the story; as usual, the reporters allowed themselves a few embellishments:

> The taking of the 27 demijohns of wine did not matter much, but I could not live there with my wife and family after the food was gone. Besides the American hams I took from New York with me, the peasants stole a hogshead of olive oil and raided my prize chicken farm, one of the best known in Italy, which contained 150 varieties of choice poultry.
>
> I thought that when I had invited the peasants to eat and drink of the best that I had on tables set out under the trees on the big lawn, they would appreciate my kindness, as it was many months since they had tasted such food, their leaders told me. To my surprise and disgust a large delegation appeared at my house a few days later and handed me a document with big official-looking seals attached which, they said, was a communal order to take over all my food and wine, which they proceeded to do without any tedious preliminaries. The people have always proved ungrateful to those who have been their benefactors throughout history.[6]

The reporters then asked me some questions, but being terribly self-conscious, I could barely mumble a few words. We were much amused to read the following day that "Enrico, junior, is taller than his father and speaks a little English, which he acquired while serving three months with the Italian Y.M.C.A."[7] I hadn't heard such hearty laughter from Papa all summer. "Enrico junior speaks a leetle Inglish!" he kept repeating all day. "Leetle Inglish!"

Bruno Zirato, Father's Italo-American secretary, met us at the pier. After the obligatory session with the reporters, we could disembark. As we got into the waiting car and started passing through the docks, I could not hide my disappointment.

"Is this New York?" I asked Zirato.

"Oh, no!" he laughed. "This is New Jersey. We first cross the river, then we are in New York."

"You will love it," added Dorothy. "You will have a nice room at the Knickerbocker, and there is a big cat outside the window that winks at you."

I found the hotel very nice, my room pleasant, and the much-heralded big cat, which was a giant advertisement, rather silly.

A day or two after our arrival, I went to Papa's suite in the morning to greet him. As I entered the front room, I walked into a mob of waiting reporters. Before I realized what was happening, I was surrounded and bombarded with questions. "What did I think of President Wilson?" was one of them. I don't remember exactly what I said, but I made it plain that I was unhappy about Wilson giving Trieste and Dalmatia to Yugoslavia. The next day's headline was something like "Caruso's Son Disapproves of President Wilson," and Papa hit the ceiling.

"Remember Mimmi, never say anything negative to the press, and never, absolutely never, discuss politics, religion, or other singers!"

Father always had a good time with reporters and was expert at pleasing them. He made good copy, and the reporters loved him. "They have to make a living too," he used to say, and he helped them as much as he could by being a cooperative subject, informal and charming. I saw him handle the press in Italy and again in the United States. In New York, he would say: "Ah, my friends, we had a terrrrible crossing. The sea behaved very badly." In Italy, it was: "*Abbiammo avuto un viaggio fantastico! Il mare era calmo come un specchio.* ("We had a fantastic journey! The sea was calm as a mirror.") The reporters never realized that to amuse himself, he always said the opposite of what actually happened. But I had to admire his excellent rapport with the gentlemen of the press. They all seemed eager to be his friends, and it was years before I learned how dangerous the American way of reporting could be.

CHAPTER SIXTEEN

Last Seasons

D OROTHY was quick to grasp the circumstances of my upbringing and found it absurd that a fifteen-year-old boy should be under the tutelage of a governess. Supposedly it was she who talked Father into taking me back with them to America. She wanted me to have an American education, and because I spoke English fluently, there was no language barrier. Miss Saer was to come with us. As always, she obeyed orders without voicing her preferences.

In light of the developments, I cannot understand why Lei was taken along. With the baby soon to be born, the logical thing would have been to keep her on and have her raise the child as she had raised me. This must have been Miss Saer's secret hope as well. She was devoted to my father, and as he was always satisfied with her, she had no reason to doubt that she would be the chosen governess for his next child as well. Unfortunately, Mrs. Caruso didn't care for Miss Saer at all. Dorothy felt that Lei had been with the family too long; she knew too many sordid details about the past and may have felt loyalties to Papa or to Rina which would be a disadvantage in the long run. Dorothy was too smart to show open hostility, but she soon made it plain that she did not want Lei around. To get rid of her, she first had to get rid of me.

Dorothy and her siblings had never known a home life. She was sent to a convent at the age of thirteen and remained there through her nineteenth year; her brothers were also sent away from home. It was natural for her that I, too, should go to a boarding school. At her initiative, it was decided that I should go to the boys' school her brother Romeyn had attended, along with the sons of the first families of New England. I had no choice in the matter. I sorrowfully said good-bye to Lei. This was to be the first time since I could remember that she would not be at "home" with me and I would not find her waiting each day after school.

As soon as I left for school, Miss Saer was dismissed. I don't know when this decision was made, or whether Lei knew in advance that her services would no longer be required once we arrived in New York. Conceivably, it was her preference to find employment in America rather than returning to England. For once, I have serious doubts whether my father displayed his reputed generosity. He must have given Miss Saer severance pay or a farewell bonus, but I don't believe it was substantial. Within a short time, she was hired by a family in Meriden, New Jersey, to look after two young girls. She continued to work as a governess for a decade and a half. For her own child, Dorothy hired a Swedish nanny by the name of Helen Ridstrom. She was a competent woman but a true Nordic type, cold and remote as a fjord. To my mind, she could not compare to gentle and wonderful Lei.

Dorothy's view of Lei was entirely different. She wrote that Miss Saer "was so frightened of Enrico that she never dared address him above a whisper."[1] Dorothy had the most superficial sense of their relationship. Miss Saer was a cultured, soft-spoken woman, and she had a deep respect for Papa. But frightened of him? Never! Once, in Italy, I remember that we stopped in Pisa and went to see the Leaning Tower. Workmen were repairing one of the altars in the cathedral, and there was a heap of loose pieces from the mosaics. Father picked up a piece and slipped it into his pocket as a souvenir. Miss Saer gave him a stern look and reprimanded him in no uncertain terms:

"Mr. Caruso, don't do that! What would happen if everyone who walked by took a piece? There would be nothing left of that beautiful picture. Put that piece right back!!"

And Father sheepishly put the piece back.

Miss Saer was always polite with Papa, but she was definitely not subservient. She never hesitated to stand up to him. Shortly after we arrived in New York, for instance, Father got the idea that I should

type some letters for him. When I protested that I didn't know how to
type, he said:

"You play the piano, don't you?"

"Yes, sort of," I replied.

"Well, then, why can't you type?"

Miss Saer happened to be within earshot. She was as dismayed by
the absurdity of Father's reasoning as I was, but I was afraid to say so
and she was not.

"Mr. Caruso, that is a foolish thing to say. Typing has nothing to do
with piano playing, and you know it. Or are you just trying to pull the
boy's leg?"

Papa half smiled, half grunted, and dropped the subject. But I was
impressed that Lei came to my defense and stood up to almighty Papa.

I WAS still in New York when Father was scheduled to go to Camden
for a recording session on 8 September 1919. He offered to take me
along, and I jumped at the opportunity. We drove to Camden in his
powder-green Lancia, and I was surprised that he was no more apprehensive than any clerk or plumber on his way to work. He didn't talk
much on the way, but when he did, it was obvious that he was not
trying to spare his voice. Another thing I found amazing, not then but
many years later: He did not warm up before the session, or at least I
have absolutely no recollection that he did. He just turned toward the
recording horn and sang.

When we walked into the studio, he introduced me to the
orchestra and the conductor, Joseph Pasternack: "This is Mimmi, my
son." The entire orchestra stood up, and the violinists beat their bows
on their instruments in a gesture of greeting. I grinned, blushed, and
could have gone through the floor with embarrassment. The engineer
showed me the recording equipment before the session began. Later,
it was covered from view by a canvas curtain and I could not see the
mechanics of recording, but I enjoyed watching the whole process.

Father recorded multiple takes of a group of Italian songs. I had
never before heard him sing at full voice at such close range. The
sound that filled the studio was a marvel that finally made me sit up and
respond to the miracle of Father's singing. He sang magnificently. The
volume and the beauty of his voice were overwhelming. The voice had
such aural solidity that one felt the sound itself had a physical presence
and could somehow be touched. I soon forgot all about the machinery,
cutting needles and the rest, and listened to Father transfixed. I could

not understand then or in the years since why so many of the takes were considered unsatisfactory. They sounded positively wonderful to me. Thinking back on this session, I believe it was at this time when my mind truly opened up to vocal music. I finally felt the splendor of my father's singing.

It struck me that Father was not merely delivering a tune but was living each song. His face was animated, and he acted out the words as he would on the concert stage, so that I not only heard but also *saw* the song. The only particular number I remember was " 'A vucchella." He sang it several times, and each take was better than before. He had a good time singing it too: He would smile and pucker up—one could swear he actually saw some lovely girl smiling back at him from the recording horn—and he closed the song with a flirtatious wink. I think the released take admirably captures the spirit of D'Annunzio's playful little poem as well as Father's ability to create a mood with sound and inflection. The recording he made that day is one of my all-time favorites.

Fred Maisch, who was a recording engineer for the Victor Company for thirty-six years and who made thirty thousand master discs in his time, said in 1944 that when Caruso recorded the "Quartet" from *Rigoletto,* he had to stand "back six feet from the other singers so as not to blast the recording apparatus."[2] Reading that comment and remembering the session of 1919, I am certain he was not exaggerating.

I SPENT my first school year in America at the Gunnery School in Washington, Connecticut, where I was enrolled under the Anglicized name of Henry Caruso, Jr. The school had nothing to do with firearms but was so named after its founder, Mr. Gunn. After Mr. Gunn's death, the school was run by his daughter and her husband, Mr. and Mrs. Brinsmade. Their sons Fred and Chapin were on the faculty: Fred taught languages, and Chapin mathematics and science.

I had a wonderful time at the Gunnery, although the boys gave me a terrific hazing. Having survived my initiation, I was accepted. I participated in winter sports, and when spring came I played baseball well enough to become manager of the team. I had come a long way from the solitary little British boy at Cricklewood! The spirit of the place was congenial, and the Brinsmades treated us as if we were all their own children.

Father was in Mexico City, and his letters to Dorothy contained many references to me. I realized many years later, when Dorothy published his letters, that my welfare was often on his mind. He tried to stay in touch through correspondence, admonishing me to study hard; and I dutifully answered him. But I thought he wrote only out of obligation, and I was still too young to sense or appreciate his sensitivity. My coolness hurt him. In his expressive and charmingly misspelled English, he wrote to Dorothy on 14 October 1919: "I receive a letter from Mimmi, not ver expansive. I will answer him in the same way."[3] And on October 23: "Mimmi wrote me, but without affections—so cold. This hirt me very much."[4] It seems we were both waiting for a show of affection from the other one, and we remained in a standoff.

Father called me after he got back to New York; and on one occasion, when he was scheduled to sing in Hartford, he sent a car to get me. Unfortunately, a tremendous snowstorm spoiled our plans. The car could not get through, and we missed our chance to spend an evening together.

I went to New York for the Christmas holidays. We all looked forward to the imminent birth of the baby. My half-sister Gloria arrived on 18 December 1919. She had four Christian names, but soon after her birth Father began to call her *Puschina,* and he never referred to her by any other name.

In spite of his feeling that he already had too many women in his life, as he had commented to Maestro Tanara the year before, Papa decided long before the baby was born that it had to be a girl. He was beside himself with joy when he laid eyes upon his little daughter. The baby was healthy and beautiful (with neither long ears nor a harelip), and her features were the very image of Papa's, which he never failed to point out to anyone who would listen. There was no end to the calls, telegrams, and well-wishers.

During the holiday, Father took me around to meet some of his friends at the opera house. I met Scotti, Amato, Matzenauer, Gatti-Casazza, and others. Many times, he took me along to his favorite restaurants, Doctor Pane's and Del Pezzo's on Forty-sixth Street, and a couple of times we went to dine at the home of the Garcias. They were wealthy Cuban "sugar barons," absentee landlords who preferred the cosmopolitan life of New York to that of Havana. Papa was very much at ease in their home. He enjoyed cooking, and I can still see him preparing a pasta dish in their kitchen on one of our visits. Another time, he cooked dinner at the Vanderbilt Hotel for a small group of friends. He made the spaghetti sauce so hot that no one else could eat it, but he shoveled it into his mouth without blinking an eye. To this day, I don't know whether he made the sauce hot by accident or because he liked it that way.

The Garcias had two sons and a daughter, Corina. She was a typical Spanish beauty with shiny, long black hair, large, luminous eyes, and skin as white as alabaster. I was very much attracted to Corina Garcia. Unwilling to wait until Father was ready for another visit, I decided to invite Corina to tea at Schrafft's. That, of course, required money—certainly more cash than my weekly allowance of one dollar.

"Papa, I would like to have five dollars."

"You got good shoes?"

"Yes, Papa."

"Are you well dressed?"

"Yes, Papa."

"Does it rain in your room?"

"No, Papa."

"Then why do you want five dollars?"

"I would like to take Corina Garcia to tea."

"Young man, you will have tea with Corina when I take you along to their house. You will sit straight on your chair and behave like a gentleman. Now go."

I left, my hopes for a wonderful afternoon with Corina dashed by an apparent whim of my father's. A few minutes later, Zirato came bringing twenty-five dollars from Papa. Dorothy, who had witnessed the scene between Father and me, followed him.

"Don't ask your Father for anything," she said. "If you want something, ask me, and I will get it for you."

"Why did I get that lecture? I only wanted to take Corina to tea!"

"That's all right, don't worry about it. Now I will call the Garcias and invite Corina on your behalf. I will also have a table reserved for you at the *thé dansant,* and the two of you can enjoy Paul Whiteman and his orchestra."

I was grateful to Dorothy for her help.

This was one of many occasions when I learned that one was not to ask Papa directly for anything. It was his nature to want to take the initiative himself; otherwise, he would become contrary for no discernible reason. Dorothy learned this in a short time. If she did not want to go out, she would say:

"Rico, let's go out to Del Pezzo's."

"Why do you want to go to Del Pezzo's? We have a perfectly good chef. He will cook a fine meal and we can have a quiet evening at home."

If she wanted to eat out, she would say:

"Rico dear, what shall I tell the chef to fix for dinner?"

"I am tired of his cooking. Let's eat out. We don't go out enough. We'll go to Doctor Pane's."

I don't know whether Father was at all aware of what he was doing, but his *spirito di contraddizione* surfaced very often. He was argumentative by nature as far back as I can remember. When it came to giving, he had to initiate the gesture and was extremely resentful when he felt pressured. On this subject, Richard Barthélemy, his long-time accompanist, once told me a story about a very elegant Parisian society lady who came to invite him to take part in a benefit concert in Paris *after* Father had seen his name listed in the morning papers.[5] He was so annoyed that he made the lady beg then demanded an exorbitant fee. After the public announcement, the organizers could not afford *not* to have him participate, so they paid. When he had the check in hand, he endorsed it as his personal contribution for the cause. In short, he was willing to help or to give, but if forced, he became downright obstinate. All the same, he probably sang in more charity events and benefit concerts than any other singer with the exception of Beniamino Gigli.

"DO you want to go to a movie?" Father asked me one day. I was happy to join him, and off we went to the Capitol Theater. Not wanting to be late, I asked him to hurry.

"I want to be late," he answered. I couldn't understand why on earth he would want to miss the beginning of a movie, but I soon found out. The silent movie houses in those days had an organist or a small orchestra that played music appropriate to the action on the screen. The moment we entered the theater, Father was recognized. Word must have spread like wildfire that Caruso was there, because no sooner were we in our seats than the orchestra began to play "Ridi Pagliaccio!" The entire audience stood up, turned toward us, and broke into applause. Father graciously acknowledged the spontaneous demonstration, but he felt uncomfortable and embarrassed. I finally understood why he preferred to slip into a movie house after the lights were down and dart out the moment the show ended.

During my first few weeks in New York, complete strangers often asked me to give their regards to Papa. Every one of them was "a friend" of his. When I would deliver the message and say to Papa, "I met Mr. Smith, a friend of yours, who sends you his regards," he would say, *"Sono tutti amici miei, ma io non li conosco."* ("They are all my friends, except I don't know them.")

IN 1919 De Segurola left the Metropolitan, and in May of that year, he became the first director of the Gran Casino de la Playa de Marianao in Havana. It was a gambling casino and turned out to be an enormously lucrative venture; the roulette tables yielded $1,400,000 in three months, the amount projected for twelve. With this kind of revenue, De Segurola could afford to think big. In order to bring in more customers, he offered to underwrite nine performances of grand opera if Adolfo Bracale could bring Caruso to Havana.

After signing Papa in 1895 for his first opera season in Cairo, Bracale became a full-time operatic impresario. Now, with the backing of the casino, he became obsessed with the idea of presenting Caruso in Cuba. Father maintained that he would not go there and decided to set a price so high that Bracale could not meet it. The two men met in New York and in a test of nerves that lasted only minutes, negotiated a contract for ten performances—including two matinées—at $90,000. When word of the terms spread through the musical community, everyone thought that Bracale was crazy. As it turned out, not only did he make a handsome profit, but the casino, which had expected to end up $40,000–50,000 in the red according to De Segurola, netted a $90,000 profit.

Father left for Atlanta on his way to Cuba in April 1920, Zirato traveling with him. Within days of his departure, the Knickerbocker Hotel, his New York home for ten years, was sold. It was to be converted to an office building, and all the occupants had to move out. Father was annoyed that James B. Regan, his "landlord" for over a decade, did not tell him about the sale before he left New York and so give him the chance to decide where to move and handle the arrangements himself. Now the task was left to Dorothy. Through cables and correspondence, they weighed the alternatives. Father contemplated moving to the Hotel Biltmore but in the end decided on the Vanderbilt at Thirty-fourth Street and Park Avenue. He rented a large and spacious apartment on the top floor with an entrance hall, a reception room, a dining room, a large drawing room with a piano, a bedroom with twin beds, an adjacent nursery, a practice room, baths, a kitchen, and a room for the Swedish nanny. Additional rooms were opened up when we had family visitors or when I was there.

Immediately after his last appearance in Atlanta, a performance of *L'Elisir d'amore* on 1 May 1920, Father traveled on to Cuba. He wrote to Dorothy en route from Jacksonville, Florida, and arrived in Havana on May 5.

With Father away, Dorothy had to cope with the details of the move. Papa's return to an unfamiliar apartment was extremely unpleasant for him. The furniture was the same, but the building, the rooms, and the layout of the apartment were different. Father adjusted easily to hotel living on his travels; but in his home life, he needed order and a sense of permanence.

The move upset Father tremendously for still another reason. In Neapolitan tradition, a forced change of home or residence is an omen of misfortune to come. He mentioned this to Dorothy more than once, but she did not share his typically Italian superstitions. When she took the idea lightly, he just shook his head—he knew better.

Superstition or not, all his troubles began immediately after the move.

AFTER our dreadful experiences of the previous summer, and with the situation in Italy still deteriorating, a summer vacation at Bellosguardo was out of the question in 1920. Shortly after Father left for Atlanta in April, Dorothy moved to East Hampton on Long Island with Gloria, the servants, her brother Park Benjamin, Jr., and his wife and children. The house was rented from Albert Herter, and Dorothy and Papa planned to stay there all summer so that he could rest after the strenuous Cuban tour. It was a large, rambling house on Lake Georgica with a separate guest cottage, which became my home when the school year ended in May. Papa wrote to Dorothy on May 14: "I hope the coming of Mimmi dont trouble you—tell him to be a gentleman and not a boy."[6]

To protect the family at East Hampton while Father was away, George W. Fitzgerald, our chauffeur, was given a handgun. "Fitz" was a tall, pleasant man of forty or so, and a crack shot. Once, as he sat cleaning his revolver, I asked him to show how well he could shoot. He set up five cans at some twenty-five paces and without pausing hit every one of them in the middle.

Father's accompanist, Salvatore Fucito, used to come to East Hampton even in Father's absence. Fucito was an excellent musician with impeccable credentials. A graduate of the Accademia di Santa Cecilia in Rome, he was an assistant conductor at the Met from 1915 to

1917, and he served as vocal coach to a long line of outstanding artists which included Giulio Crimi, Rosa Raisa, Margaret Romaine, Mary Mellish, and Luca Botta. He was a well-mannered, congenial man who was always welcome at the house. To keep him busy, Father gave him the assignment of trying to improve my skills at the piano. He tried, but I had little interest in the piano. Instead, we used to wrestle in the spacious living room, having a good time.

We all enjoyed East Hampton, and it would have been a pleasant vacation, except for a couple of harrowing incidents. While Father was still in Cuba, someone broke into the house and took Dorothy's jewel box, which contained almost all her jewelry. At the sound of the alarm, Fitzgerald came to the room. He then ran after the burglar or burglars, firing three shots in the dark, but the chase was to no avail. All he found was the empty jewel box in the garden, along with a couple of small pieces the burglars had dropped. The rest of the jewelry was gone.

The burglary occurred Tuesday night, June 8, and ended our peaceful existence for the rest of the summer. A never-ending stream of policemen and detectives roamed the house and grounds for weeks, looking for clues, and examining and cross-examining everyone. *The New York Times* reported on developments daily. According to the first report, "Mrs. Caruso told the police that all of the servants were trusted by her and that she would not for an instant consider the possibility of an 'inside job.' " She added: "All of the stolen jewelry was set in platinum. It included many gifts which were doubly prized for sentimental reasons."[7]

One police theory was that the jewels were actually stolen sometime between Sunday night, when Dorothy put them away upon returning from New York, and 10 p.m. Tuesday. Thus the robbery was staged to cover up the theft, and in fact the box was empty when the robbers took it. E. M. Gattle, a jeweler at 630 Fifth Avenue in New York, was able to provide purchase records and descriptions of the stolen jewelry, and the June 11 issue of *The New York Times* published a complete list, giving the total purchase price as $118,068. At the time of the theft, it was estimated that the jewelry had an appreciated market value of $236,000.

Because of his position, poor Fitzgerald, described in the *Times* as "a direct, square-looking chap," found himself the center of police attention. In a public statement, he said to reporters that he knew he was "under suspicion," but his conscience was clear. He added that Mr. Caruso had been "wonderfully kind" to him, paying him $180 a month plus board for his family. When Fitz last drove him to the train, Father had given the chauffeur fifty dollars, saying, "Here, Fitz, play poker with this when I'm gone."

In the week after the burglary, Dorothy made a complete turnabout. The following Tuesday, 15 June 1920, *The New York Times* reported that Mrs. Caruso and other members of the family held the "conviction that the thief is of their household." Then we were momentarily distracted by the news of a bomb explosion during *Aida* in Havana that occurred the day before. Apparently the terrorist act was not aimed at Father, and he was unharmed.

In the meantime, the hundred-acre estate was invaded by detectives representing two insurance companies, the Caruso family, Suffolk County, and East Hampton. Ten extra detectives commenced a systematic search on June 15. The police, eager to solve the burglary in a hurry, found Fitzgerald a convenient scapegoat. By this time, Fitzgerald had wisely hired an attorney and refused to talk further with reporters.

On June 15, Fitz was arrested and charged with having violated the Sullivan law by carrying the gun he had fired three times on the night of the robbery. He told the newsmen that Dorothy had given the gun to him when the family arrived at the East Hampton estate on May 8, and that she had told him he "did not need any permit, that Mr. Caruso had made the arrangements with the police in New York City."[8] Henry J. (or L.) and Frederick E. Goldsmith, lawyers for Fitzgerald, called the chauffeur's arrest a "cheap frame-up by the detectives."[9]

This it certainly was. Dorothy seemed to believe that Fitz had been, at the very least, an accomplice in the burglary. More than once, she expressed the fear that Fitz would vanish from East Hampton before the matter was settled; thus the police found a pretext to take him into custody. After his arrest, Fitz cabled Father: "ENRICO CARUSO, SANTA CLARA, CUBA. ARRESTED FOR HAVING GUN YOU GAVE ME. MADAM REFUSED TO GO MY BAIL. FITZ."[10] Dorothy's only comment was that "she had nothing to do with his arrest."[11]

Fitz, ever loyal to Father, said: "I think Mr. Caruso is the finest man that walks this earth. I know that he does not know half of what has been happening here. That is why I sent him the cable message today." As for Dorothy's fear that he might vanish, Fitz called the idea "ridiculous. I won't leave Mr. Caruso or his place through my own volition until I receive orders from him."[12]

All the servants were upset about Fitz's arrest. His $1,000 bail was posted by John Easer, caretaker and gardener of the estate. The other servants and members of the family were subpoenaed to testify in court, but the inquiry produced no evidence. On June 18, Fitzgerald's name was cleared. Detective Thomas J. Corrigan declared: "I have absolutely eliminated the chauffeur. Fitzgerald, I am convinced, is innocent of any part in the crime."[13]

On July 3, when Father arrived home, the place was still a madhouse. We waited for him at the train station in New York and arrived in East Hampton in the afternoon. He shook hands with Fitz with an inscrutable expression on his face which even the reporters were unable to classify with adjectives. But on July 8, *The New York Times* carried this report:

> George Fitzgerald, for seven years chauffeur for Enrico Caruso, was discharged last night, but his dismissal did not become known until this afternoon. . . . Mrs. Caruso insisted that there was no connection between the gem robbery and Fitzgerald's discharge. She said that she had not liked the chauffeur and his dismissal had been a subject of conversation between herself and Caruso for some time.

In the end, Dorothy succeeded in pushing out Fitz, another oldtimer in Papa's entourage. Father paid him an extra month's salary, a distinctly ungenerous gesture toward a man who had served him faithfully for seven years and whom the police had cleared of any involvement in the burglary. Fitz was deeply hurt and left on the first train in the morning.

The jewels were never recovered. One piece Dorothy had believed to be among the stolen jewelry was later found in her bank safe. Insurance broker Nathan M. Guinsburg handled Father's claim against the Federal Insurance Company. According to Guinsburg, "Mr. Caruso would not permit a claim to be filed until he returned from Cuba, some time after the robbery. Within five days of the filing of the claim, the Federal Insurance Company turned over to me a check covering the loss, which amounted to $75,735."[14]

AS if the commotion about the robbery were not enough, soon after his return from Cuba, Father received a letter from the Black Hand threatening to kill him, Dorothy, and Gloria unless he paid them $50,000. Father instructed Dorothy not to let anyone know about the blackmail letter. According to Dorothy's later account,[15] on the day the money was to be delivered, Father arranged a casual outing by car for Dorothy, Gloria, the nanny, and himself. Instead of returning home, they met the Long Island train, which made an unscheduled stop as previously arranged by detectives, and traveled to the city. They stayed in New York a few days until Father felt it was safe to return. An Italian detective accompanied them to East Hampton and stayed to provide protection.

I knew nothing of this. The only thing I recall is that I stayed at the neighboring villa of my friend, Henry Huddlestone Rogers, Jr. The Rogers family had a Mediterranean-style palace at South Hampton, and Millicent Rogers was Dorothy's long-time friend.

The jewel theft and the ransom note produced a flurry of unwelcome visitors. Papa, finding himself surrounded by his wife's family, a staff of eleven servants, policemen, detectives, investigators, insurance agents, and nosy reporters who barraged him with questions from morning to night, began to have second thoughts about the situation he had gotten himself into. One day I walked in on him as he sat on the edge of his bed, his head in his hands. Looking worn and dejected, he mumbled to no one in particular: "*Chi me l'ha fatto fare? Chi me l'ha fatto fare?*" ("Who made me do it?")

Dorothy recognized Father's distress and did her best to shield him from the intruders. During this period, he was suffering from frequent, intense headaches which only the passage of time could help. When he was prostrate with pain, he needed quiet and seclusion, both of which were elusive this summer.

Once in a while, in an attempt to escape the commotion at the house, Papa and I took a little motor boat, crossed the lake, and walked to a sandbar by the ocean. He would wade out in the water and swim à la Neapolitan—with more effort than style. There were no other bathers in sight, and we could enjoy a leisurely swim undisturbed. We would frolic in the water; he would let me climb on his shoulders, hold me by the ankles, then flip me into the water. He loved the sun and the sand, and after a swim we would lie on the sloping, sandy shore. He would sunbathe, or I would bury him in the sand from head to toe. He believed that the heat of the sand combined with the iodine of the sea was beneficial for the body and very relaxing. I wish I had a picture of him with only his large, grinning face showing above the sand. We must have been a sight to behold: a teenage boy on a mound of sand conversing with a live head.

Being alone with Papa was an unusual situation that summer. On the sandbar, I had him all to myself, and I was his only audience. He was glad to be able to talk to me in Italian. He spoke English quite fluently by this time. Still, Italian was his native tongue and the language above all others whose beauty and musical sound he enjoyed. As he lay there immobile and relaxed, we had quiet talks punctuated by long silences—not conversations so much as monologues prompted by my questions. He would reminisce and tell me little stories from his youth. For instance, he told me how he used to go barefoot to spare his only pair of shoes. When I remarked that it must have been painful, he said, lapsing into his Neapolitan dialect:

"Eh! Uno ce fa l'abitùdënë! 'A suola d' 'o piede ricresce, ma 'a suola d' 'a scarpe se consuma e costa soldi rimetterla." ("Eh! One gets used to it! The sole of your foot grows back, but the sole of the shoe wears out and it costs money to fix it.")

Father said he always wore shoes to church, *pe' rispetto,* out of respect. They had enough to eat; but he was a young and active boy, and no matter how much food his mother put on his plate, it was never enough. When he would say he was still hungry, his father would tell him, *"Va, bevi nu bicchiërë d'acqua."* ("Go, drink a glass of water.") It began to dawn on me why he had given me the long litany of questions when I asked for five dollars. To his way of thinking, I had food, shelter, and clothing—I had everything I needed, so why should I have asked for money?

His mind wandered back to his beloved Naples. He talked about the bay, the sunset, the thousands of stars lighting up the night sky. At sunrise, he told me, the fishermen went out in the bay with their *arizza,* their dragnet, about six feet deep and two hundred or more yards long. The net hung in the water, suspended by floating corks. Then the boats pulled the net all the way to the shore, and the men closed it and drew it from the water. "You could see the striped bass jumping, their silvery sides sparkling in the sunlight. Then the women loaded the catch on rattan trays and carried them on their heads into town, crying through the streets *'Péscë fresco! Péscë fresco!'* Those were fresh fish!"

Then he told me how he used to go "lamp fishing." He would stand in the bow of the boat, which was lit by a torch, and when a fish attracted to the boat by the light swam nearby, he would spear it with a trident. Others would attach lines with hooks to floating corks, leave them overnight, and pull in the fish in the morning.

It was wonderful to have such talks with Father, and I was sorry each time the sun began to set and we had to go back to the house.

Lake Georgica was full of fish, and Dorothy tried to interest Father in fishing. He and I went to the end of the pier, dangled our feet in the water, and waited. I put the worms on the hooks, for Papa wouldn't touch them. He said they reminded him of the worms in the bellies of the eels that his stepmother used to cook for Christmas. The eels tasted wonderful, but it was distasteful to watch them being prepared.

I taught Papa how to "cast," to watch the floating cork on the line, and to "strike" when the cork dipped under. He became quite proficient at this method of fishing, but when he caught a little fish, I had to take it off the hook for him. We didn't catch enough to make a meal, and in the end we threw our fish back. Papa concluded that this was fun but a waste of time, and he felt sorry for the fish. After a couple of outings, he lost interest in fishing.

At the house, Father and I played the Italian card games *scopa* and *bazzica*. When I won, which was much too often to his way of thinking, his paternal pride at my skill was greatly tempered by the fact that he was the one I had beaten.

When Father needed peace and quiet, he would retreat to one of the rooms and work on a bas-relief model of himself in the role of Eléazar. After that project was finished, he worked with his stamps, incorporating the latest acquisitions into the collection. Sometimes I joined him, and we sat together, silently pasting stamps into our respective albums. Dorothy joined us from time to time or kept Father company without me, helping him to arrange the stamps. On these occasions, neither Dorothy nor I was allowed to talk, and only Father's voice broke the silence as he now and then pointed out a particularly beautiful specimen and commented on it.

Father had a beautiful and valuable collection. He spent hours and hours arranging the stamps in albums. Although he knew a lot about philately, I am certain that he did not collect stamps for their value but rather for their beauty of color and design. A beautiful commemorative block worth fifty cents gave him more pleasure than an ugly but rare stamp worth thousands of dollars. He bought stamps wherever he went, and his collection was wondrous and well organized, consisting of mint and cancelled stamps of great value. It contained sets from all the British colonies, from the half-penny up to the pound sterling, all in booklets. He had a complete or near-complete collection of all Italy's stamps from the very beginning, also extensive collections of German, French, Spanish, Russian, and U.S. sets. I remember the commemorative issues of the various expositions, all in mint condition, as were the British and Italian stamps.

As it happened, on the boat trip over from Italy, I had stumbled upon a small trunk pushed under the bunk bed in my cabin. Out of curiosity I opened it, and my eyes grew wide. There were stamps by the millions, or so it seemed. I must admit that the sight of such a treasure trove was too strong a temptation. I was no more ethical than my brother had been on similar occasions, and I helped myself to as many stamps as I dared to filch. Perhaps it was just as well; when Papa died, Dorothy took possession of the whole collection, which had a value placed at a six-digit figure.

WRITER and music critic Pierre V. R. Key was a professional friend of Father's. Key was a year older than Papa, and they got along well. Father, who had a pet name for everyone he liked, used to call Key "Pietro Chiave," translating his name into Italian. After many years of acquaintance, Key persuaded him to tell the story of his life for a future biography. They began to collaborate in late 1919, and the New York correspondent for the *Daily Express* reported on 28 November 1919 that Caruso said he was writing his biography for publication after his death. In the previous summer, Dorothy consented to the printing of extracts from some of the letters Father had written to her from Mexico City.

According to the agreement, Key was given a series of interviews between February and July of 1920. These sessions took place anywhere and anytime that Father could fit them into his schedule. The two men met in his suite at the Knickerbocker, in Atlantic City, in the drawing room of the New York Central train between Detroit and New York, and at the summer house on Long Island. Key visited us at East Hampton more than once, sometimes adding to the bedlam in the aftermath of the burglary.

Father always graciously made himself available. I remember that on one of Key's visits to East Hampton, Papa had a terrific headache. In addition, there had been some misunderstanding about the time of Key's arrival, and we delayed our lunch until two o'clock, a great concession on Papa's part. Then we could wait no longer, and we were in the middle of lunch when Key showed up, explaining that he thought he was expected to arrive "after lunch." When the meal was over, Papa had to excuse himself and lie down in the boathouse, his headache was so unbearable. For Key's sake, however, he rejoined us an hour later and obligingly resumed the narrative of his youth.

On July 15, Papa's name day, Dorothy arranged a surprise dinner party, inviting Pierre Key as well as several of the wealthy neighbors. Father was in a good mood; he told stories and did some imitations after dinner. Everyone had a good time, then the men sat down to play poker. In his articles, Key mentioned that Caruso lost sixteen dollars that night. But one wonders about his reliability for details, for he also mentioned that in East Hampton, he met the rest of the household, including "Rodolfo Caruso—the tenor's eldest son, now 16."[16] *The New York Times* made the same mistake a few months later, so at least Key was in good company.

Papa talked to Key about his childhood and his early years, the time of struggle until he established himself. Key quoted him as saying:

> Perhaps I should separate into their distinct period the four phases of my career. The first period ended in April 1897, at Palermo. The second covered the ten years between the years 1898 and 1908. The third period extended between the years 1909 and 1918. My fourth period, which began in 1919, will go on for I cannot say how long.[17]

In fact, Father brought his life story up to 1909 and refused to go beyond that, saying that the rest of his career was already widely known and a matter of public record. The year 1909 marked the beginning of the "third period," the years without Ada, and he may have preferred not to talk about that. It is also possible that he had grown tired of the interviews and chose an arbitrary cutoff date. In any case, realizing he was not going to get anything more from his subject, Key went into print with what he had. Between 5 June and 11 September 1920, he published Father's recollections in twelve installments in the *Daily Telegraph* of London under the title "Enrico Caruso, Singer and Man." I believe Key had the articles syndicated in United States newspapers too; and before the year was out, he published an essay in a ten-page booklet entitled *Enrico Caruso Souvenir Book*. Papa must have approved of that project too, because he drew several self-caricatures specifically for the publication.

These writings were mediocre efforts in Key's labored style, with occasional factual errors and without a discernible plan beyond the constraints of chronology. The contents were largely anecdotal. Key was apparently inept at drawing a narrative from his subject. His *modus operandi* was to pose questions and let Papa answer or not answer then drift in other directions according to his mood of the moment. Papa told his story in English peppered with Italian phrases, which Key must have understood then rephrased in English.

Key's admiration and respect showed in his behavior in Father's presence and also in his writing. His desire to be Father's first biographer was based on his wish to pay tribute to an artist he greatly admired, not solely on monetary considerations. The extensive notes he had taken in the course of his conversations with Caruso formed the nucleus of the biographical volume which, in collaboration with Bruno Zirato, he was to publish in 1922, within a year of Father's death.[18] Another biography, entitled *Caruso and the Art of Singing*, written by Salvatore Fucito, Father's accompanist from 1915 to 1921— and so billed on the title page—appeared in the same year.

TOWARD the end of the summer, Father resumed work with Fucito. He was studying the title role of *Andrea Chénier*. Although he sang it twice in London, in 1906, it is amazing that this successful opera of the *verismo* period, premièred in 1896, never became a permanent part of the Caruso repertory. It was not produced at the Met until 1921. As in the year before with the role of Eléazar in *La Juive*, Father threw himself heart and soul into his work on Giordano's music. His good spirits returned, and he became less tense and irritable. When Bain Photographic Service sent one of their men to East Hampton to take publicity pictures, he was willing to clown for the camera. I watched him in action, and I was surprised to see that he, rather than the photographer, made all the suggestions for various poses. The result was a series of amusing pictures, most of them unabashedly staged: Caruso painting the boat, fishing with a string tied to a long branch, mock-playing a tennis racquet like a guitar, pushing a wheelbarrow, blowing out a lamp, cranking a Packard automobile (with very worn tires!) The same photographer took several shots of the family. My favorite of the lot is one that Guido d'Onofrio brought to my attention after more then sixty years: a snapshot of Papa playing a fierce game of *scopa* with me on the patio. It is the last picture taken of the two of us together.

CHAPTER SEVENTEEN

Sickness

A UNTIE RINA had wanted me to go to a technical school because I
had shown some aptitude in things mechanical. I was always good
with my hands, a quality I inherited from my grandfathers on both
sides. I wanted to become a naval engineer; at least that was my ambition as a youngster. Yet I was sent to the *ginnasio* to get a classical education, presumably upon my father's instructions. Papa once said to
Rina: "We'll make an ambassador out of him."

Recalling Father's remark, I was surprised, in the fall of 1920, by his
consent to send me to Culver Military Academy in Indiana. The school
Fofò had attended was not a military school, even though the students had to wear a uniform. But at Culver, we were R.O.T.C. cadets
who graduated as second lieutenants in the reserves and went on to
West Point. I had no intention of going to West Point nor the slightest
inclination toward a military career. To this day, I cannot fathom why I
was sent to Culver. Dorothy maintained that the training would help
me when I returned to Italy to do my military service. I must admit that
she was right on that count: Five years later, the Italian army turned
out to be a breeze after the hellish time I spent at Culver as a plebe. All
the same, the East Coast was home to many fine schools with excel-

lent academic programs—schools closer to New York City and without the harsh military aspect. But Dorothy sincerely believed in what she preached. It was taken for granted that I would return to New York for every vacation.

As at the Gunnery School the year before, I was enrolled at Culver under the name of Henry Caruso, Jr. Why it was decided that I should not go by the name of Enrico is one of the many oddities of my life for which I have no explanation. At the height of my father's renown, to be the bearer of his name was a great distinction, not a handicap. In fact, the school Commandant, Colonel L. R. Gignilliat, was only too happy to number me among his students. In a letter to Dorothy, he hastened to point out that "George [Washington] Schumann, youngest son of Madame Schumann, Heincke [*sic*], has been a student at Culver and we had the pleasure of several visits from Madame herself."[1]

The Colonel's official notice of my admission was dated August 31; I was to report to school on my sixteenth birthday, 7 September 1920. Even before I left New York, Dorothy wrote to the Colonel asking for a special favor. Father was giving a recital in Chicago, and he wanted me to be there. Her handwritten letter was exceedingly polite:

1 September 1920

My dear Colonel,

Henry will arrive at Culver on September 7th. Mr. Caruso will sing in Chicago on October 1st, on Sunday afternoon.

He suggested to me to ask you if it would be advisable to permit Henry to go to Chicago for the concert. He does not wish Henry to miss any of his classes nor to be allowed a privilege that another boy would be refused. Also, if you consider it too soon after his arrival, Mr. Caruso would be grateful to know before he makes any arrangements. In case you permit his going, Mr. Caruso thought that one of his instructors might accompany him to the city and be Mr. Caruso's guest at the concert.

Tho [*sic*] it seems rather previous to write of these things, reservations for tickets must be made far in advance.

Mr. Caruso wishes to do in this matter, that which you think is best for Henry.

Yours very truly,
Dorothy Caruso[2]

It spoke not only for the school's rigid discipline but also for the integrity of its leaders that they refused to make an exception to the rules, even for Enrico Caruso. The privilege was denied by return mail, with reasoning both sound and prophetic. The letter, from Acting Superintendent Glascock, read in part:

> I regret to say that leave of absences are strictly contrary to the school regulations, except in cases of the most urgent necessity, such as the serious illness or death of an immediate member of the family. If we grant one leave of absence, we are immediately besieged with many others and, if we grant one and decline to grant another, we are placed in an inconsistent position which causes no end of trouble. I am sure that you will understand our position.
>
> We will look forward with much pleasure to seeing you and Mr. Caruso here this fall.[3]

Culver was military through and through and prided itself on strict discipline. The freshmen, or "plebes," as they were called, were not only treated as servants of the upperclassmen but were quite often mistreated and abused. I found the senseless, self-serving military discipline humorless and hard to endure, and I was very unhappy. I wrote to Dorothy begging her to take me out of Culver. Dorothy knew better. She advised me to let my letters sleep overnight before sending them. I was getting a good education, she admonished, and that was the most important consideration. I survived that awful first year, and I concede that the academic standards at Culver were high; but I doubt that the experience built my character, made me a better person, or produced any feeling in me other than the most profound resentment. I have retained no fond memories of the time I spent at Culver.

The only amusing incident I recall was in my freshman year, when I was called upon to sing at the final presentation of the school year. I protested that I could not sing at all and had never sung in my life, but no one believed me. Caruso's son could not sing? Nonsense. They insisted that I participate in the program. Unable to beg off, I worked out the necessary arrangements to play a joke on the audience.

The stage had a deep curtain. My roommate and I set up a Victrola and got hold of Father's recording of "Vesti la giubba" with piano accompaniment. I planned to go through the motions of singing and have my roommate do likewise at the piano. I practiced lip-synchronizing the aria for days. All would have gone well, except for my roommate's wicked sense of humor. He substituted another record, and when I opened my mouth pretending to sing, out came Galli-Curci's brilliant soprano singing "Caro nome" from *Rigoletto*. The joke was on me, and I ran red-faced from the stage.

FATHER was unable to fit a side trip to Culver into his tight Chicago schedule, so I did not see him until Christmas. When I returned to New York for the holidays, I had an unpleasant surprise. He was not at all himself. He looked ill, and he was in constant discomfort, complaining about a pain in his left side, just below the kidney. A piece of scenery had hit him at exactly this spot during the last act of *Samson et Dalila* on December 3. The two gigantic pillars Samson pulls down at the end of the opera were made of huge woven basket rings. They were fairly light, but not when falling from the height of three stories. When Samson pushed the columns, the cast members threw themselves to the floor. The stage hands in the wings then pulled on the ropes attached to the topmost baskets to direct the fall of the rings sideways and away from the cast. Something went wrong on this occasion, and one of the baskets struck Father in the back just below the left kidney. This was the first of a series of mishaps that made December 1920 one of the worst months of his life.

Father did not complain of the pain in his side after the accident. Anyone else would have sued the company, but to him it was unthinkable to blame the Metropolitan for the injury. The pain grew steadily worse. Five days later, on 8 December 1920, as he sang "Vesti la giubba" at the end of the first act of *Pagliacci,* he felt such agonizing pain in his side that he nearly blacked out and he tripped as he staggered up the steps of Canio's wooden stage. It has been variously reported in print that he fainted, that he collapsed onstage into the arms of Scotti (who was not in the cast that night), or that he collapsed offstage into Zirato's. Oscar Thompson's report in the December 18 issue of *Musical America* was correct:

> [Caruso] was long in coming out for the curtain call, though the audience clamored for him. A rumor spread that he was hurt. Finally he appeared, and, guided by De Luca, the Tonio of the performance, crossed the stage without looking at his audience, one hand clasping his head, the other his left side.

Dorothy told me the same story, adding that he indeed had to be held up in the wings by Zirato, so acute was his pain. After a long interval, he was able to continue, but Gatti sent William J. "Billy" Guard, the Met's publicity director, to announce that Mr. Caruso "had strained his side in a fall on the steps in entering the little theater" but would finish the performance.

Following this incident, Pasquale Simonelli sent Father a get-well note. Father's reply of December 11 read: "Dear don Pasquale, Many thanks for your kind letter and affectionate concern. The terrible pain, fortunately, is now gone and God be thanked."

Ironically, this was the very day that Father performed *L'Elisir d'amore* at the Brooklyn Academy of Music, the theater he and Farrar had inaugurated with a performance of *Faust* on 14 November 1908. Shortly after the performance began, Papa began hemorrhaging from the throat. He sang the entire first act of *L'Elisir* wiping the blood from his mouth as one handkerchief after another was passed to him by the chorus and the Adina of the evening, soprano Evelyn Scotney. Because Father had seen a few drops of blood as he gargled before the performance, Dr. Philip Horowitz had been called to the theater. Fortunately, he was there when Father came offstage. The doctor forbade him to go back on, and Guard had to face an apprehensive audience for the second time in three days, this time to inform them that the performance would not continue. Zirato had the presence of mind to send me a telegram telling me not to worry.

On December 13, only two days after the incident, Father insisted on appearing in *La Forza del destino* to quell the rumors that he was finished; then, on the 16th, he sang *Samson et Dalila* to confirm his vocal health. Both performances showed him in excellent form, much to the relief of the public and critics alike. Aldrich wrote of the first performance that "he carried the role of Don Alvaro with no apparent unusual effort and was in as easy voice at the end of the third act as at the start of the first."[4] At the end of the famous duet "Solenne in quest'ora," Don Alvaro is carried off on a stretcher, but the audience kept applauding until Danise, the Don Carlo of the evening, dragged Caruso back onstage. The ovation lasted until he was dragged back several more times.

Although the two performances went well, Father canceled another *L'Elisir* on December 22. So that the public would not speculate about further health problems, a special notice was placed in *The New York Times* announcing that on December 24, Caruso would sing Eléazar in *La Juive,* with Florence Easton taking over the role of Rachel from Rosa Ponselle.

I watched Father prepare for the Christmas Eve performance; he was visibly ill. Dorothy gently tried to persuade him to cancel the performance, but Father would not hear of it. He could have coined the phrase "the show must go on." He would not let his public down. As long as he was able to move and open his mouth, he was going to meet his obligations.

I heard him say: "It is Christmas Eve, Doro. People want to be happy. Unless I am dead, they will hear me sing."

Father was a man of many contradictions. Apart from throat specialists, he would not see a doctor if it was at all avoidable. Like many Italians, he thought going to a doctor brought *scarogna,* bad luck, and one went to a hospital only to die. Thus I was able to gauge the magnitude of his discomfort when he asked Dorothy to call the house doctor of the Vanderbilt, Dr. Francis J. Murray. Zirato and I watched with apprehension as the doctor tightly taped Father's sides, strapping him all around as they do football players. I was shocked when Dorothy told me that he had sung the last few performances bandaged in this way. It gave him support and lessened the stabbing pain in his side. He went to the theater with Mario, his valet, and I stayed with Dorothy a while longer. She was worried, but the poor woman had been in that state ever since the series of mishaps began. Partly from a sense of social obligation, partly to keep her mind off Father's condition, she went on supervising arrangements for the Christmas Eve party Papa wanted to give for a circle of close friends, which was to follow the performance. Except for the time when Gloria was born, I believe this was Father's only performance in New York that Dorothy missed.

It turned out to be his last.

Dorothy urged me to stay with him until curtain time, so I went to the theater earlier than usual. I climbed the flight of stairs to Father's dressing room and knocked on the door. A voice called "*Avanti!*" and I entered. The dressing room was long and narrow; it had a big table with makeup paraphernalia, a shelf with a mirror and two lamps, a washstand, a coat rack with costumes, and a window at the end. When I entered, I saw Mario. To his right, by the window, stood a very tall, ancient man, with a hooked nose, a long beard, and droopy eyes.

"Good evening, Sir," I said to the strange gentleman. Then, turning to Mario: "*Dov'è Papà?*" ("Where is Papa?")

The old man looked at me and said: "*Sono quà, Mimmi.*" ("I am here, Mimmi.")

Turning to Mario, he added with a satisfied smile: "*Se mio figlio non mi riconosce, la truccatura deve essere buona!*" ("If my own son doesn't recognize me, the makeup must be good!")

Only then did I notice the familiar cigarette and holder in the old man's hand. But even the exceptional makeup did not conceal Father's true condition. His warm and wonderful voice sounded tired. I asked him if he felt all right. He told me not to worry, everything was going to be just fine. Although I did not feel reassured, I was not alarmed and expected the performance to go like any other. I stayed with him until almost curtain time, kissed his hand as usual, and went to take my seat.

The first two acts seemed to go without difficulty. Mostly on account of his acting, I did not realize how much the sheer mechanics of singing were hurting him. At this period in his career, he did not like to be disturbed during intermission, and only Dorothy was admitted to his dressing room. I did not go backstage. I found out much later that when the conductor, Bodanzky, went to see him between acts, Papa was sitting in his chair weeping with pain.

In the third act he was noticeably worse. Knowing his condition, I could see that he was not play-acting, he was in agony. Then came his big aria, "Rachel, quand du Seigneur." He usually sang this seated, with Rachel at his feet, while gently caressing her head. This time he sang it standing, clutching her very close. He knew he would not be able to deliver the difficult aria seated and asked Easton to hold him as tightly as she could. Throughout the song, he clung to her with all his strength. The embrace was taken as a show of paternal affection for the daughter he was about to sacrifice. Ironically, some critics remarked the following day that they never heard Caruso sing with such pathos as on this occasion. After the last phrase of the aria died away and the applause exploded, Father closed his eyes. I could see tears streaming down his face from under the closed lids. He was trembling, barely able to stand.

After the performance, he took his curtain calls, smiling gratefully at his adoring public even though he was drained to the point of exhaustion. Once this last obligation was fulfilled, he bade everyone within earshot a merry Christmas. Then Mario bundled him up in his fur-lined coat and Zirato whisked him into our car, which was waiting with the engine running and the heater on. His face was sallow, and he looked terrible without the makeup. We rode back to the hotel in silence. He went straight to the bathroom and into the tub. After relaxing for half an hour or so, he dressed and dutifully played the role of the gracious host at the party. He was deeply moved by the Nativity scene Dorothy had set up for him in the fireplace as a surprise, to compensate for the beautiful *presepio* he had left behind at Bellosguardo.

The next morning, Christmas Day, as Father was getting ready to go to the theater to distribute his Christmas presents to the Met staff and musicians, he had his first attack of pleurisy. His left side still hurting, he got into the bathtub. The warm water must have caused fluids accumulated in the chest cavity to expand, and he was suddenly struck by an attack of such agonizing pain that, as he wrote to his brother Giovanni, he was "letting out howls like a wounded dog, so loud they heard me on the street from the eighteenth floor and throughout the whole hotel."[5] I don't know if his screams were heard on the street, but I certainly heard them and went running to his apartment. He was surrounded by the entire household and kept on moaning and screaming until Dr. Murray could be located.

And so his calvary began.

DR. MURRAY gave him an injection of morphine which made the pain subside. It was Christmas Day, however, and no reliable diagnostician could be found; the good doctor stayed with him through the night. The next day, Dr. Evan M. Evans was called in, and he diagnosed acute pleurisy. Then came a succession of doctors: Samuel Lambert; the lung specialist Antonio Stella; and the surgeon John F. Erdmann. Another doctor, Philip Horowitz, had dismissed most of Father's complaints since the *Samson et Dalila* episode as intercostal neuralgia. Horowitz disagreed with all the other doctors, insisted on the wrong diagnosis, and prescribed questionable medication. When his interference became intolerable, Dorothy ordered him to leave and never come back. To save face, he later claimed that he was obliged to withdraw from the medical team after suffering a head injury in a fall from his horse in Central Park.

Dr. Erdmann considered it a matter of life and death to operate as soon as possible. The necessary medical equipment was brought in and the library converted into an operating room. According to newspaper reports, two operations were performed that first week, but in fact there was only one, on December 29. Father was kept sedated with painkillers until the operation, which was performed under local anesthetic; fluid and pus were drained from his chest. *The New York Times* carried the news on its front page, top center, on 30 December 1920, quoting the doctor's report of the previous evening: "Mr. Caruso has developed suppurative pleurisy necessitating a surgical operation. This has been successfully performed and he is now resting comfortably."

In the weeks ahead, more abscesses formed in Father's pleural cavity; one after the other, they were located and drained. Between operations, Father's fever would subside and he would seem to recover, only to suffer another relapse.

I overstayed my Christmas leave. After the first series of surgeries, when Father appeared to be out of danger, I returned to Culver. Then, in mid-February, his condition took a turn for the worse. The doctors rushed Dorothy to his bedside thinking he had as little as ten minutes to live. Two priests came to his room, but Father said, "rather testily," according to *The New York Times*: "What are you doing here? I am not going to die."[6]

The extreme crisis passed for the moment, but on February 16 I received a frantic phone call from New York: Father was dying, I must come immediately. The Commandant of Cadets, Major McKinney, came to fetch me at the stables where we were doing cavalry drills. This time there were no questions about leaving school in mid-term. I hastily threw a few essentials into a suitcase and, still in my riding outfit, was driven to the railway station at Plymouth, where I caught the Twentieth Century Limited. After a day's travel, I arrived in New York early the next morning, on February 17. Zirato met my train, and we took a cab to the hotel. He told me that Father was comatose and the doctors thought he might die. I was to be very quiet and not stay with him long.

Father's heavily curtained room was dark and smelled of antiseptics. I went in and found Father lying motionless, his breathing labored and loud. He had been barely conscious for some time. I knelt at his bedside, gently took his hand, and kissed it several times.

"Papa, son quà" ("Papa, I am here"), I said in a trembling voice. His eyes flickered for a moment. I waited.

"Papa, caro, son io, Mimmi." ("Father, dear, it is I, Mimmi.")

There was a long silence. I wasn't at all sure that he heard me or was even aware of my presence. Then his lips moved, and in a very soft and weak voice he said:

"Figlio mio, puzzi." ("My son, you smell.")

I realized only then that I was still in my riding outfit, boots and jodhpurs, reeking of horse sweat. I had washed my hands and face in the lavatory on the train but had not bathed for a day and a half. But it was a good sign that Father was aware of his surroundings. A faint smile passed over his face, and his hand in mine gave a gentle squeeze.

My heart went out to him. He looked much, much worse than he had in January when I left. I was overcome by a sense of compassion and frustration at not knowing how to ease his suffering. There was nothing I could do. I would have been happy to stay there for hours just holding his hand, but I was asked to leave.

Before noon, Rolando Ricci, the Italian ambassador, visited Father. He was a bit better by then, and he said to the ambassador in a weak voice: "*Voglio morire in Italia . . . al mio paese!*" ("I want to die in Italy . . . in my own country!") He was able to carry on a brief conversation, and he reminisced about a performance of *The Pearlfishers* he had sung twenty-three years earlier in Genoa, which the ambassador had attended. Later in the day, around 5 p.m., Giulio Gatti-Casazza stopped by for a short visit, and Father was glad to see his "*padrone.*"

That day was a turning point in Father's illness, and he took solid food for the first time in days. My visit and that of Ambassador Ricci came to be romanticized for their beneficial effect on his condition. On February 18, Zirato said to the reporters: "I believe the turning point came with the arrival of his son yesterday. The boy's smile coming at the psychological moment inspired his father with a new will to live."[7] He was happy to see us both, but I don't think that either Ricci or I could have lowered his fever, blocked the formation of a new abscess, or induced the wound in his side to drain more readily through the tubes the surgeon had inserted. Still, it is a fact that within a few days he rallied, and this gave us hope that the worst was over. Even the newspapers were hopeful. On February 19 one headline read: "Although Danger Is Over for the Present, Another Relapse Is Possible."[8]

In the following week, the medical bulletins claimed that the inflammation of the pleural cavity was under control. During most of his illness, Father was aware of his condition. He knew he was fighting for his life, and he often talked about dying and wishing to die in Italy. When he felt better, he changed his tune and said he wanted to recuperate in Italy, but the theme remained: back to Italy. Dorothy and the medical team tried to dissuade him from this plan, all in vain. To keep him under medical surveillance for a period of convalescence, they began to talk about moving him to Atlantic City or to Lakewood, New Jersey, before undertaking the sea voyage.

Father's forty-eighth birthday was approaching, and we were overjoyed to have the opportunity to celebrate. Because some musical dictionaries listed his birthday as February 25 and others as February 27, telegrams, letters, flowers, and gifts poured in all week. Even Zirato and the publicity director at the Met, Billy Guard, thought Caruso's birthday was the 27th, and Papa, looking forward to having two birthdays, chuckled about the mistake he helped to perpetuate. On the 25th, we all congratulated him and wished him many happy returns, but our celebration was subdued, on doctors' orders.

On February 16, and again on the day between the birthdays, Father was allowed a short visit from his Met colleagues. Beniamino Gigli later recalled his visit:

> There was a heartrending scene on February 26th when, feeling that he had not much longer to live, he asked to see all his Metropolitan colleagues once again to say good-bye. We stood round his bed, trying desperately to be cheerful, but most of his old friends—Lucrezia Bori, Rosa Ponselle, Scotti, De Luca, Didur, Rothier, Pasquale Amato—were unable to restrain their tears. I had, of course, known him very little; but after each of our few meetings, even this last one when he lay struggling with pain, I came away feeling enriched by the generous warmth of his overflowing personality. Everything was exceptional in him, not only his voice.[9]

Just nine days later, on March 7, Gigli, who in the years ahead was destined to assume many of Father's roles at the Metropolitan, sang the title role of *Andrea Chénier*. This was the first Metropolitan production of the opera, and it had been mounted for Caruso. Under the circumstances, the honor fell to Gigli, who was relieved that he did not have to follow Caruso in the role. He had a well-deserved success and in the years ahead made the role his own. Father did not begrudge Gigli his success, but it hurt him that the revival meant for him was taken by another tenor. In the recesses of my memory lies a comment Father made upon hearing about the performance: "*Poteva almeno aspettare che fossi morto.*" ("He could at least have waited until I was dead.")

The day after Father's "second" birthday, his rally came to an abrupt end. His fluctuating fever began to rise, and on the morning of March 1, he underwent another operation to drain the pus that had accumulated in the lower part of the pleural cavity. In the following days, Father's fever was lower than it had been for weeks, and we again had reason to hope he was out of danger.

It was decided not to disclose every medical detail to the press. Indeed, a great deal of information was withheld from the public until after Father's death. Only then did Zirato disclose to *The New York*

Times that, contrary to the medical bulletins that had been issued, there were six operations rather than three—three major ones performed by Dr. Erdmann himself, and three lesser ones. The second operation was on February 9, the third on February 12, and the fourth on March 1. Father's condition improved after that, but on March 12, a blood transfusion was deemed necessary. The newspapers withheld the donor's name, but Dorothy later identified him as Everett Wilkinson of Meriden, Connecticut. Although the transfusion had accelerated Father's recovery, he complained that he no longer had pure Italian blood. The young man, on the other hand, said: "I wouldn't change places today with the King of England!"[10] Two lesser operations followed on March 15 and 25. By April, it seemed that Father was on the long road to recovery.

I was in Indiana, back at Culver, from early January until the third week in February, so I was not present at the second and third operations. I heard from the family that on one occasion, the pocket of liquid beneath the incision burst with such force that fluids hit the opposite wall. One can imagine the pain and the pressure such an abscess had caused within the body! During one operation, the abscess was inaccessible without the partial removal of a rib; the surgeons excised a four-inch section. This took place on 12 February 1921; the 31 December 1920 edition of *The New York Times* carried Zirato's explicit—and at the time honest—denial of such a rumor. The fact had been concealed from Father, as he would instantly have known that his singing equipment, the bellows that provided that astounding column of air, had been permanently weakened. The operations were increasingly dangerous, and the last ones were performed with only local anesthesia, because the doctors felt that Father's heart could not take another full anesthesia. His moans and screams were simply frightful. All the household wanted to run beyond earshot, yet we stayed mesmerized in the adjacent rooms, unable to leave. It was agony for us all to stand by helpless, unable to ease Father's suffering.

During these difficult months, Dorothy showed great courage and human fortitude. She had the support of the medical and household staff, her brothers Park and Romeyn, and her sisters Torrance and Mrs. Marjorie Glenny, together with their respective spouses. In spite of the large staff at her command, she had to be wife and mother, moving between the sickbed and the nursery. When the doctors allowed her to stay with Father, she never left his bedside. She scarcely slept, and when she was not with Papa, she was just a room away from him, ready to rush to his side. No man was ever surrounded by more love in his hour of need—love from his family, his friends, and his faithful public.

For some reason, no one seems to have considered calling Fofò and Uncle Giovanni to New York. Attached as they both were to Papa, they remained in Italy, depending on long-distance reports for any word of changes in Father's condition.

During Father's illness, the whole city of New York was preoccupied with his fluctuating condition. Day after day, *The New York Times* carried articles on his progress, mentioning every detail: whether Caruso had said anything to the nurse, what he had eaten, whether he had a good night's rest, and whether he sat propped up in bed or remained prostrate. The concern and regard of the public was boundless. At one point, the streets around the hotel were covered with straw to muffle the beat of horses' hooves. Taxis and motorists were asked not to use their horns in the neighborhood, and the infernal cacophony that went along with traffic in those days was toned down to a drone. Telegrams and cablegrams arrived by the hundreds each day, inquiring about Father's condition and assuring us of the sender's good wishes and constant prayers. During the crisis periods, the attending physicians issued medical bulletins daily, sometimes several times a day. These were posted in the hotel lobby and diligently copied by the press.

Hundreds of strangers stopped in each day to inquire about Mr. Caruso. Friends, acquaintances, admirers, fans, and newspaper reporters kept calling, by phone and in person. To keep the well-meaning multitude away, Alfonso Iacoletti, Giovanni's brother-in-law (my Aunt Bettina's brother), posted himself at the entrance of Papa's suite like a watchdog and slept on a couch in front of the door. He was totally devoted to my father, asking and receiving nothing for this service. Perhaps he was one of the relatives Father helped with a monthly check, but I do not know this. He just stayed at the door to help as he could. When Alfonso had to return to his job, Dorothy asked old Schol to be the official screener of callers. The old man, head of the Met claque and a devoted fan of my father's, was most happy to oblige.

There were a few callers who were always admitted to the suite: Pasquale Amato; Geraldine Farrar; Father's best friend, Antonio Scotti, who went by the affectionate nickname of "Totonno"; the "boss," Giulio Gatti-Casazza; and Calvin G. Child of the Victor Talking Machine Company, a personal friend for eighteen years. Papa was always happy to see them, and they did their best to show how much they cared.

GRADUALLY Father regained his strength and was able to move around in the apartment. He looked worn and emaciated and had deep circles under his eyes. Dorothy records that X-rays taken at this time revealed his left lung had contracted, and there was a persistent numbness in his right hand, which trembled and had shrunk and lost its strength. During his ordeal, the muscles in Father's entire body lost their tone; one of his shoulders drooped, and he could not fully straighten up. He seemed to have aged a decade in the span of ten weeks. It was shocking to see a man who had been so alive—so strong and exuberant and alert—completely drained of energy. We were saddened by his condition; but he was most pained and frustrated by the fact that he had become an invalid, dependent on the assistance of others. His impatience with his circumstances added to the difficulty of the situation. During his recovery, as in the months of his illness, we could judge Father's condition by his moods. When he was irritable and domineering, we knew he was feeling better. His two nurses, Muriel Lamalfa and Alice Updegrove, endured the brunt of it, but we all got our share of abuse on the good days. Any little thing could irritate him, and we had to take great care not to annoy him.

Once, I remember, one of the nurses asked Father whether he wanted the window open or closed. Because he seemed uncomfortable and half-asleep, I answered the nurse.

"Lasciami stare! Posso rispondere da me stesso!" ("Let me be! I can answer myself!"), Father snapped.

I remember that instead of being upset by his outburst, I felt happy. "Good!" I thought to myself. "Papa has got his roar back, he must be feeling better."

During a lull in the series of relapses, Father told Giovanni about his struggles in a long letter dated 1 February 1921. The moment he received the letter, Uncle Giovanni made arrangements to come over to take Father back to Italy for his convalescence. Giovanni left Naples on February 19 on the Cunarder *Caronia* and arrived in New York March 4. The brothers had not seen each other since the summer of 1919. Although Giovanni had had ample warning, the shock of seeing Papa in such a state was too much for my uncle. He was a very emotional man, as most Neapolitans are, and when he left Father's bedside, he sat in the salon sobbing like a baby. Papa was more than a brother or a benefactor to Giovanni. For him, his brother "Erri" was a hero in the absolute sense of the word: a person larger than life, better, greater, and more accomplished than anyone else, a veritable human monolith, invincible and indestructible. Seeing what the illness had done, Giovanni was distraught at life's unfairness. Could he have done so, my uncle would gladly have taken all Father's pain and suffering upon himself. To my mind, whatever faults Giovanni may have had, they were balanced by his boundless and unconditional love for my father. In New York, he hardly budged from Father's side. Only when the collective medical opinion declared him entirely out of danger did Giovanni sail home, to make the necessary arrangements for Papa's arrival in Naples.

Father's condition improved beyond expectation. The fever did not return, and he gradually grew strong enough to get out of bed, walk around the apartment, and look after himself. When he was well enough to go outside for a walk, he visited the Metropolitan. There is a famous photograph taken of him on this first outing on 26 April 1921. It shows him holding onto Dorothy with one hand while with his free hand showing how loose his collar had become around his skinny neck. Compared to his former self in robust health, he looks pitiful in that picture, yet ten times better then he had looked just a few weeks earlier. For me, the most shocking aspect of the photograph is the bewildered look in his eyes and the complete absence of his customary, self-assured swagger. He has the look of a sick and frightened man, a man unsure of himself, holding on to his wife for support like a child clinging to its mother.

Around the middle of March, I returned again to Culver. When it was time for me to leave, Father and I said our farewells without any premonition of the tragedy to follow. I think we both wanted to believe our world was in order and that his life, and mine along with it, would soon return to normal. Thus, if our good-bye was more emotional than usual, it was only on account of the ordeal Papa had been through. I kissed his hand and left the apartment without any sense that this would be the last time I saw my father alive.

In the weeks that followed, I called New York regularly to stay informed about his progress. Sometimes I spoke to him; other times, if I happened to call when he was resting or asleep, I spoke to Dorothy or Zirato. Even before I left New York, *The New York Times* of March 18 and 20 mentioned that Father planned to go back to Italy in May. I asked Dorothy about this on the phone, and she told me with grave apprehension that it was still the plan. Papa stubbornly insisted on going to Italy for the summer, and he spoke about it so much and with such determination that she felt it was impossible to dissuade him. He refused to listen to her reasoning, to friends' advice, or to doctors' recommendations, steadfastly maintaining that only "in his country" could he get well. All thoughts of renting a house in Atlantic City or Lakewood had been abandoned, she said, and preparations for the trip had begun.

In late May, Father called me.

"Mimmi, we are going back to Italy for the summer. I am calling to say good-bye."

"Papa, please take me with you."

"No, no. *Hai già perduto troppo tempo* (You have lost too much time) at school on my account. You better stay there for the summer session and try to catch up."

"Please, Papa, let me come after you when the school year is over," I pleaded. "I would like to be near you. Maybe I could be of some help to you."

"Don't worry, Mimmi. I am well taken care of. Dorothy will be with me and Fofò will join us in Naples. And there are Giovanni, Mamma Maria, and the others. I will be all right."

"Papa, please let me go with you," I begged him in vain.

"*Non temere, figlio mio. Sii bravo. Ci rivedremo a settembre.*" ("Don't worry, my son. Be brave. We will see each other in September.")

This time I was filled with apprehensions. Italy was far away, and I would be unable to call to find out how he was. I felt abandoned and more alone than ever before: I was thousands of miles from anyone I could call a friend, and now I would be an ocean away from my family. I have never understood why I was left in America, but once again, I could only resign myself to a decision that was made for me.

Before leaving New York, Papa went to the doctor's office for a final set of X-rays. The physician, not previously connected with the case and unaware of the implications, remarked that the X-ray showed his rib had grown half an inch at the incision. Father was shocked. He was shown the X-ray. Confronted with the irrefutable evidence of the damage done to his singing apparatus, he must have endured one of the most agonizing moments of his life. He realized that even if he could sing again, his lungs could never sustain the mechanical demands of his craft as before. Dorothy, as she later said, stood by helplessly.

Before Father left New York, Geraldine Farrar and her husband, Lou Tellegen, stopped in to say good-bye. (Although Tellegen places this visit on the day before Father sailed, it had to be earlier, because he mentions that he met Giovanni. According to Fofò, my uncle was with him in Naples at the time of Papa's arrival.) Father was glad to see his friends. Pointing at his chest, he told them: "They have hurt me so,

these great doctors—cut and cut and cut! But I shall be all right again—
just the sun and *Italia* and I shall sing as I never sang before!" Tellegen
writes that he "begged him not to undertake the voyage, to rest quietly
in the South here—no travel, no excitement, no more operations, just
to be a plain human being drinking in the warmth of Nature. But no;
he was determined to return to his beloved *Italia!*"[11] After they left the
apartment, Tellegen turned to Farrar and said: "I am afraid we shall
never see Enrico again on this earth."[12]

Father's journey to the dock on May 28 was a triumphal march.
Special guards were necessary at Pier 7, Bush Docks, in Brooklyn, to
hold back the enormous throngs who came to bid him farewell. He
was accompanied by Dorothy, Gloria, and numerous servants. *The
New York Times* reported that the suite of rooms cost $35,000, and the
Caruso party carried seventy-two pieces of hand baggage and forty-six
trunks of luggage—certainly a long way from the days when Caruso
carried all his earthly belongings from Livorno to Florence in a paper
bag. Hundreds of telegrams and floral tributes from admirers were
awaiting him as he boarded the liner, S/S *Presidente Wilson,* en route to
Italy.

As was to be expected, reporters were also on hand. "During his
interview with newspaper men Caruso insisted on standing, but Mrs.
Caruso overruled him and he sat down on a deck chair."[13] When he was
asked "whether he had done any singing since his convalescence, he
burst into one of his golden notes—a particularly high one—and held
it without apparent difficulty."[14] In reference to his weight loss, he
mentioned that he now weighed 174 pounds, "adding that before he
became ill he tipped the scales at 215."[15] Of course, by this time he had
regained many pounds since his illness.

"Good-bye, America, my second home," he shouted, leaning over
the ship's railing. "I will be with you again soon, and will sing, and sing,
and sing."[16]

Everyone hoped so, but none more fervently than Caruso himself.

Zirato was very kind and occasionally called me at Culver. Perhaps
he was instructed to check on me from time to time. I was glad to hear
his friendly voice and to receive some news from overseas. I received a
couple of postcards from Italy, but they were not enough to put my
mind at ease. I counted the days until September, when I would see my
father again.

CHAPTER EIGHTEEN

The End

IN faraway Culver I tried to remember Father's comforting words
that in Italy he would be surrounded by relatives and friends. At
least I was happy for Fofò. During the critical spells that last spring, he
never knew whether the next news item would bring word of Father's
death. Now he was given the opportunity to see Papa once more.

Fofò's description of Father's last summer in Italy captures the
mood of his arrival and his last days.

In May of 1921, I came down from Florence to Naples.
After his long, near-fatal illness, my beloved father was
returning home from America. We had not seen each other
since he left Bellosguardo at the end of his summer vacation in
August 1919. Now, once again, I could embrace him.

Arriving in Naples, I checked in at the Santa Lucia Hotel
on the waterfront where Papa and I had stayed many times
before. I asked for a room on the top floor facing the water.
From the balcony I had a panoramic view of the Bay of Naples,
with the islands of Ischia and Procida on the horizon to the
right of the entrance of the bay. It was between these two

islands that the S/S *Presidente Wilson* was due to appear the next morning, bringing back to his native land my father, the world-famous tenor, Enrico Caruso.

It was strange that the phrase "world-famous tenor" should fill me not only with admiration for his achievements and pride at being his firstborn son, but with a great aversion as well. It is easy to understand the reason for the former; the cause for the latter was my perception that his fame was to blame for all the anxiety in his life, which had kept him away from me for long periods of time all my life.

The sun had barely begun to gild the peak of Mount Vesuvio when I jumped out of bed. I got ready to meet the ship that was scheduled to dock around eleven in the morning. I was on the balcony at nine, scanning the distant horizon and impatiently awaiting the thin wisp of smoke announcing the ship's approach: a dot first small, then rapidly growing in size. As the time drew near, Uncle Giovanni arrived to pick me up, and together we hurried down to the pier.

We arrived as the ship was being nudged to its moorings by tugs. The decks and the promenades were crowded with people waving hats and handkerchiefs. But no matter how much I strained my excellent eyes searching the faces in that multitude, I was unable to pick out my father. With all the happiness I felt, this delay had given me an added sense of anxiety. The pier had become a madhouse. People in tears were running, shouting, calling names, waving handkerchiefs, quarrelling and cursing each other, with heads high in the air trying to catch a glimpse of their loved ones. The first-class gangplank was finally put in position. Struggling against a sea of humanity trying to get ashore, Uncle Giovanni and I finally managed to get on board. A deck steward took us to Papa's suite.

Although I had been toughened by all I had seen in the trenches during the war, the sight of my father, the way he looked after his long illness, almost took my breath away—only for a second, because I did not want to upset him. Yet I could not hold back my tears as I threw myself in his arms. Fortunately he mistook my emotion for joy, although it was pain for the suffering he had endured. I was alarmed by his emaciated look and the ashen color of his face. He had the appearance of a sick man, which all of us took to be the last stage of his illness before a full recovery.

After our long embrace, I greeted Dorothy and the others. Dora, my stepmother, was most kind and solicitous. Before we had first met at Bellosguardo, she had written several letters declaring that she wanted to become a second mother to us. Next, I was led to a small cabin where my baby sister Gloria was playing on the floor under the vigilant eyes of a Swedish governess, who was gruff to the point of making me feel unwelcome. The little ball of rosy flesh and blonde hair was the very image of Papa. I was immediately drawn to that graceful and innocent creature, and I wanted to hug, kiss, and cuddle her, and hold her on my lap. But the icy stare of the Swede, looking at me as if I were some sort of barbarian, froze all my expansive affection.

When everything was in order, all the baggage collected, customs and immigration formalities cleared, we went ashore. To my surprise, we drove to the Hotel Vesuvio instead of the Santa Lucia, and to the regret of the management, I had to move next door.

A happy month went by. The air of Naples brought life and color back to Papa's face. Each day I became more attached to the little one who, in her turn, grew to like me, and I gradually overcame even the strange hostility of the gruff Swedish governess.

Needless to say, Papa's life during this period was anything but restful. From morning till night, innumerable friends, admirers, and petitioners came and went all day long. No request for an audience was ever denied. It was either the baritone who had sung with him at Caserta, or the impresario who had engaged him in Salerno, or his Metropolitan Opera colleagues, or reporters, or close and distant relatives. Everyone came for a visit except those who should have—the doctors.

Doctors! That was a bogey word. At the first hint of these professionals, Papa's usually jovial mood would darken, so much so that we all avoided even mentioning them. One day when we were alone, he told me all about his illness and the operations. He showed me the scars of the incisions on his back. A three-inch-long wound just below the shoulder blade was still not completely healed. It was covered by a pad of gauze, held in place with strips of adhesive tape. At that sight something snapped in me, and that image has remained with me to this day. I held back the sobs that welled in my throat as I tightly embraced him. He insisted that he felt well and did not want any more doctors around.

Days passed. One day Father called a family council consisting of Uncle Giovanni; an old friend, the brother of the baritone Missiano; and myself. Father turned to me and said [approximately]:

"Rodolfo, you are now twenty-two. I have developed a strictly American outlook on life, and it is my wish that my children should have an art or a trade, just like the sons of American families, rich as they may be. *Signor* Missiano is the director of a large spaghetti factory, and he is willing to take you on with a starting salary of 450 lire per month. I will add to that 2,000 lire and a clothing allowance. I would like you to accept this employment for two or three years and learn the business of manufacturing all types of pasta. Then you and I will form a partnership, set up a large factory, and export real 'Enrico Caruso' pasta."

I was stunned! I was deeply touched by the offer and the trust Father placed in me. I said with all my enthusiasm that I would accept the offer, and along with it all that he might demand of me.

In the meantime, Dorothy, I, and Papa's intimate friends began to worry about the strain the activities in Naples imposed on him. To ensure a more complete rest, which he badly needed, it was decided that he should spend a month at Sorrento. Arrangements were made with the owner of the Hotel Vesuvio to rent one of the small villas he owned in Sorrento in addition to the Hotel Vittoria. After a month there, Father planned to return to Bellosguardo at Signa.

When I accepted the job at the pasta factory, I failed to consider one drawback: If Father moved to Sorrento I could not be near him. When I learned about the intended transfer, this reservation must have showed in my face, because he said:

"As long as we are staying in Sorrento, you can take the ferry over Saturday nights and spend Sundays with me."

I found a furnished room near the office where I worked. Since I was the son of "the" Enrico Caruso, they charged me rent of 400 lire per month instead of 200, with the excuse that the room belonged to a very distinguished family and had all the modern conveniences, including a bath and a flush toilet! I didn't quibble because it was convenient and clean. Also, Father's generous allowance made the price hike of little importance.

During that first week of work, I wished the time would fly so that I could rejoin Father in Sorrento. I spent an enchanting Sunday with him, never leaving his side for an instant. I helped him with his correspondence, and I remember a letter from the Manhattan Opera [*sic*] offering him 1,000,000 lire (about $50,000) for singing there the very first performance in the United States following his recovery. I still recall Father's smile as he had me answer that although he was greatly honored by the offer made by the administration of the Manhattan, he was unable to accept the munificent offer because he was morally committed to the Metropolitan. I answered many more letters. About three-fourths of them asked for money, some courteously, some rudely, others with threats, with credible stories, or with such overblown tales that we could not help but laugh. Nevertheless, a good many of them received something if not all they asked, and their requests were generously satisfied.

Family members and some close friends were invited the following Sunday to celebrate Father's name day, the day of Saint Enrico (July 15). It was an unforgettable day, and even though my memories are somewhat hazy, I still remember Father radiantly happy with little Gloria at his side—but only for a few minutes, because her governess was scandalized by all the fuss made by the guests. Father sang a few brief phrases in magnificent voice which made him happier than ever, because he was terrorized by the possibility of losing his voice. He was greatly preoccupied by his responsibility for his fame and his art with respect to the public and the press. If a newspaper so much as hinted at the possible darkening of his voice or at vocal problems, it made him physically ill and put him in a bad mood for days. Later that day when we were alone, he said to me:

"You'll see, tomorrow all the newspapers will say I sang in full voice, and this will destroy all the rumors that have been circulating lately about my voice."

When I left Papa the following morning, I had an inexplicable ill feeling, and he must have felt something as well. Mario, who was with him, told me later that when I went aboard the fragile little boat that was to take me to the ferry to Naples, Father, leaning on the balustrade, followed me with his eyes until the boat vanished on the horizon. Was it premonition?

As for myself, I leaned on the ship's railing in a state of depression. I watched the promontory of Sorrento vanish in the morning fog. The white square of the villa grew smaller and smaller. I never imagined that Father too was following me with his eyes.

TO quell any speculations to the contrary, the general manager of the Met, wily Gatti-Casazza, included Caruso's name in the list of artists to appear in the fall of 1921 at the Metropolitan. He visited Papa in Sorrento on July 6. Reassured by what he saw, he sent a cable to New York about Father's condition, concluding with the confident statement: "He will sing surely coming season." Soon after Gatti's visit, Father wrote to assure his old friend Marziale Sisca, publisher of *La Follia di New York,* that "my health is improving daily and I hope within a few more weeks I will be completely well."[1] On July 17, he wrote to Salvatore Fucito: "I am in good health, thanks to the sun and the sea baths. I have voice to sell for still a score of years."[2] And on July 19, he received a reporter for the *Chicago Tribune.* This may have been the last interview he ever gave; it was also carried by *The New York Times* on 3 August 1921. He tried his best to convince his visitor that he was well, that his illness was behind him, for he wanted desperately to be depicted as a healthy man. When the reporter commented on his smoking, he snapped:

"Of course I smoke. What do you think? That I am sick?"

Father said his voice was unimpaired and that he planned to sing again when he felt fully recovered. He added that his muscles were becoming firm, but the reporter observed that his walk was "a trifle shaky. He fully looked the man convalescing from a most serious illness. His good nature was the same, however, and his determination to recover his strength bespoke a great deal."[3] While Dorothy and other friends went for a swim, Father, his friends Amedeo Canessa and Dr. Niola, and the reporter rowed out some distance in a boat. Father took off the upper part of his old-fashioned bathing suit to let the sun hit the "four ugly gashes remaining from his operations for pleurisy."[4] After they rowed back to the pier, Papa went in the water for the second time since coming to Sorrento. Presumably the wound that was still open at the time of his arrival in Italy had healed by then.

During the interview, Father described his daily routine, emphasizing that he led "quite a normal life, you see. Doctor? I have no doctor. I take care of myself, or rather Mrs. Caruso or my valet takes perfect care of me."[5] He admitted that his diaphragm was weak and the wounds had to heal fully before he could sing again without pain. He added,

> But I am gaining strength every day. Besides, one needs a year to recover completely from pleurisy. When my wounds are quite healed and my strength recovered I shall sing. For my voice and my throat are the same as ever. I am my own master and I shall not sing again until I am completely able and recuperated.[6]

Papa then told of a turning point in his illness. One night, he said, he dreamt that he was dead and buried, and he saw himself carved in bas-relief on the top of his tombstone. "It seemed so calm and peaceful to be dead, no more suffering."[7] The honking of an automobile horn brought him back to consciousness. Later, he told an anxious Dorothy that "one experience beyond the grave would be sufficient for me for some time, and from that moment I have been improving. It's very agreeable to be dead, but it's a great deal nicer to be alive."[8]

Father did seem to improve during the summer, and this gave him a false sense of strength. He acted as if he were healthy. Not wanting to appear henpecked by Dorothy, who tried in vain to restrain him, he exerted himself more than he should have. His constitution could not take it, and Fofò had a bad surprise on his next visit.

> When I returned to Sorrento a week later, I found Papa very worn. I learned that during the week he took an excursion to Capri and a few days later went with Dorothy, Amedeo Canessa, and other friends to Pompeii, to give thanks to the Madonna of Pompeii for his recovery. They visited the excavations too, and I also learned that he had gone to see a notary in Castellammare, but the purpose of his visit was never established or discovered. Later on many conjectures were advanced about this, but without concrete foundation. [The visit to the notary also served as a basis for a rumor that he had had a new will drawn up.]
> On Sunday afternoon I had an argument with him,

because he wanted me to enjoy myself and go swimming with the rest of the young people. Dorothy, who was playing tennis, was only a few years older than I, and Father was amazed that I insisted on staying with him and refused entertainment suitable for persons of my age. Considering how sports-oriented and active I was, his amazement was quite appropriate. But as I approached manhood, my attachment to him took on gigantic proportions, and it grew even stronger when I saw him so dispirited.

When we sat down to tackle the correspondence as usual, I at the desk and he stretched out on the bed, he seemed to be uncomfortable but did not want to show it. Observing him with a sideways glance, I noticed light pearls of perspiration on his forehead. It is true that near the end of July, the days were muggy, but those droplets seemed suspect. I stopped writing and approached his bed as if to caress him. I wiped his forehead with a handkerchief, and it felt hot. I didn't say anything, but, excusing myself to get a glass of water, I ran to find Dora to tell her about it. She was very upset and burst into his room, and in spite of all his protests, she took his temperature. The thermometer showed a high fever.

From that moment on, our life was filled with anxiety. Papa absolutely insisted on calling his old friend Dr. Niola, who had been his family doctor since his childhood. The old man lived in Naples, and it took him a full day to get to Sorrento. As soon as he saw Father's condition, he disavowed all responsibility and called in several famous professors from Naples for a consultation. Another day of waiting.

Naturally, I did not return to work. When the luminaries of medical science arrived, they huddled for a long time then advised us to turn to the famous doctors, the Bastianelli brothers of Rome! I was growing desperate. Father's fever continued to rise, and it was apparent that he was suffering. At the news of his worsening condition, Uncle Giovanni rushed to his sickbed, and with him relatives and friends. The latter, with all due respect for their devotion to Father, were a great nuisance. There was too much confusion; both Dora and I were young and inexperienced and in that madhouse did not know how to handle the situation.

Dorothy's memories of these turbulent days are somewhat at variance with Fofò's. For one thing, in both her published memoirs, Dorothy largely ignores Fofò's presence on the scene, although Fofò referred frequently to her. Perhaps, because the language barrier allowed no communication between them, Dorothy simply blocked Fofò out of her memory. Also, the unexpected and rapid worsening of Father's condition brought all those around him to near-hysteria. Trying later to reconstruct what had happened, it is probable that both Dorothy and Fofò remembered some details and condensed or forgot others. For example, neither took note of the other relatives or of two musicians mentioned by the papers: Vincenzo Bellezza and Paolo Longone. Further, for literary or editorial reasons, Dorothy may have felt obliged to omit some facts at the expense of historical accuracy. The chronology of events suggests that Fofò did not leave Papa's side after July 25. Yet he failed to mention one of the most dramatic incidents of the last days, which Dorothy preserved. The story concerned a young man who came to Father for an audition.

I heard the boy's voice singing the first bars of "M'apparì," Caruso's famous aria from *Martha*. He stopped. There was a pause and all at once the music began again. I held my breath in astonishment. What a lovely voice—and then I leaped to my feet and rushed up the stairs. There was only one voice that could sing "M'apparì" like that! I flung open the door of the studio and there, beside the piano, stood Caruso, his arms outstretched, a divine light of happiness in his face as the last note of the song died away.

When he saw me he shouted, "Doro, Doro, did you hear? I can sing! I can sing as well as ever! Better than ever! I can sing! Oh my God, I can sing!" . . .

That night the fever returned. I knew that something would have to be done at once, but after the happiness of the day I did not know how to break the news to him that a doctor should be sent for. Giuseppe de Luca was staying in Sorrento, and that evening I slipped away and went to see him. Between us we made a little plot that he should come to call upon us and ask me about Enrico in his presence. I would admit that I was worried by the return of fever that came now and then, and De Luca would then suggest having a doctor in, if only to put my mind to rest. We did it all as we planned. Enrico protested irritably that it would be 20 lire thrown away for nothing, but our point was gained and I immediately telegraphed for the famous doctors, Giuseppe and Raffaele Bastianelli, to come to Sorrento. After their examination, they said there was undoubtedly an abscess close to the kidney and advised us to come to Rome so that X-ray pictures could be taken.[9]

There can be no doubt that if Dorothy remembered the words "an abscess close to the kidney," that was precisely what the doctors had said to her. Communication was not a problem in this instance, as both Giuseppe and Raffaele Bastianelli had married American women and "spoke perfect English."[10]

Fofò gave this account of the doctors' visit:

> The Bastianelli brothers came by plane to examine him. Let us remember that this was in 1921. It took them longer to drive from Naples to Sorrento than to fly from Rome to Naples. Still, the moment I saw them, I felt my hope for a speedy recovery reborn. The Professors Bastianelli consulted with the other physicians at length and examined Papa, who seemed increasingly annoyed by all this coming and going of doctors. After a long and thorough examination, the Bastianellis gave their verdict:
>
> "He must have an operation as soon as possible. You must bring him to our clinic in Rome."
>
> They felt sorry for us; they did not want to tell us the truth and gave us this merciful last hope, but they probably knew already that Father would never reach Rome.

PAPA could not contradict the Roman specialists. He finally had to concede that he was ill and in need of immediate medical attention. The examination and apparent encouragement of the most respected surgeon and internist team in Italy gave him hope and reassurance. However, he had no inkling that his life was in grave danger, and he considered the whole episode as a setback that could easily be reversed with a little more discomfort and perhaps another surgery. He wrote to Sisca on 29 July 1921:

> I am certainly still passing through a nasty period of convalescence, because I feel acute pains at every moment that worry me, and as recently as this morning I was visited by the Doctors Bastianelli of Rome, and to have a better diagnosis

they invited me to go to Rome to make an X-ray and to hear
from their mouth and from the results of the X-ray the last
word: the coming Wednesday, August 3rd, I will be in Rome.

The voice however has nothing to do with my sickness, in
fact a few days ago I sang to the surprise of everybody the
romance from *Martha* and the Bastianellis assure me that in
four or five months I will be able to resume my work.[11]

The letter was typed by Fofò, but the signature, written with a
trembling hand, must have told volumes to Sisca. It bore no
resemblance to the firm, round letters that characterized Father's
calligraphic handwriting, nor even to the signature on his letter of July
17. His failing control of his right hand, along with his increasing
infirmity and constant pain, is tragically reflected in these angular,
jerky lines, so unlike his usual signature as to fail even for a forgery.
Father seized every opportunity to insist his voice was unimpaired.
But he was feeling worse by the hour, and by this time he must have
been aware of the gravity of his condition. Yet his actions suggest that
if he thought he might die, he expected it to be during or after the
operation in Rome and not before. He had a long talk with Giovanni
about that eventuality, but he did not want to alarm his household. He
showed no signs of despair and remained the good trooper to the end,
continuing his daily routines as the family made preparations for the
trip.

As usual, he kept up his correspondence. He sent a check for
lottery tickets to the organizing committee for the benefit of war
orphans,[12] and on July 31 he wrote what may well have been his last
letter—a note to Maestro Silvestri, the librettist of an opera Father had
sung at the Teatro Bellini.

> Esteemed *Sig.* Silvestri,
> Your kind letter, which has recalled so many memories to
> my mind, arrived at the very moment I was about to leave
> Sorrento going North. I thank you for your courtesy and I am
> sorry I cannot have the pleasure to shake your hand. My con-
> valescence has its highs and lows, but I hope that in a few
> months I will be fully recovered.
> With most cordial greetings, your devoted
> Enrico Caruso[13]

Incredibly, this letter was supposedly written in Sorrento and
dated July 31, fully two days after the Bastianellis' visit, and following a

night of high fever. Dorothy decided to wait no longer. She called Giovanni and asked him to make a reservation in the Hotel Vesuvio in Naples for the night and to engage a private train for the following day to take Father to Rome. Fofò wrote of the fatal trip:

> Feverish preparations for the trip began. In half a day we were ready to depart. In that dreadful situation Father remained calm. His main preoccupation was to be able to show himself in public in such a way that the press could speak of him as a man on his way to recovery. In fact—and I don't understand why it was allowed—he insisted on taking the ferryboat the following morning, although we could have driven him a lot faster in an ambulance to Naples and to the train for Rome.
>
> He rose early in the morning, still with a very high fever, and dressed in a sport suit. During the entire crossing of about two hours, he sat on a wooden bench on the promenade deck of the ferryboat. With good spirit, he joked with the innumerable tourists of all nationalities who, unaware of his condition, gathered around him. Neither my scowls, nor Dora's annoyed expression, nor the grumbling of Uncle Giovanni could drive off these unwelcome admirers. Father smiled, and his responses were somewhat tired. What concerned me most was the color of his skin, which was turning increasingly grey.
>
> Finally we arrived in Naples and rushed to the Hotel Vesuvio. We had to make a rest stop there because Father was tired, and we did not want to exhaust him by going directly on to Rome. During the entire day, there was an incessant coming and going of doctors and relatives.

Dorothy described the details of the next hours. Without any warning, Father began to scream. The hotel manager notified all the hospitals, and Mario rushed to find a doctor and sent the bellboys to find one, but most were away from the city on their summer holidays. Father went on screaming for four hours before the first doctor arrived. Because he brought no morphine, he had to go out for some; and then, on his return, he was so agitated that his hand trembled, and Dorothy took the syringe from him to make the injection. Soon several other doctors arrived. Following an examination, they concluded that Father's kidney must be removed right away and without full anesthesia, because his heart could not take it. With the operation, his chance of survival was one in a thousand, but without it he would certainly die. Dorothy begged them to probe for an abscess first and then, if they found none, to operate. But after further consultation, the medical team concluded it would be useless to operate and sent for a tank of oxygen.

Fofò was apparently not present at this discussion. He narrates:

In the meantime, the fever kept rising. Uncle Giovanni had a long talk with Papa in private, and when it was over, my uncle asked me to help him find an oxygen tank. When I heard this, I felt something grip my heart, but my optimism didn't allow me to give in. I did not panic, nor did I have the perception of an imminent catastrophe. During the trip, Giovanni repeated what Father had said to him the previous day in Sorrento.

"Giovanni, I will go to Rome tomorrow. I will probably be operated on, but I don't know what may happen. In the meantime, before I leave, I will go to the Bank of Naples and deposit a million lire for each of you: you, Rodolfo, and Mimmi, so that you all can await with reassurance the outcome of the inheritance proceedings if I should meet with some misfortune. Dorothy already has a safe-deposit box in her name, yet the three of you have nothing. I am quite confident that my heirs will be in agreement. However, I also do this to ward off the evil eye."

It must be remembered that Father was good-naturedly superstitious. My uncle tried to protest, but Father's mind seemed made up.

When we returned to the hotel with the oxygen, indescribable confusion reigned in the suite. Father's fever would not fall, yet he maintained a phenomenal lucidity without ever losing control of his thoughts. He was sweating so profusely that he had to be moved from one bed to the other every half-hour to replace the soaked-through bedding with dry linen. His thirst would not subside, and he drank large quantities of chilled mineral water.

"*Mi sento molto male. Sarà difficile scamparla stavolta*" ("I feel very ill. It will be difficult to escape this time"), he said.

Evening came, and I refused to leave Father's room. Mario and I spent the night carrying Father from one bed to another, trying to fit in short naps stretched out on the floor between the two beds. Dorothy was mercifully attended by Father's friends, who tried to hearten her.

Around five in the morning, I began to notice a strange smell, like the odor of decay. At a certain moment, Amedeo Canessa, an old friend of the family, with gentle force dragged me out of the room, and I saw *Monsignor* Tonello enter. He, too, was a great friend of Papa's who, as I learned later, received the confession of the dying man and gave him final absolution. In the meantime, in the adjoining salon, I was in a state of stupor, as much from exhaustion as from anguish. Until the very last moment, I placed my hope in God's miracle. It seemed impossible to me that my father, such a good man, so dear, so fundamentally humble and spontaneously charitable, could be in mortal danger. While I was nearly semiconscious, building up hopes, I heard a suffocated scream from Dora: "Rico! Rico!" In a flash I understood the catastrophe. Pushing aside those who tried to hold me back, I rushed to the room just in time to see Papa close his eyes. I felt as if struck on the head by a club. I did not understand anything any more. I recall only that both Dora and I were dragged outside by force, because I was clinging to the headboard howling like a madman, and she had fainted.

ON the first day of August, I received at Culver the first print of the last photograph taken of Papa on the terrace of the Hotel Vittoria in Sorrento. On it he had written, "*Al mio piccolo Mimmi con tanto affetto, Papa. Sorrento, 1921.*" ("To my little Mimmi with much love, Papa.") I scrutinized the photograph, trying to determine Father's condition. He was erect, trim, and tanned, outwardly a healthy man in every respect. It was a nice photo, and I was tremendously pleased at the affectionate dedication.

The following night, in the morning hours of August 2nd, I had a strange dream. I saw my father lying in bed, covered with a white sheet. I saw his face; he was very pale, almost as white as the sheet. For a moment, I thought he was dead. Then he spoke in a feeble voice: "*Figlio mio, sii bravo.*" ("My son, be brave.") Afterward he was still.

I awoke, shaken by the dream, and looked at the clock. It was a few minutes after 2 a.m. My movements awakened my roommate.

"I just dreamed about my father. I saw him lying on his deathbed."

"Oh, come on! You are so worried about him you are having nightmares. Go back to sleep."

Eventually I fell asleep. In the morning we had reveille at 5:45. The corps of cadets was going to Chicago for several days of exercises on the shores of Lake Michigan. We packed our belongings and went to Plymouth, Indiana, to catch the train. We had a twenty-minute wait until the Twentieth Century Limited arrived. I had nothing to read, so I went to a nearby newsstand and bought a handful of magazines. My footlocker was full already, and after I added the magazines, I had difficulty closing the lid. A lady stepped up to me and said, "Let me help you." As she pressed down on the lid, her eyes fell on my name, which was painted on it in large white letters. Impulsively she threw her arms around me. "Oh, you poor boy!" she said, and hurriedly walked away. I was puzzled. Why was I a poor boy if I had trouble closing my footlocker?

Just then the train to Chicago pulled in. I was about to board when I heard the stationmaster calling my name.

"Cadet Caruso! Cadet Caruso!"

"Here, Sir. I am Cadet Caruso."

"Wait here, the Commandant is on his way to get you."

"But I will miss the train!"

"I just received a phone call asking me to tell you to wait for the Commandant. Please stay right here; he is coming to get you."

The train pulled out, and I was left alone in the waiting room wondering what I could have done wrong. Before long Colonel Gignilliat arrived with Major McKinney. They were very solemn, at the same time extremely courteous, almost solicitous toward me. They asked me to get into the car. I sat between them, and we drove off. On the way back to Culver, Colonel Gignilliat told me, as kindly and gently as he possibly could, that he had just received word that my father had died in Naples at 9:07 in the morning. There was a seven-hour time difference between Indiana and Italy. At the very time that Father lay dying in the Hotel Vesuvio, I saw him on his deathbed in my dream.

I cannot explain this telepathic link I seem to have had with my father in his final moments. While he was alive, I never experienced anything comparable. Yet I sensed his presence many times after his death, in different places and in the strangest manner, at completely unexpected times.

I was shocked and numbed by the news. Father had sounded so strong on the phone in May when he called to say good-bye! Perhaps I wanted to believe he was completely out of danger and the Italian trip was nothing more than a badly needed vacation. I had not imagined that Father would really die, and I was looking forward to seeing him in September, just as he had said.

The officers were very kind, but I wanted to be alone. Fortunately, to my frame of mind, the school was deserted. I went to my room, put the photograph of my father in front of me, wound up my Victrola, and put on his records. I played one record after another, listening to that wonderful, miraculous voice, and cried. For the first time in my life, I was fully aware of my feelings toward my father: I loved him, really loved him. Every now and then, the colonel or the major would stop by to ask if I was all right. I would silently nod and put on the next record.

FROM the newspapers I learned what I could about Father's final hours and the events of the following days. The Associated Press reported that according to Dorothy, Father's last words were "Let me sleep."[14] On the morning of his death, Grandmother Maria came to the hotel to inquire about her beloved stepson. She was met at the entrance by the impresario Giulio Staffelli, who told her of the tragedy. She broke down crying, then she entered the improvised chapel, knelt beside the body, and prayed. Gloria, too, went in to see Father's body. At her young age, she knew only that something dreadful had happened because Papa could not speak to her. The newspaper report added that "Mrs. Caruso is bearing her sorrow with fortitude."[15] Giovanni was beside himself with grief. He remained by the corpse, crying inconsolably, until his brother's body was removed to be embalmed. In addition to the family, there was a constant procession of artists, friends, and admirers. Before Father's body was moved from the Hotel Vesuvio, Filippo Cifariello, the sculptor who had made at least two busts of Papa a decade earlier, prepared a death mask and a cast of his hands.

The funeral was as glorious as such a sad event could possibly be. All activities ceased that day in Naples, as the city put on deep mourning for its celebrated son. The shops were closed, buildings were draped in black, and the tricolor flew at half-mast. As a demonstration of affection, the people of the city lined the streets from the Cathedral of San Francesco di Paola to the cemetery, the Cimiterio del Pianto. Political and musical dignitaries came from afar for the services, and Titta Ruffo rushed down from Fiuggi to serve as a pallbearer. The entire family was there. To my enduring sorrow, only I was denied the opportunity to be with my father during his last days and to honor him as he was laid to rest. The fastest way to get to Naples from Indiana was by ship; but the trip would have taken two weeks at the very least, and such a postponement of the funeral was unthinkable. And so I was absent from the crowd of 80,000 who paid their last respects to my father.

The tragic event was not beyond commercial exploitation. Within a very short time, a double-sided recording of the funeral appeared on the Okeh label.[16] Allegedly, the services were recorded "live," complete with bells, speeches, and interviews. Capitalizing on the presence of Titta Ruffo, the recording even purported to contain a brief eulogy spoken by the baritone. The record, clever and atmospheric as it sounds, is a fake. There is no way this recording could have been made "live"; in fact, it was staged and recorded in the New York studios of the General Phonograph Corporation. Until the advent, in 1925, of electrical recording which used a microphone, a recording such as this could not have been produced. Dr. Ruffo Titta, Jr., owns a copy of the record and states unequivocally that neither the voice nor the vocabulary of the eulogist is that of his father.[17]

The Associated Press cable from the funeral on August 4 was carried by *The New York Times* the following day. The services, conducted by the Bishop of Naples, were held in the cathedral by permission of King Victor Emmanuel, who sent a special representative to attend the ceremony. A choir of hundreds of singers assisted in the high requiem mass. The crystal coffin, encased in a wooden casket, rested on a catafalque in the center surrounded by hundreds of candles and countless floral offerings. A large wreath carried the inscription: "From the City of New York."

Before the church was opened to the public, the family viewed the body once more. Dorothy placed beside it a large bunch of roses. *The New York Times* reported:

> Others of the grief-stricken relatives gathered in the basilica and looked for the last time upon the face of the dead, which seemed to be that of one sleeping peacefully. Giovanni, brother of Enrico, first knelt beside the coffin, then, rising, invoked Caruso to breathe again. Rodolfo, the son, was equally affected.[18]

Fofò narrates:

> The events of the following days were like being in a haze

for us. I vaguely remember that there seemed to be a disagreement as to whether or not to have him embalmed. In the end it was decided to call in an embalmer, who had great reservations about the success of the process because septicaemia had invaded Father's entire body, and he was not sure that he could do his work with lasting results. But all this is but a vague memory for me, as I was semiconscious from grief.

I can still see the imposing funeral at the Cathedral of San Francesco di Paola where, until that day, funeral services were held only for the remains of kings and members of the royal family. This honor was accorded to Father as one of the late great glories of Italy. At the end of the funeral mass, I could no longer restrain myself and finally broke into a flood of tears, comforted by Uncle Giovanni and others I don't recall; they held me on each side and led me out of the church. I cannot describe the bitter effort and obligation of following his remains during the imposing funeral through all of Naples, where an enormous crowd of sad and crying people watched the funeral cortège pass carrying one of the most illustrious sons of their city. The procession lasted hours. It was only about one kilometer long but an eternity for me. Members of all branches of the army and navy headed the cortège. Ministers of the government, representatives of the Holy See, ambassadors, and admirers preceded the large group of the clergy who prayed in front of the funeral carriage. On the four sides, the most intimate friends held the cordons; behind them followed Dora, Uncle Giovanni, and I. After us came other relatives and dignitaries, and finally a sea of the Neapolitan people, which, I was told, made a most impressive sight. While the cortège wound its way up Via Toledo, low-flying planes of the Royal Air Force scattered laurel leaves. Naples could not render a greater tribute to the glory of its deceased son.

I did not have the courage to follow the coffin into the cemetery, where it was temporarily laid to rest in the Canessa chapel, to remain until our own family chapel was built. I stayed in the carriage with Dorothy, towards whom I felt an incipient affection that I could not show until then. Weeping, she tried to comfort me, saying she had promised Papa to be a mother to us, the mother we had not had for so many years.

It was the 4th day of August, 1921.

Newlyweds Enrico Caruso and Dorothy Park Benjamin, 1918. Courtesy of Francis Robinson Collection, Special Collections, Vanderbilt University.

The Carusos boarding the S/S *Presidente Wilson* en route to Europe. *Left to right,* jeweler E. M. Gattle, Enrico, Dorothy, and Mr. and Mrs. Romeyn Park Benjamin (Dorothy's brother and sister-in-law). Photography by Bain News Service.

Dorothy and Enrico Caruso waving good-bye to the crowd at the pier.
Courtesy of Francis Robinson Collection, Special Collections, Vanderbilt
University.

Dorothy Caruso
in the garden at
Bellosguardo, 1919.

Snapshot of the Carusos in the garden at Bellosguardo in 1919, taken by
Enrico, Jr. *Left to right,* Rodolfo, Giovanni, Dorothy, Enrico.

Snapshot of the
Carusos in the garden at
Bellosguardo in 1919,
taken by Rodolfo. *Left
to right,* Dorothy,
Enrico, Sr., Enrico, Jr.,
and Giovanni.

Enrico, Jr., with his
uncle, Giovanni, at
Bellosguardo, 1919.

The Carusos returning from Europe in 1919. *Left to right,* Enrico, Jr., Dorothy, and Enrico, Sr.

Opposite, Caruso in Cuba, autumn 1920. Embossed a lower right are the words "Foto. Kiko"—perhap Caruso's whimsical byline based on his nicknam "Chico."

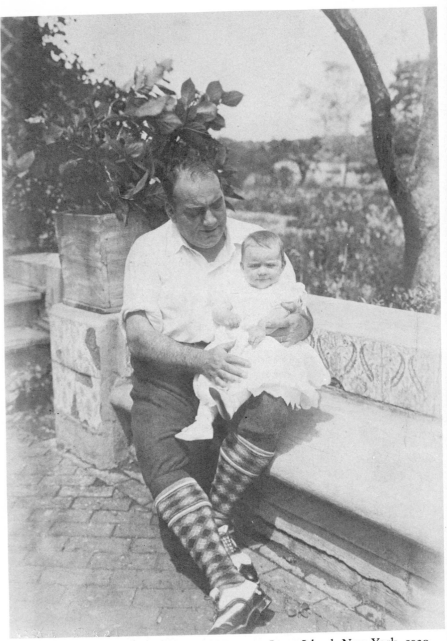

Caruso with baby Gloria at East Hampton, Long Island, New York, 1920.
Photography by Bain News Service.

Dorothy, Enrico, Sr., Gloria, Enrico, Jr., Mrs. Park Benjamin, Jr. (Dorothy's sister-in-law), and her two children, East Hampton, 1920. Photography by Bain News Service. Reproduced from the collection of the Library of Congress.

Caruso clowning for the camera, East Hampton, 1920. Photography by
Bain News Service.

The two Enrico Carusos playing *scopa*. This is the last picture taken of father and son together. Photography by Bain News Service. Courtesy Metropolitan Opera Association.

Dorothy and Enrico Caruso on their first outing after the tenor's illness, 26 April 1921. Caruso is showing how big his collar has become after his weight loss.

Enrico, Gloria, and Dorothy Caruso en route to Europe in May 1921. Wide
World Photos. Courtesy of Francis Robinson Collection, Special Collections,
Vanderbilt University.

Opposite, Cadet Enrico Caruso, Jr., at
Culver Military Academy in Indiana,
Easter 1921. This is the photograph En
sent to his mother in Buenos Aires.

Caruso in Sorrento, July 1921, a photograph used by the Victor Company for
its 1923 catalog. Courtesy of Francis Robinson Collection, Special Collections, Vanderbilt University.

Caruso on the terrace of the Hotel Vittoria in Sorrento, July 1921.

The last photograph of Caruso, taken at the urging of his friend R. Carbone on 29 July 1921, a few hours before the arrival of the Drs. Bastianelli. Reproduced from the collection of the Library of Congress.

Caruso on his catafalque. Courtesy of Francis Robinson Collection, Special
Collections, Vanderbilt University.

Caruso's funeral in Naples.

Enrico Caruso's great admirer, Guido d'Onofrio, at the Caruso chapel in Naples on the 116th anniversary of Caruso's birth, 25 February 1989.

CHAPTER NINETEEN

My Father, Enrico Caruso

FATHER was dead! As time passed, I missed him more and more. It was strange to realize that in spite of the geographical distance that had separated us most of the time, somehow he was always there, an entity with an inexplicable permanence. For my own consolation, I could have pretended that nothing had really changed—that he was still out there somewhere, in New York, or London, or Italy. However, he wasn't, and no amount of make-believe could change that. Fofò's and my papa, Dorothy's husband, Gloria's father, was no more. The only person who could protect us and keep all harm from our lives was gone. Rather than getting used to the idea of his death, I felt his absence even more with the passage of time. He was frequently in my thoughts, and I kept returning to events, incidents, details of incidents, that occurred while we were together. As my mind wandered back in time, I put together all the little bits and pieces, assembling a composite picture of my father that has stayed with me all my life.

Regardless of Father's relationship with the rest of the family and with me, no matter how we thought of him, he was first and foremost a singer. Dorothy recorded a remark he made to her before we left Bellosguardo: "Remember, Doro, my art will always come first, even before you." Thus he echoed what her father had told her before they were married.[1]

That was absolutely true. For Father, singing was not a career but a calling, his sole purpose in life. He could not imagine life without it. In the dark days of his illness, he must have struggled against the idea of not being able to perform for the rest of his life, however long or short his remaining time might be. I don't think he ever came to grips with that eventuality.

My brother told me that on one of the last weekends in Sorrento, he asked Papa what he would have done had he been born without a singing voice. Papa said that many people had asked him that question over the years and he had given many pat answers, but the truth was that he never even considered the possibility. From the moment he discovered the beauty and pleasure of singing, he never had any doubt that he would become a professional singer, whatever the extent of his eventual success. He confessed having had dreams of a singing career, but "it was probably hope rather than a determination," he said. After he went to Father Giuseppe Bronzetti's school, he never gave serious thought to any other profession. He was determined to become a singer, and a good one. In later years, he never attributed his acclaim to the vocal equipment he was born with, but rather to what he did to and with the inborn voice, which he tried to improve from year to year, just as he tried to improve his delivery from performance to performance. He attributed his success to hard work, and accordingly, he practiced for hours daily to keep his instrument in good working order and to improve his art.

Once someone asked Father in my presence who had taught him to sing. "I taught myself!" he snapped. What he meant was that he had perfected his own technique. It was Guglielmo Vergine who gave him a solid foundation, and in the many autobiographical statements journalists coaxed out of him, he never failed to give the maestro due credit. He also acknowledged conductor Vincenzo Lombardi's help with learning to conquer the high notes that gave him so much trouble. The one person whose contribution he never mentioned was my mother.

Yet it was not coincidence that Father's career began to blossom after Ada came into his life. In the words of Emil Ledner, Father's longtime European impresario:

> At Livorno the woman who laid the cornerstone of his career entered his life—the woman to whom he owed a great

deal and who was his great happiness, perhaps the only woman whom he ever truly loved. . . . Ada Giachetti was . . . probably unconsciously, an excellent and very energetic teacher. Under her instruction and wise guidance Caruso evolved from a chorister into a true opera singer. She studied his parts with him, trained his voice, gave him dramatic instruction. . . . Ada Giachetti! Caruso's great fortune and misfortune![2]

It seems that Father had Ada to thank for a great deal, but he was too "macho" to admit it during the years they were together, and he certainly was unwilling to mention it after their scandalous breakup. But he was man enough to admit it to Key in 1920: "I can say very definitely that from the time of my Livorno engagement began the fortunate period of my career—from which I have had much pleasure, success, and . . . sorrow."[3]

Father took his calling seriously and worked in every way he could to perfect his craft. One Friday afternoon in Hamburg, for example, he asked Ledner to go with him to a Jewish synagogue. They took a cab to the temple on Grindelallee, and after the service, Father explained:

I have discovered that the Jewish cantors employ a peculiar art and method of singing in their delivery. They are unexcelled in the art of covering the voice, picking up a new key, in the treatment of the ritual chant, and overcoming vocal difficulties that lie in the words rather than in the music. For this reason I visit the Jewish synagogues whenever I have the opportunity and the time.[4]

In the course of the years, the two of them spent every free Friday evening and every rehearsal-free Saturday at Jewish services in Vienna, Berlin, Budapest, Frankfurt, and Paris. "Caruso listened attentively," remembered Ledner. "He would prick up his ears at every solo by the principal cantor. Then we would drive home and practice for half an hour the effortless attack and modulation of tone which seemed so precious to him."[5]

Father knew what worked for him and what did not. What evolved as his own method of singing became second nature to him, a process that was all but instinctive, like speech to an ordinary person. He was no longer conscious of how he did it and could not communicate his technique to others. He once tried to teach a young man and was unsuccessful. After a few months of fruitless efforts, his accompanist Fucito said to him:

"*Commendatore,* you are a singer, not a teacher. Stick to singing."

First page of a four-page composition in Caruso's hand, possibly his own composition. It should put to rest the romantic rumor that Caruso could not read music; he would surely not write or copy a score just to pass the time.

FATHER was a dedicated professional to the core. He took care of himself, his health and his voice, as an athlete takes care of his body: It was an obligation to his public. He felt that if the audience paid to hear Caruso, he had better be the Caruso they paid to hear. He was aware that his way of life and his self-esteem depended on his public: It was they who gave him glory, success, and wealth. He felt an indebtedness which he repaid in installments each time he stepped to the footlights and sang, giving his all.

Pierre Key once posed the question: Which is more difficult, getting to the top or staying there?

"Staying at the top," Father replied.

> Before one gets there, one wonders if he will ever make it, and once that objective is reached, you wonder, "When shall I fall?" Never do I prepare for a performance that I am not moved to ask myself: "Will I get through all right?" The best must eventually slip. Until the audience is before you and you are before the audience one can never be sure. The people constitute the fourth dimension of the theatre. And they are quick either to approve or condemn. Then the time comes when the voice begins to fail. It may be while we are apparently at our zenith. But we are capable of only going so far; we arrive there, remain for—nobody knows how long. Finally the descent begins; though we may not at once be aware, or the public. Little by little we drop, imperceptibly at first. Then some night or at an important matinée someone notices; then someone else. A whisper runs round: "Is he slipping?" The scales you have held so long in perfect balance are starting to swing to the wrong way. Almost in a flash it is over. Oh yes, I think staying at the top is much more difficult, surely harder on the nerves than getting there. . . . Each time I sing I feel as if there were someone waiting to seize my position from me, to destroy Caruso, and I must fight, fight like a bull to hold my own.[6]

Father often spoke about the burden of the responsibility his fame placed upon him. Although he phrased it differently in each interview, the message was always the same. The *Daily Citizen* quoted him as saying:

> I am the unhappiest of mortals. Whenever I sing I cannot forget that I have a great reputation to sustain; a single slip,

five minutes of hoarseness . . . and something of my reputation would go.[7]

In 1908, he said to an interviewer for the London *Star:*

> In my present position, at the point at which I have
> arrived, I am forbidden to have the least weakness. I am in the
> case of a man who must, cost what it may, be continually at the
> pitch of his reputation. . . . I was happier when I was earning
> ten francs a night. I spent seven francs, kept three, and knew
> my reputation was not ruined if I happened to give a croak.[8]

In 1913, he said:

> When I was unknown I sang like a bird, careless, without
> thought of nerves. But now my reputation is made, my
> audiences are more exacting. Here I am today bending
> beneath the weight of a renown which cannot increase, but
> which the least vocal mishap may compromise.[9]

A similar statement was quoted after his death: "I am the man who
will never be pardoned for the slightest falling off!"[10] By 1918, he was
clearly bitter about the golden trap he had wrought for himself:

> I am not a man at all, I am just a money-making machine,
> an apparatus that produces dividends. They compel me to live
> in a glass case, not that they value me, Caruso, but only
> because of my throat, which I have sold to managers as Faust
> sold his soul to Mephistopheles.[11]

Father paid a high price for his fame and success. Onstage, he was
invariably measured by a yardstick reserved only for him. He once
said: "Is it any wonder that I am nervous before an appearance? The
people expect from me the very best; the best I may have given on
some one occasion and which perhaps I can never again duplicate."[12]
Offstage, wherever he went, every eye was fixed upon him. He
attracted crowds on the street, in restaurants, train stations, and
theater lobbies. He was hounded by souvenir hunters, hero-
worshippers, cranks, con men, blackmailers, newspaper reporters,
and aspiring singers. The solitude and quiet of his hotel suite was a
refuge as much as it was a home.

The universal acceptance that became his did not come easily. As
he told Key:

> I had to fight with both the critics and the public, because

in 1903 there was a memory of "another." Every time I sang, some of the critics would write: "Yes ... a beautiful voice, wonderful quality, velvet, everything which is required in an Italian tenor voice, but Jean!" But I went on just the same, because I could not forget that some years before, this 'Jean' [de Reszke] had said something in Salsomaggiore which made me very happy. It was in the presence of his brother [Edouard] that Jean said: "This is the boy who will some day turn the world upside down with his voice."

Nevertheless, for three years after I joined the Metropolitan it did not seem as if the part of the world in which New York lay would be turned upside down by my voice; some of the critics continued to write: "A beautiful voice, but white, like an Italian ... and we don't particularly like it."

"But you never sang with what we know as 'white' voice," remarked Key.

Oh, yes, I sang "white" then. The voice, however, was growing rounder, getting more color, more of what you call "body," a stronger voice, which is the kind the American public likes best. I realized how much was expected of me, and because the standard was so high, and I was always compared only with the greatest artists, I worked hard to become one of those. I don't believe I ever felt satisfied with a performance, no matter how much praise it brought; I always had the wish to make what I had done a little better the next time I tried, so I studied and practiced, and thought a good deal about everything connected with my art.[13]

Someone asked Father what the requirements of a great singer were. He gave his classic reply: "A big chest, a big mouth, 90 percent memory, 10 percent intelligence, lots of hard work, and something in the heart."[14] He certainly had all these qualifications, but the physical attributes of his vocal equipment were unique too. Dr. William Lloyd, Father's throat specialist and the London caretaker of many singers' vocal apparatus, gave an interview on the Caruso voice, entitled "The Perfect Singing Machine." He said, among other things:

I have made several examinations of *Signor* Caruso's throat. Perhaps the most striking single feature is the abnormal length of his vocal tube. For example the distance from his front teeth to the vocal cords is at least half an inch longer than that of any other great tenor I know. Another point is the extreme length of his vocal cords, which are at least an eighth of an inch longer than those of any other tenor I have ever examined. His phenomenal chest capacity is another physical attribute which goes towards the production of a unique singing machine. The other day the great tenor stood up in my drawing room with his back against the wall, and when he emptied his lungs of air we pushed my large Steinway concert grand piano close up against his chest. He drew in a deep breath, expanding his chest, and pushed the piano some inches along over the carpet. This tremendous power accounts for his ability to sustain a note for forty seconds or more.[15]

Greatness cannot be measured in absolute terms but is a comparative value attributed to a person of exceptional attainment in some field of endeavor. I am certain that the consensus of those competent to judge vocal art is that Enrico Caruso was a great singer. Even by his colleagues, he was considered *hors concours*.

At a party in Palo Alto, California, on 8 February 1967, prodded by his close friend Eddie Smith, the tenor Giovanni Martinelli recalled a time when someone said to him that Caruso's greatness rested not on his voice but on the enormous publicity he generated in the press.

"I grabbed the man by the lapel," recalled Martinelli, "looked him straight in the eye, and said: 'You can take Gigli, Pertile, Lauri-Volpi, and me, roll us all into one, and we would still be unfit to tie Caruso's shoelaces!' "

Since my father's death, every promising new tenor has been hailed as a second Caruso. Apart from the inanity of such labeling, it is a great disservice to an emerging star, whatever his gifts. Beniamino Gigli, who during his years at the Metropolitan was the first to be subjected to comparisons with my father, had the good sense to keep repeating to reporters: "I don't want to be another Caruso; I just want to be Gigli."[16] The endless speculations in the newspapers as to who would be Caruso's heir began two days after he died. British reporters mentioned Edward Johnson, Joseph Hislop, and even John McCormack; entries in America were Beniamino Gigli, Giovanni Martinelli, Giacomo Lauri-Volpi, or Aureliano Pertile. On 29 November 1921, Gigli, showing commendable integrity, penned the following letter to *Musical America:*[17]

To speak of Caruso's successor is a sacrilege, profanation

of his memory, violation of a tomb sacred to Italy and the entire world!

Every artist today should aim to gather and preserve the artistic heritage of the Great Departed, not with vain exhibitions but with persistent study to the triumph of [what is] pure and beautiful.

This is how he strove, and for the glory of art we must follow his example with dignity.

Beniamino Gigli

The day after Father's death, Scotti publicly stated: "As Caruso succeeded no one, there can be no successor to him. He is and always will be supreme, the greatest tenor."[18] Yet the line of second Carusos seems endless. There was Tom Burke, the Lancashire Caruso; Jussi Björling, the Swedish Caruso; Miklós Gafni, the Hungarian Caruso; Mario Lanza, the American Caruso; and more recently Richard Tucker, whose voice Dorothy considered closest to Father's. These are all outstanding singers, with beautiful voices and solid techniques; yet the fact remains that there has never been another Caruso. My father had a musicality that blossomed from within. His physical and emotional attributes, intellectual gifts, and ability to project the essence of his very self into his roles made his singing unique. Consistent, lifelong study made his technique flawless; constant practice made his delivery impeccable. In the end, Caruso was a paragon that probably never will be duplicated. The legendary Russian bass, Alexander Kipnis, called him a "real genius of an artist," on a level with Battistini and Journet; Tullio Serafin named him, with Ruffo and Ponselle, one of the three "miracles of singing" he had known in his life. Arturo Toscanini referred to Caruso as one of the four "vocal phenomenons" of his lifetime, placing him in the company of Tamagno, Tetrazzini, and Ruffo.

It is a fact that in the more than six decades since his death, my father's fame and appeal have remained undiminished. Each decade seems to have belonged to a succession of favorite tenors active in his repertoire: Gigli, Martinelli, Björling, Tucker, Corelli, Pavarotti, Domingo. But none has eclipsed Enrico Caruso, who somehow belongs to all decades of the twentieth century. It may have been trite publicity that dubbed him "King of Tenors" and "Voice of the Century." But it is true that he had an artistic intuition and a style that left its mark on operatic singing. He had no successors among operatic tenors, only descendants.

As the first modern singer of the century, Caruso stamped his musical personality on successive generations of singers. A review of his repertoire of more than sixty roles shows that over half the operas in which he appeared were new works and world premières or works composed within a decade or two before his birth. He was born only fourteen months after the world première of *Aida*. He made his professional debut in 1895, three years after Leoncavallo's *Pagliacci* was first performed; and he sang his first Canio in 1896, the year when Giordano's *Andrea Chénier* and Puccini's *La Bohème* had their premières. *Adriana Lecouvreur, L'Arlesiana, Fedora, Tosca, Madama Butterfly, Fanciulla del West,* and *L'Amore dei tre re*—to name a few of the operas which Caruso later sang or whose tenor role he created—were yet to be composed! Although he dropped many roles in later years (a matter of choice as well as lack of demand for the operas involved), his active repertoire remained fairly large until the end. He denied that he had a favorite role. "The singer who has a favorite role," he once said, "is not an artist but a specialist. It is the public that makes the favorite roles."[19]

Father had an individualistic style. He was able to combine the emotionalism of *verismo* with the roots and traditions of *bel canto,* and he continued to grow and develop with changing musical tastes. The evolution of his interpretations is well documented by his recordings. The earliest, which date from 1902, already show a degree of individuality. Remarkably, his delivery sounds fresh and musically valid today, while the same selections recorded by many of his exact contemporaries seem stylistically dated. Most authorities concur that a handful of his many records rank as the all-time best renditions of the given operatic selections. His *Pagliacci* arias have never been equaled in dramatic intensity or prodigious outpouring of lustrous tones. Likewise, the last two versions—1908 and 1911—of his six recordings of "Celeste Aida" can compete only with each other. The 1908 *Rigoletto* arias are also as close to perfection in delivery as one could wish. Among the popular songs, his "Addio a Napoli," " 'A vucchella," and "La danza" are paragons of singing and interpretation.

The magic of my father's singing was inseparable from his person and personality. The combination of man and artist gave him the communicative powers that held his listeners spellbound; past and beyond the wondrous voice, this combination was the key to his enormous appeal. On the occasion of the last Caruso performance in the 1917 Met season, the critic for *Musical America* wrote:

As the years roll by there is no diminution whatever in Caruso's popularity. He has absolutely won the favor of the opera-loving public. . . .

The regard for Caruso has increased. It is coming to be understood that he stands for something more than a wonderfully beautiful voice. The press, musicians, music teachers, who bring their pupils to the opera to hear him, have gradually formulated public opinion to appreciate the fact that Caruso today, while no longer in what may be called the "golden period" of his voice, is singing with greater charm, and certainly with greater artistic effectiveness than ever.

Among the reasons which have strengthened his popularity with the public is his democracy. Caruso, while accepting invitations from prominent people, has never been a social climber. Then, too, he now speaks English with considerable fluency; he understands it; can write it. To all of which he adds a *bonhomie,* as the French call it, which is very pleasing to the mass of the people. Through this he has established a personal bond of sympathy between himself and the public. ("Mephisto's Musings," *Musical America,* 28 April 1917)

In the last decade of his life and for years after his death, it was sometimes said that Caruso owed his great popularity to inflated publicity and to a large personal staff that functioned as a public relations machine. The fact is that whatever my father did, wherever he went and whenever he sang, it was a news item of surefire interest. It was the reporters who sought Caruso out and not vice-versa. Editors were eager for anything written about him. During the second half of his life, one could pick up at random the daily newspaper of any major city in Europe or America and find at least one news item about him. For this reason, the compilation of a complete bibliography of newspaper articles about Caruso will remain a task beyond any researcher's ability.

As for publicity agents, my father had none. Over the years, he had a succession of "men of affairs": Armand Lecomte, Felice Caramanna, Errico Scognamillo, and a few others. These men helped with the details of his daily life, made travel arrangements, handled routine business correspondence, or ran errands. Bruno Zirato, whom he hired in 1917, was as close to a professional secretary as anyone in my father's employ, but he certainly did not function as a public relations staff. When Zirato made statements on Father's behalf, it was only to help him discharge his obligations to his public and to protect his privacy. Even organizers of his tours, like Emil Ledner in Europe, had an easy job. As Ledner wrote: "His advertising came of itself, without any effort. When he arrived in a large city, a battery of movie cameras was ready to receive him."[20] In addition, hundreds of men and women gathered at the station to catch a glimpse of the famous singer, to follow him around, to talk to him and to talk about him. That Caruso's fame rested on his artistry is well attested by the habits of the record-buying public of over eight decades. Even in this age of digitally recorded compact discs, Father's records continue to sell internationally, and engineers devote considerable talents and formidable technical resources to improving the original recordings, trying to get every decibel out of the old grooves which the diaphragm and cutter, attached to the acoustical horn, engraved over three-quarters of a century ago.

Speaking personally, I must say that until my late twenties, I could no more tell whether my father was an extraordinary singer than Louis XV could have told whether he had a nice home. The palace of Versailles was the only home he knew, and my father was the only tenor divo I knew. Except for a *Pagliacci* in Montecatini in 1912, I never heard another singer in a leading tenor role in my father's lifetime; thus I had no basis for comparisons. Of course there were the *comprimario* roles—the Messengers, the Arlecchinos—but they were in the background, and the great Caruso shone even brighter in contrast.

Although as a youngster, I did not pay much attention to Father's vocalizing or even to his performances in the theater, my musical taste had improved by the time Father took me to America, and I remember well the magnificent performances I attended. Whenever I was in New York, home from school for the Thanksgiving or Christmas holidays, I went to the opera every time Father sang. I recall seeing him at the Met in *Aida, L'Elisir d'amore, Pagliacci, Martha, Samson et Dalila, La Forza del destino,* and *La Juive,* and at the Brooklyn Academy of Music in still another *Martha.* I also remember that on one occasion, after spending a day and a night on the train from Indiana, I went straight to the theater, collapsed in my seat, and promptly fell asleep. I slept through the entire first act of *Martha,* thus becoming possibly the only person in Metropolitan Opera history who slept while Caruso sang. Later, when Papa asked how I liked the performance, I praised it more extravagantly than usual!

FATHER'S was an uncommon speaking voice. It was not particularly voluminous or resonant, but it had a musical sound. A stranger with a trained ear could peg him for a singer. I began to appreciate its quality much too late. To me it was just my father's voice, until during the months of his illness, it took on a weak, hollow, sheenless sound. Only then did I become aware of its innate beauty, and with everyone, I rejoiced when Father got better and the familiar richness of his voice slowly returned. In our last telephone conversation, his voice was strong and clear and sounded very much like the old voice I knew so well.

I have little recollection of my Uncle Giovanni's speaking voice. I believe it resembled Father's, and it had a Neapolitan sound. My brother's voice lacked these qualities. However, I was often told by my father's friends that my speaking voice was very close to Papa's.

His singing voice was quite a different matter. It was clear, with a glow and color that were described in every language with the same two adjectives: "velvety" and "golden." The noble, metallic ring in his voice had an ingratiating softness. It also had the power and resonance of a perfectly cast bell. The evenness of the voice was especially noticeable when Father vocalized, almost exclusively *mezza voce:* His voice had a unity, an aural homogeneity. His breath control was machine-perfect. The tone sat on a solid column of air, unwavering in pitch or intensity. I often heard him practice in the summers of 1916 and 1919, and also in New York. He never vocalized up to a B or B-flat; he knew the top notes were there and felt it was pointless to strain himself. All he was doing was giving a daily workout to the throat muscles and vocal cords, and going over his music in the process.

Father had an uncanny ability to color his voice. He vocalized according to the role he was about to sing next, giving it a shading and texture appropriate for the part. He could lighten or darken his voice at will. If he was preparing to sing Eléazar or Samson, as he was about to leave for the theater, his standing joke was to ask Mario:

"Nel terzo tiretto del casettone, prendimi la voce pesante." ("From the third drawer of the chest, bring me my heavy voice.") Or, if he was to sing Nemorino, he would ask for *"la mia voce leggera dal primo tiretto di sopra"* ("my light voice from the top drawer").

Before going onstage at the Met, Father always warmed up, singing some scales and a few phrases *mezza voce.* Then, just before leaving the dressing room, he would let out a phrase with the top note at full voice—*"A ventitre ore!"* or *"Un trono vicino al sol!"* or *"Dalila! Je t'aime!"* to test "the instrument" and to remove any phlegm that might remain after the ritual gargling, and gargling only, with whiskey. The power of his voice in the confined space of a small dressing room was painful to the ear.

In every performance, he gave his utmost. His voice had an amplitude that seemed to fill the auditorium and envelop the listener in sound that was alternately soft and caressing, when he sang at *mezza voce* or *piano,* and wild and alarming, when he opened up. I am quite certain that anyone who ever heard his bloodcurdling scream at the end of *Pagliacci*—"*Il suo nome o la tua vita! Il nome! Il nome!*" ("His name or your life! His name! His name!")—could never forget its chilling horror.

It is a shame that Father did not live a few more years, past 1925, into the era of electrical recordings. However, experts have generally agreed that the acoustic properties of his voice and the capabilities of the primitive equipment of the early recording process were a perfect match. A person listening to a Caruso record, even to one of the less successful takes, can formulate a fair idea of the Caruso sound. Theoretically, listeners familiar with his voice only from recordings could walk into the opera house blindfolded and instantly recognize his singing. For those who heard him in the flesh, the records are a wonderful souvenir of the live experience. For those who did not, they give a faithful impression of how he sounded. But the full richness, color, modulation, and dynamics of his voice, skillfully tuned to the mood and demands of the music, are inadequately captured by the old records. Inevitably, they leave a great deal to the listener's musical imagination. Also, his expansive phrasing is often destroyed by the confines of the two- to four-minute segments that a ten-inch or twelve-inch record could accommodate.

Caruso's critiques show a general agreement that his acting, which was crude or nonexistent at the beginning of his career, improved with each season. Father, always most critical of himself, knew that in his youth he was clumsy onstage.

> When I read, now, what some critics write of my singing and acting in performance ... at the Metropolitan I sometimes wish they knew how hard I worked to be able to do those things they like. Some of these men say: "Caruso improve in his acting; once he did not act well." What do they expect? A great artist of the young Caruso when he come first to this country?[21]

Aware of his deficiency, he worked very hard through his entire career to improve his acting. He made a conscious effort to project a character rather than merely singing a role. "I try really to impersonate the character I am representing in an opera," he said to Key. "One is always acting, of course, but the reality is suggested in proportion to the degree of feeling that is in the artist's heart."[22] The results were obvious and readily acknowledged by audiences and critics. A London newspaper wrote in 1914:

> Caruso no longer steps to the front and sings for all its worth. His voice has become an acting voice—that is to say, he never sacrifices sense for sound by putting vocal values before the values of the words. Indeed, Caruso the artist is now a more prominent personality than Caruso the singer.[23]

The culmination of Father's stagecraft was the role he essayed last, that of Eléazar in *La Juive*. The reviewers agreed that in this opera, his acting approached the level of his singing. In the 28 November 1920 issue of *The New York Times,* Richard Aldrich wrote: "He showed in *La Juive* . . . perhaps the finest manifestations of his art in certain ways that can be recalled in recent years." Analyzing the confrontation between Eléazar and Cardinal Brogni in the last act, Aldrich continued:

> Here Mr. Caruso is a tragic actor and discloses resources of tragic power that he has never before disclosed in the same potency. It is a scene that he has evidently studied seriously; and his composition of it in pose, gesture, facial expression . . . is matched by the poignant intensity of his declamation in the baleful color he imparts to the musical phrase. It is operatic acting of a high order.

I found his impersonations wonderfully effective, *especially* because I knew him so well. Time and again, for example, I had to remind myself during a performance that Eléazar, the dignified old Jew with the stooped shoulders and long beard that I saw onstage, was actually my own father. And yet, when Father sang Nemorino, despite his age he gave the impression of a young yokel. He pranced around with springy steps playing the lovesick peasant boy to perfection, and especially in his tipsy scene, he got as much laughter as applause. He had a grand time playing the country bumpkin, and the audience loved every minute of it.

The role of Father's that lives most vividly in my memory is Canio, not only because it was by all accounts his best role, but perhaps because I saw him perform it in Rome before I saw it at the Met. The first performance left a deep impression on me, and the one at the Met reinforced those memories. I can still see him in the first scene, entering the Calabrian village with his troupe, the carefree, white-faced comedian trying to drum up an audience for his evening performance. He was the quintessential simple, open-hearted Italian, whose brimming friendliness flooded the scene. Furiously, he beat the big drum, as the applause of the villagers, intermingled with that of the audience, gave the proper prelude for his first line: "Allow me to speak!" He proceeded to invite them all to the "spectacle" that night; then, his work done, he wiped the white powder from his face, signaling that the comedian was now an ordinary person. The welcome of the crowd put him at ease, and he gladly accepted their invitation to the tavern, until one of the villagers jokingly suggested that Tonio, the clown of his troupe, was staying behind to court Canio's wife, Nedda. He turned with a jolt, and his face darkened. "You think so?" he asked with a menacing edge to his voice. "The theater and life are not the same thing. I am speaking to Tonio and a little to you all," he warned. If he were to catch Nedda with someone, not in the comedy on the stage but in real life, the story would have a different ending. And his ominously raised hand clutching an imaginary knife stopped in mid-air, pausing long enough to let the listener complete the image of the execution of his threat. The choristers, caught up in his acting, reacted with fear and embarrassment. He used the applause that followed the aria to soften his features, and Caruso-Canio snapped out of his dark thoughts. He was all smiles again as he left with the peasants for the tavern.

In the next scene, he surprised his wife with her lover, the villager Silvio. When the young man escaped his pursuit, he tried to force Nedda to reveal her lover's name. He drew a knife, and the brutality and jealous rage with which he grabbed her by the wrist made it clear she had to fear for her life. Beppe, another actor in the troupe, grabbing his raised arm, forced the knife from his hand, and he collapsed on the steps, totally shattered.

He was a different man now. There was not a trace left of the friendly, good-natured comedian who had arrived in town only a few hours before. He was only a man now, and his world had collapsed. Only a man? No, only Pagliaccio. His "Recitar!" and his inimitable lament, "Vesti la giubba," drew the audience into the heart of his personal drama. It seemed that every listener in that vast audience suffered with him. Sobbing, his shoulders trembling, he mounted with unsteady steps the platform of Canio's improvised stage, and the curtain fell. The audience exploded in a roar of applause that would not end, celebrating the artist and at the same time releasing their own pent-up tensions. Father could bring the character of Canio to life because it was so real to him, especially after 1908.

One night Pierre Key watched *Pagliacci* from backstage. After the first act, he saw Father walking upstairs to his dressing room.

> [Caruso moved] laboriously, taking each step slowly, and holding partly to the hand-rail that runs along one wall. I thought I heard a sort of choking sound. Looking more closely at the tenor I was astonished to see a real tear on one cheek.
> "What's the matter? Anything wrong?"
> He turned his face upward, brushed a hand almost roughly across it, and replied:
> "No! Caruso only a damn fool. He feels too much when he sings."[24]

I am mystified as to what theatrical means Father used to convey the duality of the character in the last scene, the play-within-the-play. Yet it was clear to everyone in the audience how the mind of his character was swaying back and forth between reality and make-believe. Having to enact a comedy with his unfaithful wife turned his Canio into a seething volcano. It finally erupted in his "No, Pagliaccio non son!" "No, I am not Pagliaccio!" he sang. "If my face is pale, it is from shame and from craving revenge! The man reclaims his rights, and the bleeding heart wants blood to wash away the disgrace, damned woman!" In the second, more lyric part of his outburst, he reminded her: "I happily endured every sacrifice of the heart, and trustingly believed in you more than in God himself! But only evil dwells in your wretched soul; you have no heart. . . . Only the senses are your law. Go, you do not deserve my grief."

The sound of his voice was hot and vibrant, his singing impassioned, the words exploding as if they were his own. What thoughts, what memories must have passed through his mind each time he sang these lines!

The end of the opera came swiftly, with tragic inevitability. After he stabbed both Nedda and Silvio, he half-spoke, half-sang his last words: "The comedy is over!" The audience was stunned and drained of emotion, and there was a notable pause before the applause, erupted. In *Pagliacci,* Caruso was Canio and Canio was Caruso, because Father *lived* this role.

After the curtain fell, the ovation lasted at least a quarter of an hour. As Father took his endless curtain calls, he spotted me standing in the wings. Dripping with perspiration, he turned to me and asked in an anxious tone: *"Com'è andata? Com'è andata?"* ("How did it go?") I told him it went superbly; to me it sounded wonderful. And now I know for certain: It was the best *Pagliacci* one could ever hear.

I HAVE often been asked: "Did your father sing for pleasure?"

No, my father sang for money. He sang for the pleasure of others, and although he enjoyed it, he got paid for it. Laymen cannot realize the amount of energy a singer expends in a performance, what hard work singing is and what labors the pursuit of a singing career entails. Yes, Papa sang all the time in his younger years for his chums, for himself, for the sheer pleasure of singing. But this was the exuberance of youth. As far back as I can remember, I never heard him sing "socially," neither at family gatherings nor for himself. Very rarely did he sing offstage and outside his studio. I remember him humming as he was building the *presepio* at Signa in the summer of 1919, but that too was work: He was going over some passages he had just practiced with Bruno Bruni.

In 1920, Pierre Key asked Papa over dinner at East Hampton why he no longer sang in the impromptu way he once had. As Key recorded, Papa explained that "it is for the singer much as it is with the candy-store clerk: After eating a certain amount of sweets the taste for it goes. It is the same with the singer . . . singing gets finally to be a business."[25]

Instead of volunteering to sing for his guests, Father gave record recitals. He took a great deal of pride in his recordings. Not only was he fascinated by the miracle of having his voice preserved, but he was quick to see the value of the recordings as a learning device. When Papa played his latest records for friends, it was not to fish for the inevitable compliments but rather to gracefully avoid having to sing and to have the opportunity to judge from the listeners' reactions how good his delivery really was. He could gauge the sincerity of praise; he knew human nature well and could not be deceived. (Supposedly, he once played a minor singer's records pretending they were his own, and his listeners voiced extravagant praises. Caruso was distressed to have this proof that his name rather than his voice commanded accolades.)

On the other hand, I don't remember Father ever playing the records of other singers, and it is entirely possible that he didn't own any. When I returned to Le Panche in 1922, the only non-Caruso records I found were "The Whistler and His Dog" and Harry Lauder's "Roamin' in the Gloaming." In this respect, Father was the very opposite of Titta Ruffo. The baritone hardly ever played his own recordings but preferred those made by others. As a matter of fact, Ruffo never owned a complete set of his own records, and when he retired he gave away those he had to friends and admirers.[26]

Papa also knew what to expect of his public and had no illusions about their limited understanding of vocal artistry. Albert Reiss, a respected Metropolitan Opera artist, a great Mime, and a celebrated Witch in *Hänsel und Gretel,* could not understand why he never received much applause for his offstage serenade in *Pagliacci,* although he was convinced he sang it well. Once, while on tour in Boston, Reiss prevailed upon Father to sing it for him. Amused by the challenge, he did so. To his consternation, he received no more applause than his colleague. Reiss asked him to do it again, but Papa refused, until two years later, when he sang it once more in Chicago. As Reiss told the London *Daily Telegraph,* "he sang like a god, and took great pains with the special intention of calling forth applause. Yet no hand moved. He then said that he would never do it again."[27] But the experiment must have irked him, because he tried it at least once more, in Berlin. This time he sang the serenade in place of Walter Kirchhoff, another international artist of the first rank, who should have been well received on his own merits. Yet the result was the same. He was obliged to recognize, yet again, how little his hearers understood the qualities of his voice and singing that set him apart from his colleagues.

His high fees and his sense that singing was a business notwithstanding, I doubt that after his apprentice years, Father ever performed purely in order to make money. Dr. William Lloyd, his throat specialist in London, once said to a *Daily Mail* reporter:

> Despite the fact that he demanded thousands of pounds in fees, he really cared very little for money. I have known him to refuse 2,000 pounds to sing a Sunday afternoon concert at Albert Hall, with the remark: "No, I feel too tired." On another occasion I made him the offer of 4,000 pounds on behalf of Sir Oswald Stoll to sing in London, but he waved it aside with a smile, saying: "Too much."[28]

In 1909, Father turned down an offer of 20,000 pounds from Harry Rickards for twenty concerts in Australia. Then there is the story of J. Pierpoint Morgan offering him 1,200 pounds to sing at an evening party he was giving at Prince's Gate, but Father excused himself saying he could not possibly break a long-standing dinner engagement with his old friend Leoncavallo on the very night of the party.[29] In January 1912, Oscar Hammerstein offered him "any figure he cared to name" to appear in his summer season in London. This was after Hammerstein had signed an agreement with the Metropolitan not to produce operas in New York. By accepting the offer to sing in London, Father would not have placed his home company in an awkward position, yet he turned it down.

He simply enjoyed the profession for which his talents predestined him, and he derived pleasure from the pleasure he gave his listeners. If money had not been an obvious measurement of his artistic worth, he would probably have sung just as gladly for no fee. Still, there is no denying that he enjoyed the material fruits of his labors and delighted in being able to afford anything he wished and also to help others.

Father's acts of generosity are legendary, from his regular support of needy friends and relatives to impulsive acts like taking off a ring or a tie pin and giving it to someone who could never afford it just because the person had admired it. Soprano Frieda Hempel, eyewitness to the incident, wrote in her memoirs that once, in the middle of winter, Caruso encountered a beggar shivering in a ragged jacket in front of the Hotel Knickerbocker. Father took off his fur-lined coat and, with a significant "it is yours" gesture, put it over the man's shoulders and without a word walked into the hotel.[30]

His own needs and demands were more like those of an exceptionally well-to-do bourgeois than those of a spoiled millionaire. He bought the best clothes and furnishings; he lavished gifts on his friends and jewelry on the women he loved. But he had no extravagant desires for himself. He did not buy bigger and better cars, yachts, or race horses. His villas were spacious homes, large enough to receive invited guests and relatives, but not showpieces of ostentation. From 1903 until his death, he spent more than half of each year in New York City, yet he never bought a house or an apartment where he could have entertained sumptuously or flaunted his wealth. In spite of the attachment and gratitude he felt toward the United States, and toward New York in particular, he remained an Italian to the end. America was his place of work; Italy was his home.

Father was a one-man mint. There was a well-known cartoon showing him singing, with sheet music in hand, as the notes floating from his open mouth turned into a cascade of gold coins. In fact, all his income came from singing, as opposed to investments. In the best years of his career, his income amounted to hundreds of thousands of dollars annually, and this in the happy days before income taxes. Until the 1907–08 season, the Metropolitan paid him in francs. At the prevailing exchange rate, in 1903–04 he received $960 a performance. This amount was raised to $1,440 by 1906–07 and jumped to $2,000 in the following year. Starting in 1914–15, he was paid $2,500 a night. Most biographers mention that this fee was established when Gatti put a blank contract in front of his star tenor, inviting him to fill in whatever amount he deemed appropriate. It was said that it was Caruso who set his fee at $2,500 for each appearance, and that he never asked for more. However, I have it on good authority that toward the end, Gatti, on his own initiative and insistence, paid Father an extra $500 "under the table" for each appearance. It was an arrangement that served the ends of the crafty manager: On the one hand, he showed his appreciation to his star attraction, and on the other, he could say to a demanding prima donna, "Even Caruso gets only $2,500—I cannot possibly pay you more." Father's highest single year of earnings at the Metropolitan was 1907–08, when he received $140,000 for sixty-eight opera performances and two concerts.[31]

Father's concert fees were usually higher than his fee at the Met, and he often sang at the homes of the super-rich for large honorariums. Then there were the legendary payments for his South American, Mexican, and Cuban engagements, some of which rose as high as $15,000 a performance, paid in gold, at a time when the average weekly salary in the United States was about $10. As if all this were not enough, *My Cousin* and *A Splendid Romance,* the two movies he made for Jesse L. Lasky's Famous Players Corporation in 1918, brought him an extra $100,000 each.

IN addition to income from his public and private appearances, Father had a lucrative recording contract with the Victor Talking Machine Company, which became the longest-running money machine in recording history.

Caruso's association with the recording company predated his association with the American-based Victor. Early in his career, he made three (and possibly four) recordings for the Anglo-Italian Commerce Company[32] and seven sides for Zonophone. When he appeared at La Scala on 11 March 1902 in the world première of Franchetti's *Germania,* the enterprising young recording technician of the Gramophone & Typewriter Company, Fred Gaisberg, went to hear him on the recommendation of the company's Milan representative, Alfred Michaelis. Gaisberg's enthusiasm was such that he asked Michaelis to find out what fee Caruso would accept for ten songs. Maestro Salvatore Cottone brought the message that Caruso wanted one hundred pounds, and that all ten selections would have to be recorded in one afternoon, as that was all the free time he had. Gaisberg transmitted the terms to his superiors in London, strongly recommending their acceptance. The London office cabled its oft-quoted reply: "FEE EXORBITANT FORBID YOU TO RECORD."

Gaisberg was a recording technician working in the field, and he had enough experience to trust his own judgment. "It was only by being on the spot that one could grasp the urgency of the opportunity," he wrote in his memoirs.[33] He decided to go ahead with the plan. Disregarding the cable from London (or possibly writing before its arrival), Michaelis wrote to the head office on Gramophone Company Italy Limited stationery on 10 April 1902: "Caruso sings ten songs tomorrow for £100. Pinto, the soprano you heard in *Germania*, sings ten for £40. Gaisberg requires £60, and I also want money for the Zurich records. . . . I confirm my telegram: 'Please cable 300 pounds Caruso Pinto Zurich Gaisberg reply Tamagno tomorrow.'"

The ten sides were made on April 11, with Maestro Cottone providing piano accompaniment in an improvised studio in Gaisberg's suite in the Grand Hotel di Milano. The session took two hours.

The records were rushed into production and became an instant success. It can be said without exaggeration that the rest is history. It has sometimes been claimed that the gramophone made Caruso, but historical perspective shows the reverse to be the case: It was Caruso who made the gramophone, or, at the very least, accelerated its coming of age. An indication of the speed of manufacture and breadth of distribution of that first batch of Caruso's records is a letter from St. Petersburg on the stationery of the Obshchestvo Grammofon' v Rossii (The Gramophone Company in Russia) dated "June 12/25th 1902" (the date reflects both the Gregorian and the Russian calendars):

> We have in due time received the Red Label Records, and have had great pleasure in hearing the Caruso ones. They are splendid indeed, and, certainly, will be in considerable demand. We have, therefore, issued a special circular (three copies of which we send you under separate cover) and hope to be able to use a great many of them.[34]

As for the economic side of Gaisberg's gamble, it should be noted that Father made these records for the flat fee of one hundred pounds sterling; no subsequent royalties were paid to him. If Gaisberg was "stunned at the ease with which such a vast amount was earned,"[35] Papa would have been even more stunned had he known the exact amount of the revenue he produced for the Gramophone & Typewriter Company. Gaisberg observed: "I heard 15,000 pounds net profit mentioned as a result of the venture."[36] At the prevailing exchange rate of about six dollars to the English pound, this totals about $90,000—not a bad return for a hundred-pound investment and a two-hour recording session!

Immediately after the records hit the market, sales exceeded all expectations. Even the cautious executives of the Gramophone Company took notice, and their most urgent concern was how to lure Caruso back into a recording studio. They first approached the composer Umberto Giordano about accompanying the tenor at the piano for a recording of "Amor ti vieta" from his own *Fedora*. In a letter of 14 November 1902 to W. B. Owen in London, Michaelis gave the translation of Giordano's note to him, dated 12 November 1902, which read in part: "I consent with pleasure to comply with your demand to make my friend Caruso sing my *Fedora,* presiding myself at the pianoforte." Next it was necessary to obtain Caruso's services. In the same letter, Michaelis wrote: "Besides this settles the question about Caruso singing for us again as he cannot possibly refuse the request of the composer. Of course we must pay him, and I hope also to get out of him the promise not to sing for anyone else—though this latter I cannot promise."

Papa was pleased with the records. The Gramophone & Typewriter Company officials tried hard to persuade him of the company's ability to faithfully preserve his voice. They sent him a complimentary machine, which he acknowledged with the following note (in Michaelis's translation of 7 December 1902): "Thanks for the Gramophone 'Monarch,' the effect of which, from one room to another, is so magnificent that some of my friends have had the impression that they heard me sing while I was engaged in conversation with them."

Michaelis was apparently successful in coaxing Father before the recording horn again. He sang another ten selections on 12 November 1902, and Michaelis sent this telegram to London: "Caruso sang yesterday please send cheque 200 pounds Michaelis."[37] In a subsequent letter of 7 December 1902 to Owen, Michaelis devoted a long paragraph to Caruso.

I have had him sing over again "Dai campi, dai prati" which is defective, and Aida which had that bad note at the end, and eight new pieces, amongst which several songs sung by him during the Covent Garden Coronation season in the houses of Rothschild, Astor, etc., and some others of which we shall send you a complete list, because they will of course have to buy machines with these records as will all the Aristocracy invited to these concerts. It was on this occasion that Astor shocked his English guests by posting up a notice in his salons reading something like this: "Ladies and Gentlemen are requested to be silent during the concert." Caruso asked for lire 3000 for the "Amor ti vieta" with Giordano's accompaniment, or 5000 lire for 5 songs. The most I could obtain was that he would repeat Mefistofele and Aida gratis. We thus had 7 songs for 5000 lire [about $1,000]. During the execution on Sunday Giordano promised to get his friend the composer Cilea to accompany Caruso & De Luca for us in *Adriana Lecouvreur* and Caruso gave us to understand that he would do it gratis.

After much discussion and correspondence, an exclusive contract between Caruso and the Gramophone & Typewriter Company was finally concluded in 1904. Alfred Clark of the Compagnie Française du Gramophone, the Paris branch of the company, wrote to T. B. Birnbaum at the London headquarters on 17 May 1904:

> In view of the fact that since Caruso's debut in Paris and his enormous success some weeks ago, his name is on every tongue, Pathé have profited to advertise greatly their Caruso records.
>
> We have today received two samples of new records of Caruso from Hanover, and when announcing these records it would be well for us to say that they are newly made under our exclusive arrangement. At the same time it would interest us to know whether there are any more new Carusos coming out in the near future.

Clark's letter reached London in two days. Birnbaum was in Berlin at the moment, and an unnamed assistant drafted a reply on May 19. Regarding the Caruso contract, he stated that "Caruso was bound up by the Victor Talking Machine Company whilst in America, and he can only sing for Victor and for us. I have published this to my trade here."

The letter made reference to the first twelve-inch record made by Caruso, the tenor aria from *The Pearlfishers,* or *I Pescatori di perle,* as it was recorded in Italian. It also stated that Michaelis had made arrangements with Leoncavallo, Mascagni, Franchetti, Giordano, and Puccini to compose one song each expressly for the gramophone. The writer stated that "Caruso has sung Leoncavallo's ['Mattinata'] and is going to sing Mascagni's and Puccini's here in London." According to the recording logs, he never recorded the last two numbers.

When Father returned to London in the fall of 1904, he refused to record for the Gramophone & Typewriter Company unless they were "able to show him in writing or by cable that he was permitted to do so" under the terms of his contract with the Victor Company. The London executives were very disappointed that Victor did not cable permission to Caruso at the Hotel Cecil in time for him to make any recordings during his stay in London. Trevor Williams of the Gramophone & Typewriter Company wrote a panicky letter to Eldridge R. Johnson of the Victor Talking Machine Company. The latter answered with a four-page letter on 10 November 1904, touching upon a number of topics. The passages that relate to the Caruso contract cast an interesting light on the fees involved.

> My dear Mr. Williams,
>
> Your letter of October 28th, concerning Caruso contract received. I have just read over the Caruso contract, and am sending you enclosed copy of same. It is quite true that Caruso charged us at the rate of 80 pounds per song. It is also quite true that he might refuse to sing again at that rate, and ask more. Mr. Child, however, assures me that Mr. Caruso will sing at the same rate, providing we give him at least ten songs for an engagement.
>
> I quite agree with you that there should be some stipulation in the contract whereby the price is fixed during its continuance, but the agreement was the best that we could get. The Columbia people were after Caruso, and were willing to pay him more money than we paid him. We found him rather difficult to deal with, although he was very nice after the contract was executed.

The contract stipulated a fifty cents royalty per record and a sizable advance against royalties.[38] It also called for $2,000 to be paid on January 28 "of each year for five years so that he will not sing for any other talking machine company or party for the purpose of making

Talking Machine records (excepting the Gramophone & Typewriter Limited of London) for the period of five years, to wit, from January 28th, 1904, to January 28th, 1909."

This contract remained in force for its full term. Eldridge Johnson signed it for the Victor Talking Machine Company, and it was witnessed by Calvin G. Child and Emilio de Gogorza, the baritone who was responsible for obtaining Red Seal artists for Victor.

The contract was amended on 15 January 1906. The amended contract specifically left the original contract in force, giving Father and a company representative the right to reject and remake any recording that did not meet their joint approval, and giving Father the right to examine his account on the company's books. The contract reconfirmed his exclusive commitment to Victor and the fifty cents royalty to be paid per record. Then, under Item Four, a sentence was added in Calvin Child's hand and initialed by the signatories: "The royalty to continue as long as the records are sold." The concluding sentence stipulated: "This agreement to bind the heirs, executors, administrators, successors and assigns of the parties hereto."

By 1908, Victor was routinely making twelve-inch records as well as ten-inch, and the directors of the company felt it was time to make a distinction between the two sizes with respect to royalties. Father agreed to the readjustment the company proposed. In a "Supplemental Agreement," which again stipulated that the original contract remain in force, it was specified that after January 1908, Father was to receive twenty-five cents for each ten-inch record and fifty cents for each twelve-inch record sold.

When the first contract expired, a new contract was drawn up, this time to run for a twenty-five-year period, from 1 January 1909 to 1 January 1934. While the company remained obligated to pay Caruso royalties due under the previous arrangement, the new contract superseded all previous agreements. This supersedure was specified as a matter of legal form, for the new contract reaffirmed all the important points previously agreed upon: Father would make records only for the Victor Company unless permission to record for another firm was granted in writing; he would make records when his health permitted and when the recording session did "not interfere with his operatic and concert engagements." Father and a designated company representative had the right to approve or reject any recordings. Again, Father was to receive a royalty of twenty-five cents for each ten-inch record and fifty cents for each twelve-inch record sold. Notable changes in the contract were the absence of any reference to Caruso's right to examine the account books, and the company's guarantee of a minimum of $10,000 in royalties in each year when he made at least three recordings approved for sale. The important stipulation concerning royalty payments was expanded to read:

> It is understood and agreed that the royalties provided for in this agreement shall continue as long as any records of Enrico Caruso are sold by the Victor Talking Machine Company, or its successors and assigns, and that the payments thereof shall be made to Enrico Caruso during his lifetime and after his death to the legal representative of his estate.

The document was signed on 3 April 1909 by Eldridge Johnson for the Victor Talking Machine Company and witnessed by Calvin G. Child and Armando [*sic*] Lecomte, Father's current "man of affairs." The contract was renewed on 29 January 1912, probably to include a codicil which granted Caruso $2,000 in travel expenses should he make a trip to New York solely in order to fulfill his commitment to Victor.

Of course, the records continued to sell, making a small fortune for Caruso and a large fortune for Victor. Reflecting on the first recordings in Milan, Gaisberg wrote that he could not foresee that "Caruso would earn close to $5,000,000 in the next twenty years and the industry twice that amount."[39] So much income was produced by the Caruso records that by 1919 it was decided to renegotiate the contract. The new contract, which was to run from 1 January 1919 until 1 January 1934, required Father to record forty solos during that time span. His royalty was set at 10 percent of the catalog price regardless of whether his recordings were solos or ensembles, and Victor guaranteed him an annual minimum payment of $100,000. He was to remain exclusively a Victor artist, and if he were to record his voice for any other company, the breach of contract would automatically release Victor from any obligation of future payments to him. The concluding statement specified that this new agreement superseded all previous ones, and that "the covenants of and rights granted by this agreement shall apply to, bind and be for the benefit of the heirs, executors, administrators, successors and assigns of the parties hereto."

This was the final contract drawn up between my father and the Victor Talking Machine Company. Father could rightly believe that he had assured financial security for himself and his family. His earnings from record royalties continued to rise and were the subject of endless speculation during his lifetime. A close friend once asked him how much his gramophone records brought in.

"Guess," replied Papa.

"$10,000," the friend said tentatively.

"Right," he answered. "Only I make that monthly, you know."[40]

THOUGH money for its own sake had little importance to my father, he did not lose sight of the value of a dollar. He never paid more than its true value for anything, and he was generous but not lavish with tips. My own allowance in New York was a dollar a week, which went a long way in the days when a movie was fifteen cents and a banana split fifteen or twenty.

Father helped over a hundred people with monthly checks, but it was he who determined the amount, and woe unto the one who dared to ask for more. He gladly supported his brother all his adult life, but when Giovanni asked for money, which he did from time to time, Papa grumbled. On the memorable occasion at Signa when Fofò asked for a million lire, Papa yelled at him:

"Me li mangio! Me li mangio io, non vi lascio niente!" ("I will eat them! I'll eat them myself, I'll leave you nothing!")

Outsiders could request anything freely; it was only members of his family who aroused his wrath, for he felt that they always wanted something from him. Many of them did, it is true—Giovanni in particular. But Father's spontaneous gifts—the money he would sneak into the pocket of a wig-man at the Met, or the piece of jewelry he would offer to a stagehand who had admired it—never occurred within the family. The notable exceptions to this rule were his women. He lavished gifts on my mother, he was generous with Rina, and he was particularly magnanimous with Dorothy. I am told that he also opened his wallet to the many ladies who came between. He did this as much out of love and innate generosity as out of self-serving pride: Caruso's women were his showpieces and had to have the best of everything.

His attitude with the family was: I will give, but don't ask. The trick was to influence his thinking so as to get what one wanted without making a direct request. When I wrote to him after the war from Florence and asked for permission to buy a bicycle, Papa said no. After I came to New York, I still wanted a bicycle. Dorothy said no this time, adding that only delivery boys had bicycles in New York, and she would rather buy me a car. Father nixed the car, so I ended up with neither.

Despite his feeling that his family was always ready for a handout, he remained loyal to them. The expense involved was enormous; he often said that he spent more than $80,000 a year on his family. When Livorno became his summer home, he invited my grandparents, Guido and Teresa, their son Umberto, and their granddaughter Mimma to live with us at his expense. *"Tu vivrai con noi. Sei di famiglia"* ("You will live with us. You are family"), he said to Guido. Except for a couple of years after Mother left him, Father always treated the Giachettis as his own family. Papa regarded Guido and Grandmother Giuseppina—and later Teresa—as his inlaws. He never forgot that when he was flat broke after the Livorno season, the Giachettis lent him money, and when he and Ada settled in Milan on Via Velasca, they pawned their valuables to help him pay the rent. When Father began to earn money in earnest, the Giachettis enjoyed all the benefits of belonging to the Caruso household and were added to the Caruso payroll. As far as I know, their relationship was friendly, and Father accorded Guido the respect due to an older man. What part of his thoughts and private concerns Papa shared with my maternal grandfather I am unable to say. But a couple of years after Mother left, he met with Guido, and it was this or subsequent meetings that finally led to his engagement to Rina.

Father was invariably generous with his friends. Friendship had a special meaning to him that transcended all else. Dorothy summed it up quite accurately:

> Friendship was another matter. In that he was inflexible, judicious, monumental. He discussed neither the faults, virtues, manners nor behavior of his friends. His standards were based on certain rules of human dignity; if the rules were broken he withdrew his friendship, offered no explanation, made no comment, simply continued on his way. He had no thought of revenge, neither did he "forgive and forget." "I forgive and remember," he said.[41]

He was unconditionally devoted to his friends. While a friend was a friend, he or she could do no wrong, and Papa would tolerate no criticism of his friends. In his mind, friendship entitled a person to ask for anything, money or favors, and he seldom refused a request.

Marziale Sisca was the owner and publisher of the Italian newspaper *La Follia di New York*. He published his paper for the Italian immigrants, those who had not yet learned English or those who had but preferred to read Italian. He knew everyone in Little Italy, and the Italian businessmen were his friends and advertised in his paper.

Father met Sisca within weeks after his arrival in New York in 1903, and a close friendship developed between them.

One of Sisca's friends was a Sicilian fellow, the owner of the Atlantic Macaroni Company. I met him, but I have forgotten his name. Perhaps I intentionally blocked it out of my memory after he told me with ludicrous arrogance:

"Io e mettido u nomme e Caruso in goppa du mappamunde!" ("I have put the name of Caruso on the map of the world!")

It seems that the Atlantic Macaroni Company was veering toward bankruptcy. The Sicilian asked Sisca to approach Caruso and ask him to endorse his pasta. Sisca was willing and went to see Father at the Knickerbocker. When Sisca said the Sicilian was a friend of his, Father said with his typical largess:

"Un amico tuo è un amico mio." ("A friend of yours is a friend of mine.")

Then and there he wrote on the hotel's stationery a statement authorizing the Sicilian to use his name, photograph, and signature on his products.

The Enrico Caruso name first appeared on pasta, as expected—then on olive oil, salami, canned tomatoes, and other "products." Later on the man sold his business, selling each "product," together with the right to bear the Caruso name, to a different food company, and getting more for the license of the name than for the product itself! Father never got a cent from it, not even a complimentary case of spaghetti. Sisca told me how embarrassed he was about the whole affair, but by then it was too late to back out of it.

Some of the hangers-on came frequently to Father's New York apartment, but an even broader circle tried to catch him after a performance at one of his favorite restaurants. When he entered Del Pezzo's or Doctor Pane's, all the guests would greet him. He usually gave a general salutation and proceeded with his meal. After dinner, some cronies would come around with a *"Commendato', baciamm'i mani"* (*"Commendatore,* I kiss your hand") and would actually kiss his hand. He tolerated this, but not out of ostentation, for he never lorded his status over anyone. All the same, I think he felt he was entitled to a certain adulation. After all, he was who he was, and it is likely that many of the cronies were actually thanking him for his monetary support. Because Father was aware of his own worth, it would be an exaggeration to call him humble; but as a private person, apart from his artistry, he came very close to it. He knew that a beautiful voice does not turn a nobody into a somebody. He expected respect and recognition, not for his voice, but for the hard work that made it such a perfect musical instrument and that made him the artist he was.

At these post-performance meals, just about anyone could walk up to Caruso. At times the scene was like that of a mafia *padrino,* a godfather, holding court. Father would patiently listen to every man's story. "Ah, *Commendatore,* my wife is so-o-o sick, and I have lost my job." There were always some with special requests. They knew he might not give them all they asked, but he would always give them something, and he could be generous even with strangers. Father took no particular pride in supporting so many people. His attitude was that God had been kind to him in giving him a voice and enormous earning power, and it was his obligation to share his wealth with those less fortunate.

It has been said that Father ate too much. This idea got into early articles and biographies, and the writers responsible for the vast Caruso literature have been borrowing it from one another ever since. In fact, it is not true. On a normal day, when Father was not performing, he ate at regular mealtimes and neither more nor less than an average person with a healthy appetite. He drank only wine with meals, never hard liquor, and never to excess. But on the days when he performed, he ate very lightly; then, when he sang, he perspired so heavily that he routinely lost four or five pounds during the performance. By the time the opera was over, he was famished and needed to replenish his energy and his lost fluids. If food seemed more important at the moment than a hot bath, his chauffeur would drive him down to Mulberry or Spring Street, in New York's Italian section, and he would fill up on a spectacular helping of spaghetti and salads. When fans or friends tagged along, he would buy dinner for them also. The sight of a hungry Caruso stuffing himself with pasta gave birth to the legend that an oversize appetite was responsible for his oversize girth.

Part of Father's problem with weight was that while he did not mind hard physical work, exercise for exercise's sake was anathema to him. At East Hampton, I remember that he played tennis one afternoon and was ready to collapse. Thereafter he picked up a racket only to pose for a picture; he would rather spend his free time organizing his clippings or his stamp collection or playing with baby Gloria.

Father was never good at small talk except in the company of his Neapolitan cronies. As for routine social intercourse, Emil Ledner wrote:

> In a large or small circle, his ability to carry on a conversation, to immerse himself in an exchange of ideas, failed com-

pletely. Even though on such occasions people were considerate, placing "the center of attention" so that French- or Italian-speaking persons would be nearby, the success rate remained negative. He filled the pauses by drawing caricatures at which he became proficient, signing autographs which were always in demand, and in a very short time every gathering would break up.[42]

In Naples, however, it was an entirely different matter. Family and friends often piled into several cars and drove to *I Promessi Sposi,* Father's favorite restaurant on the Vomero, or to *Zi' Teresa* at Posillipo or *A Bersagliera* at Santa Lucia. When we were in Naples, these were daily outings, and a meal could last from early afternoon until midnight. At *I Promessi Sposi,* we would sit at long tables set up on the *terrazzo* overlooking the beautiful Bay of Naples, Vesuvio with its white plume looming in the background. The tables were under a pergola laden with grapes and buzzing flies, the whole illuminated by Chinese lanterns and a full yellow moon once night fell. The dinner party would begin with the family; then friends of relatives and friends of friends would join us, and the party would swell to thirty or forty people. Papa tremendously enjoyed these impromptu dinner parties, and he also knew that many at the table were having their first decent meal in a long while. Although he was the host and the focus of attention, Father did not dominate the boisterous gatherings; instead, everyone talked at once. Father knew how to stand out in a crowd, but he also knew how to blend into a group. He was skilled at putting people at ease, just as he was skilled at keeping strangers at arm's length.

He was neither a loudmouth nor a showoff. If he dressed well, gave generously, or entertained lavishly, it was from a simple desire to please himself and others, not from the wish to impress anyone.

I HAVE great respect for my Father's artistry, for his beautiful voice and his unique delivery. But when I look objectively at his private life, my admiration falters. The only women he treated well were Dorothy and Gloria. By the time he married Dorothy, he was forty-five, ready to settle down and lead a nearly normal family life. He was simply crazy about his baby girl. Unfortunately, Gloria was barely a year and a half old when he died, so she never got to know her father. Of all Caruso's children, Gloria lost the most, for no child could have had a more loving parent. Fate should have been kind to Father and let him enjoy the fruits of his labor and grow old with his children and family at his side. I remember his remark when he heard the sad news that Alfredo Pane, the restaurateur, had died:

"A man works all his life to make something and then he dies before he can enjoy it."

Papa did not know it then, but he could have been talking about himself.

In private life, Father's behavior left a good deal to be desired. Publicly, he was most ethical with others; he was scrupulously honest in his business dealings, steadfast in his friendships. He was a man of his word: A handshake or a nod of his head was as good as a written contract. Yet privately, and especially in his love life, he was irresponsible and often callous. Several of his affairs with the scores of women who passed through his bedroom—or he through theirs—made headline news, nationally or internationally, and some ended up in the courts. Father liberally, shamelessly, and carelessly used his celebrity to indulge himself with women. Billy Guard told me many years after his death that Papa had the pick of the women at the Metropolitan, and he exploited his privilege like a feudal lord exercising his *ius primae noctis*.

Between his involvements with Elsa Ganelli and Mildred Meffert, Father formalized his relationship with my Aunt Rina. She was very much in love with him. I was too young to observe such matters, but my brother said that every time she looked at Papa, "she went completely gaga." Father was kind and affectionate toward his women, but he was not demonstrative in public. I don't recall any kissing or caressing in my presence; his sense of propriety reserved that for behind closed doors. Yet even I felt the warmth and strong attachment between Papa and Rina, something intangible yet real, a certain sense of belonging together that I did not sense at all in Father's relationship with Dorothy.

Of course, Rina was Italian and much more outgoing and emotionally expressive than her American successor. Furthermore, Father and Rina had shared the same language, a common cultural heritage, and an artistic and personal past that spanned nearly two decades. Father was seven years older than Rina, whereas he was twenty years older than Dorothy. Whatever their legal status, it seems to me in retrospect that Father and Dorothy acknowledged he was in many respects her surrogate father. It is beyond any doubt that he loved Dorothy and was very gentle, protective, and good to her. But the husband I met in 1919 was a serious, middle-aged gentleman compared to the light-hearted, often playful man I knew before the war. I searched in vain for the young man who used to bounce me up in the air as I rode on his tummy in the mornings at Clarendon Court in London when I was five.

Before the war "to end all wars," Papa was riding the crest of success, and he was not particularly concerned about his physical condition. He swam often, ate and drank anything he pleased, and took no special precautions with respect to his throat. He was a different man in 1919. He worried about drafts, would not drink cold water, and religiously cleaned "the instrument" every morning. Apart from his incessant smoking, he avoided anything that could harm his singing apparatus.

Analyzing his behavior and reading his public statements, it is apparent that he realized he could rise to no greater heights; now his task was to cling to his present glory and hold his place in the operatic world as long as possible. The inevitable years of decline were nearing, and he was terrified at the prospect of a precipitous collapse of his career. Beginning with the South American tours of 1915, the critics did not hesitate to remind him of the passage of time. He must have had dark thoughts about the approaching time when Caruso would not be Caruso any more. The ovation at the end of each successful performance must have reassured him that he could still do it, he could still sing wondrously, he was still preeminent among his peers . . . but for how much longer?

CARUSO "is simple enough to be big, and big enough to be simple,"[43] Pierre Key observed. Edward L. Bernays, organizer of a brief 1917 concert tour, referred in his memoirs to Caruso's complex personality, which he found in turn "tempestuous, whimsical, childlike, primitive, friendly, distant, warm, and ingratiating."[44] While agreeing with these observations, I would add that Father had three distinct personalities: one for his public, one for his friends, and one for his family. Although these personalities overlapped, they were clearly defined. He could slip from one into the other as easily as he turned from an admirer to Dorothy, or from me to a guest at the dinner table. Dorothy also noticed this division of personalities. Fofò captured some of the characteristic behavior in his description of the boat ride from Sorrento to Naples the day before Papa died, when he spent his last energies in exchanges with "innumerable tourists."

The public image of Caruso drawn from popular anecdotes and

biographies is that of an immensely likable overgrown child, full of fun, always ready for some prank. Yes, he was often light-hearted and cheerful. But in his private life, he was basically serious. He often said in interviews that he was a serious man. His preoccupation with his work, and the many daily concerns with which even a great star must contend, forced him to be so. He was also a very private person and lived in a world of his own making. Dorothy magnificently zeroed in on this quality in her earlier biography:

> He never inflicted his low spirits upon us; he simply went quietly away by himself and let no one come close to him. I do not think that anyone ever came close to Caruso. He had a way of retreating into a world of his own, from which he would look upon even those dearest to him as though they did not exist.[45]

Even his sense of humor had a domestic and a public variety. At home he sometimes teased Fofò and me or traded quips with Auntie Rina. But he was "on" only when we had company or when he had an audience of friends, fans, or reporters. Then he would tell jokes, clown around, make funny faces, draw caricatures.

Father's sense of humor was broad and down-to-earth: He enjoyed practical jokes, gags, slapstick, and mischievous pranks. He would gleefully recount some of his pranks, like the time he slipped an egg into Giraldoni's hand in *La Gioconda*. The baritone was unable to dispose of it, and the choristers were in on the joke and refused to take it from him. Poor Giraldoni had to carry on gesturing till the end of the scene with an egg in his hand he did not dare to squeeze or drop. Ironically, as much as Father liked to play practical jokes on others, he was deeply resentful when he himself was the butt of one.

At home, Father would occasionally amuse us with impersonations of his fellow artists, exaggerating their mannerisms without malice, very much in the spirit of his caricatures. I can still remember his imitation of Alessandro Bonci, whom he called *il nuotatore* (the swimmer) because Bonci, when he sang, made motions with his arms like a man doing the crawl. (The fact is that the much-ridiculed operatic arm-waving of the old school helps the breathing, and Bonci belonged to the old school in the best sense of this classification.) Father never made an adverse comment about Bonci's voice or singing, and his impression of his colleague was just innocent fun. Pierre Key observed: "Throughout my long acquaintance with the great tenor I have never heard him speak unkindly of any other person." Along the same lines, John McCormack once commented: "For the fourteen years I have known him I never knew him to say an unkind word of or to a colleague."[46]

In his younger years, Papa also dabbled in ventriloquism. In the restaurant of the Hotel Cecil in London, he drove some waiters batty by talking and laughing in a little boy's voice that seemed to come from various directions, even from under the table. But on one occasion, the joke was on him. In the Seligmans' garden in London, he prepared to start a conversation with an imaginary person hiding in the branches of a tree.

"Are you there?" he asked.

To his astonishment, a real person answered: "Yes, but don't tell Father or I shall be whipped."

Father's experiments must have been related to his ability to produce a falsetto tone. One night, when a certain Miss Hall, the leading lady of the musical *The Prince of Pilsen,* was a member of the dinner party, he sang her number "Every morn I bring thee violets" in a beautiful falsetto soprano.[47]

Papa's verbal fun was usually limited to puns and bilingual word plays, like pronouncing the words "ice cream" in Italian as "*i ce cream-me,*" which in the Neapolitan dialect means "here we create ourselves." He had a whole string of these dubious terms and added to it as new ones popped into his mind. But being funny, being a prankster, was merely Papa's perception of what was expected of him in public. The play-acting of the celebrity was reserved for strangers, while in the family circle he was not a showman but was natural, relaxed, and informal to the point of embarrassment. I remember one morning going to his room to greet him and finding him in the bathroom, sitting on the toilet. This didn't bother him in the least, though I was deeply embarrassed.

Although he was generally good-natured and even-tempered, Father was a man of many moods. Dorothy's perception was that in the last years of his life, he was a "melancholy man, with a habit of dropping into periods of sadness and silence."[48] While this was true, his moods never changed without a cause, usually a quite obvious one. Bad press always upset him, often for the entire day. He did not have erratic mood swings or long periods of depression, but he was susceptible to the ups and downs of everyday life.

Father did not like doctors. Apart from his final illness and the operations in Milan for the nodules on his vocal cords, he avoided the members of the medical profession. Except for his terrific headaches, I don't believe he ever took medicines. When he had a cold, he relied on the curative powers of his vaporizer. He did visit Dr. Pasqual Mario Marafioti, his throat specialist, with some regularity, but that was more like calling on a friend than consulting with a doctor.

While still a practicing physician, Dr. Marafioti concocted and marketed a cough tablet called "Cough Drop of the Stars." It came in a small metal box with a picture of all the prominent Met artists on the top. This was yet another venture of a friend which Father helped to finance. Soon after Father died, the cough drops of the stars melted away.

In 1922 Dr. Marafioti published a book on singing, entitled *Caruso's Method of Voice Production; the Scientific Culture of the Voice*. Allegedly, it was based on Father's singing method. This book, his friendship with Caruso and other prominent singers of the Metropolitan Opera, his medical specialty, and his fascination with the human voice led him to give up his medical practice in the late twenties and become a voice teacher. In March 1930, he moved to Hollywood and became studio voice coach at MGM. At the time his engagement was announced in *The New York Times* (2 March 1930), his pupils included Gertrud Lawrence, Marguerite d'Alvarez, Maria Kurenko, Julia Culp, Grace Moore, and Gloria Swanson.

FATHER had the collector's instinct and loved to assemble beautiful things. He started with postcards and moved on to stamps, rare coins, snuff boxes, and exquisitely enameled or engraved pocket watches. During his years with my mother, he accumulated an enormous post-card collection. He bought cards himself and also asked friends around the world to buy them for him. The many postcards he wrote to Mother, and vice-versa, were added to the collection; many of these now reside in private and institutional libraries. Reflecting his compulsion for order in every aspect of his life, the cards were organized by subject into hundreds of albums. In addition to scenic groups, there was a superb collection relating to British history and another dealing with Napoleon and the Napoleonic Wars. He also had a big album of French postcards depicting couples performing the sex act in every imaginable and unimaginable pose. This album was kept under lock and key, but my resourceful brother found a way to pick the lock. I gained my theoretical sex education from those explicit postcards.

Father had a wonderful collection of books, custom-bound in red or blue morocco, gold stamped, with gilt edges. Some of these dealt with Napoleon and Italian history; others were fine editions of the classics of world literature, such as Dante's *Divine Comedy* with Doré's engravings, *Don Quixote,* and the plays of Shakespeare. There were many bound volumes of the magazine *Corriere Illustrato.* Papa enjoyed his books, but I doubt that he ever read any of them. Dorothy wrote:

> Caruso was such a versatile person, he had so many inter-ests that it seems almost a paradox to say that he was uneducated. And yet in the accepted sense of the word, that is true. He had the knowledge that comes from wide experience of the technique of singing, of drawing, and of modelling. He knew sixty-four operas, he spoke seven languages. But he never read a book or pretended to any knowledge of litera-ture.[49]

Father had a strange interest in things Moorish. He had his study decorated entirely in the Moorish style with North African furniture. When he visited Tunis in the summer of 1908, he bought himself Moorish garb; then he returned to Naples impersonating a Turkish diplomat. In the spring of 1911, he went dressed as a Moor to a fancy dress ball in London. He made several sketches of himself in that outfit, which Sisca later published in *La Follia di New York.* He may have anticipated a future appearance as Otello and wanted to see how he would look as a Moor. I know that the role greatly appealed to him, and he did not have the slightest doubt that some day he would sing it.

Father never left the decorating of his homes entirely to the lady of the house. He carried a mental image of the layout of each room in his head, and when he saw the right piece of furniture or art object in his travels, he would say to Mother or Rina: "This piece will go well in the corner of such and such room." Occasionally he would buy a whole roomful of furniture; I was told that most of the large pieces in the Moorish room at Le Panche came in a single purchase.

Father's bedroom at Signa was very dark, Medici-style, with a high bed on a platform and red curtains on the sides. It had a connecting door to the bedroom of the lady of the house. Here the decor was entirely different. This room, which was planned for my mother, had a big brass bed. Later the room was occupied by the series of *mammina*s Papa brought home for the summer, then by Rina, and finally by Dorothy.

Father had a large number of retainers. There were the personal valets, Mario Fantini and Martino Ceccanti. For the short time Punzo was in his service, he was in charge of Papa's costumes. Giuseppe

Vecchiettini was the administrator of his Italian properties. Before Vecchiettini, Mother's cousin Giuseppe Guidalotti was in charge of Le Panche. Emilio Tani was the gardener then; later, he took over management of the villa from Guidalotti. Cesare Romati, of most unhappy memories, was the chauffeur, later replaced by Fulvio Fava. And Father had other employees I no longer recall. There was also Giulia Focosi, my wet-nurse. And Miss Saer was my governess. She was there when Mother's affair with Romati began, and she accompanied the fugitives on their mad escape, with me on her lap. Yet of all these retainers, not one was ever willing to talk to me about what happened when Mother made her break from Father. I asked them years later, and most refused to say anything. Their loyalty to my father went beyond the grave. When Emilio Tani told me the story about the jewel box, it was only to show that the *Commendatore* was innocent of "stealing" Mother's jewelry, as she had accused. Miss Saer always gave me evasive answers, saying I would find out about all that when I was old enough to understand. Everything I learned about my family's early history came to me much later, mostly from my brother and, through him, from Aunt Rina.

Father's power over the household was absolute; he laid down and maintained the law. Everyone was in awe of him, because he was a great artist and also because he paid the bills. Yet he never "ruled" the servants. They genuinely liked and respected him, and their devotion went far beyond their dependence. They were well treated and well paid. Serving in the household of Caruso carried a certain distinction, and they could have found equally lucrative employment elsewhere. Yet they all stayed on as long as they could.

Father expected each servant to attend to his or her responsibilities and to do them well. He had little patience with incompetence, laziness, or stupidity. He regarded the household staff as a service organization whose task was to keep him in top form, so that he could give his best and earn enough money to keep them employed. At times he was short-tempered and impatient, especially when things were not accomplished as he expected. He would not hesitate to issue curt orders and scold an offender for mistakes; but all the same, he treated the household staff with kindness, with respect for their human dignity, and without condescension.

Punzo, the last valet he employed, was a special case. He came looking for a job, and Papa engaged him just before his Mexican tour in 1919. Punzo had been Vergine's prize pupil and later his son-in-law, and the Maestro had predicted that "he will be the greatest tenor in the world."⁵⁰ It didn't turn out that way, because—in Papa's words—Punzo was "a proud and stupid man."⁵¹ In his way, he was devoted to my father; but unlike Mario and Martino, he was lazy, indolent, and obstinate, and moreover he was resentful of his benefactor. Papa put up with him out of kindness and took him along when he returned for the last time to Italy. He admonished Dorothy not to mention to anyone that Punzo was his servant, because "Punzo is a proud man, and here is his home."⁵² He also surprised Punzo with a house he had bought for him in Sorrento, along with a generous bank deposit. The last time I saw Punzo was in 1925 when I was stationed in Sorrento with my regiment. He was sitting at a café table on the piazza at Sorrento, basking in the role of the big impresario and singing teacher he had become. He did not seem too happy to see me. Perhaps he was afraid that I knew the closets where his skeletons were hidden.

Father was consistent about his daily routines, which he established early in his career and maintained all his life. They gave him a sense of stability and order and gave the rest of us a degree of predictability as to how the day would go. On vacations or holidays, he slept until nine a.m.; on workdays he was up at eight. Because his comfort was everybody's concern, one could hear a pin drop in the house in the early mornings. People tiptoed around and talked in low whispers.

"*Sshhhh! Il Commendatore dorme!*" ("Sshhhh! The *Commendatore* is sleeping!")

When Father's call bell finally rang signaling that he was awake, the household came alive, and we could walk and talk normally.

The moment Papa opened his eyes, he reached for his cigarette holder, inserted a cigarette, and lit up. He then rang the bell for Mario, who brought him a cup of Italian coffee, strong and sweet, along with the morning papers. Puffing on the cigarette and sipping his coffee, he read the critiques of the performance of the night before. Although he spoke his own brand of English till the end, by his third or fourth season in New York, he had no trouble reading the newspapers. If the reviews were good, he would be jovial and all smiles for the rest of the day. If the critics were unkind, he would be in a black mood. "*Imbecilli! Cretini! Bestie!*" he would yell, and he would angrily scribble his expletives on the edge of the paper. "They don't know what they are talking about!" In 1915 one of the critics wrote something negative about his performance, and Papa supposedly scrawled "LIAR. Enrico Caruso" over the article in colossal letters and posted it on the bulletin board at the Metropolitan.

He had a clipping service send him all his reviews, whether favorable or not. Then, sitting around for hours with scissors and a pot of glue, he painstakingly pasted every clipping into albums. I still have a seventy-one-page bound volume which contains all the reviews from his German tour of 1910 in Italian translation. It was prepared for him by Emil Ledner's agency and bears Ledner's stamp. In 1917, Edward L. Bernays, preparing for the 1917 concert tour, was shown the "clippings room" at the Hotel Knickerbocker, which contained dozens of thick, newspaper-sized clipping books bound in linen.

If Papa was in good humor in the morning, I would go to his bedroom to greet him, kiss his hand, make a little conversation, and leave. If he was not, I would just put my head in the door and call "*Buon giorno, Papà!*" In New York, Zirato was my weather vane. "*Che tempo fa?*" ("How is the weather?") I would ask. He would say "*burrasca*" ("stormy"), or "*bella giornata*" ("nice day"), or "*calma*" ("quiet"), so that I knew exactly what to expect.

While Father read the paper, Mario drew his bath water; then he took the first bath of the day. He loved to soak in the warm suds for a long time. It helped him to relax, physically and mentally. He only sang in the bathtub if Fucito was playing the music of the next performance in the adjacent room. (As he believed, bathroom singing is the specialty of amateurs.) As Father stepped out of the tub, Mario wrapped him in a bath-sheet of terry cloth. He dried himself, rubbed himself down with 4711 cologne, put on his hooded terry bathrobe, and dried his hair with the hood.

Now it was time to clean the vocal apparatus. He turned on the inhalator, a small boiler with an alcohol burner. The boiler was filled with water, and its atomizer at the end of a tube led into a container filled with a mixture of Dobell solution and glycerine. He would cover his head with a towel and lean over the equipment. When the atomizer began to spurt steam, it created a fine spray. He inhaled deeply, his mouth wide open. The nicotine deposits in his throat and bronchial tubes made his sputum come up in great gobs of black phlegm at first. Then with each cough it lightened, until in fifteen or twenty minutes he would bring up nothing but clear white saliva. Satisfied, he would turn off the inhalator.

"*Lo strumento è pulito*" ("The instrument is clean"), he would declare.

And he would reach for a cigarette and light up.

From then on, it was chain-smoking for the rest of the day. In his younger years, Father supposedly smoked considerably less on the days he did not sing; but on the day of a performance, there was no end to it. "If I cannot smoke I cannot sing. Smoking is the only thing that calms my nerves," he once said to Ledner.[53] Among several others, the baritone Armand Crabbé recorded in his memoirs that one of Father's valets would regularly hold a lighted cigarette in the wings, and as soon as he came off the scene, he would start smoking. Crabbé wrote that he heard Caruso sing "in *Aida* the famous final phrase of the third act 'Sacerdote, io resto a te!' splendidly in one breath while the smoke was coming out of his nose and mouth."[54] Even I saw him exhaling the last puff of a cigarette as he walked onstage. I am almost certain that he did this as much to keep his throat "liquid" as to calm his nerves. Aunt Rina used to say, "*Enrico ha una gola liquida*" ("Enrico has a liquid throat"), because he could clear his throat and remove anything that was clogging "the instrument." He knew his equipment better than anyone else; he knew the cause and effect of everything he did. That he sang with a clear, uncongested throat is a fact, and it may have been partly due to the cigarettes that he could expectorate easily, clearing his throat and bringing up all the phlegm at once.

It amazes me that Father could smoke so much without doing noticeable damage to his voice. To what extent the darkening of his voice was due to the normal aging process and to what extent it was due to the chain-smoking is anybody's guess. Smoking certainly did not "shorten" his voice. He recorded "Cujus animam" from Rossini's *Stabat mater* with the D-flat in December 1913, two months short of his forty-first birthday. Because of his premature death, we will never know what his vocal longevity could have been.

When I conjure up the image of my father, I always see him with a cigarette holder in his mouth. He had a superb collection of holders, some of amber, others of ivory and gold, inlaid with emeralds, rubies, or diamonds. He always smoked with a holder, partly because a piece of cotton stuffed into the tip filtered out some of the nicotine, partly because it did not leave nicotine stains on his fingers. He inhaled deeply, and if the nicotine did not damage his vocal cords, it is amazing that it did not affect his lung capacity and his breathing. Who can tell? Had he lived out his normal lifespan, he could well have died of lung cancer, emphysema, or some other pulmonary disorder.

In spite of Father's constant smoking, he did not have bad breath. Being extremely particular about cleanliness, he brushed his teeth after every meal and often rinsed his mouth with Eau de Benedictine, a solution originally made by the Benedictine friars of Fécamp, France. He also scraped the mucus off his tongue with a one- by five-inch piece of flexible celluloid. He had excellent teeth, and he was very proud of them. He never had a toothache, and I am not aware of his ever going to a dentist. He gave credit for his strong and healthy teeth to his wet-nurse, *Signora* Baretti, the society lady who nursed him when his poor mother, Anna Baldini, had no milk.

Although his demands in the home were exacting, I don't remember Father ever complaining about the accommodations or discomforts on trips. He cheerfully endured the heat, dust, and dirt of travel, the crowded railway stations where everyone stared at him, and the occasional fan who accosted him when he least wanted to be bothered.

He was careful but not inordinately concerned about his health, except on winter concert tours, when a drafty train or a poorly heated hotel room could affect his health and jeopardize the entire tour. Leaving the Metropolitan after a performance in the middle of winter, when he was hot and perspiring and exhausted from the physical exertion, Father wore a scarf, a hat, and his fur-lined coat to avoid catching a cold. Because the ride from the Met to the hotel was too short for the car to heat up properly, the chauffeur would start the engine before the performance ended and have the car warmed up before Father got in. Arriving at his apartment, he always took a bath to unwind, clean up, relax, and cool off.

Bernays wrote in his memoirs that at the Shenley Hotel in Pittsburgh, Father's room was drafty and had a twin bed with only one mattress. He asked for a full-size bed with three mattresses, and eighteen pillows with which to surround himself to keep out drafts, saying that without them, he would be unable to sing the following night, when he had to give his best to a capacity audience of four thousand.[55] Thus were born the legends that he worried constantly about his health, he was petrified of drafts, he was preoccupied with the care of his voice, he demanded extra cushions and mattresses each night so as to sleep high in the air, and so on. I can unequivocally say that these tales are untrue. His respiratory organs and vocal cords were the tools of his art, and it is true that he did all he could to keep them in top condition. But his concerns were neither irrational nor excessive.

It is also true that Father took two or three baths daily. In those days, of course, there was no air conditioning. Smoke from the chimneys and incinerators polluted the air, and the buildings were always overheated in the winter. Father also perspired profusely, especially when he sang. Whenever he felt "dirty" after a walk, a performance, or even a meal in a stuffy, smoke-filled restaurant, he took a bath and changed into clean clothes. He did not shower; he preferred to soak in a hot bath filled with smelling salts. His favorite soap was

Carnation by Roger Gallet.

These excesses had their roots in Father's childhood. He must have been repelled by the filth of Naples, and as an adult, he made a point of keeping himself clean, his body and his clothes. As soon as his finances permitted, he always dressed impeccably in custom-tailored suits and shirts. More than once, he took me along to Carlson's on Forty-first street between Fifth and Sixth Avenues, and I watched the tailor take his measurements, then on subsequent visits fit him with the half-sewn suit, marking the sleeve and the collar, ripping them off, stitching them back again. We also went to Sulka's on Fifth Avenue, where he ordered a dozen or two silk shirts at a time. Accordingly, in his large wardrobe of clothes, every piece was tailored to perfection and kept in excellent condition. Yet, true to the spirit of contradiction that so typified my father, after his death we found that his underwear was old and worn, and many of his socks were darned!

With his highly developed sense of the appropriate, Father changed three times a day, choosing a different outfit for morning, afternoon, and evening. In Italy during the summer, he often wore natural silk or white linen suits. At home, he would dress casually in one of many beautiful silk lounging robes. He owned at least fifty pairs of shoes, and because of his fetish about cleanliness, he expected Mario to polish the insteps of the shoes along with the tops and sides. That way, when he sat down and crossed his legs, the bottom of his shoe would not appear dirty or worn. Most of his shoes were two-tone, many with buttons on the side. If he wore spats, they were color-coordinated to his clothes.

His outfit was topped off by a white or pearl-grey fedora and a cane, according to the occasion and the time of day. He always wore exquisite jewelry: rings, a stickpin, and a thin platinum watch with a gold chain and fob. He had top hats for special occasions; I remember Mario stroking them with a hot iron and then buffing them with a felt pad until he could see his own reflection.

"Caruso strode, never walked, to his table,"[56] Bernays wrote in his memoirs. Indeed, Papa had a straight, almost military posture, and he walked faster than one might expect of a man of his height and bulk. At about five feet, nine inches, he was not a tall man, yet he had tremendous presence. Quite apart from his immaculate dress and grooming, he was an impressive personage and would have been noticed in any group. He commanded respect wherever he went, whether he was recognized as the great Caruso or not. As I grew older, I was able to see and judge this phenomenon quite objectively. I don't think Father was aware of the lasting impression he made on others. But all through my life, people of all ages have recounted for me the wonderful experience of meeting him, or talking to him, or coming into possession of one of his caricatures, which they treasured like a precious family heirloom.

Father believed in efficiency, in himself and in others. Around his twenty-seventh year—in about 1900—he worked out a daily schedule. This became a routine to which he adhered for the rest of his life. He found that it worked well for him to get up at the same hour each day, vocalize at the same time, and eat or rest at the same time. What was at first a self-imposed schedule became a natural way of life, and it certainly made him, the "singing machine," work most efficiently. A vignette that speaks volumes has been preserved by the Australian soprano, Evelyn Scotney, whose beautiful green eyes Father likened to "the emerald sea."[58] She told how once, on tour, she came upon Caruso working at a typewriter on the train. She asked him what he was doing. He said: "I am doing three things at once: I am learning to type, I am memorizing the libretto I am typing, and I am improving my French as the libretto is in French!"[58]

Although Bruno Zirato, Father's personal secretary since 1917, was entrusted with a wider range of responsibilities than his numerous predecessors, he was not given access to information concerning Father's business affairs and estates in Italy. "Mr. Caruso was the only person who knew the extent of his estate, as far as I know," Zirato said to a *New York Times* reporter. "I had been in close contact with him during all the time I had acted as his secretary, but never once did he intimate to me the extent of his estate. He did his own bookkeeping. He alone . . . knew the amount of money he had or the value of his estate in Italy."[59] Father also preferred to take care of his own correspondence, writing his letters and telegrams in longhand rather than dictating them to Zirato.

Father was meticulous and precise about his affairs. His bad experiences with agents made him dislike the lot of them, and he preferred to deal directly with the impresari. He negotiated the terms of his contracts, kept track of his business transactions, and wrote his own checks. He kept the books relating to his personal affairs in a separate cabinet in his suite in the Vanderbilt. Father believed in the old adage that to do something right, he had to do it himself; that way, no one could swindle him out of any money. "Caruso was a shrewd businessman who knew how to look out for himself,"[60] Ledner wrote. In addition to his bookkeeping, he maintained a record of the tickets he sent as gifts to friends, so that he could not be accused of buying publicity in any way. It was not in his nature to "collect debts" or ask for return favors. He never accepted complimentary tickets from the Metropolitan but always paid for the considerable number he gave to people at all levels of the social hierarchy. Sending a ticket was a token of his friendship for the rich and a treat for his less affluent friends. He had a strong compulsion to share his art, his joy in life, and his money with his fellow men.

Father was not a prejudiced man. In his time, racial and ethnic segregation was a way of life. In the United States, especially, there were many "black jobs," for waiters and bellhops, porters and boot-blacks. Father took no notice of color distinctions, and I had ample opportunity to observe that he treated everyone he met with respect. He saw no marked differences among people and valued them for their own merits.

Likewise, in Italy and elsewhere in Europe, anti-Semitism was a mild undercurrent in daily life. But my father had no such feelings. He had many Jewish friends, in all walks of life and in many countries, and he had a very high respect for the Jewish people and traditions. For him, the religious ceremonies of *La Juive* had a deep significance. He consulted several rabbis to enable him to recreate authentically the rituals of this religion so different from his own.

I have occasionally been asked whether Father was a religious man. The answer, a qualified yes, depends on one's definition of the term. He believed in God, and he always crossed himself before he went onstage. He made many donations to Our Lady of Pompeii, carried her image, and believed in its protective power. But he had little use for institutionalized religion. He was never a churchgoer and seldom attended Mass. My mother, on the other hand, was deeply religious. I was told that Papa frequently invited Father Tonello to celebrate Mass in the little chapel at Le Panche for her. Whenever he spent enough time in Naples, he would visit the church at Pompeii and make large contributions to the orphanage of Our Lady of Pompeii, often as much as $10,000 at a time.

Except during his daily baths, Father never relaxed. It was not in his nature to be idle. He always had to be occupied with something, whether it was music, friends, women, drawing, stamps, newspaper clippings, building a *presepio,* gardening, socializing, eating, or just reading the newspapers. He was neither restless nor overcharged with nervous energy, but simply a dynamic person, full of vitality and crea-tive force which sought some outlet every minute of the day.

Two canceled checks in the hand of Caruso, one made out to Alfredo Del Pezzo (owner of the restaurant Del Pezzo's at 211 West Thirty-fourth Street) and the other to photographer Herman Mishkin.

MY Father had another talent besides his vocal endowments: He had the gifts of a master caricaturist. Making a pun on his dual talents, in 1912 some wit wrought this limerick:

> Many folks are surprised at the way
> That Caruso can sketch; but they say
>   The directors foresaw
>   Just how well he could draw—
> He can draw a full house any day.[61]

Father's caricatures are brilliantly executed miniatures that capture not only the dominant features of a face and posture, but the personality of the subject as well. Gatti's mournful gaze, Teddy Roosevelt's toothsome yet steely grin, or Verdi's blank stare are so many little masterpieces. Among the several hundred published and reprinted drawings, few are second-rate efforts. What captivates the viewer is the bold, secure line and the unmistakable originality of the Caruso touch, which makes it possible to identify a Caruso drawing even before seeing the familiar rounded signature. In fact, some years ago, William R. Moran, the internationally known collector, writer, and discographer, located a Caruso drawing in a small junkshop by this "first glance" method of identification.

Father had the ability to see the humor in the physiognomy of others, and he was merciless in depicting himself. The many known snapshots that show him mugging for the camera suggest that he was not only amused by the effects of contorting his face but he relied on these photographs for drawing himself. His humorous self-caricatures show how critically he viewed himself throughout his life. In the progression of drawings, his face and features develop, mature, and age. The later self-caricatures show deepening wrinkles, loss of hair, baggy eyes, a double chin, and an expanding girth. To his observant eye, the face in the mirror was not merely a surface to be made up in greasepaint, but a living, aging part of himself.

Drawing and painting were less a pastime or hobby for Father than a compulsion on the order of singing. In fact, according to Dorothy, "he often said that he would rather draw than sing."[62] Friends, relatives, colleagues, dinner guests, even strangers, became his willing or unwitting subjects. Although the exaggerated truths of his quick sketches seemed unflattering at times, none of the caricatures was unkind. Even Melba—a competent judge of malice if not of art—was quoted as saying that Caruso's sketches were always free from malice and that his delighted victims could smile at his jests. Only a small fraction of the several thousand drawings and watercolors Papa made in his lifetime have survived. Father was thirty years old when he came to New York, and he had acquired his skill through considerable practice. To the best of my knowledge, only three of his very early family drawings were preserved: one each of his father, stepmother, and sister. Luckily, I have salvaged all three; only one is signed and dated (with the year 1905).

Although Father had a quick hand, especially with a pencil sketch, the sheer quantity of his output shows that he devoted a great deal of time to this artistic outlet. The many published collections of his cartoons contain mostly those he drew for his friend Marziale Sisca, to be published weekly in *La Follia di New York*. Father was often asked to sell his drawings and paintings or to contribute drawings to other newspapers for large sums of money.

"Drawing is my hobby, I don't sell it," was his standard reply. "I make my living with my voice, I draw for my pleasure. It has no price."

Sisca recalled: "One day the elder Joseph Pulitzer sent one of his editors named Buranelli to Caruso, offering payment of fifty thousand dollars a year for a cartoon to be published once a week in the *World*. Caruso thanked him but refused the offer."[63] When Buranelli asked how much Sisca paid him for his caricatures, he was shocked to find out that Caruso charged nothing. "Where there is pleasure there is no loss," Caruso said.[64]

But he was proud of the public's interest in his work. He told a reporter in May 1914: "People are getting fond of my sketches. In a tiny country inn I happened to see a few days ago, beautifully framed, a piece of blotting paper on which some years ago I had dried one of my sketches. I don't think many artists have had such an honor."[65]

He drew anytime, anywhere, on any material, from napkins to menus to the walls of dressing rooms or ships. I remember he once drew a picture of a lady in a restaurant on the tablecloth. He was quite pleased with it, so he asked the waiter for a pair of scissors, neatly cut out the drawing, and had it presented to his model. (I am told that he did this on other occasions also.) He gladly paid for the tablecloth, hugely enjoying the lady's consternation and delight over the unexpected present from Caruso.

When Papa had someone sitting for him, he preferred that his model remain silent. Sometimes he used drawing as an excuse to get out of small talk at parties. In October 1910, the Berlin correspondent for a London newspaper was invited to a party given in Father's honor at Emil Ledner's home in Berlin. Afterwards, the correspondent wrote:

> Caruso is such an indefatigable caricaturist that he is a poor conversationalist at table. When, according to the established rules of society, he should be lending a polite ear to one of the ladies flanking him, or enthralling the assembled company with his brilliant conversation on music, he is bending over his sketches, elaborating their details and putting the finishing touches on them.[66]

Father sometimes drew during interviews for the same reason: He did not have to talk much, and still the reporter went away happy. In 1910, one interviewer wrote: "Caruso is by no means ungenerous with his caricatures, which he throws off as easily as his mellifluous notes. The only fact which may militate against Caruso's caricatures being some day very valuable is that there are so many of them."[67] The writer was quite wrong, of course. Once, in New York, Father spotted one of his drawings in a shop and sent Dorothy to inquire about the price. He was delighted to find out that it was seventy-five dollars—not bad for a living artist who drew only as a pastime. As for their current value, one should be so lucky as to find a Caruso drawing on the open market!

Often, Father drew or painted when he was alone, just for his own amusement. Many times at Bellosguardo, he took me by the hand and said:

"Come, Mimmi, let's draw clouds."

And off we went into the park, to lie down with our backs against some grassy slope. Sketch pad on his lap, Papa would gaze up at the clouds drifting across the vibrant blue Italian sky then begin to draw them. In his fertile mind, the amorphous patches of white would take the shape of a camel, a chariot, an old beggar, a landscape. When I would glance from his sketch pad to his model in the sky, I would be surprised that I had not seen the camel, or the chariot, or the beggar in the first place! Unfortunately, none of these wonderful little sketches survived. I have mentioned that after Papa had his fun, he would crumple up the paper and throw the drawings away. None of us had the foresight to collect his discards. They were in no way inferior to the drawings he gave away but were discarded only because he had no use for them. We were much too close to him to appreciate these charming products of his creative drive.

Others had a greater appreciation of his work. As early as 1906, a forty-seven-page collection of his drawings appeared. Then in 1908, Marziale Sisca wanted to publish a quarto-size book of the caricatures that had appeared in *La Follia*. Papa had some misgivings and wrote to Sisca from the Hotel Cecil in London on 30 July 1907:

> I see no difficulty if you would like to republish in a book my caricatures that appeared in your newspaper, however, I cannot see its success because the subjects are from the [Italian] colony. Otherwise, if you think it will be a success, go ahead. . . . I enclose a few recent caricatures . . . among which there is a small collection of the Italian Maestri resident in London.

Sisca's edition came out in 1908, and more complete collections were published several times over the years, the most complete edition appearing in 1965.

Father mostly used pencil, pen, or charcoal for his drawings and watercolors for his paintings. Mother also painted; I have several snapshots which show her wearing a painter's smock and standing in front of an easel. The hallway at Le Panche, which served as a gallery, displayed several small oils painted by my parents. The subjects were not very original, but the paintings were well done, with fine detail and attention to perspective and lighting. I recall the Rialto Bridge on the Grand Canal in Venice, the Piazza San Marco, and the port of Montevideo which were painted by Papa. I never saw a drawing by Mother, but her paintings seemed equal in quality to Father's. The two paintings of hers that I remember were a village scene with a bridge, and the park at Bellosguardo, the latter on a canvas about forty by sixty centimeters in size.

Presumably, Father wanted to preserve the little aquarelles for himself, because he had special blank postcards printed with the inscription *Collezione Carusiana*. It is impossible to tell how many dozens or perhaps hundreds of these have been lost over the years or now rest in forgotten corners of households around the world.

MY relationship with my father went through several stages. When Mother left, he promised to be both father and mother to Fofò and me. There can be no question that he did what he thought was best for us.

In many ways I revered my father. As I was growing up, I was in awe of him and a little afraid of him too. He was kind, genial, easygoing, informal; but at home he always carried an invisible swagger stick, and none of us forgot it. I never dared to question or contradict him.

When I grew out of the cuddly age, he treated me like a little man long before I was ready. I needed more outward signs of affection than he was willing to give, and I withdrew from him because I didn't understand his behavior toward me. Then, as I grew older and looked for a close relationship, he was already too old and too serious to be a chum to a ten- or twelve-year-old boy. The responsibilities of his career and his determination to stay on top weighed too heavily on his mind. In his reminiscences, Fofò laments that Father died just as he was beginning to get to know him. For me, too, it seemed that Father died just as we were becoming great friends. A warm and close relationship was never to be.

As I was growing up, I sometimes paid attention to the conversations of the adults around me. Thinking back, I don't recall that I ever heard my father discuss his colleagues. Auntie Rina, a singer herself, was certainly able to carry on a conversation on the subject of Papa's profession at his level. Yet all the time I was around Rina and Papa, matters of the theater and singing never came up. Perhaps, when Papa was on vacation with his "Rinuccia," anything related to his work was far from his mind.

I find it even more curious that Papa's singing was never discussed or praised within the family. Singing, delivering a performance, was his work. It was artistic and rewarding work, but it was a job all the same. After that glorious *Pagliacci* in Rome, we all told Father he had sung magnificently, but at home I never heard anyone exclaim, "Oh, the way Enrico sings!" By the time I was old enough to pay attention to the conversation around me, it was taken for granted that he always sang well and always had a great success. For us Papa's singing was the norm—what was there to discuss?

In his memoirs, De Segurola wrote of Father that "his name was always encircled by a halo of honesty, goodness and sincerity. Because loyal, affectionate and sincere was he, indeed, with his business associates, his friends, and most particularly his colleagues, upon whom he never tried to impose his superiority."[68] De Segurola tells of the time when a talented young soprano was to sing her first Musetta, and the management at the Met asked Farrar, Scotti, and himself to rehearse the second and third acts with her. According to the unwritten rules of the house, a singer was never asked to rehearse on the day of a performance; thus Father, who was to sing Samson that night, was not even called. When he unexpectedly showed up, his colleagues asked him why he came to rehearsal on a day when he was scheduled to perform. His reply was: "Why not? If I were a beginner, I would like to see a Caruso coming to my rehearsal."[69]

Marcella Sembrich once said: "It is a wonderful thing to be able to say of him that he was loved by all of his associates. There never were any jealousies existing between them. He was above all that, he was so big hearted, so broadminded, so much the truly great artist, the perfect gentleman."[70] Father was always considerate of his fellow artists, especially the ladies. When his partner's voice did not carry as well as his, he would hold back in the duets so as not to overpower or overshadow her—unless it was Melba or Tetrazzini. He was less careful of Melba, because he resented her dislike of him as an Italian, and of Tetrazzini, because she came close to overshadowing him! But the latter was a friendly rivalry; Tetrazzini and Papa were fast friends since St. Petersburg days at the turn of the century. Although she wanted to sing at his funeral, the Pope would not allow a woman to sing in the cathedral; instead, Fernando de Lucia came out of retirement and sang "Pietà, Signore" at the service. But Tetrazzini did sing on the first anniversary of Father's death. I attended the Requiem Mass in Naples, and afterwards Mme. Tetrazzini and I wept together, she for the loss of a great colleague, and I for not having been at Papa's side in his last hours.

After Father's death, many individuals and organizations paid him special tributes through donations to his favorite causes, the establishment of foundations, and memorial concerts. In December 1922, Filippo Cifariello delivered a bust that was commissioned by the Italian population of New York City in his honor. The bust was four times life-size, standing on a pedestal and supported by figures of the Muses, between which were medallions representing the principal operas sung by Caruso. Prior to shipment to New York, the bust with its pedestal was consigned to Giovanni in the presence of the Mayor of Naples, the Military Commander, the Municipal and Provincial Council, and delegations from various artistic societies. The orphanage, the prime beneficiary of Father's annual gifts to the Madonna of Pompeii, had an eighteen-foot candle weighing about a thousand pounds placed in the church at Pompeii in late 1921. It carried the inscription: "Offered to the Madonna of Pompeii for our benefactor Enrico Caruso. A.D. 1921." The candle is lit for twenty-four hours every year on All Saints' Day; it can burn for a thousand years. A greater memorial to his life and work is the incandescence of his voice, his art, and his warm humanity.

In the darkest days of his illness, Father kept repeating that he wanted to die in Italy. After the danger had seemingly passed and he felt reassured that he was going to live, in his mind, it was his country and his home town that would replenish his strength. He returned to Italy full of hope, and to the last minute he clung tenaciously to the notion of a full recovery and a return to the stage. At the same time, I am quite certain that had he been able to choose the exact place of his death, it would have been Naples, the city he loved above all others.

In this respect fate was kind to my father. His cradle and his grave are but a few miles apart.

CHAPTER TWENTY

The Doctors

EVER since Father died, there has been controversy about the circumstances surrounding his death. It has often been suggested that only two decades later, antibiotics, better diagnostic equipment, and other advances of medical science could have saved him.

In the minds of many, he should not have died even in 1921. They claim that had he been properly attended by physicians and treated in a major medical establishment, he could have survived his last illness as well. The blame has been laid on the doctors, sometimes those in New York and sometimes those in Italy. But in my view, all Father's doctors were doing their best. The physicians in New York unquestionably saved his life; later, the physicians in Naples, without immediate access to a modern clinic, could not.

Were any of them guilty of neglect?

Given Father's disposition, it is easy to understand why he was not moved to a hospital at the onset of the first attack. With the funds at his disposal, it was a simple matter to convert the salon of the Vanderbilt suite into an operating room sufficiently hygienic to perform the surgery he needed. Nurses and a squadron of doctors were in constant attendance or on call. It is said that he was X-rayed, but I don't know when or where. I do not remember him being moved out of the hotel suite as an invalid, and I doubt that portable X-ray machines existed in 1921. Would ready access to an X-ray machine in a hospital have helped the surgeons to locate the abscesses faster and with greater accuracy? Would additional X-rays have altered or expanded the diagnosis? We do know that when Father was well enough to leave the hotel, he was X-rayed in a laboratory, and he returned there for a final checkup before his doctors in New York allowed him to travel.

Dr. Antonio Stella held a conference of Father's physicians only a few days before he sailed. They examined the X-rays and agreed that his progress was good and his condition satisfactory. Yet the five attending physicians allegedly let him go with a wound that had not yet fully healed, protected only by gauze and tape. They sent no medical records with him, made no arrangements to line up physicians in Naples in case of an emergency, and made no recommendations to Father concerning periodic checkups. To my mind, these facts reflect the doctors' assessment of Father's condition rather than any negligence on their part. Their actions showed that in their collective opinion, precautionary measures were no longer necessary.

Pathologist Robert W. Prichard, M.D., summarized Caruso's medical history in an article in 1959.[1] Although Dr. Prichard received personal communications from some of the medical professionals who attended Caruso, by and large his article is a recapitulation of previously published details, primarily those provided by Dorothy in her 1945 biography. Dr. Prichard mentions that a four-inch portion of rib was removed on 12 February 1921 by Dr. Erdmann, who commented: "When his chest was opened, out poured the foulest pus I think I have ever seen and smelled."[2]

Dr. Prichard also noted the persistent rumors that Caruso died from a cancer of the respiratory tract.[3] He contrasted this with the opinion firmly held in Naples that the singer's abscessed kidney ruptured and led to peritonitis. He concluded that a series of complications probably caused "a subphrenic abscess, possibly a perirenal abscess, and, terminally, general peritonitis."[4]

After Father's death, reporters in New York and in Italy rushed to interview his doctors. "My information is very meager as to the nature of Caruso's fatal illness," Dr. Stella said on August 4 in an interview for *The New York Times*. He added that with what little information he had from the press dispatches, he was positive that the course of Father's sickness excluded any connection between "the recent attack and the pleurisy that had affected him last winter." He also discounted the possibility that infection had remained in Father's body.

I have never known in the history of medicine of a patient in a septic condition to gain weight and to be without fever or pain for three months. If there was an abscess forming at the time of his departure his condition would have shown it. He had been without fever for two months before he sailed. The wounds were entirely healed and Mr. Caruso was free from any symptoms that might lead to peritonitis.[5]

Yet another, unidentified member of the New York team of doctors was quoted as saying: "I and my colleagues believe Caruso never fully recovered from his illness in New York last winter. His long sickness from pleurisy weakened his resistance."[6]

The Central News Agency reported on August 4 that "the medical men of Naples having cast allegations against American doctors in their treatment of Caruso, Professor Raffaele Bastianelli, Italy's greatest surgeon, interviewed by a representative of the *Epoca,* ardently defends the American doctors." Dr. Raffaele Bastianelli said that the American doctors had done all that was humanly possible, given Father's condition.

It was undoubtedly putrid empyema which immediately put the patient in such a grave condition that it must be considered a miracle that the American doctors succeeded in saving his life. [They] showed the greatest professional skill and technique in the operation they performed. Their work commands the greatest admiration and respect, increasing the deserved fame which American doctors enjoy throughout the world. Whatever you can say in praise of American doctors, say it as coming from me.[7]

Regarding the final developments in Naples, Bastianelli said that after the examination, he and his brother agreed that "the present and past suffering of the great tenor was derived from a subrenal abscess probably in the left kidney. . . . We know with certainty that Dr. Erdmann realized the existence of the subrenal abscess."[8]

They were convinced that the X-rays they intended to order in Rome would have confirmed their diagnosis and guided them during the necessary operation, which they could only perform in a modern, well-equipped hospital.

The correspondent for the London *Evening News* of 4 August 1921 quoted Dr. Bastianelli's assessment of Papa's condition at the time of the examination:

Together with my brother Giuseppe I was called to Sorrento on July 28 to visit Caruso. Our examination proved his present and past sufferings to be due to a subrenal abscess, probably originating in the left kidney. We decided immediately to remove the patient to submit him to Roentgen rays, so that the diagnosis might be completed and also as a guide for the operation that was to follow at once.[9] This was possible, as Caruso's condition was then relatively good. Caruso joked, laughed, sang dramatically, and showed us how, the last time he appeared in public, while singing a high note, he felt an effusion of liquid in his mouth which proved to be a clot of blood. Caruso's collapse followed shortly after our departure to make preparations for his removal.

The Bastianelli brothers did not equivocate; they made it clear that Father needed to go to Rome to their clinic. Tragically, either they did not impress upon him that speed of action was a matter of life and death, or Father's entourage failed to realize the gravity of his condition. Instead of rushing him by ambulance and special train to Rome, they wasted two precious days with preparations, and another with the ferryboat ride to Naples and the rest stop at the hotel. Whether immediate access to a clinic could have saved him after the onset of the last attack is a matter of conjecture, and the answer can only be a tentative "maybe."

Curiously, there are serious discrepancies in the eyewitness accounts. Dorothy's first description of the doctors' visit, written only seven years after these events, suggests no particular haste: "After their examination, they said there was an abscess close to the kidney and advised us to come to Rome so that X-ray pictures can be taken."[10] According to her second description, which appeared in 1945, Dr. Raffaele Bastianelli said nothing to Father but told Dorothy, "Your husband must have a kidney removed."[11] According to this version, the doctor told her he planned to operate on Father a week later, and when she suggested she would rather bring him the following day, Dr. Bastianelli replied, "Next week will be time enough."[12]

The Bastianellis made no public statements to challenge Dorothy's assertions. However, in a letter of 5 October 1959 to Dr. Prichard, Raffaele Bastianelli wrote: "We urged him to come the next day to Rome [for an X-ray, a firm diagnosis, and an operation.] I don't know why he delayed to come to Rome."[13] Fofò's recollections convey the same degree of urgency. Indeed, logic suggests that two medical experts who felt it necessary to remove a kidney would not want to postpone the operation by a week.

Another puzzling statement in Dr. Bastianelli's letter to Dr. Prichard relates to the diagnosis itself. He explicitly stated that while he wanted to avoid any discussion of Mrs. Caruso's statements, he wished "to correct the diagnosis, which was not of a subrenal, but of a subphrenic abscess."[14]

The medical term "subrenal abscess" appeared repeatedly in newspaper accounts in August 1921 quoting Dr. Bastianelli and others. It is a term not commonly used, which makes one wonder whether it was simply a journalist's misquote of the term "subphrenic."

The subphrenic space is the arbitrarily defined area lying below the diaphragm and above the transverse colon. Thus, a subphrenic abscess could be located anywhere below the diaphragm, whereas a subrenal abscess would lie somewhere below the kidney, a less common location for an abscess. However, either could have been fatal in 1921, in the days before antibiotics. A perirenal abscess, as Dr. Prichard suggested, could be below the diaphragm, attached to the outside of the kidney. One concern in this academic speculation is whether the blow to the kidney region by a piece of scenery that fell and struck Caruso's back near the kidney could have contributed to the development of an abscess.

There has also been controversy about the role of the doctors in Naples. One can assume that the Italian doctors were no less capable than those in America. If Father had called them in time, they could have gotten him to a hospital quickly, and his life might have been spared. All the same, after Father's death, there was much debate about the blame that could be assigned to one or the other of the medical teams, and it was usually one's nationality that determined one's viewpoint. Puccini, writing to Sybil Seligman after she had been treated by an Italian physician, commented: "Poor Caruso! What a sad destiny! It has made me dreadfully unhappy—so an Italian doctor has cured you, and the American doctors have killed Caruso!"[15]

ONE medical opinion published in the thirties deserves attention, especially because it agrees for the most part with that of the Doctors Bastianelli. The portion of the text quoted here comes from an unidentified clipping in my possession that was sent to me by someone in the family in Italy. The article, entitled "Of What Did Enrico Caruso Die?", was written in Italian by Professor Raffaele Chiarolanza.

It will not be without interest if one of the surgeons, who had the painful privilege to attend the great patient in his last moments, would reconstruct how his illness developed, and for what reasons an ultimate effort to snatch him from death was not feasible.

When Professors Moscati, Sorge, Soda, Niola, and myself first gathered around the dying man at ten in the evening, the extreme gravity of the illness was evident. The patient presented with septic peritonitis, with septicaemia as evidenced by extreme restlessness; labored breathing; rapid pulse (over 140 beats per minute); generalized abdominal tenderness; paralytic ileus (complete immotility of the gastrointestinal tract); inability to take fluids, including water, in spite of an extreme thirst; profuse perspiration; anuria (cessation of urine production) proven by bladder catheterization; the face with sallow features and the sunken eyes circled with livid discoloration; in short the entire picture of the disease showed clear signs of generalized infection that was progressing very rapidly.

The physicians discussed whether surgery was advisable; while we all agreed in principle that in the present condition only surgery could lend some help, I did not fail to express the modest opinion that it was now too late for salutary surgical intervention directed to the center of the infection [in the presence of such general deterioration].

There are moments in a surgeon's life when the burden of the responsibility he must assume weighs heavily on his mind and conscience. The patient's fate depends on a single error in evaluating a symptom of the disease. After an exchange of ideas between internists and surgeons, we agreed to try to alleviate the patient's suffering with the available measures on hand, and to postpone any active intervention until eight in the morning. The postponement was hopeless; and alas, by seven a.m. the next day, fate had closed the case. In a few hours the great singer was dead.

One of the first things that surprised us when we gathered together to examine the patient was the complete absence of any kind of written case history. The antecedents of the case were gleaned by bits and pieces from family members; there were no records of X-rays, which, we were told, had been made only of the chest area; no records of blood or urine tests. We were assured only that tests had been made in a summary way and they showed nothing abnormal.

The patient initially had suffered for several months from pain in his left side, which was first regarded as rheumatic in nature; afterwards intercostal neuralgia on the same side; followed by one, and if I am not mistaken, by a second incident of spitting up blood.[16]

Then there was the buildup of liquid in the left pleural cavity, which was later diagnosed as empyema. Hence the first intervention in the pleura which, after shorter or longer periods of remission and apparent recovery, was followed by further attacks of fever, new buildup of pus, and more surgical interventions (seven in all, it seems).

After the last operation, a cyst remained on the left side. The patient came to Italy, weakened and feverish. He made excursions to Sorrento, Capri, Pompeii, and Naples. He was suddenly struck by abdominal pains and then by the symptoms described above.

The reconstruction of the disease presented no difficulty to us as physicians. It began as an abscess below the left diaphragmatic region. This was unusual as such abscesses are usually found on the right. There was a pleuric reaction from the very beginning, which is natural and quite ordinary for several, largely anatomical reasons. And because the morbid signs of the pressure on the pleura assumed predominance in the clinical picture, this explains why the American doctors, who at first diagnosed the initial pains as rheumatic in origin, focused their attention on the pleural cavity alone.

Clinical science can easily commit a diagnostic error; one makes a mistake especially when one does not think of a given disease. The American doctors did not think of the possibility of a subphrenic abscess, otherwise they would have found it. In all professional honesty, one must admit that it is not easy to diagnose in the beginning a subphrenic abscess, and certainly not for all doctors. One must have a certain amount of experience. I have operated on and healed a patient of Professor Evoli of the Castellino clinic who for four months had been treated at a distinguished clinic for nephritis, and had a subphrenic abscess on the left side. Another patient of Professor

Luigi d'Amato, of the clinic of Professor Cardarelli, was treated by doctors of indisputable ability for constant fever, and I found an enormous subphrenic abscess on the left with an associated empyema. I operated on this patient also and he recovered. I could bring up more examples to demonstrate that an initial diagnostic error is possible.

It is surprising that the failure of the various operations did not clearly indicate to the American surgeons in the period that followed that they were on the wrong track.

So little would have been needed. If clinical observation and common sense were not enough, an X-ray properly administered (and not only of details) would have dispelled any doubt. Unfortunately, the lack of recognition of the facts in America was followed by an incomprehensible—shall we say—fatalism. Indeed, if a proper diagnosis had been made in time in Naples, Caruso would have been saved, because he died not only on account of the abscess itself, but due to complications that certainly would have been avoided if time had not been lost and the patient had not been permitted to indulge in an exhausting lifestyle.

The peritoneum had resisted quite well for months, but one could not expect this resistance to last indefinitely. If an operation had been performed ten days earlier, Caruso could have recovered. I permit myself to make this simple declaration, with great sadness in my heart.

For those who believe in fate, things develop as they should have developed. And who knows whether the fatalists are not right. . . . But one obliged to judge human phenomena with scientific precision cannot adequately stress that no mistake has ever been more painfully expiated.

It seems that Father's determination to project the image of a man on his way to recovery, his reluctance to complain about his growing discomfort, and his stubborn refusal to place himself under medical surveillance for the duration of the summer, conspired against a timely diagnosis. Even so, with his weakened heart and his enfeebled condition, at a time when the only means of anesthesia was ether, the chance of saving his life was probably small.

The posthumous medical debate continues to this day. Dr. Adrian Zorgniotti, professor of urology and medical director of the Metropolitan Opera House, has long been fascinated with Caruso's illness.

He has given lectures on the subject, and *Opera News* reported that he plans to write a book about the singer's controversial medical history entitled *Caruso and His Doctors*.[17] Perhaps Dr. Zorgniotti will be able to shed more light on the famous case.

CHAPTER TWENTY-ONE

Life Goes On

ZIRATO was no less shattered by the news than I. Refusing to believe the first report, he cabled Italy asking for a confirmation or denial. "Alarming reports about you. Please advise."[1] He did not have to wait for a formal reply, for the multiple dispatches to every newspaper in the city confirmed what had happened. He sat for hours in the Vanderbilt suite, head in hand, silently weeping.[2] It bespeaks the character of the man that even under such trying circumstances, he thought of his obligation to his dear *Commendatore* and sent me a telegram within hours. It read: "Received no direct news did you receive cable from mother [i.e., Dorothy] wire me what you want to do all our thoughts are with you please do telegraph me at once Hotel Vanderbilt much love Zirato."[3]

I replied, telling him I had received no communication from Naples. Zirato answered immediately, insisting that I should not be alone and must join him in New York. I packed immediately, took the next train, and arrived in New York on August 3 at 7:50 in the evening. Zirato and several friends were waiting at the Pennsylvania Terminal to take me to the Vanderbilt Hotel. Reporters, who had been camping in the hotel lobby since the news of Father's death reached New York, surrounded us in an instant. Zirato gave them this statement:

> It is the boy's intention to remain in this city until he
> receives word from Italy. He expects that word of some kind
> will be sent to him as soon as Mrs. Caruso and other members
> of the family have recovered sufficiently from their grief to
> make a decision about the matter. Inasmuch as the funeral of
> his father will take place tomorrow, as reported, there would
> be no sense in him starting for Italy right away.[4]

In a couple of days, Zirato arranged that I spend the rest of the
summer with Nina Morgana's family in Buffalo. Nina, who was
devoted to my father, had been a child performer appearing under the
name of "Baby Patti." Papa heard her in 1908 and suggested she should
study in Italy. Nina became the pupil of the celebrated soprano Teresa
Arkel, in Milan. Following her return to America, Father continued to
boost her career, and he was supposedly instrumental in her joining
the Metropolitan, where she appeared from 1919 until 1935. He also
engaged her for a concert tour of American cities from March through
May 1919. It was through her association with my father that the
diminutive Morgana met the lanky, six-foot, four-inch Zirato. Father
maintained that no man could serve two masters so insisted that his
staff remain single while in his employ. But after Mario was allowed to
marry the maid Brunetta due to Dorothy's intervention, Zirato was
also excepted from the house rule. He married Nina on 15 June 1921 in
the Church of the Holy Cross in Buffalo, New York. Papa cabled his
congratulations, sent Nina a diamond ring and Zirato a large check,
and also gave the newlyweds the use of his Vanderbilt penthouse "until
his return from Italy." As it turned out, they lived in the apartment six
months, as Nina gratefully recalled in the last letter I received from
her, which was dated 25 June 1982.

I was then invited to spend some time at the home of Gaetano
Scognamiglio, Papa's old friend and a cellist with the Metropolitan
Opera Orchestra. Dorothy had not yet returned to New York, so
Zirato looked after me. My memory may be faulty on this point, but I
have no recollection of any communication from Dorothy during this
time. She must have written to me at least once, but I simply don't
recall hearing from her.

At the end of the summer, I returned to Culver, still awaiting word
of my fate from someone in my family. It seemed that while the body
of the dead was ceremoniously disposed, the living were unceremoniously ignored.

IN this turbulent year, I recommenced my quest, forsaken when I was seven or eight, for my mother. Considering how little recollection I had of her even at that young age, by 1921 she might have sat in the same room yet I would not have recognized her. Rina never talked of her, nor did others in the family, including Fofò. It is to his credit that he did not force the hatred he felt toward her upon me. She was always in the back of my mind, yet when I inquired, only evasive answers were forthcoming.

Two large photographs of Rina and Ada hung in a bedroom in Livorno, and a life-size painting of Mother was stored in the attic at Bellosguardo. When I asked who the lady was, I was told it was none of my business. I concluded, correctly, that it was my mother. When I confronted Lei with the question, she admitted:

"Yes, Mimmi. The lady in the painting is your Mamma, Ada Giachetti."

I never raised the matter with Papa and had no idea until after his death that he sent her money every month. Only during the trip to America in 1919, upon seeing "n.n." in place of my mother's name on my passport, did I understand that my parents were never married.

I first contacted my mother around Easter of 1921. Father was still alive and in New York when I wrote to her from Culver. I cannot recall what led me to write at that particular time nor where and how I obtained her address. I wrote to her in Italian, enclosed a photograph, and awaited her reaction.

The letter was delayed, but as soon as she received it, Mother cabled a short reply, and I wrote her again.

November 10, 1921

My adored Mother,

Actually, I do not know how to begin, but you can believe that my heart turns to you. After so many years I have found you again. When I received your telegram I was not able to answer you because I did not have your address. I searched for it everywhere and asked people at home, but nobody knew it.

I hope this [letter] will reach you and I will receive a reply. Did you receive my picture I sent you last Easter (1921)?

My address is [Culver Academy].

Write me soon because I can hardly wait for the day until I receive a letter from you.

With all my heart, your son,

Enrico (Mimmi)

In retrospect, it is shocking and inexplicable that I made no reference to Father's recent death, and I cannot reconstruct my motives for failing to do so.

DOROTHY returned to the United States at the end of October. On November 27, she, Gloria, and the Ziratos attended the Caruso Memorial Concert at the Metropolitan, a benefit concert for which Galli-Curci, Alda, Gigli, Martinelli, De Luca, and others contributed their talents. The receipts, more than $12,000, were given to the Giuseppe Verdi Casa di Riposo, the home for aged musicians the composer had founded in Milan. Halfway through the program, amidst commemorative speeches, New York Mayor Fiorello H. La Guardia presented a bust of Enrico Caruso to Otto H. Kahn, chairman of the board of directors of the Metropolitan Opera Association. The bust was commissioned from Onorio Ruotolo, an Italian-American sculptor, who made it from "Mrs. Caruso's favorite photograph" and from memory, as he was a friend of Papa's. I was not invited to the ceremony, even though it fell on Thanksgiving weekend. This was the first of numerous celebrations held at the Metropolitan relating to my father for which I was overlooked.

I returned to New York for the Christmas holidays. Dorothy had rented an apartment at 126 East Sixty-fourth Street, so I was quartered at the St. Regis Hotel. I was glad to see my stepmother, as she was my closest link to Papa, which gave me the illusion of belonging to somebody. But she was busy, and I did not see much of her. All the same, when Zirato invited me to spend Christmas with him and Nina, I thanked him for his thoughtfulness but said that I was spending the holidays with Dorothy. When I called her to inquire about plans for Christmas, she replied:

"I don't know what you are going to do, Dearie, but I am going to a party. You do whatever you want."

I was ashamed to call Zirato back. Uncle Giovanni was also in town, but he had his circle of friends. As I refused to wrangle an invitation from any of the few people I knew, I had to celebrate Christmas without any of my relatives.

After the holiday, I returned to Culver. Soon afterward, I received a letter from Mother, who seemed pleased by my interest in her and asked about my circumstances, my studies, and Miss Saer. I replied on 15 January 1922.

Dearest Mother,

You can imagine with what joy I received your letter, the first letter I have ever received from you.

I have changed a great deal since you last saw me. I now have black hair and brown eyes. I am five feet, eight inches tall . . . and rather strong. I weigh 159½ pounds. The Buenos Aires post office has returned my photograph, and I have now told the secretary [of the school] to send it to your new address.

Dear Miss Saer stayed with me until two years ago and then, because I had to go to college and I was a bit too big to have a governess, she found another position in the state next to New York, and we see each other often when I am on vacation. She is such a good [person], poor thing, what patience she had with me, she has been a real angel of goodness.

My studies show that in Italy I would be at the level of a *liceo*. In another year and a half I will go to a university.

I will obtain a school catalogue and send it to you so that you can formulate an idea of the beauty of this place.

Write soon, with a thousand kisses and affectionate embraces,

Mimmi

This is the last letter I have in my possession from that period (Mother kept this and my first letter to the end of her life).

Not long thereafter, Zirato informed the officials at Culver that I was scheduled to sail for Italy on April 21 and had to be in New York no later then April 16 to attend to passport formalities.[5]

In New York I stayed at the apartment of Amedeo Canessa, Father's friend and supplier of antique artworks. He was a bachelor who lived alone in a spacious apartment not far from his gallery on Fifth Avenue at Fiftieth Street. The Canessa family specialized in art and antiques; another brother, Ercole, had a gallery in Paris, and the third brother, Cesare, at the Piazza dei Martiri in Naples.

Amedeo and I sailed together in late April. When our ship docked in Naples, Fofò was waiting at the pier. Near him stood a lovely girl in a red hat, Amedeo's niece Elena, the daughter of Cesare Canessa. I also met her brothers, Guglielmo, Roberto, and Ambrogio, and her sister Natalia. In a short time, I became a regular visitor at the Canessa home. I found Elena attractive and enjoyed her company.

The settlement of my father's estate was approaching its final stages when I arrived in Italy. I joined the other heirs and the lawyers in Florence to settle the division of the estate. After Father died, a family council was convened. But because I was a minor, a guardian *ad litem* was appointed to look after my interests. This was a certain Manlio Tizzani, who was most likely one of Uncle Giovanni's friends.

The day after Father's death, a handwritten will was located in his bank safe in Naples. This was duly deposited with a notary public on 8 August 1921. It had been prepared with the help of Constant J. Sperco, a businessman and Father's friend for some twenty years. The drafting of this will had been extremely casual, and even Father's attorney, Alfred Seligsberg, was unaware of its existence.

Sperco, a frequent visitor to the apartment in New York whom Papa often consulted on business matters, told *The New York Times* that one afternoon in November 1919, about a month before Gloria's birth, he stopped by the Knickerbocker. Somehow, the conversation drifted to the disposition of Father's estate in case of his death. Papa said, "Let's not talk about that"; but Sperco continued:

> "Do you realize what would happen to your estate if you left no will?" I asked Caruso. "You know you have a large estate."
>
> "Well, how would it be divided?" asked Caruso, with his interest only feebly aroused.
>
> I explained to him that one-third of it under American law would go to his widow, while the remaining two-thirds would be divided equally by his children.
>
> "And would nothing be given to my brother?" he inquired.
>
> I informed him that the brother would receive nothing if he died intestate, and his wealth were divided under American laws. He then wanted to know whether his stepmother would receive anything from his estate if there were no will. And when he was assured that she would be disregarded, he sat in deep reflection for a moment and then said:
>
> "Well, let's make a kind of a will."
>
> Caruso got some paper and a pencil, he began writing the document and it was worded in Italian. At intervals he asked to be prompted, but the phraseology for the most part was his own. He stated clearly and concisely the terms under which he wished his estate to be divided.[6]

While there is no reason to doubt Sperco's account about the place and circumstances in which the will was prepared, he was in error as to the date when it was drawn. The will, only a page in length, bore the date 4 January 1919 and thus predated not only the birth but even the conception of Gloria! Father carried the original will with him; but he had the foresight to instruct Sperco to send the certified copy to Giuseppe Vecchiettini in Florence should the need arise. Sperco mailed this copy without delay following Father's death. The only thing that was momentarily in doubt was whether this will was indeed the last Father had prepared, for there was a rumor of a will made in Sorrento although none was ever found.

The will described by Sperco for *The New York Times* corresponded with the handwritten will. It stated, in part: "*Lascio la mia eredità ai miei figli, Rodolfo, Enrico, ed a mio fratello, Giovanni. Alla mia moglie americana ciò che le spetta per legge italiana. I miei eredi provederanno al mantenimento decoroso della mia matrigna, Maria Castaldi.*" ("I leave my estate to my sons, Rodolfo, Enrico, and to my brother, Giovanni. To my American wife that which Italian law specifies. My heirs will provide for the decorous maintenance of my stepmother, Maria Castaldi.")

According to all accounts and my own observations, Father paid meticulous and personal attention to his business and legal affairs. Given this characteristic, it is surprising, even inexplicable, that after the birth of a daughter whom he deeply loved, he did not take the trouble to replace the handwritten will with a new one to provide for her. The Italian expression "*miei figli,*" which means "my sons," in some contexts could also mean "my children." As phrased in Father's will, however, it could not have included Gloria unless she was specifically mentioned by name. Under Italian law, the birth of Gloria, another child, rendered the will a legal "nullity."

How does Italian law treat inheritance?

It divides a man's estate into two equal parts: *la legittima* and *la disponibile,* the "legitimate" and the "disposable." The legitimate half must be left to the legal heirs, whereas the disposable half may be divided *a volontà del defunto,* "according to the wish of the deceased." In other words, Italian law specifies that a man must provide for his legitimate heirs by leaving them half his estate, but he can do as he pleases with the disposable remainder. This legal provision ensures that a man will not spitefully or whimsically disinherit his children and leave all his wealth to the church, the Red Cross, or his current mistress. This division of an estate applies whether the deceased left a will or not. The law also specifies that a man is not obliged to leave his wife anything beyond the revenue from his estate.

Thus, under the law, Father's estate would have been divided among his three children and his brother, Giovanni. Dorothy would not have shared in the inheritance but would have received the income from the disposable half. In Father's case, the income the estate was to produce consisted primarily of phonograph record royalties. Although this could have been a substantial sum, it was uncertain at best, and only a fraction of the millions the estate was worth.

THE division of the estate became a legal issue. Dorothy displayed a preoccupation with Father's millions almost before his body was cold. Cables sent to *The New York Times* from Naples and London on August 4 were front-page headlines the following day: "CARUSO'S WIDOW WANTS HIS ESTATE TO GO TO GLORIA—Appeals to Courts to Enforce Statute Which Would Make Little Daughter Sole Heir." The article disclosed that Dorothy had had the apartment at the Hotel Vesuvio sealed by order of the district judge of Naples and had contacted the Italian ambassador in Washington seeking to have the Vanderbilt suite sealed as well. She was trying to keep Father's belongings out of reach of the Caruso family in Italy, and she must have wanted to protect the contents of the Vanderbilt apartment from me. As mentioned before, the penthouse suite was entrusted to the newlywed Ziratos while Father was still alive, and Dorothy trusted Zirato completely then and later, when she retained him as her personal secretary for some time after her return to America. As I was the only other person in the United States with legal access to the apartment, I must have been the one she wanted to keep away.

Under New York tax law, the estate owed no inheritance tax. The only assessable tangible property in New York—principally Father's art collection, which was worth $100,110—was valued at $106,301. The total New York debts, however, amounted to $262,518. These included $50,648 and $80,850 due in income tax for 1920 and 1921 respectively; $36,441 owed to Joseph of Fifth Avenue, the finest woman's clothier of New York, for Dorothy's wardrobe; $26,410 to E. M. Gattle & Co. for jewelry; $4,215 to the Hotel Vanderbilt; and $18,250 to the Metropolitan Opera for an unearned advance on the 1920–21 season.

Father's intangible property in New York consisted of $80,778 deposited in the Fifth Avenue Bank, $68,615 in the Columbia Trust Company, and $656 in the Hudson Trust Company. In Florence, he had a bank deposit of $277,559, and in Naples, $3,915. His collection of gold coins (of which nearly $17,000 was in United States currency) was valued at $19,610.

The most valuable piece in Father's New York art collection was a fifteenth-century marble Madonna and Child appraised at $22,000.

Father's opera costumes and accessories, valued at $1,386, included forty-three wigs, forty-two hats, fifty-two shirts, fifty pairs of shoes, fifty-five pairs of hose, eighteen silk and linen tights, five swords, and thirty-seven feathers.

On 10 August 1921, Dorothy filed a petition with the Civil and Penal Tribunal of Naples for the appointment of a special guardian for Gloria in accordance with the requirements of the Italian Civil Code. Two days later, the tribunal appointed Amedeo Canessa "to assist her [Gloria] only in those acts in which conflicting interest with her mother may arise." On 17 January 1922, Dorothy was granted the rights of administration of all assets and Father's interests in the state of New Jersey. In the United States, she retained the services of Alfred Seligsberg, and in Naples, those of Giovanni Porzio, the attorney who had represented Father in earlier lawsuits. Porzio was put in the difficult position of having to arrange an equitable settlement among family members. He tried to maintain the appearance of impartiality, but in the end he attended largely to Dorothy's interests.

I was present at the discussions in Florence only from May 1922 on; thus I learned the details of the preceding negotiations from Fofò and Giovanni. It appears that grief-stricken Dorothy did not lose her head in the forty-eight hours between Father's death and his funeral. The 4 August 21 *Evening News* reported that "according to a Milan message to *The Times,*" Father's 1919 will was located, and "*Signora* Caruso, who is an American, has made application to have the will set aside, as it does not provide for her daughter Gloria." Porzio, acting on Dorothy's behalf, explained to my uncle and my brother that Father's will was no longer valid because it predated the birth of the legitimate daughter and did not name Gloria as one of the heirs. He also stressed the point that even though Father had recognized both his sons and given them his name, we were natural children and thus ineligible to share in the "legitimate" half of the estate. To avoid complications, Porzio suggested that we declare Father intestate, draw up a contract, and divide the entire estate, revenues included, according to our own consensus. On the one hand, he said, Mrs. Caruso would not dispute the rights of the natural children to a share of the inheritance; on the other, the heirs would admit Gloria's legal standing as the legitimate child entitled to half the estate. Simply stated, Gloria's legitimacy was worth an additional quarter of the estate, since she would no longer share equally with the other three heirs to whom Father had meant to leave his fortune. Porzio's most persuasive argument was that if we accepted his proposal, the inheritance would be divided in accordance with Italian law and would thus be unassailable.

All those present agreed, primarily, I believe, out of fear.

According to Italian law, a brother does not inherit; hence Giovanni was concerned that he might be denied a share of the estate despite Father's stated intentions. Fofò was terrified that someone would again bring up Father's perjury on his birth certificate and prove him the child of an adulterous relationship, which indeed he was. I was not consulted in the matter, and my appointed guardian did as Giovanni advised. A district judge presided over the first family council, and the conclusion reached was approved by the Tribunal of Naples on 26 August 1921. The final family agreement was also submitted for approval to the Tribunal of Naples and was approved by decree on 16 June 1922. With reference to Gloria, the court ordered that "at least four months of the year should be passed in Italy by the infant." As "mother, tutor and legal administratrix," Dorothy was to receive half Gloria's share of the inheritance without restrictions until Gloria came of age at twenty-one, and she was to deposit the other half in the New York branch of the Banco di Napoli in Gloria's name. As agreed, Gloria drew the *legittima* portion of the estate, inheriting half of everything, which left the *disponibile* half to be divided three ways among Rodolfo, Uncle Giovanni, and me.

At this point, Dorothy stopped the proceedings, objecting that if the brother of her late husband was to be considered an heir, she too was entitled to a share in her own right.

Once again the parties present capitulated to Dorothy's demands. Our attitude was that there was plenty of money to go around, not only in Italy but also in America. If the brother was to be included, it was reasonable that the widow should receive a share as well. The net result of this agreement was that we all agreed to collect our inheritance on the basis of a legal contract.

Had the letter and intent of the original will been carried out, modified only by the stipulation under Italian law that half the estate must go to the legitimate heir or heirs, Gloria would have received half; Rodolfo, Giovanni, and I, a sixth each; and Dorothy, the income the estate produced. According to the new agreement, Gloria received half, and the other four of us, Dorothy included, an eighth of the estate and an eighth of all future income as well. In short, Gloria and Dorothy received five-eighths of the great wealth my father had accumulated during his lifetime.

THE contract was drawn up and submitted to the Civil and Penal Tribunal of Naples. The court found the agreement in conformance with Italian law and approved it on 21 October 1921. Later, on 16 June 1922, the same court confirmed and approved it by decree as *Il Decreto del Tribunale di Napoli*. Taking the last name of the notary who drafted and filed it, the document was often referred to thereafter as the "San Severino agreement."

After the issue of the decree, Dorothy was allowed to remove Papa's belongings. She flatly told us she was giving Father's clothes to her brothers, although they would have fit Giovanni without alterations. Before she had the valises readied for shipping, Dorothy invited Fofò and me to pick one tie each to remember our father by. It was hard to believe then, as it is hard to believe today, that she actually did such a thing, and that we did not object. Giovanni fared somewhat better. Because he, like Papa, had unusually small feet, he ended up with more than fifty pairs of shoes. Fofò had bigger feet, and mine were exceptionally large. The incident brought to mind a moment from years past, when once, at the beach, Papa was struck by the size of my feet and delivered one of his proverbial *bons mots: "Morrai povero, ma mai spiantato."* ("You may die poor, but never without a footing.")

The division of the estate provided by the family agreement in the 16 June 1922 decree of the Tribunal of Naples not only applied to the existing estate but also clearly established the ratio of individual entitlement to all current and future royalties from the Victor Talking Machine Company. We assumed that it was a matter of time until the legal formalities in the United States were worked out, and that we would thereafter receive our predetermined share of the royalties so long as Caruso recordings were sold by Victor and its affiliates.

The great majority of Father's assets were in Italy: all his real estate, a large number of government bonds, bank deposits, cash, furniture, household items, art objects, memorabilia. I seem to remember, though I am not absolutely certain, that the Italian estate was appraised at 40 million lire before taxes, which gave us each a share valued at 5 million lire, with Gloria receiving four times that amount.

When the actual division took place, Gloria received all the *palazzi,* the apartment houses Father owned in Florence, and a complete village of *quartieri popolari,* inexpensive housing Father had built for workers near Le Panche. Probably on the advice of an attorney, Dorothy refused to accept any real estate or securities, taking her entire share in cash. Around this time she also received $255,105.20 in royalties from Victor which she did not share with the other heirs on the grounds that it was income and thus due to the widow. We were unaware of the royalty payment at the time and learned about it only years later.

In her book on Father's life, Dorothy wrote that she "had given Signa to Enrico's family. . . . The Villa Bellosguardo and its many farms at Signa were too difficult for me to administer for Gloria until she should become of age."[7] Her use of the word "give" implied an act of generosity, which was not at all the case. But it is true that she stated more than once that since she was an American and in spite of the court ruling obliging Gloria to spend a part of each year in her father's homeland, she had no intention of settling in Italy. Moreover, Dorothy realized that Bellosguardo was a white elephant: It produced no income, so only an owner with the earning power of an Enrico Caruso could afford its upkeep. On the other hand, my uncle and brother saw Bellosguardo as a saleable piece of real estate and so agreed to take possession of the villa jointly. They probably received some cash as well. When I asked my brother about this, he remarked curtly: *"Non fare i conti in tasca mia."* ("Don't make accounts in my pocket.") It was also revealed much later and by accident that Giovanni received $15,000 in cash from Dorothy. Whether this was a payment in return for giving up property or rights, or perhaps for joining with her in having the existing will declared null and void, I was never able to ascertain.

Dorothy had many valuable items from Father's Italian estate shipped to America. She claimed them either because my father had "given" them to her or to Gloria or simply because she wanted them, and the rest of the family felt the bereaved widow was entitled to special consideration. She took all the linens and embroidery from Bellosguardo as well as the finer paintings and statuary and a solid gold flatware service consisting of twenty-four settings. She even arranged the removal of the large bronze mortar bearing the Medici coat of arms that stood in front of the house at Le Panche, an object weighing several tons—to where and for what purpose I never learned.

Giovanni, Fofò, and I divided pieces of Father's jewelry which he carried on his travels and had with him in Italy. I received a large star sapphire mounted in a platinum ring, several pocket watches, the beautiful gold ingot fob Father was given by Bracale after the Cuban engagement, two stick pins, and assorted cuff links and shirt studs. Dorothy kept her own jewelry worth several hundred thousand dollars, most of which had been bought to replace the pieces lost in the

East Hampton robbery. She also kept Papa's large and valuable stamp collection and his entire collection of paintings, statuettes, and other art objects. Some of this collection was on display in the hotel suite in New York, but most was stored at the Canessa Gallery on Fiftieth Street. As I have mentioned, Amedeo Canessa, the owner of the New York gallery, had been appointed Gloria's co-guardian soon after Father's death.

In March 1923, a great many memorabilia, art curios, and other of Papa's private effects were auctioned in New York for the benefit of the newly established Caruso Foundation for Needy Musicians. The London *Daily Telegraph* reported that the auction yielded over 14,000 pounds (about $68,000). Father's robe for the role of Radames fetched 10 pounds, and one of his Canio costumes (he had several) drew 5 pounds.

A month later, Papa's other collections were auctioned: the coins, medallions, watches, and other artifacts. The London *Sunday Express* of 7 April 1923 carried a report.

> Mrs. Dorothy Park Benjamin Caruso, widow of the tenor, was at first reluctant to part with any of her husband's possessions. . . . But Mrs. Caruso was not greatly interested in antiques, ancient glass, Florentine bronzes, first editions, old coins and other art objects that Caruso, an enthusiastic collector and real connoisseur, had gathered from the corners and cubby-holes of the world.
>
> And so, keeping for Gloria one costume of every role Caruso ever sang, Mrs. Caruso authorized her attorneys to sell at auction more than one thousand mementos of her husband. They ranged from fifteenth-century Limoges plaques to caricatures Caruso dashed off of himself. . . . Her own share of the proceeds, Mrs. Caruso announced, she would donate to the Caruso foundation for struggling singers.
>
> Experts worked for days arranging the display in the showrooms of the American art galleries. The cases gleamed with glass bowls, bottles, vases, jars, jugs of Greek and Roman workmanship, some of them dating as far back as 200 B.C. Graceful figurines of fauns and nymphs and satyrs were poised atop their pedestals. There were plaques of the saints, Byzantine amulets, coins of forgotten countries and dead dynasties, Greek oboles.

This auction took in over 30,000 pounds ($146,000).

DID Fofò, Giovanni, and I resent the fact that Dorothy and Gloria inherited five-eighths of Father's estate? At the time we made the division in Italy, we certainly did not. Dorothy was our father's wife, the woman he chose to marry in his middle years, and Gloria was his daughter, our sister and niece. We felt genuinely sorry that Dorothy had been widowed at such a young age, left behind by the man who protected her and apparently loved her very much. Fofò did not particularly care for Dorothy, yet he made every effort to be friendly and courteous. Giovanni saw in her a threat to his wonderfully secure, dependent existence. I liked Dorothy, even if she was not to become the mother I had longed for.

Furthermore, the estate was so large that even a one-eighth share was more than most people could hope to accumulate in a lifetime. In addition, we were all to share in future royalties. Thus, for various reasons, the specter of greed did not arise for any of us. Even Giovanni was complacent about the terms of the final contract. Although he would have liked to receive as much of the estate as possible, he realized that even his reduced share was a greater fortune than he could have expected to command if my father had lived out his expected lifespan. The same was true of Fofò. As for myself, I had no conception of money. It seemed to me that I would never want for anything as long as I lived, so questions about the actual percentages would have seemed like quibbling to me.

When it came to the division of property, I was asked whether I wanted to enter into joint ownership of Bellosguardo with either my brother or my uncle. I did not want to find myself in a partnership, so I took what was left over: the villa Le Panche, an adjacent farm, a five-acre piece of land where our tenant farmer kept his dairy cows, and a small farmhouse at neighboring Cercina with a bit of land around it. In addition, I received 500,000 lire in cash and government bonds, in equal portion, which realized only 60 cents on the dollar when I later sold them.

Le Panche held sentimental value for me. I was born there, so despite its enormous size, it seemed like a home to me. The villa had been built in three parts. The original structure had five rooms on the first floor and three on the second. It also had a tower with a crenelated battlement which dated from the thirteenth century. The second part, built centuries later, contained a very long room we called the *sala dei troni* because it had two Medici-style thrones on a dais, built for a duke and a duchess. There was a fireplace at one end of the room, which was large enough to seat forty-eight people at one long table. A surrounding glassed-in veranda was two stories high. The third part was built by Papa after he bought the property. Here were a new kitchen with a large pantry, wardrobes, a linen room, and large servants' quarters with two baths.

Le Panche was a fine piece of property, and I planned to live there happily ever after.

CHAPTER TWENTY-TWO

Marriage

DURING my stay in Florence, I met Fofò's fiancée, Armanda Comparini. She was a lovely girl who had known Fofò since she was fifteen, when she worked as a cashier in her father's restaurant and Fofò first met her. They were very much in love and had an excellent rapport. Armanda and her two sisters were the "three A's": Aurelia was the eldest and Adriana the youngest. They also had a brother, Ernesto.

All three girls were very beautiful, and at my age, it did not take much for an attractive young woman to arouse my interest. I began to pay a great deal of attention to Adriana. I was supposed to stay in Florence for only a short while, but I was developing a man-sized crush on her and showed no intention of leaving. Then a telegram arrived from the Canessa family in Naples: "Come quick," the telegram read, "Elena deathly ill." I took the telegram at face value and took the next train to Naples. I found out many years later that this was only a ruse to make me return. Elena told me how she waited for the doorbell to ring then jumped into bed fully clothed, pretending to be sick.

"You were so cute," she said. "You came rushing down from Florence, worried about me. And I was laughing my head off as I lay all dressed under the cover. But I got you back, didn't I?"

414

After my return, Elena had an amazing recovery. Everyone assured me that it was due to the attention I lavished on her, and I was naïve enough to believe it. I saw her every day, always properly chaperoned, and enjoyed her company more and more. If I had been more astute, I would have noticed that the whole family was on pins and needles waiting for me to "pop the question." Elena was nice to me, but I had no plans to pop any kind of question. Fate and Elena's relatives had something else in store.

One evening after dinner at the Canessas', Elena and I went out on the balcony. The apartment was on the top floor of the building, overlooking Piazza Municipio. As she leaned over the balustrade, I feared she might fall and took her waist with both hands. She turned around, and I found myself holding her in my arms. At that instant, her brother Guglielmo came charging from the dining room shouting:

"You have violated my sister! Mamma! Papa! Enrico has violated Elena!"

In a moment I stood before the Canessas, staring at me like so many living question marks expecting an explanation. I was young, inexperienced, and possessed of a ridiculous sense of honor.

"*Signora* Canessa," I said, with all the solemnity I felt appropriate for the occasion, "you have no cause for reproach. I will marry your daughter."

Elena flew into my arms amidst great rejoicing. My transgression was instantly forgiven, and I fell into the tender trap set by a woman six years my senior and her clever family.

Papa, who had a long-standing business relationship with the Canessas, had known Elena since she was a little girl. She also spent time in his company during his last summer in Naples and Sorrento. Fofò told me they got along well because Elena was also a heavy smoker and loved Papa's Egyptian cigarettes. Over the years, the Canessas became close friends, and I am sure Father would have approved of my marriage.

Some would have it that he did. Spiritualism was having its heyday around this time, and the Associated Press, reporting on my wedding to Elena, carried the headline, "Enrico Caruso, Tenor's Son, Weds in Naples; Father's Spirit Said to Have Approved Match." The article said that "at the time the engagement was announced a wave of spiritualism was sweeping over Naples and a great deal of publicity was given to the fact that Caruso's spirit at a number of seances gave his approval of the match."

The one person who did not approve was Uncle Giovanni. He

wanted me to marry his daughter Anna and made many obvious hints along those lines. My desirability as a son-in-law did not stem from any great affection, but rather from a thinly veiled desire to keep all the Caruso money nearby, within the family, if not quite within his reach. I had no intention of marrying a first cousin, and when I announced my impending marriage, my uncle was very disappointed. I don't think he ever forgave me for not marrying Anna. He remarked to Elena in Neapolitan:

"Tu te si' truvate nu bellillo, giovinillo, e cu vurzillo." ("You found yourself someone young, handsome, and with a wallet.")

The civil ceremony took place a week after my eighteenth birthday, on 14 September 1922, at the City Hall of Naples. It was simple and informal, except that the mayor, decked out in his morning frock-coat and tricolor sash, went into a long discourse about my father and how honored he was to officiate at the wedding of Caruso's son. Deputy Giovanni Porzio, who was then a member of the cabinet of Premier Nitti, was my best man. The religious ceremony was held the following Sunday at the Canessas' apartment and turned into a monumental affair. An altar was erected in the salon with a *prie-dieu* for each of us before it. The wedding ceremony was performed by the Bishop of Naples, with two *monsignori* in attendance. As we knelt on the hard wood, the bishop spoke interminably, eulogizing my father. In both ceremonies, I could not help but feel that Elena and I were only extras; center stage still belonged to Papa.

All Elena's relatives were present except her father, Cesare. The poor man suffered from acute diabetes and, shortly before the wedding, had to have his toes amputated. In fact, he was in bed when I formally asked for his daughter's hand in marriage. He managed to smile despite his discomfort and asked whether his sons had taken care of the dowry. I waved the issue aside, then and later—a Caruso could not take a woman's money! I did not have the presence of mind to suggest that they deposit the dowry in an account in Elena's name. Fool that I was, I even insisted on picking up the tab for the wedding!

On my side of the family, only Giovanni and Bettina were there. Fofò was in Florence preparing for his own marriage to Armanda, and Dorothy was enjoying herself in Venice. She had just spent thousands of dollars on a big bash at a plush hotel on the Lido: The party was on such a grand scale that the newspapers carried the story. It may have been a farewell party, for her father had died three weeks earlier, and she was preparing to sail home to join her brothers and sisters in contesting his will.

I came into my inheritance on my eighteenth birthday. Since Elena, born on 14 July 1898, was six years older than I, according to the law I became the legal ward of my wife until I reached the age of twenty-one.

We were still on our honeymoon when Fofò married Armanda Comparini on 25 September 1922. From Ravello, where we spent our honeymoon, we returned to Naples to spend a few weeks at the Santa Lucia Hotel before making our way to Florence. Thus we did not attend Fofò's wedding, but only sent a telegram of congratulations.

AFTER our arrival in Florence, Elena and I settled in at Le Panche. Although I did not realize it at the time, the villa and the farm around it were more a liability than an asset. Upkeep was costly, and the property produced no cash in return. Because of the renovations Father had made, the villa was in good condition. It needed only a thorough cleaning, as it had remained uninhabited since the doors were sealed in 1918. Most of the furniture was still there, but there was not a mattress, a piece of linen, or even a pillow in the whole house; these had been removed to Florence when Rina set up house at Piazza Donatelli.

Soon after our marriage, Elena became pregnant. Our first son, Enrico-Cesare Caruso, named after his two grandfathers, was born at Le Panche on 12 July 1923, in the same bed where my mother had delivered me nineteen years earlier. He, too, was baptized in the villa's chapel.

Initially all went well. I had money from the Italian settlement to buy the essentials and refurnish the house. My credit was excellent, and I expected to receive the Victor royalties from the United States shortly, as stipulated by the San Severino agreement. Confident of my position, I began to spend money like a Caruso.

I retained my father's valet, Mario Fantini, and his wife, Brunetta. Mario brought in his nephew as his assistant. We had a chauffeur, Otello; a female cook; and, when the opportunity came, we lured away the French chef of the Canessa family. (He went by the name of Monsù, an Italianized version of *Monsieur;* I may never have known his real name.) Two maids from the Canessas' also happily followed Elena; and when my son was born, I hired a nurse for him. After all, I had a governess, and Gloria had a governess; my son was surely entitled to one as well.

Being without a trade, academic degrees, or even specific ambitions, I decided to become a gentleman farmer. Here "decided" may be too strong a word—rather, I let myself drift in that direction. Had I inherited a windmill in Holland, I probably would have "decided" to become a miller. At any rate, my objective was simple and basically sound: I was going to turn my land holdings into a successful, income-producing operation. Le Panche was surrounded by farmland, as was Cercina, the small estate I inherited in the Tuscan hills some four miles from Le Panche. I had about 600 *ettari* (approximately 1,500 acres) with sixteen families living on the land and cultivating it for a share of the crops. But the farm had been neglected. Few investments had been made there after 1908, so it yielded only the small part of the harvest the tenant farmers gave my father in return for use of the land. After the communist raids of 1919, Father refused to replenish the livestock, and the expensive farm machinery he bought was never used and had rusted beyond repair.

My plans were on a grand scale, which required money, and there was only one place to obtain it: the *consorzio agrario,* the government agency in charge of agricultural affairs. I mortgaged my properties to collateralize the immense loans needed for repairs and modernization, blithely believing that the Victor royalties would enable me to repay the loans on time.

At Cercina, situated at an elevation of a little over a thousand feet with a sweeping view of Florence below, there was a dilapidated, two-story building. I had it gutted and completely remodeled with new bathrooms and modern fixtures. All in all, Cercina had the makings of a profitable enterprise, and given time, I thought, it could provide us with a comfortable living. The farm yielded vegetable crops, meat, poultry, milk, and eggs for the household. Excess produce could be sold, but that was small change compared to possible revenue from the two main cash crops: wine and oil. I imported and planted about 50,000 vine roots from California to rebuild the vineyards that had been devastated by *Phyloxera vastatrix,* an aphid which attacks and destroys most European vine roots. I planted an orchard of fruit trees. I ordered tons of mineral phosphates from Chile to fertilize the rocky, depleted soil and had wells dug for better irrigation. I purchased a thrasher and locomotive and built a garage for them; I bought a modern olive press to make olive oil and built a *frantoio,* a shed to house it. I also bought a generator to provide the farm with electricity. I had a road built to the back of the house so delivery carts could take a shortcut and save time, and I bought oxen to till the land, since the terraces were too small for a tractor. The crumbling terrace walls had to be rebuilt to prevent the further loss of fertile soil through erosion.

Inevitably, money went so fast that I could barely keep track of the zeros as enormous sums vanished from my bank account. I spent the cash I had and the money I had borrowed. I can say that I disposed of a small fortune through honest means. I didn't squander the money, I spent it. The result may have been the same, but the intent and the process were not.

Looking back on this period, I am shocked to realize how childish I was about money. I had no understanding of its source or how it could be used, preserved, or made to multiply. Money just "happened," and if one didn't have any at the moment, one borrowed it. It would always be replenished. My inexperience in financial management was to be my personal tragedy.

When I was a youngster, it was taken for granted that I had time to learn these worldly matters later, after I became an adult. Apart from my weekly allowance, I did not handle money; I never paid a bill or wrote a check. Thus I failed to realize that in the absence of a steady income, and a large one at that, the investments I was making would consume my capital. Unfortunately, Elena was as inexperienced in money matters as I, and Fofò was preoccupied with his own affairs. I also failed to consider that Father's guaranteed annual income of $100,000 from Victor lasted only during his lifetime, and only as long as he continued to make records. After his death, the heirs were to receive royalties only for the records sold.

I anticipated a large sum that would cover all my debts, and this was not an unreasonable expectation. As it happened, the sale of Caruso records peaked in 1921, and the royalties for that year alone amounted to $422,981.56, a staggering sum by any standard. No one could foresee that in a single year, sales would drop by 70 percent to produce only $125,177.66. I viewed Victor as a sort of cornucopia that would spew forth huge royalty checks and take care of any problems I might have with cash flow or credit till the end of my days. Living with that illusion, I kept on buying on credit, naïvely confident that money would soon start flowing. In fact, I wasn't entirely wrong on that account: Had I been paid my share of the royalties as expected, without delay, I could have paid off my promissory notes on time. The Victor royalties for 1921 and 1922 totaled a little over $548,000, of which a one-eighth share amounted to nearly $70,000, which was certainly more than my total indebtedness.

IT was an Italian custom to place the famous dead on view in a sarcophagus sealed in glass, so that by sliding back a marble top, one could see the embalmed body from the waist upward. As I have said, Father's remains were temporarily placed in the Canessa chapel while ours, designed by G. Cimmino and constructed by Chiurazzi,[1] was being completed. When it was ready, his remains were placed on display according to custom. Giovanni insisted that the marble top should be on rollers to expose the body under the glass top at will. He would sit in the chapel for hours contemplating his dead brother, talking to him, and finally dissolving in tears. The chapel was accessible only to the family, but on special occasions such as All Saints' Day or anniversaries, it was open to the public. Since Uncle Giovanni was the only blood relative living in Naples, he automatically assumed responsibility for seeing that the tomb was properly maintained. He also made arrangements for an annual memorial service.

Oh, my *Zi' Gioà!* (Unc' Jack!) How proudly he would roll back the lid of the sarcophagus to show off his famous brother! Father was laid out in a formal evening suit with white tie and all his decorations on the left lapel. I can still see Giovanni standing at the steps on the second anniversary of Papa's death, 2 August 1923. Elena and I came down from Florence to show our newborn son to the family and to attend the memorial mass. She wore a long-sleeved black dress with a black mantilla over her head, and I had on a dark grey suit with a black arm band and a black tie. I thought we were properly dressed.

As we approached the chapel, we saw a long queue of visitors winding up the chapel steps. Uncle Giovanni stood at the entrance to the chapel dressed all in black—black suit, black shirt, black tie, black shoes, a black fedora, and a small white handkerchief with a thin black border in his breast pocket. Like a barker in front of a tent at a village fair, he repeated in a stentorian voice:

"Vutate, Signò! Vutate!" ("Keep moving, gentlemen! Keep moving!")

He then caught sight of me in my grey suit. Pushing his way through the crowd, he confronted me.

"Comme te permette de vinì vestito accussì! Screanzato, nun tenite rispetto! Malcreato! Vattenne!! ("How dare you come here dressed like that! You boor, you have no respect! Get out of here!!")

I wanted no part of a public quarrel, so I calmly said in my best Neapolitan:

"Nun ce penzà' zi', me ne vaco. Tornerò quanno c'è meno gente." ("Don't

worry, Uncle, I'm going. I will come back when there are fewer people.")

We returned the following day. The caretaker rolled back the marble top of the sarcophagus, and under the airtight glass cover, I saw the corpse of my father for the first and last time. His face was expressionless, a death mask. The embalmers had used no makeup, and his skin had a strange, grey-white tint. I looked at him for several minutes, feeling nothing. This was not my father, but a dressed-up corpse. I do remember him in his coffin, but to my relief, when I think of Papa, that image never comes to me. My mind always projects the image of a strong, active, kind, cheerful man, vibrant and alive, as I knew him.

Father's rolltop, glassed-in sarcophagus became a tourist attraction over the years. The cemetery custodian soon realized its commercial value and kept the glass top covered with an American flag; for a lira or two, he would lift the flag to let the visitor view the body. The tourists' motives were blameless, I am sure, but this manner of paying respects was distinctly morbid. Dorothy always abhorred the idea of Father's remains being on public display, and when a motion picture company wanted to film him, she had had enough. Over Giovanni's protests, in 1927 she had the sarcophagus covered with the heavy marble top and the chapel doors locked. The doors were to be opened only once a year, on November 2, on All Saints' Day.[2]

As if the exhibit of the corpse were not enough, a weird, downright ghoulish ritual developed surrounding my father's remains. I was completely unaware of it until I read about it in the newspapers. An English-language account of the event appeared in several papers, among them the London *Daily Express*. The following report was filed from Paris on 14 November 1929:

> The bizarre custom of the late Enrico Caruso in attiring the great singer's body in a new outfit every three years was revealed here today by Tito Schipa, the Italian tenor, who organized this ceremony.
>
> "Caruso loved to be dressed up to the limit," said Schipa to me, "and so all of us who knew and loved him could think of no more appropriate plan than to make sure that he would not look dowdy or old-fashioned in death, so we gather at his tomb in the cemetery in Naples every third year.
>
> "Caruso's body has been so wonderfully embalmed that it is still absolutely life-like, and the face retains its natural colors. We say a few prayers, and then, in our presence, the

body is entirely dressed over again in a fine new suit made by one of the best Naples tailors.

"At the moment Caruso wears a smart morning coat. We have not decided what the next outfit will be."

The body of the great Italian tenor, who died eight years ago, is enclosed in an airtight glass case in a magnificent marble tomb, and many visitors to Naples are still allowed to visit the place and actually see his body.

In the course of these re-dressings, the medals that were displayed in neat order on Father's coat disappeared without a trace. Their value lay not so much in the gold but in the fact that they once belonged to Enrico Caruso. The valuable studs and cuff links also vanished from his shirt, as did the silver chalices and silver candelabra from the chapel.

This revelation in the international press caused Dorothy to intervene once more. She saw to it that there was no "next outfit," and I believe 1929 was the last time Father's remains were disturbed.

CHAPTER TWENTY-THREE

Ghosts

I T was summertime, the middle of August, and beastly hot. The day after the anniversary, we had a private memorial mass said in the chapel. Then, after saying good-bye to Mamma and Papa Canessa, Natalia, and the brothers, we returned to Le Panche.

We were glad to be home. Florence was a good deal cooler than Naples, and the evenings were almost pleasant. After freshening up from the long, dusty train ride, we retired to our second-story bedroom and went to bed. We slept with the windows open wide, closing only the *persiane,* shutters with horizontal slats that were attached to the outside of the window frame. The slats let the air through, darkened the room, and at the same time allowed complete privacy.

We had barely fallen asleep when we heard a loud knock on the shutter. This was followed by another. It sounded as if someone had thrown a rock. We sat up, listening. Then, all of a sudden, a barrage hit the shutters.

I jumped out of bed, grabbed my rifle, opened the shutter, and fired a couple of rounds in the air to frighten away whoever it was. But I saw no one in the garden or beyond the twelve-foot wall that surrounded it at a distance.

The following morning, right under our window on the paved walk encircling the house, we found a number of smooth, round stones, about the size of an American half dollar, all of them clean as if polished by the flow of a river. They didn't resemble anything we had in the garden, where the pebbles were small and round like garbanzo peas. We could not explain how those stones got there.

We thought this was an isolated incident, but the following night the same thing happened, then again the next night. This went on for months, during the entire winter of 1923–24. The flat white stones struck the villa almost nightly, always on our bedroom blinds. They never harmed anything, never broke a window. But the strange phenomenon upset Elena and the servants. I was at a loss for an acceptable explanation.

I began to carry a handgun. I also kept a gun under the mattress and a rifle near the bed. This seemed a sensible thing to do; we didn't know who or what we were up against. The servants were convinced we were being visited by a ghost that belonged to the thirteenth-century part of the house.

At Elena's urging, I contacted the *carabinieri*. I went to the police station at Il Sodo, the little town above us. It was staffed by a *brigadiere,* a staff sergeant, and five men. I explained to the sergeant what was happening at the villa and that I came to ask for his help. He listened with an expression on his face that clearly showed he thought I was crazy. Still, it was his duty to investigate, and he agreed to come down after dark, so as not to be seen by anyone when he and his men entered. They arrived around ten in the evening and settled in the dining room, which had large French doors opening onto the garden and protected by shutters on the outside. We served the men coffee and cake while we waited for the rock-throwing to begin as usual around ten-thirty or eleven o'clock.

By eleven, nothing had happened; by eleven-thirty—nothing. The men grew impatient. A few minutes before midnight, the sergeant stood up and announced with a condescending smile that he had to get his men back to their quarters. At that moment, a barrage of stones hit the shutter of the French doors on the ground floor, not the upstairs shutters as before. The men sprang to their feet, flung open the doors, and rushed into the garden. There was no one there. The *carabinieri* were baffled. Maybe someone threw the stones from beyond the wall, the sergeant suggested. I said that anyone who could throw rocks over a twelve-foot wall, hit a door or window several hundred feet away, and not break anything was a better man than I was. The sergeant thought it over and conceded that the feat was quite impossible.

This experiment produced no results, so I went down to the *fascio* headquarters in Florence and told the consul about my predicament. I said that someone must be coming into my garden, probably from the farm behind the villa. The consul was not much more receptive to my complaint than the sergeant from Il Sodo; still, he sent up fifty men of the fascist militia and stationed them around the house and farm. No one entered the garden, no one left, yet the round, polished stones kept coming. We picked them up and collected them in a bucket. After several nights of this, the men left, their disbelief changed to bewilderment and fear.

A couple of months after the *carabinieri*'s visit, the stones stopped coming. We waited anxiously to see whether they would resume, but that was the end of them. Just as we gave a sigh of relief, we began to experience other strange events. Under the circumstances, security became our main concern. Fortunately, there were no doors to the street except from the chapel. The street-side windows had heavy iron grills which made it impossible for anyone to enter, and each night we locked every door to the garden. Mario and I would start in the oldest part of the villa and work our way around until all the large French doors to the garden were secure. Since each room opened into the next one, we could work our way back to the new part of the building. As we made our nightly rounds, we inspected the rooms in succession, looking behind the heavy drapes to see if anyone were concealed there, and even lifting the visors of the two suits of armor at the bottom of the main stairs to make sure no one was hiding inside. Finally, we checked all the windows and locked the doors. Mario then handed over the keys, which I took upstairs with me.

The next morning, we would find all the inside doors unlocked. No matter how many times we locked and checked, we would find them open in the morning.

Men having failed me, I turned to beasts. I brought two mastiffs from Maremma and installed them in the garden. They were fierce dogs, and they ran to and fro at night, howling under my window. But they would only go to the edge of the new part of the building. There they would crouch, snarling and barking at something or someone not visible to us. Finally, after one or one-thirty in the morning, they would quiet down, lie beneath our window, and continue to show their agitation with low-pitched growls.

Of course, the whole household was aware of these mysterious happenings. The servants, petrified, locked themselves in their quarters and refused to venture out at night for any reason. Monsù claimed that he heard voices and loud cackling outside his room challenging him to come out; at last he couldn't take it any more and went back to Naples. Elena was terrified and started at every noise. I was much more annoyed than afraid. I did not believe in ghosts, and I was convinced that all these incidents had a rational explanation. Although I was determined to find it, I must admit that I never did.

THE villa chapel where I was baptized had two rows of pews, an altar with a picture of the Madonna and Child, and a small screened balcony where we could attend mass privately when we opened the chapel to the public. At least once a month, we had mass said. One morning, on my rounds of inspection, I found all the chandeliers in the chapel on. I asked Mario whether he had forgotten to turn the lights off. No, he said, he was quite certain he turned them off before he locked up. We then noticed that the vigil light on the altar was out, so we lit it. A few days later the same thing happened: Behind the locked doors of the chapel, we found the lights on and the little candle on the altar out. I decided to conduct a test. That night I left the candle out and turned the lights on. The next morning the lights were out and the candle was lit! Someone or something was signaling its presence.

My father's study was in the center of the thirteenth-century part of the villa. It held his beautiful collection of books—fine editions of the classics, but also many volumes by contemporary writers, including adventure stories and mysteries. It was one of these I went to fetch one afternoon.

I entered the study through the archway, which was covered by heavy drapes embroidered in Moorish designs with gold and silver threads. The archway opened into a sort of a vestibule with three more arches leading into the study proper. Father loved the rich, warm feeling of Moorish furniture inlaid with ivory, silver, and mother-of-pearl, and all the furnishings in this anteroom were Moorish. There were sofas and cushions in heavy velvet, carved, inlaid stools and tables, and, on the walls, scimitars, battle axes, suits of chain mail, helmets, and shields. Among the bric-a-brac were a *nargileh* and a small Turkish coffee machine.

The shutters were closed to keep the room cool, and it was dark inside. One had to pass through this vaulted arcade about eight feet wide by twelve feet long before reaching a light switch. I entered the anteroom, lifted the heavy drapes, and moved forward toward the light switch. Then I froze. The curtain did not drop behind me leaving me in the dark, and the dim light that came through the archway from the hall cast my shadow on the floor in front of me. I swung around. The curtain was held up as if by an invisible hand, allowing me to see my way.

I fled from the room.

When I regained my composure, I went back. The door to the study was open, just as I had left it, and the drape hung inertly. Timidly, I lifted the panel that had stayed up—it fell. I lifted it again, it fell again. There was nothing, positively nothing, it could have gotten hooked to, nothing that could have held it up. I tried to fold it to make it stay up, but it was too heavy and dropped. This incident went far beyond stones and vigil lights, and I must admit I was intimidated.

In the thirteenth-century tower of the house, there was a narrow wooden staircase that led up to the battlements. Halfway up was a landing and a small room I used as an armory. I liked to hunt quail and partridge, and I made my own shotgun shells. Here I kept gunpowder, shells, pellets, and a small pharmacist's scale. Above the little room, another flight of stairs went up to what we called the tank room because it held the pump and the water tanks that supplied the house with running water. A final staircase led to the terrace on top of the tower.

I used to spend long afternoons in the armory making rounds of ammunition. In fact, it became such a routine that Gina, the maid, would bring my coffee there around four o'clock without asking.

One afternoon around three, I heard steps on the wooden stairs. Without giving much thought to it, I assumed that Gina was bringing my coffee a little early. I expected the door to open; but instead, the footsteps did not stop on the landing outside the door but continued up the stairs. I then heard footsteps above my head in the tank room, as if someone with wooden clogs were walking there. Who on earth could it be? I went upstairs and found the door to the tank room open. I checked to see if someone was hiding behind the door, but there was no one. I went inside, looked around, looked under the tanks, which stood on iron legs—no one. Whoever had been there must have climbed onto the terrace. I climbed the last flight of stairs but found the door to the terrace barred from the inside. I opened it, but there was no one outside either. I put the bar back in place, descended to my room, closed the door, and continued my work. A few minutes later, I heard the footsteps again, coming down the stairs. When they reached the landing outside the armory, I called out loudly:

"*Nel nome di Dio, rimani dove sei e dimmi cosa vuoi!* ("In God's name, stay where you are and tell me what you want!")

There was no answer. The steps ceased, and there was no more sound. Whoever it was never budged from that spot. I waited several minutes until I could summon the courage to open the door. The landing was empty.

About half an hour later, Gina brought my coffee.

"Gina, were you upstairs this afternoon?" I asked.

"No, Sir," she said.

Once again, I found no rational explanation for the incident.

THE next occurrence, in the fall of 1924, was even more curious and inexplicable. There was an enunciator board in the servants' hall with the numbers of all the rooms in the house. This was connected to call buttons in the various rooms; when someone rang the bell anywhere in the house, the room number would come up on the call board so the servants would know where their services were required.

One night after we were in bed, I heard a knocking on the door.

"Who is it?" I called apprehensively. To my relief, it was Mario.

"*Signorino,* did you call?"

"No, Mario, I did not." I turned to Elena. "Did you ring for Mario?"

"No, Dear."

"I am sorry, *Signorino,*" said Mario, "I thought you did. Good night."

Half an hour later, Mario again knocked on the door.

"Your bell rang."

"Mario, you must be dreaming. We didn't ring. Let me see what's wrong with that board."

I went to the servants' hall and looked at the board. Numbers 2 and 5 were up, the billiard room and the library, both in the oldest part of the villa. As usual, Mario and I had locked the doors to both rooms before we retired. We looked at each other quite perplexed.

"Do you want to go and see who is ringing the bell down there?"

"Not I, Sir!" Mario said.

"Nor I! I wonder what this is all about."

"You know, *Signorino,* somebody may be trying to tell you something. Why don't you play those numbers in the lottery?"

It was Friday night, and bets could be placed until noon of the following day. By chance, Otello, the chauffeur, had to run some errands in Florence the next morning. On a whim, I told him to go to the lottery office and play for a hundred lire 2, 5, 25, and 52. Betting on four numbers in succession was called a *quaterna;* one could play as many as five numbers, which was called a *cinquina*. When the chauffeur came back from town, I asked about the lottery ticket.

"Mio Dio! Me ne sono scordato!" ("My God! I forgot!")

Otello raced back to the lottery office, arriving a few minutes after noon. The office was already closed because the drawing started at one o'clock. When we got the evening papers, I looked for the lottery results. There, neatly lined up, were my numbers: 2, 5, 25, 52.

It occurred to me only later that these were the numbers in my father's birthday: February 25. Odd as it may seem, I could only conclude that somebody was trying to tell me something. As it turned out, I came very close to winning over a million lire! Poor Otello apologized for weeks, but that didn't make up for the barely missed bonanza.

Soon after this incident, a small bill of a few thousand lire came due, and I did not have the cash to pay it. For some reason, I needed something from my father's desk in the Moroccan study. When I opened the middle drawer, I saw a small stack of thousand-lire notes, the exact amount I needed. I was stunned and looked around the room instinctively, but of course I was alone. I took the money, locked the desk, and paid my bill. A few days later, I went back to see if there were more surprises in the desk drawers. I found no more cash, but in the very spot where I found the banknotes before, there was a small, neat pile of fine grey ashes.

I was the only person who had a key to the desk. By this time, I felt convinced that something mysterious indeed was transpiring.

ONE evening I had to do the nightly inspection alone. Elena, who could not take the situation any more, had taken the baby to Naples to visit her mother and her sister, Natalia. Mario had the weekend off, so I was alone in the main part of the house. After I checked all the rooms on the main floor, locking each door as I retreated, I went upstairs by the servants' staircase. Proceeding along the second-floor gallery to the end of the house, I reached the old section. The door to the tower was already locked and bolted. I inspected the three rooms and bath in this part of the villa. Then, on an impulse, I went to the double doors that opened onto the long walnut staircase leading down to the main entrance. These were glass-paneled French doors inlaid with the Caruso coat of arms. They were locked, and the iron bar was in place. I cannot imagine to this day what possessed me, why I lifted the bar from its sockets, opened the door, and stepped onto the top landing. Only dim moonlight filtering through the stained-glass windows lit the dark stairwell.

There, on the second landing below me, was a figure—a man, or so it seemed—dressed in a formal evening suit with tails, slowly descending the stairs. As I stood there, frozen, he disappeared.

My father was buried in his black evening suit.

For what seemed an eternity, I remained transfixed; then, as if released from a trance, I quickly backed into the hall, closed the doors, and replaced the iron bar.

This was too much. The next day I went to see Fofò and told him about the latest manifestation. His first thought was that Papa was trying to contact us. He suggested that we get in touch with a woman he knew, a medium who had a good reputation. I was ready to try anything that might bring me closer to some resolution.

Fofò contacted the medium, who agreed to hold a seance at Le Panche. We made the necessary arrangements; Fofò, Mario, and I participated. The medium got off to a slow start. For a while it seemed we were wasting our time and money. Then the table she used for the seance began to rock, tapping out a message she deciphered for us. It said, in the most vulgar Neapolitan: "*Iate n'America. Doro ve sta sfuttenne.*" ("Go to America, Dorothy is 'cheating' you.")

We were stunned. With all due skepticism about seances, spiritualism, ghosts, and the rest, we agreed that even if the medium had faked the table-tapping, she could not have faked the message. Although she might have learned of Dorothy's existence, it seemed she could not possibly have known of the situation in America. We didn't suspect one another of trickery, for we were all Florentines around the table, yet the message was in the Neapolitan dialect.

AT first Fofò was against telling Uncle Giovanni about the seance. "He won't be able to handle this—he will crack up," he said. But we had no intention of doing anything behind his back so told him what had happened. He took the message of the medium more calmly than we had anticipated, but he agreed with us that it was time to stop waiting and start acting.

In 1924, my creditors were closing in, and it became clear that I would have to sell Le Panche and move to Cercina. But if the record royalties did not start coming soon, I was going to lose Cercina as well. Although Giovanni and Fofò were not in the same financial straits as I was, toward the end of 1924 we decided to go to America and see for ourselves what was holding up our money.

Having had my twentieth birthday, I was supposed to begin my military service. I asked for a deferment, which was granted with the stipulation that I would serve a year later, with the class of 1905. This gave me a breather to get my affairs temporarily in order. In January 1925, we sailed for New York. We ran into a bad storm and were happy to catch the first glimpse of the Statue of Liberty. One of the photographs taken of the three of us upon landing on January 19 shows a gay and hopeful threesome. Keeping our business to ourselves, we told waiting reporters we had come to visit friends; Giovanni declined to tell them even where we planned to stay. This was the first time I encountered the inevitable question: Did either Fofò or I plan to embark on an operatic career? We answered that neither of us had professional vocal equipment, nor any ambition to follow in our father's footsteps. With typical journalistic inaccuracy, reporters gave our ages as 19 and 21, while I was 20 and Fofò 26.

New York was familiar to Giovanni and me, but Fofò saw the metropolis for the first time and was overwhelmed by its immensity. There was not much warm feeling between our uncle and ourselves, so apart from our joint trips to the lawyers' offices, Fofò and I did not associate much with Giovanni. He dined at Del Pezzo's or Goodman's. For our simpler tastes and slimmer resources, Horn & Hardart, the famous automat, was just fine.

When we called Alfred Seligsberg at his office, he was cordial but aloof. We did not realize until later that Father's old friend was now Dorothy's lawyer. He was paid to work for her, and as we soon discovered, that meant working against us. He agreed to a meeting and suggested that as we came on business, we should hold a formal conference at his office with all parties present. He set the date for the following week. This gave us time to pay a visit to the Metropolitan, where we placed a laurel wreath against the pedestal of Father's bust. The ribbon read merely "Giovanni—Rodolfo—Enrico."

We convened at Seligsberg's office at the appointed time. It was the first time we had seen Dorothy in two years. After the obligatory exchange of greetings and small talk, during which we found her remarkably distant, we got down to business. We stated our concern that because we had seen not a cent of the Victor royalties, we had come to investigate what was holding up the settlement of this portion of the estate.

Seligsberg was smooth and deft. He said he could not understand what had prompted us to undertake this journey and what it was we expected to accomplish. There was nothing to settle, for the estate had been settled. In the United States, he explained, there was no such thing as a natural child: Children were born either in or out of wedlock, and those born out of wedlock were illegitimate in the eyes of the law. Even though our father had recognized us and given us his name, Fofò and I were considered—we should forgive his use of the term—bastards. Furthermore, in this country, neither illegitimate children nor brothers were entitled to any portion of an estate unless the deceased had no legitimate descendants. The law was quite clear and specific: Two-thirds of the estate went to the legitimate minor and one-third to the mother. There was no room for further interpretation or discussion; legally speaking, we didn't have a leg to stand on.

We were shocked and furious. We refused to accept the fact that we had made the trip for nothing. Uncle Giovanni suggested we go downtown to Little Italy to ask his friends for advice. We did, and I met Giovanni's circle. I knew he felt most at ease among the lower-class Italians, including the *mafiosi;* but I was not prepared for the rough milieu we visited, and I was surprised at the respect he commanded among his cronies. I distinctly recall our visit to Mulberry Street. Giovanni complained bitterly about Dorothy and the inheritance we felt she had commandeered. One of the men, straight out of a gangster movie, said:

"*Commendato'! Dicite 'na parola e la mettimme into a lo Hoodson!*" ("*Commendatore*! Just say the word and we'll drop her into the Hudson!")

This option, tempting as it was to Giovanni, was unacceptable. We consulted another lawyer instead. At first, he showed some interest in the case. But after we explained all the details, he agreed with Seligsberg's conclusion: We didn't have a leg to stand on. We were not in a position to hire lawyers and start a lengthy, international lawsuit whose outcome was doubtful at best, and Dorothy and her attorneys knew it. Nor did we have the money to linger in New York in the hope of finding someone who would take our case. There was nothing to do but sail home, bitterly disappointed and disillusioned with American law. An undated photo taken just before we sailed shows the three of us looking grumpy and belligerent. We certainly had nothing to smile about.

A photo of Rodolfo
Caruso inscribed to
his brother Enrico in
the mid-1920s.

Enrico, Jr.,
holding one of
the bronze
billikens
Caruso sculpted
of himself,
ca. 1911.
Photography
Bosworth.

Above, attorney Vincenzo Traballesi bound for New York, ca. 1928.
Below, Traballesi aboard the S/S *Conte Grande* with an unidentified woman,
ca. 1928.

Left to right, Rodolfo, Giovanni, and Enrico Caruso, Jr., arriving in New York in January 1925, determined to collect their inheritance. Photography Underwood and Underwood. Courtesy of Francis Robinson Collection, Special Collections, Vanderbilt University.

Geraldine Farrar
as intermission
commentator for
the Metropolitan
Opera broadcasts
in 1934–35. Farrar
is seated at a
Steinway originally
made for the private
railway car in which she
toured the U.S.

Wagnerian tenor
Lauritz Melchior,
hunter, in Alberta.
Photography Interna-
tional News Photo.

Enrico Caruso, Jr., in the Warner Brothers dining room, flanked by Edward G. Robinson and tenor Tito Schipa. Photography Bert Longworth.

Maestro Adolfo de la Huerta
and his pupil Enrico Caruso, Jr.,
ca. 1932.

Enrico Caruso, Jr., in Hollywood with Señor A. A. Cuyas, his Spanish-
language coach at Warner Brothers.

Hollywood publicity shot of Enrico Caruso, Jr., inscribed to Andrew Farkas. The photograph was taken in 1934.

Bass Alfonso Pedroza as Sandor, the gypsy chief, in *La Buenaventura,* 1934.

Count Andrès de Segurola, master of ceremonies for the opening of *La Buenaventura* in 1934.

Anita Campillo and Enrico Caruso, Jr., in the Spanish-language film *La Buenaventura*, 1934. The photograph is inscribed to Enrico by Campillo.

Enrico Caruso, Jr., singing the "Serenade" from Donizetti's *Don Pasquale* in *El Cantante de Napoles,* his second Spanish-language film, in 1934.

Enrico Caruso, Jr., costumed as Manrico in Verdi's *Il Trovatore,* in *El Cantante de Napoles,* 1934.

Carmen Rio and Enrico Caruso, Jr., in the film *El Cantante de Napoles* (*The Singer of Naples*), a romanticized version of Enrico, Sr.'s early life, 1934.

PAYRET
MAYO 2 - 3 - 4 - 5 - 6

Estreno en Cuba del más rutundo Exito obtenido por una Opereta en Español ! . . .

La voz de un ángel . . . La fortuna de un mendigo . . . Una historia de locas ambiciones . . . Dos mujeres que se disputan el amor de un hombre . . . Una, la Eva fatal y triunfadora, que le ofrece el veneno de sus caricias y la gloria de la Scala . . . ¡suprema aspiración de todo artista ! . . . La otra sólo puede ofrecerle su virtud y las primicias de sus brazos inmaculados ! . . . . . .

La vida del inmortal Enrico Caruso, llevada por primera vez a la pantalla, revivida por su propio hijo!

Colosal producción en español, orgullo de WARNER BROTHERS.

EL CANTANTE DE NAPOLES

con **ENRICO CARUSO** (HIJO)

MONA MARIS   **CARMEN RIO**

BURGAY Y Cía.—Habana.

Poster for Enrico Caruso, Jr.'s second film, *El Cantante de Napoles*.

The photograph
Rodolfo Caruso sent
to his mother in
South America
in 1931. The
inscription reads:
"To my dear
Mamma as a sign
of filial affection,
Fofò. Florence,
16 February 1931."

Portrait of Rodolfo Caruso
inscribed to Enrico, Jr., in 1938.

Nuova York.
Nov. 11, 1938

Alla mia Mamma Adorata, con tu
il mio affetto, offro.
Enrico

The photograph Enrico, Jr., sent to his mother in Rio de Janeiro in 1938. The inscription reads: "To my adored Mamma, with all my affection, from Enrico."

Ada Giachetti in Rio de Janeiro, ca. 1935. This was the first photograph Enrico, Jr., ever received from his mother.

Ada Giachetti in Rio de Janeiro in 1938, posing for an *A Noite* photographer with the photograph of Enrico Caruso he gave to her in 1917.

Edward J. Smith, whose name became a household word among record collectors, in the late 1930s.

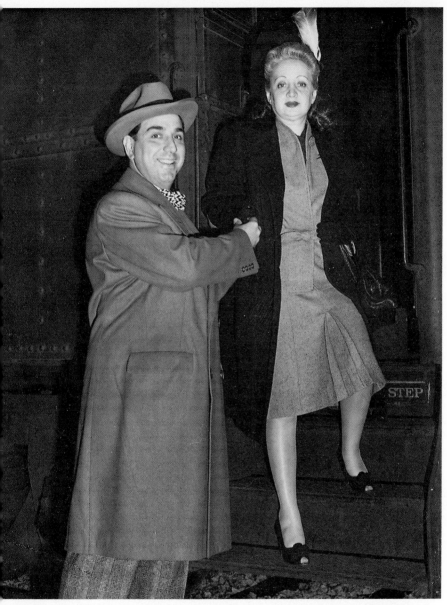

Enrico Caruso, Jr., and his wife Helen Roth Burnett arriving in Miami, October 1944.

Enrico Caruso, Jr., in 194

Enrico Caruso, Jr., singing in a nightclub in Chicago in 1945.

Enrico Caruso, Jr. (*above*), and Andrew Farkas (*left*) speaking at the Metropolitan Opera House on the occasion of the first-day issue celebration of an Enrico Caruso stamp, 27 February 1987. Photography U.S. Post Office.

Enrico Caruso, Jr., and Andrew Farkas signing programs at the first-day issue celebration of the Caruso stamp. Photography U.S. Post Office.

Brazilian soprano Bidù Sayão, Andrew Farkas, and Enrico Caruso, Jr., at the Metropolitan Opera House, 27 February 1987. Photography U.S. Post Office.

FATHER'S birthday coincided with our return trip. Uncle Giovanni went to the captain and requested that a mass be said for his brother. The captain agreed and had the event announced in the ship's bulletin. Giovanni loved to show off, especially where Papa was concerned. He announced that the brother and the two sons of the great Caruso would be present at the anniversary mass. All passengers were invited to attend.

Because religion is a strictly personal affair in my eyes, and because I thought the circumstances overdramatized, I decided not to attend the mass.

When it was over, my uncle, like an enraged bull, came to my cabin and furiously berated me, yelling at the top of his lungs.

"Where were you? Why weren't you there?"

"Uncle, I didn't want to come. I didn't feel like being there with all those people. I prayed for Papa here."

"You should have been there!" he yelled. "It was your duty! You are just the son of that whore of a mother of yours!" And he slapped me across the face.

I did not hit him back. My upbringing kept me from striking my elder, my uncle. But from that day, I never spoke to him again.

DURING my young years, I looked upon Giovanni as an uncle, just one of the family. I wasn't particularly fond of him, but I was used to him because he was always around. When he assumed the role of a surrogate father and tried to tell me how to behave, I rebelled.

Giovanni had his convictions, and one of these was that not only my mother but the entire Giachetti family had done my father wrong. After Ada left in 1908, he stayed away from the Giachettis. I don't think Rina and Giovanni ever got along. Out of respect toward Papa, he was civilized to her when we were in Naples, but I have no memory of him ever visiting us in Livorno. Before the years with Rina, however, Giovanni was always around when Father was in Italy. I remember him on our holidays at Rimini, Marina di Pisa, Montecatini, and Salsomaggiore. Papa had no illusions about Giovanni, yet he always treated him as his equal. They would embrace and kiss when they met, and it was obvious that Papa was very fond of his brother. Whatever Giovanni's shortcomings, my father felt true brotherly love for him, and my uncle, on his part, felt much more than that. He was a simple, warm, effusive person, and I am sorry that a stronger and warmer relationship did not develop between us. But we were simply not compatible.

Father and Giovanni looked as alike as two drops of water, yet as Dorothy once put it, "he looked like a caricature" of Papa. He tried to be like his famous brother, but he lacked the polish and the artistic soul. Father had raised himself from the lowest socioeconomic stratum of Naples to become a gentleman, well informed if not educated, refined if not cultured. Even when he spoke in anger, I never heard him swear or use foul language; either he never did, or he was careful in the presence of women and children. He had an instinctive sense of propriety; he may not have known the fine points of the prevailing customs of each country where he lived or performed, but he projected the image of a gentleman. To the best of my knowledge, in the vast Caruso lore, there is not one recorded story of a social gaffe or *faux pas* he committed. Considering that he had to learn manners through observation and imitation, this too speaks for his innate intelligence.

Giovanni, on the other hand, remained a *cafonesco,* a coarse Neapolitan, despite his airs as a man of the world. He was not very bright; in fact, Father considered him almost dim-witted. But he had a peasant's natural horse sense, a broad smile, and a good sense of humor. He could crack a joke or make a pointed remark, and in some ways he was like Father. But Father had multiple talents, while Giovanni had no artistic gifts or inclinations. I never heard him sing, and his speaking voice did not bear a noticeable resemblance to Father's. Papa spoke good Italian, although with a trace of a Neapolitan accent. He always spoke the Neapolitan dialect with Giovanni, for the simple reason that my uncle spoke Neapolitan almost exclusively, whether in Naples or not. In fact, until I learned Neapolitan myself, I could not understand half of what he said.

The king of Italy bestowed several titles upon my father: In 1900, he was made *Cavaliere* (Knight); in 1903, *Ufficiale* (Officer); then *Commendatore* (Commander) in 1909; and finally, in 1920, *Grande Ufficiale della Corona d'Italia* (Grand Officer of the Italian Crown). Everyone addressed him as *Commendatore.* Naturally, Giovanni wanted to be called *Commendatore* too. After all, Father shared everything with him— why not his title?

I was aware of Giovanni's pivotal role in my father's life and grateful for all my uncle had done for him. There were three years between them, and in Italy in those days, when there were only two brothers in a family and they were so close in age, only one had to serve in the army; that way both males would not perish in case of hostilities. That is why Giovanni could take Papa's place and serve out his time.

But that was not all Giovanni served in the Ethiopian War and was wounded in the Battle of Aduwa in 1896, which ended in a disastrous defeat for the Italian forces. He served again in 1912, in the war between Italy and Turkey, when the Italian forces went to Tripolitania and Cyrenaica. Then, in 1916, he was called to the colors and served with the "terrible territorials," the uniformed civil defense consisting of men too old to serve in the regular army. Had he not served, my father would have had to don a uniform, as Gigli, Pinza, Ruffo, Lauri-Volpi, and many other singers did. So my uncle earned his rights to the good life which Papa's earnings made possible. Father, who was not only generous by nature but compulsively grateful, never forgot what Giovanni did for him. Although I am told there are letters in which he complained about Giovanni's constant requests for money, he gladly supported him all his life. He felt he owed him a great deal, and he went on paying till the end.

Giovanni never worked in his life, and certainly not after Father began to earn real money. Actually, my father once tried to set him up in the automobile tire business, but it fell through. Giovanni was simply not interested in working. Once someone asked him: "Hey, Gioà! Why don't you do something? Why don't you work?" Giovanni gave his classic reply: "God gave my brother a marvelous voice, and he gave me a marvelous brother! Why should I work?"

CHAPTER TWENTY-FOUR

Vincenzo Traballesi

B ACK in Italy, I delivered the bad news to Elena. It extinguished her flickering hope that we would ever get back on our feet finan- cially. The Canessas tried to help us with advice and lawyers, but the legal opinions were unanimous: Whatever the law was in America, we had to abide by it. In a token effort to regain some part of our lost inheritance, we had the Tribunal of Naples issue a decree on 26 August 1925 stating that if its decrees were not recognized by the courts of New Jersey, the Tribunal would help us in any way it could to recover what the New Jersey court might take away from us. It was a mere ges- ture without power of enforcement; both the American heirs and the American courts knew that. Besides, Dorothy learned her lesson from our surprise visit and made sure that she would never be left vulnerable to us. She also wanted her daughter's funds under her sole control, claiming that "she, as surviving parent, is the natural and general guardian of her daughter, Gloria Caruso, during the latter's minority and until she reaches the age of twenty-one years," and as such, she should be entitled to receive all income belonging to Gloria "to use, hold, or otherwise dispose of the same without accountability." To put the money safely out of our reach, she obtained a court order on 31

March 1925 which directed her to have all the royalties she had received up to that time, and all she was to receive thereafter, deposited and retained on deposit with the Union Trust & Hudson National Bank of Jersey City. For the time being, this made the money inaccessible to all parties in the dispute.

I left the legal endeavors to Fofò and Giovanni; my own worries were more pressing. One note after another came due, and I was unable to make the loan payments. Now that I knew there would be no royalties from America, I had to accept that I must put Le Panche up for sale. I had to find a buyer, and fast. I was able to sell the villa for 400,000 lire, as I remember; because of the depressed value of the lira, this amounted to approximately $20,000. For the time being, I kept the adjoining farmland, which I sold not long afterward. In my difficult situation, I had to go along with the buyer's demands and sell the villa *a porte chiuse* (with closed doors), meaning as it was, complete with contents. Considering the urgency of the moment, I thought I was lucky to make the sale. The proceeds barely canceled my debts.

At this time in my life, I had no sense of the abstract value of objects, nor any feeling for antiques or mementos. Even before I sold the villa, I gave my father's music scores, annotated in his own hand, to my auto-mechanic friend Dino Barsanti. Dino and Mario Barsanti were the nephews of Giulia Focosi, my wet-nurse, and I spent many hours at their garage trying to improve the performance of my car. Dino was taking voice lessons, and I had no use for the scores—so why not give them to him? Now, in my old age, I cling tenaciously to any small object that once belonged to my parents.

Thus it was that I sold Le Panche not only with all its furnishings, but with a wealth of family memorabilia. Among items too numerous to mention were not only paintings of my parents but paintings by my parents, Father's magnificent book collection, and the Dick Johnson bronze by Angelo Arachite, Father's army sergeant turned sculptor. At least I salvaged a companion piece, the Pagliaccio bronze. But the study was left full of photographic mementos in silver and gold frames: the famous dedicated portrait of Teddy Roosevelt, inscribed and signed pictures of King Edward VII and Queen Alexandra, Kaiser Wilhelm of Germany, Czar Nicholas II, Puccini, Mascagni, Leoncavallo, Tosti, Giordano, Ruffo, Tetrazzini, Scotti, Chaliapin, Masini, and many, many others.

There were two paintings I did not want to leave behind. One was Mother's portrait. Fofò had no interest in it, so it was given to me when the estate was divided. I took it with me to Cercina, where Elena and I went to live after the sale of Le Panche, then to an apartment in Florence. When I eventually emigrated to America, Elena had no room for such a large canvas so gave it to Umberto, Mother's half brother. The other was a full-length painting of Papa as Vasco da Gama in *L'Africana*. This, too, I entrusted to Elena.

Those who bought Le Panche had more business sense than I did. As soon as the deal was concluded, they gutted the villa and hauled its entire contents to Materassi, the auction house in Florence. The cash netted from the sale was more than the money they had paid for the house *and* the contents!

We moved to Cercina, and I was more determined than ever to make it a self-supporting, producing farm able to sustain me and my family. At the same time, we had to dismiss most of the servants. It was a blow to them and a heartache for us. Either Elena or I had known many of them since our childhood, and it was almost like losing a part of our family. In spite of my grave financial circumstances, I gave each of them a handsome severance payment according to the number of years spent in the service of the family. Mario, of course, received the largest amount. I believe Dorothy had also given him a sizable gift after my father's death. He bought a delicatessen and did quite well.

With the sale of Le Panche, my affairs were temporarily in order. I could no longer postpone the inevitable and was inducted into the army. Soon after I reported to my duty station in Naples, my second son, Wladimiro, was born on 26 June 1925. I was allowed to return home on "paternity leave," a welcome respite from army life. My tour of duty was uneventful and unpleasant. In the end, I developed a bad case of pneumonia and was given a medical discharge. As a special inducement for my regimental commander, Lieutenant Colonel Niutta, to sign my release papers, I "donated" a custom-made mahogany dining table for the officers' mess.

UPON my discharge, I again needed money. Cercina was mortgaged to the hilt, so I went to the Banco di Sconto to try to borrow cash. The vice president expressed his regrets, but as I did not have a *castelletto,* a commercial account, he was unable to accommodate me. He suggested that I go to see a wealthy local attorney who was occasionally willing to discount a promissory note to certain clients.

He gave me the name and address of a certain Vincenzo Traballesi. He was a handsome young man about my brother's age, tall, with smooth, white skin, fine features, and dark hair beginning to thin in the front. He was then, as always, elegantly dressed. He looked me over through his monocle, which to me and everyone else signified "class." I introduced myself and told him about my predicament then asked him to discount a note for me. The encounter remained so clearly in my memory that I can still recall it almost word for word.

"Well, Mr. Caruso," he said in a most friendly manner, "what can you offer as collateral?"

"I don't have anything to offer. I own a farm and some property, but those are already heavily mortgaged."

"You have nothing else?"

"It may be hard to believe, but no, I do not. I have a few acres left where a tenant keeps his dairy cows and the farmhouse where I live. I have just about reached the end of my rope."

"Come now, Mr. Caruso, you certainly inherited more than the little farm you just mentioned."

I told him the story of how I lost Le Panche, the land holdings, and all the farm machinery.

"What about the royalties from your father's recordings? Haven't I read something about that in the papers?"

The newspapers had picked up the story of our unsuccessful attempt to collect the money due to us. I explained that the Victor royalties were not only tied up in court on behalf of Gloria, but that as far as American law was concerned, we didn't exist; only the widow and the legitimate child were recognized as heirs.

"Something is wrong here," said Traballesi. "Do you have a copy of the documents relating to your case?"

"Yes, I do."

"Would you mind letting me see them?"

"Not at all. But I must warn you, Mr. Traballesi, that you are wasting your time. My brother, my uncle, and I went to America in 1925 specifically to settle the matter. We were told by lawyers in New York and in New Jersey that American law did not recognize us at all. As far as the inheritance was concerned, we had no claims."

"They may be right. Still, if you don't mind, I would like to look over whatever you have. After that we might talk about a loan."

I was convinced that Traballesi was looking for a rainbow to chase, or perhaps was motivated by curiosity. I was equally certain that if he were searching for some collateral in my lost inheritance, I could kiss the loan good-bye. However, I had nothing to lose. Without any faith in the outcome, I took all the documents I had to his office. He asked me to give him a few days to study them and then come and see him.

When I went back, I could read in his face that he was greatly pleased with himself.

"Mr. Caruso, I am shocked that no one advised you properly. This is a very simple, I would almost say open-and-shut, case. You, your brother, and your uncle are entitled to your share of the royalties."

"How is that possible?"

"It is quite simple, obvious in fact. You all signed a contract, every one of you, including the American heirs. It has been ratified by the Court of Naples. Here is the decree of the court, and this makes you all not testamental but *contractual* heirs. This is a document that must be recognized by international law. It applies anywhere in the Western world. The American heirs don't have a legal leg to stand on!"

"But we are in Italy," I protested; "they are in America where the money is, and possession is nine-tenths of the law. What can we do about it?"

"That too is very simple. We will go to America!"

"You mean you will go to America."

"No. *We* will go. You and I."

"Come, Mr. Traballesi, be serious. How can I go to America? My farm is not producing an income to live on, I have debts I cannot pay, I have a wife and two small children to support. I couldn't possibly go."

"Then let me make you a proposition. If your brother and your uncle go along with it, I will take your case for 20 percent of whatever the three of you will receive, plus my expenses. This way you don't have to worry about out-of-pocket cash. If we lose the case, you owe me nothing, not even expenses."

"And how will I support my family in the meantime?"

"How much do you owe on your farmhouse?"

"More than it is worth!"

"Then I would urge you to sell it and move your family to an apartment. Pay only those notes that will come due in the meantime, and we will take it from there."

"And what do I do when the other loans are due?"

"We can sell your land with the fruit trees and dairy stock. But if that is not enough, I am prepared to deposit in the bank enough money for your family to live on for a couple of years or longer if necessary, for as long as it takes the courts to reach a verdict. Of course, I will also pay for your expenses while we are in America. When we win the case, you will pay me back from your share of the inheritance."

I noticed he didn't say "if" we win the case, he said "when."

"You seem very confident, Mr. Traballesi, that we will win this lawsuit," I said.

"I have no doubt about it!"

Traballesi was as capable as he was persuasive, and he soon made all the arrangements for our trip. Elena and I sold Cercina and moved into an apartment in Florence. Having momentarily regained my solvency, I could leave my wife and children behind with cash in hand and with my own conscience clear. Unfortunately, we suffered a great blow before I left: We realized that our younger son, Wladimiro, was born deaf and mute.

AS I recall, Traballesi and I sailed for New York late in 1926. We took rooms at the Prince George Hotel and headed straight to the offices of Mr. Hurd, who handled what was left of Father's estate in New York, mostly tax matters. He said there was nothing he could do for us, as all the royalty money was in the hands of the Victor Talking Machine Company under the jurisdiction of the courts of the State of New Jersey. He advised us to hire an attorney licensed to practice there and referred us to Merritt Lane, a man he held in high esteem who seemed to have all the right connections.

Our next stop was the law office of Merritt Lane. Traballesi's spoken English was adequate to order a meal or ask directions but was not up to the demands of a legal discussion. I was to serve as interpreter; but when it came to legal language, I was at a loss. Some of the terms I knew only in English, some in Italian, some not at all. In the end, the two lawyers found the obvious solution: They conversed in Latin. Unlike today's attorneys, lawyers in those days received a classical education that included foreign languages, first and foremost Latin.

Once Traballesi clarified the basic issues with Lane, the latter accepted the case, and we returned to New York City. With Traballesi's persuasive arguments, my interpreting, and the magic of my father's name, we were allowed to check out armload after armload of law books from the New York Public Library, which we hauled back to the Prince George Hotel. Traballesi spent days and the best part of many nights examining cases, precedents, all the fine points of international law. His reading vocabulary was much larger than his speaking vocabulary, and he also had the benefit of a dictionary. Now and then he would throw a pillow at me, interrupting my snoring, to ask the meaning of this word or that expression. But I wasn't much help.

"How can I tell you what it means in Italian?" I would say. "It's your language, legalese, I don't know it!"

"Well, try! I am going blind with all this reading, and all you do is sleep!"

This went on for over two months. From time to time, Traballesi consulted with Merritt Lane, then he came back to the hotel and resumed work. Finally, when he was satisfied that he had incorporated all that was necessary in the document, he took a lengthy brief to Merritt Lane's office. Lane's staff had it recast in proper form and correct English, and it was submitted to the Court of Chancery in New Jersey.

If my memory serves me, we spent close to half a year in New York.

WHEN I returned to Italy, it was again time to settle outstanding loans. I asked Traballesi to sell the little orchard with the dairy farm. No one knew until then, as no one had bothered to investigate at the *catasto* (the city planning office), that this piece of land was within city limits and already plotted for subdivision. Traballesi discovered this as soon as he made a title search, and he immediately realized the great value of the property. He found a buyer in short order, and I sold the 5 *ettari,* about ten acres, the last piece of property I ever owned in my life, at an excellent price. Traballesi, of course, collected his fee from both buyer and seller. The money I received from the sale was consumed by the outstanding loans, but at least I was free of debt.

Traballesi felt it would be a good idea to have an "outpost" in New York, someone from the family empowered to sign a document when necessary, so I assumed this charge. My marriage, which was never ideal, had suffered irreparably from the constant strain of financial pressure. I had married Elena because of my exalted sense of *cavalleria Carusiana*—because I had compromised her by putting my arm around her waist. She was a placid woman who did not inspire passion; and although she bore me two sons, I believe it was out of duty rather than love. I was grateful that she never attacked me for the hopeless situation I had gotten us into, yet I struggled with a constant feeling of guilt. In deciding to go to New York, I also decided to ease matters by removing myself from the family as much as possible.

Preliminaries to our litigation were set on 16 November 1923, when Dorothy filed a bill of complaint in the New Jersey Court of Chancery against Gloria Caruso and others in an attempt to become the administratrix of all moneys in her hands. Gloria was brought into court on 27 February 1924, and Norman Grey, clerk of the Chancery, was appointed her guardian *ad litem*. Grey soon died, and Martin V. Bergen was appointed in his stead. Bergen, a solicitor from Philadelphia, filed through counsel a litigious answer on behalf of Gloria requesting that all proceeds from Victor be decreed the property of Gloria, allowing only a portion of the income to her mother.

Dorothy made no secret of her objective. A special dispatch from Trenton, New Jersey, to *The New York Times,* published on 15 June 1926, made this statement:

> In an effort to prevent Rudolfo [*sic*] and Enrico Caruso . . . and Giovanni Caruso, a brother of the famous tenor, from sharing in royalties paid on the sales of records by the Victor Talking Machine Company, Gloria Caruso, 6-year-old daughter of the singer and his widow . . . entered protest through her guardian, in the Court of Chancery here, against her mother's accounting of the estate. . . . Martin V. Bergen of Camden, guardian of Gloria, argued the document on the royalty settlement had no standing before Italian law. The settlement was unjust, he added, and the sum belongs to Gloria subject to her mother's dower right.

Under the pretext of protecting the interests of Gloria, Bergen was the instrument of the law chosen to bring all the royalties under Dorothy's control.

It was actually Dorothy, seeking free access to the money, who brought suit "against Rodolfo Caruso and others, for discharge of administratrix and for distribution of moneys in her hands as such." She filed her petition for the final distribution of the funds in the Court of Chancery on 25 February 1927. Later in the year, the Prerogative Court of New Jersey, recognizing a conflict of interest, denied her petition to become Gloria's general guardian. However, with the permission of Chancellor Edwin R. Walker of the Court of Chancery of New Jersey, on 24 January 1928 she was appointed special guardian for Gloria's estate in New Jersey.

I dutifully stayed in touch with Merritt Lane's office, returning to Italy every six months, when my three-month visa and its extension expired. It soon became obvious that the mills of the legal system ground more slowly than we had anticipated. To preserve my funds and to avoid depleting my credit with Traballesi, I decided to find a job.

First, I contacted my father's old friends, Scotti, Amato, Zirato, Pierre Key, but they could offer no help. Scotti suggested that I look up the general manager of the Metropolitan, Giulio Gatti-Casazza.

When Father was alive, Gatti was exceptionally friendly toward me. On my visits backstage, he would put his arm around my shoulder and say: "*Figlio mio, come stai? Come sei bello!*" ("How are you, my son? How handsome you are!") When I went to see him, he was as friendly as always.

"*Commendatore,*" I began, "I come to you as a friend, my father's as well as mine. I need your help."

"What can I do for you, my son?"

I explained that the litigation was taking longer than I had expected. I needed a job to pay my hotel bills and to eat. I was not asking for handouts, but I was willing to move scenery, carry props, sell tickets, sweep floors, paste clippings, do any sort of work he could give me at the Met so long as I earned $25 a week.

"*Ah, figlio mio, mi dispiace tanto, ma non ho niente. Qui non c'è niente per te.*" ("Oh, my son, I am so sorry, but I have nothing. There is nothing here for you.")

This was a great disappointment. Gatti could surely have found something for me, if not out of friendship toward my father, then out of gratitude for his services to the Metropolitan. Father faithfully sang at the Met for $2,500 a night until he died, although his fees elsewhere were as high as $10,000 a performance, or even $15,000 in Mexico City according to Dorothy. The net savings of a single Caruso appearance at the Met would have paid my salary for 300 weeks. Gatti must have realized that if I went to him asking for a $25-a-week job, I needed that job. But on the entire payroll of the Metropolitan Opera House, there was no room for the son of Enrico Caruso.

I turned to the want ads. *The New York Times* advertised an opening for an Italian-speaking salesman at the Real Silk Hosiery Mills, Inc., 11 West Forty-second Street. I applied for the job and was hired. Carrying a sample case, I sold hosiery to clients throughout the city, including many members of the Metropolitan. I earned $8–9 a day plus a monthly bonus, which added up to double my targeted $25 a week.

I then had the first taste of the liability attendant to my name.

One of the New York papers—the *Mirror,* the *News,* or some other—carried a mocking headline: "Carutho's Thon Ith Thelling Thockth!"

The first thing the article produced was an invitation to the Immigration and Naturalization Service. The commissioner, Edward Corsi, politely informed me that as long as I was in this country on a visitor's permit, I was not allowed to work. I explained the dilemma to my boss, who suggested the practical solution of changing my name.

The disadvantages of my famous name clearly outweighed the benefits. More than once, I was not hired specifically because my name was Enrico Caruso, and employers felt I was "too good" for the job. So, for employment purposes, I changed my name to Henry de Costa. Remembering the love Madame Bertha Nuñes da Costa had shown me during my childhood years in London, I assumed her last name with the slight modification of changing the Spanish "da" to the Italian "di." After people began to call me "die" Costa, I changed it to "de" Costa. For purposes of income tax and social security, and above all for the Immigration Service, I remained Caruso. My colleagues called me Henry or Hank de Costa, a name that stuck with me through all my years of employment in the United States.

The newspaper article also produced a flurry of nasty letters from my father's old friends. The message was always the same: I was degrading my father's name, and it was disgraceful. They were ready to condemn, but not one had lifted a finger when I asked them to help me find a job. In their view, I was a *figlio di papà,* a "daddy's boy," a perfectly respectable status which carried the obligation of not working for wages. I was supposed to live on air. In their defense, I must say that they did not know the details of my dire financial straits. Still, in my view, working at any job was an honorable way to earn a living regardless of the name I bore.

THE next court hearing was on 14 March 1928. Although this round involved the actual amount Dorothy was to be allowed to draw for the support of her daughter, Chancellor Walker brought into the suit the validity of the Italian decree and the issue of whether the Victor royalties constituted principal or income. He conceded that personal property had no locality and that the laws of the owner's domicile should govern the disposition of such property. He then confused the matter by allowing the division of the estate in Italy to stand, insisting at the same time that the estate in New Jersey must be divided according to "our law," meaning the law of the State of New Jersey. He reasoned that since the State of New Jersey did not have a will of the late Enrico Caruso on file, the estate should be distributed according to the Orphans' Court Act of 1918. Whereas Italian law gave half the estate to the legitimate heirs, New Jersey law gave two-thirds to the legitimate heirs and one-third to their mother. Chancellor Walker held that above all, "the rights of infants must be protected by the court, while adults must protect their own." Because a relative or guardian could not surrender the rights of an infant, he judged that "the rights of the infant Gloria were not concluded by the Italian decree." In other words, the chancellor asserted that New Jersey law prevailed over Italian law in the matter of the royalties, not on the grounds of legal principles or international law, but because the former favored the infant.

Petitioning a large annual allowance, Dorothy reported an annual income of only $9,000. This was too much even for the learned chancellor. "Mrs. Caruso's income is alleged to be much greater than stated," he said. He dismissed the affidavits to the contrary and awarded her an annual allowance of $12,000 instead of the $30,500 she had requested.

From the transcripts of this hearing, I learned the exact amount Dorothy was so tenaciously fighting to keep: The payments made by the Victor Talking Machine Company to Dorothy P. B. Caruso between 1921 and 15 February 1928 totaled $741,449.20. It was a tidy sum; according to government statistics, the average annual income in 1928 in the United States was $1,384.

Since Traballesi's presence at these hearings would have made little difference, he chose to make the trip from Italy to join Merritt Lane only when they had the court transcripts in hand. I happened to be in Italy at that time on one of my periodic visits to tend to my affairs, so I sailed to New York once more with Traballesi and arrived in mid-April of 1928.

My next sojourn in New York brought a special joy. I somehow found the address of my dear Lei, and on her day off, we had a wonderful reunion in New York City. She had aged, but the gentleness and warmth were still in her blue eyes. She was with the same family, raising their three children. They had moved from Meriden to Morristown, New Jersey, some time before, which was why I was unable to contact her sooner. I told her candidly about my circumstances and what had transpired in the past six years. Inevitably, we returned to the events of my childhood. I reminded her that when I was young and posed questions about my parents, she always said, "We will talk about that when you are older." I was older now, so it was time for her to tell me what she knew.

"My dear Mimmi, please don't ask. I cannot talk about those things."

The loyalty she had shown Father while he was alive had lost none of its intensity. Lei had her inviolable code of ethics, and she would say nothing that might reduce my respect for my parents. Thus Lei, the only eyewitness of the rift that developed between them and eventually led to their separation, refused to say anything about it.

A week or so after we met, she wrote: "I would love to see you again. If you would care to come out here and could let me know a few days in advance I would arrange to have a free day." Surprisingly, she wrote a second letter on the same date, 28 May 1928. Obviously, she wanted to tell me what had come to her mind about Father's intentions regarding his estate.

> Dear Mimmi,
> Just a line to ask how you are and if you have done all you can to make the decision favourable for yourself on June 2nd.
> I don't know if you know that when you were a little boy in London your father spent a lot of time and thought arranging for you and Fofò to inherit his property. And before he married Miss Benjamin she said that she would never wish her child to have anything more than you two boys. Any children she might have should share equally with you. This of course is verbal and at this time would perhaps not have much value but that was the sort of talk that was talked at that time because your father and Mrs. Dorothy said so to me. . . .
> Good luck Mimmi and best wishes. Love from
> "Lei"

THE lawsuit was unfolding very slowly. Chancellor Walker was a deliberate man, and he took his time to formulate his opinions. Traballesi and Lane were preparing for the final round.

In the meantime, I had to find something to do. I was about to return to Real Silk when a Mr. Rush Jermon, representing the I. N. Weber Theatrical Agency, called me at my hotel. He had heard that I was in town, he said, and he wanted to hire me for a vaudeville tour through New England at $500 a week. "Could we have lunch at the Friars' Club to discuss the details?"

I had never thought of going on the stage, but the fee he mentioned had an irresistible appeal, so I agreed to meet him. The outcome of the meeting was a contract to tour in New England with the vaudeville act of Clarita and Lewis called *Echoes of the Past*. My name would serve as a drawing card. They also engaged a young tenor by the name of Vincenzo Ceccarelli. In the final script, I sang a few bars of "Laugh, Clown, Laugh" as an introduction to Ceccarelli's "Ridi Pagliaccio!" Vincenzo was a short, amiable *lucchese,* and we became good friends. He had a nice voice and sang well, although he kept his voice "covered," belying his claim that he had learned to sing from my father's records. We toured for eight weeks, performing in half-empty halls. The fine print of my contract made my salary dependent on box-office receipts, so my weekly pay never rose above $75.

When the tour was over and I returned to New York, the litigation was in its final phase. On 27 November 1928 (the court reports were dated December 4), Chancellor Walker at last stated his conclusions.

> I hold upon this final hearing that the original decree of the Italian court ordering distribution generally of the assets of the estate of Enrico Caruso, deceased, is valid here, save so far as it conflicts with the distribution declared in New Jersey for the benefit of the infant Gloria Caruso, who, under our law, acquires a far better standing than she does under the Italian decree.

He then gave vent to considerable indignation with regard to the 1925 decree of the Naples Tribunal which pledged to give "all of the aid and assistance which Italian Courts can give . . . to making reparations to Enrico Caruso, Jr., and Rodolfo Caruso for what [the court of New Jersey] may take away from them." Chancellor Walker considered this a threat and an affront. "An amendment to the decree of the Italian court is truly astonishing," he said. "It breathes defiance to the Court of Chancery of New Jersey, and declares that it will retaliate and enforce the distribution which it has decreed, out of the estate which it controls," to compensate for any losses in the division of the New Jersey assets. He added that "the Italian court should not presume that this court is in the least degree incompetent to do full and complete justice in cases that are within its jurisdiction, regarding property that is here and subject to our laws. . . . A threat of reprisal will not deter this court one iota in doing its full duty under the law of this state."

He then considered the argument posed by the guardian *ad litem,* that the court of Naples had no jurisdiction to make the decrees it did because Father was not domiciled there but in the Province of Florence, Tuscany. But Chancellor Walker's juristic arrogance had limits too; he added that he "should not assume, directly or indirectly, any appellate jurisdiction over the Italian courts." Finally, mixing Italian and American law, by his final decree of 4 January 1929 he ordered the Victor Company to distribute two-thirds of Father's accumulated royalties to Gloria "and the balance one-third to the other parties named in the Italian decree." This awarded one-twelfth of the total, more than $61,000 each, to Dorothy, Giovanni, Fofò, and me.

Traballesi could not believe the magnitude of the chancellor's incompetence and explained to us the fallacies and contradictions of his arguments. Wasting no time, our legal team filed an appeal. Much later, Traballesi admitted that he had grave apprehensions about the outcome of the appeal. If a practicing chancellor could be such an imbecile, what guarantee had he that the higher court was not populated by representatives of the same breed?

We were to find out, but it took a full year.

CHAPTER TWENTY-FIVE

Appeal and Verdict

O N one of my trips to Italy to renew my visa, I looked up Auntie Rina. During my visit, I asked her if she thought I had enough of a voice to sing.

"Voice? What voice? Don't be silly!" she said after I sang some popular song.

Undaunted, I looked up my father's old friend, Leopoldo Mugnone, the one-time conductor of all my singing relatives, my mother and aunt as well as my father. I considered him a friend by inheritance. He was most cordial, but when I told him the purpose of my visit and asked him to judge whether I had a voice worth training, he looked at me in disbelief. He said in Neapolitan:

" *'Mbè, vuo' cantà?*" ("So, you want to sing?")

He played a few scales, and I squeezed out the notes. I was as aphonic as a wooden board. Pulling on his goatee, he gave me a sad, compassionate look and pronounced his verdict:

"*Fiddu miu, è nu vero peccato che nun tenite mestiere!*" ("My son, it is a real shame that you don't have a trade!")

His opinion did not surprise me, although after my brief taste of the vaudeville stage, I was hoping for some encouragement. Well, if I had no voice, I had no voice; not every Caruso could be a singer. Mugnone was very kind, invited me to stay for dinner, and entertained me with some of his ribald stories. He was well known for his foul mouth, quick wit, and affairs with lesser talents who sought to advance their career by gaining the favor of the conductor. The anecdotes he told from his life were true and mostly revolved around sex. Although he must have repeated his favorite stories hundreds of times, he told them with spontaneity, as if for the first time. I can still recall a fair number of them.

For example, Mugnone was greatly displeased with a woman cellist. The poor lady tried her best, but the Maestro's interruptions only made her playing worse. Finally Mugnone could take it no more and made this memorable comment:

"*Signorina! Lei ha uno strumento fra le gambe; la prego di suonarlo, non grattarlo.*" ("Miss! You have an instrument between your legs; please play it, don't scratch it.")

But Mugnone's caustic wit was not reserved for women. This story was told to me by one of the prominent tenors of the day, Amedeo Bassi.

Rehearsing a *Tosca* somewhere, Mugnone took a dislike to the Cavaradossi. He could not dismiss the tenor because he had been engaged by Ricordi, and this powerful music-publishing firm representing the composer insisted that he sing the role. Mugnone was fuming but powerless. At the general dress rehearsal, he took his revenge. In the third act, as the firing squad passed the prompter's box on its way to execute Cavaradossi, Mugnone commanded loudly in Neapolitan:

"*Ehi, Sargè! Caricate a palla!*" ("Hey, Sergeant! Load live bullets!")

ONCE back in New York, I signed up for a second vaudeville tour that continued until March of 1929. It was during this tour that I suffered a grievous loss. I carried with me Father's last photograph, the one taken on the terrace of the Victoria Hotel in Sorrento, which I kept in a silver frame; it always stood on my makeup table. During a performance in Elizabeth, New Jersey, someone stole it from my dressing room while I was onstage. I was heartbroken, for it was the only photograph my father had ever dedicated to me.

It took the New Jersey Court of Errors and Appeals nearly a year to hand down a decision. On 3 February 1930, eight and a half years after Father's death, the last portion of his estate was settled. Our appeal was reviewed by a chief justice, seven justices, and three judges; with the exception of one dissenting justice, they all agreed with Traballesi.

To put it mildly, they tore Chancellor Walker's legal opinions to shreds. They noted the absurdity of appointing an out-of-state guardian, Dorothy Caruso, over whom the court had no jurisdiction if she should prove derelict in her duties. Moreover, they maintained that the family contract, having received judicial sanction, was a final determination on the distribution of the property.

In their view, "the Victor Talking Machine Company was an unnecessary party to the proceedings"; the Italian decree clearly showed to whom and in what proportion the royalties were to be paid, which made any intervention of the courts of New Jersey unnecessary. Whether the proceeds from Victor were to be considered principal or income was deemed "wholly unimportant."

Because Father's domicile was Italy, and both Naples and Florence were in the Kingdom of Italy, the actual domicile of the deceased was "inconsequential."

They stated that "the prime question" to be decided by the litigation was whether the division of royalties was "to be governed by, and in conformity with, the decree of the Naples Tribunal, under the Italian law, or to be distributed under the statute of distribution of this state," that is, New Jersey.

Chastising the "learned Chancellor," they stated that "it is difficult to perceive upon what sound legal theory the Court of Chancery was authorized to reform the decree of the Italian court and make a decree which increases the amount that Gloria is to receive" and thereby diminishes the share of the other parties. To disregard the judgments of foreign courts on the grounds of protecting the interest of infants was "a palpable fallacy. . . . The mere circumstance of the infancy of Gloria cannot properly have a legal effect [on] the legal acts of individuals whether they be adults or minors." In their view, "the interposition of an administratrix was wholly unnecessary" to deal with the distribution of the royalties.

The Court of Errors and Appeals summed up its conclusions in one concise, unequivocal statement: "The decree of the Naples Tribunal pointed the way and it should have been followed." The decision brought about five main changes:

1. The reversal of the decree of the Naples Tribunal by the New Jersey Court of Chancery was reversed.
2. The administratrix was to account for all moneys received

from the Victor Company and distribute it as determined by the Naples Tribunal, which was "upheld by this court."

3. The order of 24 January 1928 appointing Dorothy P. B. Caruso as Gloria's special guardian was reversed.

4. The decree of 10 April 1928 fixing allowances to the special guardian was reversed and her petition dismissed.

5. The final decree of 4 January 1929 was reversed, and "the bill dismissed."

In short, Vincenzo Traballesi, with the help of Merritt Lane and his firm, won the case for the Italian Carusos. I was finally to receive that portion of my inheritance that could have saved the rest, all of which, because Dorothy had successfully blocked the distribution of royalties for seven long years, was now irretrievably lost.

THE courts notified the Union Trust & Hudson National Bank and the Victor Talking Machine Company to pay out the accumulated royalties according to the provisions of the San Severino agreement. Giovanni, Fofò, and I would each receive an eighth of the royalties, which had continued to accumulate.

Upon hearing of the impending settlement, Fofò, Giovanni, and Traballesi came to New York. If I remember correctly, Fofò and Traballesi arrived together, and Giovanni came alone in early March.

We were jubilant. In addition to the stipulated fees, Fofò and I wanted to show our appreciation to Traballesi for his efforts and ingenuity. Because he was crazy about American cars, we decided to buy him a top-of-the-line Chrysler. Since I was no longer on speaking terms with Giovanni, Fofò went to obtain his consent.

Giovanni agreed to contribute his share, and the Chrysler Imperial was duly purchased. We had a brass plaque installed on the dashboard reading "*A Vincenzo Traballesi, in ricca riconoscenza, gli eredi Caruso.*" ("To Vincenzo Traballesi, with deep gratitude, the Caruso heirs.") Traballesi was wild about the car and appreciated the gesture, but not the plaque.

"You don't think I will drive my girlfriends around with that thing on it! They will think I can't afford a car like this on my own."

So he had the plaque removed but kept it in the glove compartment.

Traballesi's concern about girlfriends was not posturing, for he was a ladies' man whose conquests were proverbial. He came from a wealthy family, was well educated, and had a fine law practice and a large income. Moreover, he was handsome, most charming, always impeccably dressed, and by 1930 fairly fluent in his accented street English. As I have mentioned, he had an aura of distinction, and his monocle and elegant cane gave him an aristocratic appearance. For some reason, women found these "props" irresistible, but he carried both for a good reason. His right eye and right knee had been injured at the front in the last months of the war. Lying on a stretcher, already wounded and waiting to be carried behind the lines, he was hit by thirty-six shrapnel fragments in an enemy raid on the banks of the Isonzo River. One of the steel shards hurt his eye, and another remained permanently lodged in his right knee. When he recovered, he was decorated for heroism.

At the conclusion of our settlement, he returned to Italy, taking his Chrysler with him. Upon his arrival, he sent me a cable: "*Ben arrivato, viaggio fantastico.*" I found out later why the trip had been so fantastic. Aboard ship, he met a tall, beautiful blonde, Sylvia C., from Dallas, who was on her way to Gibraltar to marry the attaché to the U.S. Consulate there. Her fiancé was also on board. Halfway to Europe, he lost his bride-to-be to Traballesi. When the ship docked at Gibraltar, the attaché disembarked alone, and Vincenzo sailed on with his latest conquest. The couple stayed together in Italy for many months.

As if this weren't fortune enough, Traballesi, while in New York, had bought a $3.00 ticket for the Irish sweepstakes. Fofò told me later that Vincenzo won first prize, which came to $240,000, tax-free. What a year it was for Traballesi!

Everything he touched turned to gold. True, he was a bright man, but "smarts" had nothing to do with winning the Irish sweepstakes. Apparently, my friend Vincenzo was born under a lucky star, and his luck never left him, in love or war.

During the years of litigation, jealous colleagues of the Florentine Forum often sniped behind his back, saying that he was taking the Carusos for a ride, that he knew he could never win the case and was only using the litigation to promote himself. When he returned to Italy victorious, Traballesi challenged his detractors to a duel. He was an excellent swordsman and won four duels out of four—not bad for a man with a stiff right knee!

God gave Vincenzo a long life. He was eighty-seven when I last called him in Florence from Florida. His voice, still strong and clear, recalled the Traballesi of my youth.

WE had paid high inheritance taxes in the United States and in Italy, and tax rates had risen considerably during the years of litigation. According to published sources, the estate owed over half a million dollars in taxes on the royalties because the Internal Revenue Service tried one of its inimitable dirty tricks: It attempted to collect taxes on the lump sum. This would have netted the government more than taxing the individual shares, especially since non-resident aliens were involved. We had to hire more lawyers to shuttle back and forth to Washington until that kink was straightened out.

When the case was settled, a net $800,000 remained to be divided among the heirs. Fofò, Giovanni, Dorothy, and I received $100,000, and Gloria $400,000. I paid Traballesi his 20 percent fee and $18,000 in expenses, including the funds he had advanced over the years. This left me, after ten years of waiting and litigation, with $62,000. What Dorothy's legal expenses were I don't know, but they had to be substantial. The several teams of lawyers working for all parties in tandem in New York and New Jersey had a field day with us. The combined legal fees from the time of Father's death until the ultimate settlement of his estate reached a high six-digit figure. If Dorothy had honored the San Severino agreement in the first place, we could have saved about a quarter of a million dollars in combined legal fees and other expenses.

ELENA, for her part, did not trust me with money in my pocket. To make sure that she would collect what she considered her due, she arrived in New York in the company of a young man about my age whom she introduced as her "counselor."

My bitter experiences of the 1920s put many things in new perspective and awakened some sense of responsibility. I was painfully aware of the small fortune that had passed through my fingers without a trace, although not entirely through my fault. I felt guilty for having mismanaged what I had inherited from my father, and I did not want to jeopardize what my sons could one day inherit from me. Mindful of my duties as a father, on 2 May 1930 I created a trust containing $20,000 (595,000 lire) for each of my sons, confirmed by a legal document in the New York office of an Italian lawyer, Frank Colavolpe. Elena was named the administratrix of the trust. At first the income was assigned to me, but eventually, on 15 November 1934, I relinquished all proceeds from the trust to Elena.

Although I had spent most of the past three and a half years in New

York, returning to Italy only periodically to renew my visa, Elena and I had not separated officially. We were still on friendly terms, and now that the case was settled, it seemed we might make a new start. I suggested to Elena that she bring the children to America. With the royalty money as a nest egg, we could settle down in New York, I would get a job, and we could see that the children got a good education. At the least, they could be spared the problems of the fascist regime or the next Italian war.

"Oh, no!" exclaimed Elena. "I want my children to have an Italian education! And do you think I would leave Mamma, Natalia, and my brothers?"

I was disappointed. America was a land of freedom and opportunity, and I was sure we could have made a good life here. But I wanted to try once more to save our marriage, if only for the children's sake. In late September 1930, I followed Elena back to Italy. We tried, but it was apparent to us both that we had grown too far apart. We agreed that the best thing for us was to separate and restore each other to freedom. The separation was amicable but final.

Before leaving, I counseled Elena to buy a producing farm, or to try to buy back Cercina. In that way she would always have a roof over her head, food to eat, and a modest income. My last futile efforts to make Cercina work out for us had left a bad taste, and instead she bought two small apartment buildings in Florence and a villa in Viareggio for the summer months. She lived in one of the Florentine apartments with our sons, and the rentals produced a decent income. She was a thrifty woman, a good manager of her resources, and a good mother who shouldered the responsibilities of single parenthood and coped well with the added burden of a handicapped child. I am sorry I was not there to help her; the difference in our personalities, the political polarization of Italy, and my ongoing financial problems kept my children and me apart. I recognize my loss and am filled with deep regret.

Then World War II came, and with it many additional hardships for Elena. Rents were frozen, and the cost of living skyrocketed, as did taxes. Unable to maintain the buildings in good repair, Elena sold her properties one by one at greatly depressed prices. As I understand, her brothers, who had benefited from my youthful refusal to accept her dowry, came to her rescue. Occasionally, when a royalty check left me temporarily flush, I sent her money, but during the war even that was impossible. Our deaf and mute son, Wladimiro, became a ward of the state, which helped with the expenses of his education.

Although Elena formed no permanent liaison with another companion, I am confident I was not the last man in her life. After the war she moved to Rome, where she died on 19 June 1975, at the age of seventy-seven.

CHAPTER TWENTY-SIX

Voice? What Voice?

THERE is a reference to my singing in one of Father's letters, but I can't even guess what prompted his comment. In 1919 he wrote to Dorothy: "Mimmi with a voice? I dont think."[1] In the following year, I was asked to join the Culver Glee Club. Because it involved singing, I asked for Father's permission when I went to New York for Christmas.

"What is a Glee Club?" he asked. I explained.

"Do you think you can sing better than me?"

"No, Papa."

"Then forget it. If you can't sing better than I can, don't sing. Besides, one singing Caruso is enough."

Papa's response led me to drop the whole idea. With this simple, pointed remark, he drove any thought of voice training or a vocal career from my mind. The one occupation I never contemplated pursuing was singing.

With hindsight, one can say that he was right. Because I could not expect to sing better than he could, I should never have tried. Yet hindsight might also suggest that had he given me encouragement and guidance, I could have taken my first steps in such a direction seven or eight years earlier than I eventually did and perhaps made a better

458

showing in the end.

Another thought that disturbs me at times is that perhaps Fofò had a voice too. Father never asked either of us to sing, yet with two such parents and a prima donna aunt to boot, we theoretically had a better than average chance of having some vocal endowments. I believe that Gloria had a fine voice. In the late thirties, I once heard her interviewed on the air during a Met broadcast intermission and was struck by the charm of her speaking voice, its warmth and rich texture. Recently, a recording that Gloria made when she was only ten years old surfaced on a specialist label.[2] It shows that my sister had a nice little voice at that tender age. She did study singing with Maestro Fernando Tanara, in Venice. Why her training never led to an active career I do not know.

I can trace the beginning of my own singing career to a single incident. On one of my return trips from Italy in the late 1920s, the newspapers picked up the story that Caruso's son had come to collect his inheritance. I was asked to do a Movietone newsreel, and because the producers also knew about my vaudeville stint, they asked me to sing.

"But I don't sing," I protested. "I can't sing."

They insisted that a son of Caruso, bearer of his name, must be able to sing. It was the Culver predicament all over again. "All right," I finally said. "Get me an accompanist." This they did, and I sang some Italian song—"Santa Lucia," I believe—with a good deal of verve and a good deal less voice. Once they had their film, they were happy, and I went on my way.

I WAS at a major crossroads. Once more I had some cash to plan my future, and I had to decide what to do next. Almost on impulse, I bought a Model A Ford and drove to California. Helene Packheiser, whose parents took me in as a boarder in 1929, joined me, and we had a wonderful trip. Helene was a very attractive woman, with strong yet feminine features, high-spirited, and a delightful companion.

When I registered at the Hollywood Plaza Hotel in Los Angeles, I was besieged by reporters. Their first question was: "Mr. Caruso, are you planning on a movie career?" I said I was not in the least interested in the movies. I was on a vacation.

When the interviews were published, I received a surprise call from Vincenzo Ceccarelli. He was teaching singing and performing in opera. In fact, he was singing the Duke in *Rigoletto* the following night and invited me to attend. He left a complimentary ticket for me at the box office.

The performance went very nicely, and Ceccarelli sang well. During intermission, I went out to the lobby. As I stood there, all of a sudden an arm went around my shoulder, and a deep, resonant, musical voice exclaimed:

"Mimmi! What are you doing here?"

Surprised at hearing my childhood name, I turned and came face to face with Count Andrès Perello de Segurola, better known to his friends as "Seggy." He was Father's dear old friend and had known me since childhood. He embraced me and insisted that I have supper with him after *Rigoletto*.

"Now *you* tell me," I reciprocated the question, "what are you doing here?"

"You haven't heard? I am in motion pictures. I just finished *General Crack* [1929] and *Song O' My Heart* [1930]. I am too old for the opera routine, and I must say I really enjoy working in pictures. But let's talk about you. I hear you sing."

"I don't sing."

"I read you were in vaudeville, and I heard you sing in a Movietone newsreel."

"You call that singing?"

"Maybe not, but you have a voice. A good teacher could help you become a singer. I will take you to my singing teacher."

"Singing teacher!" I was surprised. "Why should *you* need a singing teacher? You have been singing for more years than I have been alive!"

De Segurola explained that he had lost his voice, and this teacher had helped him to regain it. He then returned to the idea that I ought to sing, too. I protested, telling him about the expert opinions of Auntie Rina and Maestro Mugnone. De Segurola refused to listen. I came from a singing family, he said. Both my parents had voices, ergo I must be able to sing. I let him take me the following day to meet Señor Don Adolfo de la Huerta.

Don Adolfo was fifty years old in 1931 and had a most unusual background for a singing teacher. Born in Guaymas, Sonora, Mexico, he went into politics at an early age and was elected governor of Sonora in 1919. He became involved in a dispute over states' rights and the presidential succession, and when he and his fellow Sonorans, Alvaro Obregón and Plutarco Calles, rebelled against President Venustiano Carranza in 1920, the Sonorans triumphed. De la Huerta served as provisional president of Mexico from June through November 1920, and as Obregón's finance minister for three years thereafter. In 1923 he broke with Obregón, who supported Calles' presidential candidacy.

After the failure of an armed rebellion, Adolfo de la Huerta was forced to flee. He may have been finance minister, but he was an honest man. When he fled, he left penniless. He settled in Los Angeles in 1924, and to support himself and his family, he gave singing lessons.

De Segurola introduced us and explained in Spanish who I was and why he had brought me. Without much ado, Maestro De la Huerta gave me an audition. Señora Clarita de la Huerta played the piano, and I sang. Don Adolfo listened attentively. When he had heard enough, he said:

"How would you like to have a million dollars?"

"I would like that very much," I said, letting him make his point.

"Well, I cannot give it to you in cash. But I can give you the means to make a million dollars, or even more. I will teach you to sing."

I protested that I was almost twenty-seven, too old to begin voice training. And besides, I had it on good authority that I had no singing voice at all.

"*No se preocupe,*" he said. ("Not to worry.") "*Soy carpintero de la voz. Se la voy a hacer.*" ("I am a carpenter of the voice. I will make you one.")

He said he was willing to take me on as a pupil if I agreed to follow his instructions and work with him daily.

I went home slightly dazed by this development. After considerable thought, I decided that all I had to lose in the process was the tuition, so I plunged ahead. I never thought that Don Adolfo was interested in my money, and my intuition was proven right. Even though he was happy to have me among his pupils and publicly acknowledged the fact, he never advertised himself as the voice teacher of Enrico Caruso's son. As a matter of fact, when after my fashion I returned to a state of insolvency a couple of years later, Don Adolfo insisted on teaching me "on the cuff."

During this period, one of my more memorable fiscal fiascos was promoting "dollar opera"—every seat was a dollar—at the Greek Theater in Los Angeles. I invested $2,000 in this venture shortly after I arrived in California. The troupe sang *Rigoletto* and *Lucia* to half-empty houses, and I lost most of my investment in record time.

I BEGAN to work with Don Adolfo every day on special exercises which, initially, seemed to have little to do with singing. They were designed to get the singing equipment into shape, open up the throat, develop the diaphragm, get the tongue and the larynx into the correct position. They produced no singing at all, just noises. The other students said among themselves:

"The Maestro has gone mad. Why is he wasting his time with this Caruso? He has no voice at all! He will *never* sing."

I too became discouraged. Was this dream really worth the effort?

"Enrique, just stick to it for a couple of years," Don Adolfo said. "Then you will see the results."

A couple of years was a long time, but I decided to stick with it. It wasn't easy. My tempo was bad, but I had excellent relative pitch and good intonation; I never sang off-key. In fact, I must have had a fair amount of inborn musicality. In spite of seven years of so-called piano studies, I barely read music; yet eventually I was able to learn my repertory of two hundred or so songs and arias, in addition to the roles of Edgardo and Turiddu, essentially by ear. I was in good company; in those days my kind of musical ignorance was still common among opera singers, including the legendary greats.

Occasionally a reporter would call for an interview, and the resulting articles would bring letters from people with whom I had lost contact. In the fall of 1933, I received a letter from Miss Saer at Don Adolfo's address. It was a joy to hear from her. "I often think of you and wonder and hope that you are well, happy and prosperous," she wrote. "I wish for nothing but to hear of your welfare. Do you like California and what you are doing there? I was glad to hear you are studying music. It seems natural. Both your father and mother were so gifted in it." Lei's letters were always in character, full of good advice and caring. "Guard your health. It is the greatest asset you have. Excuse me giving you advice. Remember you were my little boy." And then the salutation: "With much love, yours as always, Lei."

A Christmas card was the last piece of mail I received from her. It read: "With love and every good wish for Xmas and always, from Louise Saer, 'Lei.' " It is my understanding that she died early in 1935. I never knew or even thought about her age; for me she was only "Lei," the fixed point in my disjointed universe, and she was permanent and ageless. I realized only in my adult years that she was the one person whose affection for me I never questioned, because it enveloped me throughout childhood and adolescence like a soft, warm blanket. I bless her memory and carry with me a deep gratitude.

DON ADOLFO labored mightily on my voice, and I followed his instructions faithfully. Miraculously, within a year I was singing, in the second year tolerably well, and into the third year I was singing well enough to consider launching a career.

One day while practicing my growing repertory in the studio, Manuel Reachi, the man in charge of the Spanish department at Warner Brothers' First National Studios, called on Señor de la Huerta. The department made "B" pictures, films of secondary interest to the company. Reachi was planning to produce a picture about General Obregón, and Don Adolfo, thanks to his personal association with the Mexican soldier and statesman, was a primary source of information.

I was singing "Spirto gentil" from *La Favorita* to Señora Clarita's accompaniment when Reachi called. The Maestro excused himself to join his visitor in the adjoining room, and I went on singing. Instead of attending to the matter at hand, Reachi asked who was singing that difficult aria. As the conversation was repeated to me later, Don Adolfo replied:

"One of my pupils, a most interesting case. The boy came here completely aphonic about two years ago."

"That is hard to believe!"

"That is the truth. Would you like to hear more?"

"With pleasure!"

Don Adolfo led Reachi into the practice room. Without any introduction, he asked me to sing another selection, whereupon I sang several arias. Unaware that Reachi had heard it the first time around, I concluded the impromptu concert with "Spirto gentil." Reachi's words still ring in my ears:

"*Este debe ser oido de rodillas!*" ("One should listen to this on one's knees!")

At that point I was introduced.

"*Es increible!*" Reachi's eyes lit up. He immediately saw the commercial possibilities of my name and voice. The General Obregón project was abandoned as he decided on the spot to make a film with me, build it around my voice, and sell it on the strength of my name.

"In English?" I asked.

"Of course not. In Spanish."

"But I don't know any Spanish," I objected.

"You speak Italian, don't you?"

"Why, certainly."

"So? Spanish, Italian—what's the difference?"

Reachi was as good as his word. He managed to sell Jack Warner on the idea of starring me in a picture, and in a matter of days, he presented me with a contract. Following Don Adolfo's advice, I signed it. The terms were not particularly generous; but it was a start, and I needed the money, as I was living on the small and ever-decreasing Victor royalties. I was to receive $1,250 for the first picture. If the company chose to pick up my option within six months after the first film was finished, I would be paid $2,500 for the second film, then double that amount for the third, and so on until I completed five movies. It was not the million dollars my Maestro had promised, but it was certainly a step in the right direction. For the fifth picture, I would earn the princely sum of $20,000.

The first film, *La Buenaventura*, was loosely based on Victor Herbert's *The Fortune Teller*. I played the role of a famous opera singer, and the score included mostly popular operatic selections and very little of Herbert's music. I overcame the language barrier with greater ease than expected, learning the Spanish text rapidly thanks to a language coach named Señor A. A. Cuyas as well as some coaching from Don Adolfo. Other members of the cast helped as well, among them a fellow student from Don Adolfo's studio, Alfonso Pedroza. A giant of a man with a huge, booming bass voice, he played the gypsy chief in the film. The filming took only a few weeks.

The fringe benefit of working in a major film studio was being surrounded by famous stars. I made the acquaintance of Edward G. Robinson, William Powell, Dick Powell, Dolores del Rio, Paul Lukas, Ginger Rogers, Guy Kibbee, Joe E. Brown, and the Mexican opera and film star José Mojica, and I often met Tito Schipa, who used to come by to visit his friends.

During my years of study, I often visited De Segurola at his home, and we became close friends. He loved Italian food, so I spent many afternoons cooking Italian pasta dishes for him. After dinner we would chat about his work, my aspirations, and the good old times. We would invariably end up talking about Papa. Seggy had boundless admiration for him, both as an artist and as a man, and had nothing but praise for his kindness, his generosity, and his bubbling good spirit.

Armed with a fine voice, good looks, a noble title, an exotic monocle, and disarming charm, Seggy was the epitome of the cosmopolitan gentleman. His excellent command of several languages made him feel at home in most countries of the Western world. Acting in films was a logical conclusion to a distinguished lyric stage career. To remain active in his primary field of music, he taught singing, and at least one of his pupils achieved celebrity, the well-known Deanna Durbin. Helene Packheiser, my charming companion since the move to California, was a fairly good pianist and often played for his students. Now, following Seggy's suggestion, she began to use

FILMARTE THEATRE

Presents

"*La Buenaventura*"

(The Fortune Teller)

First Spanish Version of Victor Herbert's Famous Operetta, Starring

ENRICO CARUSO, Jr.

SPECIAL PREMIERE, FRIDAY EVENING,
May 18th, at 8:30 O'Clock

* Stars * Stage Presentation *

ANDREAS DE SIGUROLA
Master of Ceremonies

Regular Performances After Opening Date

Daily 7 and 9	Sundays 3 to 11
Sat. Mat. 2:30	CR. 6171 HE. 4387

RESERVATIONS FOR PREMIERE NOW
All Seats Reserved $1.00 and $1.25 Tax Included
Box Office Open from 1 to 9.   HE. 4387

Announcement of the première of the first Spanish-speaking motion picture made by Enrico Caruso, Jr., *La Buenaventura* (*The Fortune Teller*), 18 May 1934.

the euphonious name Yvonne de Costa. She liked it so much that she began to call herself Yvonne, a name she retained permanently. In addition to accompanying students, she typed Seggy's memoirs, which he entitled *Through My Monocle*. Because my friend had an interesting life and sang in the so-called golden age at the Metropolitan, he certainly had a story to tell. Although the memoirs remain unpublished, the manuscript exists.

After finishing *La Buenaventura*, I had to travel to Europe to renew my visa. Upon my return, I obtained a Mexican divorce from Elena. Then Yvonne and I, who were by this time very much in love, traveled to Phoenix, Arizona, and were married on 12 March 1934. Her mother came all the way from Middletown, New York, to attend our wedding. To help me obtain permanent resident status, Mrs. Packheiser signed an affidavit of support on 27 April 1934. Now I had an American wife and an American film career; I wanted to settle in the United States permanently.

La Buenaventura opened at the Filmarte Theatre in Hollywood on 18 May 1934. Warner Brothers made it a special occasion, and the master of ceremonies, appropriately, was Count Andrès Perello de Segurola. He was greatly pleased with himself for having been the catalyst in launching my career, and I gratefully acknowledged his role.

La Buenaventura had its official première on 25 May 1934. It was well received; *The New York Times,* among other newspapers, carried a favorable review.[3] Yet hardly any critic failed to mention that I sang well but was not equal to my famous father. This observation required no more than a pair of good ears, and I was reminded of Seggy's response when I once made the same complaint to him: "Nobody could sing as well as he could. Does that mean that nobody should ever sing at all?"

Before the film was released, I was interviewed on 29 April 1934 on a Spanish-language radio station, and again on 15 May 1934 by George Fisher on the Los Angeles radio station KFWB. I sang "Questa o quella" both times; the ancient transcription discs of the interviews show that my voice was in good shape.

Roberto Guzman Esparza, private secretary to Don Adolfo and a fellow voice student, agreed. Years later, in the 31 December 1950 issue of *Impacto,* he recounted how on a bet Don Adolfo, in ten lessons, gave a singing voice to a previously hoarse Patterson Greene, music critic of the Los Angeles *Examiner*. The unbelieving Greene continued studying with him and in a year sang a difficult baritone aria in a public concert. Guzman Esparza went on to say:

> What he did with Enrico Caruso, Jr., was similar but even more difficult. The young man . . . after very arduous work got to singing in such a way that listening to records he made and comparing them with some selections performed on disc by his immortal father, Enrico Caruso, Sr., one hesitates to choose which is the better voice.
>
> The obvious mastery, technique, temperament, and the father's long experience tell decisively over the son's lack of those qualities, but the latter's voice, its timbre, its even greater power than that of his late father, his greater ease on the high notes, almost totally compensate for the qualities that he did not possess.

The film must have done well at the box office, because when the six months rolled by, Warner Brothers decided to pick up my option. Not long afterwards, I again faced the cameras. This time I played an Italian street urchin turned opera singer in a romanticized story supposedly based on my father's early life. The title was *El Cantante de Napoles* (*The Singer of Naples*). The plot was built around situations that gave the principal character opportunities to sing, and sing I did: "Una furtiva lagrima" from *L'Elisir d'amore*, "Com'è gentil" from *Don Pasquale*, "O Paradiso" from *L'Africana*, "M'apparì" from *Martha*, and "Di quella pira" from *Il Trovatore* in the original key with the high C's. I also sang several Neapolitan songs and a lively tarantella written especially for me by the music director, Maestro Alberto Conti.

The second film was at least as successful as the first. *The New York Times* praised my singing and singled out the "Di quella pira."[4] I was pleased, for if this film too was well received, then the good reviews of the first were not merely a fluke. I had finally found a direction for my life. The difficult years began to recede in memory, and I even began to think it was possible that I would bring further glory to the famous name I bore.

AFTER *El Cantante de Napoles* opened, I had a wait of another six months before Warner Brothers decided my cinematic future. Don Adolfo had accepted an invitation from the new Mexican government to visit his homeland, so I could not continue my voice lessons. Since I could not afford to sit idle, I found an agent who booked me, along with my accompanist, Edith Pengilley, for a concert tour up the California coast into Oregon. The towns where we appeared were small and the halls modest, but the audiences received us enthusiastically. It was good experience and I enjoyed it, except for the terrific stage fright I seem to have inherited from Father. He suffered because he had a reputation to maintain, and I, because I had one to build.

Apart from my brief stint in vaudeville, I had no stage experience, and I had no concert experience at all, even as a spectator. My exposure to opera was limited mostly to Father's performances. Thus I had only vague ideas of what was expected of me; and I was sufficiently aware of my limitations to feel extremely insecure. Fortunately, my audiences on this tour were made up of simple people who did not come to my concerts expecting me to sound just like my father and who could accept me on my own merits. With each recital, I gained confidence, and my delivery improved.

I returned to Los Angeles eager to tackle the next assignment. But I went to the Warner Brothers studios only to learn that the Spanish department had been closed. Hal Wallis, the man reporting to Jack Warner, explained that the market for Spanish-language films had not yielded enough revenue to sustain the department. He was sorry, but he had nothing else for me. They had Dick Powell for English-language musicals, and as I was not a known quantity, an accomplished actor with a big following, my days at the studio had come to an end.

Once more I found myself without an income. I tried the other studios but was unable to land a contract. Although I worked as an extra in several movies, I never had another leading role in a film. The lost dream of a movie career was only endurable because Yvonne and I were still together, and we nurtured high expectations for my singing career.

CHAPTER TWENTY-SEVEN

Caruso Is Not Caruso

W HEN Don Adolfo returned from Mexico, I resumed my studies with redoubled efforts, but I was no longer able to pay for them. He continued to work with me out of friendship, kindness, and unshakable faith in my eventual success. "Don't worry, Enrico," he would tell me. "Something will turn up."

Sure enough, one day I received a telegram from Havana. A certain promoter had seen my films and wanted to book me for a tour of the island; he was offering $1,000 for a month's performances in Havana, Camaguey, Holguin, Bayamo, Ciego de Avila, Matanzas, Santiago de Cuba, and Guantanamo. It sounded exciting, but when I told Don Adolfo about the offer, his immediate response was: "Don't go."

He reasoned that I would be away from him too long. If something happened to my voice, I was likely to ruin it. "You may catch a cold, you may lose the emission, and I won't be there to put it back on track," Don Adolfo said.

Convinced that I was doing the right thing and lured by the promised fee, I sailed for Cuba on 6 April 1935 with Yvonne and my accompanist, Edith Pengilley. Fate meant to make a prophet out of

469

Don Adolfo: On the trip from New Orleans I became seasick, then I developed a bad case of laryngitis. Under such conditions it is possible to sing only if one is properly trained and the vocal cords are not affected.

I felt obliged to give all I had, so in spite of my affliction, the tour got off to a promising start. I made my debut at the Teatro Campoamor in Havana on April 11 and had a respectable success. Inevitably, after the concert, every well-wisher told me worshipful stories about my father, recalling this or that occasion when they had heard him. I could sense their disappointment, implied rather than expressed, that I was not a singer of the same caliber as he. The critics plainly, if politely, observed that "Caruso is not Caruso." In the end, I began to wonder whether the applause after each concert, which sounded genuine enough, was a response to my singing or a tribute to my name.

Although I recovered from the laryngitis, I was not at my best through the entire trip. All the same, I finished the tour without a single cancellation, and my stay in Cuba left me with pleasant impressions. The outgoing warmth of the Cuban audiences put me at ease, and I still have fond memories of the halls where I sang. Each little community boasted a miniature opera house built of wood in the Spanish style. These were little jewels with superb acoustics, and it was a pleasure to perform in them for such friendly and expressive people.

At the end of the tour, I was paid in silver dollars. The thousand coins were an impossible hoard to haul around, so I converted them into paper money at the first opportunity. In addition to the uplifting feeling of being once more loaded with cash, I had a pleasant surprise upon my return to Havana. I received a telegram from a Mr. Liebeskind of FIRNATEX, the First National Export branch of Warner Brothers in Rio de Janeiro, offering me a five-week tour in Rio and São Paulo at $500 per week!

During the Cuban tour, a new government in Mexico had asked Don Adolfo to return to take up a post, and he had accepted. With my teacher gone and no further prospects in the movie industry, I saw no reason to return to Los Angeles in pursuit of a career.

More than that, a South American engagement would have enabled me to look for my mother in person. Nearly a decade had passed since our last contact, for when I left Culver, our correspondence stopped as abruptly as it had begun. Yet it was important to me, as I grew older, to find her again. In the past year, I had sent a long letter to her address in Buenos Aires, but it was returned marked

"Addressee moved, forwarding address unknown." I had also engaged the Italian consulate in Los Angeles in an effort to locate her, but I knew that such a search could be tedious and uncertain. The proposed trip to Brazil was a wonderful opportunity, altogether too good to be true.

I wired back my acceptance on the condition that two weeks' salary be deposited in advance at a bank in New York and round-trip boat tickets issued for two. By return cable, Liebeskind agreed to my terms. However, since Brazilian government regulations did not allow the export of currency, I was to present his telegram at Warner's New York office, and the necessary arrangements would be made there. I exchanged the Havana–New Orleans–Los Angeles tickets for passage for two to New York. Yvonne and I sailed to the north, while Edith remained in Cuba to study with Ernesto Lecuona.

In New York, I presented my telegram at the Warner's office. I was sent from department to department, but no one knew anything about Mr. Liebeskind or his plans for the Brazilian tour. They were unwilling to advance me the money, so I was stranded in New York.

AS fate would have it, I heard on the musical grapevine that Alberti de Gorostiaga was in New York. The name rang a bell. Once, in Los Angeles, Don Adolfo had commented that he knew of only one other teacher who used his method. I remembered his very words:

"Enrique, if I should die tomorrow, you must do one thing: Go to Paris to study with Alberti de Gorostiaga. He is the creator of Lily Pons's voice."

It seems that Gorostiaga's star pupil, Lily Pons, had developed severe vocal problems due to overwork; she was singing off-key, and her voice had developed a wobble. Upon the recommendation of her future husband, André Kostelanetz, she had asked Gorostiaga to come to New York to get her voice back into shape. The Maestro coached her for almost a year, even traveling with her to California when she made her first movie, *I Dream Too Much*. In New York he stayed at the Ansonia Hotel at Broadway and Seventy-third Street, along with everyone else connected with the singing business. I telephoned him, and when he heard my name, he wanted to see me immediately. He was a pleasant gentleman, a high-strung Basque, and he gave me a warm welcome. When I told him about my predicament, he sat down at the piano and with no further ado gave me an audition. He listened attentively. Then he said:

"The way you use your voice shows that your Maestro knows what he is doing. But the laryngitis you had apparently affected the voice. You need a good rest and a lot of work yet."

"What do you suggest I do?"

"I am soon going back to Paris. You could come with me, and I will put your voice back on track."

"I would love to, Maestro, but I can't afford it. I couldn't even buy a one-way ticket."

"You need not worry about that. You will live in my house as my guest, and we will work together every day. You have a wonderful instrument, very much like your father's. I would gladly teach you at no charge. I always had the greatest admiration for your father. The least I could do to serve his memory is help you to have a voice worthy of his name."

It was a generous offer, somehow too generous. My pride would not allow me to accept it. I asked for time to think it over, told myself I did not want to leave Yvonne behind for an indefinite time, and never followed up on it.

Gorostiaga went back to France, and I missed an exceptional opportunity.

THUS began a particularly aimless period of my life. Jobs were scarce, I couldn't find work, and I felt that my prospects for the future were dim. I became irritable and impossible to live with, which had the worst possible effects on my marriage. In October 1935, I returned briefly to my old employer, Real Silk Hosiery Mills. Then in April 1936, I decided to try teaching Don Adolfo's singing method. Yvonne and I rented a suite in the Ansonia Hotel, and I hung out a shingle: "Voice Teacher." One of my students served as my accompanist in return for voice lessons.

I soon had a handful of students. After three years of intensive study with De la Huerta, I found I was able to help every one of them. I intended to go on teaching, but after half a year, I had to realize that the venture was leading nowhere. The number of my pupils didn't grow, and I was barely able to cover expenses. To keep food on the table, Yvonne took a secretarial job at the Warner Brothers office. By this time, we had been together for almost seven years and married for two. But since our return to New York, under the pressures of never knowing where next month's rent was coming from, our relationship had gradually deteriorated. Now there was little to hold us together.

On the bright side, living and teaching at the Ansonia gave me a reassuring sense of participating in the musical life of the city. Traditionally, most of the resident guests of the Ansonia belonged to the singing profession. The old hotel had thick walls, double doors, and small antechambers to the rooms that constituted excellent sound-proofing. The hotel went to great lengths to accommodate its guests, especially the luminaries of the music world.

A case in point was the world-famous Wagnerian tenor Lauritz Melchior. The great Dane was devoted to big-game hunting, a sport he was unable to pursue during his long New York stays. While the Met held him captive in the city, he took up target-shooting instead. Undaunted by the restrictions of his surroundings, he devised his own shooting gallery right in the hotel. Somehow or other, he obtained a piece of elbow pipe from a large water main. This he had mounted on a crate filled with sand and sealed with a target card. He then positioned it at the end of one of the long corridors and would shoot at it from the other end, apparently never missing the target. The tenants on the floor were always notified in advance, and his valet stood at the elevator with a red flag to warn anyone coming on the floor that the firing range was open.

In January 1937, I was asked to participate in a revue entitled "Broadway Juniors" which featured the sons and daughters of famous stage personalities. Among the juniors were Eddie Foy, Frank Tinney, Eddie Leonard, Joe Cook, and Joe Dorris; Ruth Howard, June Carroll, and Lois Lait also appeared. The show opened in the Hippodrome Theater in Baltimore on January 29 and also played in Detroit and Philadelphia. The revue appearance was fun and produced a bit of income, but it too led nowhere.

After a good deal of soul-searching, I decided that the best alternative left to me was to return to Italy, alone. I contacted the Italian embassy and, through their consular repatriation program, was given a one-way ticket. In April, I sailed for Genoa on the *Conte di Savoia*.

On 1 May 1937, I arrived in Italy. I telephoned Elena; she was out, and my son Enrico answered the phone. I said that I was a friend of his father's, and that I was going to call on them when I reached Florence. He delivered the message to his mother but added, "I know that was Papa!" When I arrived and rang the doorbell, Elena opened the door and greeted me with a robust "*Ah, sei tu, farabutto!*" ("So, it's you, scoundrel!") In spite of this reception, we remained on friendly terms while I was in Florence. I was delighted to see my growing boys, and we had some wonderful times together. I also hoped to see my brother again, but I learned that he had just left for Abyssinia.

Contrary to my expectations, the situation in Italy took a turn for the worse. The *fascisti* ran the country with an iron hand. Without funds, connections, or party membership, I was unable to find employment. The country was on a dangerous path toward economic and political self-destruction, and job opportunities simply did not exist for a repatriate. I found the political atmosphere oppressive; the intimidating presence and occasional violence of the ubiquitous blackshirts made me long for the freedoms of the United States. I decided to make a last effort to find a job in Italy, and I departed for Rome.

WHEN I had moved to Italy in 1922, I hesitated to resume my relationship with Auntie Rina. The years I had spent under her wings were not rich in pleasant memories, and the echo of her resounding slaps still rang in my ears. I also remembered that Father had not wanted us to have anything to do with the Giachettis, but Fofò kept urging me to let bygones be bygones and insisted that I go to visit her.

"Rina loves you," he assured me, "and after all, she is your aunt. She will be happy to see you."

In the end I paid her a visit, and thereafter I saw her and Dr. Pierallini from time to time. She was a gracious hostess, and I behaved as a dutiful nephew should. I remember that on one of these occasions, I noticed a partial coffee and tea service on her sideboard.

"Oh, Auntie, you have the rest of my set!" I exclaimed.

"No, *caro,* you have the rest of mine!" she retorted.

We did not argue over whose set it should be, but it was significant that the two halves were never reunited.

Now, in 1937, I decided to look Auntie Rina up in Rome. Before I left Florence, I managed to obtain her address, and I called on her as soon as I reached the capital.

After Grandfather Guido died in 1935, Grandmother Teresa found herself alone. Rina, too, was alone since the death of Pierallini, in the late 1920s, I believe, but I am not certain. In order to earn a living, the women had opened a *pensione* for artists in Rome. Actually, *pensione* may be too elegant a word to describe their establishment, which was just a large flat with several rooms which they rented to artists who lived and ate there. Grandmother Teresa did most of the work: She did the shopping, supervised the maid, cooked, and generally kept the place running. Rina served more as a figurehead and spent most of her time sitting in her room reading penny-dreadfuls. When I arrived in Rome, all the rooms in the *pensione* were rented, so I took a room at a nearby hotel and ate my meals at their *pensione* as a paying guest. We talked about old times, but only in general terms, without going into any of the tempting topics. Rina had an "easy come, easy go" attitude and did not seem particularly downcast about her reduced state in life. Teresa kept begging her to open a voice studio, but she would not hear of it.

"Rina, why don't you teach singing?" Teresa would plead with her. "With your name and experience, you could attract many students!"

But Rina just went on reading her penny-dreadfuls and smoking her cigarettes. Their exchange sounded like a conversation they had had a dozen times before.

In the summer of 1937, during my stay in Italy, I received an envelope from Yvonne. She was kind enough to forward a letter I had received from the Italian consulate in Los Angeles. It had taken the consulate officials two years to locate my mother, but they had found her, still living in South America, and sent me her current address. Why, after eighteen years, she made the major move from Buenos Aires to Rio de Janeiro, a move which necessitated crossing yet another language barrier, I can only surmise. Much later, I heard from a different and not entirely reliable source that Mother, who was not the sort of woman to live alone, had found an affluent "protector." Perhaps it was due to this gentleman friend that she moved. The story of this alleged liaison is another missing piece in the puzzle of her life in South America.

At any rate, I was elated to have her address. When I mentioned the good news to Rina, she showed no interest at all. I then asked Grandmother Teresa if she had any message for my mother.

"Tell Ada that her father died," she said.

Succinctness where Ada was concerned ran on both sides of the family. Many years later, I found a letter Giovanni wrote to Mother on 22 April 1925, possibly his first communication with her since she left Father in 1908. He dictated the letter to his son, Marcello, and purported to send news of Fofò and me. In two sentences, he finished with his subject:

I speak now a little about your sons. As you know, they have always been headstrong, because after the tragedy of their father I tried to put them on the right track and they told me it was none of my business. Mimmi now has two sons, Rodolfo has one.

I TOLD Rina about my movies and that in spite of her earlier verdict, I had learned to sing after all. She was curious to hear me and took me to the studio of a singing teacher who must have been over eighty years old. I sang "Che gelida manina," not particularly well. The old man mumbled something, and Rina made only one comment: "You have a good top, but you need work."

Although our relationship was still based more on courtesy than anything else, a good deal of our initial awkwardness disappeared after a few days of seeing each other regularly. In fact, Rina felt comfortable enough with me to ask me to lend her 50 lire, which was about three dollars at the time. I gladly gave it to her, reflecting on the irony of our circumstances.

But Rina was not destined to die in poverty. Soon afterward, she and Teresa gave up the *pensione*. Teresa moved in with her son Umberto, and Rina's faithful friends, the Fontanellas, invited her to live with them. Rina accepted the invitation and moved to Cecina. To spare Rina the embarrassment of having to ask for money, Tina Fontanella made a substantial deposit in her name, and the interest paid for all her personal expenses. After Mr. Fontanella died, my aunt stayed on with Tina as a friend and companion. The lady was quite elderly by then, and because she had no descendants, she made Rina her sole heir. Upon her death, Rina inherited her entire estate, which supposedly included houses, farmland, timberland, jewelry, bonds, and cash. She was well set for the rest of her life. Rina died at Cerreto Guidi, at the age of seventy-nine, on 1 June 1959.

Because of the circumstances of our births, Fofò and I were not related to Rina in the eyes of the law. At the time of her death, she had only one living, legally recognized blood relative—her half brother, fifty-nine-year-old Umberto Da Vela Giachetti. Umberto had been penniless all his life, barely able to make ends meet. The only one of my generation of the Caruso-Giachetti clan to learn a trade, he was a bookkeeper married to an extremely frugal wife (according to Fofò) and had lived in modest circumstances for many years. As Rina's heir, literally overnight, he found himself rich. Better with money than the Carusos, he was reportedly able to hang onto the wealth that fell into his lap.

CHAPTER TWENTY-EIGHT

Eddie Smith

GOING to Rome from Florence in the hope of finding employment was not just a stab in the dark. I had heard that someone was planning to make a movie about Father and hoped to take part in the project. Unfortunately, it was still in an embryonic stage and held no possibilities for me either on- or off-screen. In the end, I bought passage to America and left Italy, for the last time, on 1 August 1937. Unaware of the wisdom of my choice at the moment, I thus escaped entering World War II on the wrong side of the conflict. I arrived in New York on August 12, once again, back at square one.

During the Depression, it was almost impossible to find work; for every dishwasher's job, there were fifty applicants. Because I was not a citizen, I could not be employed on a government-sponsored work project like the WPA or CCC. My resources dwindled until I was flat broke. I went hungry for days, trying to find a friend who would buy me a meal. At times I joined the group of hungry men at the "B & W," which was advertised as the Bottomless Cup. One could buy a cup of coffee and sit there all day, and the waitress would refill the cup as many times as one's system could stand it. With some luck, another, more affluent customer would leave a half-finished doughnut or bagel on his plate, which one could furtively snatch before the busboy cleared the table. The men hanging around the place took turns grabbing the leftovers.

Just as it seemed I had reached the end of my rope, I received a call on the common phone of the boarding house where I had taken a room. The caller identified himself as Edward J. Smith. He said he had seen my movies and liked my voice. If he could arrange a singing engagement on Robert Ripley's "Believe It Or Not," would I be interested?

Of course I was interested! I suggested we discuss the matter in person and agreed to meet him at his office. Mr. Smith was a friendly, likable young man fairly bubbling with ideas. For an accurate description of our meeting and its preliminaries, I turn the narrative over to Eddie.

In 1937 I was on the New York staff of the *Hollywood Reporter,* a daily paper devoted to motion pictures. I was a jack of all trades, from meeting personages coming in from Europe on boats, ranging from Kipling through H. G. Wells to Marjorie Lawrence, to writing a weekly musical column, mostly related to opera, since by that time Hollywood had signed and used Lawrence Tibbett, Grace Moore, Nino Martini, Ernestine Schumann-Heink, Gladys Swarthout, Jan Kiepura, Lily Pons, and others.

I was approached by a man named Burnet Hershey, a World War I correspondent, who had written a film script based on the life of Enrico Caruso, mostly dealing with the events of his life from 1918 to 1920. The basis for the chronological limitation of the script was Dorothy Caruso's tentative approval, provided she could stay in control and received adequate payment. Hershey had approached me for some guidance in doing the story and to help him in offering it to a film studio, because he had no experience or connections in the film industry. I read the script and felt it was a travesty; it contained nothing about Caruso's early years. When I asked him what tenor he had selected for the role of Caruso, he said he did not know but would welcome my suggestions.

I felt that if it was to be done at all, it should be done right. I wanted the whole life story of Caruso to be used from his infancy, including the story of Ada Giachetti and their life together. I suggested that I would approach RCA Victor and get them to electrify more Caruso records, i.e., re-record electrically more acoustic originals with an overlaid orchestra. We also decided that an actor, rather than a singer, should play Caruso in the film. We thought that Edward Arnold looked enough like Caruso from 1910 on to be able to represent him on the screen. An additional consideration was that Arnold spoke Italian, so he could synchronize his lips with the electrified Caruso records. I then turned to my close friend, Gladys Swarthout, who was making films for Paramount at that time and whose husband, the baritone Frank Chapman, was also a close friend. I wanted Swarthout to play Ada Giachetti.

When I approached them, they were most enthusiastic, and we started to make plans. But we needed a blood relative of Caruso's to gain permission for the film, since Dorothy Caruso and her daughter Gloria, who was eighteen at the time, would not want to authorize a film in which they could only be a small part. As if by coincidence, I received a release notice from Ripley's "Believe It Or Not" radio program wanting some publicity on the next week's promotion of Caruso. Ripley's theme was that Caruso—Believe It Or Not—was a failure in his first operatic appearance.

In the course of reviewing films, I had come across a film with Enrico Caruso, Jr. It was in Spanish, and I found it quite good. I remember that I was much impressed with his singing of "O Paradiso" from *L'Africana*. I made some inquiries in Mexico and in Hollywood and found that Caruso Jr., was in New York City. I phoned him and asked if he would be prepared, if I could arrange it, to sing on the Ripley program. He agreed, and I called Robert Leroy Ripley himself. Here was a real Believe It Or Not: The singer would not be announced, and at the conclusion, Ripley would say: "Believe it or not, the tenor you have just heard was none other than Enrico Caruso." A howl of protest would rise from the studio audience; after all, Caruso had been dead for sixteen years. "Yes, but this man you heard singing was Enrico Caruso, Jr., son of the late tenor."

Ripley went for it, hook, line, and sinker. "Can he sing?" he asked. I told him of the Spanish films. "How much?" I asked for $500 an appearance, with two appearances guaranteed. He agreed at once, and believe me, for 1937, that amount was the equivalent of $5,000 an appearance today.

Rico came to the office of the *Hollywood Reporter* at 229

West Forty-second Street, and we met for the first time. In the course of that meeting, I also offered him $150 a week to act as "consultant" on the planned film, and he also agreed to that. With Rico's consent and endorsement, Chapman left for the West Coast, where he talked with Adolph Zukor, the president of Paramount pictures. Zukor was interested and wanted to see the script. But Hershey would not let it out of his hands, so he left for Hollywood, carrying the script himself. As a possible director, Swarthout also suggested Reuben Mamoulian, one of the best at that time, and one of the few who was also a musician.

Paramount was willing to guarantee 50 percent of the negative cost, the usual amount for an independent producer. We budgeted the film at $1,000,000, with Paramount guaranteeing $500,000. It became my task to come up with the balance of the money. To that end I approached the head of the Atlas Corporation, a multimillionaire outfit which lent money at reasonable rates or took a portion of the film in return for the investment. At that point Hershey had to come back from California, where he had been living the good life, and his script was submitted to Atlas. It was rejected as being "uninteresting."

The next question was how to improve the script. I spent long hours with Hershey, giving him data about Caruso's life and early career. The script was much improved, but the best offer we were able to get from Atlas was that if we ever decided to make a quickie, a $200,000 film, they would be willing to participate in the financing. When I got this far, I had wired and phoned Burnet Hershey, who was by then back on the West Coast, to go to the Paramount studios and ask for Adolph Zukor, who was prepared to assign someone to revise the script to bring in the earlier episodes. Hershey did not want to take a second place. He decided that I was not telling the truth, that no appointment with Zukor had been made, and that the script was fine as it was and needed no further revisions. He did not show up at the studios, and Paramount lost interest in the project. The filmed story of Caruso's young life vanished in the 1930s, and it was not revived until Mario Lanza sang Caruso for the film [*The Great Caruso*] a decade and a half later.[1]

EDDIE'S account accurately summarizes the abortive film project. The newspapers followed the developments closely; even the British papers carried announcements including such specifics as the fact that Eddie Arnold had been suggested as the actor who would play Caruso.

While the film project was gestating, a letter from Mother was a bright spot in my life. I hadn't been in touch with her for fifteen years. Now, suddenly, I felt I had a mother again.

> My adored Mimmi!
> You don't know how and how much I wanted to have news from you. I have already written a letter to Warner Brothers but I had no answer. I asked for your address in Italy but they couldn't give it to me; now I try again to see if I will have better luck.
> I have seen and heard your films, however I found that you still need to study to have more *finesse* in the attacks. The voice however is beautiful and I am proud of you because beyond a beautiful voice you are a handsome young man as you promised to become when you were a baby. You know? They all say that you are my image, especially the eyes and the mouth and the expression of your glance.
> You can imagine how happy I am! Oh! If I could only press you, my love, just once to my breast! Who knows if God will have this happiness in store for me?
> This letter, begun on May 10, was left unfinished because I was waiting for your correct [address] from someone who left without telling me anything else.
> Today, then, I had the great joy of being called to the consulate where they told me that through the Italian Consul of New York you wanted news of me. You can imagine my happiness! Now then: My adored Mimmi, I live here in Rio giving singing lessons and that is how I carry on, tolerably, my life. Certainly if I could be near you it would be my dream come true. I could just as well give lessons in New York and support myself with that. Don't you think? I would be so happy! Let us hope that God will grant this great wish of mine.
> Well, my treasure, I send you all my love and an infinite kiss, your mamma,
>
> Ada

I was thrilled to receive this loving letter. We had tried to find each other simultaneously: While I was searching for Mother by way of the

Italian consulate, she was trying to locate me via Warner Brothers.

I wrote to her immediately, resolved to be candid and truthful. I told her about the loss of my inheritance, the lawsuit, the cancellation of my contract with Warner's, and my present circumstances, and I commented that my only prospect for a change for the better was the projected Caruso film.

Although the film project that brought Eddie and me together did not materialize, it was responsible for my appearance on Ripley's. This did not go quite as Eddie had planned. Mr. Ripley wanted me to sing on the first of two programs dedicated to the opening of the Metropolitan Opera season, but my voice was in no shape to be heard publicly, and I sensibly declined. Ripley refused to let the matter drop. He said he had heard from Mr. Smith what a fine voice I had, and Eddie chimed in on cue: "He has a magnificent voice!" Ripley's towering expectations made me even more apprehensive about singing, and I remained adamant in spite of his coaxing. Finally he agreed to let me take the speaking part of my father in the first program on the Metropolitan with the stipulation that I would sing on the second. I was to receive $350 for the first, non-singing appearance on 23 October 1937 and $500 three weeks later for singing an aria in two broadcasts four hours apart. (The program was always rebroadcast for the West Coast.)

The skit for the first show was a piece of cake. I had a few lines to read with script in hand. But the singing commitment lay ahead, and I knew I was in trouble. How was I to get my voice back into shape without the critical guidance of a vocal coach? I needed a saint or a miracle.

A saint did come to my rescue, in the guise of an old friend. As I left the first broadcast, I ran into Alfonso Pedroza, De la Huerta's prize pupil, the Mexican giant who played the gypsy chief in my first movie. I told him of my predicament, and it was just the kind of challenge Pedroza liked. Besides, he had a missionary zeal about preserving and transmitting Don Adolfo's method. We began to work together every day, and in two weeks he brought my voice back to par.

During my years with Yvonne, she often served as my accompanist. Now there was no one to fill this crucial role, so Pedroza set out in search of a pianist. He found a likely candidate and set up a date at a friend's apartment.

The pianist turned out to be a petite woman with a lovely face. She was Helen Roth Burnett, a concert pianist and the first woman ever to publicly perform Gershwin's Concerto in F, first with the Milwaukee

Symphony, later with the New Symphony of Chicago. She sat down at the piano, and I set the score of "Celeste Aida" before her.

"In what key, Mr. Caruso?"

"I don't understand the question."

"Do you sing it in the original key, or do you wish me to transpose it down?"

"No, no," I said, "in the original key."

She took off her white gloves, adjusted the piano stool, and attacked the first chords of the recitative, the fanfare preceding the line "*Se quel guerrier io fossi!*" It sounded as if all the trumpets in heaven were blaring, and I instantly knew I was in the presence of exceptional talent. The hair on the back of my neck stood up, and inspired by her accompaniment, I sang as never before. Afterwards, I complimented her playing and explained that I needed her services, but I also explained, in the words of the Duke of Mantua, "*Studente sono e povero.*" ("I am a student and poor.") She said that after hearing me sing, she was certain of my success and not worried about the money.

From that meeting on, Helen became my accompanist, more often without pay than with it, and my constant companion. Our private joke was that in a few years, I ran up such a debt that it was easier to marry her than to repay her. She became the light of my life, the joy of my existence. She was a precious woman, and I loved her very much. I regard our years together as a forty-two-year honeymoon that lasted until she died in 1980.

But that is another story and must wait for the telling.

THANKS to the efforts of Pedroza and Helen Burnett, I made enough progress to face the microphone at the appointed time. When I showed up at the WEAF studio, the conductor of the orchestra solemnly admonished his players:

"Play together, men, this ain't jazz, this is op'ra!"

Ripley's advance publicity had brought several reporters to this program. Mr. Ripley, unaware of my singing during the Los Angeles radio interviews in 1934, advised his radio audience that they were about to hear the son of the great Caruso sing on the air for the very first time. I took my position in front of the microphone and began to sing "O Paradiso" from *L'Africana*. As soon as I attacked the first phrase, "*Mi batte il cor,*" a dozen blinding flashguns went off one after another, and I was barely able to continue. I regained my composure and finished the aria. Four hours later, starting at midnight New York time, we repeated the entire show for transmission to the West Coast. This time there were no reporters, no photographers or flashes. All things considered, I would say I gave a decent performance, although I did not think so at the time.

After I finished my number, Mr. Ripley asked me on the air:

"Mr. Caruso, now that you have chosen singing as your career, do you find the name of Caruso a help or a handicap?"

"It is both a help and a handicap," I answered. "I find that people want to hear me because my name is Caruso, and that's a help. But I find that they inevitably compare my singing with my father's, and that's a handicap, because I don't think there will ever be a voice like my dad's."

I read in the newspapers that Don Adolfo happened to be in California at the time of the broadcast. I wrote him a long letter, wished him happy holidays, and asked whether he had heard me on the air. His reply, written the day before Christmas, arrived shortly.

> My dear Enrico,
> I received your letter dated the 18th of this month and I was, in fact, surprised—albeit pleasantly so—that overcoming your habitual laziness, you turned your hand to writing me news of your artistic life.
> It is not fair of you to feel that your singing was very bad. Naturally I could see that your total "stage fright" did stop you from singing securely, and it probably also caused your slight loss of timbre. Generally speaking, however, I saw clearly that the organ is still open and retains its extension and flexibility, which are two very good qualities.

He proceeded to give me detailed instructions about positioning the lips to regain what my voice had lost and told me which arias to sing daily and which to sing weekly for practice. I appreciated his long-distance help, but it could not take the place of daily lessons.

I felt especially grateful to Pedroza for bringing about the minor miracle of restoring my voice. Eddie being Eddie, he tried to help Pedroza too, and the two stayed in touch. On one occasion, Eddie was witness to a humorous, if nearly tragic, incident with my friend Pedroza. I let the story stand in Eddie's own words.

> Enrico's closest friend in those days was a giant Mexican-Indian basso named Alfonso Pedroza. He had an enormous voice of good quality and a good range, but he was a very poor

musician, which I did not know. At Rico's request, I had arranged for an audition for Pedroza with Fortune Gallo. Gallo's opera company, the San Carlo, was about to come to New York for a season at the City Center, opposite the Radio City Music Hall. The building no longer exists. Pedroza went for the audition and sang "Son lo spirito che nega" from *Mefistofele* and "Il lacerato spirito" from *Simon Boccanegra*. The impresario was entranced and engaged him on the spot to sing the King in the opening night production of *Aida,* on 5 May 1938. When Gallo's company came to town, the conductor, Carlo Peroni, was furious because he saw his planned ensemble in Act I ruined. He demanded that Pedroza come to his hotel to rehearse alone with him, and I knew he planned to protest Pedroza as musically incompetent. I arrived with Pedroza, went to the Maestro's apartment on the fourteenth floor, and was ordered to wait outside. Peroni seated himself at the piano and the rehearsal began.

Now Pedroza did sing in Italian, but with a Spanish accent, and the word "*guerra*" was difficult for him; it always came out as "guwewa." Peroni's short fuse blew. He started to curse Pedroza, called him an incompetent, and screamed at him as the phrase with "*guerra*" was repeated again and again. Suddenly I heard a shuffle, a squeak, and then silence. The door was not locked, and I cautiously opened it to peek inside. The enraged six-foot, seven-inch Pedroza, weighing over three hundred pounds, had blown his top. He was holding Peroni by the neck with his right hand around the conductor's throat and was trying to open the window with the left. By all signs he intended to drop the conductor from the fourteenth floor. I tore into the room, grabbed his arm, and managed to get him to let Peroni slide to the floor half conscious. Pedroza and I left; and as we walked out, Mary McCormick, the soprano who was to sing Marguerite the following day, arrived for her rehearsal, carrying an umbrella. That night, when Pedroza sang the King, Peroni conducted, but he looked like a raccoon. Earlier that afternoon he had cursed McCormick too, but she would not take it and whacked him across the face with the umbrella. He had a black and blue throat and two black eyes. Needless to say, that ended Pedroza's career with the San Carlo Opera Company.[2]

EDDIE was pleased that my voice was serviceable again. He tried to help me capitalize on it, but without much success. In the United States in the thirties, there was no such thing as regional opera to serve as a training ground for beginners. In those days, the successful stars sang with the Metropolitan, San Francisco Opera, and Chicago. The celebrated traveling troupe, the San Carlo Opera Company, took in some of those who were not on the roster of the three big companies. And that was that.

To tide me over financially, Eddie found me a few nightclub engagements around New York and New Jersey. But nightclubs, for an aspiring opera singer, were steps below even "the provinces." I could go on singing there till kingdom come and no one would take notice. Finally, Eddie found a unique way for me to earn something to live on. According to his recollections:

> Rico in the interim had gone through the money he received from Ripley, and I had to come up with something to keep him going. On Forty-second Street and Seventh Avenue there was a large Caruso restaurant. It served Italian food and was a typical restaurant of its type. But while Caruso was a common name in Italy, the restaurant was delighted to have some legitimate tie-in with the Caruso name. They had Rico seated in a spot near the entrance at a table where he signed autographs on his father's picture and dedicated his inscription to the customers. He was expected to sit in the restaurant from six in the evening until ten nightly, seven days a week. His pay for that was $60 a week, not a large sum, but it kept him going and it was easy money.
>
> Unable to book Rico anyplace where he would have an extended stay—for nightclub work was too precarious and I wanted him in New York—I sat down and wrote a letter to Edward Johnson, general manager of the Metropolitan Opera. I told him about the magnificent raw material I had heard in the young man. I also reminded him that when he was singing under the name of Edoardo di Giovanni, he had been in the same Italian and South American companies with Caruso Sr. and that he had known Rico from the time he was eight years old. I pleaded for the chance to have him sing for Johnson.
>
> I had also discovered that Rico had reached the stage where he was afraid to sing for anyone. No matter how magnificently he sang, there would always be someone at the end

who would say, "That was wonderful, Mr. Caruso, but I remember when I heard your father sing the same aria . . ." and Rico would smile and turn away. Once, twice, a hundred times perhaps. Every time he sang it happened, and the ghost of Caruso Sr. was always there for comparison. Nobody would want to acknowledge that the voice was there, in fact a true Caruso voice, with the same timbre, the same innate qualities, the same sound that one can come by only through genetic inheritance. And nobody seemed to recognize that they remembered a singer of many decades' experience in the elder Caruso, whereas Rico had but a brief career behind him, and no operatic stage experience at all. The audience came to hear the Caruso of legend and for the best part remained unreceptive to the comparable gifts of the son.

Fully believing in Rico's potential, I told Johnson that if [Rico were] properly coached and developed, he would have a magnificent tenor on his hands, and one whose name would have a tremendous draw, not a negligible consideration in view of the dwindling box-office receipts at the Metropolitan. When Johnson did not respond to my letter, I decided to approach Lucrezia Bori and solicit her help. I wrote to her on 21 September 1937, and her reply, with an apology for the delay, came dated 26 October 1937. In it she promised to submit my letter to the board of directors. She must have done so, because shortly thereafter Johnson agreed to hear Enrico, and an audition was set up at the old Met. Aware of Rico's fear of an audience ready to compare him with his father, and knowing that for just about anyone connected with the Metropolitan, Caruso was a living memory, I asked Johnson to keep the time and place of the audition a secret. He agreed, but he broke his promise only once: He told Lucrezia Bori, who also had known Rico since he was eight years old. Bori also broke the promise of secrecy only once and told Edward Ziegler, assistant general manager of the Met, about the audition, who told Earl Lewis, box-office treasurer, who in turn told others. By the time Rico arrived for his audition, he was greeted by a score or more of his father's old friends, all of whom had known him as a child or since 1919, when as a boy of fifteen he came to the U.S. for the first time with his father and stepmother.

Rico did not blow up. He was polite and courteous to all in

spite of being in a terrible state because of the ordeal he was
about to face. He walked out onstage with his accompanist.
For a moment he was blinded; the house was totally dark, and
there was just a little light over the piano at the far end for the
accompanist. Rico hesitated. He may have been afraid that a
false step would project him into the orchestra pit. Suddenly
he moved forward with confidence and faced the unseen
audience. He announced he would start with "Recondita
armonia" from *Tosca*. He then turned toward the wings as if to
say something to an invisible person, turned back to the
auditorium, and sang. He sang the *Tosca* aria, the "Flower
Song" from *Carmen,* and "Che gelida manina" from *La Bohème*.
He then thanked Johnson and came off. When we were alone,
he turned to me and said in an awed voice:

"Did you see that?"

"What?" I asked him.

"I could not see where to go," Rico said. "I was blinded.
Then someone came up, took my arm, and led me to the
center of the stage in front of the prompter's box. I turned to
thank him, and I saw my father's back vanishing into the
wings."

Rico sang well in the audition and I asked Johnson to help.
He said he would secure vocal training for him and have him
study five operas. Then he would place him in Italy under
another name to let him gain stage experience and would
bring him back to the Met when he was ready, in a year or so
from then. He said he would assign Gennaro Papi, who had
conducted for the elder Caruso, to give some musical training
to the young man. But that was the end; we never heard from
Johnson or the Metropolitan again.[3]

I am not surprised that despite the passage of time, Eddie remembered this incident as clearly as I did. The apparition left us both in
awe. I must have felt it augured well for the audition, otherwise I might
not have found the courage to sing. I think it was fitting that this incident occurred on the stage of the Metropolitan Opera House.

I will never know why the audition, which went well, led nowhere.

CHAPTER TWENTY-NINE

Family Ties

I N the years that followed and until the outbreak of World War II, I maintained a correspondence with my mother. Each letter from her was a miniature portrait—a curious mixture of simplicity and sophistication which mirrored the experience of a long and troubled life. In our steady exchange of letters, I did not hide my difficulties. Mother, too, would write about her problems, and she would bemoan my lack of progress and give me advice about singing technique and repertory.

Shortly before Christmas, on 3 December 1937, I received her sorrowful reply to my own detailed letter.

> My adored Mimmi,
> Your letter saddens me a little because of all the explanations you have given me regarding the infamy they committed with the division of the inheritance. . . . To think that your poor father worked all his life (and even lost it for that) to accumulate a fortune which in a few years should vanish like a puff of smoke! Was it worth suffering so much as he suffered for such results?

489

In addition to finding a handful of nightclub engagements for me, Eddie Smith, my inventive friend, came up with a promotional scheme. He decided I needed some recordings to use as musical calling cards. My father's Metropolitan Opera contract had supposedly been clinched by a recording—who knew what a record might do for me?

Now there was an important question to decide: Should I record something my father had not, or should I borrow his repertory and suffer the inevitable comparison? Eddie maintained that I should sing the same music to show the similarity of our voices. I went along with this judgment, which was probably a mistake. In those days, I could go up to an E-flat and had a good high C; in the long run, it may have been wiser to capitalize on my range and sing "Nessun dorma" from *Turandot,* or some other piece with an exposed high C that Father had not recorded.

To finance the recordings, Eddie persuaded his friend Jack Caidin, owner of the Record Collectors' Shop at Fifty-third Street and Seventh Avenue, that he needed some publicity for his store. As Eddie tells the story:

Looking for a way to promote his store, Jack wanted to record Rico. We went to the RCA Victor studios on Twenty-third Street, and he recorded with the piano accompaniment of J. Konstantin four numbers: "Questa o quella," "Recondita armonia," "Core 'ngrato," and "Deserto sulla terra" from *Il Trovatore,* the last being an aria his father had never recorded. It was not as good as the others, and Caidin released the *Tosca* on a single-sided record and "Core 'ngrato" and the *Rigoletto* aria back-to-back on a ten-inch 78 rpm disc. The whole recording session was done on a shoestring, thus there was no question of multiple takes. It was decided that the *Trovatore* being less satisfactory than the rest, it should not be issued.

"Questa o quella" and "Core 'ngrato" were recorded on March 1 and the other two on 14 March 1938. I doubt that Caidin sold more than a hundred copies of the records. He did not know how to promote them, he did not send out review copies, and the records died. They were not without merit, as they showed more than just the promise of Rico's voice. But there were two strikes against him: The listeners expected to hear the vocal reincarnation of his father, and none of the listeners realized that they were hearing a singer with only three years' training and no musical education. There can be no doubt that young Enrico had outdistanced his father's accomplishments at the same stage of his career.[1]

I sent a copy of the record to Mother, for hers was the opinion I valued most. On 25 June 1938, she wrote:

> You have a beautiful voice and most beautiful high notes; however you must close a little more the middle and must soften and perfect your diction. At certain points it is too colorless and lacks brilliance, and those are the marks of a trained singer.... Sing with more sweetness and try not to open even the high notes. Remember that your voice resembles a little that of your poor father, so with perseverance and patience you should be able to become *somebody*.

I asked her to clarify her remark about diction, and in a letter of July 9, she replied: "Your diction lacks elegance, it lacks that certain thing one doesn't learn except from great teachers and great artists. It's a fact. 'Recondita armonia' is better than the Rigoletto. What exercises do you do to reach such top notes?"

Mother naïvely asked whether my record royalties brought me enough to live on. In fact, only well-meaning friends and a handful of collectors bought copies. At Eddie's urging, Caidin finally sent out some review copies, and the records were reviewed in the *New York World-Telegram, La Follia di New York,* and *The New York Times.* In the 1 May 1938 issue of the *Times,* Compton Pakenham wrote that I had "a musical sense above the average and a fine, evenly built tenor, which, however, [I was] inclined to overtax in the upper reaches." What he meant by "overtaxing" I could not imagine, for none of the released numbers contained a high C, and my B's came without effort. Pakenham added that being overshadowed by my father was inevitable and concluded that nature should have made me a baritone!

IN a letter of 30 January 1938, Mother enclosed a photograph. "I have changed a lot, haven't I?" she asked. "But my spirit is the same." I made no comment about the picture. What could I say? That she looked the same as in the old photos I had seen? My silence did not pass unnoticed. "In your last letter you say nothing of the little picture I sent," she wrote. "Did you find it so ugly?" I reassured her that I found her photo lovely.

In one of my letters, I told her the little I knew about Fofò's affairs. She replied:

My adored Mimmi,
My dear son, (without wanting to) you have brought sadness to my life. I thought that at least the two of you were doing well, especially financially, instead of having to struggle. One in Abyssinia, and you not settled either. . . . you give me the impression of a boat lost on the high seas without oars and without a compass. . . . Ah! Enrico! You, who should take the place of your poor father, instead there you are unsettled, out of balance.

Inadvertently, I caused Mother even more distress. At the time of the recording sessions, Eddie induced a reporter to write an article about me. It was published in the *New York World-Telegram* on 8 March 1938. The reporter, eager to stress my wretched circumstances, began with a hard-hitting statement: "In the back basement of 153 West 78th St., where he is living with and on his singing coach, Pietro Della Rosa, . . ." In fact I had a basement apartment, but I was living neither with nor on my singing coach, whose name was Pedroza, not Della Rosa. The direct quotations, however, were accurate enough. "Ah, at the mention of my father's name, all doors are open to me, but once I get inside . . . well, I am not the old man, you know."

The interview was picked up by the foreign press, and Mother came upon it in Brazil. She wrote:

An article appeared in a newspaper here that speaks accurately about your situation! That is, that you live in the home of someone who calls himself a maestro and who is supporting you and your girlfriend. You can understand that this cannot make me happy, and what is more, it is degrading for a son of Caruso. Try to have it retracted because it has made a bad impression here.

Through the Italian-language newspapers, the article reached Abyssinia as well. Fofò read it and sent me a long letter from Addis Ababa dated 9 April 1938. Fofò too commented on the damning aspects of the article. He told me of the problems in his life and said he was preparing to return to Florence, where he asked me to write to him in care of Vincenzo Traballesi.

Knowing how Fofò felt about Mother, I was hesitant to tell him about our correspondence. In the end I did and enclosed her address.

To my surprise, my brother's reaction was entirely positive. He wrote to her for the first time in many years. His letter did not bring much joy to Mother, who plainly said so: "Fofò's letter did not make me happy: I sense between those lines something I do not like; it seems to me that he is somewhat of an egoist and completely debauched. For the time being I will not write to him."

The same letter from Mother contained a revealing comment: "To live well one must be diplomatic and think before acting, one should not be impulsive! Take it from me. . . . If I had reflected before acting, I would not find myself as I am." In a letter of 15 April 1938, she mentioned that she was having heart trouble. "I have suffered and struggled a lot, and thus I now suffer the consequences," she wrote. She also asked what had happened to her music, exclaiming: "How I need those scores!" I had guilty visions of Dino Barsanti; her scores must have been in the pile I had given away so lightly. She wanted to have Umberto's address, "to ask him certain things," and closed with the theme that was to become the leitmotiv of our correspondence: "Well, my heart, keep me calm and try to put your life in order! This is what sorrows me the most. I embrace you and kiss you with all my soul, your Mamma."

I sent her not only Umberto's address, but Rina's as well. Her reply contained her first reference to Rina. "I will write to Umberto to have some news of them, but certainly not about my sister, who was the principal cause of my ruin. I don't wish her ill, but God knows what we do, and who does wrong sooner or later will pay for it."

IN a letter of 9 July 1938, Mother surprised me with the question:

> Tell me: Wouldn't you like to spend three or four months with me? I would take care of the trip, and we would adjust ourselves quite well to living here because I have a comfortable house that could give you a decent accommodation. You could restore your health and spirits. If you want this, write me and I will try to arrange your coming here. Can you imagine what a revolution you would make? It would be most advantageous for both of us. . . . At least we could stay a little together, and who knows? One thing may lead to another.

I replied that I could not possibly accept her offer to travel to Rio at her expense. In her next letter, Mother explained that it was not her money that would pay for my trip. The linchpin in an elaborate scheme was Gabriella Besanzoni, the famous mezzo-soprano, Father's one-time partner, Arthur Rubinstein's former lover, and now the wealthy widow of a Brazilian millionaire. Mother explained the details in eight handwritten pages.

> My adored Mimmi,
>
> The offer I made you was an idea that occurred to Madame Gabriella Besanzoni, who would like you to come here, unknown to anybody, and then [she would] prepare you to sing next season at the [Teatro] Municipale here for the main opera season. She would like you to study with her, with the understanding that thereafter she would take the credit for having discovered you. I mind and don't mind all that; so long as I can see this dream realized, I would accept the proposal. She (so she says) would give you enough [money] each month for your expenses until you can make your debut here. But since she is a very volatile woman, I have not yet put much faith [in this offer]. In any event, I would make her sign a contract wherein she would commit herself to all this.

This tempting offer put me in a quandary. Accepting it would have meant a long separation from Helen, for surely I could not ask Mme. Besanzoni to support us both. Mother's attitude only confused the issue, for her letters showed annoyance about my involvement with Helen. She plainly told me that in order to succeed, I had to be alone, committed to no one and responsible only for myself. In the end, though Helen was willing to make the sacrifice for my career, I was not, so I turned down the offer. Mother did not try to persuade me to change my mind. I suspect that she had very limited faith that the volatile Besanzoni would live up to her part of the bargain.

Around this time, I wrote to Mme. Da Costa in England, telling her about the Ripley broadcast and my efforts to establish myself. The sweet lady's answer was most affectionate, as always. "My dearest Mimmi, You cannot imagine the joy and pleasure your 'sign of life' gave us," she wrote. Her next letter, acknowledging a photograph I had sent her, contained the following comment about Father:

> Thousands of thanks for lovely photograph received some days ago. Dear boy, it's just you & I still see my wee Mimmi looking at me through those soft eyes, & as I look I always remember something your Papa told me when I asked him about Fofò. He said, "I *love* Mimmi because he looks like *his mother.*"

Another letter came from my brother. In the summer, I sent a copy of my record to Elena to show what her "scoundrel" of an ex-husband was doing. She was pleasantly surprised, liked my singing, and commented that my voice resembled Papa's. In late fall, she ran into Fofò, now back in Florence from Abyssinia. She mentioned the record, and Fofò was curious to hear it. He was greatly shocked and dispatched a letter to me on 2 November 1938.

> When your voice began to vibrate, my Mimmi, I felt a rush of blood and two large salty drops rolled out of my eyes, and I remained with mouth open. I felt an infinity of contrasting sensations! It seemed as if I were hearing the voice of poor Father. In my mind I went back many years, I saw again our childhood, and it took a profound effort to remind myself that it was you who were singing! My dear brother, how happy I am!

When I told Mother of Fofò's emotional reaction, her comment was: "Don't pay attention to what Fofò says regarding your voice; what does he know?"

Fofò's ambivalence toward Mother became apparent when he asked to see the photo she had sent. I mailed it to him, and he returned it with a letter.

Florence, 1 February 1939

Dear Enrico,

> I am infinitely grateful to you for having sent the picture of our mother; I had a certain desire to see it. Frankly, I don't remember her. Neither the portraits nor the miniatures I have help my memory. I only have a vague, most faint idea of having had a mamma, and it seems almost impossible that I still have one. Don't be scandalized by my harsh words—what do you expect? A bit of Africa, a bit of age, I am no longer the same. In any case, I will soon write to her and will also send a photo of myself which will surely please her. She is our mother after all.

I was surprised to see that Fofò signed himself as "Rudy." I could only assume that my opportunistic brother meant to turn his Italian "Rodolfo" into the German "Rudolph."

I wrote to Mother around Christmas, mentioned that I was in touch with Fofò, and asked whether he had written to her. Commenting on her statement that she did not want to know anything about Rina, I felt it only fair to tell her that while we lived with our aunt, she took good care of us. I wrote something to the effect that her reasons, since after all, Rina was her only sister.

This time she waited a long time before replying. In a letter post-marked 22 March 1939, she wrote:

> My dear son,
> I delayed writing to you because I was a little annoyed. It will be best if you never speak to me again of my sister who usurps such a sweet name (sister); do you understand? I do not hate her, I have forgiven her. But for me she is more than dead, because for the dead, one reserves a certain reverence, whereas *for me* she is gone up in smoke.

A month later, in a letter postmarked 18 April 1939, Mother again spoke of Rina.

> My Mimmi dear,
> I received your letter together with that of Fofò. The tone of Fofò's does not surprise me because he was always close to his aunt and could not help learning to be dishonest and egoistic. I don't blame him because he has heard her accusations without knowing the true drama that unfolded at that time. If not for her wickedness, perhaps your father would not have died, and we would all be together.

In the meantime, as our letters passed back and forth, gingerly turning over pieces from our past, my singing career made scarcely any headway. After much effort, Eddie found an important engagement for me at a prestigious night club, Leon & Eddie's, at 33 West Fifty-second Street. The nightclub did a good job with advance publicity, and on my opening night, the place was packed with reporters. The following day, 23 July 1938, reviews appeared in several New York papers, including the *New York Journal and American,* the *New York World-Telegram,* and the *New York Sun.* On the whole, they were complimentary, and I had hopes that the show would lead to something bigger. But the going was slow, and as usual, it seemed the whole world knew it. On September 14, Leonard Lyons wrote in his column "The Lyons Den" in the *New York Post* that "Enrico Caruso Jr. still hasn't succeeded in finding a singing job for himself."

Finally, in the spring of 1939, an agent booked my only real singing engagement since Cuba. I was to give two recitals, in Montreal and Quebec City, at Easter. The newspapers didn't hesitate to exploit Father's name, announcing the concerts with the headline "Caruso's

Son Is Singing."

The Montreal concert on 8 April 1939 went very well. According to the April 11 review of the *Montreal Star,* I had *"un très grand succès"* at the Théâtre Château, and Helen's accompaniment received special mention. I sang "Lolita," "Amor ti vieta" from *Fedora,* "For You Alone," " 'A Vucchella," and several encores. In short, I sang my father's repertoire.

In the damp Canadian winter, I caught a bad cold, and I was hoarse by the time we reached Quebec City. Coincidentally, the organizers were unable to attract a sufficiently large audience, and the concert was cancelled. I received my fee all the same, which I counted as a bit of good fortune.

Following my return to New York, Eddie assured me with irrepressible optimism that because of the good press notices, more concert offers would follow. I was eager to believe him. But despite our combined efforts, I was unable to earn a living by singing. Finally, in August, I went back to my old standby, Real Silk Hosiery Mills, this time with a green card and a working permit in my pocket, so that I could work under my own name. My clientele included many celebrities, among them Kirsten Flagstad, Grace Moore, Helen Hayes, Talullah Bankhead, Tito Schipa (who complained in a long letter about the color of the stockings he received), Marjorie Lawrence, and Kitty Carlisle. Once I boldly made a sales call to the White House. Mrs. Roosevelt saw me during a visit to New York and made several purchases for herself and for the president. She was a gracious lady and even took the trouble to send a cordial thank-you note.

EDDIE kept cheerfully repeating that my big break was just around the corner. As he tells it:

> I was still determined to try to get Rico some singing engagements. As a promotional device I took him to another private recording studio [at WEMC] run by an old German tenor, Paul Normann-Ehrenfels. We recorded "Nessun dorma" from *Turandot,* "L'Alba separa dalla luce l'ombra" and "Amor ti vieta" from *Fedora* on 25 June 1939, and "Che gelida manina" from *La Bohème* and "Je crois entendre" from *The Pearlfishers* on 27 September 1939. On each occasion, Rico ripped them off one after another, with no fears or difficulty, and again without the benefit of retakes. He was singing for friends who would not criticize, nor draw comparisons."[2]

One day Eddie said to me with a wink:
"I am taking you to a concert you will never forget."
"A singer?"
"You'll see."

I wondered what the mystery was about, and I soon found out! We went to the ballroom of one of the large New York hotels. It was jam-packed with people, all chattering in cheerful anticipation. Then the concert began. A stout, improbably dressed woman walked out, positioned herself in the bend of the piano, and began to screech, shriek, scream, and cackle. I had never heard anything like it in my life. The audience started to giggle, then laugh at every twisted phrase, squeal with delight at each aborted trill, and howl at the yodeled, hooted high notes she missed with predictable consistency.

The performer was the legendary Florence Foster Jenkins. She was immune to the audience's reaction. In fact, her imperturbability was only accentuated by her gracious acceptance of the applause that exploded after each barely recognizable number, delivered in her inimitable manner. When the roar of applause died down, she vanished from sight for overlong intervals only to return wearing a costume as outrageous as before, which in her mind suited the theme and mood of the next number. Her costumes ranged from a Spanish outfit complete with fan and shawl to silk and lace, a sumptuous evening gown, an Austrian dirndl, and a shiny satin dress with large angel wings attached to the back. She would "act" each song, which made her presentation even more grotesque. For "Clavelitos," she brought out a basket of carnations which she tossed to the audience as she sang. Her public, better acquainted with her routine than I, screamed, howled, and applauded, demanding an encore, until she was forced to repeat the song. This, of course, necessitated that the flowers be gathered up in her basket so that she could throw them again with the graceless gestures of an overweight lady of sixty or so impersonating a delicate flower girl. I could not believe my eyes and ears, and by the time this musical circus act was over, my sides hurt from uncontrollable laughter.

After Madame Jenkins had massacred a dozen songs and arias, she gave the obligatory encores. When the musical slaughter was over, her fans formed a queue to thank her for a truly unforgettable recital.

Eddie dragged me to the receiving line. When my turn came to invent a complimentary remark, I introduced myself and told her that although my father had sung with the greatest prima donnas of his generation, he had never sung with anyone like her. As soon as

Madame Jenkins heard my name, her layers of rouge and lipstick parted in a huge smile, and she insisted that I join her in the receiving line. It was impossible to say no without offending her, so I dutifully stood at her side as she passed every well-wisher on to me with an effusive introduction. No one knew why I was there, and certainly neither did I. Eddie watched my discomfort with an offensive grin on his face.

On another occasion, Eddie played a deliberate prank on me, which he described in a memorable letter.

> There is another story connected with Jack Caidin. I used to visit his store quite often, and Enrico came with me on several occasions. He met a number of record collectors and entertained them with stories about his father. On one such occasion I printed on an 8 × 10 piece of paper "World's Greatest Tenor." It was winter and he was wearing a heavy coat; I slipped the sign on the back of his coat, under the collar. Rico was unaware of it, of course, but everyone else in the store saw it. After more jokes and kidding he left. He stopped and turned to wave good-bye to the men in the store from the outside, through the front window. A woman had just started to come in. She read the sign on his back, and we saw her question him in front of the door. He responded and she sidled away from him as if in fear. Rico turned toward us and behind her back gestured to us with a finger to his head, giving the international sign for "crazy," and walked on. The woman then entered.
>
> "Do you know you had a lunatic outside?" she asked the laughing customers.
>
> "Indeed, Ma'am," said Caidin innocently. "What makes you think so?"
>
> "He had a sign on his back 'World's Greatest Tenor,' and when I asked him who he was, he said, 'I am Enrico Caruso!' "[3]

DISILLUSIONED about my possibilities in New York and lured by the promise of a job in Chicago, Helen and I packed our belongings and left the city in February 1940. The only person I regretted leaving behind was my friend Eddie Smith.

Eddie was a remarkable person and a walking encyclopedia of operatic facts and lore. In 1983, he released one of my private recordings in a long-playing record featuring a potpourri of tenors, and it was the rediscovery of my few recordings that brought us together again after forty-four years. We reestablished contact in several telephone conversations. My collaborator, Andrew Farkas, who was also a long-time friend of Eddie's, asked him to write down a few incidents he remembered from the days we spent together. Although Eddie was in the last stages of a painful terminal illness, with his customary enthusiasm and good cheer, he labored two days on a long letter, which he followed up with telephone calls. Reminiscing about my unsuccessful struggle to gain a foothold in the world of opera, he observed:

"Look, Enrico, you were in a no-win situation. Had you made it, had you become a great singer, people would have said 'Big deal! It's easy for him. He is the son of Caruso!' "

THROUGH his record releases of live performances of the recent and distant operatic past, Eddie was known to collectors around the world. I believe I am doing a service for opera lovers everywhere if I devote a few paragraphs to what he told me of his background and career.

He was born Edward Joseph Smith in Brooklyn, New York, on 17 June 1913. His father, Dr. Joseph Smith, born in 1876 in Philadelphia, was the last of seventeen children. Dr. Smith's father—Eddie's grandfather—was in the diplomatic service, and at the age of six, young Joseph was taken to Europe. He grew up in turn-of-the-century Vienna, spent a year in St. Petersburg with his grandfather, and studied with Sigmund Freud. In 1897, he returned to the U.S. fluent in German, which gave a heavy accent to his native English for the rest of his life. In the Spanish-American War, he served in the medical corps as a sergeant attached to Roosevelt's Rough Riders. He later earned his degree from Jefferson College in Philadelphia and joined the staff of the Brooklyn State Hospital as neurologist and psychiatrist in 1904. When British surgeons were afraid to operate on King Edward VII, Dr. Smith performed the operation and pulled him through. In memory of the kind King whose life he prolonged by the successful operation, he named his son Edward. In addition to being an eminent physician, Eddie's father was an accomplished amateur violinist.

Eddie's mother was also a person of unusual talent. Born Sophia Sagere, she studied to become a concert pianist. She was a pupil of Rafael Joseffy and Josef Hofmann and made her debut with the New York Symphony in 1904, playing the Grieg A Minor piano concerto under the baton of Walter Damrosch.

With such parents, it is small wonder that the boy grew up with a profound interest in music and musicians. His parents took him to the Met from the age of three onward. They had been subscribers since before Eddie was born, and from the programs his mother had saved, Eddie was able to reconstruct that by the age of seven, he had heard Caruso forty-seven times.

In his teens, Eddie spent the summers in Europe or South America with his mother, visiting concert halls and opera houses. Because of his mother's social position and musical standing, he had entry into the highest musical circles and became friendly with many great performers of the period, among them Farrar, Ponselle, Gigli, Battistini, Hofmann, Kreisler, Pinza, and Rethberg. He first met Martinelli as a little boy at a party, and later in life, the tenor became a second father to him. He was teeming with anecdotes about these legendary artists, and musical literature is the poorer because he never wrote them down.

"How could I?" he said in our last telephone conversation, only weeks before he died. "These are historical personages by now, and I could never tell the truth about them. If I can't tell the intimate details, why write?"

Upon graduation from Columbia University, where he earned his B.A. and M.A. in journalism with a minor in music, Eddie became a professional baseball player. He left baseball in 1934 to join the staff of the *Hollywood Reporter;* then he became a reporter for *Variety* in 1938 and stayed with the magazine until 1942. From 1942 to 1945, he served in the Counter-Intelligence Corps of the Army Special Services. After the war, he worked for a publicity agency and served on the editorial staff of *Musical Digest* and as editor-in-chief of *World Wide Music Syndicate,* a syndicated weekly musical column.

Finally, in 1949, he went into the record business, founding the classical music department of Continental and Remington Record Companies. From this point on, he devoted all his time to recordings, first working for other firms, then making monthly releases under The Golden Age of Opera, Unique Opera Records (UORC), and A.N.N.A. Record Company labels. Culled from a variety of sources and often released with the consent and encouragement of the artists involved, these records were the first to acquaint collectors worldwide with operatic performances sung by legendary casts from the thirties and forties. They were the first so-called pirated records, and his large-scale, pioneering work made Eddie the Pirate King. Edward J. Smith became a household name among collectors. Through his tireless efforts, the off-the-air recordings from the personal archives of many famous artists gained wide circulation. Thanks to Eddie, opera buffs could own recordings of live performances of Tibbett, Martinelli, Schorr, Flagstad, Melchior, Pinza, Rethberg, Ponselle, Gigli, Sayão, Lehmann, Jeritza, Marjorie Lawrence, Björling, Kipnis, De Luca, Sved, Warren, Rothier, Crooks, Kullmann, Pons—the list goes on and on.

The 78 rpm recordings Eddie arranged for me were his first involvement with record production. He had great faith in me and in my future as a singer, and he did everything within his power to promote my career. Once, when I was feeling low, he went to the trouble of writing a glowing report of my future debut at the Met, which he had printed in the typeface used by *The New York Times*. Expressing the hope that I would someday be treated to such a review, he presented me with the printed piece—an absurd, touching gesture from a sensitive friend. For all his help, Eddie never asked for anything in return.

Eddie struggled with three primary cancers in his life, first in 1972, then in 1980, finally in January 1984. His last illness was diagnosed as Adens carcinoma of the lung, and his valiant fight was not prolonged. His wife, Anna, telephoned to let me know that on 11 July 1984, he quietly slipped away. With him vanished a vast store of twentieth-century operatic history. I wish I could offer a more fitting tribute to his memory than this brief summary of the enterprising, productive life he devoted to vocal art and artists. I, among many others, was greatly privileged to call him a friend.

CHAPTER THIRTY

Chicago

IN Chicago I held a succession of jobs which kept me barely above the poverty line. Only the dwindling royalty payments brought periodic relief. The state of my finances was such that I was unable to pay my 1939 income tax. In October 1940, the Office of the Collector of the Internal Revenue Service sent me a final notice saying that a "warrant for distraint" had been issued against me for nonpayment of taxes for the year 1939. I had one last chance, the notice added: "Execution of this warrant will be suspended until five days from date; and if payment is not received on or before that time, it will be necessary to proceed with an enforced collection of the amount due." I don't remember how I came up with the money, but I did. The amount I owed was a grand total of $12.36.

My correspondence with Mother continued. "Whatever happened to that film they wanted to make?" she asked on 1 May 1940. "It would be a wonderful thing because that way I could have a nice sum and would arrange something for the two of us." To my amazement, she added: "I received a letter from Rina, very affectionate. I answered, but I cannot be very expansive because I cannot forget that all my troubles were her fault. I forgive, but I cannot forget."

On 18 April 1940, I gave a memorial lecture to the Chicago College Club entitled "Reminiscences of My Father." It was so well received that it gave me the idea of writing a series of radio programs about Father's private life. If I gathered enough details that were as yet unknown, the programs could give a fascinating glimpse of the famous Caruso. Mother was an invaluable source of just such information. I told her about my plans and asked her to help me with material. Her reaction was unequivocally negative. On 31 July 1940 she wrote: "I ask you not to do what you tell me regarding the radio. Leave your father's private life in peace; it is not right for you to speculate about all that. It is not right and I do not approve."

The conspiracy of silence I encountered all my life now extended to Mother. I could gather the basic facts and the sequence of events from secondary sources; but the thoughts and feelings that consti-tuted the heart of the matter —the matter of the heart—Mother refused to divulge.

I replied to Mother that if she was unwilling to talk about private matters, very well then, at least she could send me some anecdotes about Papa. The objective of my programs, I told her, was not only to earn money, but also to help keep his memory alive. I also asked if she had a photograph taken with him.

"Regarding data and anecdotes about Papa," she replied, "I don't have any besides those you already know. As far as being forgotten, have no fear, everybody will always remember him. I have no photographs with him. If some little fact should come to my mind, I will write it down and send it to you."

Her unwillingness to tell me anything about my father was a great disappointment. If only I could talk to her! But the possibility of a trip to South America remained as remote as ever. I asked her what my chances would be of arranging a concert tour in Brazil, and in a letter of 6 October 1940, she wrote: "This is not a country to give concerts! Only for those who have a great name. Schipa is here, but I don't know him; he sang with Bidù Sayão." She also advised me to "try to take lessons from Tito Schipa, who is the only one who could give you artistic guidance and a perfect technique, because he is the only one who sings indeed with great schooling. Try to gain his friendship and his advice."

Her suggestion made sense but was impractical. Schipa and I were acquainted, but he was an internationally acclaimed tenor domiciled in Italy, while I was struggling in Chicago.

DURING our years in New York, Helen became friends with a singing teacher, Elisabeth Kriger, a former pupil of Lilli Lehmann. Helen often played the piano at Miss Kriger's coaching sessions, and Miss Kriger in turn let me practice in her studio. After we left New York, the ladies stayed in touch. In the early summer of 1941, one of her pupils was engaged to sing at a café on the Copacabana Beach in Rio de Janeiro. As she was to accompany the young soprano, she offered to call on my mother and take her anything I wished to send. Being a voice teacher herself, she was eager to meet Mother and perhaps learn some technical points from someone representing the old Italian school of singing.

In the letters that followed, Mother acknowledged "two visits from Miss Elisabeth. She is very nice and I found her most pleasant. I gave her an explanation of diaphragmatic breathing, which she does almost identically. . . . The *Signorina* Elisabeth will bring you a tie I made for you. I hope you will like it."

Upon her return, Miss Kriger gave me a detailed report, first by telephone, then in a letter. Mother looked well, she said, and lived comfortably. She had a nice little apartment and seemed healthy, considering her age. She thought of me all the time and wanted to see me very much.

Mother's next letter was late in coming and stamped in large black letters: "Opened by the censors." The international political situation was deteriorating rapidly, and a few months later came the Japanese attack on Pearl Harbor. Within days, Mother wrote an anxious little note, also censored, as was every subsequent letter until the end of the war.

13 December 1941

Dear Mimmi,

Answer immediately to let me know if I can still write to you at the same address.

I am very worried about you all.

May God allow peace to return soon to the world. I bless you and I send you a big kiss,

Mamma

She had more cause to worry than she knew. Immediately after the bombing of Pearl Harbor, I tried to enlist in the army, but I was rejected due to my age and my status as an "enemy alien." Determined to make some kind of contribution, in early 1942 I broadcast a program in Italian on WGES, calling on the Italians living in the

United States to help the war effort. The broadcast went well and produced a flurry of approving letters. Arnold B. Hartley, station manager of WGES, informed me that he had written to the Office of Facts and Figures in Washington, advising them that the station intended to make a special transcription, with me as the speaker, "on the duties of all Italian-Americans to American democracy." Mr. Hartley continued:

> This transcription will be distributed to all stations carrying Italian-language programs throughout the country. It is my feeling that the son of Enrico Caruso should have great influence among Italian-Americans in strengthening their loyalty to our democracy, which I know your father greatly admired and respected.
>
> We also have under consideration a symphonic hour, with you as commentator. I will talk to you later about this.[1]

When we had our talk about the symphonic hour, Mr. Hartley made a commitment to produce the program. I proposed a series of shows entitled "Contemporaries of the Great Caruso," which would feature one or more of the artists who had sung with my father. Mr. Hartley's assurance gave me enough confidence to begin collecting material in earnest.

MY starting point was Father's friend and colleague, Geraldine Farrar. In a polite letter, I asked her to be good enough to answer fourteen questions relating to her career. I worried needlessly about her reaction; Gerry Farrar did not disappoint me. Her letter of response, with the many dots characteristic of her style, radiated kindness. It was obviously typed by her, as were the three long pages appended to it, in which she answered each question at length.

> My dear Mimmi;
>
> What happy memories your letter called to mind; and I am glad to send the enclosed, hoping that the material will meet your needs for the radio series you have in mind . . . may they be all you hope . . . and that all your father's many comrades will have some interesting notes to give you.
>
> It had to be done in haste as I have so much here on hand, and no time for research. . . . nor the wish to keep you waiting for a reply.

It seems only yesterday that you were a little chap, just over from London, and your father brought you to see me at the Elysée Palace hotel, in Paris . . . and then I lost track of you in all the many years that changed so many lives.

Your father was always such a generous comrade, and from the first days when he came to Berlin, and had the musical world at his feet, my family cherished a real affection for him. . . . . that later period at the Met. found us all in many years of happy association. . . .

I saw your father the day before he sailed for Naples, and am glad I did have that last glimpse of him.

He passed away in the full bloom of incontestable triumphs, and so we all love to remember him . . . the vocal miracle of his age, knowing no defeat or rival.

With every good wish to you,
believe me
Very Sincerely,
Geraldine Farrar

5 July 1942

Her answers to my questions dealt mostly with the widely known details of her own career. She also made personal observations reflecting her artistic views and her opinions of other singers. On the subjects of her great teacher, Lilli Lehmann, and her colleague, my father, Farrar wrote:

[Lehmann] was unrelenting in her desire for perfection, in herself and in her students. She left nothing to chance, but conceded that inspiration sustained by a complete mastery of one's instrument, was the acme of desirable combination for fine performances.

For this reason too, your father was notable; he was not content to just employ his endowment of miraculous beauty, but studied all the time, to bring to the fullest, the marriage of song and art.

He could have easily remained a supreme singer, as far as voice was concerned, but to the phenomenal instrument, he added the final grace of art . . . an indifferent performance was never the aim, but the best his unceasing interest.

I recall in the first years of his assumption in French, of the role of FAUST; he labored to obtain the proper pronunciation, and at the same time, not change the flow of the truly beautiful melody. . . .

Since the gift of song is at its best in the flush of physical prime, I personally feel the retirement from public stage is incumbent on good taste and pride; never to have to apologize for the arrival of those years that should interest one in other ways; but always to have been a peak of fine endeavor, and thus leave one's public wishing for more, and *not* painfully aware of fading powers.

Your father, in my estimation was a favorite of the gods, since he passed away in his prime, with no human ear able to discern any waning of that glorious instrument.

Thus my own retirement came about very naturally, at the time when I felt other interests, not of public nature . . . and being zealous of the name I had worked hard to keep to a standard of high endeavor, that standard must never be lowered . . . nor was it.

As for teaching, I do not engage in it; with the advent of the many mechanical avenues of entertainment, I find that standards would have to be revised, and such changes admitted as would offend my taste.

Having had the association of truly great personages, I cannot enjoy nor accept, seriously, what is now the current exposition of song and art . . . as I have known it. This is a field for the younger generation who make music? and compose its noisy tunes. . . . and so the same generation will understand the idiom of these, and give their expression to the output; I can be content with no lesser plane than that I have known.

The world changes, and it is for the newcomers to follow their bent, as we of another epoch, watch from the sidelines.

The material she had sent captured and projected her personality so well that it required no editing. I was delighted, assured her of my deep gratitude, and asked for her permission to read it over the air. I also asked whether she preferred to be called "Miss" or "Madame." Once more the reply came by return mail.

My dear "Mimmi";

Your letter is just here, and of course you may read my missive to you, over the air; I am generally called "Miss," as most professionals are. So this manner will be the usual address, and the most familiar to the public. . . .

If ever you are in my neighborhood, it would give me

pleasure to see you ... tho I live in the country, I *do* come to
New York, and thus the distance need not be a barrier to an "a
rivederci."..... I can still see you in Paris, and recall the many
sweet things your proud father had to say of you. . . . . you
were the most mannerly little chap I ever saw.

> With all good wishes,
> Very Sincerely,
> Geraldine Farrar

11 July 1942

Encouraged, I wrote to ask her for the addresses of Father's former
colleagues. Again she replied immediately, enclosing addresses for
Bori, Amato, De Gogorza, Homer, Ponselle, Galli-Curci, Hempel,
and Alda. I collected addresses from other sources too, then I wrote all
the singers at the same time. The replies said something of the character of these operatic celebrities.

Alda's reply was typically terse. I knew she was reputed to be
outspoken to the point of rudeness, and I had met her before, when I
was selling hosiery in New York. She berated me then for being "just a
salesman," which, in her view, was a disgraceful occupation for a son of
Caruso. At least her caustic note was prompt!

July 1942

Dear Mr. Caruso:

I regret that while I am under contract, for radio broad-
casting, myself, I cannot allow anything from my book to be
used; nor can I give my name in conjunction with another program. I am sorry.

Gloria Caruso stayed with me for five days a few weeks
ago. You should try to do something serious and uphold the
name of your father.

> Sincerely yours,
> Frances Alda

Pasquale Amato sent a brief, handwritten letter which, as it turned
out, was one of his last. He passed away a few days later, on 12 August
1942.

New York, August 6, 1942

Dear Mimi [*sic*]:

Your letter was forwarded to me when I have taken ill with
arthritis which keeps me suffering in bed for the last three
weeks.

It is physically impossible for me in such condition to attempt anything that you ask at this moment as the doctor just allow [*sic*] me to do what is strictly necessary and only few minutes daily. Hope to be able to do so in the near future when, returning to Baton Rouge and hope in good health I can dictate to the secretary.

With all best wishes,

Truly yours,
Pasquale Amato

In a six-page manuscript letter, Mabel Garrison wrote, among other things:

I entered the Met in 1914 and made my debut as Frasquita in *Carmen*. The cast: Farrar, Bori, Garrison, Braslau, Caruso, Amato—Toscanini conducting. A few weeks later I went on with no rehearsals to do the Page in the 1st performance of the season [of] *Huguenots* (I was to take someone's place who fell down on the job) and was literally dragged around the stage most amiably by Caruso and Scotti. So my 1st two performances were with your father. And I was the Adina in *L'Elisir d'amore* in Brooklyn when he was taken ill after the 1st act. . . .[2]

In my 3rd year at the opera I was told to prepare Martha and I did, trying it out at Ravinia Park with Orville Harrold who was also at the Met. When I came to do it with Caruso—he was indisposed and couldn't come to any rehearsals. I was rather nervous because I had never seen him do the role and wasn't at all sure that what *I* did would be agreeable to him. I spoke to him before the first act and in his generous way—to put me completely at ease—he said "Listen, my dear, you forget Caruso and do exactly as you please—if you look for him over there (pointing to the right) he'll be there; if you look for him over there (to the left) he'll be there." And he was.

Lucrezia Bori was out of the country, but her secretary contacted her and replied on her behalf. Bori reminded me that she had made both her debut in Paris in 1910 and her debut at the Met in 1912 as Puccini's Manon opposite my father. They sang together many times, at the Met and on tour. Once, when they were performing in New Haven, Bori arrived at the theater, but her costumes did not. She was to sing Nedda in *Pagliacci* but refused to go on. Father went to her dressing room and begged her on his knees to sing the performance. In the end she relented, using the chorus girls' shawls to improvise a costume that was held together with ordinary pins. Father did not dare touch her all evening because of the pins; but after the performance, he went down on his knees again and kissed her hands to express his gratitude. The next day, the press reported that Miss Bori's costumes were the most original they had ever seen.

In addition to sharing this little story, Bori authorized her secretary to lend me the only extant copy of her press book. Among the broad range of responses I had from Father's old friends, there were several such acts of generosity and trust.

Emilio de Gogorza wrote twice. The first letter, dated 10 August 1942, was somewhat formal and contained autobiographical highlights along with a few references to my father. He wrote:

> It might be of interest to you to know that as a child I sang in the choir of the Carmelite Church in London with Gayarré and Santley! I also brought to your father his first contract with the Victor and it was my good fortune to interest him in a royalty contract. That was when Mr. C. G. Child my treasured friend was at the head of the record department and I was his first lieutenant in contacting the artists which I did for several years.
>
> Your father sent me a picture of "Mimmi" which is still in my possession and I knew you as a child.

It was generous of De Gogorza to say that it was his good fortune to interest my father in a royalty contract. It was entirely Father's good fortune to receive De Gogorza's counsel: It made him a wealthy man. Had he been paid in full every time he recorded an aria or song, neither he nor his heirs would have reaped the ongoing benefit from the sales of his records. His good friend and esteemed colleague, Titta Ruffo, like Richard Tauber after him, was more interested in being paid in full and on the spot. Ruffo signed a royalty contract fairly late in his recording career; if he had been properly advised by someone like De Gogorza, perhaps he would have had a steady income in his long years of retirement.

A second letter from De Gogorza, dated August 15, was a postscript to the first. He talked about Tosti, whom he knew well in London, and added:

> It came to my mind that the last time that I saw you was on

the Rue de Castiglione in Paris and I was struck by your beautiful English pronunciation and your looks which overjoyed your paternal parent who was leading you by the hand, the year if my memory is correct was 1911. [De Gogorza is off by a year: This had to be either 1910 or 1912.] It is always a pleasure to remember a cure at Salsomaggiore in 1914 with your father in July of that year, a most pleasurable memory.

Margaret Matzenauer was equally gracious. I wrote to her in New Jersey on July 1, and her reply was dated July 3. This speaks not only for her cooperative spirit but also for the legendary efficiency of the U.S. Postal Service in the days before airmail. Her letter, composed in endless sentences without punctuation, was a graphologist's delight, written in strong, large, angular letters in heavy black ink. She was prepared to offer even more help than the other artists.

> Dear Mimmie [*sic*]!
>
> I am greatly interested in your plan of presenting the contemporaries of your great father my dear friend Enrico. Is there a chance, that you would want me actually there at the broadcast and have me talk and also sing a few numbers as you will see from the material mailed that I am still singing before the public and going also into a show on Broadway as a comedienne! I do feel it would be so much more interesting to listeners to hear the actual voices instead of records. [At this point she gave a list of her favorite records.]
>
> I cannot tell you how much I am looking forward to paying this tribute to my beloved colleague and friend and I only wish I can come to Chicago in person and talk about my experiences with your father.

I also tried to contact some artists in person. Taking advantage of their presence in Chicago, I interviewed Edith Mason, and also Rosa Raisa and Giacomo Rimini. Raisa entertained me with stories about her childhood in Romania; and Rimini volunteered to give me singing lessons. I was grateful for the help so generously offered, but I soon realized that his teaching method was fundamentally different from De la Huerta's and thought it wiser not to "retool" my voice with a new technique that could destroy the good results already obtained with the old. Offering some polite excuse, I discontinued the lessons.

THE enthusiasm shown by these distinguished artists convinced me that I could assemble a fine series of programs. Although some letters produced disappointing results or none at all, I received enough interesting information to get started on the typescripts. I submitted the first script to WGES. The executives were enthusiastic, and a trial program of "Contemporaries of the Great Caruso" was aired. When the audience response was enthusiastic, a date was set for the following week to sign a contract. Unbelievably, by the time the appointment rolled around, the executives had changed their minds. The series was not to be.

I then submitted three scripts to H. C. Darnell at RCA Victor, explaining that each script was designed to present a singer and that without difficulty, I could produce programs for twenty-six to fifty-two weeks without repeating.

To my great disappointment, Mr. Darnell replied on August 27 that his company was "unable to use such a program, or script, at the present time."

Although I had to set the radio project aside, I stayed in touch with Gerry Farrar through correspondence. In 1943, I sent her a copy of her autobiography, *Such Sweet Compulsion,* for an inscription. She replied with a letter on 2 October 1943:

> My dear MIMMI;
>   I am mailing, insured, the book with a little word of greeting on the front page for you; it seems so odd to know you as a young man, when I can recall you so vividly as a very nice little boy . . . in whom your father took such pride.

The book arrived in due course with a gracious inscription reading: "For Mimmi Caruso: —whom I remember well as a little chap coming to see me with his father, and my friend. . . . With every good wish, Sincerely, Geraldine Farrar. Ridgefield, October 1943."

CHAPTER THIRTY-ONE

New York Again

HELEN BURNETT and I were married in Chicago on 5 June 1944.
Although we had been living together for five years, legalizing
our union gave us the illusion of a fresh start. We decided to take our
$600 savings and return to New York City. I could afford to concen-
trate on singing, and my immediate objective was to establish myself
in the city's music world.

Soon after our move to New York, I came upon a full-page advertisement in the June 25 issue of one of the newspapers: "Gimbel's Fifth
Floor sells Enrico Caruso mementos." The ad continued in detail:
"Out of the Villa Delle Panche, Caruso's home in Florence, Italy, and
from Mrs. Caruso and from one of the singer's life-long friends has
come a fascinating collection of mementos. An editor of a newspaper
to which Caruso sent his clever caricatures has given Gimbel's a stack
of the precious things, done in pencil, in pen and ink. And Gimbel's
has bronzes *by* Caruso. There was practically no limit to the man's
talents." The editor in question was Marziale Sisca, who had in his
possession an enormous cache of Father's caricatures. A partial listing
of the items for sale included a bronze of Caruso in *La Favorita* by O.
Cosentino, done in New York in 1906; a bronze self-portrait plaque; a

portrait plaque of an old man signed and dated in New York in 1905; and a signed bronze plaque identified as Caruso and his teacher, two men in profile side by side. I went to the sale. Seeing these familiar objects brought back memories and saddened me deeply.

In New York, I went to the Chase Manhattan Bank to open a savings account. Upon hearing my name, the clerk referred me to the vice president, and the latter escorted me to his office.

"And how much money do you intend to deposit, Mr. Caruso?" the vice president asked.

"Six hundred dollars."

"Do you also wish to open another account?"

"No, Sir."

"Perhaps you plan to transfer money from your accounts with other banks?"

"No; this is all the money I have," I said, regretting the fact more than he did. His solicitous smile became strained.

"In that case one of our account executives will take care of it, Mr. Caruso. Follow me, this way please."

And he politely ushered me out of his office.

The state of my career was more difficult to assess than my finances. I was thirty-nine, not too old for a singer, but much too old for a beginner. I had not used my voice professionally in a long time, and I badly needed coaching.

I looked up my old friend Pedroza, who by this time was concentrating on teaching and had many students. We began to work. It was not a case of the blind leading the blind, for no matter how well a singer remembers his maestro's teachings, he can never hear his own voice as it sounds to others. I firmly believe that Father used his own records as a learning device, both those that were released and the unpublished takes which he would listen to and then have destroyed. I needed Pedroza to coach me and correct my mistakes.

When we both felt I was ready to face an audience, Harry Stanley's agency booked me for a trial engagement. I opened on 8 November 1944 at the Kitty Davis Theater Restaurant, a supper club on Miami Beach. "Enrico Caruso, Jr., singing American songs in a modern manner," declared the program. I would be hard pressed to explain what that pretentious phrase meant but can only disclaim being its originator. I sang fairly well "in a modern manner," and the stint gave me confidence. My agent, reassured that I could take on further engagements, booked me for a string of one- and two-week appearances in fashionable nightclubs and hotels.

I opened on January 8 at the Town Barn in Buffalo. A singing Enrico Caruso was again a news item, and the event was written up in many eastern and midwestern newspapers on January 11; I even made the 22 January 1945 issue of *Time* magazine. The tour was on.

DID I enjoy singing? That is hard to answer. I wanted to sing, and I wanted to sing well. At the same time, I knew that I was inadequately prepared, even when I was at my best, when I left De la Huerta. Pedroza's coaching was a tremendous help; but try as I might, I could not surpass the level I had reached under Don Adolfo's tutelage. Every time I sang before an audience, I worried not only about how I would sound but also about how I would be received. Would I crack on the high C? I never did. Would I be compared again to my glorious father? I always was.

I was locked into a vicious circle. I needed engagements to earn money, those who hired me were interested *only* if I used my real name, and when I did, the audience found that I did not measure up to my father.

Before I went on, I was always a nervous wreck. Yes, I enjoyed singing after I had sung, when I knew it went well and the audience response was good. Sometimes, when I heard my voice soar, I was proud to be able to produce such sounds. But it was never an exhilarating physical sensation to open up and sing. I did not have the necessary experience or self-assurance to just relax and sing. The better evenings would bring a handful of fan mail, which did not reduce my apprehension about the next night and the next. I regarded every performance as a test for which I was not quite ready, and the only thing I would really look forward to was finishing the tour and getting back home.

Mother wrote on 30 April 1945: "I am happy that finally you are working and earning money! At least for that I can be tranquil. Let us hope that now you will be able to go forward and have a little material relief." She added: "I see you got married again! Will it last? Let us hope so. You were born to a fate of Helens!" The conclusion of the letter was the usual theme: "May God grant me the happiness to see you again, I will never ask anything else of the Creator. My adored son, if you knew how many sad moments I have spent thinking of you!"

Mother's repeated wish to see me set my mind in motion. I had to find a way to get to Rio and finally, finally see my mother! I asked Harry Stanley to get me a nightclub engagement and explained why I wanted to go to Brazil. He promised to cable the prominent nightclubs, while I was to take care of the legal end of the trip. Since I was not an American citizen, I needed an exit visa and reentry permit. It should have been a routine matter; the war in Europe was nearly over, and travel to South America from the East Coast was no longer a problem.

I asked Mother for advice about fees and repertory, suggesting that perhaps Gabriella Besanzoni could help me obtain a contract or line up additional bookings once I arrived. I mentioned that there was talk again about a Caruso film and reminded her that we had discussed it a few years earlier. I concluded by saying that I could hardly wait to embrace my beautiful mother.

She was elated at the prospect of my visit and wrote with great anticipation.

May 26 1945

My dear Mimmi,

I am answering yours of the 16th which I received with immense joy as you can imagine. . . .

May God want you to be able to obtain a good contract and come here and [may I] thus have the joy to embrace you before I die, and take with me the memory of your face. . . .

My dear Mimmi, even though I have completed my 70th year, I have, thank God, a colossal memory. I remember all the segments of my life all the way back when I was only a few years old. I remember very well my portrait and I remember very well the deal on the film they wanted to make about the life of our dear Enrico, and furthermore that you mentioned they offered a thousand dollars that I found insignificant. I alone could give the fabric of his entire life, from the time when he began to study with Maestro Vergine. But we will talk about that if there is an opportunity. . . .

I must warn you of one thing. I am no longer a friend of Gabriella Besanzoni because she has done a formidable dirty trick (which I will tell you if you come). Suffice it to say that she is the most wicked and false woman who exists in all mankind.

I am *entirely white,* but they say I resemble a princess of the 15th century—what do you think? As for being beautiful, I don't think I am.

I have been very sick! I had a touch of diabetes and a little uremia, but I am very strong and I cheerfully endured it all.

Very well then, my adored son. I trust in God [that I will
be] able to embrace you and have the happiness of knowing
you are in a good position.

I send you, along with a big kiss, my blessings.

Your Mamma, Ada

I was in luck. Stanley received not one but two offers from
nightclubs, and the contract terms were acceptable. I felt the long-
awaited visit would finally come to pass.

Between March 26 and June 6, I took fifty lessons from Pedroza at
three dollars a lesson. I worked very hard, and at the end of these
lessons we both agreed that my voice was in good shape. In the
meantime, Stanley lined up a month-long engagement at the
Roosevelt Hotel in New Orleans, where I gave one to three shows
daily from June 21 through July 18. Even *Musical America* carried a notice
about the engagement.

On June 22, while in New Orleans, I sent my application for an exit
visa and reentry permit to the Immigration and Naturalization
Service.

When I left New Orleans on July 23, I still had no answer. Stanley
had to cable a response to Rio, and when it became clear that I would
be unable to arrive in time to fulfill the engagements, the offers were
withdrawn. I never received an acknowledgement of my application,
nor an answer to further inquiries. The opportunity to visit my mother
was lost.

IN September I resumed my nightclub engagements. During 1945, I
sang in Buffalo, Cleveland, Milwaukee, Minneapolis, Chicago, New
Orleans, and Newark. In some cities, I appeared twice as I was called
back for a return engagement. Although I was warmly received everywhere, the tour was a nightly replay of my previous experiences,
beginning with the Cuban tour of 1935. Caruso's son who sang was a
curiosity; the name attracted attention, and I could fill a nightclub.
Then a curious thing would happen: The audience, both those who
had seen Father and those who knew his voice only from records,
would desperately want to see and hear a reincarnation of the great
Caruso. After the performance, a throng of well-wishers would surround and reminisce about my late father, the roles in which they
saw him, and what he said to them backstage.

"Ah, Mr. Caruso, I remember when I heard your father sing this
aria!"

"You know, Mr. Caruso, your top notes sound so much like your father's, but the middle . . ."

Or, "You have your father's low register, but not his top!"

The critics would add their two cents' worth, never failing to observe that the old man sang better than his son, yet never mentioning that the old man sang better than anybody's son. At times my listeners made comments about my voice within my earshot, drawing the customary comparisons while I was still singing. I grew so accustomed to these remarks that I could go on performing. Some people even complained that I did not look like my father, and I would patiently explain that I inherited my physiognomy from my mother. I was expected to match my father's singing note for note. But in the endless singing contest with my dead father, I could never hope to win.

The strain took its toll. After the second engagement in Chicago, I felt terribly ill. We took the night train to New York, and the following day, on 15 December 1945, I was rushed to the West Side Hospital with an acute case of diverticulitis.

It was time to face facts, to give up the dream that I would follow in my father's footsteps. I was wasting my time in nightclubs for fees that barely exceeded my expenses, and my pursuit of a singing career was ruinous for my health.

Around Christmas of 1945, I packed away my music, and that was the end of Enrico Caruso, Jr., tenor.

MOTHER was unaware that I had given up singing and with it any hope of a South American engagement. When I didn't hear from her for a while, I became worried about her health and sent a cable. She cabled back on February 27:

> HEALTH IS GOOD WAITING LETTER ANXIOUSLY
> WHEN ARE YOU COMING. MAMMA

We kept up our correspondence, and I tried to sound encouraging about a possible visit to Rio. Then, in the fall, I received word from the Italian embassy that after a short illness, Mother had died on 16 October 1946. Apparently, she developed nephritis, complicated by uremia and diabetes. Without antibiotics, and possibly without adequate medical care, she never recovered. I don't know whether she could have been saved, and it is better that I do not know. Her last letter gave no indication that she was gravely ill.

During the decade of our correspondence, my love for my mother grew with each letter, and the news of her death was a great shock. Beyond the tragic fact, I knew nothing about the circumstances of her death. Miss Kriger suggested that I write to a friend, Mrs. Correa, who had written to her the year before at Mother's request. I did so, seeking information and consolation. Mrs. Correa replied with a typed letter composed in fluent English.

She told me that Mother, who had become gravely ill in September, died almost painlessly, and "how everyone grieved, and how beautiful and noble she looked in her black coffin, *tutta di bianco vestita* [dressed all in white] and covered with flowers she loved so much." She also spoke of Mother's life in her later years:

> [Ada] lived by herself for years a simple and busy teaching life with the only company of a faithful negro woman named Paula, and a dog, both entirely devoted to her. To improve her economic life, she used to let the upper rooms of her comfortable house, but she scarcely had contact with people living there. Friends she had many, and she was admired and beloved by everyone.

Mrs. Correa mentioned that she was coming to New York at Christmastime. "When I will be there in USA," she wrote, "I will be very pleased to meet you and talk about our dear one who is no more." My Mother had left "a few memories" for me with her closest friend, a Mrs. Azamôr. I asked Mrs. Correa to bring these mementos with her. She answered again in English.

Rio, November 22, 1946

My dear Mr. Caruso,

I just had your last letter, and reading it was both gratifying and very sad. My mother and Mrs. Azamôr both cried when I read it to them with tears in my eyes. *La Signora* Azamôr, to whom I read your letter by telephone, said: "*Lui è veramente il suo caro figliuolo, come lo chiamava lei.*" ["He is indeed her dear little boy, as she used to call him."]

Please, don't be so distressed. She wouldn't like it at all. She used to say that she was ready to go now, because her time was over and she craved for her place of rest and peace, but we wouldn't hear of it, because she was always so gay and looked still so full of life, strength and grace. Her head was a study of beauty haloed by white silken curled hair. Yes, we'll certainly have memories to talk over, when we'll meet.

I am informed that my ship will depart on December 5, and we'll arrive in New York exactly by Christmas, 25. . . . I decided to take with me what Mrs. Azamôr has for you. . . .

Looking forward to meet you at the dock, I remain here sincerely yours,

Santinha Martins Lopes Correa

True to her word, Mrs. Correa brought me a few pieces of jewelry, the letters Mother had kept over the years, and her photographs. That was all that remained to me of a mother I had never really known. When I saw Mrs. Correa in New York, she confirmed what she had said in her letters. Mother was a wonderful, warm woman, kind-hearted and gracious. She talked about me often and never stopped hoping to see her "little boy" once more.

I learned that Mother had dictated a will on 21 September 1946 and signed and dated it the following day. Written in pencil on two sheets of paper, it read:

I, the undersigned, of sound mind and completely of my own volition decide and claim to dictate my last wishes.

The money that has been deposited on this house and the interest thereof should be used to buy a small corner in the cemetery. The amount deposited is 3.450$ [contos] exclusive of the equity.

All the furniture and household utensils are to be sold and the proceeds to be given to the poor of Bottafogo.

The money placed in the drawer of the long chest is to be given to Paulina Melo [Mother's friend and servant, "Paula"].

My jewelry, that is, the platinum plaque with diamonds and my topaz pendent, should be sold and the proceeds given to my son Enrico Caruso Junior.

My music is to be given as a souvenir to my students, as well as my photographs to my son.

These are my last wishes after those of God.

Ada Giachetti
Rio Janeiro—22 September 1946

BEFORE Mrs. Correa's visit, I had written to Mother's intimate friend, Mrs. Azamôr. If it were possible, her emotional reply increased my sense of loss.

Rio de Janeiro, 28 November 1946

Signor Enrico Caruso,

I was very pleased to receive your letter of the 17th.

I can well imagine your sorrow upon receiving the sad news. We, who knew that she was ill, we, who expected the fatal moment, also felt a stab in our heart. I can imagine you, the son! ... far away! ... without fate permitting you to embrace her.

Weep, *Signor* Enrico, for not having had the chance to be near your mother! ... For not having been able to press her to your bosom, to cover her with caresses and kisses. You don't know what you have lost! You don't know the kind of person your mother was! ... You don't know how much she loved you!

She never forgot her adored son in her prayers.

When someone mentioned that you, *Signor* Enrico, were far away, she never had a word of reproach for her little son.

In her prayers she asked Heaven every day: "My God! My beautiful and good Madonna! Don't let my sons suffer; give their pain to me!" ...

Refined soul! She knew how to forgive everyone, particularly those who were responsible for her sad end.

And ... if you should have the opportunity to find or communicate with your aunt (the sister of your mother), reassure her, tell her that Ada has forgiven her and always asked God that even He should forgive her. ...

I will impose on the kindness of *Signora* Correa to have her bring you the mementos your mother had entrusted to my care that should be yours.

I advise you to retain a lawyer whom you can trust to take care of your interests here. Otherwise years and centuries will pass before you receive any satisfaction. If possible, [obtain] a document proving that you are indeed the son of Ada Giachetti. In the hope of making your acquaintance in person one day, respectfully,

América Lignini Azamôr

Mrs. Azamôr's final words were the ultimate irony. In order to collect my maternal inheritance, I needed to prove that I was the son of Ada Giachetti! Yet all my documents gave my mother as "n.n.," not known. By law, Ada Giachetti and I were not related.

The last twist of fate in our shipwrecked lives, hers and mine, was the disposition of her estate. The Italian consulate was obliged to track down the next of kin. The closest legitimate, living relative of Ada Giachetti was Lelio Botti, her firstborn son, whom she had not seen since he was an infant. I learned later, from Fofò, that Lelio collected the money Mother had willed to me and supposedly passed it on to Rina. I only hope this posthumous gift helped him to muster some compassion for this mother he, too, had never known.

Ada Giachetti was buried in Rio de Janeiro in the cemetery of *San João Batista*. May my beloved mother's restless soul find eternal peace.

CHAPTER THIRTY-TWO

My Brother Fofò

ALL my relatives save my mother were in Italy, and I lost contact with them during the war. As soon as the international situation returned to normal, I resumed correspondence with Elena and my younger son Wladi. I learned that Grandmother Maria had passed away of natural causes in 1939,[1] and Uncle Giovanni had died of a heart attack in 1940; the other members of my family were unharmed. After Mussolini's fall, the Germans interned most of the Italian army in Germany, and Enrico (my older son) and Roberto (Fofò's son) were taken prisoners of war. In a letter of 9 May 1945, Elena asked for vitamins, sugar, shoes for Wladi, and cigarettes. She asked whether my mother was still alive and acknowledged newspaper critiques I had sent her from my tour. In a letter of July 5, she complained that Enrico was still not back from the POW camp; he was not repatriated until late in 1945. Elena also wrote: "Do you know that Dino Barsanti has a most beautiful voice and will soon make his debut?" The war had delayed his career, but my auto-mechanic friend had stuck to his singing. Giving him Papa's scores was not a waste after all.

I knew my family in Italy was in dire need. I sent what money I could and helped them with food parcels. However, Elena, then and until her death, was convinced that I was drawing fabulous sums from Victor, from my films, concerts, and records. Nothing could convince her to the contrary, and she wrote many acrimonious letters over the years. Despite the Mexican divorce and my remarriages, she considered herself Mrs. Enrico Caruso, Jr., and thus entitled to a portion of Father's record royalties. After the divorce, I kept any royalties received, so in 1953 Elena tried to sue me for what she considered her just share. I wrote to her lawyer in Rome, Gennaro Leone, that I had no intention of defending myself. I had no money for the out-of-pocket expense of hiring a lawyer, and if she won the case, there was nothing to collect, for I had no assets and nothing to give. I asked Leone to advise her to drop the suit.

The other person who reentered my life was my brother. At war's end, Fofò lived near Trieste and was worried about living in a territory controlled by Marshall Tito. In addition to his political concerns, Fofò found himself in a peculiar financial situation. His share of the Victor royalties had been accumulating since 1941 and now exceeded $10,000. But because he was a citizen of a formerly hostile country, the money could not be transferred from the United States to his account in Italy. If he wanted to collect it without excessive delay, he had to come to the U.S. and claim it in person. It became my lot to help him make the trip.

My brother and I had an unusual relationship. We did not grow up together; except during the summers, we had lived apart until 1914, when he was sixteen and I was ten. My memories are few prior to the summer of 1910; the frequently reproduced picture showing the heads of Papa, Fofò, and me, one behind the other like organ pipes, was taken that year on the beach at Rimini.

When I was a toddler, Fofò used to play with me as if I were an animated toy he could put into his cart and drag around the garden. I was always glad to see him, but I didn't miss him particularly when we were apart. An attachment developed between us only during the years in Livorno and Florence. After that time, we thought of each other with the casual affection of two boys who happened to grow up in the same family.

As Fofò grew older, he tried to spend as much time with Papa as possible. They had long conversations, about what, I neither knew nor cared. Fofò's respect for Father grew as he matured, reaching such proportions that I can only call it adulation. That Fofò was closer to him than I never bothered me. Before the first great war, I was too young to have much interest in Father; and when I was in America with him, Fofò was not around, so the idea of competing for his attention or affection did not even arise.

After I moved back to Italy and married Elena, Fofò considered me an adult to be dealt with on an equal footing. Being older and streetwise, he could have helped me to avoid some of my blunders. But he was concerned with his own affairs and offered no advice on the handling of my affairs. Our association during our early adult years did little to promote a real bond, though we always felt a fair degree of brotherly caring and remained on good terms.

After we both married, Fofò often came for visits and usually stayed for dinner. We would talk about Papa, play cards, and discuss our common concern: the money delayed in America. Otherwise, for the most part, our lives moved in separate orbits.

Fofò was an opportunist of the first order. He disliked Dorothy for her legal maneuvering, yet he was always very friendly to her. "Politics!" he would explain. There was an angle to everything he did. When I asked him why he continued his friendship with Rina after Papa's instructions to have nothing to do with the Giachettis, he first said, "Because Auntie Rina is, after all, Auntie Rina." He paused for a moment then added, "and if I am nice to her, she may leave her beautiful pearl necklace to Armanda." He disliked Mother all his life, yet in November 1924, he obtained her address from Grandfather Guido or from Giovanni and wrote her a charming letter.

The letter was a masterpiece of calculated melodrama. He set the tone by stating that although he barely remembered what she looked like, "something in my heart calls out every now and then, 'Mamma!'" He mentioned that he was married and had a son, then complained that he could not afford a trip to see her. "Are we destined never to see each other again?"

After this buildup came the true reason for the letter. "My capital is Signa, and it is worth three or four million [lire] today, but it takes time to find a buyer." This was followed by a detailed description of the real estate at Signa and the suggestion that Mother might know some South American millionaire in a position to buy Bellosguardo. He dangled the bait: If she found a buyer, they could live close to each other again, she could "get to know his little one" and his wife, and someday "your Fofò could embrace his mother again."

He followed up the letter with a lovely studio portrait of Armanda and Roberto, inscribed: "*Alla mia cara Mamma in ricordo di mio figlio e mia moglie, Rodolfo. Firenze 1925.*" ("To my dear Mamma as a memento of my son and my wife, Rodolfo. Florence 1925.") I do not know whether he wrote to her again, but he sent her another portrait six years later inscribed with the dedication, "*Alla mia cara Mamma in segno di figliale affetto, Fofò. Firenze, Feb–16–31.*" ("To my dear Mamma as a sign of filial affection, Fofò. Florence, 16 February 1931.") Our astute mother was not taken in by these attentions; she once commented that Fofò was "*veramente falso*"—truly phony.

Fofò used a large vocabulary and spoke pure Italian; he often criticized my Tuscan accent. He graduated from high school and attended the *liceo,* which gave him a sound basic education. He knew French and a little English, was well read in the classics and in Italian and world literature, was at home in history, and was sufficiently well acquainted with the high points of Western civilization to hold his own in most company. He had no academic or artistic ambitions and no interest in higher education. Fofò was always careful about his clothes, a preoccupation he picked up from Papa. He had pleasant manners and the bearing, presence, and conversational manner of a gentleman. He was always enormously proud of being Enrico Caruso's firstborn son, and if the situation allowed, he flaunted and exploited this fact shamelessly.

In Florence, Fofò's friends belonged to the upper middle class. The circumstances of his birth and his lack of a title kept aristocratic circles closed to him. In the twenties, he became involved with a fast crowd, experimented with drugs, and in one escapade contracted syphilis. It was a very bad case, but after his recovery he boasted about it as if it had been some heroic accomplishment. Indeed, he boasted of everything dangerous, illegal, or immoral in which he was involved.

Father's older valet, Martino Ceccanti, was the caretaker of the villa at Signa after 1915 or so. (Following Father's death, he became the administrator of Gloria's properties in Florence.) After Fofò was discharged from the army in 1919, he stayed at Bellosguardo, where he managed to get hold of the keys to the vault where Father's gold coins were kept and took a handful. He hid them in the crack of one of the sofas, and Martino accidentally found the hoard. Confronted with the evidence, the culprit confessed, which put Martino in an awkward position. Should he report to his employer that his son was stealing from him? Should he cover up the crime? Martino ordered Fofò to put the money back and did not tell Papa about the incident, but he made sure that Fofò never gained entry to the vault again. When Fofò told me about this years later, he added that he still managed to filch a gold piece every now and then from the superintendent's office. His motto was "*Pochi, maledetti, ma subito!*" which freely translated means "A little, damn you, but now!" I believe his pilfering did not go unnoticed but was tolerated for the sake of family peace. Again, Fofò not only talked about his little dishonesties then and later, but was apparently quite proud of them.

Around 1914, while we were living at Le Panche, Rina suddenly dismissed one of the maids. Miss Saer took me to visit her, instructing me in advance to be nice to the girl because she was very unhappy. I assumed she was disconsolate because she had been let go and did not learn the real story until much later. The maid had been caught in bed with Fofò, and since the son of the family could not be fired, the maid was dismissed. She became pregnant and had a baby girl. When Fofò was in New York in 1948 and this incident came up, he looked back on even this sad adventure as some kind of heroic deed.

I never had any illusions about my brother's less-than-sterling character. But Fofò also had a gentle side. This was reserved for his wife, Armanda, whom he deeply and passionately loved, despite his passing infidelities, and always treated with effusive tenderness.

Fofò learned to drive in Rina's car in Livorno in 1914 and eventually became an excellent driver. He loved to drive fast, yet I don't think he ever had an accident. Cars and stock-car racing were his hobby. He raced in the *Circuito del Mugello,* and in 1934 he won the great Italian automobile race, *il giro delle Mille Miglia.* This was a grueling course of 1,000 miles, and Fofò arrived two hours ahead of the second car in his category. Of a total of 187 cars, only 120 finished the race; eleven drivers died and forty were injured. Fofò had asked several auto manufacturers to back him, only to be turned down because he was an "amateur" with no chance of winning. It must have given him great satisfaction to prove them wrong. He received the winner's trophy from Mussolini himself and was always very proud of that honor.

I never knew exactly what my brother did for a living. He was an *affarista*—a wheeler-dealer—and was reticent about his affairs, which no doubt often strained the limits of the law. In any event, steady employment was not Fofò's métier. In the early 1930s, I urged him to come to the United States and start some business here. He had money from the sale of Bellosguardo and had just collected his share of the Victor settlement. He was in a position to emigrate but was disinclined to do so, for he felt more at home on his native soil and in his native language. In the mid-thirties, he went into partnership with the husband of Armanda's older sister, Aurelia—a gilt-edged crook named Alberto Panerai. They opened a Fiat dealership in Florence, but the business did not do well, and they sold it around 1936.

In letters of November 1938 and September 1940, he told me about his African adventures. He first went there with Armanda's brother, Ernesto. They made a good deal of money but lived like pioneers in the African heat that at times reached 122 degrees in the shade. He had to shoot at crocodiles to keep them at bay in order to bathe, and at night he was kept awake by the howling of hyenas and jackals. But he found it a big and beautiful country and returned once more, this time with Panerai. For two years, they ran a trucking service between Eritrea and Addis Ababa under "infernal conditions." Fofò was also fighting liver disease and malaria. The investment was mostly his, so he stood to lose the most if the venture failed. During one of his worst attacks of malaria, Panerai disappeared, taking with him not only one of the trucks, but also their money. Fofò sued his brother-in-law but never recovered his investment.

He returned to Italy in 1938. For a time, he smuggled gold across the border into Switzerland, a capital crime in those days. During World War II and for some time afterward, he worked as office manager and bookkeeper for the firm Snia Viscosa in the town of Torre Viscosa, near Trieste. This was a German affiliate making synthetic fibers and other war materials, and a prime target for Allied bombing raids. The plant was struck more than once; Fofò and Armanda lived in constant fear for their lives.

After the war, Fofò planned to collect his share of the accumulated Victor royalties and to export reproductions of Italian artworks to America. I wrangled with the authorities to secure the release of the money and was partially successful: The government authorized the transfer of a monthly living allowance of $150, with payments starting in March 1947. Later they authorized a payment of $1,000 for medical expenses and a travel advance, which made Fofò's plans for a trip to America viable and left him with a credit of $8,300 at the end of 1947.

A LETTER dated 27 December 1947 projected a sick and disillusioned Fofò with no trace of the old swagger. To my surprise, he suggested that he might wish to settle with Armanda in the United States:

> I don't have much pretense left; I have a heart condition
> and can no longer do any work that requires movement. I
> would be fine in a little village on the Atlantic in the south
> where it is warm, cheap, and relatively close to you, the only
> blood relative I have left on Father's side!! Our poor family!
> Even Mother is dead, and although I did not have much affec-

tion for her, now that I know she is no more, I feel lost. I believe she left several thousand pesos that went to Botti who says he wants to pass them on to Aunt Rina. I really hope so for the sake of that poor old lady. . . . Roberto is engaged and will soon have a family of his own, and the two of us could vegetate there on some seashore in our last days. To be reunited with you would be a beautiful dream come true!

In a letter of 9 January 1948, he repeated his wish to finish his days in peace near me, because "even with some grey hair around the temples, I feel the same affection for you as I did when you said *'thuto thera'* . . ." He wrote again the following day, mentioning that "Auntie Rina is with *Signora* Tina Fontanella, at Crespina (Pisa), and she would be happy if you wrote to her. *Signor* Fontanella has been dead for about five years." I had never corresponded with Rina, so I am sure that I did not respond to Fofò's suggestion.

IN 1945, Dorothy published her second biography of Papa.[2] It was a respectable effort, considering that she had known him only in the last three years of his life and that he had spent the final eight months as an invalid. The book dealt primarily with their years together, giving only a sketchy outline of his life prior to their marriage. It was a success due to the inclusion of the many letters Father had written to Dorothy, which she shared with a grateful reading public.

Then, in 1947, Eugenio Gara published a full-scale Caruso biography in Italy.[3] Gara borrowed liberally from published sources. His book contained little original material and few insights, but was an amalgam of previous works—those written by Dorothy, Pierre Key, and Nicola Daspuro. Gara sent me an inscribed copy through Fofò, but I was very disappointed. Papa again appeared wreathed in the halo of the limelight, and beyond the familiar anecdotes, his human side was nowhere to be seen. Apparently, my old friend De Segurola shared this view. In a series of three articles entitled "My Hall of Memories,"[4] he wrote:

"Two or three books have been published about Enrico Caruso, but in not one of them have I found the man, the real man I knew intimately, and the artist, the real artist that he was."

Each generation of writers relied almost exclusively on the ample and often faulty documentation of Father's career in the international press. Focusing increasingly on the career of the singer, the professional performer fulfilling engagements, they moved farther and farther away from the man. Yet I firmly believed that only a performer who drew on his life experiences could become an artist. To understand and assess an artistic personality, one had to know something of those experiences. A large portion of Father's story was missing and deserved to be told.

This realization prompted me to consider writing a family biography. The idea of a book was not new. Eddie Smith was the first to suggest that I write one, fleshing out Father's life story with the details of his private life. I did not have the facts to do so, but my brother did. He had lived with our parents, had memories of our mother, and had witnessed some of the momentous turning points in Father's life. He also had access to Aunt Rina, who could supply some of the important details that Mother was unwilling to divulge. When it appeared that Fofò would have to come to New York to collect his royalty money, I saw an opportunity for the two of us to jointly author the book no one else was in a position to write. I presented the idea in my next letter to Fofò:

> I have many letters from Mamma, but they don't say much. They say enough, however, to cast a light on the several fundamental reasons that led to the separation of our parents. Rina has the key. If you, who were always close to her, could convince her to unburden her soul and merit the forgiveness of our mother, you will have a story you would hardly expect. Rina, and perhaps Grandmother Teresa, if she is still alive, could give you the truth of all that happened that destroyed our parents' happiness.

Fofò's next letter, dated 28 January 1948, was written after a visit to Naples and Father's tomb.

Dear Mimmi,

So many years have passed since we were boys, but I always remember you as a little toddler, very willful and determined, at the same time very attached to your older brother, which made him proud. I cannot remember you otherwise and I wish it to remain so. You are the memory of our childhood now irretrievably gone, of the most beautiful years of our life, our lost possessions, everything that was our family. You will say I carry too great a burden, but it is a burden that never weighed you down, and I am glad for that. What you say of

poor Mamma makes no difference to me. Our father loved her
immensely, and even if she could not stay with him, the fact
remains that she abandoned us not only physically but
spiritually as well. Remember that I was at the front in the previous war, at the disposal of those who called themselves our
relatives and administrators; and when I was struck by malaria
and the Spanish flu and lay on the naked ground among the
wounded and the dying, I did not have one comforting word
from anyone, especially our mother! You did not live through
my miseries, you don't have the moral pains; but I cannot
forget. The transgressions of my father, although he did
commit them, did not exceed those that you, I, and thousands
of others commit, while moral offenses are more grave for me.
I don't want to condemn Mamma by this, nor Papa or the
others; I only egoistically think that the way we—you and I—
have gone was because all this happened while I was old
enough [to understand, while] you understood nothing.

Fofò's attitude toward Mother did not surprise me. At the same
time, I believed that Mother must have had her reasons for doing what
she did. This I said in a letter of February 15, and I also returned to the
notion of the book:

There have been many books written about Enrico
Caruso, the tenor . . . but we should have new material, that to
date has never been shared with the public. I mean the true
story of Papa, Mamma, Rina, you, and me. This is essential in
order to depict our father as a man, not only as an acclaimed
singer or a public idol. You . . . you are the one, the only one
who can gather all the details and materials we need. You must
research the facts, the truth . . . You must talk to those who are
still with us and know something: Rina, Emilio the gardener of
Le Panche, his wife, and others. Try to find out who the
servants were at the time Mamma left. That she left is not
important, the whole world knows that. But why? Why? We
want to know. The reasons must have been tremendous. From
the letters Mother sent me over the years, I could gather that
the biggest reason was Rina, the fact that she accepted our
father's amorous advances while they were all living at Le
Panche, and that she continued the liaison in London when
they sang together at Covent Garden. Mind you, I don't

condone the past, I have simply forgiven it. Perhaps it was easier for me than for you, because I did not suffer as you did.

I maintained that it was our obligation to present the facts as we knew them, without any attempt to cast Papa in a more favorable light than truth permitted. "I am with you all the way," my brother replied on February 21. He was in full agreement that we should approach Father's life story with absolute candor. As he wrote:

> The naked truth of his life story will make the most fascinating biography written to date about a man who has by now passed on to immortality. . . . As far as Mamma is concerned, I can tell you that the truth will not flatter her, especially that she had always disliked me and had often brutally abused me, provoking the intervention of Papa and others. As for Rina, she had known Father before Mamma did, and if there were amorous relations between them, it should not have entitled our mother to abandon three sons, one of whom was alien to all that! . . .
>
> Papa, with all the faults he may have had, always thought of supporting Mamma and shortly before his death told Dora to send to the "mother of his sons" 25,000 lire annually, an amount more than sufficient in those days to live decently. I was present at this discussion in Sorrento. As for our being bastards, as you say, it is not our concern, because our father was free and young, he legitimized us, and we always bore his name. If there was ever an uproar about this, it was due to the base jealousy of our Neapolitan relatives (Giovanni, Bettina, and the others) and the celebrated lawsuit of Milan in which Mamma jeopardized our name and paternity, but was defeated.
>
> As far as the famous chauffeur is concerned, it is not worthwhile to go fishing for him. He was a good-looking man, a bit of a "bull," and a typical seducer of women. I know enough about him without looking for him, which would be painful and disconcerting.

This was the first time I heard that Father had explicitly asked Dorothy to send 25,000 lire a year to my mother. Because Mother had to support herself with singing lessons, it was obvious that Dorothy had declined to honor yet another of her husband's wishes with respect to the disposition of his fortune.

Fofò's comment about Romati prompted me to tell him what Mrs. Correa had said to me about the relationship. On 28 February 1948, I wrote:

> I was told by one of the Portuguese pupils who had known our mother in the last thirteen years of her life that Romati was a member of the mafia, that he always had plenty of money which he gave to our mother, and he threatened to kill Papa and us if she left him. Supposedly he wasn't a nobody but came from a good family. One fine day he disappeared and was never seen again. But before he left, he sent a wallet with several thousand pesos (or contos, or whatever) to Mother for her support.

In the same letter I told Fofò the biggest news of the day in the recording industry: A test pressing of "Vecchia zimarra," where Papa sang bass, had been located and would soon be released by both Victor and His Master's Voice. The discovery of the recording was a sensation, and collectors eagerly awaited the release.

A search for the record had begun almost a year earlier. Bruno Zirato, Father's former secretary, wrote to De Segurola on 17 March 1947 asking for "a tremendous favor." He continued:

> For the sake of our old friendship, I am sure you will not refuse it. As you probably know, you and I are getting older and we have to think of future generations' pleasure, and therefore I am asking you if you could do me the favor of allowing the Victor people to copy the famous record "Vecchia zimarra" that our great friend, Caruso, recorded in 1916 after that memorable incident of singing the "zimarra" at the Academy of Music in Philadelphia.[5]

Zirato added that he wanted Victor to make copies "so that Mrs. Caruso and I might have a copy of it." He wrote that his own copy of the recording "was lost someplace," and when he made inquiries at the Victor Company, he was told that the matrix had been destroyed.

De Segurola replied on March 27:

> The copy that Mr. Child gave me at the time of that memorable incident got lost together with other contents of the two trunks that when I came to Hollywood I left with Vladeck Zbyszko, owner of the building 3 West 69th in which I was then living. He sold the house without taking care of the

two trunks in which I had other precious things, a rare violin by Gaspar de Saló, among them. But what is even more strange is that Victor destroyed the matrix of such an unusual and meaningful record, and that Dorothy neglected it too.[6]

Zirato next tried Father's old friend, Dr. Mario Marafioti. Marafioti was just recovering from a heart attack, and neither he nor his wife was interested at the time in letting Zirato have the precious record to be copied. Now that the release was imminent, I was curious to learn the circumstances, so I wrote to Dr. Marafioti in Los Angeles for information.

I received a reply from Dr. Marafioti's wife:

25 February 1949

Dear Mimi [*sic*],

Excuse my delay in answering your letter, but Doctor has been quite ill. He had a heart attack about nine months ago—from which he has never fully recovered—and since then has not been actively interested in anything pertaining to business. If he is well enough by spring, he hopes to go to Italy.

In regard to the record which you wrote about, Doctor was never very anxious to do much about it in the past. He kept it principally as a souvenir to which he attached great sentimental value rather than commercial value, for after your father sang "Vecchia zimarra" in Philadelphia, it was the Doctor who suggested that he make a record of it to commemorate the event—unique in vocal history—in which a singer sang as tenor and basso in the same opera.

It was for this reason, in fact, that he was reluctant to give it to Victor until last year; but then we never came to any agreement with them. . . .

With kindest regards from Doctor and myself, I am

Sincerely yours,
Clara Marafioti

When *The New York Times* announced the impending release of the record, Zirato felt obliged to pen a memorandum to Carter Brown of the *Times* on 22 September 1949. He recounted his version of the incident as published in the 1922 book he coauthored with Key, adding the following:

Caruso was many times asked to give his permission for the release of this record and he always refused. I think that his wish should be respected even today, so I am amazed to read that the Victor Company has decided to publish this recording.

This was certainly a curious statement from a man who only two years earlier was thinking of "future generations' pleasure" in having the record copied.

Encouraged by the resurfacing of this record, I asked Fofò to seek the assistance of the His Master's Voice offices in Milan to track down the matrix of the "Prologue" from *Pagliacci*. If it existed at all, it had to be somewhere in the company vaults in England, and the Milan office could initiate a search. There was a rumor in the family that Father did record the prologue, although I never met anyone who had seen or heard it. That he had thoughts of recording the piece is quite clear from a conversation quoted by Calvin G. Child, director of the recording laboratory of the Victor Company and Father's long-time friend. This appeared in *The New York Times* on 4 August 1921, only two days after Father's death. Child recalled:

> Once I visited him at the old Knickerbocker Hotel while he was being shaved, and I am not so sure that there was not a manicurist working at his hand, too. He said to me:
> "Some day I will make a record just for me and you alone, and I will sing it for you now. Fucito, the piano!"
> And he sang the baritone prelude [the prologue] to *Pagliacci* with infinite richness. I had never heard it sung better.
> "Why make that record for us?" I asked. "Why not for everybody?" His reply was:
> "If I did, then there would be a baritone war."

The article went on to quote Child's version of the "Vecchia zimarra" incident in Philadelphia, but curiously, Child failed to mention that Caruso had recorded the aria, even though he knew about it. True, it was a "private" record: Papa gave away five pressings to friends, then the matrix was destroyed. This take was entered in the log books of the Victor Company; but another unusual take, the introductory tenor solo of the *Rigoletto* "Quartet," was not. The latter is a ten-inch disc, which in itself is an indication that it was meant to be a test record only, as a ten-inch side could never accommodate the full four minutes of the "Quartet." Whether more than one copy was pressed is not known. Papa wrote on the label of the surviving disc in bold letters: "To Caruso by Enrico."[7]

I thought it was possible that Papa also recorded the "Prologue" from *Pagliacci* strictly for himself, and that is why there was no trace of it in the recording logs of the Victor Company. I hoped that Fofò would either find proof of its existence or permanently put the *canard* to rest. As I later learned, Zirato, in his memorandum to *The New York Times,* stated unequivocally with reference to the prologue: "This aria was never recorded, however."

To further our plans for a biography of Papa, I asked Fofò to take color pictures of the portrait of Mother that Elena had given to Umberto, the painting of Papa as Vasco da Gama I had left with Elena, and portraits Father had had Stragliati paint of the two of us; I also asked him to bring me back two caricatures I had lent to Rina when she and Teresa had the *pensione* in Rome. I suggested that he borrow other memorabilia from our relatives to illustrate the book.

Fofò assured me that he would visit our relatives and collect as many facts, insights, and documents as possible, but I grew increasingly impatient with him for postponing the most important interview of all. In April 1948, I wrote: "When are you going to see Rina? Are you waiting for her to go to the other world with her secrets?"

Fofò never did visit Giovanni's widow, Aunt Bettina, and our family history is the poorer for the many details she took to the grave. But he did go to the offices of His Master's Voice in Milan. In a letter dated April 26, he reported:

> That they should have the matrix of the "Prologue" of *Pagliacci* can be absolutely ruled out, this having been a most private recording of Papa's of which he made them destroy the shell. Therefore there is no hope of finding it except with some old collector friend of Papa's.

His phrasing suggests that the record did exist at one time. Frankly, I doubt that either he or the officials of His Master's Voice in Milan had any basis for this assumption.

Fofò wrote on May 26 that he would be leaving from Genoa on the *Vulcania* in "exactly forty-three days."

He left his visit to Rina to the very last minute, for he was extremely reluctant to undertake this delicate mission. In a letter of June 14, he let me know what he had accomplished.

> My dear Brother,
> I delayed answering your last because I was in Crespina at

Auntie Rina's. . . . Our encounter was more or less embarrassing, because I posed questions to Auntie that certainly no
one has ever asked in her entire life, and of such confidential
nature that I had difficulty formulating the questions. But, as I
foresaw, the outcome of the meeting was such as I more or less
expected, interesting and very serious for the various
protagonists of our turbulent family history. . . . I have taken
notes, and we will sort them out together.

THE time couldn't pass fast enough as I waited for Fofò's arrival. The
last time I had seen my brother was in Nice in 1934, fourteen years earlier. I came to agree with him that the times we had spent together
were the best and happiest of our lives. For each other, we were living
souvenirs of our youth.

When Fofò arrived in New York in the summer of 1948, it was a
great shock to see him. The trials of Africa, the war, and his disorderly
life had left their mark; he had aged far beyond his years. He was thin
and suffering from heart trouble, which demanded a lifestyle entirely
different from the one he had been living. I had aged too; but we recognized each other without difficulty, and our reunion was tearfully
happy.

After Fofò settled into a hotel, we went to RCA Victor to collect
his accumulated royalties, which came to around $8,000, a substantial
amount in 1948. I can still see him sitting on the bed in his room,
counting out the hundred-dollar bills one by one. He sent Armanda
half and kept the rest.

His financial worries were ended for the moment, but his health
problems were of major proportions. It did not take me long to realize
that his whole system had been ravaged by the hardships he endured in
Africa and during the war. To make things worse, he was an alcoholic.
Ignoring his heart condition, he often retired at night with a bottle of
Four Roses, which would be empty by the following morning. I tried
to dissuade him from destroying what remained of his health, but to
no avail. Within a few months, he suffered a mild heart seizure. I spent
the remaining year of his visit on tenterhooks, never knowing from
one day to the next whether I would find him dead or alive. To my
alarm, he had a second heart attack, another mild one. Our family
doctor, Dr. Adler, prescribed some pills for him which relieved his discomfort and helped to regulate his heart.

We tried to make Fofò as comfortable as possible. Helen did his laundry, and he ate his evening meals with us. After dinner, we played cards as in the old days at Le Panche, talking about our family and the book we were to write. Thanks to Fofò, bit by bit the story of our parents unfolded to me. I learned many details about our family, and the disjointed pieces I had collected from here and there began to fit together. Gradually, a clear picture formed in my mind. A great deal of vital information was salvaged through these after-dinner talks with my brother.

At the time of his visit, I was working again for Real Silk and had to make daily sales calls. Fofò passed his days roaming the streets, going to the movies, or visiting with friends in the Italian section of New York. He befriended Riccardo Cordiferro, the lyricist of the popular song "Core 'ngrato." In fact he was Marziale Sisca's brother Alessandro, and a columnist for *La Follia* under the pen name "Cor di Ferro" ("Heart of Iron"). Fofò was a frequent guest at his home in Brooklyn, where he became friendly with several businessmen in the import-export trade, among them Giuseppe Gatti, the commercial attaché of the Italian consulate in New York.

When he did not go out, Fofò worked on the book in his room until I returned home in the evening. He used my battered old typewriter and would slowly peck away at our project whenever the mood struck him, when he had nothing better to do, or when he did not go to bed early with a bottle of Four Roses. I set about preparing an English translation of his manuscript. We alternated on our only typewriter; he wrote in the daytime, and I repossessed the machine in the evening and worked on the translation until late every night. With the rough translation of the rough draft in hand, we began to make the rounds of publishers.

Francis B. Hamlin, a lawyer with whom I had been in contact, introduced us to the executives at Random House. They seemed interested in the project and offered to assign a professional editor to it. Later, however—in a letter dated 15 September 1949—the offer was withdrawn. The only concrete result of the discussions with Random House was a $150 bill from Hamlin for services rendered! We tried other alternatives without results. After this setback, Fofò's enthusiasm waned, and he worked less and less on the manuscript. Finally, he began to talk about going home and leaving the project to me.

While he was still in New York, we decided to proceed with his plans to export replicas of Italian artifacts. I easily sold the samples he had brought from Italy, and we took this as an indication that we could sell them in quantity. Taking syllables from our names, RODolfo and ENrico CaruSO, we incorporated under the name RODENSO. We anticipated a bright future for our venture; a Christmas greeting we recorded in a private studio for Armanda in December 1949 reflected our high spirits. Referring to ourselves as president and vice president of the company, to Helen's piano accompaniment we sang "Merry Christmas to You" first in English, then in Italian. The recording engineer cut two copies simultaneously on two turntables; Fofò sent one to Armanda, and I kept the other. This is the only surviving recording of my brother's voice, and the only record on which the sons of Enrico Caruso sing together.

In February 1950, Fofò was ready to sail home. As he was clearing customs at the pier, the customs officer demanded a form certifying that he owed no taxes. Fofò had no such form for the simple reason that Victor had made a single payment to him without withholding taxes, and he had not filed an income tax return. A series of frantic phone calls followed, and an RCA Victor officer had to come to the dockside and guarantee payment of the back taxes before Fofò was allowed to board ship. The customs officer then stamped his passport with the word "Delinquent."

The Italian equivalent, "*delinquente,*" means "felon." At the sight of the stamp, Fofò exploded. He began to scream at the top of his lungs that he was not a delinquent, and it was some time before I could calm him down enough to explain that the stamp only meant he was behind in his taxes.

The incident completely exhausted him. As we took our last farewell and I watched Fofò make his way up the gangplank with uncertain steps, I knew with a great sadness that I would not see my brother again.

RCA VICTOR soon notified Fofò that his future royalty payments would be withheld until the back taxes were repaid in full. Unable to work because of his heart condition, he thus found himself without an income for two, possibly three years, as the RODENSO venture was only in its infancy. On Fofò's behalf, I began to correspond with RCA Victor, pleading with them to take out the back taxes in installments so that Fofò and his family would receive some income in the interim.

From this time on, his letters were uniformly depressing. His heart condition grew worse, aggravated by financial worries, domestic problems, and the business arrangements he had to make for the shipments of the artifacts. He wrote:

> I should go to Rome to obtain the import permits, but I have no money and I don't even know how to keep my family going. Could it be that the spirit of our father has been offended by our desire to divulge his affairs of the heart? . . . Dear Mimmi! If you don't give me some good news soon, I will go to meet the Creator. I have never felt so bad as in this month since my return from America. I always feel my heart in my throat and I am slightly dizzy all the time.

He finally made the rounds of the various artisans, and the shipments began to arrive. I began traveling in New England for an import firm and RODENSO simultaneously, selling for both companies. While I became more optimistic with each sale, Fofò grew more and more dispirited. He wrote that his heart trouble showed no sign of improving. "Get on with the book!" he urged, and he asked me to tell him what I could about the Caruso film MGM was reportedly making.

With respect to our book, there wasn't much to "get on with." In March 1950, I had received a refusal from Doubleday. "We have sent the material on your father and the Giachetti sisters to Mr. Irving Stone," wrote Assistant Editor Betty Arnoff, "and he has just written us that he doesn't feel that he wants to work on this subject. I am awfully sorry because I think there is certainly some wonderful stuff there." Foulton Quesler, the man who had arranged my introduction at Doubleday, promised to call some friends at Simon and Schuster. But this firm had published Dorothy's book and was disinclined to invest so soon in a second book about Caruso. By the end of the year, my efforts to contact publishers had not produced a contract. I did not have the heart to tell my brother the truth but tried to keep up his spirits with false hopes.

Fofò's contacts in Italy continued to dispatch shipments for RODENSO. I managed to move the merchandise and received orders for more; but the profits were modest, and Fofò's share was not enough to keep his living and medical expenses from consuming the remainder of his capital. Armanda made a brief trip to Rome to arrange for a move to her brother Ernesto's house. She wrote:

> Dear Mimmi,
> Fofò is very ill, and the doctor recommends a more tranquil life. It is so essential that we receive an advance from Victor. I beg you to do everything possible. These misfortunes and his illness have cost so much money!

A letter to Fofò was already in the mail, carrying the good news that RCA Victor was about to agree to deduct the tax payments at the rate of only 25 percent per year. Fofò was deeply grateful. But in his next letter, written 12 January 1951, he again complained of pain in his chest, adding that he needed "tranquillity, rest, rest, and rest." He hoped to find quiet in Rome, and he asked me to send more of the pills Dr. Adler had prescribed for him in New York. The medicine had helped him before, and he was convinced that it would help again.

About this time, Fofò came across a lengthy review in *Il Tempo* of *The Great Caruso,* which had just been released. He wrote me that he "flew into quite a rage." The article recounted the plot of the movie, which Fofò called "hogwash." I could understand his outrage; the factual distortions of that film were too many to enumerate. To see herself depicted in the best possible light, Dorothy had endorsed a script that flew in the face not only of the facts of Father's life as she knew them, but of both her own books as well.

Fofò wrote on the day he and Armanda left Florence, then two days later from Rome. Although they arrived on January 20, after snow-covered Florence, the clear Roman skies and the mild weather felt like spring. Still, Fofò's nightly coughing fits continued, and he began to spit blood. He complained that everything tired him. Three days later, on January 25, he wrote that his coughing was aggravated by a bad case of the flu. This was the last letter written in his own hand. He dictated the next one, dated February 10, to Armanda. By this time they were both bedridden with the flu, although he claimed he was recovering.

Then the letters stopped, and I grew alarmed. I wrote on March 7: "If your health were not as it is, I would not be concerned about your silence, but as things are, I am really worried."

The very same day, Armanda's sister Adriana was writing a letter to me.

> 57 Via Sistina, Rome
> March 7, 1951

Dear Mimmi,

I am writing to you on behalf of Armanda and Roberto to give you the grave and most painful news. Yesterday, while it seemed that Rodolfo was somewhat recovering from the crises of the past few days, he serenely passed from life. We wanted to cable you at first, but then we decided we would rather give you the particulars in a letter, so that you may know more about the dear departed.

A few days ago he received the medicine and seemed greatly pleased by your caring. He showed it to the doctor, saying how much faith he had in this medicine that you sent him. He stayed in bed all the time, but he was almost normal and even spoke of getting up as soon as possible. He read the newspapers and conversed with Armanda and me; I visited him every day, bringing him meals. He ate little, but knowing that he felt a pressure on the heart, we did not insist that he eat more. Two days ago he twice had very high fever, which the doctor thought might be a new attack of malaria, but it is obvious that the fever was very exhausting for him. Yesterday at 16:30, while he was sitting in bed playing cards with Armanda, his head suddenly fell back, and he expired instantly. Aurelia and Roberto arrived tonight from Florence and are with him now. Elena arrived too, greatly stricken by the news, and even Lillo [my son, Enrico III] is coming to see him. Only you are missing, dear Enrico, whom he loved so much, to give him a last farewell. But you will regard it as if you had been with him. Pray for his blessed soul. He was so good and generous and kind, and the Lord will bless him and the earth where he lies.

Forgive me for bringing this sorrow to you. I embrace your wife, and for you, an affectionate embrace,

Adriana

Rodolfo was not yet fifty-three when he died on 6 March 1951. His death affected me deeply, and I mourned his passing.

Elena sewed a silk burial pillow for him. His body was transported to Naples and buried in the family chapel in the Del Pianto Cemetery. "Now he is resting together with your Papa," Armanda wrote after the funeral.

This was only proper. Fofò never loved a human being more than he loved our father.

CHAPTER THIRTY-THREE

Finale

I N 1923, Dorothy married a Captain Ernest Ingram. According to her account,[1] the marriage was a failure and lasted in reality only three months; they were divorced in 1925. Shortly after Dorothy's thirty-first birthday on August 6, her second daughter, Jacqueline, was born on 18 September 1924.

In July 1927, the newspapers carried an announcement of her engagement in Venice to Alexander Pollock Moore. Upon embarking at Le Havre on October 5 for her return to America, she confirmed the engagement to reporters and projected the wedding for January 1928.

Born in 1867, Moore was thirty years Dorothy's senior. He was a widower, the fourth and last husband of the celebrated actress Lillian Russell, who died on 6 June 1921. Moore was also a prominent newspaper man. He was part owner of the *Pittsburgh Telegraph* and *Pittsburgh Chronicle Telegraph;* and in 1928, he purchased the *New York Daily Mirror* and *Boston Advertiser*. Between 1923 and 1925, he was Ambassador Extraordinary and Plenipotentiary to Spain, and from 1928 on, he held the same position in Peru. His diplomatic career and post of service may have been a stumbling block for Dorothy. In any case, the wedding never took place, and Moore died two years later on 17

February 1930.

Dorothy remained single for a few years; then on 5 July 1933, she married another elderly widower, Dr. Charles Adam Holder. The civil ceremony, lasting five minutes, took place in Paris at the *mairie* (the town hall) of the Sixteenth Arondissement. Dorothy was forty years old and Dr. Holder sixty. He was a wealthy retired diplomat and banker who lived in a country house near Fontainebleau, thirty-seven miles from Paris. He served as the American consul at Rouen in 1909 and later in the U.S. State Department. After his retirement from the diplomatic corps, he became president of the Guaranty Trust Company. According to the newspapers, the ceremony took place in the presence of a small group of friends; Peggy Holder, one of Dr. Holder's three daughters, and thirteen-year-old Gloria Caruso served as witnesses.

This marriage lasted seven years. It was dissolved in September 1940, "both parties agreeing not to contest the decision."[2] Dorothy lived in Italy and France until 1942 then moved back to the United States due to the war.

In spite of her two subsequent marriages, she continued to use the Caruso name. It looked much better than either Ingram or Holder on the title page of her second biography about Father, published in 1945, and it also gave her a firm negotiating base when she sold film rights to her book to producers Jesse E. Lasky and Walter MacEwen. Louella Parsons reported in the *New York Journal-American* of 30 July 1945 that "Mrs. Caruso has set her heart on having Joan Fontaine play her, and it looks as if she'll get her wish." The role of Dorothy was the easy one to cast, for in 1945, there was no one on the cinematic or operatic horizon who could do justice to the title role. Plans for a film were shelved until the fortuitous emergence of Mario Lanza. He was approved by both Dorothy and the movie moguls, and the cameras began to roll. Dorothy's *Life and Death of Enrico Caruso* went through a remarkable metamorphosis and emerged as *The Great Caruso*.

The film project was strictly Dorothy's. The Caruso name and story were valuable property, and as Father's widow, she considered herself the rightful heir to the Caruso legend. Although members of the Caruso family appear as extras in her book, they were summarily excised from the film script. In addition to engraving the name of Enrico Caruso in the minds of millions around the world, the film unintentionally made both Fofò and me non-persons. After *The Great Caruso,* well-meaning people would say in all sincerity to me or to my wife:

"Come now! Caruso had no sons, he only had a daughter. I saw it in the movies."

The film was rife with distortions and did a disservice to my father's memory. All the same, it made a star of Mario Lanza and through him performed an invaluable service to opera. Lanza became a household name; thanks to him, opera was no longer an art form for an elite group of eggheads, but was acceptable entertainment for all. Vocally and musically, *The Great Caruso* is a thrilling motion picture, and it has helped many young people discover opera and even become singers themselves. José Carreras is one of them.

It was Lanza who made the picture a success. While the crowds idolized him, the experts and purists insisted that he was a far cry from the real thing, that he had no business impersonating the great Enrico Caruso, that he was no more than a gifted amateur who never learned to sing properly.

In my opinion, this was a facile and unfair dismissal. Mario Lanza was born with one of the dozen or so great tenor voices of the century, with a natural voice placement, an unmistakable and very pleasing timbre, and a nearly infallible musical instinct conspicuously absent in the overwhelming majority of so-called "great" singers. His diction was flawless, matched only by the superb Giuseppe di Stefano. His delivery was impassioned, his phrasing manly, and his *tempi* instinctively right—qualities that few singers are born with and others can never attain.

Musically speaking, Lanza grew up on records, including my father's, yet he imitated no one; his recordings of operatic selections are original interpretations. Let it not be forgotten that Mario Lanza excelled in both the classical and the light popular repertory, an accomplishment that was beyond even my father's exceptional talents. Lanza's acting may have been elementary, but his innate charm and sincerity compensated for any awkwardness. In addition to these attributes, Lanza bore a passing physical resemblance to my father. I can think of no other tenor, before or since Mario Lanza, who could have risen with comparable success to the challenge of playing Caruso in a screen biography. As one London reviewer put it: "It says something for Mario Lanza that in impersonating this living cathedral of sound, he never once (while he is singing, anyway) makes the performance seem embarrassing or inadequate."[3]

I only regret that Lanza was not given a script faithful to the facts to immortalize the Caruso story and through it his own art. The reviewer for the *Sunday Express* of 13 May 1951 observed: "Mario Lanza has been endowed with a fine voice, but he has been saddled with a story that is without art, without subtlety, and without conviction. Caruso deserved a better biography than this." Paul Dehn wrote in the *Sunday Chronicle* of the same date:

> Biographically it [*The Great Caruso*] is a twice unnecessary lie; first, because if MGM insists on telling lies, they should at least admit to having told them; secondly, because in any case, they have so concentrated on the music that they never *needed* to lie about the life at all.

Paul Holt's review was even more brutal. "I have sat through many stodgy screen biographies," he wrote, "full of funeral parlour dialogue and the pious sludge of beneficiaries' conversation. But never before, I think, have I seen a great man newly dead so smothered."[4]

Marziale Sisca, whose friendship with Father dated back to his New York debut in 1903, carried a bilingual editorial in the 15 May 1951 issue of his Italian-language *La Follia di New York*. He called *The Great Caruso* a "biographical travesty," asking: "Where is Caruso the man?" He bemoaned the damage done to the younger generation, which would rightly ask if this was the man who became a legend, the glory of the lyric stage. Answering his own rhetorical question, he wrote:

"No! The Caruso of this film has nothing, absolutely nothing in common with the immortal artist who animated and dominated the stage of the Metropolitan during the Golden Age of our greatest lyric theater!"

The film that elicited such critical reactions had a predictable effect on the Caruso family. As already mentioned, Fofò was appalled by the reviews. After his death, the family in Italy was sufficiently upset to contact a lawyer in Rome about the possibility of suing Metro-Goldwyn-Mayer for falsifying Father's life story. Three weeks after Fofò's death, Armanda sent me two letters in the same envelope, both dated 31 March 1951. One, a handwritten note, acknowledged my condolences. The other was a typed copy of her lawyer's opinion, with a note urging me to contact an attorney in New York.

I replied to Armanda in April, advising against a lawsuit. We had to consider the legal expenses, I wrote, and MGM would welcome a court action that would give the film free publicity through the scandal it might create.

The family thought it over. They may have pursued the matter no further, had the movie industry not committed another affront.

In the wake of the success of *The Great Caruso* and seeking to capitalize on its omissions, Tirrena Film Associata of Rome rushed into production with another movie entitled *Enrico Caruso: La leggenda di una voce*. (In English-speaking countries, it was shown under the title *The Young Caruso*.) Here the considerable beauty of Gina Lollobrigida as the young Caruso's love interest was combined with the considerable vocal gifts of the young Mario del Monaco, but the script itself was an abomination. The movie purported to cover Father's early years, ending the story roughly where *The Great Caruso* began. Adding myth to fiction, it was another admixture of inventions, conjectures, and distorted facts. Coming as it did on the heels of the MGM movie, this was simply too much for my family. I received the following telegram from my son on 27 September 1951: "I have legally obtained a private viewing horrible Italian film began action of injunction [and] damages give me urgently power of attorney to continue action [and] get favorable results wire me Enrico."

We sued Tirrena Film for violation of rights of the person, the image, and the voice under the provisions of Italian law. It took us two years to win the case in the Roman courts, in 1953. The film company was ordered to eliminate certain parts of the dialogue along with the objectionable scenes, specifically: Caruso shown as a child of drunken parents; shown as a child in abject poverty; shown as a drunkard himself; shown as a would-be suicide. Tirrena Film was enjoined from exporting the film unless these cuts were made. But the film was shown in the United States in its unexpurgated version, so I hired a lawyer in New York, Chester S. Mandel, to look into the matter.

Concurrently with this lawsuit, the family sued MGM for the damage done to them through the falsification of Father's life story.

In 1953 the courts decided in our favor, ordering MGM to pay five million lire in damages to the heirs of the tenor Enrico Caruso for the "offence to their honour and private life"[5] caused by the company's film *The Great Caruso*. MGM was also ordered to pay all court costs and to withdraw all copies of the film from circulation in Italy. As was to be expected, the film companies appealed the verdict, but in May 1955 the Roman court of appeals upheld the lower court's decision. The higher court also confirmed the decision ordering Tirrena Film Associata to pay Caruso's heirs two million lire on the same grounds.

A third lawsuit the Caruso family waged during this period was against Coca-Cola. Someone at the soft-drink company had picked up on the fine tradition of coining money from the Caruso name, and the giant posters advertising *The Great Caruso* in Italy began to sport a huge Coca-Cola emblem. The claim of the Carusos against Coca-Cola was described in both *Time* and *Life* magazines in their 5 May 1952 issues. The case, handled by Gennaro and Adolfo Leone of Rome, was heard in 1954. When Coca-Cola claimed they had meant to help young singers with part of the revenue the advertising campaign produced, the family went one better: The Carusos made the commitment that if they won the case, they would donate their entire monetary award to the Casa di Riposo Giuseppe Verdi in Milan, the retirement home for singers set up in the composer's will.

We won the case and honored our commitment.

Another situation that stopped just short of litigation arose in the United States. In 1953, someone at RCA Victor came up with the bright idea that the company could increase the profits made on the Caruso records if they reduced the royalties paid out to the Caruso heirs. (This had nothing to do with the shift from 78 rpm to long-playing records; the royalties were still paid on a per-disc—not a per-band—basis.) Early in 1954, I was notified of the proposed reduction by Alan Kayes, manager of the Red Seal Artists and Repertoire. The company requested "our consent" but summarily withheld the royalty payments that were due in February.

Lincoln W. Lauterstein, the lawyer I hired for this matter, discussed it separately with Gloria and Dorothy and with me. In this case, we were of the same mind and instructed Lauterstein to communicate our unanimous rejection of the company's request for a reduction in the royalty rate. He wrote to RCA extremely courteously:

> It is obvious, particularly in view of the fact that relations between the Victor Company and the Caruso family must extend for an infinite duration under the Caruso contract, and in view of the unique position held by the Caruso records, that the maintenance of harmonious relations and mutual good will is desirable to all parties.

In a response to Lauterstein dated 12 October 1954, Mr. Kayes conceded defeat. "I have issued instructions that the payment be made as per your request," he informed us tersely. Another effort to delay or withhold the royalty payments—this time on the part of the company that coined many millions of dollars from the Caruso records—had failed.

Dorothy was still living when the various judicial decisions were handed down and the appeals upheld in Rome. But soon afterward, on 16 December 1955, she died of cancer at the Union Memorial Hospital in Baltimore. She was survived by her daughters and grandchildren and by her sister, Torrance (Mrs. Frederick) Goddard.

THE GREAT CARUSO continued to be shown everywhere except in Italy and its producer, Jesse E. Lasky, recouped many times over the money he had lost on Father's silent films in 1918! An unexpected spinoff of the film, a two-record set combining Lanza and Caruso records, sold so well that I received $10,000 in royalties.

I sent some of the money to Elena and the boys in Italy and used the rest to stay in business. After Fofò died, I renamed our firm "Italian Artcrafts" and continued for a time with the help, in Italy, of my nephew Roberto. But I did not have the resources to build up stock or warehouse merchandise, and operating on a per-order basis meant the artisans had to wait for their money. If a tourist came by and bought the pieces they had made to fill my orders, they sold them for ready cash. The merchandise ceased coming in a timely and orderly fashion, and I abandoned the venture within a couple of years.

After a series of lesser jobs, I took a position as customs clerk at Dunnington & Arnold Inc., a customs brokerage firm. My own business had taught me a great deal about customs operations, and I was to work for nearly two decades in the import-export business, moving to D. C. Andrews Co. then back to Dunnington & Arnold. I retired at the end of the year in 1970, as Helen's health was beginning to deteriorate, and I wanted to spend our remaining time at her side.

During all these years, I used my "working name," Henry de Costa, and was one among many employees who earned a modest living and built up social security benefits. My colleagues called me Hank or Henry. None of them knew my real name, which usually invited the wrong reactions and was only good to get a better table at a restaurant or a good room in a hotel because it carried the promise of a big tip.

Moreover, Henry de Costa did not have to live up to his father's image.

THE Caruso family had one more encounter with Mario Lanza, or, to be exact, with his corpse. He died in Rome on 8 October 1959, and several papers immediately reported that Lanza would be buried in the Caruso chapel. We had nothing against Lanza, living or dead, but his screen impersonation of Caruso gave him no more claim to a burial place in the family chapel than playing Lincoln gave Raymond Massey claim to burial in Arlington Cemetery. My cousin Marcello, Uncle Giovanni's son, wrote from Naples on 13 November 1959:

The death of Mario Lanza has caused me a lot of headaches, because even though I did not know him, the word got around that he was to be buried in the Caruso chapel as that was his last wish. I was never able to find out who started this rumor, but the reporters certainly gave me a run for my money. In spite of my denials, they kept saying that since it was his last wish, we could not refuse! To which I replied that if I were to leave instructions that upon my death I wish to be buried next to Saint Peter in the Vatican, according to that line of reasoning, the Pope could not refuse. You cannot imagine the interest of the custodian of the cemetery, who got wind of a superb deal; he phoned me even at night to ask about my decision. Finally, the departure of the remains to America set everyone's soul at rest and closed the open wallets.

Due partly to reverence and partly to self-interest, Father's chapel, the Caruso burial place, has always been a concern to the family. Fofò visited it in 1948 and found everything in order. After he died, my cousin Marcello and his sister Anna looked after it, but they could only do so much, and it fell into neglect. In Marcello's November 1959 letter, he gave me a bleak account of the situation:

> I went to the cemetery on All Saints' Day to perform my sad duty. As Anna has already told you, to enter the chapel I was obliged to track down the custodian and ask him to be good enough to open it. It seems grotesque, but that's how it is. . . .
>
> Apart from the matter of the key, which I will resolve, I would be glad to bring to a conclusion the project that is very dear to my heart. I don't know if you remember the chapel; it has two sides separated by a wall, and between these and the sides of the chapel, a walkway leads to the cemetery proper. Now, you must know that at the moment the authorities are not furnishing the cemetery with proper hygienic services (urinals and commodes) to serve either those working in the cemetery or the visitors. So what better spot to use than the side of the Caruso chapel?
>
> I brought this unconscionable irreverence to the attention of the authorities only to be told (and perhaps not without reason) that nothing can be done. One could not expect them to post a guard; nor could the gardeners be expected to clean up, because they are not even paid to trim

the hedges or to sweep up.

To avoid all the above, I thought of erecting little gates at the two ends of the walkway to keep the traffic out, but I understand I cannot take the initiative without consulting the other heirs.

So this is the situation with the chapel. It is maintained and cleaned only by Anna and me. I felt obliged to inform you. My father once told me that a fund for the upkeep of the tomb had been set up, a fund that became funds in somebody's pocket; therefore I believe it would be useless to pursue this option.

Disturbed by this situation, I asked my sons to look after the chapel. From time to time they did, but Wladi lives in Florence, and Enrico, who lives outside Rome, has been in poor health. The Neapolitan authorities did nothing to alleviate the situation, despite my urgent letters. It is difficult to understand why the city of Naples would not invest the truly negligible amount of money needed to maintain the tomb of one of its most prominent sons, if not out of respect, then out of the desire to provide a place of interest for the operatically inclined tourist.

My friend Fred Manning, an executive officer of the Federal Reserve Bank system and a Caruso devotee, contacted the Italian consul in Philadelphia about the condition of the chapel. In 1985, I received word that the outside had been cleaned and the surrounding area was no longer being treated like an outhouse. It seems that Naples finally did its civic duty.

That left the matter of the interior. Guido d'Onofrio, another good friend and my father's most devoted admirer, hired two helpers at my request and expense. Working together, the three of them removed years of grime from the altar and the tombs. I was pleased to receive photographs showing the white marble of the lovely chapel gleaming again for All Saints' Day of 1985, and I greatly appreciated Guido's efforts. Since this time, Guido d'Onofrio has made an annual pilgrimage to the tomb on Caruso's birthday, on All Saints' Day, and on August 2nd, the anniversary of Father's death. All the Caruso family members are deeply grateful for this devoted service.

MY half sister Gloria has kept her distance from me all her life, which I can only attribute to her mother's influence. Once, in 1948, when Dorothy and Gloria were living in Greenwich Village in New York, I called at their house and asked the maid to tell Gloria her brother had come to see her. The maid soon returned with the message, "Miss Gloria has no brother." I never learned whether these were Gloria's words or Dorothy's. Since her infancy, I saw Gloria only once: She graciously accepted my invitation to my wedding in 1982. My dear Helen had died two years before, leaving a great void in my life. Now I found happiness in the twilight of life in marriage to Harriett Covington, a loving lady from the Carolinas who was two years my junior. Gloria helped us to celebrate the occasion, but it was clear that at this stage of her life, she wanted to keep the Caruso legacy at arm's length.

In contrast, others around the world have eagerly embraced a so-called family relationship with my father, sometimes in the most humorous fashion. My cousin, Marcello, wrote on 27 December 1967:

> Now I want you to laugh. A few days ago, a Yugoslav from Ljubljana showed up at my house. In very broken Italian, he informed me that he was convinced he is the son of Enrico Caruso and wanted to know whether the inheritance has been fully divided yet. He also wanted your address and Gloria's, which I was not about to give him. Yours I did not remember, and Gloria's I never knew. You can imagine how I handled him; I did my best to shorten the conversation, in part due to the difficulty of understanding him, because he spoke mostly Slovenian. In fact, the moment he asked if there was any money left, I was immediately on the defensive. My wife was also present and scolded me for the unkind manner in which I treated this new cousin of mine.
>
> As you can see, fifty years after the death of my dear uncle, there are still people who try to fish in the muck.

Marcello's experience was by no means unique. I have met and heard of several others who say they are direct descendants of Enrico Caruso. A gentleman from south Florida contacted me recently, claiming to be a son of Enrico Caruso. I also met a middle-aged man from Utah who steadfastly maintains that his mother, adopted at birth, was my father's illegitimate daughter. And a young man in Jacksonville, Florida, reportedly claims to be Caruso's great-grandson.

Considering Father's international travels and his many affairs, I may well have a few half brothers or sisters somewhere in the world.[6] For the record, however, I must mention that my nephew, Roberto, who died in 1986, had only one child, a daughter. My younger son Wladimiro never married; thus only my son Enrico III, his two sons,

Federico and Riccardo, and his one grandson, Tommaso, carry the Caruso name as direct descendants of my father. They all live in Italy.[7]

IN 1956, I published a short piece about Father in *Hi-Fi Music at Home*.[8] Shortly thereafter I received a letter from Francis Robinson, assistant manager of the Metropolitan Opera.[9] He invited me to lunch to discuss the possibility of borrowing photographs and other graphic material for a book he was preparing on Caruso. I called to tell him that I did not want to part with my photographs because I planned to use them in my own memoirs. I expressed my hope that he would be able to obtain material from other sources and wished him good luck with his book.

Immediately after my call, he sent a second letter, dated 26 June 1956, which said, in part: "Thank you for telephoning me today and I hope we can get together in the next week or so. It will be enormously helpful if I can see your material even if you still withhold it." He went on to say that "this subject is bigger than any of us and what helps one helps the other. . . . It may be presumptuous of me to suggest but it's just possible there might be some things here which might be of interest to you and it would never occur to us not to cooperate in any way possible." Robinson was polite in his demands, but I was wary of helping him, for too many people had borrowed my memorabilia and neglected to return them. One example that sprang to mind was a youthful picture of Father that he gave me in London. It was partially damaged because I once spilled ink on it and tried to wash it off. I lent this picture to Pierre Key for his book, but he never returned it. To my utter amazement, the very same photograph—with the damaged portion visibly restored—showed up in Francis Robinson's book, which credited Gloria as the source of the picture![10]

THE year 1971 marked the fiftieth anniversary of Father's death. In January of that year, the Met mounted an exhibit of his costumes in one large exhibit case, and costumes that had belonged to Kirsten Flagstad in another. Gloria was invited to the opening of the exhibit; *The New York Times* carried the story on 20 January 1971. When a few months later my son Enrico and his wife visited me in New York, I took them to the Metropolitan to see the exhibit. Francis Robinson met us and gave us a tour which included the Cifariello statue of Papa. He was quite civil, and I thanked him for his attentions. Then, in the spring of

1973, the Met gave a gala performance of *Aida* to commemorate the centennial of Father's birth. The next day's papers mentioned that the distinguished guests at the event included the daughter of the great tenor, Gloria Caruso. This time I could not resist making a point, and I called Robinson.

"Mr. Robinson, I read in the paper about the gala performance in honor of my father. May I ask why I was not invited?"

Robinson was not accustomed to being put on the spot. After a brief pause, he said with equal directness:

"You didn't want to help me when I needed you, so why should I think of you now?"

This cultivated man known for his polish and his kindness had harbored a petty grudge for seventeen years! I was so angry at his response that I replied with the first expletive that came to mind, which happened to be in Italian, and hung up. I hope his Italian was good enough that he understood what I called him. To be excluded even from the centennial celebrations of my father's birth did rankle.

AFTER Fofò returned to Italy, I simply shelved the idea of the book. I was too tired in the evenings to work on it, and the draft I had to show was insufficient; every publisher I approached wanted to see a finished manuscript. Helen wanted me to revive the project, saying it was my obligation to remind the world that contrary to the Hollywood fiction, Father had a family long before Mario Lanza, a.k.a. Enrico Caruso, gazed into the pretty eyes of Ann Blyth, a.k.a. Dorothy Park Benjamin.

At last I dictated three reels of tapes which she transcribed. Then personal concerns forced me to set the project aside, this time permanently. Yet I had the notion that not only the information I carried in my head, but Fofò's notes, my drafts, and all the scraps and documents I had been guarding for years had come my way for a purpose. Even if I was not able to write the definitive biography of my father, I could not allow them to vanish, for no one coming after me could write a definitive biography without them! And so, in my seventy-ninth year, through a series of coincidences I met the very person I needed, a man thoroughly versed in music and opera lore and able to organize disorganized reminiscences into a readable narrative.

Andrew Farkas became my much-needed collaborator, writer, researcher, and resident critic, and a dear friend. He devoted endless hours to this project, which was a labor of love. The likelihood that our paths would cross was so small that I am prepared to believe he was sent to me by my father. With his assistance, I began to work on this book in earnest. No one knows better than I the gaps I was forced to leave in the narrative through lack of trustworthy information. Yet the many facts I was able to accumulate about Father and my family contribute essential detail to the existing picture of them, and I hope to have answered some of the questions other biographers were compelled to ignore. To Father's countless admirers, I offer this most personal memoir.

Father had a distinguished, God-given talent, and he became a consummate artist, the unalloyed gold of the period remembered as opera's Golden Age. But he also led a life beyond the public eye. In his personal story, like so many extras, we came and went: my mother, my aunt, my brother, and I. If we come across in these pages as characters marred with weakness and imperfection, so be it—Enrico Caruso and his family, like any other, were richly human.

In Memoriam: Enrico Caruso, Jr.

by Andrew Farkas

"I WILL never live to see this book finished!" Enrico, Jr., said more than once.

My standard reply was that I had no control over editors' schedules or publishers' deadlines. The one thing I could promise was to forge ahead so that he would see the finished manuscript.

I kept that promise.

I handed over the final draft on 9 December 1986. Enrico was elated and began to work on it immediately. His eyesight was poor, so it was a slow and strenuous process. He read the book straight through, then reread it from beginning to end. He made many stylistic changes, corrected some details, added a sentence here and there, and rearranged a few paragraphs. His phone calls multiplied—some days we had five or six consultations. Because of his advanced age and a serious heart condition, he knew his days were numbered, and he wanted to do all he could to ready the manuscript for publication.

In January 1987, Mr. Hugh McGonigle of the U.S. Postmaster General's office invited Enrico and me to attend the first-day-issue ceremony for a commemorative Enrico Caruso stamp, which was to be held in New York at the Metropolitan Opera House. Enrico was thrilled by the prospect. We agreed that I would give the keynote address about Caruso, and Enrico would follow it with a brief speech.

The U.S. Postal Service gave us red-carpet treatment. As I checked us in at the Plaza Hotel, the desk clerk read the name on the reservation slip and suddenly looked up:

"Do you know that you carry a most distinguished name, Sir?"

"It is not my name," I replied. "It belongs to the gentleman over there, leaning on his cane. He is the son of the great tenor."

The desk clerk's eyes grew big, and he was momentarily speechless. He then called his colleagues over, and they all gazed at Enrico in awe. To see the son of Enrico Caruso was like seeing an apparition.

The ceremony was held on the Grand Tier of the Metropolitan Opera House at eleven in the morning on 27 February 1987. About four hundred people gathered for the occasion. The celebrated Brazilian soprano, Bidù Sayão, was present to meet and greet Enrico. Of course, the two revived the story of the great Caruso singing the *Pagliacci* "Prologue" in the place of her late husband, Giuseppe Danise, in Buenos Aires. They were joined by Michael Sisca, Marziale's son and Enrico's old-time friend.

Master of ceremonies John M. Nolan, New York Postmaster, introduced James A. Marcus, Chairman of the Metropolitan Opera Association. My turn was next. After I spoke about Caruso, I introduced Enrico, giving a brief summary of his life and career.

In his speech, Enrico said:

> First, I wish to thank all concerned for inviting me to take part in this ceremony—a ceremony that is a thrilling and memorable occasion. To accept on behalf of my father this token of the esteem in which he is held by the American people is an unbelievable and great privilege. I do not think any of you realize what this means to me, to be able, finally, after all these years, to participate in a ceremony honoring my father.

No one in the audience could have known how sincerely these words were spoken. It was the very first time in his long life that Enrico was invited to represent his father, and it was a highly emotional occasion for him.

Without a doubt, Enrico was the star attraction of the event. The easy flow of his delivery, his natural charm and dignity, and the aura of his famous father held his audience captive. When he finished, they spontaneously rose and gave him a standing ovation. I saw him fighting to control his tears. As people later remarked, the applause was meant as much for him as for his father.

Jim Sharpe, designer of the stamp, sat on the dais but did not speak. The program concluded with a few words from Postmaster General Preston R. Tisch.

After the ceremony, Enrico remained the focus of attention. The cameras did not stop clicking, and he was interviewed by ABC Television, National Public Radio, and Radiotelevisione Italiana (RAI) for same-day broadcast in Italy. Later he spent two and a half hours signing programs, first-day-issue envelopes, and other memorabilia.

Soon after our return to Jacksonville, Florida, Enrico received a congratulatory letter from President Ronald Reagan. The local post office held its own celebration on 9 March 1987, and we were asked to repeat our speeches. The Mayor of Jacksonville proclaimed it Enrico Caruso Day, and Enrico again gave television and newspaper interviews and signed programs and envelopes with the Caruso stamp for nearly two hours. But he was pale and visibly tired.

Exactly one month later, on April 9 around 1:50 p.m., Enrico felt a sudden chest pain, and he died within minutes. He had a two-inch aneurism in the wall of his heart; his doctors believed it had burst. In accordance with his wishes, he was buried in Jacksonville, Florida. The burial spaces in the Caruso chapel in Naples, originally designed to hold the immediate family, were already filled with Enrico's relatives who had died before him.

I knew Enrico only in the twilight years of his life. As his own words have conveyed, we became very close friends. Our work on this book fostered our mutual attachment, but simple friendship was our primary bond. I think of him often, and when I do, it brings a smile to my face. He was a lovable, easy-going man, not self-effacing but without pretense, optimistic, wise yet child-like, gallant, and generous to a fault. He had engaging manners, a superb sense of humor, and a streak of the "ham" that made his many stories delightful to hear.

After Eddie Smith and Enrico resumed contact, Eddie had a long-playing record made of Enrico's original 78-rpm recordings, which he had guarded for forty-six years. It was an only copy, so I asked Enrico to make a tape for me. He did so on the occasion of his father's birthday, on 25 February 1984, introducing the music with these words:

"Beyond dedicating this tape, I dedicate to you my heart and my profound affection, with the wish that you should be able to fulfill all your dreams in a long and healthy life. Remember me always, Andrew, because I will always remember you, even from beyond the grave."

My dear friend may be assured that I will never forget him and our wonderful friendship, one of the most memorable of my life.

Andrew Farkas
9 April 1989
Jacksonville, Florida

Notes

CHAPTER ONE

1 As late as 1988, Michael Scott repeated the myth of twenty-one children on page 3 of his *The Great Caruso* (New York: Knopf; London: Hamish Hamilton), as did Daniele Rubboli in 1987 on page 11 of his book about Caruso entitled *Lo "scugnizzo" che conquistò il mondo* (Naples: Liguri Editore).
2 Key, Pierre V. R. *Enrico Caruso: A Biography.* Boston: Little, Brown, 1922, p. 10.
3 This fact has also been established by Guido d'Onofrio, working directly from contemporary records.
4 *The New Grove Dictionary of Music and Musicians* (London: Macmillan, 1980) gives, erroneously, the date of February 27.
5 *The New York Times,* 3 August 1921.
6 Key, Pierre V. R. *Enrico Caruso: Souvenir Book.* New York: Francis C. Coppicus, 1920.
7 Key, Pierre. "Enrico Caruso, Singer and Man." *Daily Telegraph,* 12 June 1920. The majority of quotations attributed to Pierre Key throughout this volume appeared in a series of articles published in the *Daily Telegraph* in 1920. Although Key incorporated this material into his 1922 book on Caruso (op. cit.), these articles contain the original versions of the biographical details supplied by Caruso. The singer was still alive when they were first published, so he could have taken Key to task for any inaccuracies or embellishments. Key also asserted that "the words quoted in these articles are Caruso's own, partly those spoken in English, the rest translated from his Italian." The latter fact explains phrasing that is clearly in Key's style.
8 Ibid.
9 Ibid.
10 Ibid.
11 Ibid.
12 *The New York Times,* 12 November 1905.
13 Key, Pierre. "Enrico Caruso, Singer and Man." *Daily Telegraph,* 12 June 1920.
14 *The New York Times,* 12 November 1905.
15 Key, Pierre. "Enrico Caruso, Singer and Man." *Daily Telegraph,* 12 June 1920.
16 Ibid.
17 Ibid., 19 June 1920.
18 Ibid.
19 Ibid.
20 Ibid.
21 Ibid.
22 Ibid.
23 Ibid.
24 This information was only recently discovered by Professor Michael E. Henstock, who passed it on to Caruso chronologist Thomas G. Kaufman.
25 Daspuro, Nicola. *Enrico Caruso.* Milan: Sonzogno, 1938, p. 12.
26 Ibid., p. 13.

27 Actually, Caruso was twenty-two. Earlier biographies gave the date of this performance as 16 November 1894; but Caruso chronologist Thomas G. Kaufman accepts the findings of the Centro di Studi Carusiani of Milan.
28 Key, Pierre. "Enrico Caruso, Singer and Man." *Daily Telegraph,* 3 July 1920.
29 *The New York Times,* 12 November 1905.
30 Key, Pierre. "Enrico Caruso, Singer and Man." *Daily Telegraph,* 10 July 1920.
31 Ibid.
32 According to some accounts, Caruso's affair with the ballerina began in Salerno, hence his broken engagement to Giuseppina Grassi.
33 Key, Pierre. "Enrico Caruso, Singer and Man." *Daily Telegraph,* 10 July 1920.
34 Rodolfo Caruso's unpublished manuscript.

CHAPTER TWO

1 This date, handed down by the family, has not been verified.
2 This information was supplied in a letter from Luciano Pituello to Enrico Caruso, Jr., dated 4 November 1982.
3 Key, Pierre. "Enrico Caruso, Singer and Man." *Daily Telegraph,* 17 July 1920.
4 Ibid.
5 Ibid.
6 Key, Pierre. "Enrico Caruso, Singer and Man." *Daily Telegraph,* 17 August 1920.
7 Ibid., 17 July 1920.
8 Ibid.
9 Quoted in *Gazzetta dei Teatri,* 3 February 1898.
10 Ibid.
11 Quoted in *Gazzetta dei Teatri,* 10 February 1898.
12 *Gazzetta dei Teatri,* 3 March 1898.
13 From Rodolfo Caruso's notes taken during an interview with Rina Giachetti in 1948.
14 Key, Pierre. "Enrico Caruso, Singer and Man." *Daily Telegraph,* 17 July 1920.
15 *Gazzetta dei Teatri,* undated clipping.
16 Key, Pierre V. R. *Enrico Caruso: A Biography.* Boston: Little, Brown, 1922, p. 104.
17 I have held those eggs in my hands: One of them had a little singing bird inside.
18 This information came from Rina Giachetti. The date or place of the performance could not be traced.

CHAPTER THREE

1 Several of these have been preserved in private and institutional collections.
2 *Gazzetta dei Teatri,* undated clipping.
3 *Gazzetta dei Teatri,* undated clipping.
4 These words are taken directly from Rodolfo Caruso's record of his 1948 interview with Rina Giachetti.
5 Key, Pierre. "Enrico Caruso, Singer and Man." *Daily Telegraph,* 9 August 1920.
6 The postcards are now in the Francis Robinson Collection of Theater, Music, and Dance at Vanderbilt University, Nashville, Tennessee.
7 Ibid.
8 Quoted in *Gazzetta dei Teatri,* 8 November 1900.
9 Ibid.
10 Ibid.
11 Key, Pierre. "Enrico Caruso, Singer and Man." *Daily Telegraph,* 17 August 1920.

12 Ibid., 23 August 1920.
13 Ibid.
14 Ibid.
15 Ibid.
16 Ibid.
17 *Rassegna Melodrammatica,* 7 December 1900.
18 *Daily News,* 20 May 1912. The comment was repeated later in the *Sunday Express,* 24 October 1920.
19 This and other excerpts narrated by Rodolfo Caruso are taken from the typescript of his unpublished memoirs.
20 *The New York Times,* 4 August 1921.
21 *Monthly Musical Record,* 1 June 1902.
22 Enrico Caruso to Marziale Sisca, 28 January 1914.
23 Enrico Caruso to Pasquale Simonelli, 9 September 1903.
24 Key, Pierre. "Enrico Caruso, Singer and Man." *Daily Telegraph,* 17 August 1920.
25 Enrico Caruso to Pasquale Simonelli, 9 March 1903.
26 Ledner, Emil. *Erinnerungen an Caruso.* Hannover: Paul Steegemann Verlag, 1922, p. 13.
27 *The New Grove Dictionary of Music and Musicians,* Volume 3 (London: Macmillan, 1980), p. 839, erroneously gives the year of Caruso's Metropolitan Opera debut as 1902. As the *New Grove* is destined to become the primary authority for one or more generations of musicologists, such a crude error should not be allowed to establish itself in the literature.
28 *The New York Times,* 4 August 1921.
29 Caruso, Enrico. *The New Book of Caricatures.* New York: La Follia di New York, 1965, p. i.
30 *Les Annales du Théâtre,* Paris, 14 April 1904, pp. 242-43.

CHAPTER FOUR

1 *The New York Times,* 12 November 1905.
2 Ibid.
3 Enrico Caruso to Pasquale Simonelli, 8 August 1905.
4 Ibid.
5 Heylbut, Rose, and Aimé Gerber. *Backstage at the Metropolitan Opera.* New York: Thomas Y. Crowell, 1937, pp. 188-89.
6 *Express,* London, 12 May 1906.
7 Unidentified clipping, 23 April 1906.

CHAPTER FIVE

1 Ledner, Emil. *Erinnerungen an Caruso.* Hannover: Paul Steegemann Verlag, 1922, p. 30.
2 Seligman, Vincent. *Puccini Among Friends.* London: Macmillan, 1938, p. 159.
3 *Rassegna Melodrammatica,* 22 May 1900.
4 Quoted in *Rassegna Melodrammatica,* 7 February 1902.
5 Ibid.
6 *Rassegna Melodrammatica,* 7 March 1902.
7 Ibid.
8 Ibid., 22 April 1902.
9 Quoted in *Rassegna Melodrammatica,* 14 November 1902.

10 *Rassegna Melodrammatica,* 14 November 1902.
11 Quoted in *Rassegna Melodrammatica,* 14 February 1903.
12 Ibid.
13 Quoted in *Rassegna Melodrammatica,* 7 March 1903.
14 Ibid.
15 Quoted in *Rassegna Melodrammatica,* 22 May 1903.
16 *Rassegna Melodrammatica,* 22 July 1903.
17 Ibid., 31 December 1903.
18 Ibid., 14 February 1904.
19 Ibid.
20 Quoted in *Rassegna Melodrammatica,* 31 March 1904.
21 Ibid.
22 Ibid.
23 *Rassegna Melodrammatica,* 22 April 1904.
24 Ibid., 30 April 1904.
25 Ibid., 7 May 1904.
26 *Times,* London, 4 November 1904.
27 Ibid., 9 November 1904.
28 Quoted in *Rassegna Melodrammatica,* 14 April 1905.
29 *La Prensa,* 28 July 1905.
30 Ibid., 16 August 1905.
31 *Times,* London, 11 October 1905.
32 Ibid., 1 November 1905.
33 *Rassegna Melodrammatica,* 14 April 1906.
34 *Times,* London, 30 June 1906.
35 Ibid., 19 July 1906.
36 Ibid., 8 October 1906.
37 Ibid., 6 November 1906.
38 Ibid., 26 November 1906.

CHAPTER SIX

1 Enrico Caruso, Jr., first heard this detail from his brother, Rodolfo, but hesitated to publish it without corroborating evidence. Such evidence has recently surfaced and was communicated to me by Professor Eduardo Arnosi of Buenos Aires. According to his letter of 29 June 1987, Ada Giachetti confided to Thea Vitulli, an Italo-Argentinian soprano, this intimate incident. Vitulli, who made her debut in Rome in 1920 and sang at the Colón from 1922 onward, became Ada Giachetti's pupil in Buenos Aires. *Andrew Farkas*
2 *Neues Wiener Tageblatt,* 7 October 1906.
3 Ibid.
4 *Daily Telegraph,* 20 November 1906.
5 Reuter's Special Service, published in a London newspaper (clipping unidentified) on 29 November 1906.
6 Ibid.
7 *Daily Express,* 23 November 1906.
8 Seligman, Vincent. *Puccini Among Friends*. London: Macmillan, 1938, p. 97.
9 In reference to Fofò and me, Emil Ledner wrote in his *Erinnerungen an Caruso* (Hannover: Paul Steegemann Verlag, 1922) that he got to know "the charming little fellows intimately in London. Caruso loved them passionately." Ledner is wrong about meeting Fofò, at least, for he was never in London. If Ledner ever met him, it had to be in Italy.

10 *Daily Telegraph,* 4 October 1907.
11 Ibid., 14 November 1907.
12 Unidentified clipping from a New York daily, 1914. This quotation, like others cited without reference to a specific source, came from my collection of newspaper clippings or that of the British Library (London), many of which were unidentified or undated. Those from the British Library carry a rubber-stamped date, and in the absence of evidence to the contrary, I have cited these dates.
13 Key, Pierre. V. R. *Enrico Caruso: A Biography.* Boston: Little, Brown, 1922, p. 255.
14 This is mentioned in the *Corriere della Sera,* 27 October 1912.

CHAPTER SEVEN

1 Rodolfo Caruso wrote down this conversation forty years after it took place. He is obviously in error about the precise sequence of events, as detailed in the previous chapter. It is also possible that in concisely informing his ten-year-old son, Caruso did not go into details regarding his London–Paris–Naples–London trip.
2 There were so few luxury automobiles in use in those days that by driving around Europe, Ada would have broadcast her whereabouts. She did not know whether Caruso would have her followed or not, so she chose to leave the car behind.
3 *The New York Times,* 13 September 1908.
4 Seligman, Vincent. *Puccini Among Friends.* London: Macmillan, 1938, pp. 158–59.
5 Lou Tellegen was an actor, ladies' man, Sarah Bernhardt's on- and offstage lover, for a short time Geraldine Farrar's husband, and Rodin's one-time assistant and model for the sculptor's celebrated "Eternal Spring." He had a villa outside Florence, where Caruso visited him many times.
6 Tellegen, Lou. *Women Have Been Kind: The Memoirs of Lou Tellegen.* New York: Vanguard, 1931, pp. 143–44.

CHAPTER EIGHT

1 Ledner, Emil. *Erinnerungen an Caruso.* Hannover: Paul Steegemann Verlag, 1922, p. 38.
2 Ibid.
3 Caruso himself mentioned this circumstance in the trial that followed in Milan in 1912.
4 The newspaper quotations relating to the events on New Year's Eve 1908 are those supplied by Leonard Petts.
5 Ibid.
6 Bolig, John R. "A Caruso Discography." In: Michael Scott, *The Great Caruso.* New York: Knopf; London: Hamish Hamilton, 1988, p. 275.
7 Ledner, Emil. *Erinnerungen an Caruso.* Hannover: Paul Steegemann Verlag, 1922, p. 30.
8 Ibid., pp. 53–54.
9 Kleinsteuber, Else Trauner. "Erinnerungen an Caruso: Erlebnisse einer Frankfurterin." Unidentified clipping supplied by Mrs. Nanne Bruns.
10 This was quoted in a conversation that took place between Mrs. Ilse Trauner Mittermair and Mrs. Hildegard Ernecke in June 1987, and repeated in a letter to me from Mrs. Ernecke, dated 6 June 1987. *Andrew Farkas*
11 Ledner, Emil. *Erinnerungen an Caruso.* Hannover: Paul Steegemann Verlag, 1922, pp. 46–47.

12 Ibid., pp. 47–49.

13 Ibid., pp. 67–68, 70.

14 Ibid., pp. 59–60.

15 Key, Pierre. "Enrico Caruso, Singer and Man." *Daily Telegraph,* 23 August 1920.

16 *Daily Mail,* 20 October 1909.

17 This is *The New York Times*' version of the story. The January 29 issue of the *Morning Telegraph* claims that Ada barged into the suite while Caruso was taking a bath.

18 *Musical America,* 17 April 1909.

19 Cable of New York correspondent for the *(Daily?) Mail,* 14 April 1909, published on 15 April 1909.

20 *Musical America,* 17 April 1909.

21 Ibid.

22 Ibid.

23 Report filed by the Milan correspondent for the *Daily Telegraph* on Thursday, May 27, and published in London on 28 May 1909.

24 *Daily Telegraph,* 2 June 1909.

25 Ibid.

26 The statement was made on solid grounds. An unidentified clipping from a London newspaper dated 10 May 1911 carries the report that "Professor Della Vedova warned Caruso against overtaxing and straining his voice, and predicted a repetition of the disease. As the advice was not heeded, a third surgical operation is now necessary. Its success is assured, says the professor, and the famous tenor will completely recover his lost voice, as after previous operations." Whether the third operation actually took place I have been unable to ascertain. *Andrew Farkas*

CHAPTER NINE

1 All the quotations relating to Mildred Meffert have been taken from an unidentified newspaper clipping from 1914.

2 Unidentified clipping, 20 September 1909.

3 Seligman, Vincent. *Puccini Among Friends.* London: Macmillan, 1938.

4 Gianni Bettini dabbled in acoustics and improved the diaphragm of Edison's cylinder machine. As a nobleman and society figure, he befriended many important artists. They often sang for him just for the fun of it, and the sound quality of their efforts was so good that they encouraged him to "go commercial." Eventually he did, with a short list of recordings.

5 Victor Bettini to William R. Moran, 17 December 1965.

6 Seligman, Vincent. *Puccini Among Friends.* London: Macmillan, 1938, pp. 15–60.

7 De Segurola, Andrés. *Through My Monocle.* Typescript, p. 480.

8 *Chronicle,* 3 February 1912.

9 *The Reader,* 31 August 1911.

10 Ledner, Emil. *Erinnerungen an Caruso.* Hannover: Paul Steegemann Verlag, 1922, p. 50.

11 Ibid., p. 50.

12 Ibid., p. 51.

13 Ibid., p. 51.

14 Ibid., p. 52.

15 Ibid., p. 52.

16 Ibid., p. 52.

17 Ibid., p. 53.

CHAPTER TEN

1 *Times,* London, 4 July 1907.
2 Ibid., 9 October 1907.
3 Ibid., 11 October 1907.
4 Gatti, Carlo. *Il Teatro alla Scala,* 2 volumes. Milan: Ricordi, 1964.
5 Enrico Caruso to Marziale Sisca, 2 June 1908.
6 Key, Pierre. V. R. *Enrico Caruso: A Biography.* Boston: Little, Brown, 1922, p. 10.
7 Ledner, Emil. *Erinnerungen an Caruso.* Hannover: Paul Steegemann Verlag, 1922, p. 37.
8 *Corriere della Sera,* 25 October 1912.
9 Ledner, Emil. *Erinnerungen an Caruso.* Hannover: Paul Steegemann Verlag, 1922, p. 36.
10 *Corriere della Sera,* 26 October 1912.
11 Ibid.
12 Report of Central News, *Daily Telegraph,* 12 December 1913.
13 *Daily Telegraph,* 16 May 1913.
14 Unidentified clipping (*Daily Telegraph?*), 21 May 1913.
15 Unidentified clipping, 19 June 1913.
16 De Segurola's statement that he received the record "a few days later" is incorrect. In light of the known facts, one can assume he meant a few "years" later. *Andrew Farkas*
17 *Giornale d'Italia,* 21 October 1914, p. 4. I am indebted to Caruso biographer Michael Scott for calling this important source to my attention.
18 The *Philadelphia Inquirer* carried a review of the performance in the 24 December 1913 issue. There is a brief mention of the secondary cast members without critical comment: "Colline, Andrès Segurola." The *Evening Bulletin*'s review of the same day does not even mention De Segurola! Neither of the two reviews nor subsequent issues of these newspapers note any unusual occurrence at the performance.
19 This and subsequent quotations in this chapter relating to Mrs. Meffert have been taken from an unidentified newspaper clipping from 1914.
20 Ibid.
21 The account of this incident is from memory. I do not have a copy of the article.

CHAPTER ELEVEN

1 Ledner, Emil. *Erinnerungen an Caruso.* Hannover: Paul Steegemann Verlag, 1922, p. 21.
2 *Giornale d'Italia,* 21 October 1914.
3 De Segurola, Andrès. *Through My Monocle.* Typescript, pp. 472–75. Unaware that this anecdote was included in De Segurola's memoirs, I published it as "Stopover at Gibraltar" in *Liberty Magazine,* 29 March 1941.

CHAPTER TWELVE

1 De Segurola, Andrès. "My Hall of Memories." *The Etude,* November 1947, p. 646.
2 Titta Ruffo was still in New York and appearing in a concert at the Manhattan Opera House on 3 June 1915.

3 Sanguinetti, Florentino V. "Caruso en Buenos Aires." *Ayer y Hoy de la Opera,* no. 3 (September–October 1979), p. 66.
4 Ibid., p. 14.
5 Sanguinetti's letter regarding the key in which Caruso sang the prologue is unequivocal, using the words *"elevando el registro"* ("raising the register") to describe Caruso's masterful performance. However, the phrasing of the pertinent passage in *La Nación* is open to interpretation. In Spanish it reads: *"Caruso . . . canto entonces el famoso "pezzo" . . . en su 'tessitura' propia,"* which can mean that Caruso sang the famous piece *in his* or *in its* proper *tessitura.* In the absence of any other reference to the key in which the aria was sung, this ambivalent phrasing is insufficient to refute Sanguinetti's observation that the register was raised; thus one is obliged to interpret *La Nación*'s passage as meaning "in his own *tessitura,*" i.e., in the tenor key.

   This is puzzling, however, in view of the fact that the range of the aria was within Caruso's compass. He sang onstage and recorded "Vecchia zimarra" from *La Bohème* in the original key. This aria, written for a high bass, goes down only to a C-sharp below middle C. The *"Prologo"* in question has a single note a full tone lower, a B-natural, but the rest of the music lies in a range quite comfortable for the Caruso voice, and that single note should not have been a deterrent.
6 Las Damas Argentinas to Enrico Caruso, 28 June 1915.
7 *O Estade do São Paulo,* 9 January 1911.
8 Ibid., 13 January 1911.
9 Ibid., 20 January 1911.
10 *La Prensa,* 19 March 1911.
11 Fenston, Joseph. *Never Say Die: An Impresario's Scrapbook.* London: Alexander Moring, 1958, p. 109.

CHAPTER THIRTEEN

1 Kolodin, Irving. *The Metropolitan Opera: 1883–1939.* New York: Oxford University Press, 1940, p. 226.
2 Ibid.
3 Caruso's attacks of vertigo were mentioned in the "Mephisto's Musings" column of *Musical America,* 26 February 1916, p. 15.
4 Key, Pierre. "Enrico Caruso, Singer and Man." *Daily Telegraph,* 19 June 1920.
5 Readers may wonder why the son of Titta Ruffo is called Ruffo Titta, Jr. The celebrated baritone was baptized Ruffo Cafiero Titta, and before his debut, an impresario recommended the more euphonious inversion of his name. His son chose to retain the original form.

CHAPTER FOURTEEN

1 Undated clipping.
2 Unidentified clipping, 7 September 1918.
3 *The New York Times,* 30 August 1922.
4 Seligman, Vincent. *Puccini Among Friends.* London: Macmillan, 1938, p. 280.
5 Ibid., p. 281.

CHAPTER FIFTEEN

1 Caruso, Dorothy, and Torrance Goddard. *Wings of Song: An Authentic Life Story of Enrico Caruso*. London: Hutchinson, 1928, p. 131.
2 Ibid.
3 Marcello Caruso to Enrico Caruso, Jr., 13 November 1959.
4 Caruso, Dorothy. *Enrico Caruso: His Life and Death*. New York: Simon and Schuster, 1945, p. 38.
5 *The New York Times* of 4 August 1921 made a special mention of this ring. It stated that Caruso "spent several years collecting immensely valuable, vari-colored diamonds for a unique ring, which he lavishingly congratulated himself was 'as unique as my voice.'"
6 *The New York Times,* 4 September 1919.
7 Ibid.

CHAPTER SIXTEEN

1 Caruso, Dorothy. *Enrico Caruso: His Life and Death*. New York: Simon and Schuster, 1945, p. 38.
2 *Star,* 31 March 1944. According to unconfirmed rumors, because of his privileged position, Fred Maisch accumulated a secret hoard of unpublished test pressings of records, among them some Caruso recordings.
3 Caruso, Dorothy. *Enrico Caruso: His Life and Death*. New York: Simon and Schuster, 1945, p. 118.
4 Ibid., p. 129.
5 This may have been the 18 May 1907 concert at the Trocadéro in Paris. Caruso had to spend the day traveling, as he sang at Covent Garden in London the night before.
6 Caruso, Dorothy. *Enrico Caruso: His Life and Death*. New York: Simon and Schuster, 1945, p. 173.
7 *The New York Times,* 9 June 1920.
8 Ibid., 16 June 1920.
9 Ibid.
10 Ibid., 17 June 1920.
11 Ibid., 22 June 1920.
12 Ibid., 17 June 1920.
13 Ibid., 18 June 1920.
14 Ibid., 30 March 1921.
15 Caruso, Dorothy. *Enrico Caruso: His Life and Death*. New York: Simon and Schuster, 1945, pp. 205–06.
16 Key, Pierre. "Enrico Caruso, Singer and Man." *Daily Telegraph,* 17 August 1920.
17 Ibid., 17 July 1920.
18 Key, Pierre V. R. *Enrico Caruso: A Biography*. Boston: Little, Brown, 1922.

CHAPTER SEVENTEEN

1 Colonel L. R. Gignilliat to Mrs. Enrico Caruso, 11 August 1920. From the archives of Culver Military Academy.
2 Dorothy Caruso to Colonel L. R. Gignilliat, Commandant of Culver Military Academy, 1 September 1920. From the archives of Culver Military Academy.

3 H. G. Glascock, Acting Superintendent, to Dorothy Caruso, 3 September 1920. From the archives of Culver Military Academy.
4 *The New York Times,* 14 December 1920.
5 Enrico Caruso to Giovanni Caruso, 1 February 1921.
6 Unidentified clipping, 19 February 1921.
7 *The New York Times,* 19 February 1921.
8 Ibid.
9 Gigli, Beniamino. *The Memoirs of Beniamino Gigli.* London: Cassell, 1957, p. 117.
10 Caruso, Dorothy. *Enrico Caruso: His Life and Death.* New York: Simon and Schuster, 1945, p. 254.
11 Tellegen, Lou. *Women Have Been Kind: The Memoirs of Lou Tellegen.* New York: Vanguard, 1931, p. 145.
12 Ibid.
13 *The New York Times,* 29 May 1921.
14 Ibid.
15 Ibid.
16 Unidentified clipping of a London newspaper quoting its New York correspondent, 4 August 1921.

CHAPTER EIGHTEEN

1 Enrico Caruso to Marziale Sisca, 17 July 1921.
2 *The New York Times,* 3 August 1921.
3 Ibid.
4 Ibid.
5 Ibid.
6 Ibid.
7 Ibid.
8 Ibid.
9 Caruso, Dorothy, and Torrance Goddard. *Wings of Song: An Authentic Life Story of Enrico Caruso.* London: Hutchinson, 1928, pp. 251, 252-53.
10 Caruso, Dorothy. *Enrico Caruso: His Life and Death.* New York: Simon and Schuster, 1945, p. 268.
11 Enrico Caruso to Marziale Sisca, 29 July 1921.
12 *Il Mattino,* 5-6 August 1921.
13 *Il Mattino* published a facsimile of the letter on 3 August 1921.
14 *The New York Times,* 5 August 1921. Dorothy stated in her first biography, *Wings of Song* (1928), page 255, that Caruso's last words were: "Doro—Do-ro, Do-ro!" In her second biography, *Enrico Caruso: His Life and Death* (1945), on page 272, she wrote that his last words were: "Doro—I—can't—get—my—breath—."
15 *The New York Times,* 5 August 1921.
16 "Il Funerali di Enrico Caruso a Napoli" was written and recorded by "Fercor and Company," Okeh 86001-A/86001-B, matrix numbers S-70113-a/70114-b. Fercor was the *nom-du-disque* of the baritone Ferruccio Corradetti (1866-1939), who at the time taught singing in New York. He also made Fonotipia and Odeon records under the Fercor pseudonym. It is doubtful that Corradetti intended the recording to be taken as an on-the-scene recording of Caruso's funeral, although record collectors came to regard it as such.
17 In a letter of 20 August 1986 to me, Dr. Titta wrote: "I assure you that it is a crude fake, fabricated by an ill-advised greenhorn who never heard Titta Ruffo speak. I will be pleased if you say so in your book. I have been tormented for years by people who write me to inform me of the sensational discovery." Dr. Titta said

essentially the same thing in greater detail in a conversation in Rome in May 1985. *Andrew Farkas*

18 *The New York Times,* 5 August 1921.

CHAPTER NINETEEN

1 Caruso, Dorothy, and Torrance Goddard. *Wings of Song: An Authentic Life Story of Enrico Caruso*. London: Hutchinson, 1928, p. 178.

2 Ledner, Emil. *Erinnerungen an Caruso*. Hannover: Paul Steegemann Verlag, 1922, p. 30.

3 Key, Pierre. "Enrico Caruso, Singer and Man." *Daily Telegraph,* 17 July 1920.

4 Ledner, Emil. *Erinnerungen an Caruso*. Hannover: Paul Steegemann Verlag, 1922, p. 57.

5 Ibid.

6 Key, Pierre. "Enrico Caruso, Singer and Man." *Daily Telegraph,* 17 July 1920.

7 *Daily Citizen,* undated clipping.

8 *Star,* London, 18 June 1908.

9 Unidentified clipping, London, 14 May 1913.

10 *The New York Times,* 3 August 1921.

11 *Gaulois,* Paris, August 1918.

12 Key, Pierre. "Enrico Caruso, Singer and Man." *Daily Telegraph,* 5 June 1920.

13 *Daily Telegraph,* 11 September 1920.

14 Caruso, Dorothy. *Enrico Caruso: His Life and Death*. New York: Simon and Schuster, 1945, p. 146.

15 *Daily Mail,* 20 May 1913.

16 Gigli, Beniamino. *The Memoirs of Beniamino Gigli*. London: Cassell, 1957, p. 121.

17 A copy of Beniamino Gigli's letter, dated 29 November 1921, was enlarged and reproduced on page 18 of the 17 December 1921 issue of *Musical America*. The enlargement, along with a translation, filled the page.

18 *The New York Times,* 4 August 1921.

19 Ibid., 3 August 1921.

20 Ledner, Emil. *Erinnerungen an Caruso*. Hannover: Paul Steegemann Verlag, 1922, p. 85.

21 Key, Pierre. "Enrico Caruso, Singer and Man." *Daily Telegraph,* 9 August 1920.

22 Ibid., 5 June 1920.

23 Unidentified clipping, 15 May 1914.

24 Key, Pierre. "Enrico Caruso, Singer and Man." *Daily Telegraph,* 5 June 1920.

25 Ibid., 4 August 1920.

26 Wishing to own a complete set, Dr. Ruffo Titta, Jr., had to assemble the entire collection of his famous father's recordings from scratch. *Andrew Farkas*

27 *West End,* undated clipping (1913?).

28 *Daily Mail,* 3 August 1921; *The New York Times,* 4 August 1921.

29 *The New York Times,* 4 August 1921.

30 Hempel, Frieda. *Mein Leben dem Gesang: Erinnerungen*. Berlin: Argon Verlag, 1955, p. 161.

31 Kolodin, Irving. *The Metropolitan Opera: 1883-1939*. New York: Oxford University Press, 1940.

32 Only three of these were released. The fourth, the "missing number" of the series—84005—is believed to be "Recondita armonia" from *Tosca*.

33 Gaisberg, Fred W. *The Music Goes Round*. New York: Macmillan, 1943, p. 47.

34 All quotations from the Gramophone & Typewriter Company and Victor correspondence concerning Enrico Caruso were taken from photocopies of the

originals provided by the International Classical Division of EMI Music,
London.

35 Gaisberg, Fred W. *The Music Goes Round*. New York: Macmillan, 1943, p. 48.

36 Ibid.

37 Translation of Alfred Michaelis dated 7 December 1902. The manuscript original
as issued by the Finsbury Square Post Office in London is puzzling because of
the postal stamp it bears. The letters "DE 02" are clearly legible, preceded by a
vertical line which because of its position and appearance should be taken as the
number "1." If the telegram reporting that Caruso sang "yesterday" was indeed
postmarked the first day of December, then published sources pinpointing the
date of the Milan recording session as November 12 are in error.

   The telegram unquestionably refers to the November session. Following
the actual text of the handwritten telegram, the figure "5000" is repeated in a
note; Michaelis mentions Caruso's fee of 5000 lire in his subsequent letter of 7
December 1902.

38 All information and direct quotations from Caruso's contracts were taken from
photocopies of the originals provided by RCA Records.

39 Gaisberg, Fred W. *The Music Goes Round*. New York: Macmillan, 1943, p. 48.

40 Clipping marked in pencil *PMG* (*Pall Mall Gazette?*), 17 September 1913.

41 Caruso, Dorothy. *Dorothy Caruso: A Personal History*. New York: Hermitage
House, 1952, pp. 63–64.

42 Ledner, Emil. *Erinnerungen an Caruso*. Hannover: Paul Steegemann Verlag, 1922,
p. 72.

43 Key, Pierre. "Enrico Caruso, Singer and Man." *Daily Telegraph,* 5 June 1920.

44 Bernays, Edward L. *Biography of an Idea: Memoirs of Public Relations Counsel Edward
L. Bernays*. New York: Simon and Schuster, 1965, p. 132.

45 Caruso, Dorothy, and Torrance Goddard. *Wings of Song: An Authentic Life Story of
Enrico Caruso*. London: Hutchinson, 1928, p. 217.

46 *The New York Times,* 3 August 1921.

47 *Daily Graphic,* 18 February 1921.

48 Caruso, Dorothy, and Torrance Goddard. *Wings of Song: An Authentic Life Story of
Enrico Caruso*. London: Hutchinson, 1928, p. 113.

49 Ibid., p. 98.

50 Caruso, Dorothy. *Enrico Caruso: His Life and Death*. New York: Simon and
Schuster, 1945, p. 85.

51 Ibid.

52 Ibid., p. 259.

53 Ledner, Emil. *Erinnerungen an Caruso*. Hannover: Paul Steegemann Verlag, 1922,
p. 74.

54 Crabbé, Armand. *Conversation et conseils sur l'art du chant*. Brussels: Schott, 1931.
Translated by E. Dansard and originally published in the *Gramophone,* November 1931, p. 213.

55 Bernays, Edward L. *Biography of an Idea: Memoirs of Public Relations Counsel Edward
L. Bernays*. New York: Simon and Schuster, 1965, pp. 141–42.

56 Ibid., p. 133.

57 *Daily Express,* 3 February 1925.

58 *Sunday Express,* 26 November 1933.

59 *The New York Times,* 4 August 1921.

60 Ledner, Emil. *Erinnerungen an Caruso*. Hannover: Paul Steegemann Verlag, 1922,
p. 22.

61 Mathewson, Anna. *The Song of the Evening Stars*. Boston: Richard G. Badger, 1911,
p. 29.

62 Caruso, Dorothy. *Enrico Caruso: His Life and Death*. New York: Simon and

Schuster, 1945, p. 75.
63 Caruso, Enrico. *The New Book of Caricatures*. New York: La Follia di New York, 1965, p. i.
64 Ibid.
65 *Evening News,* 19 May 1914.
66 *E. S. (Evening Standard?)*, 31 October 1910.
67 Unidentified clipping, 16 June 1910.
68 De Segurola, Andrès. *Through My Monocle*. Typescript, p. 476.
69 Ibid., p. 477.
70 *The New York Times,* 4 August 1921.

CHAPTER TWENTY

1 Prichard, Robert W. "The Death of Enrico Caruso." *Surgery, Gynecology and Obstetrics,* July 1959, pp. 117-20. Dr. Prichard was an affiliate of the Bowman Gray School of Medicine of the North Carolina Baptist Hospital, Winston-Salem, N.C.
2 Ibid., p. 118, quoting a personal communication from Dr. John F. Erdmann to Dr. Prichard, October 1951.
3 Ibid., p. 117.
4 Ibid., p. 119.
5 *The New York Times,* 4 August 1921.
6 Ibid.
7 Ibid., 5 August 1921.
8 Ibid.
9 An Associated Press report carried in the 5 August 1921 *New York Times* quotes the same interview, giving Dr. Bastianelli's words almost identically: "We immediately decided that Caruso should be taken to Rome and submitted to an X-ray examination in order to complete our diagnosis and also as a guide for the operation which was to have been performed immediately after."
10 Caruso, Dorothy, and Torrance Goddard. *Wings of Song: An Authentic Life Story of Enrico Caruso*. London: Hutchinson, 1928, p. 253.
11 Caruso, Dorothy. *Enrico Caruso: His Life and Death*. New York: Simon and Schuster, 1945, p. 269.
12 Ibid.
13 Mouchon, Jean-Pierre. *Enrico Caruso: His Life and Voice*. Gap, France: Editions Ophrys, 1974, p. 47. Facsimile reproduction of Dr. Raffaele Bastianelli's letter to Dr. Robert W. Prichard, 5 October 1959.
14 Ibid.
15 Seligman, Vincent. *Puccini Among Friends*. London: Macmillan, 1938, p. 238.
16 Dr. Chiarolanza was referring to the single incident of hemorrhaging onstage at the Brooklyn Academy of Music.
17 "Doctor in the House." *Opera News,* September 1985, pp. 24-25.

CHAPTER TWENTY-ONE

1 *Daily Mail,* 3 August 1921.
2 *The New York Times,* 3 August 1921.
3 Telegram from Bruno Zirato to Enrico Caruso, Jr., 2 August 1921.
4 *The New York Times,* 3 August 1921.

5 Bruno Zirato to Colonel L. R. Gignilliat at the Culver Military Academy, undated.
6 *The New York Times,* 5 August 1921.
7 Caruso, Dorothy. *Enrico Caruso: His Life and Death.* New York: Simon and Schuster, 1945, p. 281.

CHAPTER TWENTY-TWO

1 The names of the architect and builder of the Caruso chapel were researched and supplied by Guido d'Onofrio.
2 *Musical America,* 19 March 1927.

CHAPTER TWENTY-SIX

1 Enrico Caruso to Dorothy Caruso, 11 October 1919.
2 "Holy Child" (Luther; Esthope Martin), piano accompaniment by Edwin Schneider. Matrix number BVE 41560–2. Recorded on 17 January 1928.
3 *The New York Times,* 15 September 1934.
4 Ibid., 25 February 1935.

CHAPTER TWENTY-EIGHT

1 Edward J. Smith to Andrew Farkas, 18 April 1984.
2 Ibid.
3 Ibid.

CHAPTER TWENTY-NINE

1 Edward J. Smith to Andrew Farkas, 18 April 1984, with some changes made as a result of subsequent telephone conversations.
2 Ibid.
3 Ibid.

CHAPTER THIRTY

1 Arnold B. Hartley to Enrico Caruso, Jr., 27 May 1942.
2 Garrison's memory must have been playing tricks on her. According to published records (among them the *New York Times* announcement and review of the performance and Quaintance Eaton's *Opera Caravan*), the Adina in that performance was Evelyn Scotney. The other possibility, though quite remote, is that there was a last-minute cast change that did not find its way into the printed records, and Garrison sang the role after all.

CHAPTER THIRTY-TWO

1 Family sources maintain that Maria Castaldi Caruso died on 20 September 1939 at the age of ninety-two, at her house at Via Kerbacher 53, Naples-Vomero.

However, according to *The New York Times* of 12 August 1940, she died on 10 August 1940 at San Martino. I believe the first date to be more reliable.

2 Caruso, Dorothy. *Enrico Caruso: His Life and Death*. New York: Simon and Schuster, 1945.

3 Gara, Eugenio. *Caruso: storia di un emigrante*. Milan: Rizzoli, 1947.

4 De Segurola, Andrès. "My Hall of Memories." *The Etude,* September, October, and November 1947.

5 Bruno Zirato to Andrès de Segurola, 17 March 1947. Courtesy of The Francis Robinson Collection of Theatre, Music, and Dance, Vanderbilt University, Nashville, Tennessee.

6 Andrès de Segurola to Bruno Zirato, 27 March 1947. Courtesy of The Francis Robinson Collection of Theatre, Music, and Dance, Vanderbilt University, Nashville, Tennessee.

7 The *Rigoletto* "Quartet" recording was made on 23 February 1916. A microgroove dubbing at 33⅓ rpm was issued on a seven-inch disc by the Stanford Archive of Recorded Sound (StARS 1000 A) in 1973. Caruso's dedication on the original label was reproduced on the reissue.

CHAPTER THIRTY-THREE

1 Caruso, Dorothy. *Dorothy Caruso: A Personal History*. New York: Hermitage House, 1952, p. 84.

2 *Evening Standard,* 30 September 1940.

3 Unidentified clipping, London newspaper, 11 May 1951.

4 Unidentified clipping, 11 May 1951.

5 *Manchester Guardian,* 30 May 1955.

6 In 1989, the Italian radio broadcast a thirteen-part program entitled "Enrico Caruso Was My Grandfather." The script was written by a certain Amleto Micozzi. The program claims that a dancer by the name of Adelina, with whom Caruso had an affair in Palermo, became pregnant. Adelina married immediately after her two-month romance with Caruso ended, and she made her husband believe that their child was born prematurely, after seven months, on 11 February 1898. The baby was named Enrico, and his daughter, making the claim in the title of the radio drama, is called Enrica.

    I am indebted to Guido d'Onofrio for this information. *Andrew Farkas*

7 Wladimiro Caruso died in Montaione, near Florence, on 1 June 1988, the anniversary of the deaths of his great-aunts, Assunta (in 1915) and Rina (in 1959). His great-grandmother, Anna Baldini Caruso, died one hundred years and one day before, on 31 May 1888. As this volume was being prepared for publication, I received word that Enrico Caruso III died in Sacrofano, near Rome, on 13 June 1989. *Andrew Farkas*

8 *Hi-Fi Music at Home,* May-June 1956, pp. 29, 64-65.

9 Francis Robinson to Enrico Caruso, Jr., 13 June 1956.

10 Robinson, Francis. *Caruso: His Life in Pictures*. New York: Studio Publications, 1957, p. 25.

576

Luigi Caruso
Rosa Lenna

Pasquale Palumbo
Maria Tancasia

Giovanni Caruso
1804–?
Maria Onorata Palumbo

Vincenzo Giuseppe Baldini
20 October 1812–?
Carmela d'Onofrio

Salvatore Caruso

Giovanni Caruso

Enrico Caruso

Marcellino Caruso
8 March 1840–20 May 1908
Anna Baldini
9 May 1838–31 May 1888
Maria Carmina Castaldi

Pasquale Caruso
6 January 1869–18 January 1876

Antonio Caruso
6 January 1871–5 July 1873

ERRICO (ENRICO) CARUSO
25 February 1873–2 August 1921
Vittoria Matilde Ada Giachetti
1 December 1874–16 October 1946
Dorothy Park Benjamin
6 August 1893–16 December 1955

Rodolfo Marcellino Giuseppe
2 July 1898–6 March 1951
Armanda Comparini
?–2 September 1960

Gloria Caruso
18 December 1919–
Michael Hunt Murray

Eric Dunmore Murray
26 March 1945–
Lynne Margaret Vendetti

Colin Duncan Alexander Murray
9 January 1949–
Elizabeth Ann Kaufold

Roberto Caruso
8 October 1923–29 August
Marisa Toscani
12 December 1920–

Jennifer Suzanne Murray
7 June 1971–

Eric Brandon Murray
14 May 1974–

Margaret Frances Murray
22 April 1975–

Gloria Letizia Caruso
19 January 1954–

Genealogical Table of the Caruso Family

Researched by Guido d'Onofrio

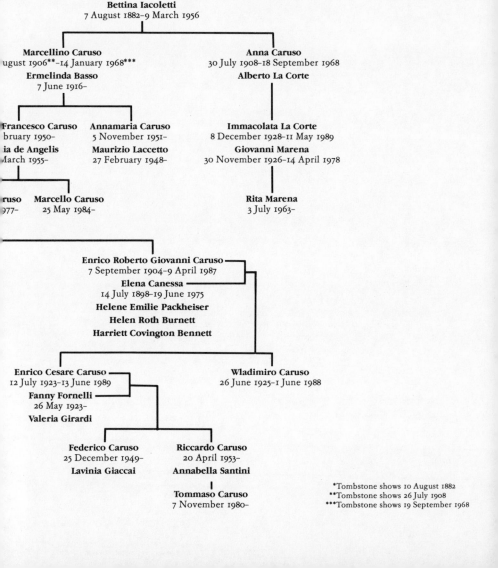

ɔmo Caruso
4–23 October 1876

Giovanni Giuseppe Caruso
6 January 1876–13 April 1940
Bettina Iacoletti
7 August 1882–9 March 1956

Francesco Caruso
15 December 1877–17 December 1878

Assunta Caruso
13 August 1881*–1 June 1915

Marcellino Caruso
ugust 1906**–14 January 1968***
Ermelinda Basso
7 June 1916–

Anna Caruso
30 July 1908–18 September 1968
Alberto La Corte

Francesco Caruso
bruary 1950–
ia de Angelis
March 1955–

Annamaria Caruso
5 November 1951–
Maurizio Laccetto
27 February 1948–

Immacolata La Corte
8 December 1928–11 May 1989
Giovanni Marena
30 November 1926–14 April 1978

uso
977–

Marcello Caruso
25 May 1984–

Rita Marena
3 July 1963–

Enrico Roberto Giovanni Caruso
7 September 1904–9 April 1987
Elena Canessa
14 July 1898–19 June 1975
Helene Emilie Packheiser
Helen Roth Burnett
Harriett Covington Bennett

Enrico Cesare Caruso
12 July 1923–13 June 1989
Fanny Fornelli
26 May 1923–
Valeria Girardi

Wladimiro Caruso
26 June 1925–1 June 1988

Federico Caruso
25 December 1949–
Lavinia Giaccai

Riccardo Caruso
20 April 1953–
Annabella Santini

Tommaso Caruso
7 November 1980–

*Tombstone shows 10 August 1882
**Tombstone shows 26 July 1908
***Tombstone shows 19 September 1968

Bibliography of Sources

Newspapers and Periodicals

ARGENTINA
Ayer y Hoy de la Opera (periodical)
La Prensa
La Nación

AUSTRIA
Neues Wiener Tagblatt

BRAZIL
A Noite
O Estade do São Paulo

CANADA
Montreal Star

CHILE
El Mercurio
El Sur

ENGLAND
Daily Chronicle
Daily Citizen
Daily Express
Daily Graphic
Daily Mail
Daily News
Daily Telegraph
Evening News
Evening Standard
Globe
London Opinion
Manchester Guardian
Monthly Musical Record
Morning Post
Pall Mall Gazette
Pearson's Weekly (periodical)
The Reader
Sporting Life
Star
Sunday Express

ENGLAND (continued)
Sunday Times
Times
West End
Westminster Gazette
Yorkshire Post

FRANCE
Les Annales du Théâtre (periodical)
Le Figaro
Gaulois

GERMANY
Berliner Allgemeine Zeitung
Berliner Morgenpost
Berliner Tageblatt
Frankfurter General Anzeiger
Frankfurter Zeitung
Hamburger Nachrichten
Münchener Post
Münchener Zeitung
Der Tag

HUNGARY
Alkotmány
Budapest
Budapester Tageblatt
Budapesti Hirlap
A Nap
Pesti Napló
Az Ujság

ITALY
Adriatico
Corriere della Sera
Corriere Italiano
Corriere Toscano
Don Marzio
Fieramosca

ITALY (continued)
Fortunio
Gazzetta dei Teatri
Gazzetta del Popolo
Gazzetta di Torino
Gazzetta di Venezia
Gazzetta Livornese
Gazzettino
Giornale d'Italia
Il Giorno
Indipendente
Il Mattino
Messaggero
Il Mondo Artistico
La Nazione
Osservatorio Triestino
La Perseveranza
Il Piccolo della Sera
Il Pungolo
Il Resto del Carlino
Rassegna Melodrammatica
Rivista Teatrale Melodrammatica
Roma
La Sera
Teatro Illustrato
Telegrafo
Tirreneo
Tribuna
Triester Zeitung
Il Trovatore

MEXICO
Impacto (periodical)

POLAND
Kurier Warszawski
Kurjer Poranny
Tygodnik Warszawski

PORTUGAL
O Mundo
O Secolo

UNITED STATES
American Weekly
Chicago Herald
Chicago Herald-American
Chicago Sun
Daily News
Daily Times
The Etude (periodical)
Evening Bulletin
Hi-Fi Music at Home (periodical)
Life (periodical)
Living Age (periodical)
Morning Telegraph
Musical America (periodical)
Musical Courier (periodical)
New York Journal-American
New York Post
New York Review
New York Sun
New York Times
New York World Telegram
Opera News (1909–20)
   (periodical)
Philadelphia Inquirer
Surgery, Gynecology and Obstetrics
   (periodical)
Time (periodical)

URUGUAY
El Dia

Monographs

Bernays, Edward L. *Biography of an Idea: Memoirs of Public Relations Counsel Edward L. Bernays*. New York: Simon and Schuster, 1965.

Bolig, John R. "A Caruso Discography." In: Michael Scott, *The Great Caruso*. New York: Knopf; London: Hamish Hamilton, 1988.

Caruso, Dorothy. *Dorothy Caruso: A Personal History*. New York: Hermitage House, 1952.

_____ . *Enrico Caruso: His Life and Death*. New York: Simon and Schuster, 1945.

Caruso, Dorothy, and Torrance Goddard. *Wings of Song: An Authentic Life Story of Enrico Caruso*. London: Hutchinson, 1928.

Caruso, Enrico. *The New Book of Caricatures*. New York: La Follia di New York, 1965.

Crabbé, Armand. *Conversation et conseils sur l'art du chant*. Brussels: Schott, 1931.

Daspuro, Nicola. *Enrico Caruso*. Milan: Sonzogno, 1938.

De Segurola, Andrès. *Through My Monocle*. Typescript, n.d.

Eaton, Quaintance. *Opera Caravan*. New York: Farrar, Strauss and Cudahy, 1957.

Fenston, Joseph. *Never Say Die: An Impresario's Scrapbook*. London: Alexander Moring, 1958.

Gaisberg, Fred W. *The Music Goes Round*. New York: Macmillan, 1943.

Gara, Eugenio. *Caruso: storia di un emigrante*. Milan: Rizzoli, 1947.

Gatti, Carlo. *Il Teatro alla Scala,* 2 volumes. Milan: Ricordi, 1964.

Gigli, Beniamino. *The Memoirs of Beniamino Gigli*. London: Cassell, 1957.

Hempel, Frieda. *Mein Leben dem Gesang: Erinnerungen*. Berlin: Argon Verlag, 1955.

Heylbut, Rose, and Aimé Gerber. *Backstage at the Metropolitan Opera*. New York: Thomas Y. Crowell, 1937.

Key, Pierre V. R. *Enrico Caruso: A Biography*. Boston: Little, Brown, 1922.

_____ . *Enrico Caruso: Souvenir Book*. New York: Francis C. Coppicus, 1920.

Kolodin, Irving. *The Metropolitan Opera: 1883-1939*. New York: Oxford University Press, 1940.

Ledner, Emil. *Erinnerungen an Caruso*. Hannover: Paul Steegemann Verlag, 1922.

Mathewson, Anna. *The Song of the Evening Stars*. Boston: Richard G. Badger, 1911.

Mouchon, Jean-Pierre. *Enrico Caruso: His Life and Voice*. Gap, France: Editions Ophrys, 1974.

The New Grove Dictionary of Music and Musicians. London: Macmillan, 1980.

Robinson, Francis. *Enrico Caruso: His Life in Pictures*. New York: Studio Publications, 1957.

Rubboli, Daniele. *Lo "scugnizzo" che conquistò il mondo*. Naples: Liguri Editore, 1987.

Scott, Michael. *The Great Caruso*. New York: Knopf; London: Hamish Hamilton, 1988.

Seligman, Vincent. *Puccini Among Friends*. London: Macmillan, 1938.

Tellegen, Lou. *Women Have Been Kind: The Memoirs of Lou Tellegen*. New York: Vanguard, 1931.

Caruso Bibliography

by Opritsa Popa

PART I
Monographs by Enrico Caruso

Caruso, Enrico. *L'altro Caruso* (The other Caruso). Milan: Eiot-Nuova Editrice Internazionale, 1961. 159 pp.

──── . *Caricatures by Enrico Caruso.* New York: La Follia di New York, 1908. 182 pp.

──── . *Caruso and Tetrazzini on the Art of Singing.* New York: Dover Publications, 1975. 71 pp.

──── . *Caruso's Book: Being a Collection of Caricatures and Character Studies from Original Drawings of the Metropolitan Opera Company.* New York: R. G. Cooke, 1906. 47 pp.

──── . *Caruso's Caricatures.* New York: Dover Publications, 1977. 214 pp.

──── . *How to Sing: Some Practical Hints.*[1] London: John Church & Company, 1913. 61 pp.

──── . *How to Sing.* Reprint edition. Brooklyn: Opera Box, 1973. 61 pp.

──── . *The New Book of Caricatures.* New York: La Follia di New York, 1965. Unpaged.

──── . *Wie man singen soll: praktische Winke* (How to sing: practical hints). Translated by August Spanuth. Mainz: B. Schott's Söhne, 1914. 61 pp.

How to Become a Successful Singer. By Madame Clara Butt, Madame Melba, Signor Caruso, Mr. Ben Davies. London: George Newnes, 1912. 64 pp.

Tetrazzini, Luisa, and Enrico Caruso. *The Art of Singing.* New York: Metropolitan Company, 1909. 71 pp.

──── . *The Art of Singing* [and] *How to Sing,* by Luisa Tetrazzini. Reprint edition. New York: Da Capo Press, 1975. 71, 136 pp.

Note

1. Since the book *How to Sing* was originally published, translated, and reprinted showing Caruso as its author, the compiler found its inclusion in this bibliography inevitable. However, modern audiences must understand that Caruso was not its author. The following quoted passages clarify this matter.

> London, August 3rd. Signor Enrico Caruso may be the greatest tenor in the world, and he certainly knows how to sing, but Mme. Meyerheim, the famous singing teacher, in a suit against Caruso and John Church & Co., the publishers, claims that the great tenor in his new book, *How to Sing,* has

copied whole chapters from her work *L'Art du Chant Technique,* and she has secured an injunction against him and his publishers prohibiting the sale of the book on the ground of infringement of copyright. Church & Co. pleaded that they bought the rights to the work from another concern and had no dealings with Caruso personally, and they were innocent parties to the infringement as well as victims. It is probable that Caruso is also a victim, for he is singularly free in giving his name to song writers and litterateurs who are anxious to coin it into money by putting it at the head of their own unsalable compositions. Caruso did not defend the suit, but let it go by default.   (*The New York Review,* 1914)

Many have wondered how much or how little Enrico Caruso had to do with the book on singing that recently appeared with his name affixed to it. Not long after it was published a singing teacher named Meyerheim, living in London, accused the Italian tenor of having appropriated entire pages from her writings for the book. Now in the *Corriere della Sera* Caruso makes reply to the charge by disclaiming all connection with the book published as his and protests against the use of his name in association with it.   (*Musical America,* 22 August 1914)

PART II
Monographs About Enrico Caruso

Armin, George. *Enrico Caruso: Untersuchung der Stimme Carusos und ihr Verhaltnis zum Stauprinzip im Spiegel eines eigenen Erlebnisses* (Enrico Caruso: an analysis of Caruso's voice and its relation to the constriction principle as reflected by a personal experience). Berlin-Wilmersdorf: Verlag der Gesellschaft für Stimmkultur, 1929. 111 pp.

Barát, Endre, and Endre Lévay. *Caruso csodálatos élete: regényes életrajz* (Caruso's marvelous life: a romantic biography). Budapest: Bibliotheca, 1957.

Barthélemy, Richard. *Memories of Caruso.* Introduction by James Camner. Translated by Constance S. Camner. Plainsboro, N.J.: La Scala Autographs, 1979. 15 pp.

Bello, John. *Enrico Caruso: A Centennial Tribute.* Providence, R.I.: Universal Associates, 1973. Unpaged.

Blanco, Eumenio. *El inmortal Enrico Caruso* (The immortal Enrico Caruso). Hollywood: Orbe Publications, 1964. 60 pp.

Bolig, John Richard. *The Recordings of Enrico Caruso: A Discography.* Dover, Del.: Eldridge Reeves Johnson Memorial, Delaware State Museum, 1973. 88 pp.

Brower, Harriette Moore. *Vocal Mastery: Talks with Master Singers and Teachers, Comprising Interviews with Caruso, Farrar, Maurel, Lehmann, and Others.* New York: Frederick A. Stokes, 1920. 292 pp.

Bruns, Paul. *Carusos Technik in deutscher Erklärung* (Caruso's technique in German interpretation). Charlottenburg: Otto Sorge, 1922. 42 pp.

Burian, Karel Vladimir. *Enrico Caruso.* "Kdo je?" Prague: Orbis, n.d.

Caruso, Dorothy Park (Benjamin). *Dorothy Caruso: A Personal History.* New York: Hermitage House, 1952. 191 pp.

_____ . *Enrico Caruso: His Life and Death.* New York: Simon and Schuster, 1945. 303 pp.

_____ . *Enrico Caruso: His Life and Death.* London: T. W. Laurie, 1946. 312 pp.

_____ . *Enrico Caruso: His Life and Death.* New York: Simon and Schuster, 1963. 305 pp.

Caruso, Dorothy Park (Benjamin), and Torrance Goddard. *Das Leben Enrico Carusos: Erinnerungen* (The life of Enrico Caruso: memoirs). Translated by Else Werkmann. Dresden: P. Aretz, 1929. 205 pp.

_____ . *Wings of Song: An Authentic Life Story of Enrico Caruso.* London: Hutchinson, 1928. 256 pp.

_____ . *Wings of Song: The Story of Caruso.* New York: Minton, Balch, 1928. 218 pp.

Centro Studi Carusiani. *Omaggio a Enrico Caruso* (Homage to Enrico Caruso). Milan: Associazione Museo Enrico Caruso, 1977.

_____ . *Testi poetici di romanze dedicate a Enrico Caruso* (Lyrics of songs dedicated to Enrico Caruso). Milan: Associazione Museo Enrico Caruso, n.d. 43 pp.

Collezione del fu Comm. Enrico Caruso, monete e medaglie in oro, Greche, Romane, Bizantine, Medioevali e moderne, Italiane e estere, Medaglie papali, Italiane e estere; La vendita avra luogo . . . Dal 28 Giugno e giorni seguenti (Collection of gold coins and medallions, etc., of the late Enrico Caruso). Paris: C. & E. Canessa, 1923. 104 pp.

Collezione Enrico Caruso monete e medaglie d'oro (Enrico Caruso's collections of gold coins and medallions). Bologna: Forni, 1970. 104 pp.

Cooke, James Francis. *Great Singers on the Art of Singing: Educational Conferences with Foremost Artists; a Series of Personal Study Talks with the Most Renowned Opera, Concert and Oratorio Singers of the Time, Especially Planned for Voice Students.* Philadelphia: Theodore Presser, 1921. 304 pp.

Corda, Alfredo. *Caruso in der Westentasche; Schmunzeleien eines Tenors: Kurzgeschichten und Anekdoten* (Pocket-book Caruso; smiles of a tenor: short stories and anecdotes). Darmstadt: Blaschke, 1977. 285 pp.

Daspuro, Nicola. *Enrico Caruso.* Milan: Casa Editrice Sonzogno, 1938. 79 pp.

_____ . *Enrico Caruso.* Translated by Arrigo Coen Anitua. Mexico: Ediciones Coli, 1943. 124 pp.

Favia-Artsay, Aida. *Caruso on Records: Pitch, Speed, and Comments for All the Published Recordings of Enrico Caruso.* Valhalla, N.Y.: Historic Record, 1965. 218 pp.

Feldinger, Heinrich. *Der Schatten des Enrico Caruso* (The shadow of Enrico Caruso). Published by Otto Eicke. Dresden: Mignon-Verlag, 1924. 32 pp.

Finck, Henry Theophilus. *The Secret of Caruso's Glorious Voice.* Philadelphia: Theodore Presser, 1929. 19 pp.

Fitzgerald, Gerald, editor. *Caruso, 1981: The Opera Engagement Calendar.* New York: Metropolitan Opera Guild, 1980. Unpaged.

Flint, Mary H. *Impressions of Caruso and His Art As Portrayed at the Metropolitan Opera House.* New York: J. P. Paret, 1917. 22 pp.

Fracassini, Gino. *Il poeta del canto* (The poet of song). Florence: s.n., 1918.

Francillo-Kauffmann, Hedwig, and Eugen-Gottlieb Hellmesberger. *Von Caruso zu dir: Gesangstechnisches aus der Praxis und für die Praxis von Kammersängerin Hedwig Francillo-Kauffmann* (From Caruso to you: singing techniques from practice and for practice by *Kammersängerin* Hedwig Francillo-Kauffmann). Vienna: Universal Edition, 1935. 54 pp.

Freestone, John, and H. J. Drummond. *Enrico Caruso: His Recorded Legacy.* London: Sidgwick and Jackson, 1960. 130 pp.

_____ . *Enrico Caruso: His Recorded Legacy.* Minneapolis: T. S. Denison, 1961. 130 pp.

Fucito, Salvatore. *Caruso and the Art of Singing.* Reprint edition. New York: Gordon Press, 1976. 219 pp.

Fucito, Salvatore, and Barnet J. Beyer. *Caruso and the Art of Singing, Including Caruso's Vocal Exercises and His Practical Advice to Students and Teachers of Singing.* New York: Frederick A. Stokes Company, 1922. 219 pp.

_____ . *Caruso: Gesangkunst und Methode* (Caruso: art and method of singing). Translated by Curt Thesing. Berlin: E. Bote und G. Bock, 1924. 60 pp.

Gara, Eugenio. *Caruso.* Translated by Concepcion Valero. Barcelona: Ediciones G. P., 1959. 128 pp.

_____ . *Caruso: storia di un emigrante* (Caruso: the story of an emigrant). Milan: Rizzoli, 1947. 282 pp.

_____ . *Caruso: storia di un emigrante* (Caruso: the story of an emigrant). Milan: Cisalpino-Goliardica, 1973. 282 pp.

Gragnaffini, Arnaldo. *Caruso: Note biografiche ed aneddotiche* (Caruso: biographical and anecdotic notes). Parma: Freschig, 1923. 38 pp.

Greenfeld, Howard. *Caruso.* New York: G. P. Putnam's Sons, 1983. 275 pp.

Hacker, Werner. *Enrico Caruso: ein Lebensroman* (Enrico Caruso: a life story). Berlin: P. Neff, 1944. 182 pp.

Huefner-Berndt, Bernhard. *Die praktischen Winke Carusos an Hand von Schallplatten* (Caruso's practical hints illustrated by his records). Leipzig: Selbstverlag, 1927. 52 pp.

_____ . *Die praktischen Winke Carusos an Hand von Schallplatten* (Caruso's practical hints illustrated by his records). 2nd edition. Leipzig: Hug, 1928. 86 pp.

Illustrated Catalogue of the Rare and Beautiful Antique Art Treasures, American and Foreign Gold Coins and Many Operatic Costumes, the Property of the Late Enrico Caruso, to Be Sold at Unrestricted Public Sale at the American Art Galleries. New York: Canessa, 1921. 172 pp.

Jackson, Stanley. *Caruso.* New York: Stein and Day; London: W. H. Allen, 1972. 302 pp.

_____ . *Caruso.* Iván Kertész. *Appendix: Caruso bukása Budapesten a korabeli sajtó tükrében* (Caruso's failure in Budapest in the contemporary press). Translated by Mária Borbás. Budapest: Gondolat, 1976. 447 pp.

Key, Pierre Van Rensselaer. *Enrico Caruso: A Biography.* Boston: Little, Brown, 1922. 455 pp.

_____ . *Enrico Caruso: A Biography.* Reprint edition. New York: Vienna House, 1972. 455 pp.

_____ . *Enrico Caruso: Souvenir Book.* New York: Francis C. Coppicus, 1920. Unpaged.

Key, Pierre Van Rensselaer, and Bruno Zirato. *Caruso.* Salvatore Fucito and Barnet J. Beyer. *Carusos Gesangmethode* (Caruso's singing method). Translated by Curt Thesing. Munich: Buchenau und Reichert, 1924. 395 pp.

Kronberg, Max. *Pucini un Karuzo dzives romans: melodijas uzvara* (The life stories of Puccini and Caruso: the triumph of melody). Translated by Tulkojis E. Feldmanis. Riga: Gramatu Draugs, 1936. 232 pp.

_____ . *Der Sieg der Melodie: ein Puccini-Caruso-Roman* (The triumph of melody: a Puccini-Caruso novel). Leipzig: Koehler und Ameland, 1935. 267 pp.

Ledner, Emil. *Erinnerungen an Caruso* (Remembering Caruso). Foreword by Leo Blech. Hannover: Paul Steegemann Verlag, 1922. 91 pp.

Lehrmann, Johannes. *Caruso singt! Ernstes und Lustiges um Caruso und die Gastspielzeit vor 30 Jahren in Wort und Bild* (Caruso sings! The serious and the gay with respect to Caruso and the guest-appearances 30 years ago, in word and picture). Berlin: Lehrmann, 1940. 80 pp.

Lévai, Endre, and Endre Barát. *La vie fantastique de Caruso: roman* (The fantastic life of Caruso: a novel). Paris: Editions Artistiques et Documentaires, 1946. 227 pp.

Marafioti, Pasqual Mario. *Caruso's Method of Voice Production: The Scientific Culture of the Voice.* Preface by Victor Maurel. New York: D. Appleton, 1922. 308 pp.

_____ . *Caruso's Method of Voice Production: The Scientific Culture of the Voice.* Preface by Victor Maurel. Reprint edition. Austin, Texas: Cadica Enterprises, 1950. 308 pp.

Maria y Campos, Armando de. *El canto del cisne (una temporada de Caruso en 1919): recuerdos de un cronista* (Swansong [a season with Caruso in 1919]: memories of a reporter). Mexico: Arriba el Telon, 1952. 159 pp.

Marone, Silvio. *Caruso: aspectos de sua personalidade psicodinamica, suas atividades em São Paulo* (Caruso: aspects of his psychodynamic personality, of his activities in São Paulo). São Paulo: Grafica Gentleman, 1973. 25 pp.

Metropolitan Opera Association, New York. *Special Gala Performance Celebrating the Twenty-fifth Year in the Career of Enrico Caruso, Metropolitan Opera House... March the 22nd, 1919.* New York: Theatre Magazine Company, 1919. 32 leaves.

Mouchon, Jean-Pierre. *Enrico Caruso, 1873–1921, sa vie et sa voix: étude psycho-physiologique, physique, phonétique et esthétique* (Enrico Caruso, 1873–1921, his life and his voice: a study in psycho-physiology, physics, phonetics and esthetics). Langres, France: Imprimerie du Petit Cloitre, 1966. 106 pp.

_____ . *Enrico Caruso: His Life and Voice.* Translated by the author. Gap, France: Editions Ophrys, 1974. 74 pp.

_____ . *Enrico Caruso: l'homme et l'artiste* (Enrico Caruso: man and artist). Ph.D. dissertation, the Sorbonne, Paris, 1978. 1605 typescript pp.

Museo teatrale alla Scala. *Enrico Caruso.* In English and Italian. Milan: Arti Grafiche E. Milli, n.d. Unpaged.

Narciso, Adolfo. *Enrico Caruso e i vermicelli a vongole. . .* (Enrico Caruso and the *vermicelli a vongole. . .*). Naples: s.n., 1935. 31 pp.

Niemand, Szymon. *Enrico Caruso 1873–1921 (w. 40 rocznice smierci)* (Enrico Caruso 1873–1921 [on the 40th anniversary of his death]). Katowice: s.n., 1961. 29 pp.

Omaggio a Caruso: nel centenario della nascita (Homage to Caruso: on the centenary of his birth). Naples: Teatro Di San Carlo, 1973. 8 leaves.

Paul, Barbara. *A Cadenza for Caruso.* New York: St. Martin's Press, 1984. 146 pp.

Petriccione, Diego. *Caruso nell'arte e nella vita* (Caruso in art and life). Naples: Edizione Santojanni, 1939. 61 pp.

Reis, Kurt. *Caruso, Triumph einer Stimme: Roman nach Zeitgenossischen Quellenwerken und Memoiren frei bearbeitet* (Caruso, triumph of a voice: a novel freely compiled from contemporary sources and memoirs). Berlin: Deutsche Buchvertriebs- und Verlags-Gesselschaft, 1955. 350 pp.

Reitsch, Gertrud. *Kann man die ideale Tongebung Carusos lehren? "Stimm-turnen," der kürzeste und schwerste Weg zum Ziel* (Can Caruso's ideal tone-production be taught? "Voice gymnastics," the shortest and most difficult way to the goal). Munich: Buchenau und Reichert, 1924. 29 pp.

Robinson, Francis. *Caruso: His Life in Pictures.* New York: Branhall House; New York: Studio Publications, 1957. 160 pp.

Rubboli, Daniele. *Lo "scugnizzo" che conquistò il mondo: vita di Enrico Caruso* (The urchin who conquered the world: the life of Enrico Caruso). Naples: Liguri Editore, 1987. 129 pp.

Scott, Michael. *The Great Caruso.* New York: Knopf; London: Hamish Hamilton, 1988. 322 pp.

Steen, Hans. *Caruso: eine Stimme erobert die Welt* (Caruso: a voice con-quers the world). Essen-Steele: W. Webels, 1946. 105 pp.

Suardon, P. *Enrico Caruso.* Milan: Sonzogno, 1938. 79 pp.

Thiess, Frank. *Caruso in Sorrent: Roman* (Caruso in Sorrento: a novel). Vienna: P. Zsolnay, 1949. 461 pp.

_____ . *Caruso: Roman einer Stimme* (Caruso: the story of a voice). Vienna: K. H. Bischoff, 1942.

_____ . *Caruso: Roman einer Stimme* (Caruso: the story of a voice). Hamburg: P. Zsolnay, 1952. 719 pp.

_____ . *Caruso: Vortrag gehalten am 26. Februar 1943 in der Deutsch Italienischen Gesellschaft in Frankfurt am Main* (Caruso: Lecture given on 26 February 1943 at the German Italian Association in Frankfurt am Main). Berlin: K. H. Bischoff, 1943. 55 pp.

———. *Neapolitanische Legende, [der Junge Caruso]: Roman* (Neapolitan legend, [the young Caruso]: a novel). Frankfurt am Main: Fischer, 1952. 208 pp.

———. *Neapolitanische Legende: Roman* (Neapolitan legend: a novel). Berlin: K. H. Bischoff, 1942. 356 pp.

———. *Der Tenor von Trapani* (The tenor from Trapani). Leipzig: P. Reclam, 1942. 74 pp.

———. *Der Tenor von Trapani, Novelle: mit einem autobiographischen Nachwort* (The tenor from Trapani, a short story: with an autobiographical postscript). Stuttgart: Reclam, 1952. 93 pp.

———. *Il tenore di Trapani* (The tenor from Trapani). Translated by Anita Rho. Turin: Frassinelli, 1942. 195 pp.

Tortorelli, Vittorio. *Enrico Caruso nel centenario della nascita* (Enrico Caruso on the centenary of his birth). Rimini: Artisti Asociati, 1973. 188 pp.

———. *Enriko Karuzo (Enrico Caruso)*. Moscow: Muzika, 1965. 176 pp.

Wagenmann, Josef Hermann. *Enrico Caruso und das Problem der Stimmbildung* (Enrico Caruso and the problem of voice training). Altenburg: S.-J. Rade, 1911. 73 pp.

———. *Enrico Caruso und das Problem der Stimmbildung* (Enrico Caruso and the problem of voice training). Leipzig: A. Felix, 1924. 107 pp.

———. *Umsturz in der Stimmbildung (Lösung des Stimmbildungs- und Carusoproblems): Schrift für Sänger, Schauspieler, Redner und Jedermann* (Collapse of voice training [solution to the problem of voice training and of Caruso]: a paper for singers, actors, lecturers and everyone). Leipzig: A. Felix, 1922. 37 pp.

Ybarra, Thomas Russell. *Caruso: The Man of Naples and the Voice of Gold.* New York: Harcourt, Brace, 1953. 315 pp.

———. *Caruso: The Man of Naples and the Voice of Gold.* London: Cresset Press, 1954. 230 pp.

PART III
Selective Bibliography of Journal and Magazine Articles About Enrico Caruso

"A propos de Caruso, le phénomène vocal" (Apropos of Caruso, the vocal phenomenon). *Musica* (Chaix), no. 106 (1963): 46–47.

Alain [Emile Chartier]. "Singt Caruso noch für uns?" (Does Caruso still sing for us?) *Phono* 9, no. 2 (1962): 36.

Altobell, D. "The Legend of Enrico Caruso (Includes LP Discography)." *Audio* 55 (November 1972): 64–65.

"Applause After 'Una furtiva lagrima' Caused Trouble: Incident Recalled by Nathan Drigand." *Opera News* 17 (January 12, 1953): 23.

"The Archivist." (Enrico Caruso's San Francisco performance on the night of the 1906 earthquake.) *San Francisco* 27 (April 1985): 40.

Ardoin, John. "Namara: A Remembrance." *Opera Quarterly* 1, no. 4 (1983): 74.
Armin, Georg. "Benjamino Gigli og Enrico Caruso" (Beniamino Gigli and Enrico Caruso). *Nordisk Musikkultur* 7 (June 1958): 36–38.
Ashbrook, W. "E lucevan le stelle: Perspectives on an Aria." *Opera News* 44 (January 19, 1980): 28–29.
———. "Perspectives on an Aria: Vesti la giubba." *Opera News* 44 (February 23, 1980): 32–33.
Barthélemy, Richard. "Love's Torment: Waltz." *Ladies' Home Journal,* June 1909, 21.
Bellows, H. A. "Musico-Economic Phenomenon." *Bellman* 26 (May 17, 1919): 550-51.
Berger, I. "Caruso by Computer (Restoration of Wire Recordings through Digital Computer)." *Saturday Review,* October 4, 1975, 47-48.
Bergman, A. "Problems of Voice Training in Connection with a New Interpretation of Enrico Caruso's Vocal Method." *Voice* 7 (March–April 1951): 10–11.
Bernays, E. L. "Musician's Relation to the Public." *Etude* 54 (April 1936): 256.
———. "On Tour with Caruso." *Variety,* January 5, 1955, 274.
Birdoff, H. "Enrico Caruso in 'My Cousin.'" *Hobbies,* November 1966, 36; December 1966, 36.
Blyth, Alan. "A Trio of Tenors." *Opera* 31 (May 1980): 442–45.
Bollew, J. A. "Is the Falsetto False?" *Etude* 72 (July 1954): 14.
Bourgeois, J. "Rééditions des anciennes cires de Enrico Caruso" (Reissues of the original records of Enrico Caruso). *Disques,* no. 104 (December 1958): 992–93.
Brandt, L. J. "Rubini Records: Voices from the Past." *Fanfare* 4, no. 3 (1981): 40-42.
Brewster, T., and E. Haas. "The Ageless Met: An Intimate Look at the Famous Opera Company on Its 100th Anniversary." *Life,* October 1983, 136.
Brunet, F. "Le drame d'Enrico Caruso, enfant de Naples" (The drama of Enrico Caruso, child of Naples). *Musica* (Chaix), no. 96 (March 1962): 30–37.
Bruun, C. L. "A Caruso Discography." *Record Collector* 4 (June 1949): whole issue.
———. "Enrico Caruso." *Record Collector* 4 (May 1949): 82–95.
Cantor, E. "'Greatest Voice I Ever Heard.'" *Variety,* January 9, 1963, 5.
"Carnegie Hall: Bronze Plaque for 50th Anniversary of His Victor Recording." *Opera News* 18 (March 1, 1954): 2.
"Caruso." *Nation,* August 17, 1921, 165–66.
"Caruso." *Literary Digest,* August 20, 1921, 24–25.
"Caruso and the Major." *Literary Digest,* November 4, 1922, 31–32.
"Caruso at Rehearsal." *Etude* 45 (September 1927): 656.
"Caruso Comes Back." *Literary Digest* 114, November 19, 1932, 18.
Caruso, Dorothy. "My Husband Caruso." *Good Housekeeping,* March 1951, 13.

Caruso, Enrico. "Some Notes on Singing." *Musician* 20 (April 1915): 266.

_____. "Talks on Singing." *Musician* 19 (April 1914): 267; 20 (February 1915): 123.

_____. "Talks on Singing." Reprinted from *Monthly Musical Record* 1913. *Choral Journal* 14, no. 4 (1973): 31–33.

_____. "Talks on Singing." *Choral Journal* 14, no. 5 (1974): 19.

Caruso, Enrico, Jr. "Caruso, 1956: Comments on the Caruso Album, from the Man Who Knew Him Best." *Hi-Fi Music at Home,* May–June 1956, 29.

_____. "Stopover at Gibraltar." *Liberty,* March 29, 1941, 18.

"Caruso in His Off Hours (from His Notebook 'Caruso on the San Francisco Earthquake')." *Show* 2 (March 1962): 84–85.

"Caruso Is Not Dead." *Literary Digest,* August 20, 1921, 35–38.

"Caruso Lives Again in New Musical Film." *Musical Courier* 143 (May 15, 1951): 2.

Caruso, of the Golden Voice Celebrates His Silver Jubilee." *Literary Digest,* April 12, 1919, 84–88.

"Caruso on Technic and Expression." *Musician* 21 (October 1916): 631.

"Caruso, Phonography, and Art." *Outlook* 128 (August 17, 1921): 597–99.

"Caruso Recording Anniversary Observed." *Musical America* 74 (February 1954): 15.

"Caruso, the Man." *Coronet* 37 (February 1955): 92.

"Caruso Whispers at the Height of Illness." *Voice of the Victor* 187 (May 1921): 94.

"Caruso's Gallery." *Opera News* 37 (February 24, 1973): 17–24.

"Caruso's Heirs Win $8,000 Suit from MGM." *Variety,* June 8, 1955, 19.

"Caruso's Last Song." *Literary Digest,* October 8, 1921, 44–46.

"Caruso's Records Restored." *Music Educators Journal* 57 (October 1970): 79.

"Caruso's Singing Apparatus." *Literary Digest* 70 (September 10, 1921): 29.

"Caruso's $3,500,000 Royalties All-Time Victor Topper." *Variety,* October 1, 1952, 30.

"Carusos v. Caruso." *Time,* May 5, 1952, 106.

"Caruso's Voice Revived by Science." *Musician* 37 (September 1932): 6.

Cleveland, P. J. "Angel of the Opera." *Coronet* 30 (May 1951): 104–5.

Coggi, A. D. "More from Rubini." *Fanfare* 5, no. 3 (1982): 30.

Collins, B. "Caruso on the Air." *Le Grand Baton* 12 (September 1975): 45–46.

Collisson, C. F. "Out of the Caruso Wardrobe." *Opera News* 16 (March 10, 1952): 28.

Cook, Ida. "Geraldine Farrar Discusses Her Most Familiar Role, Beloved Butterfly." *Opera News* 17 (January 12, 1953): 10–12.

Cooke, J. F. "The Golden Chalices of Song." *Etude* 70 (September 1952): 15.

"Correspondence." *Gramophone,* September 1953, 118–19.

Court, L. D. "Spinning Gold." *Music Magazine and Musical Courier* 164 (April 1962): 48.

Crabbé, Armand. "Armand Crabbé on Caruso." *Gramophone,* November 1931, 213.

"Death of Caruso." *Current History Magazine of the New York Times* 14 (September 1921): 1086.

De Gogorza, Emilio. "Emilio de Gogorza Recalls His Association with Caruso." *Opera News* 2 (November 15, 1937).

De Gregorio, Sergio. "Faró ricordare Caruso" (I will make Caruso remembered). *Oggi,* March 14, 1989, 116-19.

De Schauensee, Max. "The Clown We Can't Forget." *Opera News* 15 (February 26, 1951): 12-13.

De Weerth, E. "Scenes from an Enchanted Life." *Opera News* 24 (January 2, 1960): 8.

Drake, J. A. "Letters: That Unpublished Caruso." *High Fidelity and Musical America* 24 (December 1974): 8.

_____ . "The Real Voice of Enrico Caruso?" *High Fidelity and Musical America* 26 (October 1976): 86-90.

Drigand, N. "No More Furtive Tears." *Opera News* 17 (January 12, 1953): 23.

Drummond, H. J. "Caruso's Posthumous Records." *Record News* 2 (July 1950): 5-11.

Eaton, Quaintance, editor. "Cards from Caruso (to Ada Giachetti)." *Opera News* 30 (January 8, 1966): 14-16.

_____ . "The Mouth That Could Cradle an Egg." *Opera News* 37 (February 1973): 6.

Edge, Philip. "Caruso and McCormack." *Gramophone,* February 1927.

Ellsworth, R. "The Caruso Goldmine: $40,000,000 in Fifty Years." *HiFi/Stereo Review,* July 1964, 77.

Emge, C. "MGM Does Fine Job in Movie on Caruso's Life." *Down Beat* 18 (April 20, 1951): 9.

"Emotionated Singer." *Time,* May 14, 1945, 70.

"Enrico Caruso." *Buenos Aires Musical* 26, no. 431 (1971): 4.

"Enrico Caruso: 1873-1921." *Voice of the Victor* 187 (October 1921): 186-87.

"Enrico Caruso—Fedor Chaliapin, quien mas grande?" (Enrico Caruso—Fedor Chaliapin, who is greater?) *Buenos Aires Musical* 28, no. 452 (1973): 5.

Farkas, Andrew. "Caruso and Budapest." *Record Collector* 28 (April 1984): 245-66.

_____ . "Enrico Caruso: Tenor, Baritone, Bass." *Opera Quarterly* 4, no. 4 (1986-87): 53-60.

Farrar, Geraldine. "Caruso." *Theatre Arts* 42 (January 1958): 80-81.

Favia-Artsay, Aida. "Computerized Caruso." *Hobbies,* February 1977, 37.

_____ . "Enrico Caruso." *Record Collector* 6 (October 1951): 235-39.

_____ . Gigli and Caruso and Company." *Hobbies,* December 1962, 30-31.

_____ . "Glimpses of Caruso." *Hobbies,* February 1958, 28-29.

_____ . "Greatness on Disc." *Hobbies,* April 1956, 28.

_____ . "Historical Records." *Hobbies,* February 1977, 37.

_____ . "The Impossible Dream." *Hobbies,* November 1972, 5-36.

_____ . "Thoughts and Comments." *Hobbies,* April 1977, 37.

Feinstein, R. "The Caruso-Bettini Recordings." *Record Research* no. 146–47 (May–June 1977): 12.

"50 Years After Death, Caruso Still a Major Disk Name in Italy." *Variety,* January 19, 1972, 1.

Finck, Henry T. "Secret of Caruso's Glorious Voice." *Etude* 41 (August 1923): 513–14.

Freeman, J. W. "Quick-Sketch Artist: Excerpts from Caricatures by Enrico Caruso." *Opera News* 37 (February 24, 1973): 36–40.

Freestone, John. "Collectors' Corner (a Caruso Anniversary)." *Gramophone,* March 1952, 238–39.

Fucito, Salvatore. "How Caruso Practiced Daily." *Etude* 41 (February 1923): 83–84.

Gaisberg, F. W. "Enrico Caruso." *Gramophone,* January 1944, 117–19.

"Gallery of Musical Celebrities." *Etude* 47 (September 1929): 659–60.

Gardiner, B. "Caruso Centenary (Concert in San Carlo Opera House)." *Musical Events* 28 (July 1973): 6.

Gelatt, Roland. "Records—A Time of Revival (Computerized Restoration of Caruso's Pre-Electric Recordings)." *Saturday Review,* October 16, 1976, 31.

"Giant Caruso Set in Digital Revamp by RCA Records." *Billboard* 89 (March 12, 1977): 95.

Goldberg, L. C. "Miracle." *American Mercury* 77 (September 1953): 106.

Golden, H. "More Than Nostalgia." *Opera News* 24 (January 2, 1960): 9.

Goodfriend, J. "Computers, Ghosts, and Other Talents. *Stereo Review* 37 (November 1976): 60.

Grau, Robert. "Caruso Situation and Our Opera Policy." *Overland Monthly* 59 (March 1912): 233–34.

Grubowski, J. "Enrico Caruso na scenie Teatru Wielkiego w Warszawie" (Enrico Caruso on the stage of the Wielki Theater in Warsaw). *Ruch Muzyczny* 13 (October 1969): 18.

Gualerzi, Giorgio. "Unicita della sua voce" (The uniqueness of his voice). *La Scala* no. 145 (December 1961): 58–60.

Hamilton, David. "Caruso cum Computer (Soundstream's Digital Reprocessings on RCA Recording, Legendary Performer)." *High Fidelity and Musical America* 26 (November 1976): 98–99.

Harris, D. "Caruso (Murray Hill's 'Complete Caruso' Box and an RCA Set)." *High Fidelity and Musical America* 24 (February 1974): 85–87.

"Has the War Stifled Music?" *Forum* 60 (September 1918): 313–18.

Haughton, J. A. "Opera Singers from the Golden Age." *Musical America* 69 (February 1949): 167.

Herbert-Caesari, E. "Gigli v. Caruso." *Gramophone,* September 1953, 117–18.

"Here and There in the Field of Music." *Etude* 39 (October 1921): 641.

Herendeen, A. "At the Carusos'." *Everybody's* 40 (June 1919): 23.

Hill, E. "Found!" *Record Changer* 8 (December 1949): 13.

_____ . "Perpetual Portrait." *Record Changer* 8 (January 1949): 19–20.

"Historical Records." *Gramophone,* January 1957, 306–7.

Hoeslinger, C. "Enrico Caruso 25. Februar 1873 2. August 1921" (Enrico

Caruso, 25 February 1873 to 2 August 1921). *Opernwelt,* August 1971, 42–43.

———. "Die Gastspiele Enrico Carusos an der Wiener Hofoper" (Enrico Caruso's guest performances at the Vienna Opera). *Österreichische Musikzeitschrift* 26, no. 11 (November 1971): 642–47.

———. "Wir erinnern an Giuseppe de Luca" (Remembering Giuseppe de Luca). *Opernwelt,* March 1968, 47–48.

Hoeslinger, C., and R. Teuchtler. "Primadonna des Jahrhunderts: ein Hinweis auf Rosa Ponselle" (Primadonna of the century: a reference to Rosa Ponselle). *Opernwelt,* September 1967, 39–41.

"Homenaje a Enrico Caruso" (Homage to Enrico Caruso). *Buenos Aires Musical* 28, no. 450 (1973): 1.

Isaacson, C. D. "Why Great Artists Succeeded." *Etude* 49 (March 1931): 166.

"Italy, the Home of Grand Opera. An Interview with Enrico Caruso." *Etude* 30 (January 1912): 112.

Jagendorf, M. "The Rich Lore of a Rich Hotel, the Plaza." New York *Folklore Quarterly* 9 (Autumn 1953): 176–82.

Kanski, J. "Enrico Caruso w oczach swych znakomitych Polskich kolegow" (Enrico Caruso as seen by his famous Polish colleagues). *Ruch Muzyczny* 15 (August 1971): 8.

Kauffmann, S. "On Wings of Song." *New Republic,* August 8–15, 1988, 35.

Kellner, B. "All in His Voice: Enrico Caruso As Seen and Heard by Journalist Carl Van Vechten." *Opera News* 45 (July 1980): 16–21.

Kent, George. "So Kind of Them to Remember." *Readers Digest,* February 1946, 65–69.

Kerner, D. "La mort de Caruso" (The death of Caruso). Translated from *Neue Zeitschrift für Musik. Feuilles Musicales* 15, no. 6 (1962): 101–2.

———. "So starb Caruso. Zur 40. Wiederkehr seines Todestages" (This is how Caruso died. On the fortieth anniversary of his death). *Neue Zeitschrift für Musik* 122 (July–August 1961): 287–88.

Kerner, L. "Bits and Pieces." *Opera News* 37 (February 24, 1973): 42–43.

Kessler, G. "Schöne Stimmen von damals: Enrico Caruso" (Beautiful voices from the past: Enrico Caruso). *Opernwelt,* June 1979, 12–15.

Kesting, J. "Versöhnung von Technik und Ausdruck—Carusos frühe Schallplatten" (Fusion of technique and expression—Caruso's early records). *Opernwelt,* August 1971, 44–46.

Knogel, W. "Enrico Caruso und Fedor Schaljapin: Skizze und Vergleich" (Enrico Caruso and Fedor Chaliapin: sketch and comparison). *Musikleben* 7 (December 1954): 445–46.

Kobbé, Gustav. "Enrico Caruso." *Musician* 19 (January 1905): 9–10.

Kobler, John. "Bravo Caruso!" *American Heritage* 35 (February–March 1984): 104–10.

Kogel, H.-J. "Enrico Caruso, 1873–1921." *Bibliographische Kalenderblatter* 13, Folge 8 (1971): 12–15.

Ledner, Emil. "Memories of Caruso." *Living Age* 313 (April 15, 1922): 160–67; May 13, 1922): 420–26.

Lingg, A. M. "Books on the Tenor." *Opera News* 37 (February 24, 1973): 50.

Marafioti, P. M. "What You Can Learn from Caruso's Singing." *Musician* 28 (June 1923): 8; (July 1923): 11; (August 1923): 10.

Marchetti, A. "Caruso e la bella" (Caruso and the beauty). *Rassegna Musicale Curci* 26, no. 1 (1973): 29-31.

_____ . "Caruso nella fossa dei leoni" (Caruso in the lion's den). *Rassegna Musicale Curci* 29, no. 2 (1976): 37-38.

_____ . "Fumo in platea" (Smoke in the theater). *Rassegna Musicale Curci* 24, no. 1 (1971): 37-38.

_____ . "Ricordo di Enrico Caruso" (Remembrance of Enrico Caruso). *Rassegna Musicale Curci* 24, no. 3-4 (1971): 18-19.

Marek, George R. "Beneficient Ghost: Sixty Years After Enrico Caruso's Death, We Are Still Marveling at the Great Tenor's Recorded Legacy." *Opera News* 46 (August 1981): 22-24.

_____ . "A Big Chest, a Big Mouth, 90 Percent Memory, 10 Percent Intelligence and Something in the Heart." *TV Guide,* March 12, 1977, 15-16.

_____ . "Still the World's Most Popular Singer." *Good Housekeeping,* August 1951, 118.

Marx, H. "Enrico Caruso, Legend of a Voice." *Musical Newsletter* 44 (January 1952): 9.

Mayer-Reinach, U. "Die Gesangskunst Enrico Carusos und unsere Zeit" (Enrico Caruso's art of singing and our time). *Musica* 27 (November-December 1973): 563-68.

McCarten, J. "[*The Great Caruso*] The Current Cinema." *New Yorker,* May 19, 1951, 110.

Meltzer, C. H. "Caruso and the Future of Grand Opera." *Review* 5 (August 21, 1921): 171-72.

"Memories of Caruso." *Musical America* 72 (February 1952): 17.

Merkling, Frank. "A Century of Caruso: Symposium, with Editorial Comment." *Opera News* 37 (February 24, 1973): 4.

"Mexico City Braves Rain to Hear Caruso." *Voice of the Victor* 186 (March 1920): 43.

Milliman, D. "Bravo, Enrico Caruso." *Stamps* 218 (February 21, 1987): 12.

Mills, B. "Caruso in Toledo." *Variety,* February 9, 1955, 71.

Monaldi, Gino. "Enrico Caruso." *Nuova Antologia* 213, ser. 6 (July-August 1921): 369-72.

Moore, J. N. "Caruso's First Recordings (Gramophone Company's Recording Session, Milan, 1902)." *Gramophone,* February 1973, 1480; March 1973, 1670.

Movshon, George. "Enrico Caruso, Father of Us All." *High Fidelity and Musical America* 19 (September 1969): 77-78.

"NYC Debut, 1903: Notes." *International Musician* 52, no. 7 (January 1954): 26.

"Naples Finally Honors Caruso." *Variety,* November 30, 1960, 12.

"Neapolitan." *Time,* October 11, 1943, 58.

Nissim, R. "Enrico Caruso: una morte su cui ancora si discute; il grande tenore morì a soli 48 anni" (Enrico Caruso: a death still discussed; the great tenor died at the age of 48). *Rassegna Musicale Curci* 35, no. 2–3 (1982): 11.

"No Longer Quaint but Still Queenly, the Met Turns 100." *Smithsonian,* September 1983, 78.

"No Rest for Caruso." *Newsweek,* May 14, 1945, 99–101.

Osborne, Conrad L. "Instruction in Almost Every Phrase." *High Fidelity and Musical America* 11 (August 1961): 64–65.

"Passing of a Great Tenor." *Current Opinion* 71 (September 1921): 332.

Pease, E. "Computer Restoration of Caruso on McCormack Recordings: A Critical Report and the Soundstream Process." *NATS Bulletin* 35, no. 2 (1978): 8–14.

Phillips, H. E. "The Recorded Legacy." *Opera News* 37 (February 24, 1973): 44.

"Pity the Poor Singer, Says Caruso." *Theatre* 45, no. 142 (December 1912).

"Plaque on the House Where He Was Born in Naples." *Opera* 15 (October 1964): 677.

Pluck, G. "An Artist Remembers (Reminiscences of Ruha Solis)." *Hobbies,* May 1959, 28.

Pluckebaum, C. "Enrico Caruso. Vergeudete Erbschaft—Bilanz nach Vierzig Jahren" (Enrico Caruso. Wasted heritage—conclusions after forty years). *Musik im Unterricht* 52 (1961): 237–38.

Pluta, E. "Die italienische Oper des Fin de siècle" (Italian opera of the fin de siècle). *Opernwelt,* February 1983, 51–53.

Potter, Robert W. F. "Enrico Caruso." *Gramophone,* December 1930, 329–30; January 1931, 396–97; February 1931, 464–65; March 1931, 509–10; April 1931, 556.

Prichard, Robert W. "The Death of Enrico Caruso." *Surgery, Gynecology and Obstetrics* 104 (July 1959): 117–20.

Primov, V. "Little Bulgaria Will Flourish: Letters to a Bulgarian by Caruso, Enrico." *Obzor—A Bulgarian Quarterly Review of Literature and Arts* no. 76 (1986): 84–86.

"RCA Marking Caruso's Birth with 3 Albums." *Billboard* 85 (September 29, 1973): 42.

Radamsky, S. "Can Singers Avoid Colds?" *Opera* 18 (February 1967): 101–2.

"Record Artists' Fees from $5 Up." *Variety,* January 7, 1953, 246.

Rhines, H. M. "Golden Age Grandee: Andrès de Segurola Recalls Past Thrills of the Operatic Stage." *Etude* 73 (August 1955): 46.

_____. "The Timeless Turntable." *Etude* 74 (February 1956): 26.

Rivero, Pedro E. "Enrico Caruso: un paisajista del Lago de Palermo" (Enrico Caruso: landscape artist of the Lake of Palermo). *Correo Musical Argentino* no. 10 (April 1989).

Robinson, Francis. "Caruso's Other Line (Caricatures)." *Opera News* 34 (January 10, 1970): 8–12.

_____. "A Long Crescendo." *Opera News* 37 (February 24, 1973): 27–33.

Rodewald, E. B. "Day I Met Caruso." *Readers Digest,* July 1955, 51–54.

Rogers, F. "Practical Hints from Caruso." *Etude* 63 (December 1945): 675.

Ronfeldt, L. "Enrico Caruso—et problem for den moderne gram-mofonindustri" (Enrico Caruso—a problem for the modern recording industry). *Nordisk Musikkultur* 7 (June 1958): 38-39.

Rosenberg, W. "Caruso. Seine Bedeutung als Gesangsstar, Künstler und Promotor des Grammofons" (Caruso, his importance as star singer, artist, and promoter of the gramophone). *HiFi-Stereophonie* 12 (November 1973): 1264-68.

Rozensil'd, Konstantin. "Kul'tura Italii v nachale XX veka" (Italian Culture of the Early 20th Century). *Sovetskaia Muzyka* 6 (June 1974): 107-18.

Salzman, E. "Caruso's Last Drama." *New York Times Magazine,* December 4, 1960, 108-10.

_____. "Enrico Caruso (Three Memorial Albums)." *Stereo Review* 32 (January 1974): 114-15.

Sanguinetti, Florentino V. "Caruso en Buenos Aires" (Caruso in Buenos Aires). *Ayer y Hoy de la Opera* 3, no. 3 (September-October 1979): 66.

Sanguinetti, Horacio. "Enrico Caruso: vida y obra en America" (Enrico Caruso: life and work in America). *Ayer y Hoy de la Opera* 3, no. 3 (September-October 1979): 3-19.

Schonberg, Harold C. "Facing the Music." *Musical Courier* 143 (April 15, 1951): 4.

_____. "'May We Begin Now, Mr. Caruso?'" *New York Times Biographical Edition,* February 1973, 225-26.

_____. "The Trouble with Tenors." *Show* 1 (December 1961): 74-75.

Schreiber, U. "Als Schaljapin, Caruso, Lotte Lehmann und Richard Tauber sangen . . . gab es noch keinen Ärger über Fischer-Dieskau und Birgit Nilsson" (When Chaliapin, Caruso, Lotte Lehmann and Richard Tauber were singing, there was no dispute over Fischer-Dieskau and Birgit Nilsson). *Opernwelt,* January 1968, 22-23; 25-29.

_____. "Caruso und die Schallplatte" (Caruso and the record). *Opernwelt,* January 1967, 52; March 1967, 52; April 1967, 51-52.

_____. "Caruso und die Schallplatte. Versuch einer Bilanz" (Caruso and the record. Search for a conclusion). *Opernwelt,* December 1966, 29.

_____. "Ein unverausserliches Erbe?" (An inalienable heritage?) *HiFi-Stereophonie* 10 (August 1971): 622.

Schuessler, R. "Caruso, the Voice of the Century." *Modern Maturity* 26 (April-May 1983): CA2.

Schwarz, P. "I Sang with Caruso." *Opera* 24 (May 1973): 418-20.

Scott, M. "I Sang with Caruso (Mary Ellis Remembers)." *Opera News* 52 (June 15, 1988): 14.

Secrist, John B. "Caruso Discography." *Record Collector* 6 (November-December 1951): 245-80.

_____. "Caruso Discography Corrections." *Record Collector* 7 (June-July 1952): 159-61.

Sharp, F. "'A Tale of Two Tenors.'" *Royal College of Music Magazine* 69, no. 1 (1973): 25.

Simon, A. E. "The Great Caruso." *Film Music Notes* 10 (May–June 1951): 4–6.

Slonimsky, Nicolas. "Musical Oddities." *Etude* 72 (April 1954): 4.

_____. "Musical Oddities." *HiFi Review,* August 1959, 24.

Smolian, Steve. "Caruso—Legendary Performer." *Journal of the Association for Recorded Sound Collections* 8, no. 2–3 (1976): 106–7.

_____. "Da capo (Discographies)." *American Record Guide* 27 (December 1960): 339–44.

"Snub for Strauss." *Music and Musicians* 10 (July 1962): 38.

Sokol, Martin L. "Caruso Rarities." *Hobbies,* November 1973, 35–36.

_____. "The 'Pre-Victor' Recordings of Enrico Caruso." *Antique Phonograph Monthly* 5, no. 4 (1977): 3–12.

Sorel, E., and N. C. Sorel. "First Encounters (Caruso and Puccini)." *Atlantic,* May 1984, 93.

Soria, D. J. "Artist Life." *High Fidelity and Musical America* 23 (March 1973): MA8–9.

_____. "Bruno Remembered and Remembering: Caruso and the Honest Man." *High Fidelity and Musical America* 23 (March 1973): MA8–9.

"Sorrows of Caruso." *Independent* 99 (August 30, 1919): 299.

Stroff, S. "Pioneer Recording Artist: Enrico Caruso." *Hobbies,* October 1984, 62–64.

"Sunny Personality of Caruso." *Current Literature* 40 (April 1906): 379–81.

Symkins, L. O. "Caruso at the Monkey Cage." *HiFi Review,* December 1959, 28.

"Talk with Caruso." *Musician* 14 (December 1909): 550–51.

"Talk with Dorothy Caruso." *New York Times Book Review,* March 23, 1952, 25.

Taubman, Howard. "Were Singers Better in Caruso's Time?" *New York Times Magazine,* February 22, 1948, 20–23.

"10 Songs in a Session (1904)." *Billboard* 66 (February 6, 1954): 13.

Teuchtler, R. "Nichts gegen Caruso" (Nothing against Caruso). *Opernwelt,* December 1967, 6.

Thur, R. "Caruso As a Street Singer." *Etude* 45 (December 1927): 937.

"Triumphant Tenor." *MD,* July 1973, 133–39.

Tuggle, Robert. "Encore: Herman Mishkin's Photographs of Opera's Golden Age." *Connoisseur* 213, no. 860 (October 1983): 114–19.

Valenci, P. "Erinnerungen an eine herrliche Opernzeit: Caruso und Knote" (Memories of a wonderful period of opera: Caruso and Knote). *Oper und Konzert* 11, no. 4 (1973): 2.

Vernon, G. "Caruso and the Newspaper Man." *Bookman* 54 (January 1922): 422–26.

"Victor's Royalty Harvest." *Billboard* 61 (November 5, 1949): 3.

Villella, T. "Caruso: The Tenor of the Century." *Le Grand Baton* 12 (September 1975): 3–29.

Vitolo, A. "Memories of Caruso's Boyhood." *Living Age* 319 (October 6, 1923): 28–30.

"Vor 75 Jahren: Caruso in München" (75 years ago: Caruso in Munich). *Oper und Konzert* 23, no. 10 (1985): 15-16.

Warren, D. "How Many Carusos Can There Be? (Plea to Cease Hunting a 'Second' Caruso)." *The Music Magazine and Musical Courier* 164 (July 1962): 19-20.

Weidner, E. "Cost of Genius." *Coronet* 32 (August 1952): 141.

Weingartner, B. "Some Great Singers." *Musical Times* 96 (May 1955): 250-51.

Williams, T. "Enrico Caruso." *American Review of Reviews* 64 (September 1921): 311-12.

Winwar, F. "Pro Patria, 1917." *New Yorker,* January 11, 1941, 53-56.

Withrow, John B. "Reprise." Program Booklet of Massey Hall. Toronto, 1984.

Wyatt, M. "Finale at the Academy." *Opera News* 23 (March 23, 1959): 28-29.

Zhito, L. "Great Lanza Makes 'Great Caruso' Great." *Billboard* 63 (April 21, 1951): 3.

Zirato, Bruno. "My Boss, My Friend." *Opera News* 37 (February 24, 1973): 8-16.

"Zum 100. Geburtstag Carusos und Schaljapins" (On the hundredth birthday of Caruso and Chaliapin). *Oper und Konzert* 11, no. 3 (1973): 2.

The Recorded Legacy of Enrico Caruso

Discography of
Original Recordings

by William R. Moran

INTRODUCTION

The confluence of Caruso's unique career with the coming of age and respectability of the phonograph industry has long been recognized. A thorough review of Caruso's actual recorded output is thus more than a mere check list for the avid collector. Like his close relative, the bibliographer, the discographer has the responsibility to produce a well-researched and adequately documented and presented piece of work that can serve many users in many fields. The subject of discography from philosophy to format has been discussed at length elsewhere (Moran, 1977) and has no place here.

Caruso's recording career is easily divided between Europe and America, with only an inconsequential overlap of two recordings (Nos. 31 and 32 in this discography) which came just two months after the conclusion of his first Victor contract in New York. From that point on, his recording career was in the hands of The Victor Talking Machine Company of Camden, New Jersey. His European recordings were made by three companies in somewhat haphazard batches for which he was paid in cash, on the spot. His first session at Victor, arranged by Victor Artistic Director Emilio de Gogorza, can perhaps be looked upon as one of the same sort of walk-in, walk-out affairs. But after his return to the United States for the Metropolitan Opera season in November 1904, an important change took place. Caruso had no doubt met Calvin Goddard Child, close friend of De Gogorza, at the time of the negotiations for the February 1904 Victor sessions, but he probably had little hint of the important part Child would play in his fame, fortune, and phonograph records for the rest of his life.

Calvin Child had been hired by Victor founder and president Eldridge R. Johnson as "impresario" or "talent scout" when he first began to make records in 1900. Child, in turn, had obtained the services of De Gogorza when Victor decided to enter the classical field with their first "Red Seal" recordings early in 1903. Child had become "Manager of the Recording Laboratory" for Victor and was a strong member of the Johnson team. Johnson's philosophy, as expressed in his own words, is worth repeating. He wrote in February 1913:

The Victor Company is . . . in possession of many patents and secret processes, but our greatest secret process is this: *we seek to improve everything we do every day*. . . . None but the most competent can stand the fierce test of a permanent record. A single performance is heard and forgotten, but think how serious would be a mistake made in a record heard over and over again by so many. Talking machine records must be technically correct, as well as pleasing, or their educational value becomes nil, and the Victor Company would lose standing to the same extent that a publisher of textbooks would suffer through the publication of books containing inaccuracies.

Caruso was impressed by Johnson's fervent commitment to excellence and the high standards of the Victor organization shared by Child, who, as an old hand in the business of recording, was able to give the singer many hints about making records and developing ease and confidence before the horn. Child assured him that the company would never allow a flawed record to reach the public. If there were a musical accident, a false start, or a mechanical or technical defect, the record would be made over as many times as necessary in order to produce a product of which both artist and company could be proud. The two men became fast personal friends and a working team. It is said that each of Caruso's recordings, from 1905 on, was a cooperative effort between the two. Not only did Child work with repertory to be recorded, but after musical arrangements had been worked out and a piece rehearsed, Caruso always cut one or more experimental waxes which were immediately played back and discussed by the two men in detail. Only after full agreement by both Child and the singer with respect to all details would the final recordings be made. Caruso would never approve a recording for final release until it had Child's personal approval. Although not specifically written into Caruso's exclusive contract with Victor (which ran until 1933), it was understood that the singer was always to have Calvin Child as his personal company representative. Theirs was an historic association which has not been properly recognized by historians, and it explains in part the singer's lifelong loyalty to Victor, an exceedingly remunerative association for both parties.

Because of Caruso's importance to the phonograph industry in general and to Victor in particular, his entire output of Victor records has been grouped together in the following pages, along with the catalog numbers under which they were sold not only by Victor directly in North and South America, but by its world-wide affiliates. The basis for this discography is a complete transcription of the existing Victor Talking Machine Company files which the late Ted Fagan and the author laboriously compiled from the original recording sheets and other company documents over a period of some 25 years as the foundation for their *Encyclopedic Discography of Victor Recordings*, two volumes of which have been published, with further volumes in preparation. Through the years, there have been many discographies of the recordings of Enrico Caruso; a number of the more important ones are listed in the bibliography at the close of this discography. All these have been liberally consulted for checking purposes, and the author's thanks are extended to previous workers in the field. Where there have been conflicts, the original Victor data have been treated as authoritative.

Original turntable speeds were never entered in the company files, but it is recognized today that in order to reproduce these old recordings properly, they must be played at the speeds at which they were recorded. For a detailed discussion of the importance of playing speeds and how they are determined, see Fagan and Moran (1986, pp. xxxiii–xxxvi). Suggested playing speeds, as set forth in this discography, have been carefully recalculated with the use of an electronic keyboard, tuned with A' = 440 Hz.

In listing the Caruso recordings which follow, certain conventions have been established:

Titles are arranged alphabetically (in the Victor section) under the language in which they are sung, which is Italian unless otherwise noted. The European recordings are listed in chronological order, with the titles repeated (in italics) in the Victor section without full details, so that there will be one continuous alphabetical list of all Caruso's recordings in one place. The initial words used in operatic recordings are given. In the matter of alphabetization and spelling of titles in the Neapolitan dialect, the usage of De Mura (1969) has been followed.

The columns in the discography are headed as follows:

Discography Number Reference number assigned for this discography.

Matrix Number This is Victor's basic reference for any recording. It consists of three parts: the initial letter indicates size, thus B = 10"; C = 12". This is followed by the "serial," a basic number assigned to a given selection by a given artist. Theoretically, it never changed if the title, artist, and accompaniment remained the same. Individual recordings made of this title were given the following "take" numbers, no matter if the selection was repeated at the same recording session [see Discog. No. 229] or years later [166]. There were occasional errors when new numbers were assigned when earlier serial numbers should have been used [53 and 66]. When more than one "take" was made on the same day, the number printed in boldface and underlined indicates the take used for the following catalog number listings. There are a few cases where some previously unpublished take was issued for the first time on an LP or CD release. In these few cases, the take number so used is printed in italics [146, Take *1*].

Catalog Numbers   These are given in the following columns: single- and double-faced Victor, single- and double-faced Gramophone Company (HMV), followed by single- and double-faced pressings as issued by Deutsche Grammophon during and after World War I. This company was responsible for a number of "pirate" issues with such labels as "Opera Disc" which were circulated during the 1920s, usually carrying the D.G. catalog numbers. Further columns are reserved for later issues: VA and VB were HMV reissues of the 1940s; AGS and IRCC indicated special pressings for collectors' clubs. Catalog numbers which were assigned by the factory but never used for public sale are shown in parentheses [186].

Special Symbols for Dubbings   About 1915, Victor remade some of their matrices by an acoustical dubbing process which resulted in reduced sound quality. Such acoustical dubbings are generally marked "S/8" on the inner record rim. These are designated in the discography by the symbol "<" following a catalog number [40]. Earlier pressings from the original parts are to be preferred. Occasionally HMV pressings have been found made from these dubbed masters: one must watch for the S/8 symbol on the pressings. Records which have been issued in electrically re-recorded form show the symbol "rr" following the catalog number [41].

Electrical Re-Recordings of the 1930s   These recordings are discussed in a special section at the end of the discography. Their catalog numbers are shown in italics [42, shown as *17814* and *DB 2644*].

Notes   An asterisk following the discography number indicates a note on this recording in a special note section at the end of this discography.

[CR]   This is a recording of an aria or a song which Caruso created.

Acknowledgments

The author wishes to thank Ruth Edge, Manager of EMI Music Archives, for assistance with information on the HMV re-recordings with orchestra added. Thanks also to Andrew Farkas, Steve Jabloner, Richard Koprowski, and William Shaman for proofreading.

THE EUROPEAN RECORDINGS

SESSION 1: The Gramophone & Typewriter Co., Grand Hotel, Milan, 11 April 1902. Pf. acc. Salvatore Cottone. Technicians: Fred W. and William C. Gaisberg. All 10". All issued with Red Labels. All 71.29 rpm. (Matrix suffix letters were standardized some years after these recordings were made. Those used here are the later form as found in the present files of The Gramophone Co.)

Discog. No.	Matrix No.	s/f Cat. No.	HMV d/f Cat. Nos.	Victor s/f
1.*	GERMANIA: Studenti! udite (Franchetti) [CR] 1782b	52378	DA 544	(5015)
2.	RIGOLETTO: Questa o quella (Verdi) 1783b	52344	------	------
3.*	AIDA: Celeste Aida (Verdi) 1784b	52369	------	------
4.	MANON: Chiudo gli occhi (Massenet) 1785b	52345	VA 58	------
5.	ELISIR D'AMORE, L': Una furtiva lagrima (Donizetti) 1786b	52346	------	------
6.	MEFISTOFELE: Giunto sul passo estremo (Boito) 1787b	52347	DA 550	VA 7	------
7.	GERMANIA: Ah, vieni qui . . . No, non chiuder gli occhi (Franchetti) [CR] 1788b	52370	DA 544	VA 37	(5013)
8.*	MEFISTOFELE: Dai campi, dai prati (Boito) 1789b	52348	------	------
9.*	TOSCA: E lucevan le stelle (Puccini) 1790b	52349	DA 547	VA 29	5010
10.	IRIS: Apri la tua finestra (Serenata) (Mascagni) 1791b	52368	------	91009

SESSIONS 2/3: The Gramophone & Typewriter Co., Grand Hotel, Milan, 30 November 1902 (probably 1 December for Nos. 18, 19, and 20). Pf. acc. Salvatore Cottone except Nos. 12 and 19. Technician: W. C. Gaisberg. All 10". All issued with Red Labels. All 67.92 rpm.

Discog. No.	Matrix No.	s/f Cat. No.	HMV d/f Cat. Nos.	Victor s/f	
11.	MEFISTOFELE: Dai campi, dai prati (Boito) 2871b	52348x	VA 7 — DA 550	----	----
12.	FEDORA: Amor ti vieta (Giordano) (pf. acc. by composer) [CR] 2872b	52439	VA 53; VA 58 — DA 549	----	----
13.*	AIDA: Celeste Aida (Verdi) 2873b	52369x	VA 12 — DA 549	5008	91007
14.	GIOCONDA, LA: Cielo e mar (Ponchielli) 2874b	52417	VA 29 — DA 547	5009	91008
15.	PAGLIACCI: Recitar! mentre preso dal delirio . . . Vesti la giubba (Leoncavallo) 2875b	52440	VA 30 — DA 546	5016	91014
16.	CAVALLERIA RUSTICANA: O Lola ch'ai di latti la cammisa (Siciliana) (Mascagni) 2876b	52418	VA 30 — DA 545	5012	91011
17.	Non t'amo più (L. De Giorgi; L. Denza) 2877b	52441	VA 31 — DA 548	5014	91013
18.	Mia canzone, La (F. Cimmino; F. Paolo Tosti) 2879b	52443	VA 31 — DA 548	5011	91010
19.	ADRIANA LECOUVREUR: No, più nobile (Cilea) (pf. acc. by composer) [CR] 2880b	52419	----	----	----
20.*	Luna fedel (Arrigo Boito; Redento Zardo) 2882b	52442	VA 9	----	----

23.   ELISIR D'AMORE, L': Una furtiva lagrima (Donizetti)   X-1552
24.   TOSCA: E lucevan le stelle (Puccini)   X-1553
25.   GERMANIA: Ah, vieni qui . . . No, non chiuder gli occhi (Franchetti) [CR]   X-1554
26.   RIGOLETTO: La donna è mobile (Verdi)   X-1555
27.   CAVALLERIA RUSTICANA: O Lola ch'ai di latti la cammisa (Siciliana) (Mascagni)   X-1556

SESSION 5: Pathé Frères (in association with the Anglo-Italian Commerce Co.). The originals of these recordings are wax cylinders, sold both as cylinders of various sizes and in pantographed form on hill-and-dale discs (all marked Pathé). Those with black-etched labels are center-start and come in several sizes; those with paper labels are 11", outside-start. Since all copies are dubbings, made at various times in various plants, no exact playing speeds can be listed for all copies. The center-start type usually play about 87 rpm; the 11" paper-label copies were generally standardized at about 80.00 rpm. The originals were all announced—according to company advertising, by Caruso himself. Announcements were removed from the 11" product. The *Tosca* aria shows up on a pirated 6" Emerson disc. Research by the late Martin L. Sokol (1977) and further studies indicate a date in late October 1903 for these recordings, which is accepted here. Piano accompanied; pianist unknown. The first numbers given are those used for the master cylinders which are also the catalog numbers for the center-start Pathés as in issued single-faced form and in various couplings.

		Emerson	Victor
28. Tu non mi vuoi più ben (F. Carbonetti; Antonio Pini-Corsi)	84003		----
29. TOSCA: E lucevan le stelle (Puccini)	84004	Emerson 301	10009
30. UGONOTTI, GLI (Les Huguenots): Qui sotto il ciel (Meyerbeer)	84006		10009

SESSION 6: The Gramophone & Typewriter Co., Milan, 8 April 1904. Pf. No. 31 (10") by composer; No. 32 (12") by Salvatore Cottone. Speed: 74.23 rpm.

Discog. No.	Matrix No.	s/f Cat. No.	d/f Cat. Nos.	Deutsche Gram. Nos.	Victor
31.	2181h	52034	DA 546 VA 32; VA 53	74511	----
Mattinata (Leoncavallo) [CR]					
32.	268i	052066	---- VB 44	76062 85006	(92036) IRCC 61
PESCATORI DI PERLE, I: Mi par d'udir ancora (Bizet)					

RECORDINGS FOR THE VICTOR TALKING MACHINE CO. NEW YORK AND CAMDEN, NEW JERSEY, 1904–1920

(A notational entry for each of the 32 European titles has been inserted below, in italics, for convenience.)

Discog. No.	Matrix No. -Take	Date	Victor s/f	Victor d/f	G&T/HMV s/f	G&T/HMV d/f	Deutsche Gram. s/f	Deutsche Gram. d/f	Other 78 rpm Issues	Speed of Original
33.	\	\	\	\	\	\	\	\	\	\
	\	\	\	\	\	\	\	\	\	\

A Granada (F. Gras y Elias; F. M. Alvarez) (in Spanish) (Or. Pasternack)

Discog. No.	Matrix No. -Take	Date	Victor s/f	Victor d/f	G&T/HMV s/f	G&T/HMV d/f	Deutsche Gram. s/f	Deutsche Gram. d/f	Other 78 rpm Issues	Speed of Original
33.	C-22124-1	10 Jul.'18	---	---	2-062007	DB 592	---	---	17-5001 / *26571*	---
	-2,-3	26 Sep.'18	88623	6011 8038						76.00
34.	C-21773-1,-2	16 Apr.'18	89083	8038	2-064001	DB 592			VB 58	76.00
35.	B-15571-1,-2	7 Jan.'15	---	---	------					---
36.	B-23138-1,-2,-3,-4	8 Sep.'19	87304	501	7-52162	DA 103				75.00
37.	C-9747-1	29 Dec.'10	88280	6021	2-052035	DB 131	76096	85027	7156rr, *DB 3327* / *DB 1386rr*, *DB 5387*	76.0u
38.	B-23140-1,-2,-3	8 Sep.'19	---	---	------					
	-4,-5,-6	9 Sep.'19	87312	502	7-52159	DA 104			2212 / *DA 1655*	75.00
39.	C-5009-1	10 Jan.'08	88115	6006	032070	DB 116	76014	85005		80.00
40.	C-4160-1	30 Dec.'06	88054< 6007<	052157	DB 117<		76072	85015	14234 / *DB 2991*	76.60
	-2	20 Feb.'07								

34. A la luz de la luna (Anton y Michelena) (in Spanish) (w. Emilio de Gogorza) (Or. Pasternack)

35. 'A luna (Varelli) (Or. Rogers) (Tk. 1 w. mandolin: Bianculli; Tk. 2 no mandolin)

36. 'A Vucchella (Gabriele D'Annunzio; F. Paolo Tosti [1903]) (Or. Pasternack)

37. Addio (Good-bye) (S. Rizzelli; F. Paolo Tosti) (w. Orchestra)

38. Addio a Napoli, L' (Teodoro Cottrau) (Or. Pasternack)

39. Adorables tourments (Valse lente) (R. Gaël; R. Barthélemy and E. Caruso) (in French) (w. Orchestra)

ADRIANA LECOUVREUR: *No, più mobile (Cilea) [CR]: See European recording section* (19)

40. Africana, L': Mi batte il cor ... O paradiso! (Meyerbeer) (w. Orchestra)

41. Africana, L': Che dicon mai? ... Deh, ch'io ritorni (Meyerbeer) (Or. Pasternack)

AIDA: Celeste Aida (Verdi): See European recording section (3 and 13)

No.	Matrix / Title	Date									Dur.
43.	**AIDA: Celeste Aida (Verdi) (pf. acc. unknown)**										
	C-997-1	1 Feb.'04	85022	------	052074	------	------	------	------	------	78.26
44.*	**AIDA: Celeste Aida (Verdi) (w. Orchestra)**										
	C-3180-1	13 Mar.'06	(88025)	------	------	------	76080	78512	85020	------	76.60
	-2,-3	29 Mar.'08	88127	------	052224	DB 144					77.43
45.	**AIDA: Se quel guerrier io fossi . . . Celeste Aida (Verdi) (w. Orchestra)**										
	C-11423-1	27 Dec.'11	88127	6000	2-052066	DK 115	76108	85022	7770 / 8993	DB 1875 / 12-1014	76.00
46.	**AIDA: Già i sacerdoti adunansi (Verdi) (w. Louise Homer) (w. Orchestra)**										
	C9748-1	29 Dec.'10	89050	8012	2-054015	DK 115	78522	78522	15-1025	------	76.00
47.	**AIDA: Misero appien mi festi. . . Aida a me togliesti (Verdi) (w. Louise Homer) (w. Orchestra)**										
	C-9749-1	29 Dec.'10	89051	8012	2-054016 / 2-054094	DM 111	78523	78522	15-1025	------	76.00
48.	**AIDA: La fatal pietra (Verdi) (w. Johanna Gadski) (Or. Rogers)**										
	C-8353-1	7 Nov.'09	89028	8015	2-054005	DM 114	78516	78516	------	------	75.00
49.	**AIDA: O terra addio (Verdi) (w. Johanna Gadski) (Or. Rogers)**										
	C-8348-1,-2	6 Nov.'09	89029	8015	2-054006	DM 114	78517	78516	VA 40	------	74.23
50.	**Alba separa dalla luce l'ombra, L' (Gabriele D'Annunzio; F. Paolo Tosti) (Or. Pasternack)**										
	B-19484-1,-2	15 Apr.'17	87272	503	7-52104	DA 121	------	------	------	------	75.00
51.	**AMADIS DE GAULE: Bois épais (Giovanni Battista Lully) (Or. Pasternack)**										
	B-24465-1,-2,-3,-4	15 Sep.'20	------	------	------	------	------	------	AGSA 27	------	------
	-5,-6	16 Sep.'20	------	1437	------	DA 1097					75.00
52.	**Amor mio (G. E. Gaeta; V. Ricciardi) (Or. Rogers)**										
	B-14356-1	21 Jan.'14	87176	504	7-52055	DA 105	74545	80019	VA 45	------	76.00
53.	**ANDREA CHÉNIER: Un dì all'azzurro spazio (Improvviso) (Giordano) (w. Orchestra)**										
	C-4161-1	30 Dec.'06	88060	6008	052158	DB 700	76073	85016	------	------	76.60
	C-4316-1	17 Mar.'07									
54.	**ANDREA CHÉNIER: Come un bel dì di maggio (Giordano) (Or. Pasternack)**										
	B-18659-1	3 Nov.'16	87266	516	7-52094	DA 117	------	------	------	------	79.13

Discog. No.	Matrix No. -Take	Date	Victor s/f	Victor d/f	G&T/HMV s/f	G&T/HMV d/f	Deutsche Gram. s/f	Deutsche Gram. d/f	Other 78 rpm Issues	Speed of Original
55.	Ave Maria (Meditation on Prelude No. 1 of Bach's WTC 1; Charles F. Gounod) (in Latin) (violin: Fritz Kreisler; pf. Gaetano Scognamiglio)									
	C-14664-1	3 Apr.'14	.....	.....		.....			.....	.....
56.	Ave Maria (Percy B. Kahn) (in Latin) (Violin: Mischa Elman; pf. composer)									
	C-13004-1,-2,-3	20 Mar.'13	89065	8007	02472	DK 103	77500	85045	.....	76.00
	Bacio ancora, Un (Rocco Trimarchi): See European recording section (21)									
57.	BALLO IN MASCHERA, UN: Amici miei, soldati . . . La rivedrà nell'estasi (Verdi) (w. Hempel, De Segurola, and Rothier; Met. Opera Cho./Setti; Or. Scognamiglio)									
	C-14659-1,-2	3 Apr.'14	89077	10005	2-054052	DM 103	.....	.....	.....	76.00
58.	BALLO IN MASCHERA, UN: Di' tu se fedele (Verdi) (w. Met. Opera Cho./Setti and Orchestra)									
	B-11270-1,-2	19 Nov.'11	87091	512	7-52025	DA 102	74532	80009	.....	75.00
59.	BALLO IN MASCHERA, UN: Così scritto è lassù . . . È scherzo od è follia (Verdi) (w. Hempel, Duchêne, De Segurola, and Rothier; Cho./Setti; Or. Scognamiglio)									
	C-14660-1,-2	3 Apr.'14	89076	10005	2-054050	DM 103	.....	.....	16-5000	76.00
60.	BALLO IN MASCHERA, UN: Forse la soglia . . . Ma se m'è forza perderti (Verdi) (w. Orchestra)									
	C-11420-1	27 Dec.'11	88346	6027	2-052065	DB 137	76107	85031	.....	76.00
61.	Because (Parce que) ("Guy d'Hardelot" [Mrs. W. I. Rhodes]) (in French) (w. Orchestra)									
	B-12680-1,-2	7 Dec.'12	87122	506	7-32004	DA 107	74503	80002 80020	1688 DA 1380	76.00
62.	BOHÊME, LA: Io non ho che una povera stanzetta (Leoncavallo) (w. Orchestra)									
	C-11276-1	26 Nov.'11	88335	6012	2-052061	DB 122	76104	85028	15-1038	76.00
63.	BOHÊME, LA: Musette! O gioia della mia dimora . . . Testa adorata (Leoncavallo) (w. Orchestra)									
	C-11272-1	19 Nov.'11	88331	6012	2-052059	DB 122	76102	85028	.....	76.00
64.	BOHÊME, LA: Che gelida manina (Puccini) (w. Orchestra)									
	C-3101-1	11 Feb.'06	88002	6003	052122	DB 113	76066	85012	.....	76.00
65.	BOHÊME, LA: O soave fanciulla (Puccini) (w. Nellie Melba) (Or. Rogers)									
	C-4327-1,-2	24 Mar.'07	95200	.....	054129	.....	78512	78512	.....	76.60
	-3,-4	1 Apr.'07								
66.	BOHÊME, LA: O soave fanciulla (Puccini) (w. Geraldine Farrar) (Or. Rogers)									
	C-11617-1,-2	27 Feb.'12	.....	.....	.....	.....	.....	.....	AGSB 50 IRCC 61	76.00

69.* BOHÈME, LA: Vecchia zimarra, senti (Puccini) (Or. Rogers)
B-17198-1   23 Feb.'16   "87499"   D9-QB-7758-1Arr   -----   DL 100rr   -----   -----   76.00

70. Campana di San Giusto, La (G. Drovetti; Colombino Arona) (celeste: Bourdon; Or. Pasternack)
C-22514-1,-2   6 Jan.'19   88612   6011   2-052153   DB 616   -----   -----   76.00

71. Campane a sera (E. Caruso; Vincenzo Billi, arr. Paolo Malfetti) (celeste: Bourdon; Or. Pasternack)
C-22259-1,-2,-3   26 Sep.'18   88615   6024   2-052177   DB 134   -----   -----   76.00

72. Canta pe' me (L. Bovio; Ernesto De Curtis [1875-1937]) (w. Orchestra)
C-9756-1   29 Dec.'10   -----   -----   -----   76.00
B-11306-1,-2   26 Nov.'11   87092   502   7-52026   DA 104   74533   80016   76.00

73. Cantique de Noël (Adolphe Adam) (in French) (Or. Rogers)
C-17218-1,-2,-3   23 Feb.'16   88561   6029   2-032022   DB 139   -----   -----   76.00

74.* CARMEN: Parle-moi de ma mère (Bizet) (w. Frances Alda) (Or. Rogers)
C-15483-1,-2,-3   10 Dec.'14   (89083)   -----   -----   -----   75.00+?

75. CARMEN: Il fior che avevi a me tu dato (pf. acc. unknown)
C-2341-1   27 Feb.'05   85049   -----   052087   VB 57   77.43

76. CARMEN: Il fior che avevi a me tu dato (w. Orchestra)
C-8349-1   7 Nov.'09   88209   6007   2-052007   DB 117   76092   85015   *14234* / *12-1016*   *DB 3023* / *DB 3388*   75.00

77. CARMEN: La fleur que tu m'avais jetée (Bizet) (in French) (w. Orchestra)
C-8350-1   7 Nov.'09   88208   6004   2-032000   DB 130   76015   85006   75.00

CAVALLERIA RUSTICANA: O Lola ch'ai di latti la cammisa (Siciliana) (Mascagni): See European recording section (16 and 27)

78. CAVALLERIA RUSTICANA: O Lola ch'ai di latti la cammisa (Siciliana) (Mascagni) (pf. acc. unknown)
B-1000-1   1 Feb.'04   81030   521   52064   78.26

79. CAVALLERIA RUSTICANA: O Lola ch'ai di latti la cammisa (Siciliana) (Mascagni) (harp: Francis J. Lapitino)
B-9745-1   28 Dec.'10   87072   516   7-52018   DA 117   74530   80010   75.00

80. CAVALLERIA RUSTICANA: Intanto amici... Viva il vino (Brindisi) (Mascagni) (pf. acc. unknown)
B-2344-1   27 Feb.'05   81062   521   52193   DA 545   74513   80005   VA 33   77.43

81. CAVALLERIA RUSTICANA: Mamma, Mamma, Quel vino!... Voi dovrete fare (Addio alla madre) (Mascagni) (w. Orchestra)
C-14202-1,-2   15 Dec.'13   88458   6008   2-052083   DB 118   76113   85020   *15732* / *12-1016*   *DB 3023*   76.00

82. Chanson de juin (Victor Barrucand; Benjamin Godard, Op. 102, No. 6) (in French) (Or. Pasternack)
C-18658-1   3 Nov.'16   88579   6066   2-032027   DB 116   -----   VB 59   79.13

Discog. No.	Matrix No. -Take	Date	Victor s/f	Victor d/f	G&T/HMV s/f	G&T/HMV d/f	Deutsche Gram. s/f	Deutsche Gram. d/f	Other 78 rpm Issues	Speed of Original
83.	CID, LE: Ah! . . . tout est bien fini . . . Ô souverain, ô Juge, ô Père (Massenet) (in French) (Or. Rogers)									
	C-17122-1,-2	5 Feb.'16	88554	6013	2-032025	DB 123	-----	-----	-----	76.00
84.	Cielo Turchino (C. Capaldo; M. S. Ciociano) (Or. Rogers)									
	B-15569-1	7 Jan.'15	87218	504	7-52073	DA 105	-----	-----	VA 45	76.00
85.	Core 'ngrato ("Riccardo Cordiferro" [Alessandro Sisca]; Salvatore Cardillo [1911]) [CR] (w. Orchestra)									
	C-11274-1	19 Nov.'11	88334	6032	2-052060	DB 142	76103	85029	-----	76.00
86.	Crucifix (Jean-Baptiste Faure) (w. Marcel Journet) (in French) (Or. Rogers)									
	C-11442-1	7 Jan.'12	89054	6347	2-034013	DB 591	78504	78504	11-0035rr	76.60
87.	Danza, La (Les Soirées musicales, No. 8) (Pepoli; Rossini) (Or. Rogers)									
	C-11590-1	13 Feb.'12	88355	6031	2-052068	DB 141	76110	85035	15-1040	77.43
88.	Deux sérénades, Les: Sérénade française (E. Collet; R. Leoncavallo) (violin: Mischa Elman; pf. Gaetano Scognamiglio)									
	C-15683-1,-2	6 Feb.'15	89085	8008	2-032017	DK 104	-----	-----	-----	76.00
89.	DON CARLOS: Domanda al ciel dei forti la virtù . . . Dio, che nell'alma infondere (Verdi) (w. Antonio Scotti) (w. Orchestra)									
	C-12752-1	30 Dec.'12	89064	8036	2-054043 / 2-054095	DM 111	78533	78533	-----	76.00
90.	DON PASQUALE: Com'è gentil (Serenata) (Donizetti) (pf. acc. unknown)									
	C-2340-1	27 Feb.'05	85048	6036	052086	DB 159	-----	-----	VB 55	77.43
91.*	DON SEBASTIANO: Deserto in terra (Donizetti) (w. Orchestra)									
	C-5008-1	10 Jan.'08	88106	6014	052209	DB 700	76078	85010	-----	80.00
	-2	10 Jan.'08	-----	15-1037	-----	-----	-----	-----	-----	80.00
92.	Dopo (Afterwards) (Martini; F. Paolo Tosti) (Or. Pasternack)									
	C-22126-1,-2,-3	11 Jul.'18	-----	-----	-----	-----	-----	-----	-----	-----
93.	Dream, A (C. B. Cory; J. C. Bartlett) (in English) (Or. Pasternack)									
	B-24466-1	15 Sep.'20	-----	-----	-----	-----	-----	-----	S-1617 1658	75.00
	-2,-3	16 Sep.'20	87321	507	-----	DA 108	-----	-----	DA 1349	
94.	Dreams of Long Ago (Earl Carroll; Enrico Caruso) (in English) (Or. Rogers)									
	C-11616-1	27 Feb.'12	-----	-----	-----	-----	-----	-----	-----	-----
	-2,-3	18 Apr.'12	88376	6015	02396	DB 125	76000	85001	-----	76.00

97. ELISIR D'AMORE, L': Venti scudi! E ben sonanti (Donizetti) (w. Giuseppe de Luca) (Or. Pasternack)
   C-22576-1,-2   10 Feb.'19   89089   8006   2-54092   DM 107   -----   -----   -----   -----   76.00

   ELISIR D'AMORE, L': Una furtiva lagrima (Donizetti): See European recording section (5 and 23)

98. ELISIR D'AMORE, L': Una furtiva lagrima (Donizetti) (Part 1) (pf. acc. unknown)
   B-996-1   1 Feb.'04   81027   930   52065   VA 12   -----   -----   -----   -----   78.26

99. ELISIR D'AMORE, L': Un solo istante i palpiti (Donizetti) (Part 2 of No. 98) (pf. acc. unknown)
   C-996-1   1 Feb.'04   85021   -----   052073   VB 44   -----   -----   VB 16rr   -----   78.26

100. ELISIR D'AMORE, L': Una furtiva lagrima (Donizetti) (w. Orchestra)
   C-996-2 (sic)   26 Nov.'11   88339   6016   2-052064   DB 126   76106   85012   11-8112 / 12-1014rr   DB-3903   76.00

101. Eternamente (P. Mazzoni; A. Mascheroni) (w. Orchestra)
   C-11271-1   19 Nov.'11   88333   6034   2-052058   DB 121   76161   85042   VB 60   -----   76.00

102. EUGÈNE ONÉGUINE: Pour moi ce jour est tout mystère (in French) (Tchaikovsky) (Or. Pasternack)
   C-18657-1   3 Nov.'16   88582   6017   2-032028   DB 127   -----   -----   AGSB 18   -----   79.13
   -2 (in Ital.)   3 Nov.'16   -----   -----   -----

103. FAUST: Ô merveille! ... A moi les plaisirs (Gounod) (w. Marcel Journet) (in French) (Or. Rogers)
   C-8555-1,-2   16 Jan.'10   89039   8016   2-034000   DM 115   78537   78519   -----   -----   76.60

104. FAUST: Salut demeure chaste et pure (Gounod) (in French) (w. Orchestra)
   C-3102-1   11 Feb.'06   88003< 6004<   032030   DK 116<   76013   85004   -----   -----   76.00

105. FAUST: Seigneur Dieu, que vois-je! (Gounod) (w. Geraldine Farrar, Gabrielle Lejeune-Gilbert, and Marcel Journet) (Or. Rogers)
   C-8544-1   12 Jan.'10   95204   10004   2-034003   DM 102   78500   -----   -----   -----   76.60

106. FAUST: Eh! quoi! toujours seule? (Gounod) (w. Geraldine Farrar, Gabrielle Lejeune-Gilbert, and Marcel Journet) (Or. Rogers)
   C-8547-1   12 Jan.'10   95205   10004   2-034004   DM 102   78500   78500   -----   -----   76.60

107. FAUST: Il se fait tard ... Laisse-moi ... laisse-moi (Gounod) (in French) (w. Geraldine Farrar) (Or. Rogers)
   C-8533-1   6 Jan.'10   89032   8009   2-034011   DM 108   78502   78502   -----   -----   76.60

108. FAUST: Éternelle! Éternelle! Ô nuit d'amour (Gounod) (in French) (w. Geraldine Farrar) (Or. Rogers)
   C-8534-1,-2   6 Jan.'10   89031< 8009<   2-034012   DM 108<   78503   78502   -----   -----   76.60

109. FAUST: Que voulez-vous, messieurs? (Gounod) (in French) (w. Emilio de Gogorza and Félix Vieulle) (w. Orchestra)
   C-6681-1,-2   19 Dec.'08   -----   -----   -----   -----   -----   -----

110. FAUST: Que voulez-vous, messieurs? (Gounod) (in French) (w. Antonio Scotti and Marcel Journet) (Or. Rogers)
   C-8556-1   16 Jan.'10   95206< 10011<   2-034001   DO 100<   78539   78539   -----   -----   76.60

Discog. No.	Matrix No. -Take	Date	Victor s/f	Victor d/f	G&T/HMV s/f	G&T/HMV d/f	Deutsche Gram. s/f	Deutsche Gram. d/f	Other 78 rpm Issues	Speed of Original
111.	FAUST: Mon coeur est pénétré d'épouvante (Gounod) (in French) (w. Geraldine Farrar) (Or. Rogers)									
	C-8542-1,-2	12 Jan.'10	89033	8010	2-034005	DM 109	78535	78535	------	76.60
112.	FAUST: Attends! Voici la rue (Gounod) (in French) (w. Geraldine Farrar) (Or. Rogers)									
	C-8543-1,-2	12 Jan.'10	89034	8010	2-034006	DM 109	78536	78535	------	76.60
113.	FAUST: Alerte! ou vous êtes perdus (Gounod) (in French) (w. Geraldine Farrar and Félix Vieulle) (w. Orchestra)									
	C-6679-1,-2	19 Dec.'08	89001	------	------	------	------	------	------	------
114.	FAUST: Alerte! ou vous êtes perdus (Gounod) (in French) (w. Geraldine Farrar and Marcel Journet) (Or. Rogers)									
	C-8545-1,-2	12 Jan.'10	95203<	10008<	2-034002	DK 106	------	77515	16-5003	76.60
	-3,-4	16 Jan.'10					78538			
115.	FAVORITA, LA: Spirto gentil, ne' sogni miei (Donizetti) (w. Orchestra)									
	C-3104-1	11 Feb.'06	88004	6005	052120	DB 129	76064	85010	15-1036	76.00

FEDORA: Amor ti vieta (Giordano) [CR]: See European recording section (12)

Discog. No.	Matrix No. -Take	Date	Victor s/f	Victor d/f	G&T/HMV s/f	G&T/HMV d/f	Deutsche Gram. s/f	Deutsche Gram. d/f	Other 78 rpm Issues	Speed of Original
116.*	Fenesta che lucive (Giulio Genoino; Guglielmo Cottrau) (w. Orchestra)									
	C-13107-1,-2	10 Apr.'13	88439	6019	2-052077	DB 140	76112	85029	15-1040	76.00
117.	For you alone (P. J. O'Reilly; Henry E. Geehl) (in English) (w. Orchestra)									
	B-9744-1,-2	28 Dec.'10	87070	507	4-2122	DA 108	74500	80000	1658 DA 1349	75.00
118.	FORZA DEL DESTINO, LA: Della natal sua terra il padre ... O tu che in seno agl' angeli (Verdi) (Or. Rogers)									
	C-8345-1	6 Nov.'09	88207	6000	2-052006	DB 112	76091	85022	------	74.23
119.	FORZA DEL DESTINO, LA: Solenne in quest'ora (Verdi) (w. Antonio Scotti) (w. Orchestra)									
	C-3179-1	13 Mar.'06	89001	8000	054070	DM 105	78510	78510	------	76.60
120.	FORZA DEL DESTINO, LA: Nè gustare m'è dato un'ora ... Sleale! il segreto fu dunque (Verdi) (w. Giuseppe de Luca) (Or. Pasternack)									
	C-22123-1,-2	10 Jul.'18	89087	8006	2-054093	DM 107	------	------	------	76.00
121.	FORZA DEL DESTINO, LA: Invano, Alvaro (Verdi) (w. Pasquale Amato) (w. Orchestra)									
	C-11286-1,-2	26 Nov.'11	89052	8005	2-054027	DB 106	78526	78526	------	76.00
122.*	FORZA DEL DESTINO, LA: Le minaccie, i fieri accenti (Verdi) (w. Pasquale Amato) (w. Orchestra)									
	C-11286½-1	26 Nov.'11	89053	8005	2-054028	DM 106	78527	78526	------	76.00

GERMANIA: Studenti! udite (Franchetti) [CR]: See European recording section (1)

	Take	Date										Min.
	B-8713-1	14 Mar.'10	87054	508	7-52014	DA 543	74559	80022	VA 38	---	---	76.60
125.	GIOCONDA, LA: Enzo Grimaldo, Principe di Santafior (Ponchielli) (w. Titta Ruffo) (Or. Rogers)											
	C-14273-1	8 Jan.'14								---		---
	GIOCONDA, LA: Cielo e mar (Ponchielli): See European recording section (14)											
126.	GIOCONDA, LA: Cielo e mar (Ponchielli) (pf. unknown)											
	C-2343-1	27 Feb.'05	85055	6036	052089	DB 113				---		77.43
127.	GIOCONDA, LA: Cielo e mar (Ponchielli) (w. Orchestra)											
	C-8718-1	14 Mar.'10	88246	6020	2-052032	DB 696	76094	85016		---		76.60
128.*	GIOCONDA, LA: Che vedo là! il rosario! oh sommo Dio!... "A te questo rosario" (Ponchielli) (w. Emmy Destinn and Louise Homer) (Or. Rogers)											
	C-17341-1,-2	20 Mar.'16								---		---
129.	GUARANY, IL: Sento una forza indomita (Carlos Antonio Gomes) (w. Emmy Destinn) (Or. Rogers)											
	C-14730-**1**,-**2**	20 Apr.'14	89078	6355	2-054053	DB 616				---		76.60
130.	Guardanno 'a luna (Gennaro Camerlingo; Vincenzo de Crescenzo [1904]) (harp: Francis J. Lapitino)											
	B-13105-1,-**2**	10 Apr.'13	87162	509	7-52043	DA 106	74542	80020	VA 44	---		76.00
131.	Hantise d'amour (Henry Rey-Roise; Joseph Szulc) (in French) (Or. Rogers)											
	C-14357-1	21 Jan.'14	---	---	---	---	---	---	---	---		---
	C-14357-2	9 Mar.'14	---	---	---	---	---	---	---	---		---
	B-14357-1	9 Mar.'14	---	---	---	---	---	---	VA 9	---		---
	B-14357-**2**,-3	10 Dec.'14	87211	506	7-32009	DA 107				---		76.00
132.	Hosanna (J. Didiée; Jules Granier) (in French) (w. Orchestra)											
	C-12681-1,-**2**	7 Dec.'12	88403	6022	2-032008	DB 132	76018	85008	17814	*DB 3122*		76.00
	HUGUENOTS, LES (Meyerbeer): See *UGONOTTI, GLI*, Discog. Nos. 30, 257, and 258											
133.	Ideale (C. Errica; F. Paolo Tosti) (w. Orchestra)											
	C-4162-1	30 Dec.'06	88049<	6019<	052154	DB 129<	76071	85003		---		77.43
134.	I' m'arricordo 'e Napule (Pasquale L. Esposito; Giuseppe Gioè [1919]) (Or. Pasternack)											
	C-24462-1,-**2**	14 Sep.'20	88635	6009	2-052198	DB 640			VB 62	---		75.00
135.	Inno di Garibaldi (Luigi Mercantini; Alessio Olivieri) (Or. Pasternack)											
	B-22260-1,-**2**,-3	26 Sep.'18	87297	515	7-52118	DA 116				---		76.00
	IRIS: Apri la tua finestra (Mascagni): See European recording section (10)											

Discog. No.	Matrix No. -Take	Date	Victor s/f	Victor d/f	G&T/HMV s/f	G&T/HMV d/f	Deutsche Gram. s/f	Deutsche Gram. d/f	Other 78 rpm Issues	Speed of Original
136.	JUIVE, LA: Rachel, quand du Seigneur la grâce tutélaire (Halévy) (in French) (Or. Pasternack)									
	C-24461-1,-2	14 Sep.'20	88625	6013	2-032062	DB 123	-----	-----	15-1004	75.00
	KÖNIGIN VON SABA, DIE (Goldmark): See *REGINA DI SABA*, Discog. No. 201									
137.	Lasciati amar (Ruggero Leoncavallo) (w. Orchestra)									
	B-13104-1,-2	10 Apr.'13	87161	509	7-52042	DA 113	76541	80019	-----	76.00
138.*	Lolita (Spanish serenade) (Arturo Buzzi-Peccia) (w. Orchestra)									
	C-6032-1	16 Mar.'08	88120<	6003<	062005	DB 696	76153	85042	VB 60	76.00
139.	LOMBARDI, I: La mia letizia infondere (Verdi) (Or. Pasternack)									
	C-23142-1,-2	9 Sep.'19	-----	-----	-----	-----	-----	-----	-----	-----
140.	LOMBARDI, I: Qual voluttà trascorrere (Verdi) (w. Frances Alda and Marcel Journet) (Or. Rogers)									
	C-11441-1	7 Jan.'12	95211	10010	2-054029	DM 126	78542	78539	16-5002	76.60
141.	Lost chord, The (Adelaide A. Proctor; Sir Arthur Sullivan) (in English) (w. Orchestra)									
	C-11942-1,-2	29 Apr.'12	88378	6023	02397	DB 133	76001	85001	8806 *DB 2073*	76.00
142.	Love is mine (Edward Teschemacher; Clarence G. Gartner) (in English) (Or. Rogers)									
	B-11419-1,-2	27 Dec.'11	87095	510	4-2205	DA 111	74501	80000	-----	76.00
143.	Love me or not (T. Campion; A. Secchi) (in English) (Or. Pasternack)									
	C-23713-1,-2,-3,-4	29 Jan.'20	88616	6015	02891	DB 125	-----	-----	-----	75.00
144.	LUCIA DI LAMMERMOOR: Chi mi frena (Donizetti) (w. Marcella Sembrich, Gina Severina, Antonio Scotti, Marcel Journet, and Francesco Daddi) (w. Orchestra)									
	C-5052-1,-2,-3	3 Feb.'08	-----	-----						
	-4,-5	7 Feb.'08	96200	10001	054205	DQ 101	79003	79003	-----	79.13
145.	LUCIA DI LAMMERMOOR: Chi mi frena (Donizetti) (w. Luisa Tetrazzini, Josephine Jacoby, Pasquale Amato, Marcel Journet, and Angelo Bada) (Or. Rogers)									
	C-11446-1,-2	10 Jan.'12	-----	-----						
	-3,-4	19 Jan.'12	96201	-----	2-054034	-----	-----	-----	16-5000	76.00
146.	LUCIA DI LAMMERMOOR: Chi mi frena (Donizetti) (w. Amelita Galli-Curci, Minnie Egener, Giuseppe de Luca, Marcel Journet, and Angelo Bada) (Or. Pasternack)									
	C-19133-1,-2,-3	25 Jan.'17	95212	10000	2-054067	DQ 100	-----	-----	-----	76.00
147.	LUCREZIA BORGIA: Della Duchessa prieghi (Finale, Act I) (Donizetti) (w. Emmy Destinn and Antonio Scotti) (w. Met. Opera Cho./Setti and Orchestra)									

B-17123-1,2,3   3 Feb.'16   3,242   513   DA 148

Luna fedel (Arrigo Boito; Redento Zardo): See European recording section (20 and 22)

Entry / Matrix–Take	Date										Price
150. MACBETH: O figli, o figli miei!... Ah, la paterna mano (Verdi) (Or. Rogers)											
C-17197-1	23 Feb.'16	2-052112	88558	6014	DB 118	----	----	15-1038	----		76.00
151. MADAMA BUTTERFLY: Amore o grillo dir non saprei (Puccini) (w. Antonio Scotti) (w. Orchestra)											
C-8711-1	14 Mar.'10	2-054014	89043	8014	DM 113	----	78520	----	----		76.60
152. MADAMA BUTTERFLY: Un po' di vero c'è. E tu lo sai perchè?... Oh quanti occhi fisi (Puccini) (w. Geraldine Farrar) (w. Orchestra)											
C-6026-1	10 Mar.'08	054201	89017	8011	DM 110	78515	78515	----	----		76.60
153. MADAMA BUTTERFLY: Non ve l'avevo detto?... Addio fiorito asil (Puccini) (w. Antonio Scotti) (w. Orchestra)											
C-8712-1	14 Mar.'10	2-054013	89047	8014	DM 113	78520	78520	----	----		76.60
154. Mamma mia, che vo'sapè (F. Russo; Emanuele Nutile [1909]) (Or. Rogers)											
C-8344-1,2	6 Nov.'09	2-052005	88206	6009	DB 119	76090	85021	----	----		74.23
155. Manella mia (Ferdinando Russo; Vincenzo Valente [1907]) (Or. Rogers)											
C-14358-1	21 Jan.'14	2-052091	88465	6025	DB 121	76116	85021	VB 61	----		76.00
156. MANON: Manon! Avez-vous peur que mon visage... On l'appelle Manon (Massenet) (in French) (w. Geraldine Farrar) (w. Orchestra)											
C-12750-1,2	30 Dec.'12	2-034018	89059	8011	DM 110	78505	78515	----	----		76.00
MANON: Chiudo gli occhi (Il sogno) (Massenet): See European recording section (4)											
157. MANON: Chiudo gli occhi (Il sogno) (Massenet) (pf. acc. unknown)											
B-1001-1	1 Feb.'04	2-52479	81031	523	DA 125	74516	80005	VA 32	----		78.26
-2	9 Feb.'04										
158. MANON: Je suis seul!... Ah, fuyez, douce image (Massenet) (in French) (Or. Rogers)											
C-11422-1	27 Dec.'11	2-032005	88348	6020	DB 130	76017	85004	15-1004	----		76.00
159. MANON LESCAUT: Donna non vidi mai (Puccini) (Or. w. harp: A. Regis-Rossini)											
B-12945-1	24 Feb.'13	7-52039	87135	505	DA 106	74539	80013	VA 33	----		76.00
160. Maria, Marì! (Vincenzo Russo; Eduardo di Capua) (mandolin: Bianculli; Or. Pasternack)											
C-22127-1,2,3	11 Jul.'18	----	----								
161. MARTA: Solo, profugo reietto (Flotow) (w. Marcel Journet) (Or. Rogers)											
C-8546-1	12 Jan.'10	2-054010	89036	8016	DA 115	78519	78519	----	78519		76.60
162. MARTA: Siam giunti, o giovinette (Flotow) (w. Frances Alda, Josephine Jacoby, and Marcel Journet) (Or. Rogers)											
C-11437-1,2	7 Jan.'12	2-054030	95207	10002	DM 100	78528	78528	----	78528		76.60

Discog. No.	Matrix No. -Take	Date	Victor s/f	Victor d/f	G&T/HMV s/f	G&T/HMV d/f	Deutsche Gram. s/f	Deutsche Gram. d/f	Other 78 rpm Issues	Speed of Original
163.	**MARTA:** Questa camera è per voi ... Che vuol dir ciò? (Flotow) (w. Frances Alda, Josephine Jacoby, and Marcel Journet) (Or. Rogers)									
	C-11438-1	7 Jan.'12	95208	10002	2-054031	DM 100	78529	78529	-----	76.60
164.	**MARTA:** Presto, presto andiam (Flotow) (w. Frances Alda, Josephine Jacoby, and Marcel Journet) (Or. Rogers)									
	C-11439-**1**,-2	7 Jan.'12	95209	10003	2-054032	DM 101	78530	78529	-----	76.60
165.	**MARTA:** T'ho raggiunta, sciagurata! ... Dormi pur, ma il mio riposo (Flotow) (w. Frances Alda, Josephine Jacoby, and Marcel Journet) (Or. Rogers)									
	C-11440-1	7 Jan.'12	95210	10003	2-054037	DM 101	78531	78528	16-5002 -----	76.60
166.*	**MARTA:** M'appari tutt'amor (Flotow) (w. Orchestra)									
	C-3100-1	11 Feb.'06	88001	6002*	052121	DB 159	76065	85011	15-1036 -----	76.00
	-**2**,-3	15 Apr.'17	88001	6002	-----	-----	-----	-----	12-1015rr 7720 *DB 1802*	75.00

Mattinata (Leoncavallo) (pf. composer) [CR]: See European recording section (31)

MEFISTOFELE: Dai campi dai prati (Boito): See European recording section (8 and 11)

MEFISTOFELE: Giunto sul passo estremo (Boito): See European recording section (6)

Discog. No.	Matrix No. -Take	Date	Victor s/f	Victor d/f	G&T/HMV s/f	G&T/HMV d/f	Deutsche Gram. s/f	Deutsche Gram. d/f	Other 78 rpm Issues	Speed of Original
167.	**MESSE SOLENNELLE, PETITE:** Crucifixus (Rossini) (in Latin) (Or. Pasternack)									
	B-24474-**1**,-2	16 Sep.'20	87335	-----	7-52207	DJ 100	-----	-----	-----	75.00
168.	**MESSE SOLENNELLE, PETITE:** Domine Deus (Rossini) (in Latin) (Or. Pasternack)									
	C-24473-1	16 Sep.'20	88629	6010	2-052195	DB 120	-----	-----	11-0037rr	75.00

Mia canzone, La (F. Cimmino; F. Paolo Tosti): See European recording section (18)

Discog. No.	Matrix No. -Take	Date	Victor s/f	Victor d/f	G&T/HMV s/f	G&T/HMV d/f	Deutsche Gram. s/f	Deutsche Gram. d/f	Other 78 rpm Issues	Speed of Original
169.	Mia canzone, La (F. Cimmino; F. Paolo Tosti) (Or. Rogers)									
	B-15481-1,-2	10 Dec.'14	87213	503	7-52068	DA 116	-----	-----	*1688* *DA 1380*	76.00
	-3	7 Jan.'15								
170.	Mia sposa sarà la mia bandiera (Augusto Rotoli) (Or. Rogers)									
	C-17195-1,-**2**	23 Feb.'16	88555	6018	2-052106	DB 128	-----	-----	-----	76.00
171.	**MILAGRO DE LA VIRGEN, EL:** Flores purisimas (M. P. Dominguez; Ruperto Chapí) (in Spanish) (pf. acc. Gaetano Scognamiglio)									
	B-14662-1	3 Apr.'14	-----	-----	2-062002	DB 639	-----	-----	VB 56	77.43
	C-14662-1	3 Apr.'14	(88671)	6458						
172.	Musica proibita (N. Malpadi; Stanislao Gastaldon, Op. 5) ('14 and '15 Or. Rogers; '17 Or. Pasternack)									
	C-15480-1,-2	10 Dec.'14	-----	-----					-----	-----

174.* Nina (Tre giorni son che Nina) (Legrenzio Vincenzo Ciampi [1719–1762]?) (Or. Pasternack)
B-23143-1,-2,-3,-4   9 Sep.'19   87358   519   7-52234   DA 120   -----   -----   VA 40   -----   75.00

175. Noche feliz (Guillermo Posadas, from collection edited by Carmen Garcia Cornejo) (in Spanish) (Or. Pasternack)
B-24460-1,-2,-3,-4   14 Sep.'20   (87366) 958   7-52251   DA 574   -----   -----   AGSA 2   17-5001rr 26571rr   75.00
     -5,-6   15 Sep.'20   -----   -----   -----   -----   -----

Non t'amo più (L. Denza): See European recording section (17)

176. 'O sole mio (G. Capurro; Eduardo Di Capua) (Or. Rogers)
B-17124-1   5 Feb.'16   87243   501   7-52092   DA 103   -----   -----   1616   DA 1303   76.00

177. OTELLO: Nell'ore arcane della sua lussuria ... Ora e per sempre addio (Verdi) (w. Orchestra)
B-9743-1,-2   28 Dec.'10   87071< 505<   7-52017   DA 561<   74529   80013   -----   -----   75.00

178. OTELLO: Oh! mostruosa colpa! ... Sì, pel ciel (Verdi) (w. Pasquale Amato) (Or. Rogers)
C-11285-1   26 Nov.'11   -----   -----   -----   -----   -----

179. OTELLO: Oh! mostruosa colpa! ... Sì, pel ciel (Verdi) (w. Titta Ruffo) (Or. Rogers)
C-14272-1,-2   8 Jan.'14   89075   8045   2-054049   DK 114   78534   78533   -----   -----   76.00

180. Over there (George M. Cohan) (in English and French [Fr. text L. Delamarre]) (Or. Pasternack)
B-22125-1   10 Jul.'18   -----   -----   -----   -----   -----
     -2,-3,-4   11 Jul.'18   87294   515   5-2593   DA 121   -----   -----   VA 39   -----   76.00

PAGLIACCI: Recitar! mentre preso dal delirio ... Vesti la giubba (Leoncavallo): See European recording section (15)

181. PAGLIACCI: Recitar! mentre preso dal delirio ... Vesti la giubba (Leoncavallo) (pf. acc. unknown)
B-1002-1   1 Feb.'04   81032   930   52066   52066   -----   -----   -----   -----   78.26

182. PAGLIACCI: Recitar! mentre preso dal delirio ... Vesti la giubba (Leoncavallo) (w. Orchestra)
C-4317-1   17 Mar.'07   88061   6001   052159   DB 111   76074   85017   7720 12-1015   DB 1802   76.60
     -2   24 Mar.'07   -----   -----   -----   -----   -----

183. PAGLIACCI: No! Pagliaccio non son (Leoncavallo) (w. Orchestra)
C-9742-1,-2   28 Dec.'10   88279   6001   2-052034   DB 111   76095   85017   -----   -----   75.00

Parce que (d'Hardelot): See Because, Discog. No. 61

184. Parted (Frederick E. Weatherly; F. Paolo Tosti) (in English) (Or. Rogers)
B-14550-1   9 Mar.'14   87186   510   4-2479   DA 118   -----   -----   VA 39   DB 3327   77.43

185. Partida, La (E. Blasco; F. M. Alvarez) (in Spanish) (pf. Gaetano Scognamiglio)
C-14661-1,-2   3 Apr.'14   -----   -----   2-062003   DB 639   -----   -----   VB 55   -----   77.43

Discog. No.	Matrix No. / -Take	Date	Victor s/f	Victor d/f	G&T/HMV s/f	G&T/HMV d/f	Deutsche Gram. s/f	Deutsche Gram. d/f	Other 78 rpm Issues	Speed of Original
186.	Partida, La (E. Blasco; F. M. Alvarez) (in Spanish) (Or. Pasternack) C-22122-1,-2,-3	10 Jul.'18	(88670)	6458	------	------	------	------	VB 58	76.00
187.	Pecchè? (Carlo De Flaviis; Gaetano Enrico Pennino [1913]) (mandolin: Bianculli; Or. Rogers) C-15568-1	7 Jan.'15	88517	6025	2-052098	DB 119	------	------	------	76.00
188.	PÊCHEURS DE PERLES, LES: De mon amie, fleur endormie (Bizet) (in French) (oboe: Adams; harp: Francis J. Lapitino) B-18823-1,-2	7 Dec.'16	87269	513	7-32014	DA 114	------	------	VA 36	76.00
189.	PÊCHEURS DE PERLES, LES: À cette voix quel trouble… Je crois entendre encore (Bizet) (in French) (Or. Pasternack) C-18822-1,-2,-3	7 Dec.'16	88580	6026	2-032026	DB 136	------	------	7770	DB 1875
	PESCATORI DI PERLE, I: Mi par d'udir ancora (Bizet): See European recording section (32)									
190.	PESCATORI DI PERLE, I: Mi par d'udir ancora (Bizet) (w. Orchestra) C-5010-1 -2,-3	10 Jan.'08 16 Mar.'08	------	------	------	------	------	------	------	------
191.	PESCATORI DI PERLE, I: Del tempio al limitar (Bizet) (w. Mario Ancona) (Or. Rogers) C-4327-1	24 Mar.'07	89007	8036	054134	DK 111	78513	78513	------	76.60
	PETITE MESSE SOLENNELLE (Rossini): See MESSE SOLENNELLE, PETITE, Discog. Nos. 167 and 168)									
192.*	Pietà, Signore (Louis Abraham Niedermeyer [1802–1861]) (Or. Pasternack) C-22121-1,-2,-3,-4 -5,-6,-7	10 Jul.'18 26 Sep.'18	88599	6024	2-052154	DB 134	------	------	11-0036rr	76.00
193.	Pimpinella (Canzone Florentina) (Tchaikovsky) (Tchaikovsky, Op. 38, No. 6) (pf. Gaetano Scognamiglio) B-12805-1,-2	17 Jan.'13	87218	518	7-52038	DA 119	74538	80016	VA 44	76.60
194.	Pourquoi? (Tchaikovsky, Op. 6, No. 5) (in French) (Or. Pasternack) B-18656-1,-2,-3	3 Nov.'16	87271	517	7-32012	DA 111	------	------	VA 35	79.13
195.	Pour un baiser (Georges Doncieux; F. Paolo Tosti) (in French) (Or. Rogers) B-8343-1	6 Nov.'09	87042	517	7-32000	DA 118	74502	80002	VA 35	74.23
196.	Povero Pulcinella (Arturo Buzzi-Peccia) (Or. Pasternack) B-22518-1,-2,-3	6 Jan.'19	------	------	------	------	------	------	------	------
197.*	Première caresse (P. Marinier; Constantino de Crescenzo) (in French) (Or. Pasternack)					DA 1007r		------	AGSA 27rr	75.00

No.	Matrix	Date							Speed
	C-14201-1,-2	15 Dec.'13	2-032012	DB 132	88459 6022	76156 85008	14744	DB 3122	76.00
	-3	9 Mar.'14							77.43

200. Régiment de Sambre et Meuse, Le (Paul Cézano; Robert Planquette [1917]) (Or. Pasternack)

	Matrix	Date							Speed
	C-22516-1,-2,-3	6 Jan.'19	2-032042	DB 128	88600 6018	-----	-----	-----	76.00

201.* REGINA DI SABA, LA (Königin von Saba): Magiche note (Karl Goldmark) (w. Orchestra)

	Matrix	Date							Speed
	C-6062-1	29 Mar.'08	-----	-----	-----	-----	-----	-----	-----
	B-6062-1	7 Nov.'09	7-52003	DA 122	87041 520	74527 80011	VA 36	-----	75.00

202. REINE DE SABA, LA: Faiblesse de la race humaine!... Inspirez-moi, race divine (Gounod) (in French) (Or. Rogers)

	Matrix	Date							Speed
	C-17125-1,-2	5 Feb.'16	2-032021	DB 145	88552 6035	-----	15732	DB 3078	76.00

203. REQUIEM, MESSA DA: Ingemisco (Verdi) (in Latin) (Or. Rogers)

	Matrix	Date							Speed
	C-15570-1,-2,-3	7 Jan.'15	02585	DB 138	88514 6028	-----	11-0037rr	-----	76.00

RIGOLETTO: Questa o quella (Verdi): See European recording section (2)

204. RIGOLETTO: Questa o quella (Verdi) (pf. acc. unknown)

	Matrix	Date							Speed
	B-994-1	1 Feb.'04	2-52480	-----	81025 522	-----	-----	-----	78.26

205. RIGOLETTO: Questa o quella (Verdi) (w. Orchestra)

	Matrix	Date							Speed
	B-6035-1	16 Mar.'08	2-52642	DA 102	87018 500	74523 80009	-----	-----	76.00

206. RIGOLETTO: Ella mi fu rapita!... Parmi veder le lagrime (Verdi) (w. Orchestra)

	Matrix	Date							Speed
	C-11421-1	27 Dec.'11	2-052076	DB 126	88429 6016	76111 85019	11-8112	DB 3903	76.00
	-2	24 Feb.'13							76.00

RIGOLETTO: La donna è mobile (Verdi): See European recording section (26)

207. RIGOLETTO: La donna è mobile (Verdi) (pf. acc. unknown)

	Matrix	Date							Speed
	B-995-1	1 Feb.'04	52062	-----	81026 522	-----	-----	-----	78.26

208. RIGOLETTO: La donna è mobile (Verdi) (w. Orchestra)

	Matrix	Date							Speed
	B-6033-1	16 Mar.'08	2-52641	DA 561	87017 500	74522 80007	1616	DA 1303	76.00

209. RIGOLETTO: Bella figlia dell'amore (Verdi) (w. Bessie Abott, Louise Homer, and Antonio Scotti) (w. Orchestra)

	Matrix	Date							Speed
	C-4259-1	20 Feb.'07	054117	DO 100	96000 10011	79000 79000	-----	-----	81.82

210. RIGOLETTO: Bella figlia dell'amore (Verdi) (w. Marcella Sembrich, Josephine Jacoby, and Antonio Scotti) (w. Orchestra)

	Matrix	Date							Speed
	C-5053-1,-2	3 Feb.'08	-----	-----	-----	79000	-----	-----	-----

211. RIGOLETTO: Bella figlia dell'amore (Verdi) (w. Marcella Sembrich, Gina Severina, and Antonio Scotti) (w. Orchestra)

	Matrix	Date							Speed
	C-5053-3,-4	7 Feb.'08	054199	DQ 101	96001 10001	79001 79001	16-5001	-----	76.00

Discog. No.	Matrix No. -Take	Date	Victor s/f	Victor d/f	G&T/HMV s/f	G&T/HMV d/f	Deutsche Gram. s/f	Deutsche Gram. d/f	Other 78 rpm Issues	Speed of Original
212.	RIGOLETTO: Bella figlia dell'amore (Verdi) (w. Luisa Tetrazzini, Josephine Jacoby, and Pasquale Amato) (w. Orchestra)									
	C-11447-1	10 Jan.'12	——	——	——	——	——	——	——	——
	-2	19 Jan.'12	——	——	——	——	——	——	IRCC 36	77.43
	-3,-4	13 Feb.'12	——	15-1019	2-054038	——	——	79003	——	77.43
213.	RIGOLETTO: Bella figlia dell'amore (Verdi) (w. Amelita Galli-Curci, Flora Perini, and Giuseppe de Luca (Or. Pasternack)									
	C-19132-1,-2,-3	25 Jan.'17	95100	10000	2-054066	DQ 100	——	——	——	76.00
214.*	RIGOLETTO: Bella figlia dell'amore (Verdi) (Opening tenor solo only) (Or. Pasternack?)									
	No Matrix No.	25 Jan.'17(?)								76.00
215.	Rosary, The (Robert Cameron Rogers; Ethelbert Nevin) (in English) (Or. Rogers)									
	B-17196-1,-2,-3,-4	23 Feb.'16	——	——	——	——	——	——	——	——
	-5,-6	20 Mar.'16	——	——	——	——	——	——	——	——
216.	Rose, a kiss and you, A ("Souci") (Robe; Arthur) (in English) (Or. Pasternack)									
	B-22517-1,-2	6 Jan.'19	——	——	——	——	——	——	——	——
	-3,-4	10 Feb.'19	——	——	——	——	——	——	——	——
217.	SALVATOR ROSA: Mia piccirella (Carlos Antonio Gomes) (Or. Pasternack)									
	B-23150-1	11 Sep.'19	88638	6034	2-052224	——	——	——	——	——
	C-23150-1	11 Sep.'19				DB 144				75.00
218.	SAMSON ET DALILA: Je viens célébrer la victoire (Saint-Saëns) (in French) (w. Louise Homer and Marcel Journet) (Or. Pasternack)									
	C-22575-1,-2,-3	10 Feb.'19	89088	10010	2-034026	DM 126	——	——	16-5003	76.00
219.*	SAMSON ET DALILA: Vois ma misère, hélas (Saint-Saëns) (in French) (w. Met. Opera Cho./Setti; Or. Pasternack)									
	C-18821-1,-2	7 Dec.'16	88581	6026	2-032029	DB 136	——	——	15-1039	76.00
220.	Sancta Maria (J. G. Bertrand; Jean-Baptiste Faure) (in French) (cello: Rosario Bourdon; Or. Rogers)									
	C-17342-1,-2	20 Mar.'16	88559	6029	2-032037	DB 139	——	——	——	77.43
221.	Santa Lucia (Cossovich; Teodoro Cottrau) (mandolin: Bianculli; Or. Rogers)									
	C-17344-1	20 Mar.'16	88560	6032	2-052107	DB 142	——	——	——	77.43
222.	SCHIAVO, LO: L'importuna insistenza . . . Quando nascesti tu (Carlos Antonio Gomes) (w. Orchestra)									
	C-11273-1,-2	19 Nov.'11	88345	6027	2-052062	DB 137	76105	85031	DB 2991 DB 5387	76.00
223.	Scordame (Salvatore Fucito) (Or. Pasternack)									
	B-23152-1	11 Sep.'19	(87395)	1007	7-52268	DA 608	——	——	VA 43	75.00

226. Sérénade de Don Juan (A. K. Tolstoy; Tchaikovsky, Op. 38, No. 1) (in French) (Or. Rogers)

Matrix	Date									Speed
B-14355-1	21 Jan.'14	87175	513	7-32006	DA 114	74504	80004	VA 42	----	76.00

227. Sérénade espagnole (G. Ferrari; Landon Ronald) (in French) (Or. Rogers)

Matrix	Date									Speed
B-14359-1	21 Jan.'14	----	----	----	----	----	----	----	----	----
-2,-3	9 Mar.'14	87169	520	7-32008	DA 122	----	----	VA 42	----	77.43

228. Serenata (Memories of a concert) (Enrico Caruso; C. A. Bracco) (celeste: Rosario Bourdon; Or. Pasternack)

Matrix	Date									Speed
B-23151-1	11 Sep.'19	88628	6033	2-052191	DA 143	----	----	----	----	----
C-23151-1,-2	11 Sep.'19	----	----	----	DB 143	----	----	VB 62	----	75.00

229. SERSE (Xerxes): Frondi tenere e belle del mio ... Ombra mai fu ("Largo") (Handel) (harp: Francis J. Lapitino; Or. Pasternack)

Matrix	Date									Speed
C-23714-1,-2,-3,-4,-5	29 Jan.'20	88617	6023	2-052180	DB 133	----	----	8806 / DB 2073	DB 5388	75.00

230. Si vous l'aviez compris (Stephen Bordése; Luigi Denza) (in French) (violin: Mischa Elman; pf. Gaetano Scognamiglio)

Matrix	Date									Speed
C-15682-1,-2,-3	6 Feb.'15	89084	8008	2-032018	DK 104	----	----	----	----	76.00

Sole mio, 'O (Di Capua): See 'O sole mio, Discog. No. 176

231. STABAT MATER: Cujus animam (Rossini) (in Latin) (w. Orchestra)

C-14200-1,-2	15 Dec.'13	88460	6028	2-052086	DB 138	76114	85027	----	11-0036rr	76.00

232. Sultano a Tte ("Riccardo Cordiferro" [Alessandro Sisca]; Salvatore Fucito) (Or. Pasternack)

Matrix	Date									Speed
B-22515-1,-2,-3,-4	6 Jan.'19	----	1117	7-52310	DA 754	----	----	----	DA 1367	76.00
-5	10 Feb.'19									

233. Tarantella sincera (Eduardo Migliaccio; Vincenzo de Crescenzo [1911]) (Or. Rogers)

C-11472-1	19 Jan.'12	88347	6031	2-052067	DB 141	76109	85035	----	----	76.00

234. Tiempo antico (Olden times) (Enrico Caruso) (Or. Rogers)

Matrix	Date									Speed
C-17343-1,-2	20 Mar.'16	88472	6033	2-052108	DB 143	----	----	VB 61	----	77.43

235. TOSCA: Recondita armonia (Puccini) (pf. acc. unknown)

Matrix	Date									Speed
B-999-1	1 Feb.'04	81029	----	52191	----	----	----	----	----	78.26

236. TOSCA: Recondita armonia (Puccini) (Or. Rogers)

Matrix	Date									Speed
B-8347-1	6 Nov.'09	87043	511	7-52004	DA 112	74528	80010	VA 34	11-8569	74.23

237. TOSCA: Perchè chiuso? (Puccini) (w. Geraldine Farrar) (Or. Rogers)

Matrix	Date									Speed
C-11618-1,-2	27 Feb.'12	----	----	----	----	----	----	----	DB 2644	----

238. TOSCA: Or lasciami al lavoro (Puccini) (w. Geraldine Farrar) (Or. Rogers)

Matrix	Date									Speed
C-11619-1	27 Feb.'12	----	----	----	----	----	----	----	----	----

TOSCA: E lucevan le stelle (Puccini): See European recording section (9, 24, and 29)

Discog. No.	Matrix No.	-Take	Date	Victor		G&T/HMV		Deutsche Gram.		Other 78 rpm Issues		Speed of Original
				s/f	d/f	s/f	d/f	s/f	d/f		d/f	
239.	*TOSCA: E lucevan le stelle (Puccini) (pf. acc. unknown)											
	B-998-1		1 Feb.'04	81028	523	52063	DA 125	-----	-----	VA 34	-----	78.26
240.	TOSCA: E lucevan le stelle (Puccini) (Or. Rogers)											
	B-8346-1		6 Nov.'09	87044<	511<	7-52002	DA 112<	74526	80010	-----	-----	74.23
241.	TOSCA: Ah, franchigia a Floria Tosca (Puccini) (w. Geraldine Farrar) (Or. Rogers)											
	C-11620-1		27 Feb.'12	-----	-----							-----
242.	TOSCA: O dolci mani mansuete e pure (Puccini) (w. Geraldine Farrar) (Or. Rogers)											
	C-11621-1		27 Feb.'12	-----	-----							-----
243.	TOSCA: Amaro sol per te m'era il morire (Puccini) (w. Geraldine Farrar) (Or. Rogers)											
	C-11622-1		27 Feb.'12	-----	-----							-----
244.	TRAVIATA, LA: Libiamo, libiamo ne' lieti calici (Brindisi) (Verdi) (w. Alma Gluck) (w. Met. Opera Cho./Setti and Orchestra)											
	B-14729-1,-2,-3		20 Apr.'14	87511	3031	7-54006	DJ 100	-----	-----	-----	-----	76.60
	Tre giorni son che Nina: See Nina, Discog. No. 174											
245.	Triste ritorno (L. Forzati; Riccardo Barthélemy) (w. Orchestra)											
	C-4159-1		30 Dec.'06	88048	6030	052153	DB 140	76070	85005	-----	-----	77.43
246.	TROVATORE, IL: Mal reggendo all'aspro assalto (Verdi) (w. Louise Homer) (w. Orchestra)											
	C-6682-1		19 Dec.'08	-----	-----							-----
		-2	29 Dec.'10	89049	8013	2-054017	DM 112	78524	78514	-----	-----	76.00
247.	TROVATORE, IL: Perigliarti ancor languente (Verdi) (w. Louise Homer) (w. Orchestra)											
	C-6680-1		19 Dec.'08	-----	-----							-----
248.	TROVATORE, IL: Ah sì, ben mio, coll'essere (Verdi) (w. Orchestra)											
	C-6034-1		16 Mar.'08	88121	6002	052210	DB 112	76079	85019	-----	-----	76.00
249.*	TROVATORE, IL: Di quella pira (Verdi) (w. Orchestra)											
	B-3103-1		11 Feb.'06	87001<	512< / 3031<	2-52489	DA 113<	74518	80007	-----	-----	76.00
250.	TROVATORE, IL: Quel suon, quelle preci . . . Ah! che la morte (Miserere) (Verdi) (w. Johanna Gadski) (w. Orchestra)											
	C-8352-1,-2		7 Nov.'09	-----	-----							-----

253. TROVATORE, IL: Se m'ami ancor, se voce di figlio... Ai nostri monti (Verdi) (w. Ernestine Schumann-Heink) (w. Orchestra)

Matrix	Date								$
C-12804-1,-2	17 Jan.'13	89060	8042	2-054042	DK 119	78532	78818	------	76.60

254. Trusting eyes (Edward Teschemacher; C. G. Gardner) (in English) (w. Orchestra)

Matrix	Date								$
B-14203-1 (no B-2)	15 Dec.'13	------	------	------	------	------	------	------	------
C-14203-1	21 Jan.'14	------	------	------	------	------	------	------	------
B-14203-3	21 Jan.'14	------	------	------	------	------	------	------	------
-4	9 Mar.'14	87187	514	4-2480	DA 115	------	------	DA 1656	77.43

255. Tu ca nun chiagne (Libero Bovio; Ernesto De Curtis [1915]) (Or. Pasternack)

Matrix	Date								$
B-23141-1	8 Sep.'19	(87365)	958	7-52250	DA 574	VA 41	------	------	75.00

256. Tú (Habanera) (Eduardo Sánchez de Fuentes) (in Spanish) (pf. Gaetano Scognamiglio)

Matrix	Date								$
B-14663-1,-2	3 Apr.'14	------	------	------	------	------	------	------	------

Tu non mi vuoi più ben (F. Carbonetti; Antonio Pini-Corsi): See European recording section (28)

UGONOTTI, GLI (Les Huguenots): Qui sotto il ciel (Meyerbeer): See European recording section (30)

257. UGONOTTI, GLI (Les Huguenots): Ah, qual soave vision... Bianca al par di neve (Meyerbeer) (pf. acc. unknown)

Matrix	Date								$
C-2342-1	27 Feb.'05	85056	------	052088	------	VB 57	------	------	77.43

258. UGONOTTI, GLI (Les Huguenots): Ah, qual soave vision... Bianca al par di neve (Meyerbeer) (w. Orchestra)

Matrix	Date								$
C-8351-1	7 Nov.'09	88210	6005	2-052008	DB 115	76093	85011	15-1037	75.00

259. Uocchie celeste ("Armando Gill" [Michele Testa]; Vincenzo de Crescenzo) (harp: Francis J. Lapitino; Or. Pasternack)

Matrix	Date								$
C-19483-1,-2	15 Apr.'17	88587	6030	2-052149	DB 115	VB 59	------	------	75.00

260. Vaghissima sembianza (Stefano Donaudy) (Or. Pasternack)

Matrix	Date								$
B-24463-1,-2,-3,-4	15 Sep.'20	------	1117	7-52307	DA 754	------	DA 1367	------	75.00

261. Vieni sul mar (Folk song) (Or. Pasternack)

Matrix	Date								$
B-23139-1,-2	8 Sep.'19	87305	518	7-52152	DA 119	VA 41	------	------	75.00

Vucchella, 'A: See 'A Vucchella, Discog. No. 36.

XERXES: Ombra mai fu ("Largo") (Handel): See SERSE: Frondi tenere... Ombra mai fu. Discog. No. 229

262. Your eyes have told me what I did not know (F. G. Bowles; Geoffrey O'Hara) (in English) (w. Orchestra)

Matrix	Date								$
B-13106-1,-2	10 Apr.'13	87159	514	4-2375	DA 115	74599	80004	DA 1656	76.00

The Electrical Re-Recordings of the 1930s

Caruso died in August 1921; Victor began commercial electrical recording in March 1925. There were still many individuals at Victor who had been intimately involved with recording the tenor for many years, and it was their hope that somehow Caruso's acoustically made recordings could be enhanced by the then new recording process. The files show that there were unsuccessful attempts to add modern electrical accompaniments to some of the old Caruso recordings during 1927 by Victor's musical director at the time, Rosario Bourdon. It was not until August 1932 that what were considered acceptable results were obtained. The first two sides to be released were new cuts of the 1917 *Marta* (No. 166) and the 1907 *Pagliacci* (No. 182), which were placed on the market in October 1932. *Time* magazine considered the event "newsworthy" and, in its issue of October 24, described the re-recording process and gave credit for what it considered a significant event to Victor's technician Raymond Sooy and conductor Nathaniel Shilkret. Critics were generally impressed with the results, special praise coming from Compton Mackenzie and Herman Klein in the British publication *The Gramophone*. In the December 1932 issue Klein wrote:

> The resulting effect is truly marvelous—something on which to congratulate everyone concerned. . . . The success of the Caruso example in many respects exceeds my highest expectations. . . . The voice, whilst retaining all its old beauty and quality, is now brought out with abundant power. The balance between it and the orchestra is carefully preserved and discreetly graduated so as to be strong when the well-remembered tones are at their loudest; and then they are very rich and resonant indeed. . . . In both cases another great point that strikes one is the total absence of scratching or blasting or any of the mechanical blemishes of the early days.

A total of seven sides were satisfactorily reprocessed by Victor in 1932, and these, with one additional side (conducted by Cibelli) in April 1933, constituted all Victor's Camden-made releases. It was in the midst of the Great Depression; Victor must have felt that the expense involved was not warranted by total sales. The baton was then passed to HMV at Hayes which continued to produce "re-recorded" Caruso recordings (and even two by Tetrazzini) for several years. For whatever reason, Victor's techniques did not accompany the baton, for nearly all the HMV re-issues are vastly inferior to the Victor products. In all honesty, some are excruciatingly bad and can be dismissed as far inferior to the original recordings.

The question of speeds used on these re-recordings is indeed curious. Some have been corrected from their original speeds to a convenient 78.26 rpm; others were dubbed so that the speeds of the originals were retained; still others have some very peculiar speeds of their own. The following summary of this re-issue series from both sides of the Atlantic is intended to present an overview of the whole effort. Note that these recordings were all produced and sold during the "78 rpm" era and have nothing whatsoever to do with the digitally restored recordings which appeared many years later on "Long Playing" records and which did not involve the addition of new orchestral accompaniment.

Discog. No.	Abbreviated Title	Original Matrix No.	New (Electrical) Matrix No.-Take	Date of Re-recording	Victor or HMV and Conductor	New Catalog Numbers	Speed of Re-issues
31.	Mattinata	G&T 2181h	OB-5527-1,-2	20 Dec.'33	HMV/	Not issued	----
33.	A Granada	C-22124-3	BS-76050-1	24 Apr.'33	V/Cibelli	17-5001; 26571	78.26
		C-22124-3	CS-76051-1	24 Apr.'33	V/Cibelli	Not issued	----
36.	'A Vucchella	B-23138-3	BVE-23138-5 to 11	3 Nov.'27	V/Bourdon	Not issued	----
37.	Addio (Tosti)	C-9747-1	2EA 653-1 to 4	23 Oct.'34	HMV/	Not issued	----
		C-9747-1	2EA 5828-1	29 Oct.'37	HMV/Collingwood	DB3327; DB 5387	----
38.	Addio a Napoli	B-23140-6	BVE-23140-1	23 Sep.'27	V/Bourdon	Not issued	----
		B-23140-6	OEA 6751-1	9 Sep.'38	HMV/	2212; DA 1655	75.00
40.	AFRICANA: O paradiso!	C-4160-2	2EA 4012-1	8 Jul.'36	HMV/Goehr	14234; DB 2991	78.26
42.	Agnus Dei	C-12942-1	2EA 1571-2A	19 Oct.'35	HMV/Collingwood	17814; DB 2644	78.26
45.	AIDA: Celeste Aida	C-11423-1	CS-74803-1	3 Dec.'32	V/Shilkret	7770; 8993; 12-1014; DB 1875	76.00
61.	Because	B-12680-2	OB 5151-1	25 Oct.'33	HMV/	1688; DA 1380	78.26
64.	BOHÈME: Che gelida	C-3101-1	2EA 4094-1,-2	23 Oct.'36	HMV/Collingwood	Not issued	----
76.	CARMEN: Il fior	C-8349-1	2EA 4093-2A	23 Oct.'36	HMV/Collingwood	14234; 12-1016; DB 3023; DB 5388	78.26
81.	CAV. RUST.: Addio	C-14202-2	2EA 4125-1	13 Nov.'36	HMV/L.S.O. Collingwood	15732; 12-1016; DB 3023	76.00
93.	A Dream	B-24466-3	BVE-24466-1	27 Sep.'27	V/Bourdon	Not issued	----
		B-24466-3	BS-71799-1	3 Dec.'32	V/Shilkret	S-1617; 1658; DA 1349	78.26
100.	ELISIR: Una furtiva	C-996 (sic)	CS-74801-1,-2	3 Dec.'32	V/Shilkret	Not issued	----
		C-996 (sic)	2EA 8402-1	9 Nov.'39	HMV/	11-8112; DB 3903	76.00
117.	For you alone	B-9744-1	OB 5102-3	25 Oct.'33	HMV/	1658; DA 1349	78.00
119.	FORZA: Solenne	C-3179-1	CS-74802-1,-2,-3	3 Dec.'32	V/Shilkret	Not issued	----
132.	Hosanna	C-12681-2	2EA 4188-1	8 Jan.'37	HMV/L.S.O. Collingwood	17814; DB 3122	81.00
141.	Lost chord	C-11942-1	2B 3570-2A	3 Nov.'33	HMV/Organ: Dawson	8806; DB 2073	78.26
143.	Love me or not	C-23713-4	2B 5103-1,-2	29 Oct.'33	HMV/	Not issued	----
149.	Luna d'estate	B-17123-3	BVE-17123-1 to 4	23 Sep.'27	V/Bourdon	Not issued	----
		B-17123-3	BVE-17123-5 to 7	27 Sep.'27	V/Bourdon	Not issued	----
		B-17123-3	BVE-17123-8 to 12	3 Nov.'27	V/Bourdon	Not issued	----

No.	Title	Matrix	Take	Date	Label/Conductor	Catalog	Speed
166.	MARTA: M'apparì	C-3100-2	CS-58965-1A	15 Aug.'32	V/Shilkret	7720; 12-1015; DB 1802	76.60
169.	Mia canzone, La	B-15481-3	OB 5990-2	25 May.'34	HMV/Collingwood	1688; DA 1380	78.26
172.	Musica proibita	C-15480-5	OEA 6752-2	9 Sep.'38	HMV/	2212; DA 1655	75.00
176.	'O sole mio	B-17124-1	BVE-17124-2 to 7	3 Nov.'27	V/Bourdon	Not issued	----
182.	PAGLIACCI: Vesti	B-17124-1	BS-58967-1A	15 Aug.'32	V/Shilkret	1616; DA 1303	76.60
184.	Parted (Tosti)	C-4317-1	CS-58966-1A	15 Aug.'32	V/Shilkret	7720; 12-1015; DB 1802	76.60
186.	Partida, La	B-14550-1	2EA 5829-1	29 Oct.'37	HMV/	DB 3327	----
		C-22122-1	BS-76052-1 to 3	24 Apr.'33	V/Cibelli	Not issued	----
		C-22122-1	CS-76053-1 to 3	24 Apr.'33	V/Cibelli	Not issued	----
188.	PÊCH. DE PERLES	C-18822-3	CS-74804-1	3 Dec.'32	V/Shilkret	7770; DB 1875	78.26
198.	Procession, La	C-17121-3	2EA 4186-1	8 Jan.'37	HMV/L.S.O. Collingwood	14744; DB 3078	76.60
199.	Rameaux, Les	C-14201-2	2EA 4187-1	8 Jan.'37	HMV/L.S.O. Collingwood	14744; DB 3122	76.60
202.	REINE DE SABA	C-17125-2	2EA 4126-1	13 Nov.'36	HMV/L.S.O. Collingwood	15732; DB 3078	72.72
205.	RIGOLETTO: Questa	B-6035-1	OB-6072-1	28 Feb.'34	HMV/Collingwood	Not issued	----
206.	RIGOLETTO: Parmi	C-11421-2	2EA 8403-1	9 Nov.'39	HMV/	11-8112; DB 3903	76.00
208.	RIGOLETTO: La donna	B-6033-1	BS-71800-1	3 Dec.'32	V/Shilkret	1616; DA 1303	76.60
221.	Santa Lucia	C-17344-1	2EA 652-2	23 Oct.'34	HMV/Collingwood	DB 2991; DB 5387	78.26
229.	SERSE: "Largo"	C-23714-5	2B 3571-1	3 Nov.'33	HMV/Organ: Dawson	8806; DB 2073; DB 5388	78.26
232.	Sultano a Tte	B-22515-5	OB 6071-2	28 Nov.'34	HMV/Collingwood	DA 1367	72.73
236.	TOSCA: Recondita	B-8347-1	2EA 1570-2A	19 Oct.'35	HMV/Collingwood	11-8569; DB 2644	78.26
240.	TOSCA: E lucevan	B-8346-1	OEA 4011-1,-2	8 Jul.'36	HMV/Goehr	Not issued	----
254.	Trusting eyes	B-14203-4	OB 5528-1,-2	20 Dec.'33	HMV/	Not issued	----
		B-14203-4	OEA 5832-1	29 Oct.'37	HMV/	DA 1656	78.26
260.	Vaghissima	B-24463-4	OB 6070-2	28 Feb.'34	HMV/Collingwood	DA 1367	72.73
262.	Your eyes have told	B-13106-2	OB 5529-1	20 Dec.'33	HMV/	Not issued	----
		B-13106-2	OEA 6753-2	9 Sep.'38	HMV/	DA 1656	78.26

Caruso Discography Notes

1. Early copies of these recordings show the original identifications as handwritten on the wax blanks at the time of recording by the technicians. Messrs. Gaisberg apparently had a little trouble with the spelling of the name of the singer. On this, his first record, it is written "Carusso."

3. This time the singer's name was spelled "Cauroso." The record ends with the aria as written, with a *pp* B-flat, followed by two piano chords. See notes for Discog. No. 13.

8. There is a muted false entrance, two beats early.

9. Caruso begins with the wrong note in the wrong place, and there is some confusion until he and Maestro Cottone get things straightened out.

13. The singer stops abruptly before the end of the aria, thus omitting the final B-flat. The pianist also stops with Caruso's last note.

20. Thanks to Aida Favia-Artsay (1965) for the correct identification of this song, which has been variously credited to Denza and Tosti in previous discographies and on record labels. In this recording, Caruso makes a false start in the second stanza then corrects himself and comes back in where he should.

44. C-3180-1 was unpublished, but special pressings are in circulation. Like C-3180-3, there is no recitative (as in C-11423-1). In the third measure: pause and breath between "forma . . . divina." In the sixth measure, there is a portamento between "serto" and "di luce e fior" in the next measure. In the tenth measure, there is a portamento between "pensiero" and "tu sei regina" in the next measure. In the twenty-ninth measure, there is a portamento between "raggio" and "di luce e fior" in the next measure. The phrase "Il tuo bel cielo . . . del patria suol" is sung in one breath, with no portamento at the end. C-3180-3 was published. To determine which of the two versions might have been used on any given transfer, note the studio noise during the last part of "Celeste" at the opening. Third measure: no portamento. Sixth measure: no break as above. Tenth measure: a breath between "pensiero" and "tu sei regina." Twenty-ninth measure: breath between "raggio" and "di luce e fior." The phrase "il tuo bel cielo" . . . there is a break for breath between "darti" and "le dolce brezze" with a portamento from F to G-flat between "suol" and "un regal" at the end (note from Fagan and Moran [1985]).

69. The story of the making of this recording has been related in the text of this book. Only a few copies of the original were pressed at the time and presented to friends. A vinyl "78 rpm" dubbing was custom-made by RCA for a radio program in 1949 but was never listed in the Victor catalogs. The HMV shellac issue in England and elsewhere was made from the same dubbed copy and publically released for a short time. The "catalog number" 87499 was printed on the label of the RCA release, but this was a spurious number invented for the occasion and is not found in the original Victor files. The original master no longer exists.

74. The original parts for all three takes of this recording were destroyed. All versions of the duet which exist today were made from a test pressing which was in the possession of Mme. Alda, said to be Take 3. The catalog number 89083 was originally assigned, but when the record was not approved, it was later used for Discog. No. 34.

91. Both versions are sung one-half tone low to the score. Take 1, the original issue, is sung at a leisurely pace. The eight-bar orchestral introduction lasts for 20

seconds, and the playing time for the entire record is 4' 20". Take 2, issued for the first time in RCA Victor's "Heritage Series" in 1948, is rather hurried. The orchestral introduction is shortened to 4 bars (10 seconds); the playing time for the entire record is 3' 21".

116. Today this is often attributed to Bellini, but De Mura (1969) states that the song is of Sicilian origin and that the Neapolitan version "is almost certainly" by Giulio Genoino (1773–1856) with two additional verses added, in 1854, by Mariano Paolella (1835–1868). The music was composed by Guglielmo Cottrau (1797–1847).

122. The date for this recording session was changed from 21 November (when the matrix numbers were assigned) to 26 November, and it is possible that Caruso and Amato did not originally intend to record both parts of the *Forza* duet, as Parts 1 and 2 were originally assigned the same matrix number. This was never altered in Victor's files, but HMV pressings of Part 2 have a "½" added to the matrix number their copies display.

128. The Victor files first listed this recording as "Gioconda: Oh sommo Dio!" but this was corrected to read "A te questo rosario." This would be the scene in Act IV between Gioconda, Enzo, and Laura in which Gioconda (Destinn) begins "Che vedo là! il rosario! oh sommo Dio! Così dicea la profezia profonda: *A te questo rosario che le preghiera aduna . . .*". This should not be confused with the same words sung by La Cieca in Act I. No copy of this recording is known to exist, so the whole matter is rather academic.

138. This "Spanish serenade" with both words and music by the Italian composer Arturo Buzzi-Peccia (1856–1943) was dedicated to Enrico Caruso. It is sung in Italian, in spite of the Spanish language catalog number given it by The Gramophone Company.

166. C-3100-1: The final B-flat is preceded by a C within the staff. The last words are "Ah morro," followed by an orchestral postlude. This take only appeared with the double-faced number 6002 in Canada.
C-3100-2: There is no preparatory C before the final B-flat. The final words are "Sì, morrò," followed by two orchestral chords. The original 1917 version was never released in Canada nor in Europe.

174. Often attributed to Pergolesi, this song is said to have been introduced into the opera *Gli Tre Cicisbei Ridicoli* by the conductor Ciampi. Several authorities list Ciampi as the composer of this opera, which could actually be another name for his famous *Bertoldo*.

192. The Swiss composer Louis Niedermeyer (1802–1862) wrote an opera called *Stradella* in 1837, which is perhaps why this music is sometimes (as on Victor labels) attributed to the subject of the opera, Allessandro Stradella.

197. All issues are electrical dubbings from BVE-23144-6, dubbed from B-23144-4. Some pressings do not show the VE symbol, but all show Take 6R. No new orchestra was added.

201. Double-faced copies are marked Take 2 in error. There was only one 10" recording, made 7 November 1909. The error may have originated because of the unpublished 12" version (C-6062-1) made 29 March 1908.

214. The original is an unpublished 10" autographed test pressing in the author's collection. The record closes with the beginning of the contralto's first phrase. It is thought that this was made during a rehearsal for the published 1917 *Rigoletto* Quartet. The pressing carries no numbers. It has been made available as a 7"

dubbing (coupled with an unpublished 1916 Melba recording of "Songs my mother taught me") by the Stanford Archive of Recorded Sound. The Stanford edition (issued in 1973) has Caruso's original inscription, "To Caruso by Enrico," reproduced on the label.

219.   The "Metropolitan Opera Chorus" advertised on the label consists of eight men and eight women, according to the recording sheets.

249.   Recorded a semi-tone below score pitch in the key of B (rather than in the original key of C major). Thus Caruso's high notes are Bs, not Cs. This recording has been speeded up on some LP releases to make the final note a C, and some editions even had the duration of the high notes extended by tape splicing! *All releases of this title by Caruso are from the single 1906 recording listed here.*

252.   C-6036-1: Caruso ends the duet on middle B (within the staff) as in the score. C-6036-2: Caruso ends with an interpolated high G. This second edition carries a tiny letter "R" in the inner rim at the 3 o'clock position, a symbol used at the time to alert dealers to the fact that this was a newly made recording replacing an older one under the same catalog number. Copies also carry the take number, 2, at the 9 o'clock position.

Bibliography

Bolig, John Richard. *The Recordings of Enrico Caruso: A Discography.* Dover, Delaware: Eldridge Reeves Johnson Memorial, Delaware State Museum, 1973. 88 pp.

Bolig, John Richard. "A Caruso Discography." *In* Scott, Michael. *The Great Caruso.* New York: Knopf, 1988, pp. 265–93.

Bruun, Carl L. "A Caruso Discography." *Record Collector* 4, no. 6 (June 1949).

Caiden, Jack L. "Caruso Recordings: A Discography." *In* Caruso, Dorothy. *Enrico Caruso: His Life and Death.* New York: Simon and Schuster, 1945, pp. 289–301.

De Mura, Ettore. *Enciclopedia della Canzone Napoletana* (Encyclopedia of Neapolitan Song), 3 Vols. Naples: Casa Editrice Il Torchio, 1969. 1534 pp.

Drummond, H. J. "Discography." *In* Caruso, Dorothy. *Enrico Caruso: His Life and Death.* London: T. Werner Laurie, 1946.

Fagan, Ted, and William R. Moran. *The Encyclopedic Discography of Victor Recordings.* Vol. 1: *Pre-Matrix Series.* Westport, Connecticut: Greenwood Press, 1983. 393 pp.

Fagan, Ted, and William R. Moran. *The Encyclopedic Discography of Victor Recordings.* Vol. 2: *Matrix Series 1 through 4999.* Westport, Connecticut; Greenwood Press, 1986. 648 pp.

Fagan, Ted, and William R. Moran. *The Encyclopedic Discography of Victor Recordings.* Vol. 3: *Catalog Numbers, 1900–1926.* Westport, Connecticut: Greenwood Press (in preparation).

Favia-Artsay, Aida. *Caruso on Records.* Valhalla, New York: Historic Record, 1965. 218 pp.

Freestone, J., and H. J. Drummond. *Enrico Caruso: His Recorded Legacy.* London: Sidgwick and Jackson, 1960; Minneapolis: T. S. Denison, 1961. 130 pp.

Gaisberg, F. W. "Notes from My Diary: Enrico Caruso." *Gramophone* 21, 248 (January 1944).

Kelly, Alan. *His Master's Voice / La Voce del Padrone: The Italian Catalog.* Westport, Connecticut: Greenwood Press, 1988. 462 pp.

Moran, William R. "Discography: Rules and Goals." *Recorded Sound: The Journal of the British Institute of Recorded Sound,* no. 66–67 (April–July 1977).

Potter, Robert W. F. "Enrico Caruso." *Gramophone* 8, nos. 91–95 (December 1930–April 1931).

Secrist, John, "Caruso Discography." *In* Robinson, Francis. *Caruso: His Life in Pictures.* New York: Thomas Y. Crowell, 1957; reprint edition, New York: Bramhall House, no date. 160 pp.

Sokol, Martin L. "The Pre-Victor Recordings of Enrico Caruso." *Antique Phonograph Monthly* 5, no. 4 (1977).

Post-1950 Re-issues

by Richard Koprowski

INTRODUCTION

Had Caruso lived to be 78 years old, he would have witnessed a trans-formation of his recordings. In 1951 RCA Victor began to re-issue the music Caruso made for Victor, not at the old nominal (and incorrect) 78 rpm, but on discs that spun at 45 and 33⅓ rpm. Previously the pur-chase of an individual operatic excerpt sung by the great tenor was an "event"—and this was the milieu in which they had been created: Victor never issued a double-sided Caruso disc until after the singer's death. But now there was the potential to hear the voice of Caruso in a number of selections, all without changing a record.

At first RCA Victor seems to have been of two minds about how to deal with their Caruso legacy at the new slower speeds. There were a few Caruso collections, but many of the re-issues appeared only as 45s. Though these were often part of albums, individual discs still had, at the most, a coupling of Caruso selections, very much like the familiar "78s." ("Extended Play" [EP] 45s, with more than one Caruso selec-tion per side, appeared in 1953.)

But by the mid-1950s RCA was re-issuing all its Caruso material at 33⅓ rpm, on "Long Playing" (LP) albums with many selections. By 1960—only ten years after Caruso's first appearance on LP—RCA had re-issued over 60% of its Caruso material. The Caruso centennial year saw a large number of recordings devoted to the tenor, including a non-RCA "Complete Caruso" that was neither complete nor well pro-duced. It wasn't until 1978 that RCA began to publish its own "com-plete" Caruso edition. This will probably never be finished on LP (some volumes are already out of print), but the company plans to make one available on CD in the fall of 1990.

The following discography covers the period from 1951 to mid-1989. It focuses on RCA Victor's re-issuing of its Caruso material. Also included are other significant commercial American recordings and, very selectively, related releases. Quality was not a criterion; rather, the objective was to create as inclusive a listing as possible. Many re-issues are plagued with documentation and/or speed and pitch problems. In cases where these seem more than usually serious, note is made accordingly.

The producers of early re-issues usually re-recorded Caruso originals at about 78 rpm, not determining if that was the speed at which they had been recorded. Thus the pitch, tempo, and timbre may be misrepresented. Later producers paid attention to speeds, but some re-issues exhibit a startling inconsistency in this regard. The discography also makes passing reference to other reprocessing. It is probable that more work (and tampering, as in Discography Number 62E below) has been done to "improve" and "enhance" the Caruso legacy than any other segment of record history. The three selections in common on two 1985 releases (85A and 85D) provide an opportunity to hear very different RCA reprocessing of the same material, ostensibly done at about the same time.

This discography is arranged chronologically by year of issue, tracing the changing interest in Caruso's recordings; within a year, recordings are listed by label name and number, with RCA recordings appearing first. Issue dates were determined using copyright information, company catalogs, and the Schwann Catalog and *Classical Recordaid* (for the early years). Each recording is "numbered" using the last two digits for the year of release followed by a lowercase letter for 45s ("55a") or an uppercase letter for LPs ("66A"); upper- and lowercase letters for a recording released at both speeds ("51Oo"); or an uppercase letter with an asterisk for a CD ("87A*").

Before the discography proper there is an index keyed to the number of the original Caruso recording as assigned to it by William R. Moran in the preceding discography. Within the present discography, each recording is identified by title (either from the record label or the jacket) and the company name and number (for RCA recordings, only the number is given; if a recording appeared as both an LP and a 45 album, the LP number appears first). The number of LP discs, if more than one, is given in parentheses. Finally, the content of each re-issue is indicated with Moran numbers. Following the discography is a label name-and-number index.

Acknowledgments

I am grateful for assistance from the following: Andrew Farkas and William R. Moran; Ed Glazier of The Research Libraries Group, Michael Colby of San Francisco Public Library, and John D. Arnn of Baker & Taylor Books; Bernie Lozia of RCA/BMG; the staff of the Rodgers and Hammerstein Archives of Recorded Sound (The New York Public Library); and Barbara Sawka and Aurora Perez of the Stanford Archive of Recorded Sound.

INDEX KEYED TO WILLIAM R. MORAN
DISCOGRAPHY OF ORIGINAL RECORDINGS

Moran No.	Re-issues on LP (uppercase), 45 rpm (lowercase), and CD (asterisk)
1	58B, 59A, 63A, 73F, 75A, 89A*, 89B*
2	58B, 58C, 59A, 61A, 63A, 70B, 73F, 75A, 89A*, 89B*
3	58D, 59A, 61A, 63A, 70B, 89B*
4	58B, 58C, 59A, 63A, 73F, 75A, 89A*, 89B*
5	61A, 63A, 70B, 73F, 75A, 89A*, 89B*
6	58B, 59A, 61A, 63A, 70B, 73F, 75A, 89A*, 89B*
7	58B, 63A, 73F, 75A, 89A*, 89B*
8	58D, 61A, 63A, 70B, 89B*
9	58B, 61A, 63A, 70B, 73F, 75A, 89A*, 89B*
10	58B, 58C, 59A, 61A, 63A, 70B, 73F, 75A, 89A*, 89B*
11	58B, 58C, 59A, 63B, 73F, 75A, 89A*
12	56A, 58B, 59A, 61A, 63B, 70B, 73D, 73F, 75A, 89A*, 89B*
13	58B, 63B, 73F, 75A, 89A*
14	58B, 59A, 61A, 63B, 70B, 73F, 75A, 89A*, 89B*
15	58B, 58C, 59A, 61A, 63B, 70B, 72A, 73F, 75A, 89A*, 89B*
16	58B, 61A, 63B, 70B, 73F, 75A, 89A*, 89B*
17	58C, 61A, 63B, 70B, 73F, 75A, 89A*, 89B*
18	61A, 63B, 70B, 73F, 75A, 89A*, 89B*
19	58B, 58C, 59A, 61A, 63B, 70B, 73F, 75A, 89A*, 89B*
20	58C, 61A, 63B, 70B, 73F, 75A, 89A*, 89B*
21	56B, 58D, 59A, 61A, 62C, 70B, 73F, 75A, 89A*, 89B*
22	56B, 58D, 59A, 62C, 73F, 75A, 89A*
23	56B, 58C, 59A, 62C, 73F, 75A, 89A*

Moran No.	Re-issues on LP (uppercase), 45 rpm (lowercase), and CD (asterisk)
24	56B, 58C, 59A, 62C, 73F, 75A, 89A*
25	56B, 58C, 59A, 62C, 73F, 75A, 89A*
26	56B, 58D, 59A, 62C, 73F, 75A, 89A*
27	56B, 58C, 59A, 62C, 73F, 75A, 89A*
28	56B, 59A, 62C, 73F, 75A, 89A*, 89B*
29	56B, 62C, 73F, 75A, 89A*
30	56B, 59A, 61A, 62C, 70B, 73F, 75A, 89A*, 89B*
31	53K, 61A, 63B, 70B, 73B, 73D, 73F, 75A, 89A*, 89B*
32	63B, 73F, 75A, 89A*, 89B*
33	52Aa, 73D, 73F, 84B
34	56A, 73D, 73F, 84A
36	52Aa, 73D, 73E, 73F, 84B
37	65A, 73D, 73F, 80A
38	51i, 73C, 73D, 73F, 84B
39	73C, 73F, 78B
40	51P, 56A, 58A, 73A, 73D, 73F, 76A, 78A, 85D, 87A*
41	62A, 73D, 73F, 85A
42	51a, 51Nn, 73D, 73E, 73F, 82B
43	69A, 69B, 73F
44-1	73C, 78A
44-3	73C, 73F, 78B
45	51e, 51P, 53d, 56A, 58A, 60B, 62B, 71B, 73A, 73D, 73F, 76A, 77A, 80B, 84D, 85D, 87A*
46	52Bb, 71B, 73D, 73F, 80A
47	52Bb, 71B, 73D, 73F, 80A
48	61B, 62A, 62D, 71B, 73D, 73F, 79A
49	61B, 62A, 71B, 73D, 73F, 79A
50-1	73C
50-2	53K, 73A, 73D, 73E, 73F, 84A
51	56A, 58A, 73D, 73F, 85A
52	53K, 73D, 73F, 83A
53	62A, 73D, 73F, 78A, 84D

Moran No.	Re-issues on LP (upper-case), 45 rpm (lowercase), and CD (asterisk)	Moran No.	Re-issues on LP (upper-case), 45 rpm (lowercase), and CD (asterisk)
54	64A, 73D, 73F, 84A, 87A*	97	56A, 73D, 73F, 84B
56	51c, 51Kk, 53J, 73B, 73D, 73F, 82B	98	56A, 58A, 60B, 69B, 73F, 85B
57	62A, 62D, 73D, 73F, 83A, 85C	99	69B, 73F, 85B
		100	51g, 51P, 62B, 73B, 73D, 73F, 76A, 80A, 87A*
58	52Aa, 73D, 73F, 80A, 88A*	101	73C, 73D, 73F, 80A
59	51Ll, 53f, 61B, 62D, 73D, 73F, 83A, 88A*	102	64A, 73D, 73F, 84A
60	73C, 73D, 73F, 77A, 80B, 84D, 88A*	103	53H, 73D, 73F, 79B
		104	53e, 53H, 73B, 73D, 73F, 76A, 78A, 87A*
61	51Kk, 73A, 73D, 73F, 82A	105	53H, 73F, 79A
62	73C, 73D, 73F, 80A	106	53H, 73F, 79A
63	52Aa, 73D, 73F, 80A	107	51Mm, 53H, 73D, 73F, 79A
64	51P, 53c, 56A, 58A, 60B, 73B, 73D, 73F, 76A, 78A, 84D, 85D, 87A*	108	51Mm, 53H, 73D, 73F, 79A
		110	53H, 73D, 73F, 79B
65	55B, 73D, 73F, 78A	111	73C, 73F, 79B
66	56A, 58A, 60B, 73F, 82A	112	73F, 79B
67	64A, 73D, 73F, 78B	114	53f, 53H, 73D, 73F, 79B
68	73C, 73D, 73F, 78A	115	55B, 60A, 69B, 73D, 73F, 78A, 87A*
69	73C, 73D, 73F, 83B	116	56A, 73D, 73F, 82B
70	56A, 58A, 73D, 73F, 84B	117	51c, 51Kk, 62A, 73D, 73F, 79B
71	73C, 73D, 73F, 84B		
72	73C, 73D, 73F, 80A	118	53b, 73C, 73D, 73F, 79A, 84D, 87A*, 73D, 73F, 88A*
73	53J, 73D, 73F, 83B		
74	73C, 83A	119	51Mm, 53g, 56A, 58A, 60B, 73A, 73F, 78A, 85D, 88A*
75	69B, 73F	120	73C, 73D, 73F, 84B, 88A*
76	73C, 73F, 79A	121	62D, 64A, 73D, 73F, 80B, 88A*
77	51d, 51P, 53e, 56A, 58A, 73B, 73D, 73F, 76A, 79A, 84D, 85D, 87A*	122	64A, 73D, 73F, 80B
		123	64A, 73D, 73F, 79B
78	69B, 73F	124	64A, 73D, 73F, 79B
79	53a, 62A, 73D, 73F, 79B	126	69B, 73F
80	69B, 73D, 73F	127	51e, 51P, 56A, 58A, 60B, 73A, 73D, 73F, 76A, 77A, 79B, 84D, 85D, 87A*
81	52Dd, 73A, 73D, 73F, 82B, 84D		
82	53K, 73F, 84A	129	73D, 73F, 83A, 62A
83	52Aa, 56A, 58A, 62B, 73D, 73F, 83B	130	53K, 61B, 73D, 73F, 82B
84	53K, 73D, 73F, 83A	131	53K, 73D, 73F, 83A
85	62A, 73A, 73D, 73F, 80A	132	53J, 73E, 73F, 82A
86	65A, 73D, 73F, 80B	133	65A, 73D, 73F, 78A
87	51i, 61B, 62A, 73D, 73F, 82A	134	65A, 73D, 73F, 85A
		135	73C, 73D, 73F, 84B
88	56A, 73D, 73F, 83B	136	51P, 54a, 56A, 58A, 62B, 66A, 73A, 73D, 73F, 76A, 77A, 84C, 85A, 85D, 87A*
89	64A, 73D, 73F, 82A, 88A*		
90	61B, 69B, 73D, 73F	137	73C, 73D, 73F, 82B
91-1	56A, 73C, 73D, 73F, 78B	138	65A, 73D, 73F, 78B
91-2	73F, 78B	140	56A, 62D, 73D, 73F, 80B, 84D, 88A*
93	73C, 73D, 73E, 73F, 85A		
94	53I, 73D, 73F, 82A	141	51Kk, 73D, 73E, 73F, 82A
95	61B, 73C, 73D, 73F, 83B		
96	51Kk, 73D, 73F, 82B		

Moran No.	Re-issues on LP (upper-case), 45 rpm (lowercase), and CD (asterisk)	Moran No.	Re-issues on LP (upper-case), 45 rpm (lowercase), and CD (asterisk)
142	73C, 73D, 73E, 73F, 80B	182	51b, 51P, 52Ee, 53d, 55a,
143	73C, 73D, 73F, 85A		56A, 58A, 60B, 62B, 73B,
144	62D, 73C, 73F, 78B		73D, 73F, 76A, 78A, 84D,
145	73C, 73E, 73F, 82A		85D, 87A*
146-1	73C	183	53a, 55B, 60A, 73D, 73F,
146-2	51Ll, 53f, 56A, 58A, 60B,		79B, 85B
	73B, 73D, 73F, 84A, 85D	184	73C, 73F, 83A
149	56A, 58A, 62B, 73D, 73F,	185	73F, 83A
	83B, 85D	186	56A, 58A, 73D, 73F, 84B
150	55B, 56A, 73D, 73F, 83B,	187	65A, 73D, 73F, 83B
	84D, 88A*	188	73C, 73D, 73F, 84A, 85C
151	62A, 71A, 73D, 73F, 79B	189	51P, 53e, 73D, 73F, 77A,
152	52Cc, 53g, 61B, 71A, 73D,		84A, 87A*
	73F, 78B	191	61B, 62D, 73D, 73F, 78A
153	56A, 71A, 73D, 73F, 79B	192	53J, 62A, 73D, 73F, 84B
154	65A, 73D, 73F, 79A	193	65A, 73D, 73F, 82A
155	65A, 73D, 73F, 83A	194	53K, 73D, 73F, 84A
156	55B, 73D, 73F, 82A	195	53a, 73C, 73D, 73F, 78B
157	64A, 69B, 73D, 73F	197	65A, 73D, 73F, 85A
158	56A, 58A, 73D, 73F, 80B,	198	73C, 73D, 73F, 83B
	85C	199-2	73C, 73D, 82B
159	53c, 53L, 55B, 56A, 73D,	199-3	73F, 83A
	73F, 77A, 82B	200	73C, 73F, 84B
161	73C, 73D, 73F, 79B	201	53a, 61B, 73C, 73D, 73F,
162	62D, 64A, 73D, 73F, 80B		79A
163	73C, 73F, 80B	202	73C, 73D, 73F, 83B
164	73D, 73F, 80B	203	65A, 73D, 73F, 83B, 88A*
165	56A, 58A, 62D, 73B, 73D,	204	69B, 73F
	73F, 80B	205	51h, 51Oo, 53b, 56A, 58A,
166-1	73D, 73F, 76A, 78A, 84A,		60B, 73A, 73D, 73F, 76A,
	84D, 87A*		77A, 78B, 85D, 87A*, 88A*
166-2	51b, 52Dd, 53d, 55a, 56A,	206	51g, 64A, 73A, 73D, 73F,
	73A, 73F		82A, 84D
167	56A, 73D, 73F, 85A	207	69B, 73F
168	52Aa, 53J, 73D, 73F, 85A	208	51h, 51P, 53b, 56A, 58A,
169	51f, 73C, 73D, 73F, 83A		60B, 62B, 73A, 73D, 73F,
170	73D, 73F, 83B		76A, 77A, 78B, 85D, 87A*
171	73C, 73D, 73F, 83A	209	62D, 73C, 73F, 78A
172	65A, 73D, 73F, 84A	211	66A, 73C, 73F, 77A, 78B
173-1	73C	212	73C, 73F, 82A
173-2	64A, 73D, 73F, 84A	213	51Ll, 53f, 56A, 58A, 60B,
174	53K, 73D, 73F, 85A		71C, 73D, 73F, 84A, 85D
175	56A, 58A, 73D, 73F, 85A,	214	73G
	85D	217	64A, 73D, 73F, 85A
176	51f, 51Kk, 56A, 58A, 73A,	218	51Ll, 66A, 73D, 73F, 84B
	73D, 73F, 83B	219	62A, 73D, 73F, 77A, 84A
177	53a, 62A, 73D, 73F, 79B,	220	73C, 73D, 73F, 83B
	87A*, 88A*	221	73C, 73D, 73E, 73F, 84A
179	51Mm, 56A, 58A, 60B,	222	73C, 73D, 73F, 80A
	73D, 73F, 82B, 88A*	223	73C, 73D, 73F, 85A
180	56A, 58A, 73B, 73D, 73F,	224	51Kk, 56A, 58A, 73D, 73F,
	84B, 85D		84B
181	69B, 73F	225	73C, 73D, 73F, 85A

Moran No.	Re-issues on LP (upper-case), 45 rpm (lowercase), and CD (asterisk)	Moran No.	Re-issues on LP (upper-case), 45 rpm (lowercase), and CD (asterisk)
226	53K, 73D, 73F, 82B	246	70A, 73D, 73F, 80A, 88A*
227	73C, 73D, 73F, 83A	248	52Aa, 53b, 73D, 73F, 78B,
228	53K, 73D, 73F, 85A		88A*
229	51Kk, 53d, 56A, 58A, 60B,	249	51d, 52Aa, 53b, 56A, 62B,
	73B, 73D, 73F, 76A, 85A,		62E, 69B, 73A, 73D, 73F,
	85D, 87A*		76A, 78A, 84D, 87A*
230	73C, 73D, 73F, 83B	251-1	73C, 73F, 79A
231	65A, 73D, 73F, 82B	251-3	51Ll, 73D, 73F, 79A
232	73C, 73D, 73F, 84B	252-1	56A, 58A, 60B, 73D, 73F,
233	73C, 73D, 73E, 73F, 80B		78B, 85B, 85D
234	53K, 73D, 73F, 83B	252-2	70A, 73E, 73F, 80A
235	69B, 73F	253	53g, 53L, 73F, 82A
236	51Jj, 53c, 56A, 58A, 60B,	254	73C, 73D, 73F, 83A
	73B, 73D, 73F, 76A, 77A,	255	65A, 73D, 73F, 84B
	78B, 84D, 87A*	257	69B, 73F
239	69B, 73F	258	51Oo, 61B, 73D, 73F, 79A
240	52Aa, 53c, 73D, 73F, 76A,	259	53K, 73D, 73F, 84A
	77A, 78B, 84D, 87A*	260	52Aa, 56A, 58A, 73D, 73F,
244	52Cc, 53g, 56A, 73B, 73D,		85A
	73F, 83A	261	53K, 56A, 73D, 73F, 84B
245	73C, 73D, 73F, 78A	262	73C, 73F, 82B

THE RE-ISSUES

1951

51a	Agnus Dei (Bizet) (42) [with Chaliapin: Now let us depart (Strokin)] [from 51n]	17-00?
51b	MARTA: M'apparì (166-2) / PAGLIACCI: Vesti la giubba (182) [listed as 17-0122 in some catalogs]	17-0112 [re-release: 55
51c	Ave Maria (Kahn) (56) / For you alone (117)	17-01:
51d	CARMEN: Air de la fleur (77) / IL TROVATORE: Di quella pira (249)	17-01:
51e	AIDA: Celeste Aida (45) / La Gioconda: Cielo e mar (127)	17-01:
51f	La Mia canzone (169) / 'O sole mio (176)	17-01:
51g	L'ELISIR D'AMORE: Una furtiva lagrima (100) / RIGOLETTO: Parmi veder (206)	17-01:
51h	RIGOLETTO: Questa o quella (205) / La donna è mobile (208)	17-01:
51i	L'Addio a Napoli (38) / La Danza (87)	17-01:
51Jj	Composers' Favorite Interpretations 236	LCT-1; WCT
51Kk	Caruso Sings Light Music 176, 141, 117, 56, 229, 61, 96, 224	LCT-2; WCT
51Ll	Golden Age Ensembles 146(-2), 213, 59, 251(-3), 218	LCT-1003; WCT
51Mm	Golden Duets 179, 119, 107, 108	LCT-1004; WCT
51Nn	Sacred Songs 42	LCT-1005; WCT

| 51Oo | The Golden Age at the Metropolitan
205, 258 | LCT-1006; WCT-10 |
| 51Pp | Caruso Album
100, 127, 40, 64, 136, 45, 189, 77, 182, 208 | LCT-1007; WCT-11 |

1952

52Aa	Caruso in Opera and Song 58, 240, 260, 248, 249, 83, 36, 63, 33, 168	LCT-1034; WCT-35
52Bb	*Aida* of Yesterday 46, 47	LCT-1035; WCT-51
52Cc	Famous Duets 244, 152	LCT-1037; WCT-57
52Dd	Stars of the Golden Age 81, 166(-2)	LCT-1039; WCT-62
52Ee	Ten Tenors—Ten Arias 182	LM-1202; WDM-1626

1953

53a	Caruso in Five Famous Selections 79, 183, 177, 201, 195	ERAT-1
53b	Caruso: Five Verdi Arias 208, 118, 205, 248, 249	ERAT-4
53c	Caruso: Four Puccini Arias 236, 240, 64, 159	ERAT-5
53d	Caruso: The Four Caruso Best Sellers 182, 45, 166(-2), 229	ERAT-6
53e	Caruso 77, 104, 189	ERAT-7
53f	All Star Ensembles 146(-2), 114, 213, 59	ERAT-8
53g	Caruso in Duets 244, 119, 152, 253	ERAT-9
53Hh	Caruso in *Faust* 103, 104, 105, 106, 107, 108, 110, 114	LCT-1103; WCT-1103
53Ii	Old Curiosity Shop 94	LCT-1112; WCT-1112
53Jj	Caruso and McCormack Sing Christmas Music 73, 56, 168, 192, 132	LCT-1121; WCT-1121
53K	Caruso in Neapolitan Songs 130, 131, 194, 226, 31, 174, 261, 50(-2), 84, 52, 82, 234, 228, 259	LCT-1129
53L	Ten Unforgotten Stars 159, 253	LCT-1138

1954

| 54a | Four Tenors—Four Arias
136 | ERAT-26 |

1955

| 55a | MARTA: M'apparì (166-2) / PAGLIACCI: Vesti la giubba (182)
[re-release of 51b] | 447-0763 |
| 55B | 50 Years of Great Operatic Singing
1 & 2 (vol. 1, 1900–1910): 65, 115, 183
3 & 4 (vol. 2, 1910–1920): 150, 156, 159 | LCT-6701 (5) |

1956

56A   Caruso   LM-6127 (3)
       1: 45, 244, 249, 252(-1), 119, 205, 208, 213
       2: 150, 179, 140, 98, 97, 91(-1), 146(-2)
       3: 159, 64, 66, 236, 153, 12, 127, 182
       4: 77, 158, 40, 83, 136, 166(-2), 165
       5: 229, 88, 51, 116, 260, 175, 186, 34
       6: 176, 261, 20, 180, 70, 224, 149, 167

56B   Enrico Caruso, Tenor   Scala Records 825
       25, 23, 27, 24, 26, 21, 22, 28, 30, 29

1958

58A   The Best of Caruso   LM-6056 (2)
       1: 45, 119, 205, 208, 213, 252(-1), 179
       2: 229, 98, 146(-2), 64, 66, 236, 127, 182
       3: 51, 40, 77, 158, 83, 136, 165
       4: 176, 260 (from electrical re-recording), 70, 186, 175, 180, 224, 149

58B   Caruso Before His American Conquest   Eterna Records 725
       4, 12, 7, 1, 16, 10, 15, 14, 13, 11, 6, 2, 19, 9

58C   Enrico Caruso Recital   Rococo Records 2
       24, 27, 25, 23, 17, 20, 19, 11, 4, 10, 2, 15

58D   Enrico Caruso and Francesco Tamagno   Rococo Records 7
       26, 21, 22, 8, 3

1959

59A   Enrico Caruso: The First Recordings, 1901–1903   TAP Records T-307
       1: 15, 4, 1, 10, 12, 14, 3, 2, 11, 6, 19
       2: 24, 23, 26, 27, 25, 30, 21, 22, 28

1960

60A   50 Years of Great Operatic Singing: Tenors   LM-2372-c
       115, 183

60B   From *The Best of Caruso*   SP-33-75
       1: 45, 119, 205, 208, 213, 252(-1), 179
       2: 229, 98, 146(-2), 64, 66, 236, 127, 182
       [re-issue of first two sides of 58A]

1961

61A   The Young Caruso: Songs and Arias, Milan Recordings 1902–1903
       (Great Recordings of the Century)   Angel Records COLH 119
       1: 2, 5, 8, 6, 10, 3, 9, 4, 21
       2: 14, 16, 15, 18, 20, 17, 12, 19, 32, 31
       [re-released as 70B]

61B   Enrico Caruso [not released in the U.S., but part of the
       Great Recordings of the Century series]   His Master's Voice COLH 120
       90, 191, 152, 48, 49, 258, 201, 87, 130, 59, 95

1962

62A   Caruso: The Voice of the Century   LM-2639
       53, 79, 48, 49, 129, 177, 41, 219, 151, 57, 192, 85, 87, 117

62B   Ten Great Singers   LM-6705 (5)
       side 1: 249, 100, 208, 45, 182, 83, 136, 149

62C   Caruso: Complete, 1900-1904 (Volume 1)   AcoustoGraphic AG 1263
       21, 22, 23, 24, 25, 26, 27, 29, 30, 28

62D   Caruso Ensembles   Rococo Records 36
       191, 121, 209, 48, 144, 162, 165, 140, 57, 59

62E   "Di quella pira"—40 Tenors—80 High C's   TAP Records T-333
249 [The jacket notes, by Edward J. Smith, claim that this is a previously
unreleased version of the aria. This is not the case: the band consists of the
only recording Caruso made of the aria, recorded at the incorrect speed with
some interesting tape splicing.]

1963
63A   Caruso: Complete, 1900–1904 (Volume 2)   AcoustoGraphic AG 2363
2, 3, 4, 5, 6, 7, 8, 9, 10, 1
63B   Caruso: Complete, 1900–1904 (Volume 3)   AcoustoGraphic AG 31163
12, 14, 15, 16, 17, 18, 19, 20, 31, 11, 13, 32

1964
64A   Caruso Operatic Rarities   LM-2700
54, 206, 162, 121, 122, 157, 217, 102, 123, 124, 67, 173(-2), 89

1965
65A   Caruso in Song   LM-2778
255, 172, 193, 187, 133, 138, 37, 155, 134, 154, 197, 86, 231, 203

1966
66A   Opening Nights at the Met   LM-6171 (3)
     side 1: 211   side 2: 218, 136   1983 re-release: AGM3-4805

1969
69A   Unforgettable Voices in Unforgotten Performances from the
Italian Operatic Repertoire   VIC-1395
     side 2: 43
69B   Caruso: Immortal Performances   VIC-1430
1: 98, 99, 90, 115, 257, 75, 157(-2, not -1), 204, 207
2: 249, 43, 126, 235, 239, 78, 80, 181

1970
70A   Louise Homer: Profile of the Golden Age Contralto   VIC-1519
     side 2: 246, 252(-2)
70B   The Young Caruso   Seraphim 60146
     [re-release: see 61A]

1971
71A   The Met's First *Butterfly*   VIC-1600
     side 1: 151, 152   side 2: 153
71B   Golden Age *Aida*   VIC-1623
     side 1: 45   side 2: 46, 47, 48, 49
71C   Golden Age *Rigoletto*   VIC-1633
     side 2: 213

1972
72A   Great Tenors of the Century   Seraphim 60206
15

1973
73A   The Greatest Hits of Enrico Caruso, Vol. 1   ARM1-0278
205, 206, 208, 45, 249, 127, 40, 166(-2),
119, 136, 61, 50(-2), 85, 81, 176
73B   The Greatest Hits of Enrico Caruso, Vol. 2   ARM1-0279
182, 77, 64, 236, 165, 56,
244, 104, 100, 229, 31, 180, 146(-2)

73C Caruso: The Tenor of the Century ARM4-0302 (4)
1: 44(-1), 209, 68, 91(-1), 211(not 210), 144, 44(-3)
2: 118, 201, 76, 251(-1), 111, 161
3: 222, 62, 60, 163, 145, 212, 74
4: 95, 202, 69, 188, 146(-1), 173(-1), 120
5: 245, 39, 195, 101, 72, 142, 233, 262
6: 137, 199(-2), 227, 184, 254, 171, 169
7: 230, 198, 220, 221, 50(-1), 135
8: 71, 200, 232, 38, 225, 223, 143, 93
73D Enrico Caruso: Opera Arias and Songs Italian RCA LDM-70001 (12)
1a: 205, 206, 208, 213, 150, 177, 179, 140
1b: 57, 58, 59, 60, 118, 119, 120
2a: 121, 122, 246, 248, 249, 251(-3), 252(-1)
2b: 244, 89, 45, 46, 47, 48, 49
3a: 97, 100, 146(-2), 115, 90, 91(-1), 95
3b: 229, 51, 161, 162, 164, 165, 166(-1)
4a: 127, 129, 217, 222, 102, 201, 173(-2)
4b: 136, 103, 104, 107, 108, 110, 114
5a: 202, 258, 40, 41, 191, 189*, 188
5b: 77, 218, 219, 156, 157(-2, not -1), 158, 83
6a: 159, 64, 65, 67, 68, 69, 236, 240
6b: 151, 152, 153, 79, 80, 81, 182
7a: 183, 62, 63, 53, 54, 12, 123, 124
7b: 176, 187, 255, 36, 155, 223, 38*
8a: 134, 85, 72, 130, 84, 233, 234
8b: 221, 232, 87, 154, 116, 259, 225
9a: 172, 133, 138, 174, 228, 37*, 31
9b: 261, 50(-2), 193, 260*, 52, 224, 71
10a: 149, 169*, 101, 137, 245, 70, 170, 135
10b: 61, 230, 197, 195, 96, 131, 194, 226, 227
11a: 199(-2), 88, 175, 186, 33, 34, 171
11b: 94, 180, 117, 142, 93, 143, 254, 141*
12a: 203, 167, 168, 231, 192
12b: 42, 73, 86, 220, 198, 56
[* = taken from an electrical re-recording]
73E Enrico Caruso Centennial Everest SDBR 3339
141, 252, 142, 93, 221, 42, 50(-2), 132, 233, 36, 145
73F Complete Recordings of Enrico Caruso Murray Hill 920328 (14)
[RCA attempted to stop distribution of this set, which was sold
primarily in bookstores and through the mail.]
1a: 28, 29, 30, 21, 22, 23, 24, 25, 26, 27
1b: 2, 4, 5, 6, 9, 10, 7, 1, 11, 13
2a: 14, 16, 19, 12, 15, 17, 18, 20, 32, 31
2b: 204, 207, 98, 99, 239, 235, 78, 157, 181, 43
3a: 80, 90, 75, 126, 257, 249, 166(-1), 64
3b: 104, 115, 44(-3, not -1), 119, 245, 133, 40, 209
4a: 53, 182, 68, 191, 65, 91(-1 & -2), 39, 211
4b: 144, 152, 67, 208, 205, 138, 248, 252(-1), 44(-3)
5a: 195, 236, 240, 154, 118, 49, 201, 77, 76
5b: 258, 48, 251(-1, -3: not rec. 27 Dec.'09), 108, 107, 111, 112
6a: 161, 105, 106, 103, 114, 110, 123, 124
6b: 127, 151, 153, 117, 177, 79, 183, 37, 252(-2)
7a: 246, 46, 47, 58, 63, 101, 85, 222
7b: 72, 62, 100, 121, 122, 142, 45, 60
8a: 158, 86, 162, 163, 164, 165, 140
8b: 233, 145, 87, 212, 94, 141, 61, 132

9a: 66, 156, 89, 193, 253, 159, 42, 206
9b: 56, 96, 262, 137, 130, 116, 81, 199(-3, not -1), 231
10a: 179, 226, 52, 155, 227, 184, 254, 171
10b: 59, 57, 185, 244, 129, 131, 169, 84
11a: 203, 95, 187, 230, 88, 149, 176, 202
11b: 83, 198, 69, 170, 150, 73, 234
12a: 220, 221, 54, 194, 82, 102, 188, 189
12b: 219, 213, 146(-2), 50(-2), 166(-2), 172, 259, 173(-2)
13a: 224, 34, 186, 120, 180, 135, 192, 71, 33
13b: 200, 70, 232, 218, 97, 36, 261, 38
14a: 255, 174, 197, 225, 223, 228, 217, 143, 229, 175
14b: 136, 134, 260, 51, 93, 167, 41, 168
[inconsistent speed problems]

73G   To Caruso by Caruso   Stanford University StARS 1000
214 [7-inch LP, with Melba: Songs my mother taught me (Dvorak), also previously unreleased]

1975

75A   Enrico Caruso: His First Recordings   Everest SDBR 3382
28, 29, 30, 21, 22, 23, 24, 25, 26, 27, 2, 4, 5, 6, 9,
10, 7, 1, 11, 13, 14, 16, 19, 12, 15, 17, 18, 20, 32, 31
[This appears to be a re-packaging of the first 3 sides of 73F.]
[re-released as 89A*]

1976

76A   Caruso: A Legendary Performer   CRM1-1749
1: 182, 240, 205, 208, 40, 136, 64, 45
2: 127, 77, 236, 104, 100, 166(-1), 229, 249
[The first release using "Stockham/Soundstream" reprocessing (see James
A. Drake, "The 'Real' Voice of Caruso?" *High Fidelity Magazine* 26, no. 10
(October 1976): 86–90; and David Hamilton, "Caruso *cum* Computer," *High
Fidelity Magazine* 26, no. 11 (November 1976): 98–99).]
[re-issued as part of CD 87A*]

1977

77A   Caruso at the Met: Opening Nights 1903–20   Metropolitan Opera
1: 205, 208, 211 (not 210), 45, 127, 159   Met-101
2: 60, 219, 189, 236, 240, 136

1978

78A   The Complete Caruso: Volume 4, 1906–1907   ARM1-2766
1: 249, 166(-1), 64, 104, 115, 44(-1), 119, 245
2: 133, 40, 209, 53, 182, 68, 191, 65
[all vols. produced with Stockham/Soundstream reprocessing]
78B   The Complete Caruso: Volume 5, 1908–1909   ARM1-2767
1: 91(-1, -2), 39, 211, 144, 152, 67
2: 208, 205, 138, 248, 252(-1), 44(-3), 195, 236, 240

1979

79A   The Complete Caruso: Volume 6, 1909–1910   ARM1-3373
1: 154, 118, 48, 49, 201, 77, 76
2: 258, 251(-1, -3), 105, 106, 107, 108
79B   The Complete Caruso: Volume 7, 1910   ARM1-3374
1: 161, 103, 110, 111, 112, 114, 123
2: 124, 127, 151, 153, 117, 177, 79, 183

1980
80A   The Complete Caruso: Volume 8, 1910–1911   ARM1-3570
          1: 37, 246, 252(-2), 46, 47, 58, 63
          2: 101, 85, 222, 72, 62, 100
80B   The Complete Caruso: Volume 9, 1911–1912   ARM1-3571
          1: 121, 122, 142, 45, 60, 158
          2: 86, 162, 163, 164, 165, 140, 233

1982
82A   The Complete Caruso: Volume 10, 1912–1913   ARM1-4046
          1: 145, 87, 212, 94, 141, 61, 132
          2: 156, 66, 89, 253, 193, 206
82B   The Complete Caruso: Volume 11, 1913–1914   ARM1-4047
          1: 42, 159, 56, 96, 137, 130, 262
          2: 116, 231, 199(-2), 81, 179, 226

1983
83A   The Complete Caruso: Volume 12, 1914–1915   ARM1-4684
          1: 52, 155, 199(-3), 254, 227, 184, 57, 59
          2: 185, 171, 244, 129, 131, 74, 169, 84
83B   The Complete Caruso: Volume 13, 1915–1916   ARM1-4686
          1: 187, 203, 95, 230, 88, 198, 83, 149
          2: 176, 202, 170, 150, 69, 73, 220, 234

1984
84A   The Complete Caruso: Volume 14, 1916–1918   ARM1-4914
          1: 221, 194, 102, 82, 54, 219, 189, 188
          2: 213, 146(-2), 166(-1, not -2), 172, 259, 50(-2), 173(-2), 34
84B   The Complete Caruso: Volume 15, 1918–1919   ARM1-4915
          1: 224, 186, 120, 180, 192, 33, 71, 135
          2: 70, 200, 232, 218, 97, 36, 261, 255, 38
84C   RCA / Met: 100 Singers / 100 Years   CRM8-5177 (8)
          side 2: 136
84D   Enrico Caruso   Italian RCA VLS 45544
          1: 45, 182, 236, 240, 53, 206, 127, 140
          2: 150, 64, 118, 166(-1), 81, 77, 60, 249
          ["Half-speed mastering" received very favorable reviews.]

1985
85A   The Complete Caruso: Volume 16, 1919–1920   ARM1-7008
          1: 174, 197, 225, 217, 228, 223, 143, 229, 175
          2: 136, 134, 260, 41, 51, 93, 168, 167
85B   One Hundred Years of Great Artists at the Met:
          The Early Years—1883–1908   Metropolitan Opera Met-401
          side 3: 98, 99   side 4: 252(-1), 183   (2)
85C   One Hundred Years of Great Artists at the Met:
          The Gatti-Casazza Years I—1908–1921   Metropolitan Opera Met-402
          side 1: 57   side 2: 158   side 4: 188   (2)
85D   The Great Enrico Caruso   Pair PDL2-1101 (2)
          ["RCA Special Product"]
          1: 229, 136, 146(-2), 205
          2: 208, 213, 252(-1), 119
          3: 40, 45, 77, 127
          4: 182, 64, 149, 175, 180

1987
87A* Caruso: A Legendary Performer   5911-2-RC
      182, 240, 205, 208, 40, 136, 64, 45, 54+, 115+, 118+,
      177+, 189+, 127, 77, 236, 104, 100, 166(-1), 229, 249
            [incorporates 76A: additions marked with "+"]

1988
88A* Enrico Caruso Sings Arias of Giuseppe Verdi   Price-Less D 18371
      89, 179, 177, 118, 119, 120, 121,
      58, 59, 60, 203, 246, 248, 205, 150, 140

1989
89A* Enrico Caruso: His First Recordings   Bescol CD 535
      [re-release: see 75A]
89B* Enrico Caruso: Opera Arias and Songs   Angel/EMI CDH761046-2
      1, 7, 2, 3, 4, 5, 8, 6, 9, 10, 16, 31,
      15, 12, 14, 17, 18, 19, 20, 21, 30, 28, 32

LABEL NAME AND NUMBER INDEX

RCA	LCT-1039	52D
	LCT-1103	53H
	LCT-1112	53I
	LCT-1121	53J
	LCT-1129	53K
	LCT-1138	53L
	LCT-6701	55B
	LDM-70001 (Ital.)	73D
	LM-1202	52E
	LM-2372-c	60A
	LM-2639	62A
	LM-2700	64A
	LM-2778	65A
	LM-6056	58A
	LM-6127	56A
	LM-6171	66A
	LM-6705	62B
	SP-33-75	60B
	VIC-1395	69A
	VIC-1430	69B
	VIC-1519	70A
	VIC-1600	71A
	VIC-1623	71B
	VIC-1633	71C
	VLS 45544 (Ital.)	84D
	WCT-4	51l
	WCT-5	51j
	WCT-6	51m
	WCT-7	51k
	WCT-8	51n
	WCT-10	51o
	WCT-11	51p
	WCT-35	52a
	WCT-51	52j
	WCT-57	52c
	WCT-62	52d
	WCT-1103	53h
	WCT-1112	53i
	WCT-1121	53j
	WDM-1626	52e
Rococo Records 2		58C
7		58D
36		62D
Scala Records 825		56B
Seraphim 60146		70B
60206		72A
Stanford U. StARS 1000		73G
TAP Records T-307		59A
T-333		62E

Chronologies of the Appearances of Enrico Caruso and the Giachetti Sisters

by Thomas G. Kaufman

INTRODUCTION

These three chronologies were written expressly for this volume. However, through the courtesy of the authors, Enrico Caruso, Jr., and Andrew Farkas, the Caruso chronology appeared first in Michael Scott's *The Great Caruso* (New York: Knopf; London: Hamish Hamilton, 1988). Since then, additional details about the tenor's career have come to light, including information about his earliest documented appearance (provided by Michael Henstock) and his Cairo engagement (provided by Flavia Tibaldi). Thus new information has been incorporated into the Caruso chronology, and minor errors have been corrected.

As in the Scott volume, the chronologies are arranged by season rather than by calendar year since the usual engagement at the Metropolitan Opera (where Caruso spent the greatest part of his singing career) stretched from autumn of one year through winter and early spring of the next. To avoid confusion, seasons in the southern hemisphere are indicated in the same manner as seasons in the northern hemisphere. Thus the period from May to August in Buenos Aires is listed as spring and summer, though it was actually autumn and winter there. Operas are listed in chronological order, except for those performed on side trips concurrently with the main season. As far as possible, supporting casts (i.e., principal singers) are given, with registers indicated as follows:

s.	soprano
ms.	mezzo-soprano or contralto
t.	tenor
b.	baritone
bs.	bass
cond.	conductor

Only the dates of the first performance of a work during a season are indicated. The total number of performances of the same work, together with cast changes, are included where this information could be ascertained.

Since Caruso and the Giachetti sisters created a number of operatic roles and took part in a significant number of local premières as well, these are indicated as follows:

** world première
* confirmed local première

Note that the absence of an asterisk should not be construed as meaning that a given production was *not* a local première, for these could not always be ascertained with certainty.

Acknowledgments

Compiling these chronologies would not have been possible without the assistance of many persons. Special thanks are due to Michael Scott and Andrew Farkas for sharing information they themselves accumulated over the years; to Lim Lai for looking up dates and casts in his fabulous collection of books and programs; to Charles Mintzer, a walking encyclopedia of information about opera singers and opera houses; and to Robert Tuggle of the Metropolitan Opera Archives, who provided considerable assistance with respect to Caruso's appearances with the Metropolitan Opera. *Signora* Flavia Tibaldi of the Istituto Italiano di Cultura in Cairo researched Caruso's 1895 season in that city. Dr. Mario Moreau (Lisbon), Mr. Carlo Marinelli (Rome), Dr. Ruffo Titta, Jr. (Rome), Professor Eduardo Arnosi and Dr. Horacio Sanguinetti (Buenos Aires), Juan Dzazopulos (Santiago, Chile), and Michel Szurek (Warsaw, Poland) were also particularly helpful.

Equally invaluable are the contributions made by Ms. Janet Bone, Mrs. Ruth Schultz, and Mrs. Susan Rowe of the Morris County Free Library and Mrs. Josepha Cooke of the Drew University Library, who helped to locate many of the books, newspapers, and periodicals essential to creating these lists.

I would also like to express sincere thanks to the following individuals and institutions: Professor Michael Henstock, Dr. Antonino Defraia, Donald Wisdom of the Newspapers and Periodicals Division of the Library of Congress and his staff, and the staffs of the Princeton University Library, the University of Michigan Library, the University of Illinois Library, the University of North Carolina Library, the Music Division of the Library of Performing Arts, the Music Division of the Library of Congress, and numerous other research libraries across the United States. To anyone whose name I have inadvertently omitted from this list, I offer my apologies.

Finally, I am indebted to my wife, Marion, whose patience and encouragement made these chronologies possible.

> Thomas G. Kaufman
> 15 June 1989
> Boonton, New Jersey

Bibliography

Monographs

Beetz, Wilhelm. *Das Wiener Opernhaus 1869–1945*. Vienna: Amaltea Verlag, 1952.

Bracale, Adolfo. *Mis memorias*. Caracas: Editorial Elite, 1931.

Caamaño, Roberto. *La Historia del Teatro Colón, 1908–1968*. Buenos Aires: Editorial Cinetea, 1969.

Caruso, Dorothy. *Enrico Caruso: His Life and Death*. New York: Simon and Schuster, 1945.

Cerquera, Paulo de O. C. *Um seculo de opera em São Paulo*. São Paulo: Empresa Grafica Editora Guia Fiscal, 1954.

Ciotti, Ignazio. *La vita artistico del Teatro Massimo di Palermo*. Palermo: Tipolitografia Priulla, 1984.

Davis, Ronald. *Opera in Chicago*. New York: Appleton-Century, 1966.

De Brito Chaves, Jr., Edgard. *Memorias e glorias de um teatro*. Rio de Janeiro: Companhia Editora Americana, 1971.

Domanski, Piotr Jerzy. *Repertuar Teatrow Warszawskich*. Warsaw: Instytut Sztuki Polskiej Akademii Nauk, 1976.

Eaton, Quaintance. *The Boston Opera Company*. New York: Appleton-Century, 1965.

———. *Opera Caravan*. New York: Farrar, Strauss and Cudahy, 1957.

Farkas, Andrew. *Titta Ruffo: An Anthology*. Westport, Conn.: Greenwood Press, 1984.

Frajese, Vittorio. *Dal Costanzi all'Opera*. Rome: Edizioni Capitolium, 1978.

Frassoni, Edilio. *Due secoli di lirica a Genova*. Genoa: Cassa di Risparmia di Genova e Imperia, 1980.

Gatti, Carlo. *Il Teatro alla Scala,* 2 volumes. Milan: Ricordi, 1964.

Greenfeld, Howard. *Caruso*. New York: G. P. Putnam's Sons, 1983.

Kapp, Julius. *185 Jahre Staatsoper*. Berlin: Atlantic-Verlag, 1928.

Key, Pierre V. R. *Enrico Caruso: A Biography*. Boston: Little, Brown, 1922.

Marinelli Roscioni, Carlo. *Cronologia del Teatro Comunale*. Treviso: Longo & Zoppelli, 1977.

———. *Il Teatro di San Carlo*. Naples: Guidi Editori, 1987.

Mohr, Albert Richard. *Das Frankfurter Opernhaus 1880–1980*. Frankfurt: Waldemar Kramer, 1980.

Noel, Edouard, and Edmond Stoullig. *Les Annales du Théâtre et de la Musique*. Paris: 1875–1916.

Olavarria y Ferrari, Enrique. *Resena historica del Teatro en Mexico*. Mexico City: Biblioteca Porrua, 1961.

Rosenthal, Harold. *Two Centuries of Opera at Covent Garden*. London: Putnam, 1958.

Ruffo, Titta. *La Mia Parabola*. Rome: Staderini, 1977.

Salgado, Susana. *Breve historia de la musica culta en el Uruguay*. Montevideo: Aemus, 1971.
Seltsam, William. *Metropolitan Opera Annals*. New York: Wilson, 1947.
Trezzini, Lamberto. *Due secoli di vita musicale*. Bologna: Edizioni Alfa, 1966.
Walsh, Thomas J. *Monte Carlo Opera, 1879-1909*. Dublin: Gill and Macmillan, 1975.
_____. *Monte Carlo Opera, 1910-1951*. Kilkenny, Ireland: Boethius Press, 1986.
Wenzel, Joseph E. *Geschichte der Hamburger Oper 1678-1978*. Hamburg: Hamburgischen Staatsoper, 1978.

Political Newspapers

El Dia, Montevideo
Egyptian Gazette, Alexandria
La Epoca, Madrid
O Estado do São Paulo, São Paulo
El Ferrocaril, Santiago de Chile
Frankfurter Zeitung, Frankfurt
L'Imparziale, Cairo
Jornal do Commercio, Lisbon
Jornal do Commercio, Rio de Janeiro
El Mercurio, Valparaiso
Neue Freie Presse, Vienna
Neue Preussische Zeitung, Berlin
The New York Times, New York
Novoe Vremia, St. Petersburg
La Prensa, Buenos Aires
Russkaia Vedomosti, Moscow
El Sur, Concepcion
Times, London
La Tribuna, Rome

Theatrical, Literary, and Musical Newspapers and Periodicals

Allgemeine Zeitung, Munich
Ayer y Hoy de la Opera, Buenos Aires
Cosmorama Pittorico, Milan
Gazzetta Musicale di Milano, Milan
Le Guide Musicale, Brussels
Il Mondo Artistico, Milan
Musical America
Neue Musik Zeitung, Stuttgart
Der Neue Weg, Berlin
Rassegna Melodrammatica, Milan
Rivista Teatrale Melodrammatica, Milan
Signale für die Musikalische Welt, Berlin
Il Trovatore, Milan

CHRONOLOGY OF
ENRICO CARUSO'S APPEARANCES

1894 NAPLES—TEATRO EXCELSIOR
Oct. 10?   Concert   F. M. Bonini b. A. Zamparelli s.? F. Zamparelli s.?

WINTER 1895 CASERTA—CATHEDRAL
Jan. 2   *Tantum Ergo* (2 perf.)

WINTER 1895 NAPLES—TEATRO NUOVO
Mar. 15   *L'Amico Francesco*   Belvetti s. U. Ciabò b.
             (Morelli)** (2 perf.)

SPRING 1895 CASERTA—TEATRO CIMAROSA
Mar. 28   *Faust*   Ferrari-Moscati s. E. Molinari ms. E. Pignataro b.
                                    A. Sternaiolo bs.
Apr.   *Cavalleria rusticana* Ferrari-Moscati s. E. Pignataro b.
May   *Camoens*   Ferrari-Moscati s. E. Pignataro b. A. Sternaiolo
                                    bs.

SPRING 1895 COTRONE—CATHEDRAL
June   Mass

SUMMER 1895 NAPLES—TEATRO BELLINI
June 9   *Faust*   E. Pignataro b. E. Foggi bs.
July 21   *Rigoletto*   A. Pane s. C. Molinari ms. G. Ferrari b. Fari bs.
Aug. 25   *La Traviata*   A. Antinori s. G. Ferrari b.

AUTUMN 1895 ALEXANDRIA—TEATRO ALHAMBRA?[1]

AUTUMN 1895 CAIRO—EZBEKIEH GARDENS
Oct. 21   *Cavalleria rusticana* E. Bianchini-Cappelli s. V. Ferraguti b.; A.
                                    Sarmiento cond.
Oct. 23   *La Traviata*   Balvetti s. V. Ferraguti b.; A. Sarmiento cond.
Oct. 30   *Lucia di Lammermoor* Balvetti s. V. Ferraguti b. Sarti bs.; A. Sarmiento
                                    cond.
Nov. 9   *La Gioconda**   E. Bianchini-Cappelli s. M. Pantanelli ms. Bar-
                                    chetta ms. V. Ferraguti b. Sarti bs.; A.
                                    Sarmiento cond.
Nov. 15   *Manon Lescaut**   E. Bianchini-Cappelli s. V. Ferraguti b. Sarti bs.;
                                    A. Sarmiento cond.

AUTUMN AND WINTER 1895-96 NAPLES—TEATRO MERCADANTE
Nov. 29   *La Traviata (15* perf.) K. Bensberg s. (later A. Franco s. then Castelriva
                                    s.) L. Magni b. (later F. M. Bonini b.); C.
                                    Sebastiani cond.
Dec. 7   *I Capuleti ed i*   A. Franco s. E. Carelli s. R. de Falco bs.; C.
             Montecchi (15 perf.) Sebastiani cond.
Dec. 25   *Rigoletto* (10 perf.) A. Franco s. V. Ferraguti b. (later F. M. Bonini b.);
                                    V. Galassi cond.
Jan. 11   *Faust* (10 perf.)   A. Franco s. E. Riso ms. F. M. Bonini b. L.
                                    Rossato bs.; V. Galassi cond.

CARNIVAL 1896 CASERTA—TEATRO CIMAROSA
Feb.   *Faust*

LENT 1896 TRAPANI—TEATRO GARIBALDI
Feb. 15   *Lucia di Lammermoor* A. Franco s. G. La Puma b. Franchetti bs.; O.
                                    Anselmi cond.

Mar. 10   *Cavalleria rusticana*   E. Cavalieri s. E. Pignataro b.; O. Anselmi con«
Mar. 21   *Malia* (Frontini)
Mar. 24   *La Sonnambula*   A. Franco s. G. La Puma b.; O. Anselmi cond.

SPRING 1896 MARSALA
           Rigoletto
May 2?   *Cavalleria rusticana*   A. Franco s. E. Pignataro b.; O. Anselmi cond

SPRING 1896 NAPLES—TEATRO BELLINI
May 20?   *Rigoletto*   Ariberti s. E. Riso ms. V. Ferraguti b.; (
                                     Scognamiglio cond.

           La Traviata?
           Faust?
June 23   *Mariedda* (Bucceri)   A. Scalera s. E. Riso ms. V. Morghen b.

SUMMER 1896 SALERNO—TEATRO MUNICIPALE
Sep. 10   *I Puritani*   A. Franco s. V. Ferraguti b. R. Di Falco bs.;
                                     Lombardi cond.

Sep. 17   *Cavalleria rusticana*   A. Franco s. V. Ferraguti b.; V. Lombardi con

AUTUMN 1896 SALERNO—CATTEDRALE SAN MATEO
Sep. 27   Concert

AUTUMN 1896 SALERNO—TEATRO MUNICIPALE
Oct.   *La Traviata*
Nov. 22   *La Favorita*   M. Masula ms. E. Pignataro b. C. Gagliardi bs.;
                                     Lombardi cond.

Nov. 23   *A San Francisco*   M. Masula ms. E. Pignataro b.; V. Lombardi con
           (Sebastiani)
           Pagliacci[2]   A. Franco s. E. Pignataro b.; Bossi cond.
Dec. 6   *Carmen*   A. Scalera s. M. Masula ms. E. Pignataro b.

CARNIVAL 1896-97 NAPLES—TEATRO MERCADANTE
Dec. 16   *La Traviata*   N. Barbareschi s. F. Guarini b.; A. Siragusa cor
Dec. 30   *La Favorita*
Jan. 19   *La Gioconda*   A. Penchi s. A. Dombrowska ms. A. Nava ms.
                                     Guarini b. E. Brancaleoni bs.; Scalisi cond
Feb. 1   *Un Dramma in*   Ducci s. A. Dombrowska ms. Salvi ms. F. Guar
           vendemmia   b.; V. Fornari cond.
           (Fornari)
Mar. 6   *Celeste* (D. Lamonica   N. Barbareschi s. F. Guarini b.; Scalisi cond.
           and G. Biondi)**

LENT 1897 SALERNO—TEATRO MUNICIPALE
Mar. 11   *La Traviata*   C. Zucchi-Ferrigno s. (later A. Franco s.)
                                     Pignataro b.
Mar.   *La Favorita*   M. Masula ms. E. Pignataro b. R. Di Falco bs
Mar. 24   *Manon Lescaut**   A. Franco s. E. Pignataro b.; V. Lombardi co
Apr. 8   *Il Profeta Velato**   A. Franco s. M. Masula ms. E. Pignataro b.; Bo
           (Napolitano)   cond.
Apr. 18?   *La Gioconda*   C. Zucchi-Ferrigno s. M. Masula ms. E. Pignata
                                     b. R. Di Falco bs.; Bossa cond.

SPRING 1897 PALERMO—TEATRO MASSIMO
May 29   *La Gioconda* (13 perf.) M. Borelli s. E. Borlinetto ms. M. Paolicc
                                     Mugnone ms. T. Terzi b. P. Wulmann bs.
                                     Mugnone cond.

SUMMER 1897 LIVORNO—TEATRO GOLDONI
July 7?   *La Traviata*   A. Giachetti s. (later F. Rapisardi s.) A. Pini-Cc
                                     b.; V. Podesti cond.

| Aug. 14 | *La Bohème* | A. Giachetti s. A. Campagnoli s. G. Pini-Corsi t. R. Galli b. A. Silvestri bs.; V. Podesti cond. |

AUTUMN AND WINTER 1897-98 MILAN—TEATRO LIRICO

Nov. 3	*La Navarrese*	M. de Nuovina s. E. Dufriche b. L. Aristi b. M. Wigley b.; R. Ferrari cond.
Nov. 10	*Il Voto* (Giordano)**	R. Storchio s. O. Synnerberg ms. L. Aristi b.; G. Barone cond.
Nov. 23	*Cavalleria rusticana*	Passeri s. L. Aristi b.
Nov. 27	*L'Arlesiana***	M. Tracey s. L. Casini b. L. Aristi b.; G. Zuccani cond.
Dec. 31?	*Pagliacci*	L. Cassandro s. L. Casini b. L. Aristi b.

CARNIVAL 1898 GENOA—TEATRO CARLO FELICE

| Jan. 20 | *La Bohème* (Leoncavallo) (13 perf.) | E. Corsi s. R. Storchio s. R. Angelini-Fornari b. A. Pini-Corsi b.; A. Pomè cond. |
| Feb. 3 | *I Pescatori di perle* (8 perf.) | R. Pinkert s. G. de Luca b. O. Carozzi bs.; A. Pomè cond. |

CARNIVAL 1898 GENOA—TEATRO PAGANINI

| Feb. 14 | Concert | |

LENT 1898 MILAN—TEATRO LIRICO

Mar. 8	*La Bohème* (Leoncavallo)	A. Sedelmayer s. A. Santarelli s. R. Angelini-Fornari b. A. Rossi b.; G. Zuccani cond.
Mar. 16	*Carmen*	P. Leone s. I. Monti-Baldini ms. L. Aristi b.
Apr. 2	*Hedda*** (Le Borne)	Garnier s. E. Lorini ms. L. Casini b.; F. Le Borne cond.

SPRING 1898 FIUME—TEATRO COMUNALE

Apr. 10?	*La Bohème*	A. Giachetti s. V. Novelli s. P. Giacomello b. L. Contini bs.; G. Cimini cond.
Apr. 19?	*La Traviata*	A. Giachetti s. A. Nava b.; G. Cimini cond.
May 4	*Mefistofele*	A. Giachetti s. L. Contini bs.; G. Cimini cond.

SPRING 1898 TRENTO—TEATRO SOCIALE

| June 4 | *Sapho** (Massenet) | A. Pandolfini s. S. Aifos s. A. Borda ms. L. Aristi b.; G. Zuccani cond. |
| June 13? | *Pagliacci* | S. Aifos s. R. Angelini-Fornari b.; G. Zuccani cond. |

SUMMER 1898 LIVORNO—POLITEAMA LIVORNESE

| July 27? | *Pagliacci* | M. Ticci s. E. Barbieri b. S. Arrighetti b.; E. Martini cond. |
| Aug. 4 | *Cavalleria rusticana* | A. Antinori s. S. Arrighetti b.; E. Martini cond. |

AUTUMN 1898 MILAN—TEATRO LIRICO

Oct. 22	*L'Arlesiana*	A. Santarelli s. I. Timroth s. E. Pignataro b.; G. Zuccani cond.
Nov. 8	*La Bohème* (Leoncavallo)	A. Santarelli s. B. Sorel s. D. Menotti b.; G. Zuccani cond.
Nov. 17	*Fedora***	G. Bellincioni s. A. Barone s. D. Menotti b.; U. Giordano cond.
Dec.	*Sapho*	G. Bellincioni s. (later F. Strakosch s.) I. Timroth s. M. Manfredi s. L. Aristi b. G. Frigiotti bs.; G. Zuccani cond.

CARNIVAL 1899 ST. PETERSBURG—GRAND THÉÂTRE DU CONSERVATOIRE

| Jan. 27 | *La Traviata* (2 perf.) | S. Arnoldson s. M. Battistini b.; V. Podesti cond. |
| Jan. 30 | *La Bohème** (4 perf.) | S. Arnoldson s. L. Tetrazzini s. M. Battistini b. V. Brombara b. V. Arimondi bs. A. Silvestri bs.; V. Podesti cond. |

Feb. 22   *Cavalleria rusticana*   A. Giachetti s. T. Carotini ms. V. Brombara
             (2 perf.)
Feb. 22   *Lucia di Lammermoor*   L. Tetrazzini s. V. Brombara b. A. Silvestri bs
             (2 perf.)   Podesti cond.

LENT 1899 MILAN—TEATRO LIRICO
Mar. 20   *Fedora* (8 perf.)   G. Bellincioni s. A. Barone s. Salvati b.;
                                             Zuccani cond.

SPRING AND SUMMER 1899 BUENOS AIRES—TEATRO DE LA OPERA
May 14   *Fedora** (4 perf.)   G. Bellincioni s. D. Menotti b.; O. Anselmi c
May 24   *La Traviata* (2 perf.)   G. Bellincioni s. I. Tabuyo b.; E. Masche
                                             cond.
June 4   *Sapho** (2 perf.)   G. Bellincioni s. R. Angelini-Fornari b.;
                                             Anselmi cond.
June 8   *La Gioconda* (1 perf.)   E. Petri s. E. Lorini ms. I. Tabuyo b.
                                             Mascheroni cond.
June 22   *Iris** (7 perf.)   M. de Lerma s. R. Angelini-Fornari b. R. Erco
                                             bs.; E. Mascheroni cond.
July 4   *La Regina di Saba**   M. de Lerma s. E. Lorini ms. I. Tabuyo b. A. D
             (6 perf.)   bs.; E. Mascheroni cond.
July 25   *Yupanki* (Berutti)**   E. Petri s. I. Tabuyo b. R. Ercolani bs.
             (3 perf.)   Mascheroni cond.
Aug. 8   *Cavalleria rusticana*   E. Petri s. I. Tabuyo b.; E. Mascheroni cond
             (1 perf.)

AUTUMN 1899 ROME—TEATRO COSTANZI
Nov. 4   *Iris (9* perf.)   E. Carelli s. E. Moreo b. R. Galli bs.; L. Mugn
                                             cond.
Nov. 11   *La Gioconda* (5 perf.)   M. D'Arneyro s. I. Monti-Baldini ms. S. Care
                                             b. G. Balisardi bs.; L. Mugnone cond.
Nov. 22   *Mefistofele* (8 perf.)   E. Carelli s. I. Monti-Baldini ms. E. Borucchia
                                             L. Mugnone cond.

CARNIVAL 1899–1900 ST. PETERSBURG—GRAND THÉÂTRE DU CONSERVATO
Dec. 28   *La Traviata* (2 perf.)   S. Arnoldson s. M. Battistini b.; V. Podesti c
Jan. 3   *Aida* (3 perf.)   S. Kruszelnicka s. A. Cucini ms. M. Battistini
                                             Arimondi bs.
Jan. 11   *Un Ballo in maschera*   S. Kruszelnicka s. L. Tetrazzini s. T. Carotini
             (4 perf.)   M. Battistini b.; V. Podesti cond.
Jan. 17   *La Bohème* (3 perf.)   S. Arnoldson s. L. Tetrazzini s. V. Brombara
                                             Arimondi bs.; V. Podesti cond.
Jan. 22   *Mefistofele* (3 perf.)   S. Kruszelnicka s. T. Carotini ms. V. Arimond
Feb. 13   *La Risurrezione di*   S. Kruszelnicka s. T. Carotini ms. M. Batti
             Lazzaro (Perosi)   hb. A. Silvestri bs.; V. Podesti cond.
             (2 perf.)
Feb. 13   *Stabat Mater* (2 perf.)   S. Kruszelnicka s. A. Cucini ms. T. Carotini m
                                             Silvestri bs.; V. Podesti cond.
Feb. 28   *Lucia di Lammermoor*   L. Tetrazzini s. V. Brombara b.
             (1 perf.)
Mar. 2   *Maria di Rohan*   S. Kruszelnicka s. T. Carotini ms. M. Battisti
             (1 perf.)

CARNIVAL 1899–1900 ST. PETERSBURG—IMPERIAL THEATRE
(Concurrent with season at the Grand Théâtre du Conservatoire)
Dec. 30   *Aida* (1 perf.)   S. Kruszelnicka s. A. Cucini ms. M. Battistini
                                             Arimondi bs.
Feb. 10   *La Traviata* (1 perf.)   S. Arnoldson s. M. Battistini b.